English

Writing and Skills

CORONADO EDITION

HOLT, RINEHART AND WINSTON
COMPLETE COURSE

Critical Readers and Contributors

The authors and the publisher wish to thank the following people, who helped to evaluate and to prepare materials for this series:

Charles L. Allen, Baltimore Public Schools, Baltimore, Maryland
Kiyoko B. Bernard, Huntington Beach High School, Huntington Beach, California
Sally Borengasser, Rogers, Arkansas
Deborah Bull, New York City, New York
Joan Colby, Chicago, Illinois
Phyllis Goldenberg, North Miami Beach, Florida
Beverly Graves, Worthington High School, Worthington, Ohio
Pamela Hannon, Kirk Middle School, Cleveland, Ohio
Carol Kuykendall, Houston Public Schools, Houston, Texas
Wayne Larkin, Roosevelt Junior High School, Blaine, Minnesota
Nancy MacKnight, University of Maine, Orono, Maine
Catherine McCough, Huntington Beach Union School District, California
Kathleen McKee, Coronado High School, Coronado, California
Lawrence Milne, Ocean View High School, Long Beach, California
Al Muller, East Carolina University, Greenville, North Carolina
Dorothy Muller, East Carolina University, Greenville, North Carolina
Arlene Mulligan, Stanley Junior High School, San Diego, California
John Nixon, Santa Ana Junior College, Santa Ana, California
Jesse Perry, San Diego City Schools, California
Christine Rice, Huntington Beach Union School District, Huntington Beach, California
Linda C. Scott, Poway Unified High School District, Poway, California
Jo Ann Seiple, University of North Carolina at Wilmington, Wilmington, North Carolina
Joan Yesner, Brookline, Massachusetts
Seymour Yesner, Brookline Education Center, Massachusetts
Arlie Zolynas, San Diego State University, San Diego, California

Classroom Testing

The authors and the publisher also wish to thank the following teachers, who participated in the classroom testing of materials from this series:

David Foote, Evanston High School East, Evanston, Illinois
Theresa Hall, Nokomis Junior High School, Minneapolis, Minnesota
Carrie E. Hampton, Sumter High School, Sumter, South Carolina
Pamela Hannon, Proviso High School East, Maywood, Illinois
Wayne Larkin, Roosevelt Junior High School, Blaine, Minnesota
Grady Locklear, Sumter High School, Sumter, South Carolina
William Montgomery, Hillcrest High School, Jamaica, New York
Josephine H. Price, Sumter High School, Sumter, South Carolina
Barbara Stilp, North High School, Minneapolis, Minnesota
Joseph Thomas, Weymouth North High School, East Weymouth, Massachusetts
Travis Weldon, Sumter High School, Sumter, South Carolina

Teachers of the Huntington Beach Union High School Writing Program

Cassandra C. Allsop
Eric V. Emery
Michael Frym
Barbara Goldfein
Joanne Haukland
Don Hohl
Sandra Johnson

Carol Kasser
Patricia Kelly
Stephanie Martone
Lawrence Milne
Richard H. Morley
John S. Nixon

Catherine G. McCough
Kathleen C. Redman
Christine Rice
Michael D. Sloan
S. Oliver Smith
Glenda Watson

Dorothy Augustine, District Consultant in Writing

English

Writing and Skills

CORONADO EDITION

W. Ross Winterowd
Patricia Y. Murray

HOLT, RINEHART AND WINSTON

AUSTIN NEW YORK SAN DIEGO CHICAGO TORONTO MONTREAL

The Series:

English: Writing and Skills, First Course

English: Writing and Skills, Second Course

English: Writing and Skills, Third Course

English: Writing and Skills, Fourth Course

English: Writing and Skills, Fifth Course

English: Writing and Skills, Complete Course

Also available for each title:

Teacher's Edition

Workbook

Test Book

Teacher's Resource Binder

Computer Test Generator

Computer Scoring Program

W. ROSS WINTEROWD is the Bruce R. McElderry Professor of English at the University of Southern California. Since 1975, Dr. Winterowd has traveled widely as a writing consultant for numerous schools in North America.

PATRICIA Y. MURRAY is Director of Composition at DePaul University in Chicago. Dr. Murray taught junior and senior high school English in the Los Angeles city schools. She is also a consultant in curriculum development and teacher training.

Printed in the United States of America

ISBN 0-03-014667-4

Contents

1 Writing

3   Writing Paragraphs

4   Writing Exposition

5   Imaginative Writing

6   Critical Writing

7   *Writing the Research Paper*

8   *Logic and Writing*

9 Persuasive Writing

10 Business Letters and Forms

2 *Grammar and Usage*

11 Nouns

12 Pronouns

13 Verbs

14 Adjectives

15 Adverbs

20 The Phrase

21 Clauses

22 Usage and Style

3 Mechanics

23 Punctuation

28 Preparing for Tests

29 Speaking and Listening Skills

1
Writing

1 Using the Writing Process

The Writing Process

A troubled character in Albert Camus' novel *The Plague*, Joseph Grand, spends years of his free time writing and rewriting the first sentence of a book he dreams of publishing. Of course you don't want to take years to write your essays, as did this eccentric man, but you do need to think of writing as an ongoing process. Professional writers know it is the *process* of writing that allows them finally to discover and refine what they have to say—to arrive at the final product. It is not an orderly progression, however. Rather, it is messy (creativity usually is), sometimes moving ahead smoothly, sometimes falling back to start again. But it is a procedure you can follow to make your writing clearer and more precise. The process involves three stages: *prewriting*; *writing*; and *postwriting*. There will be times when these stages overlap, times when you may shorten one or skip it altogether. However, it will be useful for you to understand and master the overall process and each of its three stages.

Prewriting

Prewriting involves amassing material for your writing. This is a stage of experimentation and rehearsal—dredging up from memory or developing from experience and observation ideas, details, suggestions: words and phrases that will become your final piece of writing. Picture, for example, Mark Twain listing memories of his days on the Mississippi River or Ray Bradbury recalling childhood incidents for use in *Dandelion Wine*. From these prewritings came excellent writings. In prewriting you will jot down all your ideas, no matter how trivial they may seem. Some will be discarded later; some will be valuable. The prewriting techniques you will learn will usually provide more than enough material for your writing.

Writing

Once you have gathered (on scraps of paper, in your mind, or on neat, lined paper—it doesn't matter how) enough material that you feel you have something to say, you are ready to enter the second

stage of the process—writing. In this stage you will complete your first draft, composing your ideas in sentences and paragraphs. Professional writers recognize that their first drafts are just a beginning. (Ernest Hemingway rewrote the final paragraph of *A Farewell to Arms* twenty-five times before he was satisfied with it.) Because of this, you shouldn't censor yourself in the writing of a first draft. Instead, simply put your thoughts on paper, to be rearranged and organized later.

Usually during the course of writing your first draft, you will discover your own voice—that is, if you involve yourself in this writing process, you will find yourself writing what you really want to say.

Postwriting

Postwriting, the last stage of the writing process, includes writing all later drafts and the final piece. You may find yourself repeating techniques from prewriting and writing. This last stage may involve several additional drafts before you arrive at the final product (remember Hemingway and his twenty-five drafts).

After you have a first draft, it is helpful to get the responses of other readers. In some postwriting exercises you will learn to use response groups for guidance in rewriting. Through sharing your draft with other students, family members, and teachers, you will gain valuable insight on how to improve the piece of writing. With these suggestions in mind, you may make some decisions about revising the piece. True revision involves "rethinking" the writing—including more information to clarify a point, changing the order of some paragraphs, leaving out extraneous material.

Postwriting also involves proofreading, the cleanup part of writing. Again, you may be aided by other people, or you may rely on yourself. In this chapter you will learn to use a checklist to help proofread your writing. Proofreading includes attention to such details as grammar, spelling, and punctuation. It helps clean up the mistakes that lessen the effectiveness of what you want to say. Once you have completed this last stage of the writing process, you will have a finished piece of writing ready to share with others.

It's a mistake to think of the writing process as orderly and linear, or to assume that you have to know precisely what you are going to say before you ever put pencil to paper. Writing is a creative process in which you start writing things down from the very beginning—even before your total meaning is clear to you. Then you allow your words gradually to change and evolve. Only at the end will you discover exactly what you want to say and how you want to say it. The writing practices and assignments in this book will guide you in using the writing process to make your own discoveries.

Prewriting to Generate Ideas

This section presents two prewriting methods, brainstorming and clustering. They are especially useful for generating writing subjects and basic details about those subjects.

Brainstorming

Brainstorming is the process of stimulating creative thinking by letting your mind wander freely over a subject.

Brainstorming is primarily a group activity in which everyone shares ideas as quickly and freely as possible, making no judgments about which ones are good or bad, sensible or silly. The initial purpose of brainstorming is to come up with as many ideas as possible, not to judge them as serious or trivial. Legend has it that

Albert Einstein asked himself a seemingly trivial question: "What would the universe be like if I perceived it from a streetcar going at the speed of light?" From this question resulted the theory of relativity, not to mention the atom bomb and nuclear power. Creative thinkers must allow themselves to think about the trivial and the impossible—and the purpose of brainstorming is to bring about this kind of freethinking.

For group brainstorming the procedure is to decide on a general subject to explore and then to focus attention on it, contributing ideas, associations, and suggestions quickly and freely. To brainstorm alone, sit quietly with a sheet of paper in front of you and concentrate on the subject you have chosen. Letting your mind roam freely, jot down the ideas, impressions, and associations that come to you.

Writing Practice 1: *Brainstorming*

Decide on a subject for brainstorming. (You may select one from the list of subjects included with this writing practice or create one from your imagination.) If you brainstorm alone, sit quietly by yourself and let your thoughts wander over your subject. On a sheet of paper, jot down ideas and impressions as they come to you. Do not discard ideas if they seem silly at the time. Remember that your purpose is to accumulate ideas. If you brainstorm as a group, use the following directions.

1. Form groups of four or five.

2. Choose one member of the group to be the recorder. He or she will write all of the ideas on the board or on a sheet of paper.

3. Let one member of the group start the session by stating one idea concerning the subject. Remember that no one is to judge this idea.

4. After the session has begun, members should state ideas or call up associations as quickly as possible. Have the recorder keep a list of these thoughts.

5. As more and more ideas are brought out, group members should find it easier to suggest new thoughts. Continue to record all ideas until time is up.

Subjects for Brainstorming

Improving the cafeteria	Popular music
Alternate energy sources	Computers
Plot for a soap opera	Combating inflation
Pros and cons of a college education	How to be happy

Clustering

Clustering is a more organized version of brainstorming.

While brainstorming works best as a group activity, clustering is a technique that you can use either with a group or by yourself. For example, assume that you are part of a group that is exploring what the word *education* means to the members. The first step is to put that word in the center of a sheet of paper or on the blackboard.

Now begin to brainstorm. As you think of ideas, write them around the first word. Show how the ideas relate to each other by circling them and drawing lines. After a few minutes you might have a diagram that looks like the following one.

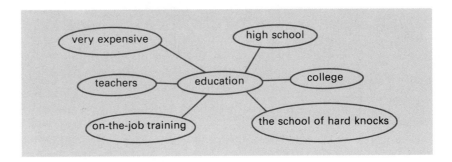

As with brainstorming, one idea will suggest another, so after fifteen minutes or half an hour, you might have developed something like the diagram on the next page.

The only limits to clustering are time and space!

The clusters around *education* would probably give you many ideas about the subject—more than enough to get you started on an essay, which might have six sections: high school education, college education, learning through experience, on-the-job training, teachers, costs, and so on. Or it might be that you would choose to write a whole essay on one of those subjects. If you chose to write on the costs of a college education ("very expensive"), you would need to do research in the library to find what costs are at various colleges and universities, what scholarships are available and what the requirements are, how to get financial aid, and so on. If you chose to write on "useful subjects," you could draw on your own experience. You might even want to make "useful subjects" the center of your cluster and add more ideas.

Through clustering, you may discover that you have more ideas about your subject than you ever imagined. Clustering can also point to aspects of the subject that you know most about, and thus suggest ways for you to limit a broad topic.

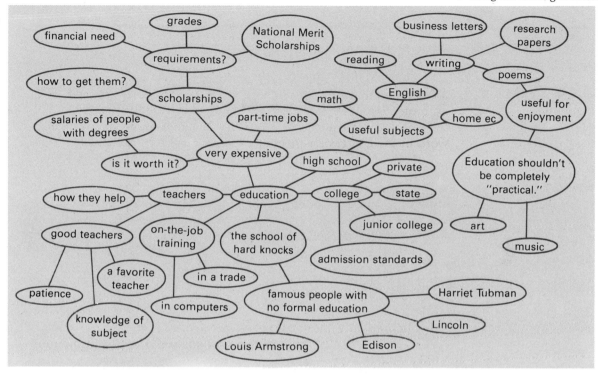

Writing Practice 2: *Clustering*

No one in the world knows more than you about how you write a paper for your English class. You probably have never thought about what you do, however—how you get ready to write, your favorite place for writing, or how you organize your writing. For you, writing papers is probably something like riding a bicycle: you can do it, but you have never tried to explain how. Use the following diagram as a starter for a cluster exercise on the subject "How I Write Papers." Put down as many ideas as you possibly can. Save your cluster for later use.

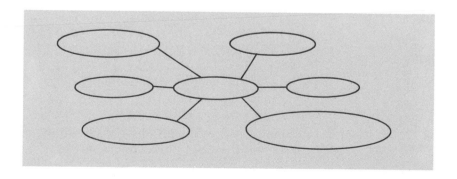

Prewriting for Greater Depth

Generating written material is often a matter of asking the right questions. Questions can help you find out how much you already know about a subject, as well as how much you need to learn before you can begin to write. Part of your task in gathering information for writing is learning which kinds of questions are most appropriate.

After you have used brainstorming or clustering to start a piece of writing, you may want to explore your topic in greater depth. The *Six Basic Questions*, the *Pentad*, and *Changing Viewpoints*, three intensive prewriting approaches, can help. Each will guide you in generating and organizing specific details about your topic.

The Six Basic Questions

When a reporter writes about an event in the news, he or she tries to answer a standard set of questions: *Who? What? When? Where? Why?* **and** *How?* **When you are writing about events, these questions can help you gather the ideas that you need to report what happened.**

When using the six basic questions, remember that these are not short-answer questions. Instead, use them to explore the event thoroughly, thinking of as many details as possible about the event. For example, the following report is not a very good one even though it answers all of the questions.

Because he detests chores, Anthony Walters avoided doing the dishes after dinner at his home last night by claiming that he had three hours of studies to complete.

Who?	Anthony Walters
What?	Avoided doing the dishes
When?	Last night
Where?	At his home
Why?	Detests chores
How?	By claiming that he was overloaded with homework

If that is all there is to be said about the event, then it is not worth writing about. However, the answers to the questions can be more detailed, creating a piece of writing that might interest readers, such as the essay on the following page.

Model: Using the Six Basic Questions

My younger brother, Anthony John Walters, has always detested household chores, and he is always at work on new techniques for avoiding them. He appears to be a completely normal twelve-year-old who tries to set records for length of time gone without bathing and whose idea of cleaning up his room is to throw all his old school papers, comic books, dirty T-shirts, and unwanted records into the closet. My parents tend to overlook these qualities, though, because Anthony truly likes schoolwork as much as he detests chores. Mom and Dad are happy that he is a good student and encourage him whenever they can.

Since we were young, our parents have taught Anthony and me responsibility by giving us alternating chores. One week I take out the garbage, the next week I set the table, and every other Saturday one of us helps with general housecleaning or special "projects" Mom or Dad dreams up for us. We're also supposed to take turns doing the dishes. For some reason Anthony hates doing the dishes more than all other chores combined, and he is a master of inventing excuses to avoid doing his duty. The excuse I liked best was his scheme for a friend to telephone him with a desperate request for help in preparing for a test. It worked fine the first three times, but after that even my trusting mother became suspicious and called the parents of my brother's accomplice. I liked that one best because my brother had to do the dishes by himself for two weeks as punishment.

Last night, however, I found that my brother had used all that time scrubbing away to dream up a new routine. As we were eating, he knitted his brow and talked about schoolwork, complaining that his teachers had all given him huge assignments due the next morning—a theme for English, a chapter of American history to be studied for a quiz, and a dozen tough math problems. He shook his head sadly and sighed, "I wish all the teachers would get together so they didn't all give so much work at the same time."

I glared at him from across the table, but he looked back with an expression of perfect innocence.

Supper ended, and Anthony jumped up from the table to clear the dishes. "I'd better do the dishes now so I can begin studying," he said earnestly.

Mom and Dad looked at one another, and I had a sinking feeling in my stomach. Dad looked at Anthony and declared, "Since you have so much to do tonight, I'm sure your brother will do the dishes for you this time. You can do the same for him when he needs extra study time." Dad smiled at me. My study habits were a sore point between us. I opened my mouth to argue, but I knew that it was no use. Fate had caught up with me—Fate and the scheming mind of my little brother.

Think and Discuss

1. With what specific details does the author answer the questions "Who?" and "How?"

2. Which of the six basic questions does the author use fewest details to answer?

Writing Practice 3: *The Six Basic Questions*

Even a simple event, such as the one in the preceding example, can be interesting if the writer supplies enough details. The six basic questions can help you gather such details.

At the top of each of six sheets of paper, write one of the six questions. Now, think of a favorite paper you have written for English. How did you write it? For ideas, reread your cluster from Writing Practice 2. Then, under the appropriate headings, list as many details as you can about the *who, what, when, where, why,* and *how* of the way you wrote your paper. Save your work for later use.

—or—

In a literature anthology, find a short story or poem. After you have read it, answer the six questions about it. Underline the parts of your answers that could lead to an interesting paper or discussion.

The Pentad Questions

Another set of questions, called the *Pentad*, can help you to investigate a subject or an event in greater depth and to organize your information.[1]

The Pentad questions can be posed about any subject in the following manner.

1. **What is the action?** What is happening, has happened, or will happen?

2. **Who are the actors?** Who are the people responsible for or involved in the action? What are these people like?

3. **What is the scene?** Where and when does the action happen?

4. **What is the method or agency?** By what means or with what instrument is the action performed?

5. **What is the purpose?** Why does the action happen?

An *action* is any physical or mental thing that has happened or is happening. An event, such as walking to school, is an action. (An event of nature, such as a tornado or an earthquake, is not considered an action; instead, it is an occurrence. An *action* is committed with a purpose in mind.) All creative works (such as poems, stories, plays, paintings, and pottery) are actions because they have happened as the result of someone's mental and physical efforts. Concepts and ideas are actions because they have happened or taken place in someone's mind.

Those who perform actions are called *actors*. When you ask the question *Who?* you are really inquiring about the actor or actors who made something happen.

The time and place of an action is called the *scene*. Therefore, when you ask *Where?* and *When?* you are asking about scene.

Most actions are performed by means of some thing or things. For example, in a murder mystery the detective always looks for the murder weapon—the means with which the crime was committed. When you talk with a friend, you use language as your means. When you drive a nail, you use a hammer. When you ask your teacher to excuse you from turning in a paper, you probably use "psychology." All of these "things" through which actions are accomplished are *agencies*. An *agency* is something that is used to make an action possible. When you ask *How?* you are really asking about an agency.

---

[1]This section was based on ideas from *A Grammar of Motives* by Kenneth Burke (Berkeley and Los Angeles: University of California Press, 1969).

Finally, actions are performed for some reason—for a *purpose*. When you ask *Why?* you are asking questions about purpose.

Using the Pentad for Research

The Pentad questions can guide you in researching and writing about topics that are outside your general knowledge. For example, assume that you are writing a paper on Stonehenge, the prehistoric arrangement of stones on Salisbury Plain in England, as a research project. To help narrow your subject to a specific topic, you gather as much information as possible by reading, by talking with teachers who know something about the subject, and, if possible, by consulting with someone who has visited Stonehenge.

To guide you in your research, you might ask yourself the Pentad questions, taking notes as you answer them. The following examples show how one writer did this. As you follow the example, notice that each of the Pentad questions has been broken down into more specific questions.

Questions About the Action

1. What is it?

    Stonehenge is a circular formation of huge, upright stone slabs and cross-piece stones located on Salisbury Plain in Wiltshire, England.

2. What happened?

    Stonehenge was constructed over a period of 200 years during the second millennium (somewhere between 1900–1700 B.C.) as a place of worship or as a sophisticated astronomical observatory.

3. What is happening?

    Research is still being conducted by scientists in order to learn more about the origin and purpose of Stonehenge. In addition, Stonehenge is a world-famous tourist site.

4. What will happen?

    Investigations of Stonehenge, including future excavations, will continue. The mystery and beauty of Stonehenge will continue to attract visitors.

5. What could happen?

    Archaeological evidence could be uncovered to throw more light on the builders of Stonehenge, on the connection between Stonehenge and the more than 50,000 prehistoric stone monuments across Europe, or on the reason for the apparently abrupt stop to the building of the megalithic structures.

Notice that the first action question is, *What is it?* Although this might seem a simple question to ask, it can help you discover important information about your subject that you might otherwise have not included. The remaining four action questions cover actions that are happening now, those that have happened in the past, and those that will or could happen in the future. Not all of these questions are relevant to every topic, and often you will generate overlapping information. When you apply the action questions to your own topic, use only the ones that are relevant. Use these questions to generate ideas for your topic.

Writing Practice 4: *Action*

Select one of the photographs on this page and write a notebook entry describing what you see. To discover ideas for your notebook entry, apply the action questions to the photograph.

Questions About the Actors

1. Who or what is responsible for the action?

    Three separate groups of people were involved in the construction at Stonehenge. The first construction was started by people known to archaeologists as the Windmill Hill People, native hunters and farmers who dug a large circular ditch at the site and piled earth into steep banks on either side. Scientists date this first construction somewhere around 1900 B.C.

    The second wave of construction, by a group known as the Beaker People, began around 1750 B.C. These were the people who brought the enormous stones—megaliths weighing up to five tons each—and organized them in two concentric (arranged around the same center) circles.

    The third wave of construction, by a group called the Wessex People, began in approximately 1700 B.C. and finished the construction with more complex alignments of stones, perhaps for observing the skies.

2. What are the actors like?

    The Windmill People are believed to have been peaceful and productive, with a strong religion. They left pottery and tools such as adzes, arrowheads, axes, scrapers for leatherwork, and millstones for grinding.

    The Bronze Age wave of builders, the Beaker People, are known for their custom of burying beakers (pottery drinking cups) with their dead. They are thought to have been powerful and energetic people, better organized and less peaceful than the Windmill Hill People.

    The Wessex People, also during the Bronze Age, appeared around 1700 B.C. Although their graves contained daggers and bows, their weapons seem more ceremonial than the battle-axes of the Beaker People. Because Baltic amber, Egyptian bead, Scottish jet, and Normandy-styled bowls were found in their graves, these rulers are thought to have been international traders, bartering for various luxuries from the Baltic to the Mediterranean.

    The writer has collected detailed information about the actors involved in the building of Stonehenge. When the writer actually prepares the report, he or she might decide that some of the information is not relevant to the restricted topic and so will not use it in the report. In the beginning stages of writing, it is always best to collect more information than one can probably use.

Writing Practice 5: *Actors*

Imagine that you know the people involved in the action of one of the photographs on this page. You can imagine that they are related to you, that they are friends or acquaintances you work with, or that you have some other association with them. Then write a descriptive paragraph describing the people in the photograph that you chose. To gather information and generate ideas for your entry or paragraph, apply the actor questions from the Pentad.

Questions About the Scene

1. Where is the action happening? (Where did the action happen? [for past action] Where will the action happen? [for future action])

    Stonehenge is in Wiltshire, England, on Salisbury Plain.

15

2.   When did the action happen? (When will the action happen? [for future action])

Stonehenge has been a feature of the landscape on Salisbury Plain for over 3600 years.

3.   What is the place like?

The great megaliths of Stonehenge are enclosed within a circular ditch and are approached by a wide roadway called the Avenue. There are four series of stones within the trench: (1) a circle of sandstones with connecting lintels, (2) a circle of bluestone megaliths, (3) within that, a horseshoe-shaped arrangement surrounding an oval-shaped group of stones, and (4) the Altar Stone at the center. The Avenue points northeast to the Heel Stone, a megalith that marks the midsummer sunrise.

4. When did the action begin?

   The first construction at Stonehenge is thought to have begun around 1900 B.C. and continued, through two new groups of builders, over the following 200 years.

5. What is the historical background of the action?

   The building of Stonehenge did not follow a direct evolution, with one construction building up from the previous one. The first stage included a large circle of holes surrounding an arrangement of circular ditches and elevated mounds; the circle opened up on a pathway to a special area marked with a large standing stone called the Heel Stone, which marked the exact point of the midsummer sunrise.

   During the second stage the circular enclosure was surrounded by megaliths arranged in two concentric circles; this structure also left an opening directed toward the Heel Stone.

   The third builders of Stonehenge removed the double circle of megaliths (no one has discovered where they were taken) and replaced them with eighty-one boulders of the same stone as the Heel Stone. The builders also added four boulders within the circle to mark sunrise and sunset, moonrise and moonset.

Not all of the preceding scene questions will be appropriate to every topic, and some questions will produce similar information. However, asking yourself about the past, present, and future scene will help you understand your subject more fully. As you write, you can eliminate irrelevant or repetitious information.

Writing Practice 6: *Scene*

Assume that you have just returned from a place in one of the photographs on page 16 and then write a description of the place or a letter to a friend in which you describe the scene. To discover ideas for your entry or letter, apply the Pentad scene questions to the scene that you have chosen.

Questions About the Method (Agency)

1. What methods were used to build Stonehenge?

   There is still much scientific speculation about how the enormous boulders of Stonehenge were transported there. Most experts believe that (as in the building of the pyramids of Egypt) humans were used to drag the boulders from their far-distant source, without the benefit of wheels or horses.

2.   What methods were used to predict the movements of celestial bodies at Stonehenge?

   The intricate series of stones in Stonehenge III can be used in a number of different ways, sighting the heavens from one particular viewpoint or another, to observe or predict the movement of heavenly bodies.

Writing Practice 7: *Method*

Apply these method questions to a topic of your choice. Think of two or more questions that you could ask about your topic that have to do with the method in which the action was performed. Write the appropriate questions and their answers on a separate sheet of paper. (You may wish to continue using a topic from a previous Writing Practice assignment.)

Questions About Purpose

1.   What was the purpose of Stonehenge?

   The main purpose of Stonehenge seems to have been the prediction of sun and moon movements at crucial alignments. Stonehenge was an astronomical observatory capable of yielding precise calculations, most probably used as a calendar for determining when to plant crops. Moreover, it was probably also a temple; religious leaders may have used knowledge of the movements of the skies to maintain their power. They could call worshippers together to observe the midsummer sunrise over the Heel Stone, knowing exactly the day on which it would come. They could assemble people for eclipses and for the midwinter sunrise through another configuration at Stonehenge. Furthermore, since the progression of structures at Stonehenge reveals an increasingly sophisticated knowledge of astronomical observation, Stonehenge's builders probably enjoyed the mental exercise of watching and predicting the movement of the stars and planets, just as people do today.

Writing Practice 8: *Purpose*

Imagine what archaeologists 2,000 years from now would make of some of the structures and objects of our contemporary American culture. Using the Pentad purpose question, ask and answer a question about the use of one of the objects pictured on page 19, suggesting its possible purposes to a scientist colleague of the future.

Changing Viewpoints

A helpful method for discovering ideas for writing is to change your viewpoint, or way of looking at a subject. In the following sections you will learn to look at a subject from three viewpoints: (1) as it appears frozen in time and space, (2) as it changes or varies over time and space, and (3) as it is made up of working parts that together fit into a much larger background. These three viewpoints can be expressed by means of the following questions:

1. What is it?

2. How does it change or vary?

3. What are its relationships? (How do its parts work together? How is it related to a larger background?)

Viewpoint 1: What Is It?

When you ask *What is it?* about a subject, you are asking about its identity. Look first at its features. The features of a subject—whether it is a concrete one (such as a pencil or a television set) or an abstract

one (such as education or sports)—are the characteristics that distinguish it from other objects or ideas like it. When you study the features of a subject, you "freeze" it in time and space, just as you would if you photographed it, to observe it minutely.

If your subject is a person or an organization, the *What is it?* question focuses on description. Assume, for example, that your subject is *trade unions*. From this viewpoint you would define the subject *trade unions*, asking yourself who composes them, what they do, and what their purpose is.

Using comparison and contrast is another good way to gather information about a subject's identity. For example, how do present-day trade unions compare with the craft guilds of medieval Europe? Was their basic purpose the same? Did they represent similar types of workers? By exploring these similarities and differences, you can broaden your understanding of the nature of the trade union.

Even abstract ideas and concepts can be examined with the *What is it?* question, since the first step in describing a concept is to make a definition. Assume, for example, that your subject is *tragedy*. Most dictionaries define *tragedy* as "a drama with a serious theme that is brought to an unhappy conclusion." You can broaden this definition by examining a particular kind of tragedy, such as Elizabethan tragedy, or you can describe your concept further by relating tragedy to one particular drama, such as *Hamlet*.

Writing Practice 9: *What Is It?*

Select one of the following ideas or concepts as your subject for this assignment, or use a similar one of your choice. Then select one of the *Questions to Ask Yourself* that follow the list of subjects, jotting down your answers on a sheet of paper. Finally, use the information that you gather to write a detailed description of your idea or concept.

Ideas and Concepts

1. Middle class
2. Honesty
3. Empire
4. Courtesy
5. Individualism

6. Art
7. Ecology
8. Progress
9. Comedy
10. Freedom of speech

Questions to Ask Yourself

1. What is the definition of the subject? (First write your own definition and then check the dictionary definition.)

2. What are the similarities between the subject you have chosen and other similar subjects?

3.   What are the differences between this subject and other similar subjects?

Viewpoint 2: How Does It Change or Vary?

Asking yourself how your subject has changed over time or how it can change (or vary) without losing its identity is another way to discover ideas.

To apply this question to a concrete topic like *trade unions*, you would first ask yourself how the nature and purpose of trade unions have changed over time. For example, you might want to study the Knights of Labor in the early nineteenth century through the real growth of the unions around the turn of the century, or you might want to study the change in unions from the turn of the century to the present. You would then ask yourself how the unions can vary without becoming something other than trade unions. For instance, if unions began opening and running factories themselves rather than representing people who worked for those factories, would they still be trade unions?

You can also apply the same questions to an abstract concept. In studying tragedy, for example, you would learn that in the Middle Ages *tragedy* referred not to drama but to narratives about how people of high rank fell to low estate and that not until the sixteenth century was tragedy associated with the theater in England. You could also ask how tragedy can change without losing its basic identity. For example, some scholars believe that real tragedy deals only with heroic figures and that twentieth-century drama about ordinary people should not be defined as tragedy. Other scholars believe that tragedy is a reflection of the beliefs and values of various societies and that definitions of tragedy must change as societies change. (There will often be disagreement about the extent to which a subject can vary without losing its identity.)

Writing Practice 10: *How Does It Change or Vary?*

Select one of the subjects on the next page or use one of your own choice (perhaps the subject you used for the previous Writing Practice). Gather information about your chosen subject by asking yourself the question *How does it change or vary?* Use this information to write a paragraph describing how your subject has changed or is in the process of changing. If appropriate, include information about how it can vary without losing its identity. The specific *Questions to Ask Yourself* that follow the list of subjects will help you explore your subject.

Subjects

1. Protein
2. Money
3. Language
4. The Great Lakes
5. Magic

6. Fashion
7. Trains
8. The Supreme Court
9. Basketball
10. Jazz

Questions to Ask Yourself

1. How has the subject changed over time? (If appropriate, select a specific time period to address.)

2. Is the change caused by natural or internal forces?

3. Is the change caused by outside forces, such as the influence of other people or forces of nature?

4. What is the most significant factor in the change?

5. To what extent can the subject change without losing its identity?

6. How does the subject vary?

7. To what extent can the subject vary without losing its identity?

Viewpoint 3: What Are Its Relationships?

The third viewpoint about a subject can be expressed by the question *What are its relationships?* This viewpoint concerns the parts of the subject and how they work together, as well as how the subject fits against a larger background. In other words, you are considering the subject as both a system in itself (parts that work together) and as part of a larger system.

To understand trade unions, for instance, you must know their parts and know how these parts work together to form a system. Trade unions are generally composed of members and leaders who form various committees through which most of the work is accomplished. Then you would ask yourself how these parts work together to accomplish the purpose of a trade union. For example, you would want to know how workers join, how leaders are elected, and how decisions are made. To understand the subject *tragedy* you would first need to know that it has the following elements: a character who is the central figure, a struggle against opposing forces of some sort (often fate), and a disastrous end for the character. Then you would need to know how these parts work together to produce the tragedy.

In addition to having internal systems, subjects themselves can also be placed into larger systems. One larger system of which trade unions are a part is the economy in general. How do trade unions

affect other parts of the economy? What role do they play in the economy? Another system might be the political system. What influence do trade unions have as a political force? The larger system of which tragedy is a part might be drama, or it might be entertainment in general. To put the subject of tragedy into a larger context, you could examine the role of tragic plays in Greek, Elizabethan, or contemporary drama, or you could look at tragic drama as it relates to other forms of entertainment.

Writing Practice 11: *Viewpoint–What Are Its Relationships?*

Select one of the subjects on the next page or use one of your own choice. (You may want to continue with a subject from a previous Writing Practice.) Then use the *Questions to Ask Yourself* that follow the list of subjects and write your answers on a sheet of paper. Finally, write two paragraphs about your subject, one describing how the parts of the subject work together and another explaining how your subject relates to a larger background.

1. Poetry	5. Conservation
2. Your high school	6. Rock music
3. Television	7. Public transportation
4. A particular fad	8. The U.S. space program

Questions to Ask Yourself

1. What are the different parts of the subject?

2. What are the most significant parts of the subject?

3. How do the parts of the subject work together to accomplish its purpose?

4. How does the subject fit into a larger system or systems?

5. How do these other systems work with the subject?

Changing Viewpoints to Analyze Problems

Often you know that all is not right with some process or some thing but cannot state concisely and exactly what the problem is; therefore, you cannot recommend solutions. Consider, for example, the following situations:

An employee at a fast-food restaurant knows that the operation is not as efficient as it might be and would like to suggest ways to increase efficiency.

A group of students complains about the intramural sports program in their school. The principal challenges them to prepare a report analyzing the problem in detail and recommending solutions.

A student is dissatisfied with one of her research papers and wants to find ways to improve it.

Another student wants to "turn over a new leaf"—to understand what has been wrong with his study and work habits in the past and to make improvements for the future.

For situations such as the preceding ones, the "viewpoints" technique can be of great help both to generate ideas and to organize them. Using the "viewpoints" technique requires three blank sheets of paper to start with.

At the top of the first sheet of paper, write the question that will help you explore your subject from the first of the three viewpoints: *What is it?* Then record ideas about the identity and features of your subject. What is the definition of your subject? What does it mean to you and to others you know? What is the dictionary definition of your subject? If appropriate, what are its physical characteristics, such as colors, dimensions, sounds, smells, tastes, textures, temperature, dampness, or dryness? How do these features differ from those of other similar subjects?

At the top of the second sheet of paper, write the question that will help you discover ideas about your subject from the third viewpoint: *What are its relationships?* (For this assignment consider the second viewpoint—*How does it change or vary?*—last.) What are the major parts of your subject? How do these parts work together? (Try drawing a diagram.) Are human actions involved? If so, what are they? Machines? Natural forces, such as winds or tides? Speeds: slow or fast? Nature of movement: jerky or smooth? Other questions about operation?

On the second sheet, also, record ideas about how your subject fits into or relates to a larger system. For example, the recreational program of a community is one system within the whole system of the community, which also includes systems such as police and fire departments, schools, and health care. The can opener in your kitchen is a system within the system of food preparation in your home. The Supreme Court of the United States is a system within the American system of justice.

Does your subject fit into its larger system well or poorly? Why? How could the relationship be changed? Different chain of command? Better communication? Should the subject be removed from its present system and be placed within another? What are other questions regarding the larger system of your subject?

It may take you several days, or even weeks, to gain all of the ideas possible about your subjects. You may want to do research, conduct interviews, or visit some place for a close inspection. However, before you proceed to the remaining viewpoint, complete your research.

When you have completed your research, consider the possible changes that will result in an improvement. At the top of a third sheet of paper, write the question that will help you to discover ideas for changes: *How does it change or vary?* On the basis of ideas and data that you have gathered, what changes would you recommend for improvement? The recommendations that you make must be possible to carry out and must not change the identity of your subject. For example, if you are suggesting improvements in your school's extra-curricular programs, you should not make recommendations that would cost more money than is available.

Purpose and Audience

Two important considerations in writing are *purpose* and *audience*. Your purpose—the reason you are writing—determines what requirements your writing will have to fulfill. Are you writing primarily to entertain, to persuade, to inform, to explain, or to describe? The answer to this question will determine many of the choices you make as you write. For example, if you were writing a school newspaper article about your drama class, and your purpose were to entertain, you might give an account of a play rehearsal in which everything went wrong, using informal language and highlighting the humorous aspects of the incident. However, if your purpose were to explain how hard it is to put on a play, you might describe the same rehearsal in a different way, using more formal language and focusing on all the hard work involved. Clarify your purpose before you begin your first draft.

Just as a knowledge of your purpose guides many of the decisions you make as you write, so too does an understanding of your audience. Who will your readers be? To see how audience affects your writing, imagine that you have just seen an excellent action-adventure film and want to convince others to see it. If your audience were your ten-year-old brother, you would probably emphasize the larger plot elements of the movie and focus on excitement and action. You would keep your vocabulary concrete and your sentences short and simple. However, if your audience were your parents, you would be able to address more complex issues, such as quality of the script and the acting. Your vocabulary would include more abstract words, and you would use more complex sentences. Finally, if you were talking to a film buff, you would try to point out the film's special features (fine cinematography, taut direction). You would use more technical terms and make comparisons to other films acknowledged as masterpieces. As you can see, you must adjust your information, and your way of conveying it, to suit your audience.

Even during the prewriting stage, it is not too early to ask yourself the following questions about your intended audience.

1. Is my audience simply myself? Am I writing for my own pleasure and satisfaction, or to discover something? Can I let the ideas flow without worrying about logic or the conventions of standard spelling and punctuation?

2. Is my audience my teacher? How can I gain his or her interest in this subject? How much background information do I need to supply, and how much can I assume he or she already has? What level of vocabulary is appropriate?

3.   Is my audience a group of my peers? What are their interests, and how can I tie in my topic with their interests? What terms do I need to explain, if any? How informal should my language be?

4.   Is my audience a large group of people I don't even know? If so, are they a general readership with varied backgrounds and interests, or are they a specialized readership, sharing similar tastes, interests, and knowledge? How much background in this subject can I expect them to have? Is my content or vocabulary too specialized for a wide reading public, or not precise enough for a knowledgeable readership?

When you know the answers to these questions, shape your writing to your chosen audience. Use appropriate vocabulary, and select formal or informal language, as the situation calls for. As you think about your readers, put yourself in their place. Are you losing them by failing to supply background information? Do you need to prove your credibility by presenting facts, statistics, and quotations? Is your vocabulary at the proper level for your intended audience? Is your tone appropriately formal or informal?

Writing Practice 12: *Purpose and Audience*

Write a short piece about a favorite (or most-hated) entertainment figure. You may also use a figure from history or literature if you wish. Your purpose is to convince your readers that your admiration (or hatred) of the figure is justified.

First, make a cluster of the admirable (or despicable) qualities of the figure you have chosen. Next, determine who your audience will be. At the top of a piece of paper, write a sentence describing your audience. Then write the answers to the following questions.

1.   What are my audience's interests?

2.   How can I appeal to those interests?

3.   What level of formality should I use, and why?

4.   What background information might I need to explain?

Finally, write a draft. Refer to your prewriting cluster as you write, and keep your audience and purpose in mind.

When you have finished, exchange drafts with a partner. Try to guess each other's intended audience. Tell each other which parts of the writing give clues about the audience and which parts would be most convincing to them. Save your work.

Postwriting: Revising

Often, changes will improve a thing, an idea, or a piece of writing. For example, you might want to think about changing a common bathtub to make it more practical, comfortable, and useful. As a writer you want to revise your essays, stories, and poems to bring them to their best form. When you change anything, there are only four possible actions you can perform:

1.   You can *add* something.

       You might add a padded headrest to the bathtub to make it more comfortable.

       You might add specific details to make your writing more lively.

2.   You can *delete* something (take it away).

       You remove the shower curtain around your bathtub because you never use the shower and the curtain gets in the way.

       A sentence in your essay is irrelevant. You cross it out.

3.   You can *substitute* one thing for another.

       You substitute a rubber plug in your bathtub for the mechanical one that did not work very well.

       For the irrelevant sentence in your essay, you substitute one that relates directly to your topic.

4.   You can *rearrange* parts.

       You put the water controls of your bathtub on the side, where you can reach them when you are lying down.

       You rearrange the paragraphs in your essay so that your discussion is more logical.

Writing Practice 13: *Revising*

Think about your own writing process. How might you improve your ability to write by making additions, deletions, substitutions, and rearrangements? You can apply these questions to *places, equipment, feelings, planning, getting started, revising, purposes,* and *"props."* Jot down your ideas on a sheet of paper under the headings *Add, Delete, Substitute,* and *Rearrange.* Then, considering your partner's comments, revise your draft from Writing Practice 12. Save your work.

Postwriting: Proofreading

The term *proofreading* generally means "correcting a manuscript before submitting it to another reader."

The process of proofreading is simple, but it requires concentration. When you proofread a composition, you examine each line carefully for errors in grammar, spelling, punctuation, and style. Many proofreaders recommend using a ruler to scan a work from the bottom to the top of the page and from right to left. This backward manner of reading forces you to examine each word separately, making it easier to catch mistakes.

Proofreaders use a set of symbols to make corrections. The list on page 30 shows commonly used proofreading symbols and their meanings. You can learn to use them in your own work to save time during the proofreading process.

Since proofreading is the final stage in the writing process, it is your last chance to make improvements in your manuscript. The Checklist for Proofreading on page 31, which reviews features of Edited Standard English (ESE), will help you make full use of the proofreading process. Each time you complete a writing assignment that should conform to ESE, check your writing carefully against each item on the checklist. Make corrections on your final copy or draft only if you can do so neatly; if the corrections are messy or make your paper difficult to follow, copy your paper over, including your corrections.

For more information on Edited Standard English (ESE), see page 611.

The section For Extra Help that follows the Checklist for Proof-reading tells you where features of Edited Standard English are explained in this textbook.

Writing Practice 14: *Proofreading*

Use the Checklist for Proofreading to proofread the piece you wrote for Writing Practice 12. (Your teacher may want to check your revision before you begin the proofreading process.) Using the proofreading symbols shown below, make any necessary corrections in your manuscript. If necessary, rewrite your paper, incorporating the changes you have marked.

Symbols for Proofreading

Symbol	Meaning	Example
Cap ≡	Capitalize	*Cap* everglades
lc /	Lowercase letters	*lc* a National Park
¶	New paragraph	¶ The Everglades covers an area of about 5,000 square miles.
no ¶	No new paragraph	*no* ¶ Once the home of the Seminole Indians, the Everglades today is a haven for such endangered species as the crocodile and the egret.
∧	Insert letter, word, or phrase; called a *caret;* also used to indicate where a change is to be made	The survival of the Everglades depends on a constant supply of fresh water. The large amount of construction in the Miami area may have endangered this supply.
stet	Leave as is (from the Latin phrase meaning "let it stand"); used to indicate that a marked change is not to be made	Ramps built over the marshy areas enable visitors to come close to the wildlife and unusual vegetation which fill the area. *stet*
∩	Transpose	As it blows across the sawgrass, the wind makes a low sound moaning.
⌒	Delete space	Signs throughout the park remind visitors that the park belongs to the wildlife, and that it is the humans who are the visitors.
#	Insert space	A delicate balance must be preserved for wildlife to survive.

Checklist for Proofreading

1. Sentence structure is accurate. There are no fragments or run-on sentences.

2. Participial phrases, prepositional phrases, and dependent clauses are clearly attached to the words they modify, to avoid misunderstanding.

3. Verb tenses are correct, and verbs agree with their subjects.

4. Pronouns are the correct subject or object forms and agree with their antecedents. Singular pronouns such as *either, each, anybody, everybody,* or *nobody* are used with singular verbs.

5. The writer avoids unnecessary shifts in pronouns, such as *I* to *you,* or *they* to *you.*

6. Capitalization, punctuation, and spelling are correct.

7. Slang and other words or phrases not a part of Edited Standard English are used only when appropriate.

For Extra Help

Sentence Structure	Chapter 19
Subject-Verb Agreement	Chapter 13
Pronoun Reference	Chapter 12
Pronoun Form	Chapter 12
Indefinite Pronoun Agreement	Chapter 12
Pronoun-Antecedent Agreement	Chapter 12
Irregular Verbs	Chapter 13
Confusing Verbs	Chapter 13
Noun Plurals and Possessives	Chapter 11
Misplaced and Dangling Modifiers	Chapter 20
Capitalization	Chapter 24
Spelling	Chapter 25
Punctuation	Chapter 23
Contractions	Chapter 23
Words That Sound the Same	Chapter 25
Punctuating Dialogue	Chapter 23
Using Edited Standard English	Chapter 25

Writing Assignment I: *Discovering Ideas and Writing*

Write an essay explaining your own writing process.

A. Prewriting

One important decision that you must make when gathering information for writing is which discovery technique to use. Brainstorming and clustering are most useful, for example, when you are just beginning to explore a subject and have no specific ideas about how to investigate it. The six basic questions are helpful when you want a formula for gathering basic, specific information about an event. The Pentad helps you to investigate many subjects in greater depth and to organize the information you find. And the viewpoints technique is useful when you must analyze a problem and recommend solutions.

To gather material for your essay, use any or all of the discovery techniques presented in this chapter. You may also want to use material from Writing Practices 2, 3, and 13.

B. Writing

You can organize your essay in any way that you choose, but if you can discover no other way, you might want to use the following informal outline.

Introduction: Your attitude toward writing essays

A description of what you do when you write

Planning
Writing
Revising

The influence of your background and personality on your writing

The place or places where you write

Description of them
Their effect on your writing
Your best times for writing
Your favorite writing equipment
Props (such as snacks or music)

C. Postwriting

Use the information on Revising on page 28 to revise your essay. Then share your essay with other members of your class. Discuss any new ideas you get from reading one another's essays.

Sentence Combining:
Using Connectors

Creative ideas alone do not make for good writing; the combination and arrangement of the ideas in sentences, and of sentences in paragraphs, are equally important. Partly through arranging and combining sentences, you give your writing the variety and fluency that appeal to readers. In these lessons you will learn several ways to combine sentences for variety and fluency.

Using Connectors to Join Sentences

For more information on coordinating conjunctions and using conjunctions to join sentences, see pages 432 and 435-438.

You can use certain kinds of words, called *connectors*, to join sentences of equal importance. This process is called *coordination*.

Study the following list of connectors. Each connector signals a certain type of relationship between ideas.

Connector	Relationship
and	similarity
but	opposition or contrast
yet	opposition or contrast
or	choice
nor	negation
so	cause and effect
for	an explanation

In each of the following sentence sets, the word in parentheses indicates which connector is to be used to join the sentences. Notice that commas precede the joined sentences.

Sentences: Michael ordered the concert tickets.
Jason picked them up. *(and)*

Joined: Michael ordered the concert tickets, *and* Jason picked them up.

33

Sentences: Luis received a scholarship to nursing school.
Anna's request was denied. *(but)*

Joined: Luis received a scholarship to nursing school, *but* Anna's request was denied.

Notice that joining sentences with the negative word *nor* requires a change in word order and the deletion of the word *not* in one of the sentences.

Sentences: We did not feel comfortable sitting in the elegantly furnished room.
We could not decide how to eat the delicate cucumber sandwiches. *(nor)*

Joined: We did not feel comfortable sitting in the elegantly furnished room, *nor* could we decide how to eat the delicate cucumber sandwiches.

Exercise 1: Using Connectors to Join Sentences

After studying the examples, combine the following sentence sets. In the first five sets the connectors to be used are given in parentheses. For the last five, choose the connectors you think work best.

Examples

a. Michael wants to attend one of the community colleges next year.
First he must explore the programs each offers. *(but)*
Michael wants to attend one of the community colleges next year, but first he must explore the programs each offers.

b. The recruits did not have the time to write long letters home.
They did not have the energy to do much more than fall exhausted into bed. *(nor)*
The recruits did not have the time to write long letters home, nor did they have the energy to do much more than fall exhausted into bed.

1. Should we harvest the grapes now?
Should we take a chance on fair weather next week? *(or)*

2. The Democratic party has traditionally appealed to organized labor.
The Republican party has traditionally appealed to the interests of big business. *(and)*

3. The audience anticipated a rousing musical.
   The acoustics in the theater were poor. (*but*)

4. The striking workers voted to accept the proposed contract.
   It was in their best interests. (*for*)

5. We wanted to see the movie before it closed.
   We were reluctant to drive on the icy roads. (*yet*)

6. The doctors did not prescribe special drugs.
   They did not offer any other medical treatment.

7. Lisa was not satisfied with her performance.
   She knew she could have done much better.

8. Using an electric saw requires caution.
   Serious injuries can easily occur.

9. Elizabeth did not want to marry Mr. Collins.
   She did not want to marry Mr. Darcy.

10. Long before kickoff a large crowd filled the stadium.
    We knew our chances of getting last-minute tickets were remote.

Writing Practice: *Connectors to Join Sentences*

Choose one paragraph from the personal essay you wrote for Chapter 1. Using the techniques you have just learned, revise the sentences in your paragraph. Use various connectors to join your shorter sentences. Strive for a balance of short sentences and long ones.

2 Personal Writing

Personal Writing

The purpose of *personal writing* is to re-create experiences, ideas, and impressions that are valuable to you.

One important characteristic of personal writing is its natural style. Personal writing is not stiff and formal; instead, it uses the language of daily speech. Good personal writing is filled with specific details and vivid descriptions that re-create experiences for readers. In general, personal writing is lively and colorful.

In this chapter you will read about two types of personal writing: the *Writer's Notebook* and the *personal essay*. You will learn how to use the skills of personal writing to improve your powers of observation, descriptive abilities, and natural writing style.

Model: Personal Writing

The following passage by the Welsh poet Dylan Thomas comes from an essay titled "Reminiscences of Childhood." As you read, listen to the natural, conversational language and notice the specific details.

Never was there such a town as ours, I thought, as we fought on the sandhills with rough boys or dared each other to climb up the scaffolding of half-built houses soon to be called Laburnum Beaches. Never was there such a town, I thought, for the smell of fish and chips on Saturday evenings; for the Saturday afternoon cinema matinees where we shouted and hissed our threepences away; for the crowds in the streets with leeks in their hats on international nights; for the park, the inexhaustible and mysterious, busy red-Indian hiding park where the hunchback sat alone and the groves were blue with sailors. The memories of childhood have no order, and so I remember that never was there such a dame school as ours, so firm and kind and smelling of galoshes, with the sweet arid fumbled music of the piano lessons drifting down from upstairs to the lonely schoolroom, where only the sometimes tearful wicked sat over undone sums, or to repent a little crime—the pulling of a girl's hair during geography, the sly shin kick under the table during English literature. Behind the school was a narrow lane where only the oldest

36

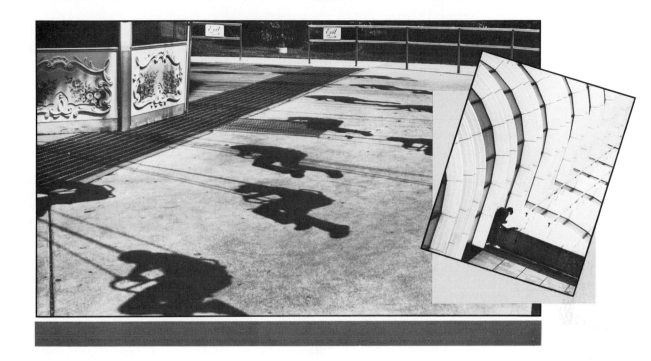

and boldest threw pebbles at windows, scuffled and boasted, fibbed
about their relations—

"My father's got a chauffeur."

"What's he want a chauffeur for? He hasn't got a car."

"My father's the richest man in the town."

"My father's the richest man in Wales."

"My father owns the world."

And swapped gob-stoppers for slings, old knives for marbles,
kite strings for foreign stamps.[1]

Think and Discuss

1. In the excerpt from "Reminiscences of Childhood," Dylan
   Thomas recounts specific childhood activities and the sights and
   sounds he associates with them. For example, he recalls the
   smell of fish and chips and the shouting and hissing in the

---

[1]From "Reminiscences of Childhood" from *Quite Early One Morning* by Dylan Thomas. Copyright
1945 by New Directions Publishing Corporation. Published by J.M. Dent & Sons, England.
Reprinted by permission of New Directions and David Higham Associates Limited.

movie theater on Saturday afternoon. What other specific activities does he recall? What sensory details—details of sight, sound, taste, smell, and texture—does he use?

2. Dylan Thomas combines natural language with poetic observations to make his descriptions interesting. For example, there is a casual tone in the opening sentence, "Never was there such a town as ours." What other examples show the use of natural, or conversational, language?

Writing Practice 1: *Personal Writing*

Select a place from your own childhood, such as your town or school; the park where you used to play; the beach, woods, or fields; or the streets of your city. Write your memories of this place.

Prewriting: Dylan Thomas writes that "The memories of childhood have no order, . . ." Begin thinking about a specific place from your childhood. You will note that bits of remembered scenes and experiences come to you at random. One way to retain all of these experiences is to record them on a list.

Find a place where you can sit quietly, and then let your mind wander over your experiences. If, for example, you have chosen to write about a street of the city where you grew up, visualize yourself doing what you used to do with your friends: playing catch, skipping rope, or just sitting on the steps and talking with your best friend. At the top of your list, write the specific activity as it comes to you.

Sitting on the Steps

Next, ask yourself what sensory details you associate with that activity. Where were the steps? What were you looking at? Add such details to your list.

Sitting on the Steps

Cracks in the concrete, grass growing through
Looking at the store windows across the street
Green and white awnings
Paint chipping off the lettering; Estelle's Beauty Salon

Then ask what sounds you associate with those steps, perhaps conversations with friends or just the sounds of the city:

Car horns, sometimes yelling drivers, "Get out of the streets, kids"

All the kids laughing and yelling back

Slap, slap, slap of the jumping-rope game down the block
Kids' mothers calling them, "Judy! Paul! Dinner!"
"I heard Lisa has a crush on you." "Does not." "You wanna
bet?"

Then try to recall the various smells, both pleasant and unpleasant, that you associate with the place you write about:

Smells of dinners cooking, coming out of the windows and
down to the street
The steamy, spicy smell when the sausage vendor came by with
his cart
The smell of rain on cement
The smell of the garbage trucks going by

The senses of taste and smell are closely related. Write the tastes you recall from this childhood experience:

After playing all afternoon, ice water so cold it hurt my teeth
Walking home past the fruit stand, buying a warm, yellow
banana
Sitting on the steps, eating roasted pumpkin seeds at Halloween

Finally, the sense of touch and texture is important. Try to recall how vivid even everyday things felt to you as a child, and add those details to your list:

Playing jacks, sweeping the jacks up off the rough cement
The spongy, hard feel of a softball and the tingle as it hits my
hands
Stair railings made of metal, ice-cold in the winter
Edges of library books poking me in the stomach as I walk home

As you think of specific sensory details, other memories will come to you. Include on your list all the associations you can recall.

Writing: From your list, choose the parts that most completely describe the experience you've decided to write about. Describe the memories in simple words and natural, conversational language, using *I, my,* and *we.* Include details of smells, tastes, and textures to bring the experience alive for your readers.

Keeping a Writer's Notebook

A *Writer's Notebook* **is a record of the writer's experiences, thoughts, and observations.**

Many writers keep notebooks as sources of ideas for future writing, using them as storehouses of personal reactions and impressions of people they encounter, places, new experiences, and ideas.

The notebook you will keep in this chapter is a public notebook, to be shared with your classmates and teacher. (If you wish to write about private thoughts and feelings, do so in a private notebook you keep at home.) Your teacher will tell you how to keep your Writer's Notebook, perhaps in a loose-leaf or spiral binder or in a special section of your English notebook.

Model: Writer's Notebook

In 1973 John Coleman took a leave of absence from his job as president of Haverford College to work as a manual laborer because he was disturbed by the lack of understanding between the academic community and the other working communities in America. The following entry is from a notebook that he kept about that experience, published under the title *Blue–Collar Journal*. As you read, notice how John Coleman uses specific, descriptive details to make vivid observations about what he sees, thinks, and feels.

Monday, April 9

A dump is not a pretty place. To a novice there is a fascinating rhythm about it as the steady streams of trucks flow in and out and the two heavy tractors dart back and forth leveling out the new loads of trash. But to find beauty it is necessary to look up at the blue sky above and the flocks of seagulls gliding back and forth in effortless flight over their food.

At this time of year, a garbage man's job doesn't smell nearly as much as I had expected. A few backyard cans made me turn up my nose, but most smells were more varied than strong. The dump is different. The noxious odors hang heavy in the air, rich and full. Nor is it possible to turn one's head away, as I could with the more objectionable cans. There was nowhere to find lighter air once we got into those vast acres of waste. The only escape was in dropping the load and getting out of there fast.

That relief is impossible for the attendant who patrols the dump and shows each of the many trucks where to deposit its load. His red plastic cape both identifies him as the traffic man and keeps the seagull droppings off his clothes. If I saw this forty-five-year-old white man on the street, with his clean-cut face and well-greased hair, I would never connect him with this job. I wonder how he got there and what pride he is allowed from his work. Someone has tried to elevate the task by giving it a fancy name: he is called a landfill inspector. That's about like calling those of us on the truck environmental control agents.

The dump is so new a world to me that today I just stood gaping while our load dropped to the ground. The volume and variety of what is thrown away are enough to leave me both frightened and sad. My picture of affluence in America is no longer going to be one of all those young people eating in the Oyster House or even of those elegant homes in the Main Line where I live. It will be a livelier, uglier scene: an unending line of refuse trucks spilling their loads of half-used goods on the ground and rushing back to get more before dark . . .

Today I brought back a single souvenir from the mountains of refuse on the dump. I spotted a pile of bold blue-and-white cards with words so fitting for the job I am doing—and the one I'll go back to soon—that I had to take one along. It says: "IF WE DID SOMETHING WRONG, TELL US. IF WE DID SOMETHING RIGHT, TELL US."

I wonder who tells the landfill inspector when he does something right . . .[1]

Think and Discuss

1. What sensory details does the writer use to convey his impressions of the garbage dump? For example, he talks about feeling the rhythms of the trucks that "flow in and out." What visual details does he use? What details of smell?

2. John Coleman's notebook entry contains many comments on the garbage dump itself. Why do his observations there leave him "frightened and sad"?

3. What other direct observations does he make?

4. Though he writes in the first person, Coleman gives almost no description of himself in this excerpt. Yet his personality is revealed by what he observes. How would you describe John Coleman? Which parts of his writing offer clues?

5. Basing your opinion on this excerpt, do you think *Blue-Collar Journal* will improve understanding between the academic community and other working communities? Why or why not?

---

[1]Excerpt from *Blue-Collar Journal: A College President's Sabbatical* by John R. Coleman. Copyright © 1974 by John R. Coleman (J. B. Lippincott Co.). Reprinted by permission of Harper & Row, Publisher, Inc. and Collier Associates.

Writing Practice 2: *Writer's Notebook Entry*

The photographs above show unusual, or exotic, settings. Select one of the photographs and examine it closely; then write a notebook entry about it. First, imagine that you have just returned from a walk through the scene or from an exploration of the scene. Then, describe in your entry what you saw, heard, smelled, and touched while visiting the scene. Include your reactions to being there by describing your impressions of the place.

Using Specific Details

Specific details **re-create sights, sounds, tastes, smells, and textures for the reader.**

For information on adjectives, see pages 398-411.

A s you develop your skills as an observer, you also need to develop your ability to "translate" your observations into precise language. Using specific details is one important way to give the reader an accurate, vivid description of your observations.

Model: Specific Details

The following excerpt is from "The Gastronomical Me," by M. F. K. Fisher. The year she recalls is 1912. As you read, pay attention to the visual and other sensory details that Fisher uses to describe the scene.

The first thing I remember tasting and then wanting to taste again is the graylsh-pink fuzz my grandmother skimmed from a spitting kettle of strawberry jam. I suppose I was about four.

Women in those days made much more of a ritual of their household duties than they do now. Sometimes it was indistinguishable from a dogged if unconscious martyrdom. There were times for This, and other equally definite times for That. There was one set week a year for "the sewing woman." Of course, there was Spring Cleaning, and there were other periods, almost like festivals in that they disrupted normal life, which were observed no matter what the weather, finances, or health of the family.

Many of them seem odd or even foolish to me now, but probably the whole staid rhythm lent a kind of rich excitement to the house-bound flight of time.

With us, for the first years of my life, there was a series, every summer, of short but violently active cannings. Crates and baskets and lug-boxes of fruits in their prime and at their cheapest would lie waiting with opulent fragrance on the screened porch, and a whole battery of enameled pots and ladles and wide-mouthed funnels would appear from some dark cupboard.

All I knew then about the actual procedure was that we had delightful picnic meals while Grandmother and Mother and the cook worked with a kind of drugged concentration in our big dark kitchen, and were tired and cross and at the same time oddly triumphant in their race against summer heat and the processes of rot.

Now I know that strawberries came first, mostly for jam. Sour red cherries for pies and darker ones for preserves were a little later, and then came the apricots. They were for jam if they were very ripe, and the solid ones were simply ''put up.'' That, in my grandmother's language, meant cooking with little sugar, to eat for breakfast or dessert in the winter which she still thought of in terms of northern Iowa.

She was a grim woman, as if she had decided long ago that she could thus most safely get to Heaven. I have a feeling that my father might have liked to help with the cannings, just as I longed to. But Grandmother, with that almost joyfully stern bowing to duty typical of religious women, made it clear that helping in the kitchen was a bitter heavy business forbidden certainly to men, and generally to children. Sometimes she let me pull stems off the cherries, and one year when I was almost nine I stirred the pots a little now and then, silent and making myself as small as possible.

But there was no nonsense anyway, no foolish chitchat. Mother was still young and often gay, and the cook too . . . and with Grandmother directing operations they all worked in a harried muteness . . . stir, sweat, hurry. It was a pity. Such a beautifully smelly task should be fun, I thought.

In spite of any Late Victorian asceticism, though, the hot kitchen sent out tantalizing clouds, and the fruit on the porch lay rotting in its crates, or readied for the pots and the wooden spoons, in fair glowing piles upon the juice-stained tables. Grandmother, saving always, stood like a sacrificial priestess in the steam, ''skimming'' into a thick white saucer, and I, sometimes permitted and more often not, put my finger into the cooling froth and licked it. Warm and sweet and odorous. I loved it, then.[1]

Think and Discuss

1. The specific sensory details that M. F. K. Fisher uses in the preceding passage help make the scene, over half a century old, come to life. She describes the "grayish-pink fuzz" from the "spitting kettle of strawberry jam" and the "opulent fragrance" of fruit waiting in "crates and baskets and lug-boxes . . . on the screened porch." What other specific details does Fisher use to describe the kitchen, the women in it, and the work of canning?

2. Which of the senses does Fisher emphasize most in the passage?

Writing Assignment I: *Using Specific Details*

Write a notebook entry about an experience you have had while working with other people. Perhaps, like John Coleman, you might write about an experience at work and how you felt as a worker. Perhaps you will write about working at a task with a friend or relative.

---

[1]From ''The Gastronomical Me'' in *The Art of Eating* by M. F. K. Fisher. Reprinted with permission of Macmillan Publishing Co., Inc. and Lescher & Lescher, Ltd.

A. Prewriting

Use the clustering technique to jot down at random everything you remember about the experience you've chosen. Include how you felt about what you were doing. Using specific sensory details, describe where you were and the people you encountered.

B. Writing

Organize your details chronologically. Add your explanations where they seem best to fit. Use a natural tone in your writing, as if you were relating your experiences to a friend.

C. Postwriting

Use the following guidelines to revise your notebook entry.

1.   The entry has a natural, conversational style.

2.   The entry is interesting to the general reader.

3.   People, places, and events that might be unfamiliar to the general reader are explained.

4.   The writer makes exact observations about the people, places, and experiences he or she describes.

5.   The entry uses specific sensory details in its descriptions.
When you have completed a satisfactory revision, you are ready for the final stage, which is proofreading.

Further Uses for Your Writer's Notebook

Each of the remaining chapters of this textbook contains suggestions for further Writer's Notebook entries. In addition, you may want to use your notebook as a kind of practice field for other types of writing. Many writers who keep notebooks use them to jot down ideas for compositions, quick impressions of people or places they will write about in greater detail later, beginning lines or images of poems, opinions about current events, and so on. You may also find it valuable to use your Writer's Notebook to keep a daily account of a subject or activity over a period of time.

Writing the Personal Essay

The *personal essay* is the most structured type of personal writing. It sets forth comments on one theme, sometimes relating to a series of connected events in the life of the writer.

Like an entry in a Writer's Notebook, the personal essay records experiences, thoughts, and impressions in a natural writing style. Unlike an entry in a Writer's Notebook, the personal essay always concentrates on and develops one specific theme. Many of the same skills you learned in notebook writing, however, also apply to writing a personal essay. You will need to observe accurately and to convey your observations using specific details. Your Writer's Notebook can be a source of ideas to develop in personal essays.

Structuring the Personal Essay

The term *personal essay* applies to a wide range of personal writing: essays that grow out of ideas, essays that are inspired by specific experiences, essays that are written in response to public events or private emotions. You will find that most personal essays are structured around five elements: the *central theme*; the *descriptive details* (describing setting, action, characters, and ideas); the *narrative element* (the action or actions illustrating the theme); the *narrator and characters*; and the *commentary*.

Central Theme

The *central theme* is the main idea that the writer develops in the personal essay.

The theme that the writer chooses to focus on in a personal essay always relates personally to the writer's life. For example, imagine that you were assigned to write a personal essay on the subject of books. Your central theme could relate to your own reading habits, to the role that books played in your childhood or play in your present life, or to some other direct personal experience with books. It would not be appropriate to write about the reading habits of Americans in general or about how books get on the best-seller list. The theme of the personal essay relates to you, the writer, and to your own direct experiences.

Model: *Personal Essay–Central Theme*

The following excerpt is the first paragraph of a personal essay written in 1926 by British novelist E. M. Forster. Its title, "My Wood," gives you a general idea that the essay will deal with a piece of property that the writer owns. E. M. Forster uses the introductory paragraph to set forth the specific theme of the essay.

A few years ago I wrote a book which dealt in part with the difficulties of the English in India. Feeling that they would have had no difficulties in India themselves, the Americans read the book freely. The more they read it the better it made them feel, and a cheque to the author was the result. I bought a wood with the cheque. It is not a large wood—it contains scarcely any trees, and it is intersected, blast it, by a public footpath. Still, it is the first property that I have owned, so it is right that other people should participate in my shame, and should ask themselves, in accents that will vary in horror, this very important question: What is the effect of property upon the character? Don't let's touch economics; the effect of private ownership upon the community as a whole is another question—a more important question, perhaps, but another one. Let's keep to psychology. If you own things, what's their effect on you? What's the effect on me of my wood?[1]

Most writers introduce the theme of the essay in the introductory paragraph so that the reader knows from the outset what to expect. In E. M. Forster's essay the theme is stated in one sentence: "What's the effect on me of my wood?" You may formulate the theme of a personal essay as a question or as a statement, but in general you should include it as one clear sentence somewhere in the first paragraph.

Notice that Forster himself avoids the general application of the theme of his essay when he writes, "Don't let's touch economics; the effect of private ownership upon the community as a whole is another question . . . ." He is focusing his essay specifically on his own reactions to ownership. He uses contractions—"Let's keep to psychology"—and he uses simple, conversational language.

Writing Practice 3: *Central Theme*

Write two sentences that introduce the themes of two personal essays you would like to write. You may formulate each theme either as a question or as a direct statement. The topic for each sentence should

---

[1]Excerpted from "My Wood" in *Abinger Harvest*; copyright 1936, 1964 by E. M. Forster. Reprinted by permission of Harcourt Brace Jovanovich, Inc. and Edward Arnold Ltd.

be different. Do not write general themes about opinions on current events. Write about your personal experience. Save your work.

You may use the following suggestions to help find essay themes, or you may use your Writer's Notebook entries as a source of helpful ideas.

–The effect that having (or not having) something has had on you
–How a particular habit you have affects your life
–The impact a particular person has made on your life
–An interest you have that sets you apart from others (for example, an unusual hobby, an interest in another culture, etc.)
–Your feelings about a particular place and its effect on you
–The effect an important past event has had on your life
–The effect a choice you have made has had on your life

Descriptive Details

Descriptive details **help make the subject of a personal essay seem real and vivid.**

Specific observations about people, places, ideas, emotions, and objects are all made more precise for the reader through descriptive details.

Using descriptive details in the personal essay is similar to using them in notebook writing and in other types of personal writing. However, you must remember to describe in detail only when the description is integral to the central theme. Your descriptions should never be simply ornamental in the personal essay.

Model: Personal Essay–Descriptive Details

Descriptive details can also be used in personal essays to illustrate the ideas of the writer. Instead of simply stating ideas, the writer uses specific details to make those ideas clear to the reader. In the following passage from "My Wood," notice how E. M. Forster uses details to describe the effect that owning property has on him.

> In the first place, it makes me feel heavy. Property does have this effect. Property produces men of weight, and it was a man of weight who failed to get into the Kingdom of Heaven. He was not wicked, that unfortunate millionaire in the parable, he was only stout; he stuck out in front, not to mention behind, and as he wedged himself this way and that in the crystalline entrance and bruised his well-fed flanks, he saw beneath him a comparatively slim camel passing through the eye of a needle and being woven into the robe of

God. The Gospels all through couple stoutness and slowness. They point out what is perfectly obvious, yet seldom realised: that if you have a lot of things you cannot move about a lot, that furniture requires dusting, dusters require servants, servants require insurance stamps, and the whole tangle of them makes you think twice before you accept an invitation to dinner or go for a bathe in the Jordan.[1]

Think and Discuss

1. E. M. Forster uses a humorous description of the "unfortunate millionaire" getting stuck because of his enormous size as he tries to enter the Kingdom of Heaven. What specific, descriptive words portray this scene? (For example, look at the word *crystalline* and contrast it with the words describing the rich man.)

2. What other details does Forster use to illustrate his idea that property makes him feel heavy?

Writing Practice 4: *Personal Essay–Using Descriptive Details*

Write one paragraph of a personal essay, illustrating observations of a scene, person, event, or idea, by using descriptive details. Use the clustering technique to help you get started. You may use one of the theme statements you wrote for the previous Writing Practice or you may write on another theme of your choice. (Look through your Writer's Notebook for suggestions on subjects that interest you.) Save your work.

The Narrative Element

Personal essays often contain *narrative passages*, passages that relate incidents or experiences in chronological order.

You will often find narrative passages mixed in with descriptive passages or commentary in a personal essay. For example, in the following paragraph from "My Wood," E. M. Forster explains the effect his wood has on him by relating an incident that took place there.

---

[1]Excerpted from "My Wood" in *Abinger Harvest*; copyright 1936, 1964 by E. M. Forster. Reprinted by permission of Harcourt Brace Jovanovich, Inc. and Edward Arnold Ltd.

Model: Personal Essay–The Narrative Element

In the second place, it makes me feel it ought to be larger.

The other day I heard a twig snap in it. I was annoyed at first, for I thought that someone was blackberrying, and depreciating the value of the undergrowth. On coming nearer, I saw it was not a man who had trodden on the twig and snapped it, but a bird, and I felt pleased. My bird. The bird was not equally pleased. Ignoring the relation between us, it took fright as soon as it saw the shape of my face, and flew straight over the boundary hedge into a field, the property of Mrs. Henessy, where it sat down with a loud squawk. It had become Mrs. Henessy's bird. Something seemed grossly amiss here, something that would not have occurred had the wood been larger. I could not afford to buy Mrs. Henessy out, I dared not murder her, and limitations of this sort beset me on every side. Ahab did not want that vineyard—he only needed it to round off his property, preparatory to plotting a new curve—and all the land around my wood has become necessary to me in order to round off the wood. A boundary protects. But—poor little thing—the boundary ought in its turn to be protected. Noises on the edge of it. Children throw stones. A little more, and then a little more, until we reach the sea. Happy Canute! Happier Alexander! And after all, why should even the world be the limit of possession? A rocket containing a Union Jack, will, it is hoped, be shortly fired at the moon. Mars. Sirius. Beyond which . . . But these immensities ended by saddening me. I could not suppose that my wood was the destined nucleus of universal dominion—it is so very small and contains no mineral wealth beyond the blackberries. Nor was I comforted when Mrs. Henessy's bird took alarm for the second time and few clean away from us all, under the belief that it belonged to itself.[1]

Think and Discuss

1. In the preceding paragraph Forster narrates the incident involving the bird to explain what he means about feeling that the wood should be larger. How does this incident help you understand his point? What specifically is he saying about his property and the bird?

2. The story about the bird is woven into Forster's commentary about the age-old desire to conquer. He mentions (King) Canute, who tried to give orders to the ocean, and Alexander (the Great), who tried to conquer the world. How does Forster then use the incident of the bird to tie his thoughts together at the end of the paragraph? What is he implying in the final sentence?

---

[1]Excerpted from "My Wood" in *Abinger Harvest*; copyright 1936, 1964 by E. M. Forster. Reprinted by permission of Harcourt Brace Jovanovich, Inc. and Edward Arnold Ltd.

Writing Practice 5: *Personal Essay—The Narrative Element*

Imagine that you are going to write a personal essay that you will illustrate with a narrative passage: an incident or experience that you will tell in chronological order. You may use one of the theme statements you wrote for Writing Practice 4 or invent a new theme to write about. If, for example, you wrote about a person who had an important influence on your life, you might relate an incident illustrating this person's importance to you. Write a paragraph including the narrative account of the incident or experience you choose. Remember to use chronological order to make your narration clear to the reader. Save your work.

The Narrator and Characters

In fiction the narrator can be the writer or one or more of the characters within the story; in personal essays the narrator is always assumed to be the writer.

In many personal essays the narrator is the central or the only character.

The writer describes other characters in a personal essay only when they figure importantly in the essay as a whole. Unlike notebook writing, which is less structured and may follow the writer's inclination for describing people or places that come to mind, the personal essay must stay focused on its main theme and may introduce characters only when they relate directly to it.

Model: *Personal Essay–Character Development Through Physical Description*

There are many different methods for presenting and describing characters. One method is to tell about the characters chiefly through physical details, a method used by Virginia Woolf's niece Angelica to describe her famous aunt in the following passage.

> She was the most enchanting aunt that anyone is ever likely to have . . . To start with there was her beauty, her rare and special physical beauty which reminded one of the most aristocratic and nervous of racehorses or greyhounds and which fascinated me and possessed me even as a child. Her face with its vulnerable narrow

temples and deeply hooded grey-green eyes shutting at an unexpected moment like the eyes of a bird and then opening to pierce me with a glance of amused intelligence. Above all her sensitive and sardonic mouth with a very pronounced downward curve, expressive often of the most intense amusement. Then her gestures which were somewhat jerky, her long hands waving a still longer cigarette-holder. She would puff the smoke out of the corner of her mouth and chuckle at some secret and intimate joke that we shared between us.[1]

Think and Discuss

1. The preceding passage presents a kind of portrait of Virginia Woolf. The descriptive details, such as her "deeply hooded grey-green eyes shutting at an unexpected moment like the eyes of a bird," give the reader a clear visual impression. What other descriptive details does Angelica Bell use to portray Virginia Woolf?

2. The description of Virginia Woolf piercing her niece with "a glance of amused intelligence" shows a woman who is quick-witted and observant. What other impressions of Virginia Woolf's character does this physical portrait convey?

Model: *Personal Essay–Character Development Through Personality Description*

The following description, also of Virginia Woolf, uses a different method of presenting a character. Here the writer, David Garnett, is talking directly about Woolf's character rather than her physical description.

> There was a strange contradiction in Virginia. She was so beautiful, so tall, so aristocratic and in many ways so fastidious. But she had a sense of humour that would stick at nothing, like Shakespeare's, or Chaucer's. And she had an appetite and a relish for life that one finds most often in market women.
>
> Nothing made her wish to avert her eyes and cross to the other side of the street. Like Rembrandt she could have found the subject for a work of art in a side of beef.
>
> Because of this there were no doors closed to her: she could pluck the secret from the heart of an old dried-up lawyer, a charwoman or a young actor enjoying his first triumph. Whenever Virginia appeared she brought a new treasure trove with her,

[1]From David Garnett, *Great Friends*. Copyright © 1979 by David Garnett. (New York: Atheneum 1980). Reprinted with the permission of Atheneum Publishers and Angelica Garnett.

something that she had heard in the street, been told over the counter, found in an old letter. After she had been to a party she would come round and regale her sister with an account of it, and what she said might have been written by Thackeray if he had been a poet with a completely uninhibited sense of humour. She was vain and sensitive to criticism, but she liked making herself into a ridiculous figure and laughing at herself.

Almost all her stories had one point, one object: to catch the unique living self that makes one human being different from another.

When she went into the street, she saw the same crowds that we all do, hurrying and scurrying along like disordered sheep. But for her the spectacle was, I think, an illusion. She never forgot that each figure was not a unit in a mass, but an individual with a secret. So that even on Oxford Street there was no crowd, and on the Downs the sheep were not a flock: the shepherd or his dog could tell each one apart.[1]

Think and Discuss

1.   In the preceding passage are many specific, descriptive details, but they have primarily to do with Virginia Woolf's character— her personality and attitudes about people and herself—rather than her physical presence. Notice that although Garnett writes about her personality in general, he illustrates his main points about Virginia Woolf with specific examples and details. How does he illustrate what he calls "the strange contradiction" in her personality?

2.   How does he illustrate her "relish for life"?

Writing Practice 6: *Personal Essay—Using Character Development*

Imagine that you are writing a personal essay that focuses on a theme concerning one central character and yourself, the narrator. Write one paragraph about the central character as if the paragraph were from your essay. You may describe the character through a physical portrait that tells something about your character's personality, or you may talk about the personality directly. In either case, use specific details and examples to aid description. Save your work.

---

[1]From David Garnett, *Great Friends*. Copyright © 1979 by David Garnett. (New York: Atheneum 1980). Reprinted with the permission of Atheneum Publishers and A. P. Watt Ltd.

Commentary

The *commentary* a writer makes in a personal essay includes direct comments, as well as reflections and observations about the central theme.

The purpose of commentary is to communicate directly with the reader about the theme of the essay. The commentary has a single focus, just as the essay has a single, central theme. In most personal essays, commentary is interspersed throughout the essay, as in the paragraphs by E. M. Forster.

55

Model: Personal Essay–Commentary

The following paragraph is the conclusion of an essay on working in a hospital by Richard Wright. His commentary about working in the hospital as a black man overseen by whites is also woven into the rest of the piece. The commentary here relates to an incident he has just described in which a fight broke out between two hospital workers, and all the experimental animals were thrown from or escaped from their cages. The workers sorted them out as best they could, but no one reported what had happened. Wright worries about the experiments but decides not to tell anyone.

> I brooded, of course, upon whether I should have gone to the director's office and told him what had happened, but each time I thought of it I remembered that the director had been the man who had ordered the boy to stand over me while I was working and time my movements with a stop watch. He did not regard me as a human being. I did not share his world. I earned thirteen dollars a week and I had to support four people with it, and should I risk that thirteen dollars by acting idealistically? Brand and Cooke would have hated me and would have eventually driven me from the job had I "told" on them. The hospital kept us four Negroes, as though we were close kin to the animals we tended, huddled together down in the underworld corridors of the hospital, separated by a vast psychological distance from the significant processes of the rest of the hospital—just as America had kept us locked in the dark underworld of American life for three hundred years—and we had made our own code of ethics, values, loyalty.[1]

Think and Discuss

1. The preceding passage clearly shows Richard Wright's conflict of feelings about what happened: his sense of responsibility toward his work and his resentment at being treated as a menial. What is Wright's attitude about the director of the hospital?

2. How does he describe his thought process and final decision not to go to the director and report what happened?

Writing Practice 7: *Personal Essay— Commentary*

Select one of the theme sentences you have already written or use a new theme topic. Remember that your theme should relate to a

[1]Excerpt from pp. 58–59 in *American Hunger* by Richard Wright. Copyright 1944 by Richard Wright. Copyright © 1977 by Ellen Wright. Reprinted by permission of Harper & Row, Publishers, Inc.

personal experience. Write at least one paragraph of a personal essay on this theme, paying special attention to the commentary. Your comments should convey your thoughts, feelings, and reactions to the theme of the essay. (As you write, remember to follow chronological order if narrating an incident, to describe important characters, and to use descriptive details.) Save your work.

Model: The Personal Essay

The following personal essay, "The Death of the Moth," was written by Virginia Woolf, British novelist, essayist, and critic. (Descriptions of her appear earlier in this chapter.) As the title indicates, the essay deals with the death of a moth: a drama that the writer observes. As you read, notice how Woolf combines narration, description, and commentary.

Moths that fly by day are not properly to be called moths; they do not excite that pleasant sense of dark autumn nights and ivy-blossom which the commonest yellow-underwing asleep in the shadow of the curtain never fails to rouse in us. They are hybrid creatures, neither gay like butterflies nor sombre like their own species. Nevertheless the present specimen, with his narrow haycolored wings, fringed with a tassel of the same colour, seemed to be content with life. It was a pleasant morning, mid-September, mild, benignant, yet with a keener breath than that of the summer months. The plough was already scoring the field opposite the window, and where the share had been, the earth was pressed flat and gleamed with moisture. Such vigour came rolling in from the fields and down beyond that it was difficult to keep the eyes strictly turned upon the book. The rooks too were keeping one of their annual festivities; soaring round the tree tops until it looked as if a vast net with thousands of black knots in it had been cast up into the air; which, after a few moments, sank slowly down upon the trees until every twig seemed to have a knot at the end of it. Then, suddenly, the net would be thrown into the air again in a wider circle this time, with the utmost clamour and vociferation, as though to be thrown into the air and settle slowly down upon the tree tops were a tremendously exciting experience.

The same energy which inspired the rooks, the ploughmen, the horses, and even, it seemed, the lean bare-backed downs, sent the moth fluttering from side to side of his square of the window-pane. One could not help watching him. One was, indeed, conscious of a queer feeling of pity for him. The possibilities of pleasure seemed that morning so enormous and so various that to have only a moth's part in life, and a day moth's at that, appeared a hard fate, and his zest in enjoying his meagre opportunities to the full, pathetic. He flew

57

vigorously to one corner of his compartment, and, after waiting there a second, flew across to the other. What remained for him but to fly to a third corner and then to a fourth? That was all he could do, in spite of the size of the down, the width of the sky, the far-off smoke of houses, and the romantic voice, now and then, of a steamer out at sea. What he could do he did. Watching him, it seemed as if a fibre, very thin but pure, of the enormous energy of the world had been thrust into his frail and diminutive body. As often as he crossed the pane, I could fancy that a thread of vital light became visible. He was little or nothing but life.

Yet, because he was so small, and so simple a form of the energy that was rolling in at the open window and driving its way through so many narrow and intricate corridors in my own brain and in those of other human beings, there was something marvellous as well as pathetic about him. It was as if someone had taken a tiny bead of pure life, and decking it as lightly as possible with down and feathers, had set it dancing and zigzagging to show us the true nature of life. Thus displayed one could not get over the strangeness of it. One is apt to forget all about life, seeing it humped and bossed and garnished and cumbered so that it has to move with the greatest circumspection and dignity. Again, the thought of all that life might have been had he been born in any other shape caused one to view his simple activities with a kind of pity.

After a time, tired by his dancing apparently, he settled on the window ledge in the sun, and, the queer spectacle being at an end, I forgot about him. Then, looking up, my eye was caught by him. He was trying to resume his dancing, but seemed either so stiff or so awkward that he could only flutter to the bottom of the window-pane; and when he tried to fly across it he failed. Being intent on other matters I watched these futile attempts for a time without thinking, unconsciously waiting for him to resume his flight, as one waits for a machine, that has stopped momentarily, to start again without considering the reason of its failure. After perhaps a seventh attempt he slipped from the wooden ledge and fell, fluttering his wings, on to his back on the window sill. The helplessness of his attitude roused me. It flashed upon me that he was in difficulties; he could no longer raise himself; his legs struggled vainly. But, as I stretched out a pencil, meaning to help him to right himself, it came over me that the failure and awkwardness were the approach of death. I laid the pencil down again.

The legs agitated themselves once more. I looked as if for the enemy against which he struggled. I looked out of doors. What had happened there? Presumably it was midday, and work in the fields had stopped. Stillness and quiet had replaced the previous animation. The birds had taken themselves off to feed in the brooks. The horses stood still. Yet the power was there all the same, massed outside, indifferent, impersonal, not attending to anything in particular. Somehow it was opposed to the little hay-colored moth. It was useless to try to do anything. One could only watch the extraordinary efforts made by those tiny legs against an oncoming doom which

could, had it chosen, have submerged an entire city, not merely a city, but masses of human beings; nothing, I knew, had any chance against death. Nevertheless after a pause of exhaustion the legs fluttered again. It was superb, this last protest, and so frantic that he succeeded at last in righting himself. One's sympathies, of course, were all on the side of life. Also, when there was nobody to care or to know, this gigantic effort on the part of an insignificant little moth, against a power of such magnitude, to retain what no one else valued or desired to keep, moved one strangely. Again, somehow, one saw life, a pure bead. I lifted the pencil again, useless though I knew it to be. But even as I did so, the unmistakable tokens of death showed themselves. The body relaxed, and instantly grew stiff. The struggle was over. The insignificant little creature now knew death. As I looked at the dead moth, this minute wayside triumph of so great a force over so mean an antagonist filled me with wonder. Just as life had been strange a few minutes before, so death was now as strange. The moth, having righted himself, now lay most decently and uncomplainingly composed. O yes, he seemed to say, death is stronger than I am.[1]

Think and Discuss

1. In "The Death of the Moth" Virginia Woolf tells of a personal experience that had meaning for her. In your own words, explain the theme of the essay. (Think, for example, about how this incident causes the writer to reflect on life and death.) Be prepared to discuss specific observations that Woolf makes about the moth's life and death.

2. The narrative element in "The Death of the Moth" is skillfully woven in with the descriptions of the setting and of the moth, and with Woolf's commentary about what is happening. How does Woolf lead into the narrative in the first paragraph? How does she relate the description of the setting in the beginning back to the moth? Go carefully through the essay and observe how Woolf moves from description to narration to commentary, and find examples of these transitions.

3. Woolf begins to use chronological order in the second paragraph to portray the movement of the moth, describing it "fluttering from side to side" at the window-pane. Where else does she use chronological order to make the sequence of action easy to follow?

---

[1]From "The Death of the Moth" in *The Death of the Moth and Other Essays* by Virginia Woolf, copyright 1942 by Harcourt Brace Jovanovich, Inc.; copyright 1970 by Marjorie T. Parsons, Executrix. Reprinted by permission of Harcourt Brace Jovanovich, Inc., the Literary Estate of Virginia Woolf, and the Hogarth Press, Inc.

4. The two characters in "The Death of the Moth" are Virginia Woolf (the narrator) and the moth. The narrator uses a great deal of descriptive detail to portray the moth for the reader. At first she describes it as a "specimen," with "narrow hay-colored wings, fringed with a tassel of the same color" that seems "content with life." Find other specific details that Woolf uses to describe the moth and its movements. What does she feel for the moth? How does she describe her feelings?

5. Woolf uses descriptive details throughout the essay to convey her impressions of setting, the time of day and year, and the sights and sounds of other life around her. Find examples of these details and be prepared to discuss their significance to the theme of the essay.

Writing Assignment II: *Personal Essay*

Write a complete personal essay based either on a theme that you have already used or on a new theme. You may look again at suggestions for theme sentences given in a previous Writing Practice, or consult your Writer's Notebook for ideas.

Notice that Virginia Woolf's essay "The Death of the Moth" works by taking a seemingly insignificant event and using it to

describe and comment on the process of death, and to reflect on life by way of contrast. You may also want to write about an event or experience that happens every day, but that has a larger importance for you. The key to writing a strong personal essay is to select a theme that you have experienced personally and directly. Perhaps you reacted by feeling curiosity and intellectual stimulation, as E. M. Forster did when he was moved to write "My Wood." Perhaps you felt intense empathy with another life, as Virginia Woolf did in "The Death of the Moth." Remember that you do not have to write on an unusual subject to have a good essay. Both Forster and Woolf write about fairly commonplace subjects—owning property and watching an insect die—but they relate these experiences to their own ideas and feelings and then draw conclusions about the experiences.

Review the five elements of the personal essay before you begin. Then follow these steps for prewriting, writing, and postwriting.

A. Prewriting

Gather and read your work from Writing Practices 4–7. Decide on a central theme; write a sentence or a question that states your theme clearly. Then brainstorm a list of phrases that will remind you of any descriptive details, narratives, character sketches, and commentary that can help illustrate your theme. Read the list over when you've finished it, and underline the items that seem most pertinent to the central theme you've chosen.

B. Writing

Write the first draft of your personal essay. Begin by stating your central theme in the essay's introductory paragraph. Be sure the introductory paragraph also makes it clear that you will be discussing your theme only as it relates to you.

Next, using your prewriting material as a reminder, write the paragraphs that will include descriptions, narratives, possible character sketches, and commentary. As much as possible, use sensory details and specific, concrete words. Arrange your paragraphs in a way that makes sense to you.

C. Postwriting

Revise your personal essay, using the checklist on the next page. After you have made a complete revision, proofread the essay for errors in usage and mechanics by using the Checklist for Proofreading at the back of this book.

Checklist for Revising the Personal Essay

1. The writing style is natural and informal.

2. The essay focuses on one central theme.

3. The narrative, or storytelling, element of the essay is presented in chronological order.

4. Characters important to the essay are described so that their behavior or their significance is made clear.

5. Descriptive details about characters, setting, ideas, and feelings are used to help convey the writer's experience to the audience.

6. The writer's commentary on the central theme is an essential part of the essay.

Sentence Combining:
Using Connectors

Using Connectors to Join Parts of Sentences

Connectors, as you have learned, can be used to join sentences. They can also join one sentence with parts of one or more other sentences. In the following example, notice that repeated words are left out when the sentences are joined. Notice also that no comma is necessary and that the verb in the combined sentence is changed to its plural form. (The connector to be used is given in parentheses.)

Sentences: In the Bradbury Building is elaborate wrought-iron decoration.
In the Bradbury Building is a soaring skylight. (*and*)

Joined: In the Bradbury Building are elaborate wrought-iron decoration *and* a soaring skylight.

When you combine sentences, you may sometimes need to use commas to separate the words or groups of words in a series. Study the following examples.

Sentences: Ancient Greece gave the world the foundations of democracy.
It gave the world great works of literature and important philosophic ideas. (*and*)

For more information on using commas in a series, see pages 551-552.

Joined: Ancient Greece gave the world the foundations of democracy, great works of literature, *and* important philosophic ideas.

Sentences: Mrs. Donato was unable to decide whether to order the seafood salad.
She was unable to decide whether to order the cannelloni with tomato sauce.
She was unable to decide whether to order the special turkey dinner. (*or*)

Joined: Mrs. Donato was unable to decide whether to order the seafood salad, the cannelloni with tomato sauce, *or* the special turkey dinner.

Exercise 1: Using Connectors to Join Parts of Sentences

After studying the example, join the sentences in each of the following sets. In the first five sets the connectors to be used are indicated in parentheses. For the last five, you must decide how to make the combinations.

Example

a. The family gathered around the grave.
The family joined hands to pay silent tribute to the one they had lost. (*and*)
The family gathered around the grave and joined hands to pay silent tribute to the one they had lost.

1. Requirements for this job include the ability to read two languages other than English.
Requirements for this job include extensive travel experience. (*and*)

2. Whenever Zachary feels depressed, he goes for long walks along the levee down by the Mississippi River.
   Whenever Zachary feels depressed, he hums quietly to himself.
   Whenever Zachary feels depressed, he tries to think of cheerful, pleasant things. (*and*)

3. The people were desperately poor.
   The people had little food in storage for the winter.
   The people could find no way to make the soil they tilled more productive. (*and*)

4. Rushing back and forth in its cage consumed the wild animal's entire day.
   Searching for bits of food under rock ledges consumed the wild animal's entire day. (*and*)

5. The speaker visually searched the crowd.
   She could not find the source of the noise. (*but*)

6. This new book will surely become a best seller.
   This new book will make its author justly famous.

7. The snow fell from ominously dark clouds.
   It drifted across roads and fields.
   It stopped homeward-bound commuters from reaching their destinations.

8. Marianna's ambition would not allow her to waste time in frivolous pursuits.
   Marianna's ambition would not allow her to expend her energy on worthless projects.

9. Visitors to the factory may park in the visitors' lot.
   They may park in the vacant lot next to the power plant on Ninth Street.

65

10. If the weather is favorable, the class picnic will be held in Central Park.

   If enough students sign up to attend, the class picnic will be held in Central Park.

   If we can find suitable transportation, the class picnic will be held in Central Park.

Using Paired Connectors to Join Sentences

For more information on correlative conjunctions, see pages 432-433.

Two sets of paired connectors—*either . . . or* and *not only . . . but also*—can be used to join sentences of equal importance. The paired connector *either . . . or* suggests a choice between alternatives; *not only . . . but also* indicates an additional idea. These connectors are also called *correlative conjunctions*.

In the following examples notice that words or word order may change slightly when the combination is made.

Sentences: You will have to turn up the heat in this building.
   I will be forced to complain. (*either . . . or*)

Joined: *Either* you will have to turn up the heat in this building, *or* I will be forced to complain.

Sentences: The scholarship offered her a chance to attend the college of her choice.
   It bolstered her self-esteem. (*not only . . . but also*)

Joined: *Not only* did the scholarship offer her a chance to attend the college of her choice, *but* it *also* bolstered her self-esteem.

Exercise 2: Using Paired Connectors to Join Sentences

After studying the examples, use paired connectors to join the following sentence sets. In the first five sets the paired connectors to be used are indicated in parentheses. For the last five, decide for yourself which of the two paired connectors to use.

Examples

a. Reduce the number of calories you consume.
   Increase the time you spend exercising. (*either . . . or*)

   Either reduce the number of calories you consume, or increase the time you spend exercising.

    b. This new diet will help you save money on grocery bills.
       It will make you look and feel better. (*not only . . . but also*)
       Not only will this new diet help you save money on grocery
       bills, but it will also make you look and feel better.

1. New sources of revenue will have to be found.
   Local governments will have to increase taxes. (*either . . . or*)

2. Studying for a test is important.
   It is a good idea to get plenty of sleep the night before. (*not only . . . but also*)

3. The weather forecasters made a mistake in their forecast.
   What I see falling from the sky isn't snow. (*either . . . or*)

4. We will have to find a new system for keeping the books.
   This company faces financial ruin. (*either . . . or*)

5. Computer crimes are increasing.
   This form of white-collar crime is expected to continue climbing in the future. (*not only . . . but also*)

6. We have the kitchen left to clean up.
   Someone has to find a way to get the kitten out from behind the refrigerator.

7. Michelangelo was a great painter.
   He was a sculptor, poet, and architect.

8. I did not get the job I wanted.
   The personnel manager is waiting a long time to notify me to come to work.

9. We must find a way to feed the world's growing population.
   We must face the prospect of worldwide famine.

10. We will have to raise money through car washes and bake sales.
    We will have to ask each band member to pay his or her own expenses.

Writing Practice: *Using Connectors and Paired Connectors*

Revise two paragraphs of your personal essay about your own writing process. Join some of the sentences in the paragraphs by using connectors or paired connectors. The revised paragraphs should contain sentences of varied lengths.

3 Writing Paragraphs

Expository paragraphs may be developed by several different methods or by a combination of methods. In the following sections, you will study the *Topic-Restriction-Illustration* (TRI) pattern and its variations. You will also study paragraphs developed by means of *comparison, analogy,* and *cause and effect*. You will then learn how to improve paragraph coherence, and, finally, how to revise your expository paragraph.

Developing Paragraphs: The TRI Pattern

One method of paragraph development that is particularly useful in expository writing is called the *Topic-Restriction-Illustration* pattern.

In a TRI paragraph, the *topic sentence* states the general topic of the paragraph. The *restriction sentence* limits, or restricts, the general topic to the specific topic that the paragraph will discuss. The *illustration sentences* develop the main idea of the paragraph by providing examples, reasons, data, descriptive details, or other information.

Model: The TRI Pattern

In the basic TRI pattern the topic sentence comes first, as in the following example by W. H. Auden from an essay "The Almighty Dollar."

> Political and technological developments are rapidly obliterating all cultural differences and it is possible that, in a not remote future, it will be impossible to distinguish human beings living on one area of the earth's surface from those living on any other, but our different pasts have not yet been completely erased and cultural differences are still perceptible. The most striking difference between an American and a European is the difference in their attitudes towards money. Every European knows, as a matter of historical fact, that in Europe wealth could only be acquired at the expense of other human beings,

either by conquering them or by exploiting their labor in factories. Further, even after the Industrial Revolution began, the number of persons who could rise from poverty to wealth was small; the vast majority took it for granted that they would not be much richer nor poorer than their fathers. In consequence, no European associates wealth with personal merit or poverty with personal failure.[1]

The preceding paragraph begins by introducing the idea that while in the future people may share a global culture, for the present there are still perceptible cultural differences among nations. This statement (the first sentence) is the general topic of the paragraph. The restriction sentence (the second sentence) limits this general idea to specific comparison of attitudes toward money in America and

[1]Excerpt from "Postscript: The Almighty Dollar" in *The Dyer's Hand and Other Essays* by W. H. Auden. Copyright © by W. H. Auden. Reprinted by permission of Random House, Inc.

Europe. After restricting the topic, Auden then explains the European attitude toward money in three illustration sentences (the third, fourth, and fifth sentences). Each one adds a new piece of information about the restricted, not the general, topic of the paragraph.

Although most statements of topic and restriction are expressed in one sentence each, there is no general rule about the number of illustrations to include. Use as many as you need to make your point clearly and thoroughly.

Writing Practice 1: *The TRI Pattern*

Select two of the following topic sentences for an expository paragraph or, with your teacher's permission, substitute two similar sentences of your own. For each topic sentence write a restriction sentence followed by three or four illustration sentences. When you have finished, write each TRI in regular paragraph form.

1. Sports may be hazardous to your health.

2. Over the years I have perfected the art of (studying/avoiding work/amusing myself/etc.)

3. I believe in patriotism.

4.   The United States should be (more/less) active in aiding needy or developing countries.

5.   The wilderness is a precious resource.

Developing Paragraphs: The TI Pattern

One variation of the TRI pattern is the *Topic-Illustration* (TI) pattern. The TI pattern combines the topic and restriction parts of the pattern into one sentence.

Model: The TI Pattern

The TI pattern presents the general topic and restricts it in the same sentence. The writer then uses the rest of the paragraph for illustrations, as in the following example from an essay on food in Elizabethan England by M. F. K. Fisher titled "A Pigges Pettie Toes."

Restricted Topic

Illustrations

Even in the lusty days of Elizabeth's long reign, when England's blood ran, perhaps, at its fastest and finest, there were melancholy observers of what seemed signs of weakening in the nation's appetite. Who could tell where things would end, when already the most reputable of rich merchants were copying an effeminate Italian mannerism, and carrying their silver and gold forks about with them instead of eating with their fingers and knives as good Englishmen had been glad to do for centuries? And the ladies, lying in bed until six o'clock in the morning! When they arose, they breakfasted like babies, thinking they could start the day decently on a pot of ale and but one meager pound of bacon. The Queen, God be thanked, paid no attention to the new-style finicking, and made her first meal of the day light but sustaining; butter, bread (brown, to stay in the stomach longer and more wholesomely than white), a stew of mutton, a joint of beef, one of veal, some rabbits in a pie, chickens, and fruits, and beer and wine to wash all down in really hygienic fashion.[1]

Think and Discuss

In the preceding paragraph the topic and restriction are combined in the first sentence. This sentence restricts the general topic, *Food in Elizabethan England*, to the more specific topic of what some contemporary observers saw as "signs of weakening" in English appetites.

---

[1]From "Serve It Forth" in *The Art of Eating* by M. F. K. Fisher, Copyright © 1937, 1943, 1954, 1971 by M. F. K. Fisher. Reprinted with permission of Macmillan Publishing Co., Inc. and Lescher & Lescher, Ltd.

These tendencies are illustrated by the remaining sentences.

1. What specific examples does Fisher cite as evidence?

2. What information does the final illustration provide?

For Your Writer's Notebook

After reading the paragraph from "A Pigges Pettie Toes" in the preceding section, perhaps you reflected on your own eating habits or on those of others. Are there foods or combinations of foods you enjoy eating that others find strange? Have your parents ever remarked on your eating habits? What food memories from your childhood stand out most? Do you recall the dull flavor of strained peas, the tartness of a fall apple, your first experience with a gloriously sticky pizza? Write a notebook entry or entries about experiences from the present or the past involving food. Use specific details to help the reader share your experience.

Developing Paragraphs: The Reverse TRI Pattern

Another way to vary the basic Topic-Restriction-Illustration pattern is to change the position of each part within the paragraph.

For example, you could write a paragraph with the topic sentence in the middle rather than at the beginning. You could also invert the order completely and write a Reverse TRI paragraph.

The *Reverse TRI* pattern begins with illustration sentences and works from them to conclude with the topic or topic-restriction sentence.

Model: The Reverse TRI Pattern

The following paragraph from an essay by Nora Ephron, titled "Bernice Gera, First Lady Umpire," uses the Reverse TRI pattern. The topic-restriction sentence is underlined.

It took four years for Bernice Gera to walk onto that ball field, four years of legal battles for the right to stand in the shadow of an "Enjoy Silver Floss Sauerkraut" sign while the crowd cheered and young girls waved sheets reading "Right On, Bernice!" and the manager of the Geneva Phillies welcomed her to the game. "On behalf of professional baseball," he said, "we say good luck and God bless you in your chosen profession." And the band played and the spotlights shone and all three networks recorded the event. Bernice Gera had become the first woman in the 133-year history of the sport to umpire a professional baseball game.[1]

The illustration sentences in the preceding paragraph give information about the background and the setting for the main topic, or idea: *Bernice Gera became the first woman umpire in the history of baseball.*

Writing Practice 2: *The Reverse TRI Pattern*

Select one of the following topic-restriction sentences or substitute one of your own. Then write a paragraph using the Reverse TRI pattern. Include at least three illustration sentences and end the paragraph with a topic-restriction sentence.

1. Revision is an essential part of the writing process.

2. Penalties for driving while intoxicated are/are not severe enough.

3. Active participation in student government is/is not essential.

Developing Paragraphs: Comparison and Contrast

Comparison **and** *contrast* **identify ways in which items are similar and ways in which they differ.**

When you use comparison and contrast to develop a paragraph, you liken and contrast two things or ideas. Such paragraphs help the reader understand more about both items by showing them in relation to one another, and by discussing the significance of their similarities and differences.

In a comparison and contrast paragraph, the things being compared and contrasted must share some common element. For

---

[1]Excerpt from "Bernice Gera, First Lady Umpire" in *Crazy Salad: Some Things About Women* by Nora Ephron. Copyright © 1975 by Nora Ephron. Reprinted by permission of Alfred A. Knopf, Inc.

example, you could compare the British Parliament with the U. S. Congress because each is a legislative body. Furthermore, the individual points within any comparison and contrast must be similar. Suppose, for example, that you are comparing and contrasting British and American football. It would not be appropriate to discuss game strategies for one and the history of the other. Each major point that you make must be discussed for both: the history, players, and method of scoring of British football must be accompanied by a discussion of the history, players, and method of scoring of American football.

The nature of your subject will tell you whether it is more appropriate to emphasize likenesses or differences. If, for example, you are writing about the painters Mary Cassatt and Edgar Degas, you might emphasize the similarity of their styles, as Degas was a great influence on Cassatt. On the other hand, in writing about Elizabeth I of England and Mary, Queen of Scots, you would probably emphasize the differences in their power and personalities.

Two basic comparison and contrast methods are the *block method* and the *point-by-point method*.

With the *block method*, each item is discussed separately; ideas about each item are grouped together. The block method is used most frequently to contrast, rather than to liken.

Model: *Comparison and Contrast–Block Method*

In the following passage from *Zen and the Art of Motorcycle Maintenance*, Robert M. Pirsig compares and contrasts a romantic view of the world and a classic viewpoint, using the block method.

Restricted Topic
Illustrations

The romantic mode is primarily inspirational, imaginative, creative, intuitive. Feelings rather than facts predominate. "Art" when

Illustrations

it is opposed to "Science" is often romantic. It does not proceed by reason or by laws. It proceeds by feeling, intuition and esthetic conscience. In the northern European cultures the romantic mode is usually associated with femininity, but this is certainly not a necessary association. The classic mode, by contrast, proceeds by reason and by laws—which are themselves underlying forms of thought and behavior. In the European cultures it is primarily a masculine mode and the fields of science, law and medicine are unattractive to women largely for this reason. Although motorcycle riding is romantic, motorcycle maintenance is purely classic. The dirt, the grease, the mastery of underlying form required all give it such a negative romantic appeal that women never go near it.[1]

Think and Discuss

1. Pirsig states in the preceding paragraph that the romantic way of looking at the world is based on feeling rather than fact. How does this contrast with the classic viewpoint?

2. What other points of comparison does Pirsig make between the romantic and classic modes? For example, how does he use the terms *masculine* and *feminine* to describe the different viewpoints?

In a *point-by-point method* of comparison and contrast, the items being compared are not separated. Instead, both likenesses and differences are discussed for each item before the writer moves on to the next point. This method is useful when there are many specific points of comparison, when the differences between the two parts are subtle and need special explanation, or when you are emphasizing the similarities between the two parts of the comparison.

Model: Comparison and Contrast–Point-by-Point Method

The following paragraph uses a point-by-point comparison to discuss the silent film comics Charlie Chaplin and Buster Keaton. As you read, notice each specific point in the comparison of the two stars.

Topic

Restriction

Illustrations

Both Charlie Chaplin and Buster Keaton began as vaudeville comics and later moved on to successful careers in silent film comedy. Both were known to millions for film characters who projected a unique comic vision of the world. Chaplin's "Little Tramp," with his bowler, twirling cane, and teetering walk, was an appealing figure of impoverished gentility and innocence whose only assets

---

[1]Excerpt from *Zen and the Art of Motorcycle Maintenance* by Robert M. Pirsig. Copyright © 1974 by Robert M. Pirsig. By permission of William Morrow & Company and The Bodley Head.

were his decency and his faith in an orderly universe. The film personality of Keaton, called the "Great Stoneface," was distinguished by the somber, stony expression of a man who has seen everything and is beyond ordinary surprise, joy, or sorrow. Chaplin and Keaton's humor grows from the incongruity between a situation and their comic character's response. In Chaplin's world, the Little Tramp is happily ignorant of danger, maintaining a daffy optimism and grace in the face of harsh reality. Starving during a bitter Alaskan winter, the Tramp cheerfully boils his shoe and serves it up with a gentlemanly flourish. In Keaton's world, the comic imbalance grows from his character's stone-faced stoicism confronting an absurd world. When his house collapses around him, he watches soberly, picks up the walls, and begins again. As the catastrophes mount, Keaton's deadpan response becomes more hilarious; he has transcended everything, even despair. When romance appears in Chaplin's films, the Little Tramp's heroine stays above the silly pratfalls and comic convolutions of his world. Significantly, his goodness and faith triumph and he usually wins her in the end. Keaton's world, however, immerses the delicate heroine in its catastrophes, and she is as likely as anyone else to be the victim of ignoble tumbles in the mud. In this world, fate provides no reward for good intentions and the hero often winds up having offended and lost the woman he hoped to win.

Think and Discuss

1. The preceding paragraph compares the comic characters of Chaplin and Keaton by examining their similarities and differences. The first point of the comparison looks at the personality of each character. What characterizes Chaplin's Little Tramp as opposed to Keaton's Great Stoneface?

2. The second point of the comparison focuses on how Chaplin and Keaton create humor for their characters. How are their attitudes toward the world different?

3. What is the final point of the comparison?

Writing Practice 3: *Developing Paragraphs— Comparison and Contrast*

Select one of the following suggestions for comparison/contrast paragraphs or write a similar comparison/contrast topic of your own. You may focus on the similarities or on the differences between the two parts of your comparison/contrast. Use whichever comparison/contrast method, block or point-by-point, is more appropriate to your topic.

1. Compare and contrast two United States presidents (or other historical figures, such as rulers, inventors, artists, or writers).

2. Compare and contrast two types of relaxation or entertainment.

3. Compare yourself (getting up in the morning, going to school, or in another situation) on your best days as opposed to your worst days.

Developing Paragraphs: Analogy

An *analogy* is a type of comparison. The purpose of analogy is to explain a difficult or unusual concept by comparing it with something simpler.

An analogy in expository writing is similar to a metaphor in imaginative writing. Both the analogy and the metaphor make comparisons of seemingly unlike items rather than making a standard comparison of like items. Consider, for example, the following analogy by Sylvia Plath.

> If a poem is concentrated, a closed fist, then a novel is relaxed and expansive, an open hand: it has roads, detours, destinations; a heart line, a head line; morals and money come into it. Where the first excludes and stuns, the open hand can touch and encompass a great deal in its travels [1]

It is not usual to compare a poem to a closed fist, or a novel to an open hand; but making this comparison helps the reader understand their differences.

Model: Developing Paragraphs–Analogy

Like an extended metaphor in a poem or novel, an analogy will often be followed through an entire piece of writing. In the following excerpt from an essay titled "Feeding the Mind" by Lewis Carroll, the analogy carried throughout is the feeding of the body compared with the "feeding," or education, of the mind. As you read, notice the specific points of comparison that Carroll describes.

Restricted Topic

> Considering the amount of painful experience many of us have had in feeding and dosing the body, it would, I think, be quite worth

---

[1] Excerpt from "A Comparison" in *Johnny Panic and the Bible of Dreams* by Sylvia Plath. Copyright © 1956, 1962 by Sylvia Plath. Published by Faber & Faber of London, copyright © 1977 by Ted Hughes. Reprinted by permission of Harper & Row, Publishers, Inc., and Olwyn Hughes as agent for the author.

Illustrations

our while to try to translate some of the rules into corresponding ones for the mind. First, then, we should set ourselves to provide for our mind its *proper kind* of food; we very soon learn what will, and what will not, agree with the body, and find little difficulty in refusing a piece of the tempting pudding or pie which is associated in our memory with that terrible attack of indigestion, and whose very name irresitibly recalls rhubarb and magnesia; but it takes a great many lessons to convince us how indigestible some of our favorite lines of reading are, and again and again we make a meal of the unwholesome novel, sure to be followed by its usual train of low spirits, unwillingness to work, weariness of existence—in fact by mental nightmare. Then we should be careful to provide this wholesome food in *proper amount.* Mental gluttony, or overreading, is a dangerous propensity, tending to weakness of digestive power, and in some cases to loss of appetite; we know that bread is a good and wholesome food, but who would like to try the experiment of eating two or three loaves at a sitting? I wonder if there is such a thing in nature as a fat mind? I really think I have met with one or two minds which could not keep up with the slowest trot in conversation, could not jump over a logical fence to save their lives, always got stuck fast in a narrow argument, and . . . in short, were fit for nothing but to waddle helplessly through the world . . .

Think and Discuss

1. Lewis Carroll states that people should provide the "proper kind of food" for their minds: Books are to the mind what food is to the stomach. How does he carry through with this analogy in the paragraph? What specific points of comparison does he make between physical eating and mental feeding?

2. The paragraph goes on to discuss feeding the mind with the "proper amount" of food. What specific comparisons does Carroll make between an overweight person and one with a "fat mind"?

Writing Practice 4: *Developing Paragraphs–Analogy*

Select one of the following suggestions for paragraphs developed by analogy or write a similar topic of your own. First list the specific points of comparison your analogy will contain. Then write a paragraph developing the analogy on a separate sheet of paper.

1. Explain your reading habits by analogy.

2. Explain by analogy how a car engine (or other mechanical device) works.

3. Explain how to play tennis (or basketball or how to ride a horse, etc.) by analogy.

4. Use the life process as an analogy to describe the rise and fall of a nation, an empire, or a sports team.

Developing Paragraphs: Cause and Effect

A good deal of expository writing explores the *causes* of an event, action, or situation and the resulting *effects*.

When you think in terms of *cause and effect*, you ask the questions, *Why did this occur?* and *What was the result?*

Because cause-and-effect paragraphs pose questions, you will often find them presented in a question-and-answer format. The writer will state the topic as a question about cause, such as "How did the Beatles influence American culture?," and then discuss in the rest of the paragraph the effects the Beatles had.

Analysis by cause and effect can be subdivided into smaller categories. First, you can examine either the immediate (or precipitating) cause, or the underlying cause or causes. For example, the

immediate cause of World War I was the assassination of Archduke Francis Ferdinand of Austria-Hungary in 1914. The underlying causes, however, included territorial and economic rivalry among the nations of Austria-Hungary, Russia, Germany, France, and Great Britain, going back almost half a century.

Second, you can examine the direct or immediate effects of an event, an action, or a situation, or you can look at its long-range effects. One immediate aftereffect of World War I, for example, was the Treaty of Versailles that forced Germany alone to assume guilt for the war. In terms of long-range effects, some historians believe that the peace treaties signed after World War I were responsible for the economic misery in Europe. This misery led to a new spirit of nationalism in Germany and ultimately contributed to the causes of World War II. (As this example shows, the study of cause and effect is seldom clear-cut. The effects of one action can in turn become the causes of another.)

Model: *Developing Paragraphs—Cause and Effect*

The following paragraph from George Orwell's famous essay "Politics and the English Language" uses a cause-and-effect approach to the language of politics.

Restricted Topic
Illustrations

In our time, political speech and writing are largely the defense of the indefensible. Things like the continuance of British rule in India, the Russian purges and deportations, the dropping of the atom bombs on Japan, can indeed be defended, but only by arguments which are

Illustrations   too brutal for most people to face, and which do not square with the professed aims of political parties. Thus political language has to consist largely of euphemism, question-begging and sheer cloudy vagueness. Defenseless villages are bombarded from the air, the inhabitants driven out into the countryside, the cattle machine-gunned, the huts set on fire with incendiary bullets: this is called *pacification.* Millions of peasants are robbed of their farms and sent trudging along the roads with no more than they can carry: this is called *transfer of population* or *rectification of frontiers.* People are imprisoned for years without trial, or shot in the back of the neck or sent to die of scurvy in Arctic lumber camps: this is called *elimination of unreliable elements.* Such phraseology is needed if one wants to name things without calling up mental pictures of them. Consider for instance some comfortable English professor defending Russian totalitarianism. He cannot say outright, "I believe in killing off your opponents when you can get good results by doing so." Probably, therefore, he will say something like this: "While freely conceding that the Soviet regime exhibits certain features which the humanitarian may be inclined to deplore, we must, I think, agree that a certain curtailment of the right to political opposition is an unavoidable concomitant of transitional periods, and that the rigors which the Russian people have been called upon to undergo have been amply justified in the sphere of concrete achievement."[1]

Think and Discuss

1. In the preceding paragraph George Orwell states that politicians use vague and euphemistic speech. What does Orwell cite as the cause of this vagueness in politicians' language?

2. Name some euphemistic words or phrases that are commonly used in other fields than politics.

Writing Practice 5: *Developing Paragraphs—* *Cause and Effect*

Select one of the following suggestions for cause-and-effect paragraphs or write one of your own. First, write a clear statement of the cause in one sentence and list the effect or effects. Then write a cause-and-effect paragraph on a separate sheet of paper. Decide before you write whether you will focus on the immediate or underlying cause and on the immediate or long-term effects.

---

[1]Excerpted from "Politics and the English Language" in *Shooting an Elephant and Other Essays* by George Orwell. Copyright 1946 by Sonia Brownell Orwell, copyright 1974 by Sonia Orwell. Reprinted by permission of Harcourt Brace Jovanovich, Inc., A. M. Heath & Company, Ltd. as agents for the estate of the late George Orwell, and Martin Secker & Warburg.

1. What are the main causes and effects of a historical event (such as the Battle of Hastings, the attack on Fort Sumter or Pearl Harbor, the signing of the Yalta Pact, Watergate)?

2. What, in your opinion, are the chief causes of dissatisfaction with public education?

3. Draw on your own observation or reading to describe the chief effects of racial prejudice.

4. Draw on your own observation or reading to describe the chief effects of television viewing on daily life.

Using Transitions for Coherence

In a *coherent* paragraph, the links between sentences are made clear to the reader.

The next sections of this chapter offer several methods for improving paragraph coherence, including the use of *transitions* (words that show links between sentences), *paraphrase*, *repetition*, and *parallel structure*.

Transitions Showing Chronological Order

Use transitions showing chronological order for paragraphs that present events or sequences of ideas as they happen in time.

Model: *Transitions Showing Chronological Order*

In the following paragraph from an essay titled "We've Never Asked a Woman Before," biographer Catherine Drinker Bowen uses chronological order to give the readers historical perspective on the achievements of women. Words that indicate chronological organization are underlined.

Topic

Without a clear view of their capabilities, men and women cannot function. Convince a two-legged man that he has but one leg, and he will not be able to walk. A writer must know her horizon, how wide is the circle within which she, as artist, extends. The

Restrictions

world still professes to wonder why there has been no female Shakespeare or Dante, no woman Plato or Isaiah. Yet people do what society looks for them to do. The Quaker Meeting House has existed

Illustrations

for centuries, but it has produced no Bach and no B Minor Mass. Music was not desired by Quakers, it was frowned on. Poetry, fiction, playwriting have been expected from women only recently, as history counts time. Of the brilliant, erratic Margaret Cavendish, her husband, the Duke of Newcastle, remarked, circa 1660, "A very wise woman is a very foolish thing." As lately as 1922, Christina Rossetti's biographer wrote of her, that "like most poetesses, she was purely subjective, and in no sense creative." What a beautiful triple sneer, and how it encompasses the entire second sex![1]

In the preceding paragraph Bowen uses a chronological progression to show what society expects and has expected from women. The examples she gives to support her idea occur in a historical framework; they are ordered in time.

Transitions Showing Spatial Order

Use transitions showing spatial order to describe the location in space of people or objects.

Model: Transitions Showing Spatial Order

In the following paragraph from an essay titled "An Englishman's Outrageous View of Texas Football," the writer J. B. Priestley describes his first experience at an American football game. As you read, notice which sentences tell about the location of the people and things that Priestley observes.

Illustrations

The professor and I carried our cushions to the top of the stand and then found places among a group of his colleagues, of both sexes, belonging to the departments of language and literature. Nodding and smiling a welcome, Middle English, Romance Languages, Modern Novel and Elizabethan Drama pleasantly acknowledged my presence, with that slight archness and hint of the deprecatory which scholars display when discovered attending some unscholarly college function. From this height, the whole stadium was spread below us, all open to our view. The scene had more color than we find in our football grounds. The crowd opposite, mostly students in colored shirts and blouses, looked almost like a vast heap of those tiny sweets known in my childhood as "hundreds and thousands." Two large students' military bands, one in orange uniforms, the other in purple, the colors of their respective teams, could just be distinguished,

---

[1]From "We've Never Asked a Woman Before" by Catherine Drinker Bowen, from *The Atlantic Monthly*, March 1970. Copyright 1970 © by Catherine Drinker Bowen. Reprinted by permission of Harold Ober Associates, Incorporated.

Illustrations

massed together, on the lower slopes, where the sousaphones gleamed and blared. In the space between the touchline and the stand, there were cheerleaders in white, men and girls, already beginning to signal to and encourage, with enormous rhythmical gestures, their obedient sections of students. One end of the ground, to my right, was dominated by an illuminated electric clock, ready to mark off every second of play. Above the crowd at the other end, lower than we were, I could see ranks of parked cars, extending apparently into far, open country, glittering, glimmering and then fading into the haze, like some plague of gray and green beetles unaccountably stricken with death. Down on the turf a host of players, enough to make a dozen teams, all uniformed, leather-armored, numbered, were throwing passes and punting the balls and loosening up. Other men, mostly in white, not cheerleaders but athletic directors, coaches, referees and linesmen, trainers and first-aid men, were gathering along the touchlines. From somewhere behind us, voices through loudspeakers, harsh and appallingly amplified, made

Restricted Topic announcements, called doctors to the telephone. The bowl, you might say, was busy.[1]

Think and Discuss

1. From the "top of the stand" where Priestley sits, he has a panoramic view of the entire football field and stadium. The first observation he makes is of the "crowd opposite" him dressed in bright colors. Next, he describes the bands located "on the lower slopes." What other sentences in the paragraph give details about people or things from Priestley's vantage point or as they are placed in relation to one another?

2. Which other words and phrases indicate spatial order in Priestley's paragraph?

For Your Writer's Notebook

J. B. Priestley's essay "An Englishman's Outrageous View of Texas Football" is interesting partly because it gives the view of an outsider about an experience that many people have had: attending a football game. Think about another common event or experience and take a moment to reflect on how you would view it if you were a visitor from another country or even from another planet. In your Writer's Notebook write a description of this event or experience from the point of view of an outsider. Be sure to include descriptions of the sights, sounds, and other sensory details that relate to your event or experience.

Transitions Showing Order of Importance

Use transitions showing order of importance to indicate order by rank or significance.

A writer may use order of importance to list ideas, facts, reasons, or other illustrations. The most common sequence for order of importance is from least important to most important point. Order of importance is sometimes called *climactic order*, because the paragraph builds to a climax.

---

[1]From "An Englishman's Outrageous View of Texas Football" from *Journey Down a Rainbow* by J. B. Priestley and Jacquetta Hawkes. Reprinted by permission of A. D. Peters & Co., Ltd.

Model: *Transitions Showing Order of Importance*

The following paragraph from an essay by E. B. White organizes its information by order of importance.

There are roughly three New Yorks. There is, first, the New York of the man or woman who was born here, who takes the city for granted and accepts its size and its turbulence as natural and inevitable. Second, there is the New York of the commuter—the city that is devoured by locusts each day and spat out each night. Third, there is the New York of the person who was born somewhere else and came to New York in quest of something. Of these three trembling cities the greatest is the last—the city of final destination, the city that is a goal. It is this third city that accounts for New York's high-strung disposition, its poetical deportment, its dedication to the arts, and its incomparable achievements. Commuters give the city its tidal restlessness, natives give it solidity and continuity, but the settlers give it passion. And whether it is a farmer arriving from Italy to set up a small grocery store in a slum, or a young girl arriving from a small town in Mississippi to escape the indignity of being observed by her neighbors, or a boy arriving from the Corn Belt with a manuscript in his suitcase and a pain in his heart, it makes no difference: each embraces New York with the intense excitement of first love, each absorbs New York with the fresh eyes of an adventurer, each generates heat and light to dwarf the Consolidated Edison Company.[1]

Think and Discuss

1. Which words and phrases indicate the order of importance?

2. E. B. White states that the last New York that he describes is the greatest. What reasons does he give for the feeling that this particular New York is the greatest?

Transitions Showing Logical Connections

Besides showing chronological order, spatial order, or order of importance, some transitions indicate logical connections. Still others introduce illustrations, comparisons, or conclusions. Transitions are also sometimes referred to as transitional devices, linking expressions, or connectives.

---

[1] Excerpt from p. 121 in "Here Is New York" from *Essays of E. B. White.* Copyright 1949 by E. B. White. Reprinted by permission of Harper & Row, Publishers, Inc.

Model: Transitions Showing Logical Connections

The following paragraph from Catherine Drinker Bowen's essay, "We've Never Asked a Woman Before," uses three common transitions: *yet, therefore,* and *but.* As you read, notice how each transition helps you follow her train of thought.

> For thirty years I have been writing about lawyers and the law. And for almost as many years I have been the recipient of invitations to stand on platforms and address large assemblies of legal experts. I enjoy receiving these invitations; it shows that people are reading my books. *Yet* I often hesitate; the program means serious preparation. A non-lawyer—and a non-man—cannot stand up and talk drivel for thirty minutes or fifty (as specified) to a hall bristling with five hundred or so hardminded professional gentlemen. *Therefore* I hold off, saying into the telephone that I haven't the time; I am writing a new book and must stay home by myself, where writers belong. Perhaps the committee will send a letter, giving details? "Mrs. Bowen!" says an urgent voice from Houston or San Francisco. "This is our law society's big annual celebration. We've had Senator Fulbright as speaker, and Wechsler of Columbia, and the Lord Chief Justice of England [and God and Santa Claus]. *But* we've never asked a woman before."[1]

In the preceding paragraph Bowen uses transitions to make her writing more coherent. The first transition, *yet,* introduces a contrasting statement: The writer enjoys receiving invitations to speak, *yet* she often hesitates about accepting. The second transition, *therefore,* sets up a conclusion to a train of thought: The writer thinks about how much work it is to prepare a speech and *therefore,* as a result, she holds off accepting the invitations. The final transition, *but,* introduces another contrasting statement: The various law societies have asked many important figures, *but* they have never invited a woman before. These transitions all serve to link and connect ideas within the paragraph, making its sequence of ideas clear and easy to follow.

Choosing Transitions According To Their Use

The particular transition word or phrase that you use depends on its purpose within the sentence or paragraph. The following list of

---

[1] From "We've Never Asked a Woman Before" by Catherine Drinker Bowen, from *The Atlantic Monthly,* March 1970. Copyright 1970 © by Catherine Drinker Bowen. Reprinted by permission of Harold Ober Associates, Incorporated.

transitions is organized according to use; one group of transitions is appropriate to show chronological order, another to show spatial order, and still another to indicate order of importance. Other groups are appropriate to introduce ideas, to continue with a sequence of ideas, or to present contrasting ideas.

Transitions	Uses
for example, for instance	to introduce illustrations
also, and, another, besides, furthermore, in addition, moreover, too	to add illustrations
although, but, despite, however, in the same way, in spite of, nevertheless, nonetheless, on the other hand, similarly, still, yet	to show comparisons and/or contrasts
first, second, third, eventually, finally, later, meanwhile, next, now, presently, then, thereafter	to show chronological order
about, above, across, around, at the top, behind, below, beyond, far, far away, here, near, on the left, on the right	to show spatial order
first, second, third, least important, more importantly, most important	to show order of importance
as a result, because, finally, for this reason, in conclusion, therefore, thus, so	to make a conclusion, to indicate purpose or a result

Writing Practice 6: *Transitions*

The following topics are suggestions for paragraphs. Select one or choose a similar topic of your own. To find and organize ideas for your paragraph, use one of the methods presented in the first part of this chapter. Then, on a separate sheet of paper, write your paragraph, paying special attention to the transitions. Use at least four transitions from the preceding list.

1. Getting to school on time on Monday morning takes great organization.

2. The problem of groundwater pollution has increased over the last fifty years.

3. When you open the hood of your automobile, note the locations of the following basic parts.

4. Reading different works by the same author allows you to learn a great deal about the author's basic attitudes and concerns.

5. From the top of the (building/mountain/bluff) I looked down on an almost indescribable scene.

More Methods to Improve Coherence

You can also improve the coherence of your writing by using such devices as *connecting pronouns*, *paraphrase*, *repetition* and *parallel structure*.

For more information on pronouns, see pages 332-357.

Connecting Pronouns

Connecting pronouns help coherence by referring to nouns in a previous sentence, thus emphasizing the connection in thought from one sentence to the next and avoiding unnecessary repetition.

Model: Connecting Pronouns

You will find that substituting connecting pronouns for nouns is one of the most widely used methods of improving coherence. In the following paragraph, notice how the underlined pronouns help link the thoughts from one sentence to another.

Topic

        Agatha Christie was a British author known throughout the world for her intriguing mystery novels. When she died at the age of eighty-six, she had published more than ninety-four volumes. Many of them were translated into several languages. Although the famous

Restriction

author rarely accepted requests for interviews, writer Gwen Robyns has pieced together some of Agatha Christie's personal ideas about writing in a biographical study called *The Mystery of Agatha Christie.*

Illustrations

For example, in its earliest stages a new mystery was for Mrs. Christie a process of mental organization. Only after perceiving a plot clearly in her mind was she ready for the commitment of beginning to type her new work. As she wrote it, often in her long walks across the fields near her home, Mrs. Christie tested the effectiveness of characters' conversations by repeating their speeches aloud. When she was worried by problems in <u>her</u> writing, <u>she</u> busied <u>herself</u> with humdrum household chores. <u>She</u> let <u>her</u> mind wander as <u>she</u> worked until solutions to the problems popped into <u>her</u> head.

Think and Discuss

1. The connecting pronoun *she* in the second sentence refers to Agatha Christie mentioned in the first sentence; the pronoun connects these two sentences and avoids unnecessary repetition. What nouns do the other underlined pronouns in the paragraph replace?

2. What sentences do these pronouns link?

Paraphrase

The purpose of *paraphrase* (rewording) is to remind the reader of a thought from one sentence by rephrasing it in a subsequent sentence.

Model: *Paraphrase*

Paraphrase connects ideas between sentences and helps avoid unnecessary repetition of words and phrases. In the following paragraph the paraphrasing is underlined and explained in brackets.

Mrs. Christie often wrote the concluding chapter of a mystery first since <u>this procedure</u> [paraphrase of <u>writing the concluding chapter first</u>] permitted her to gather the clues together, to alter minor details, and to tie up any loose ends in the <u>story</u> [paraphrase of <u>mystery</u>]. Because her principal involvement with the mysterious entanglements of plot superseded her other concerns about each <u>work</u> [paraphrase of <u>mystery</u>], Christie described characters briefly in one or two sentences and trimmed description of setting to a few well-chosen sentences. The <u>master mystery writer</u> [paraphrase of <u>Mrs. Christie</u>] admitted that she wouldn't discuss a new novel until the <u>who-dun-it</u> [paraphrase of <u>mystery</u>] was completed. She believed that if she discussed her <u>work-in-progress</u> [paraphrase of <u>new novel</u>], she would grow dissatisfied with it. Initiating each new novel with enthusiasm, Mrs. Christie conceded that she often wanted to desert a <u>project</u> [paraphrase of <u>new novel</u>] halfway through it. In spite of her many achievements, the <u>famous novelist</u> [paraphrase of <u>Mrs. Christie</u>] once commented: "People think that writing must be easy for me. It isn't. It's murder . . . I never have much faith in my writing—I am always scared that people will find out that I really can't write."

Paraphrasing in the preceding paragraph made the writer's train of thought easy to follow and also avoided the overuse of words such as *Mrs. Christie, mystery,* and *new novel.*

When you use paraphrasing in your own writing, remember never simply to substitute a more-impressive-sounding word for a simple word. Also, do not try to use paraphrase when repetition is acceptable. For example, if you write an essay about the effects of drinking coffee, you do not need to paraphrase the word *coffee* each time you use it. Substituting *steaming black liquid* or *caffeinated beverage* for *coffee* could sound pretentious or artificial.

Repetition

Properly used *repetition* can be an aid in linking ideas within a paragraph. It is not always necessary to use pronouns or paraphrase to avoid repeating the same word: in some cases selective repetition of a word or phrase can help emphasize an important point or help connect ideas in a paragraph. But choose your repeating words and phrases carefully. If you are not careful, the repetition can become monotonous and detract from coherence. Always reread your work to make sure that the words you repeat help improve coherence.

Model: Repetition

The following paragraph by sportswriter Roger Angell uses repetition to emphasize the main idea of his paragraph, which is the dimension

of time in baseball. In contrast to the Agatha Christie paragraph, in which the writer uses paraphrase to avoid repeating the words *mystery* and *Mrs. Christie*, Angell repeats the word *time* throughout to give his paragraph coherence.

> The last dimension is time. Within the ballpark, time moves differently, marked by no clock except the events of the game. This is the unique, unchangeable feature of baseball, and perhaps explains why this sport, for all the enormous changes it has undergone in the past decade or two, remains somehow rustic, unviolent, and introspective. Baseball's time is seamless and invisible, a bubble within which players move at exactly the same pace and rhythms as all their predecessors. This is the way the game was played in our youth and in our fathers' youth, and even back then—back in the country days—there must have been the same feeling that time could be stopped. Since baseball time is measured only in outs, all you have to do is succeed utterly: keep the rally alive, and you have defeated time. You remain forever young. Sitting in the stands, we sense this, if only dimly. The players below us—Mays, DiMaggio, Ruth, Snodgrass—swim and blur in memory, the ball floats over to Terry Turner, and the end of this game may never come.[1]

Think and Discuss

The repetition of the word *time* is effective in the preceding paragraph because time is its theme. Moreover, there is no effective paraphrase for the word *time* that would have been appropriate to the paragraph. Why is *time* as a repeating word more interesting than *copywriter* or *pet food* as repeating words?

For Your Writer's Notebook

> After reading Roger Angell's paragraph on the sense of time, perhaps you recall an experience of time that seemed different from other kinds of time. It might have been an experience of feeling that time was passing swiftly or the experience of a few moments that felt like an eternity. As a Writer's Notebook entry, describe your experience and the thoughts and feelings you had about time.

[1]From "The Interior Stadium" in *The Summer Game* by Roger Angell. Copyright © 1971 by Roger Angell. Originally appeared in *The New Yorker* (Underlining added.)

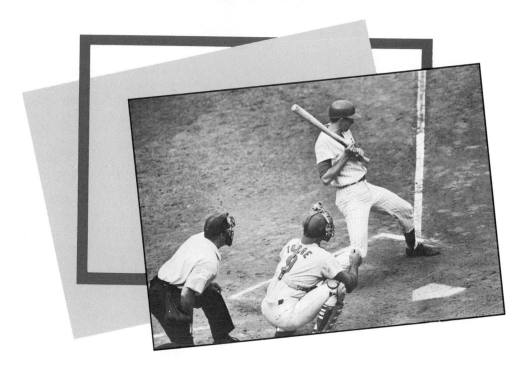

For more information on parallel structure, see pages 432 and 436.

Parallel Structure

A specific type of repetition that helps paragraph coherence is called *parallel structure*. Parallel structure means "the similar wording or arrangement of words in a sentence or series of sentences." The famous statement by Julius Caesar, "I came, I saw, I conquered," is an example of parallel structure within one sentence.

Model: Parallel Structure

Parallel structure draws the reader's attention to the thoughts being expressed with similar wording and reinforces their similarity.

Notice the underlined examples of parallel structure in this paragraph on publicity by John Berger.

> It is important here not to confuse publicity with the pleasure or benefits to be enjoyed from the things it advertises. Publicity is effective precisely because it feeds upon the real. Clothes, food, cars, cosmetics, baths, sunshine are real things to be enjoyed in themselves. Publicity begins by working on a natural appetite for pleasure. But it cannot offer the real object of pleasure and there is no convincing substitute for a pleasure in that pleasure's own terms. The more convincingly publicity conveys the pleasure of bathing in a warm, distant sea, the more the spectator-buyer will become aware that he is hundreds of miles away from that sea and the more remote the chance of bathing in it will seem to him. This is why publicity can never really afford to be about the product or opportunity it is

proposing to the buyer who is not yet enjoying it. <u>Publicity is never</u> a celebration of a pleasure-in-itself. <u>Publicity is always</u> about the future buyer. It offers him an image of himself made glamorous by the product or opportunity it is trying to sell. The image then makes him envious of himself as he might be. Yet what makes this self-which-he-might-be enviable? The envy of others. <u>Publicity is about social relations, not objects. Its promise is not of pleasure, but of happiness</u>: happiness as judged from the outside by others. The happiness of being envied is glamour.[1]

Think and Discuss

In the paragraph by John Berger, parallel structure is used extensively for emphasis: "*The more* convincingly publicity conveys the pleasure of bathing in a warm, distant sea, *the more* the spectator-buyer will become aware that he is hundreds of miles away from that sea and *the more* remote the chance of bathing in it will seem to him [*italics* added]."

1. What is the main idea Berger develops in this paragraph?

2. How does Berger's use of parallel structure make it easier to follow the development of the main idea?

Writing Practice 7: *Coherence*

Choose one of the following suggestions as a topic for a paragraph or substitute a similar topic of your own. Decide which method of development you will use in the paragraph before you write. As you write, pay special attention to connecting pronouns, paraphrasing, and parallel structures, underlining them as you go along. To find ideas for this paragraph, consider using the Pentad approach discussed in Chapter 2.

1. Compare your ideas about success with those of a close friend or family member.

2. Explain why conservation (or a different issue of your choice) is important.

3. Explain how the Electoral College works.

4. Describe your school layout and give suggestions on how you would improve it.

5. Relate an experience that changed your mind about something.

---

[1]From *Ways of Seeing* by John Berger (Pelican Books, 1972) p. 132. Copyright © 1972 by Penguin Books Ltd. Reprinted by permission. (Underlining added)

Unity

Unity, the quality of wholeness, is essential to good paragraph writing.

A unified paragraph presents one complete unit of information or sequence to the reader; the relationship of each sentence to the main idea is clear. An important way to ensure unity is to be certain that each sentence relates directly to the main idea of the paragraph. Any idea, no matter how interesting, that strays from the main idea should not be included: instead, it can be developed in a later paragraph.

Another way to unify paragraphs is to use a *clincher sentence*. A clincher sentence is one that provides a strong ending for a paragraph. All paragraphs do not require clincher sentences; in fact, you will most often find them at the ends of essays or at the end of a distinct section of an essay. However, clincher sentences can also be used to sum up the main idea or intent of a paragraph, as in the Nora Ephron paragraph about Bernice Gera that concludes: "Bernice Gera had become the first woman in the 133-year history of the sport to umpire a professional baseball game."

A clincher sentence can also be used to add a new piece of information to a paragraph. Often this type of clincher sentence is used as a transition from one section of an essay to another, as in the previous essay on publicity by John Berger. What is the clincher sentence in that essay?

Revising Paragraphs

For more information on revising, see page 28.

Revision is the process of making improvements in a piece of writing.

For some writers revision is a continuous process; as they write, they keep rereading the previous sentences, examining each one individually and as a part of the overall work. After they have finished, they reread to be certain of the total effect. Other writers like to get all their ideas down on paper before revising; they write an entire paragraph or essay and then go back and evaluate their work. Use whichever approach to revision best fits your writing habits, but remember that revision is essential to all good writing.

The following suggestions will guide you in revising your paragraphs.

1.   **Examine each sentence individually.**

Each of your sentences, by itself, should make a clear statement about the paragraph topic. However you have positioned the topic sentence within your paragraph, remember that only the topic sentence gives general information. The other sentences proceed from the topic sentence and give specific information about it.

2.   **Examine each sentence as it relates to the paragraph as a whole.**

Each sentence in your paragraph should contribute a new piece of information. Rewrite or delete any sentences that repeat information or any illustration sentence that does not contribute specific information to the paragraph. If you find an illustration sentence that does not relate directly to the restriction sentence, rewrite or delete it.

3.   **Examine your paragraph as a whole.**

Consider each paragraph as a separate unit of information that presents and develops a topic. When you reread your paragraph, make certain that you have stated your main idea clearly and illustrated it with sufficient examples, details, data, or other information.

Writing Assignment I: *Expository Paragraph*

Choose one of the following topic suggestions for a paragraph, write a similar topic of your own, or revise a paragraph you have already written.

1.   Compare how you feel at your age now with the way you thought you would feel when you were younger.

2.   Use the analogy of a menu to describe the many choices that you face in your life.

3.   Use an analogy to describe the three branches of the United States government.

4.   Discuss two important causes of the American Revolution.

5.   Discuss the effects of television on study habits of teenagers.

A. Prewriting

On a separate sheet of paper, write a clear statement of your paragraph idea in one or two sentences (a topic-restriction sentence or both a topic and a restriction sentence). Then use the Pentad questions to help develop and organize material for your paragraph.

B. Writing

Write a paragraph developing your main idea, explaining it with illustrations, or using comparison, an analogy, or cause and effect. Be sure to include sufficient details to support your main idea. As you write, pay special attention to coherence and unity. End your paragraph with a clincher sentence.

C. Postwriting

Use the following checklist to revise your paragraph. After revising, proofread for features that are not a part of Edited Standard English by using the Checklist for Proofreading in the back of the book.

Checklist for Revising a Paragraph

1. The paragraph has a clear central idea. If appropriate, this idea is expressed in a topic sentence.

2. The central idea is sufficiently restricted to be developed in a paragraph. If appropriate, the restriction is expressed in a separate sentence or combined with a statement of the topic in a topic-restriction sentence.

3. The central idea is adequately developed with illustration sentences giving specific information about it.

4. A paragraph developed through comparison is organized either by a block or a point-by-point method, the points of comparison are similar.

5. A paragraph developed by analogy uses a simpler idea or process or other model to help explain a more complex one.

6. A paragraph developed by cause-and-effect analysis discusses either immediate or underlying causes, and immediate or long-range effects.

7. The paragraph has unity. The main idea is apparent; every sentence in the paragraph supports or develops the main idea. If a "clincher" sentence is used, it focuses the reader's attention back on the main idea or presents a final interesting piece of information.

8. The paragraph is coherent. Sentences are arranged in an orderly progression; transitions, connecting pronouns, paraphrase, repetition, or parallel structure are used to link ideas.

Sentence Combining: Using Adverbs and Semicolons

Using Adverbs to Join Sentences

For more information on conjunctive adverbs, see page 482.

The last group of words that join sentences of equal importance is made up of adverbs. These coordinators are called *conjunctive adverbs*, and they require a semicolon between the joined sentences; in addition, they are followed by a comma. The most frequently used adverb connectors are the following ones.

Conjunctive Adverbs	Relationship
however instead on the other hand nevertheless	connect opposite ideas
therefore thus consequently hence	indicate that a conclusion or result follows
besides furthermore moreover in addition	indicate that an additional idea follows
indeed in fact	indicate emphasis

In the following sentence sets the conjunctive adverb to be used is given in parentheses.

Sentences: Six inches of snow fell last night.
Chris and I will have to shovel the walkway this morning. (*consequently*)

Joined: Six inches of snow fell last night; *consequently*, Chris and I will have to shovel the walkway this morning.

98

Sentences: The price of housing has risen sharply in the last decade.

               The interest rates on home mortgages have also kept the upward pace. (*Moreover*)

Joined: The price of housing has risen sharply in the last decade; moreover, the interest rates on home mortgages have also kept the upward pace.

Exercise 1: *Using Adverbs to Join Sentences*

Join each of the following sets of sentences with a semicolon and the conjunctive adverb indicated in parentheses. Study the example before you begin.

Example

   a. Danielle had insufficient funds in her checking account. Her check bounced. (*consequently*)

      Danielle had insufficient funds in her checking account; consequently, her check bounced.

1. Ian Fleming was the author of the James Bond novels. He wrote a popular novel for children titled *Chitty-Chitty-Bang-Bang*. (*in addition*)

2. Rosie argued that she wasn't going over thirty. The officer gave her a ticket. (*nevertheless*)

3. The apartment building is an old firetrap. The city will condemn it. (*therefore*)

4. Hamlet suspected Claudius of murdering his father. Claudius was now his stepfather. (*on the other hand*)

5. Dinh Van Trieu believed the course would be a snap. He had all of his older brother's class notes from the previous year. (*besides*)

Join each of the following sets of sentences, choosing the conjunctive adverb that best expresses the relationship between the ideas presented. (Refer to the previous list of conjunctive adverbs.)

Example

   a. The Hispanic population of California is a major economic, social, and cultural force in the state.

     More Hispanics of Mexican descent live in Los Angeles than in any city in Mexico except Mexico City.

99

The Hispanic population of California is a major economic, social, and cultural force in the state; in fact, more Hispanics of Mexican descent live in Los Angeles than in any city in Mexico except Mexico City.

6. Robert put up all the storm windows.
    He was ready for the storm.

7. The officials assessed a fifteen-yard penalty against the team.
    They threw the coach out of the game.

8. A good résumé can be a door opener in the job market.
    Good interview skills are probably most important to the job hunter.

9. Comparative shopping often results in tremendous savings.
    Comparative shopping also costs time and money.

10. The horror film was billed as the scariest ever.
    It was so poorly scripted and acted that it was laughable.

Joining Sentences with a Semicolon

For more information on joining sentences with a semicolon, see page 563.

If two sentences are of equal importance *and* are closely related in thought, they can be combined with a semicolon, as the following examples show.

Sentences: The 1980 national census shows that the most dramatic population increases occurred in the southern and western states.
Collectively, these states are called the Sun Belt.

Joined: The 1980 national census shows that the most dramatic population increases occurred in the southern and western states; collectively, these states are called the Sun Belt.

Sentences: Pham completed all the assignments for the course. Tomorrow he takes the final exam.

Joined: Pham completed all the assignments for the course; tomorrow he takes the final exam.

Exercise 2: Joining Sentences with a Semicolon

Combine each of the following sets of sentences with a semicolon.

Example

a. Polio is a very rare disease today.
   Only a few cases are reported each year.
   Polio is a very rare disease today; only a few cases are reported each year.

1. Our basketball team made the final round of the playoffs.
   Our opponents, last year's champs, are favored to win.

2. Esperanza wants to buy a car.
   She begins driving lessons tomorrow.

3. Robert never puts onions and lettuce on his hamburgers.
   Sally loves everything on hers.

4. I need a ride home after school.
   My sister can't pick me up today.

5. Mr. Gonzales was promoted to plant manager.
   He had been the production foreman.

6. Jennifer wants to study law.
   Her friend Maria wants to be a social worker.

7. Charles Dickens was concerned with the living conditions of common people.
   Many of his novels deal with the working class of industrialized England.

8. Michelle's cousin lives in Dallas.
   Michelle plans to visit her cousin there next summer.

9. The gray whale is an endangered species.
   Some countries still hunt the animals commercially.

10. Daniel is entering the army in June.
    He will train in California.

Writing Practice: *Joining Sentences with Adverbs and Semicolons*

Find a practice paragraph that you have written using the TRI pattern. Revise the paragraph; combine some of the sentences in it, using conjunctive adverbs and/or semicolons.

4 Writing Exposition

Exposition is writing that explains. It may explain how to do something or how something works; it may explain facts or ideas. In this chapter you will practice several kinds of expository writing.

Writing to Give Instructions

In writing instructions, be certain that each step is clear. Each step must also be explained in its proper sequence: first do this, then do that, and then do the next operation.

Model: Writing Instructions

In these instructions from *The New York Times Cook Book*, notice how the author, Craig Claiborne, uses transitions to make the sequence clear.

High Temperature Roasting of Turkey

Season a stuffed turkey with salt and place it on its side in a roasting pan fitted with a rack. Place slices of fat salt pork over the breast and spread the bird generously with butter. Cook in a preheated hot oven (425°F.) fifteen minutes, then turn on the other side and cook fifteen minutes longer.

Reduce the heat to moderate (375°F.) and continue roasting, turning the bird from side to side and basting often with fat from the pan. If the fat tends to burn, add a few tablespoons of water.

Allow twenty minutes a pound for roasting.

Place the turkey on its back for the last fifteen minutes of cooking. Pierce the thigh for doneness; if the juice that runs out is clear with no tinge of pink, the bird is done.[1]

—from *The New York Times Cook Book*

[1]"High Temperature Roasting of Turkey" from *The New York Times Cook Book* by Craig Claiborne. Copyright © 1961 by The New York Times Company. Reprinted by permission.

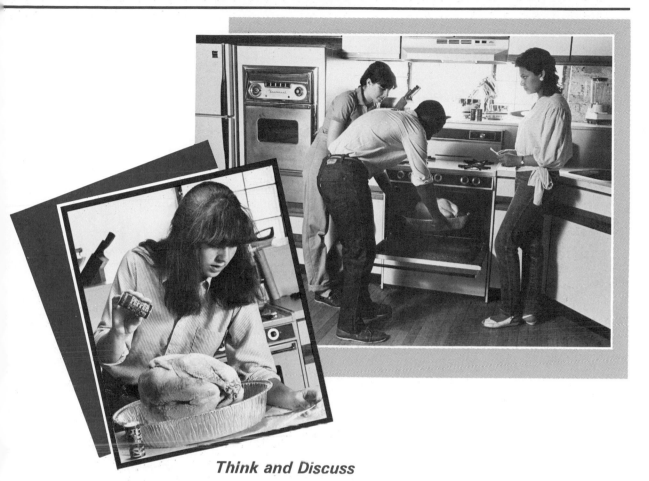

Think and Discuss

1. What transitions referring to time did Claiborne use?

2. Claiborne used a separate paragraph for each major part of the process. How does this increase the clarity of the instructions?

Writing Practice 1: *Writing Instructions*

Prepare a set of instructions. For example, you might present your favorite recipe or tell how to do something, such as how to develop a roll of film or change the oil in a car. When you finish writing, revise your instructions using the points in the following brief checklist.

1. The instructions are clear.

2. All necessary information, and no unnecessary information, is included.

3. Transitions and paragraphs make the sequence of steps easy to follow.

Facts and Opinions in Exposition

A *factual statement* relates to the physical world; it can be proved or disproved by measurements, counts, experiments, or research. An *opinion* is a belief about a subject.

It is a fact, for example, that the Constitution of the United States was amended to give voting rights to eighteen-year-olds. However, whether or not that was a good idea is a matter of *opinion*. The following are examples of factual statements and the opinions that might be formed from them.

Factual Statements	Opinions
Mount Whitney in California rises to an altitude of 14,494 feet (4,418 meters); it is taller than the other peaks in the Sierra Nevada chain.	Mount Whitney, rising above the other peaks in the Sierra Nevada chain, is majestic.
Locke High School now has an enrollment of 5,501 students and a teaching staff of 89, which yields a teacher-student ratio of one to 61.1.	The teacher-student ratio at Locke High School is far too high.
The Lincoln Memorial, a monument consisting of 164 acres (66 hectares) in Potomac Park, Washington, D.C., is dedicated to the memory of President Abraham Lincoln.	The Lincoln Memorial, one of the most moving tributes ever dedicated to the memory of a former President, represents all that is good in this country.

Expository writing can be used to explain both facts and opinions. When explaining an opinion, you should support it with facts.

Model: Fact and Opinion in Exposition

In this letter to the editor of her school newspaper, a student explains her opinion concerning the academic calendar. As you read, notice which facts she uses to support her opinion.

Joan Bremer, Editor
Bryant High *Banner*

Dear Ms. Bremer:

The calendar at Bryant High is not well planned and results in much wasted time.

This year the first semester does not end until January 15, and winter vacation lasts through January 4. This means that there are only ten days of school between the end of winter vacation and the end of the semester. During this "lame duck" period no one does any serious work; the students just mark time, and the teachers spend their class periods in review and "enrichment" activities.

It would be much more efficient to have the semester end at winter vacation. Then when students return in January, they would be ready to start serious work on new classes. Furthermore, summer vacation could begin a week or two earlier, giving students a better chance to obtain summer jobs.

Sincerely,

Jean Safier

Think and Discuss

1. What is Jean Safier's opinion of her school's academic calendar?

2. On what facts does she base her opinion?

3. In the first paragraph of her letter, Jean Safier states her opinion. In the second paragraph, she backs up her opinion with facts. To what does she devote the final paragraph of her letter?

Writing Assignment I: *Fact and Opinion in Exposition*

Think of a current issue, relating to your school, city, or nation, about which you have an opinion. Then write a letter to the editor of your school or local newspaper, explaining how you feel about the issue. Use the following steps for prewriting, writing, and postwriting.

A. Prewriting

In one sentence, write your opinion on the issue you have chosen. Beneath that sentence, jot down a list of all the facts that relate to your opinion and support it.

B. Writing

Write a first draft of your letter. If you wish, you may organize it as Jean Safier did, stating your opinion in one paragraph, backing it up with facts in the second paragraph, and offering suggestions for changes in the third paragraph.

C. Postwriting

Have two of your friends read your letter. Ask each to answer these questions:

1. What do you like best about it?

2. Are there enough facts to back up the opinion?

3. Are the facts and the opinion explained clearly enough?

4. Is any part of the letter irrelevant?

On the basis of your readers' answers, revise your letter. Check it carefully against the proofreading checklist at the back of the book. Then, if appropriate, mail your letter.

The Expository Composition

An *expository composition,* or *essay,* **usually consists of several related paragraphs that give information.**

Although you may never write an expository composition once you leave school, the process of doing so is a valuable experience. By developing an idea and discovering and arranging the information that explains it, you learn much about clear thinking and effective presentation.

In the following sections you will study the processes of developing a topic, gathering information, ordering the information, formulating a thesis, and, finally, writing an expository essay.

Subject and Topic

Very often an assignment for writing an expository essay begins with a general subject, one that covers much ground and that needs to be narrowed. Consider, for example, the subject *Poetry.* As a subject, poetry is vast, including its history from ancient times to the present, the various kinds of poetry (for example, lyric and epic, rhymed and free verse), various opinions about what makes a poem good or bad, poets, readers of poems, and countless other topics. A complete discussion of poetry would require many thick volumes.

From the enormous territory named "poetry," the essay writer must choose a small plot that he or she can cover in detail. In a brief essay of, say, 500 words, it would be possible to discuss the meaning of one poem or the difference between an Elizabethan and an Italian sonnet.

The following are more examples of general subjects and topics that might be derived from them.

Subjects	Writing Topics
Automobiles	Buying a subcompact car
Bandits	Jesse James' last robbery
Composition	Writing a good first paragraph
Democracy	The need for more democracy in my home
Environment	The problem of litter in Central Park
Final exams	How to prepare for a final exam in history
Grades	How to improve the grading system in my English class
History	The day the Mormons entered the Salt Lake Valley
Illness	My appendectomy
Knowledge	What I learned on my first job
Money	Planning a yearly budget in a time of inflation
Names	The meanings of some common American first names

The preceding topics would serve for relatively short papers. Some of them, of course, would demand research. (If you were to write about Jesse James' last robbery—in Northfield, Minnesota—you would probably need to spend some time in the library with books, magazines, and encyclopedias.) Other topics would result from your own experience and knowledge. (You are the world's greatest expert on what you learned on your first job.)

Writing Practice 2: *Subject and Topic*

On a sheet of paper, write down five general subjects that interest you. Next to each subject, write a topic suitable for a short (500-word) expository essay.

Gathering Information

You are involved in the process of gathering information about your subject from the time you first begin thinking about it. In fact, your choice of subject is probably influenced by what you already know.

Chapter 1 discusses systems of discovering ideas for writing. Such systems can be helpful to you at several stages in your writing. For example, if you have a subject but cannot think of a narrowed topic, then you might brainstorm or use clustering to find ideas for a limited topic. Having developed a topic, you might use a system such as the *Six Basic Questions*, the *Pentad*, or *Changing Viewpoints* to discover what you already know about your topic or what you need to find out through reading and other kinds of research.

Writing Practice 3: *Gathering Information*

For information on using library and reference resources, see pages 630-645.

From the five narrowed topics that you wrote in the previous Writing Practice, choose one to use as the basis for an expository essay. Using one of the systems discussed in Chapter 1, develop a list of details to use in your expository essay. If you find that you must do more reading or other research before proceeding with your essay, make a note of the areas in which you lack information.

Taking Notes

From the time that you first begin thinking about an expository essay until you actually begin writing, you may find that you have forgotten many details. If you take notes from the beginning, however, you will have a record of ideas.

Notes can be in the form of words, phrases, sentences, or even whole paragraphs. One good system is to use a separate note card for each idea. At the top of the card, you might also want to write a *slug*, or heading. For example, the following note cards represent notes made on the topic *The superwoman myth*.

Personal Experience

My aunt

Advertisements

Advertisements frequently portray women who are not only successful in business, but who are also outstanding wives and mothers.

Writing Practice 4: *Taking Notes*

Prepare a set of note cards for the topic you will develop for an expository essay. Use either the standard-sized 4 x 6 index cards or slips of paper you cut to that size. In an upper corner of each card, write a slug that will help you identify the content.

Ordering and Outlining Information

An *outline* is a listing of the main points of a book, a composition, or any other piece of writing. Outlines may be either *formal* or *informal*.

For more information on formal outlines, see pages 212-213.

Formal outlines, usually composed after the piece of writing is completed, show exactly what points the writer covers. *Informal outlines* are constructed before the writing begins, and they often change as the writing progresses. They are like road maps in that they give direction; they are unlike road maps in that the writer can change them as he or she finds new ideas.

In making an informal outline as a guide, the writer lists main points and any thoughts that he or she might have about the subject. As the writing goes on, the outline can be changed: more ideas can be added, and others can be crossed out. The following notes are for an expository essay on the topic *The superwoman myth*. As you read them over, look for general headings under which they could be arranged.

Advertisement for perfume that shows a woman coming home from her job as an executive and changing into a glamorous dress for her husband

General emphasis on success in our culture

In one way "labor-saving" devices have actually contributed to the problem. Before vacuum cleaners were invented, for example, women were not expected to clean their houses daily.

Greek mythology—Hera, Aphrodite

The Women's Movement

Wonder Woman on television and in the comics—strong, capable, yet attractive

Superb executive

Women's Movement

In many respects the Women's Movement has had positive effects: women who were not content to remain at home feel more comfortable in the business world. In other ways, however, the effects of the Women's Movement have been negative. Although more and more women are working, no one has really helped them deal with the guilt they feel at leaving their children and homes. Consequently, they feel that they must become "superwomen," equally talented on all fronts.

This problem came very close to home recently when my aunt resigned as an attorney for a large corporation. She felt that she could not be less than a perfect wife and mother, and her job did not leave her with the time or energy to accomplish this perfection.

Commercial in which a woman is shown beating her husband in a game of pool after they have both returned from work

Attitudes toward women have changed; Victorians did not expect women to succeed in business and industry

Lack of role models for women

A TV show episode showed how women did what was once considered "men's work" during World War II.

Betty Friedan

Guilt that women feel about leaving home and family

Women must realize that they cannot be perfect

Although there are many ways to organize the information in the preceding notes, five general headings suggest themselves:

Definition of the myth

Evolution of the myth

Continuation of the myth

Personal experience with the myth

Combating the myth

Developing an informal outline by arranging specific details under these general headings might help the writer decide on the following preliminary organization for the paper.

Definition of the myth

    Origins in the "Wonder Woman" story
    The modern superwoman
        Superb executive
        Excellent wife and mother
        Attractive appearance
        Good athlete

Evolution of the myth

    Victorian attitude
    Role of women during World War II
    Effect of the Women's Movement

Continuation of the myth

    Advertisements
    Lack of role models
    Guilt of women

Personal experience with the myth

Combating the myth

    Knowledge of the myth
    Acceptance of imperfections

Notice that not all of the notes were included in the informal outline. Some, such as the note on Greek goddesses and the note about modern "labor-saving" devices, did not fit and were discarded. Later, when the paper is actually written, the writer might choose to alter the outline by adding or discarding more ideas.

An informal outline, unlike a formal one, does not have a numbering system; however, in the preceding sample outline, you can easily tell which are the main ideas and which are details that develop those ideas. The writer has left space between each main idea division, and supporting details are indented (moved a few spaces to the right) under the major headings.

Writing Practice 5: *Ordering and Outlining Information*

Using the notes you already have for your expository essay, prepare an informal outline. Use the sample outline in the preceding section as a model.

From Topic to Thesis

The *thesis* in a piece of writing is the point that the writer intends to make.

The thesis is a sentence giving a clear indication of what the writer will cover in the essay. For example, consider the following subject and topic.

    Subject: Knowledge

    Topic: What I learned on my first job

From the topic, it is difficult to tell exactly what direction the writer's paper will take; what the writer learned could be skills such as operating machinery, or techniques of getting along with people. The following thesis statement, however, explains the writer's purpose in greater detail, giving a clearer indication of the essay's content: "The skills I mastered on my first job have given me a head start on an exciting career." The following are other examples of theses developed from topics.

Subject	Topic	Thesis Statement
Automobiles	Buying a subcompact car	In choosing a subcompact, you should (a) make certain that all members of your family can be comfortable riding in it, (b) be certain that service and parts are easily available, (c) compare the rates of depreciation of value among the cars that interest you.
Illness	My appendectomy	My appendectomy taught me that the care of nurses is as important as the medical knowledge of doctors when one is ill.
Pets	Spending money on pet supplies	Americans spend an enormous amount of money on food, medical care, and even clothing and toys for their household pets.

Writing Practice 6: *From Topic to Thesis*

For this activity use the topic you have used for Writing Practices 3–5. Write a thesis statement for your topic, using the ones in the preceding section as models.

Reading an Expository Essay

In many expository essays, the thesis sentence comes near the beginning. Subsequent paragraphs then explain the main points of the thesis, using facts and details. However, the thesis sentence can also be placed near the end of an expository essay. Then it functions as a conclusion toward which the reader is led by the main points in the paragraphs preceding it. Again, each paragraph contains facts and details that support its main point.

Model: Expository Essay

Aldous Huxley, a British-American author, wrote the following essay, "Time and the Machine," in 1937. Do you think his ideas still hold true today? As you read, be aware of the structure of Huxley's essay, as well as the ideas he explains.

Introduction

Time, as we know it, is a very recent invention. The modern time-sense is hardly older than the United States. It is a by-product of industrialism—a sort of psychological analogue of synthetic perfumes and aniline dyes.

Body

Time is our tyrant. We are chronically aware of the moving minute hand, even of the moving second hand. We have to be. There are trains to be caught, clocks to be punched, tasks to be done in specified periods, records to be broken by fractions of a second, machines that set the pace and have to be kept up with. Our consciousness of the smallest units of time is now acute. To us, for example, the moment 8:17 A.M. means something—something very important, if it happens to be the starting time of our daily train. To our ancestors, such an odd eccentric instant was without significance—did not even exist. In inventing the locomotive, Watt and Stephenson were part inventors of time.

Another time-emphasizing entity is the factory and its dependent, the office. Factories exist for the purpose of getting certain quantities of goods made in a certain time. The old artisan worked as it suited him, with the result that consumers generally had to wait for the goods they had ordered from him. The factory is a device for making workmen hurry. The machine revolves so often each minute; so many movements have to be made, so many pieces produced each hour. Result: the factory worker (and the same is true of the office worker) is compelled to know time in its smallest fractions. In the handwork age there was no such compulsion to be aware of minutes and seconds.

Our awareness of time has reached such a pitch of intensity that we suffer acutely whenever our travels take us into some corner of the world where people are not interested in minutes and seconds. The unpunctuality of the Orient, for example, is appalling to those who come freshly from a land of fixed mealtimes and regular train services. For a modern American or Englishman, waiting is a psychological torture. An Indian accepts the blank hours with resignation, even with satisfaction. He has not lost the fine art of doing nothing. Our notion of time as a collection of minutes, each of which must be filled with some business or amusement, is wholly alien to the Oriental just as it was wholly alien to the Greek. For the man who lives in a preindustrial world, time moves at a slow and easy pace; he does not care about each minute, for the good reason that he has not been made conscious of the existence of minutes.

This brings us to a seeming paradox. Acutely aware of the smallest constituent particles of time—of time, as measured by clockwork and train arrivals and the revolutions of machines—industrialized man has to a great extent lost the old awareness of time in its larger divisions. The time of which we have knowledge is artificial, machine-made time. Of natural, cosmic time, as it is measured out by sun and moon, we are for the most part almost wholly unconscious. Pre-industrial people know time in its daily, monthly, and seasonal rhythms. They are aware of sunrise, noon, and sunset; of the full moon and the new; of equinox and solstice; of spring and summer, autumn and winter. All the old religions have insisted on this daily and seasonal rhythm. Preindustrial man was never allowed to forget the majestic movement of cosmic time.

Conclusion

Industrialism and urbanism have changed all this. One can live and work in a town without being aware of the daily march of the sun across the sky; without ever seeing the moon and stars. Broadway and Piccadilly are our Milky Way; our constellations are outlined in neon tubes. Even changes of season affect the townsman very little. He is the inhabitant of an artificial universe that is, to a great extent, walled off from the world of nature. Outside the walls, time is cosmic and moves with the motion of sun and stars. Within, it is an affair of revolving wheels and is measured in seconds and minutes—at its longest, in eight-hour days and six-day weeks. We have a new consciousness; but it has been purchased at the expense of the old consciousness.[1]

[1]"Time and the Machine" from *The Olive Tree* by Aldous Huxley. Copyright 1937 by Aldous Huxley; renewed © 1965 by Laura A. Huxley. Reprinted by permission of Mrs. Laura Huxley, Chatto & Windus Ltd., and Harper and Row, Publishers, Inc.

Think and Discuss

1. State the thesis sentence of Huxley's essay. Where does Huxley put it?

2. What are the main points Huxley makes in explaining his thesis?

3. With what details does Huxley support the point that factories and offices make us slaves of time?

4. Do you find any ideas in the essay that do not seem to belong?

5. Where does Huxley use facts in his essay? Where does he use opinions?

For Your Writer's Notebook

It is useful to arrange the ideas in an expository essay in a cause-effect pattern, as Aldous Huxley does. After his initial statement, Huxley discusses causes for the situation: industrialism and urbanism. At the end of the essay Huxley describes the effect: while gaining a new sense of time, modern people have lost "the old consciousness."

In his essay "Time and the Machine," Aldous Huxley has some unusual thoughts on the concept of time, a subject people take mostly for granted. Think about other concepts that govern your life, but that you have never stopped to analyze, perhaps space, motion, distance, life, death, and so on. Have modern Americans changed in their approach to any of these concepts? For example, how have television and the telephone changed the concept of space and of distance? How have medical advances changed the concepts of life and death? Write in your notebook about one or more of these concepts and how you think each has changed for humanity over the past fifty years or so.

Writing Assignment II: *Expository Essay*

Using the information you have already gathered and the outline and thesis you have already written, compose an expository essay. Go through the following steps for prewriting, writing, and postwriting.

A. Prewriting

Considering Your Audience: When you talk to different groups of people, you make changes in what you say and the way you say it,

For more information on audience, see pages 26-27.

depending on your audience. Speaking to small children, you avoid long words and complicated sentence structure. When you speak to someone in authority, such as your high school principal, you are more formal and polite than when you speak to close friends. If you were talking about baseball to a British friend who did not understand the game, you would define your terms, which would not be necessary for someone who understood the game. ("Casey struck out. That is, he made three swings at the ball without hitting it.")

When you write, you must also keep your audience in mind. First, define the audience for which you are writing. (Your teacher may wish you to consider him or her or your classmates as your audience.) Think about how best to aim your language at that audience. Consider their interests as well as the extent of their knowledge about your topic. Keep these considerations in mind as you write.

B. Writing

Organization: As you begin writing, pay particular attention to the order in which you present your ideas. Usually readers will pay most attention to the first and last parts of a piece of writing; therefore, you might want to put your most important ideas in those positions. Another possibility is to begin with the least important ideas, thus creating suspense for the reader as you build to the more important thoughts. Still another approach is to proceed from the least complex to the most complex ideas.

Writing the Introduction: The first paragraph of the essay should both introduce the thesis and capture the reader's interest.

Although professional writers may not always make direct statements of their theses, including a thesis sentence in the first paragraph of your essay will give both you and your readers a sense of direction. A frequently used technique is to begin the introductory paragraph with some interesting information and to end it with your thesis statement.

You can capture your reader's attention in your introduction in any of several ways. You might begin with a bold statement, with an interesting quotation or statistic, or with a straightforward statement of the main idea. The following introductions from the expository essays of professional writers illustrate these methods.

> Time, as we know it, is a very recent invention. The modern time-sense is hardly older than the United States. It is a by-product of industrialism—a sort of psychological analogue of synthetic perfumes and aniline dyes.
>
> —from "Time and the Machine" by Aldous Huxley

The desire to hold a paid job has become so compelling that some 24 to 27 million people not now employed in full-time jobs—women, young people and old people in particular—are waiting to take jobs if they become available.

—from "The New Psychological Contracts at Work" by Daniel Yankelovich

With the onset of the vacation season the real problem of the new leisure becomes obvious. Leisure pastime in this country has become so complicated that it is now hard work.

—from "The Paradox of the New Leisure" by Russell Baker

Writing the Body: As you write your first draft, keep in mind the importance of adequate development, unity, and coherence.

In an adequately developed essay, the thesis statement is supported or explained with a sufficient number of facts and specific details. (If you have prepared a preliminary outline, each major heading might become the topic sentence for a paragraph.) To achieve unity, you must arrange details in the composition in some kind of logical order, and each detail must clearly support or develop the thesis statement.

Coherence in an essay, as in a paragraph, may be achieved by using several devices: repetition of key words and phrases, consistency of pronouns, and transition words. Aldous Huxley uses two of these techniques in his essay "Time and the Machine." For example, the following sentences are the topic sentences for each of the first four paragraphs in the essay. Notice how the word *time* is repeated in each of the sentences. In addition, the *italicized* words below are different ways of expressing the idea of the tyranny of time.

> Time, as we know it, is a very recent invention.
> Time is our *tyrant*.
> Another *time-emphasizing entity* is the factory and its dependent, the office.
> Our *awareness of time* has reached such a *pitch of intensity* that we *suffer acutely* whenever our travels take us into some corner of the world where people are not interested in minutes and seconds.

Aldous Huxley begins his essay in the first-person plural when he writes, "Time, as *we* know it, is a very recent invention [*italics* added]," and he maintains the use of that pronoun. Notice how often throughout the essay he uses the first-person plural pronouns *we, us*, and *our*. In this way Huxley includes his readers among those who are affected by this "modern time-sense." The tone that Huxley establishes at the beginning of the essay—that of the knowledgeable essayist—is maintained. Nowhere in the essay does Huxley use slang, colloquialisms, contractions, or usage features that are not a part of Edited Standard English. Notice, however, that much of his language is direct and simple: "Time is our tyrant," "The factory is a device for making workmen hurry," "This brings us to a seeming paradox," and so on.

Writing the Conclusion: The purpose of the concluding paragraph is to leave the reader with a sense of completeness.

If the essay is short, simply repeating the main points you have covered is not an effective way to end. You may, however, rephrase the main idea expressed in the opening paragraph. Russell Baker, author of "The Paradox of the New Leisure," ends his essay the following way.

> With its genius for self-adjustment, the society has turned leisure into labor. We are not far from the time when a man after a hard weekend of leisure will go thankfully off to his job to unwind.

C. Postwriting

If possible, put your first draft aside for several days before beginning the revision. This elapsed time will give you a more objective view of your own writing. Then read over the rough draft, evaluating it against the items in the following checklist. You may find that you need to add, delete, or rearrange ideas: almost all writers make substantial changes at this stage. In fact, most professional writers make major revisions several times before they are satisfied.

Checklist for Revising the Expository Composition

1. The topic is sufficiently limited for a short expository essay.

2. The introduction captures the reader's interest.

3. The thesis is clearly stated early in the essay.

4. The thesis statement is adequately developed with facts and details.

5. Ideas in the essay are logically organized.

6. The writer presents information that is not common knowledge; he or she avoids truisms.

7. Factual statements within the essay are accurate; opinions are presented as such and not as factual statements.

8. The conclusion leaves the reader with a sense of completeness.

9. The essay is unified.

10. The essay is coherent.

11. The topic and language of the essay are appropriate for the audience.

For Your Writer's Notebook

Select an audience from the following list that is different from the one for which you have written your rough draft. Rewrite at least two paragraphs of your rough draft for your new audience. Think about changes in word choice, sentence structure, and language that you will need to make. Be certain that your essay is informative for that new audience.

1. Readers of *Seventeen* magazine (audience consists primarily of teenage girls)

2. Readers of *Reader's Digest* (audience consists mostly of adults; articles are general interest)

3. Readers of your school newspaper

4. Readers of your city or county newspaper

5. Readers of *Time* or *Newsweek* magazine (audience consists mostly of adults; articles are on topics of current national interest)

Establishing Tone

Tone is the attitude the writer assumes toward his or her readers.

The choices the writer makes about diction (words), sentence length and complexity, grammatical features, and point of view will determine how the writer sounds to readers. In most exposition the writer wishes to assume an informative and knowledgeable attitude and so avoids grammatical features that do not conform to Edited Standard English. In addition, however, the writer may decide to adopt a more or less formal tone when addressing the reader.

A formal tone of writing can be achieved by writing from a third-person point of view and by avoiding slang, colloquialisms, and contractions. Also, writers using a formal tone tend to use longer and more complex sentences. For a more informal tone writers might use the first-person point of view and use features of informal English, such as colloquialisms and contractions.

Models: Tone

Each of the following pieces of writing is from an expository essay. What is the tone of the first piece? Of the second? How can you tell?

Smiling begins during the first few weeks of life, but to start with it is not directed at anything in particular. By about the fifth week it is being given as a definite reaction to certain stimuli. The baby's eyes can now fixate objects. At first it is most responsive to a pair of eyes staring at it. Even two black spots on a piece of card will do. As the weeks pass, a mouth also becomes necessary. Two black spots with a mouth-line below them are now more efficient at eliciting the response. Soon a widening of the mouth becomes vital, and then the eyes begin to lose their significance as key stimuli. At this stage, around three to four months, the response starts to become more specific. It is narrowed down from any old face to the particular face of the mother. Parental imprinting is taking place.[1]

—from "A Baby Learns to Smile" by Desmond Morris

Without being too pompous about it, I think I can say I speak for one of the largest unorganized groups in the world—the unpublished authors. We write as though our lives depended on it—yet we have long since adapted ourselves to the icy truth that we will never get into print. Why do we do it? Because it happens to please us. In my own case I enjoy it.[2]

—from "Confessions of an Unpublished Writer" by Babette Blaushild

[1]From *The Naked Ape* by Desmond Morris. Copyright © 1967 by Desmond Morris. Reprinted by permission of McGraw-Hill Book Company.
[2]From "Confessions of an Unpublished Writer" by Babette Blaushild in *Saturday Review*, 1963. Copyright © 1963 by *Saturday Review*. All rights reserved. Reprinted by permission.

The excerpt from "A Baby Learns to Smile" is written in a formal tone. The writer has distanced himself by writing in the third person. There are no slang, colloquialisms, or contractions, and although sentence length varies, the sentence structure is fairly complex. In the excerpt from "Confessions of an Unpublished Writer," however, the writer brings herself closer to readers by addressing them directly from the first-person point of view. Also, the vocabulary is not difficult, and the sentences are less complex than those of the Desmond Morris piece.

Writing Practice 7: *Tone*

Analyze the rough draft of the introduction to your expository essay for tone. First, be certain that you sound knowledgeable and informative. Then classify your introduction as having either a formal or an informal tone. Finally, if the introduction has a formal tone, rewrite it so that it has an informal one. If it sounds informal, rewrite it to give it a formal tone. When you finish, compare the two versions.

Kinds of Expository Essays

Expository essays may be divided into several categories, depending on how the writer presents the information. Two common kinds of expository essays are *definition* and *analysis*. Your entire essay may fit into one of the categories, or parts of it may be developed through each of these approaches.

Essay of Definition

One of the most important parts of communication is an understanding of the definitions of words and terms. People are especially likely to disagree about the definitions of abstract words. For example, to one person, *success* may mean having a lot of money and a job with status; to another, the word might mean inner satisfaction and happiness.

In an *essay of definition*, a word or term is thoroughly defined.

One approach the writer might take in such an essay is to give the dictionary definition of the term and then to extend that definition. An extended definition can include examples of the word or term, a discussion of its important characteristics and its history, and an explanation of variations in meaning.

Model: Expository Writing–Definition

The following sample essay, "Newspaperese" by Richard D. Altick, defines the term *newspaperese*.

Introduction

The jargon peculiar to newspapers is a combination of the cliché, dead wood, and the weak passive or impersonal construction. The great objection to it, as to all jargon, is that it is machine-made. It is written according to formula, and material written to formula inevitably loses much of its color and interest. Here is a short sampling of newspaper clichés together with their simpler equivalents:

The death toll rose to ten today in the wake of the disastrous fire . . . (*or:* Death today claimed four more victims) . . .	Four more people died as a result of the fire . . .
The mercury soared to a record high for the year (*or* plummeted to a new low) . . .	Today was the hottest (*or* coldest) day of the year
At an early hour this morning the identity of the victim had not yet been established . . .	Early this morning the body was still unidentified . . .
Traffic was snarled (*or* paralyzed, *or* at a standstill, *or* moved at a snail's pace, *or* crept bumper to bumper) as snow blanketed the metropolitan area . . .	The snowfall slowed traffic . . .
State Police, aided by local law enforcement officers, today were combing the area adjacent to Center City in search of clues that might lead to the solution of the mystery of the murder-kidnapping . . .	State and local police were looking for clues to the man who kidnapped and murdered . . .
Three persons suffered injuries when the automobile in which they were riding figured in a collision with a large truck . . .	Three persons were hurt when their car hit a big truck . . .
As he completed his investigation, the coroner said it was his opinion that death was instantaneous . . .	The coroner thought the man had been killed instantly . . .

Body   In addition, there are numerous single words, especially epithets and verbs, which are seemingly indispensable to newspaper reporting. Any better-than-ordinary fire or auto accident is *spectacular*; an accident that is more peculiar than disastrous is *freak*; when public men approve of something they *hail* it, when they disapprove of it they *attack* it, and when they want something they *urge* it; when two factions have a disagreement they *clash*; when anything is announced it is made *public*; and when men accuse others of wrongdoing they *allege*. (*Assert*, another newspaper war horse, has a slightly less negative connotation.)

The weak passive is used in newspaper writing for essentially the same reason it is used in governmental correspondence: to achieve the impersonal note, and thus, in many instances, to disclaim direct responsibility for statements that are based on hearsay. When newspapers send a reporter for an eyewitness story of a disaster or a court trial, or when they quote a press release or statements made during an interview, they can state positively that this and that are true. But much news cannot be treated in so open and confident a fashion—news based on private information picked up by reporters or on rumors circulating in the city hall or the stock exchange. Although the papers wish to relay this news, they cannot do so on their own authority; the man who gave the reporter his information refuses to be quoted, and the public will be suspicious of anything plainly labeled "rumor." The solution, then, is to use weak passives or impersonal constructions which do not require an agent: "It was revealed (*or* learned *or* reported)" (*not*: the City Commissioner told our reporter but warned him not to use his name); "indications increased" or "a survey today showed" (*not*: our reporter asked several people, and their replies, when put together, suggested). Another device of passing on news without revealing its source (or, it may be, without revealing that it has no source outside the mind of an inventive reporter) is the use of those mysterious oracles, the *officials who asked that their names be withheld, spokesmen, informed quarters, observers,* and *sources usually considered reliable.* Judged from the

Conclusion   viewpoint of clear, accurate communication, "newspaperese" has as little to recommend it as does any other kind of roundabout, machine-made language.[1]

In "Newspaperese" Richard Altick begins with a straightforward definition: "The jargon peculiar to newspapers is a combination of the cliché, dead wood, and the weak passive or impersonal construction." He then discusses each characteristic of newspaperese (the cliché, dead wood, and the weak passive), giving specific examples of each. Finally, he gives his evaluation of newspaperese.

---

[1]From "Newspaperese" from *Preface to Critical Writing,* Fifth Edition by Richard D. Altick. Copyright 1946, 1951, © 1956, 1960, and 1969 by Holt, Rinehart and Winston, Inc. Reprinted with permission of Holt, Rinehart and Winston, Publishers, CBS College Publishing.

Writing Practice 8: *Definition*

Using one of the following subjects or one of your own choosing, write an extended essay of definition. Follow the prewriting, writing, and postwriting steps outlined in this chapter for writing an expository essay. Your purpose is to thoroughly define the word or term that is your topic.

1. Feminism
2. Teenager
3. Soap opera
4. Propaganda
5. The American character
6. Cable television
7. Fads
8. A good job
9. Hero
10. "Come in from the cold" (expression used by intelligence agents)

Essay of Analysis

For more information on purpose in writing, see pages 26-27.

An essay of analysis may be either process analysis or item analysis.

In *process analysis* the writer's purpose is to explain how a process works.

In analyzing the process—creating special effects for a movie, perfecting a tennis backhand, building a log cabin, earning an *A* in English—the writer examines the individual parts of the process and how they work together. Usually this is done in the order of the steps of the process.

In *item analysis* the writer's purpose is to examine the reasons for a situation.

The situation may be inflation, a high crime rate, low school attendance, or a poor television production, but the writer looks for underlying reasons and causes that have resulted in that situation. Thus, an item analysis deals with causes and effects.

Model: Expository Writing–Analysis

In the following essay Mollie Panter-Downes analyzes a political situation in England. During the elections for representatives to the European Parliament, few British people voted. (The European Parliament is the legislative body of an association of Western European countries called the European Economic Community.) After giving background information about the election, the writer categorizes and explains the reasons for the poor showing. As you read the essay, look for these reasons.

Introduction

After last month's enormous political excitement here in Britain, the election of representatives to the European Parliament took place on June 7th in such a deep, inattentive calm that it might have been deciding something on another planet. The result, which sent Conservative winners romping off to Strasbourg in even greater preponderance than that of the Conservative M.P.s entrenched at Westminster, followed a campaign that was impersonally short of all the usual trimmings. London showed no sign of knowing that anything was afoot. In country towns to the south, which are prosperous Conservative strongholds and therefore, it is always said, contain more conscientious voters than Labour areas do, one noticed a slight blooming of party posters among the late lilacs in front gardens. There were apparently few local meetings and no door-to-door campaigning.

It was predicted all along that the turnout would be low. Yet when the melancholy figures began to trickle in—on the night of the count both television channels took part in an elaborate election-results program that went on cheerily analyzing and hooking up with other voting capitals long after the majority of this section of Europe's new constituents had certainly yawned their way to bed—the undreamed-of-faintness of Britain's voice in the European concert was a shock that the press and the political commentators castigated as "appalling."

Body

All sorts of reasons other than indifference or downright hostility were given to explain why things had turned out even worse than expected. The party organizations were tired and short of money after fighting the general election, and the public could not summon up much interest in another lot of political faces showing up so soon on their TVs, this time holding forth about Europe. The huge size of the Euro-constituencies into which Britain was carved up was daunting to many, since British election campaigns have traditionally preserved a personal, almost village character. Great slabs of the electorate were joined together willy-nilly with places beyond their normal constituency boundaries. For example, a sizable number of annoyed people who live in West Surrey found themselves pruned from the rest of the county and grafted on to part of Hampshire and all the Isle of Wight to form a new hybrid known as Wight and Hampshire East.

The lineup of candidates was unlikely to galvanize anybody. They included local-government figures, farmers, Eurocrats from Brussels, and professional men and women, with a sprinkling of past and present members of both Houses of Parliament and a few top executives who appear now and then in TV political discussions that do not attract popular audiences. Many citizens who were interested in the outcome and intended to use their vote had no idea what their candidate looked or sounded like. With one exception, the candidates were little-known players requesting to be sent out to bat for England in the unfamiliar Strasbourg field, and the lack of cheers for them—or, indeed, of any sound at all—was not surprising. . . .

Conclusion

The threatening hint in Labour's European-election manifesto that Britain might withdraw from the European Economic Community if desired reforms did not come quickly has now been shelved for the next five years or so. Pro-Europe and anti-Europe voters are united for once, however, in approving the Thatcher Government's speedy announcement that although a new cordial era has come at last, this government will be every bit as tough as the last lot in pressing for a reduction in the disproportionately hefty contribution that Britain pays into the Community's budget. The message of the fainthearted June 7th vote was clearly that for most of the British people Europe is still "them," and has not become "us."[1]

---

[1]From "Letter From London" by Mollie Panter-Downes in *The New Yorker*, July 2, 1979, p. 68. ©1979 by The New Yorker Magazine, Inc. Reprinted by permission.

Think and Discuss

1. To analyze the poor voter turnout, Mollie Panter-Downes looks at the reasons for the British voters' lack of interest. She explains, for example, that this election may have come too soon after the British national elections and that too few voters knew the candidates other than by name. What are other reasons she cites?

2. What is the thesis sentence of this essay? Where is it placed?

3. What is the topic of the essay's final paragraph?

Writing Practice 9: *Analysis*

Using one of the following ten subjects or another similar one that you select, write an essay of either process or item analysis. Follow the prewriting, writing, and postwriting steps outlined in this chapter for writing an expository essay.

1. Tuning up a car

2. Reducing urban crime

3. Why the Social Security system doesn't work

4. A successful running program

5. How cable television affects the community

6. Maintaining an all-volunteer army successfully

7. The effects of caffeine on the body

8. A bad television program

9. Why society doesn't place more value on its senior citizens

10. How to save money on clothes

The Writer's Promises

Writers of exposition make four implicit promises to readers.

First, unless there is a good reason to think otherwise, the writer promises to be *sincere* in what he or she writes.

Second, the writer promises to provide readers with all necessary information, but no more than is necessary. This promise concerns *quantity*. A writing teacher is talking about this promise when she or he says to a student, "You haven't given me enough details" or "Your ideas need further development," or, on the other hand, "You're being redundant; you've already made this point."

Third, the writer promises to express ideas as clearly as possible. This promise involves *quality*. Obscure or muddled expression of ideas annoys most readers, making them unwilling to accept the writer's message.

Finally, the writer promises that everything he or she writes will pertain to the subject; that is, everything will be *relevant*. Whenever a reader says, "I don't see what this has to do with the subject," the problem of relevance has appeared.

Writing Practice 10: *The Writer's Promises*

Find and bring to class a piece of exposition that has one or more of the following characteristics: insincerity, too little or too much information, muddled expression of ideas, or irrelevant ideas. With your teacher and classmates discuss how these characteristics affect the expository writing. Then, revise it to make it a more effective piece of communication. (You might begin your search by looking at advertisements.)

Humorous Writing

Sometimes, good writers purposely violate the rules of sincerity, quantity, quality, and relevance to achieve humor.

Model: Humorous Writing

Woody Allen violates several of the rules in the following tongue-in-cheek description of a college course.

> *Fundamental Astronomy:* A detailed study of the universe and its care and cleaning. The sun, which is made of gas, can explode at any moment, sending our entire planetary system hurtling to destruction; students are advised what the average citizen can do in such a case. They are also taught to identify various constellations, such as the Big Dipper, Cygnus the Swan, Sagittarius the Archer, and the twelve stars that form Lumides the Pants Salesman.[1]

Because no sane person could talk sincerely about the care and cleaning of the universe, the first sentence is a clue to readers that the course description will be humorous. Since everyone knows that the sun is made of gas, the second sentence violates the rule of *quantity*. The main device of humor in the description, though, is *irrelevancy*; none of the subject matter listed is relevant to a course in fundamental astronomy.

For Your Writer's Notebook

In your notebook write four humorous paragraphs, basing each one on the violation of one of the four rules.

Examples

Sincerity: I propose a new extracurricular activity for our school: demolition derbies. Money that is now spent on sports, band, and orchestra could be used to buy old cars for the derbies, which could be held on the school athletic field. If these funds were not enough to supply each student with a car, teachers' salaries could be cut.

Quantity: Darlene is the most beautiful girl I have ever known; she is my ideal. In case you have never seen her, let me describe her to you. Her fingernails are immaculately clean and neatly trimmed.

---

[1]"Fundamental Astronomy" from "Spring Bulletin," which appears in *Getting Even* by Woody Allen. Copyright © 1966, 1971 by Woody Allen. Reprinted by permission of Random House, Inc. and Rollins, Joffe, Morra & Brezner Incorporated, as agents for the author.

Sentence Combining:
Using Punctuation

Joining Sentences with a Dash, a Colon, or Parentheses

Certain marks of punctuation can be used to join sentences with special relationships. You can use a colon to join two sentences when one of them explains or restates the idea of the other, as the following example shows.

Sentences: The contract settlement was acceptable to both sides. Management held down the wage increase to 8 per cent, and the workers received improved medical benefits. (:)

Joined: The contract settlement was acceptable to both sides: management held down the wage increase to 8 per cent, and the workers received improved medical benefits.

A dash can also be used to connect two sentences when one explains or restates the idea of the other.

Sentences: The officials should have thrown a flag on the play. They could have penalized our team ten yards. (—)

Joined: The officials should have thrown a flag on the play— they could have penalized our team ten yards.

For more information on using parentheses to join sentences, see pages 568-569.

Parentheses can also be used to join sentences when one sentence explains the other. However, with the parentheses, the explanatory information is usually incidental to the idea of the sentence.

Sentences: Ambassador Okimi presented the resolution to the General Assembly.
He is from Japan. ( )

Joined: Ambassador Okimi (he is from Japan) presented the resolution to the General Assembly.

Exercise 1: Joining Sentences with a Colon, a Dash, or Parentheses

Combine each of the following pairs of sentences, using a dash, a colon, or parentheses. Use the signals given for the first five sets. For sets 6–10 you must choose which punctuation marks you think work best. Study the examples before you write your answers on a separate sheet of paper.

Examples

a. Fewer people voted in the recent presidential election than in the previous ten.
   Refer to Diagram A for the figures. ( )
   Fewer people voted in the recent presidential election than in the previous ten (refer to Diagram A for the figures).

b. Jason could have prevented the accident.
   He should have checked his brakes last week.
   Jason could have prevented the accident: he should have checked his brakes last week.

   –or–

   Jason could have prevented the accident—he should have checked his brakes last week.

1. The sunset over the mountains was spectacular.
   The yellow and orange sky was a beautiful backdrop to the snow-capped peaks. (:)

133

2. The referee stopped the fight too late.
   Thompson was already seriously injured. (—)

3. Senator McCarthy will chair the new committee.
   He is a liberal Democrat. ( )

4. Jennifer got the job at the bank.
   She was ecstatic. (—)

5. The long-forgotten trunk contained many of Grandmother's personal things.
   It contained letters, a diary, her wedding dress, and a collection of dolls. (:)

6. The use of metaphors in lyric poetry often makes this kind of poetry difficult to understand.
   A discussion of metaphors in lyric poetry begins on page 243.

7. The new synthetic material will last longer than nylon.
   It is colorfast and resistant to high heat.

8. Nicole was very upset after the swimming meet.
   Her team performed poorly.

9. The general ordered our troops to advance.
   The enemy was retreating.

10. Most department stores hold regular, seasonal sales.
    The sales include back-to-school, after holidays, and summer clearance.

Joining Parts of Sentences with a Dash, a Colon, or Parentheses

For more information on the colon, see pages 565-566.

A colon, dash, or parentheses can be used to join parts of one sentence to another. A colon can join the part of a sentence that explains, gives an example or illustration, or provides a list to the end of another sentence. The following example illustrates how this combination works.

Sentences: The overseas cargo carrier brought goods from all over the world.
It brought spices, footwear, heavy machinery, and rattan furniture. (:)

Joined: The overseas cargo carrier brought goods from all over the world: spices, footwear, heavy machinery, and rattan furniture.

For more information on the dash, see pages 567-568.

A part of a sentence that explains or restates the idea of another or that adds information can be attached with a dash or paired dashes.

Sentences: My tendency to be lazy prevents me from finishing homework on time.
My tendency to be lazy is a trait I would like to be rid of. (—, —)

Joined: My tendency to be lazy—a trait I would like to be rid of—prevents me from finishing homework on time.

When a list or illustration precedes the main part of a sentence, it is followed by a dash and a summary word, such as *such*, *these*, or *all*.

Sentences: These were the only objects the rescue team found on the frozen body.
The objects were a ration of beef jerky, a pocket knife, a pair of binoculars, and one wet match. (—)

Joined: A ration of beef jerky, a pocket knife, a pair of binoculars, and one wet match—these were the only objects the rescue team found on the frozen body.

Parentheses can also join part of a sentence to another sentence.

Sentences: Martha Yvonne Carruthers became head of a large corporation before she was thirty-nine years old.
Martha Yvonne Carruthers was a naturalized citizen. ( )

Joined: Martha Yvonne Carruthers (a naturalized citizen) became head of a large corporation before she was thirty-nine years old.

135

Exercise 2: Joining Parts of Sentences with a Dash, a Colon, or Parentheses

Join sentence pairs 1–5 using the signals indicated. For unsignaled sets, choose the punctuation you think works best.

Examples

a. On the line hung three quilts my grandparents had made years ago. The quilts were a blue-and-white crisscross pattern, a rose bouquet on a white background, and a patchwork design with bright red borders. (:)

On the line hung three quilts my grandparents had made years ago: a blue-and-white crisscross pattern, a rose bouquet on a white background, and a patchwork design with bright red borders.

b. I hope that a good mechanic will be able to diagnose what is wrong with my car and repair it quickly. My car is definitely a lemon.

I hope that a good mechanic will be able to diagnose what is wrong with my car (definitely a lemon) and repair it quickly.

—or—

I hope that a good mechanic will be able to diagnose what is wrong with my car—definitely a lemon—and repair it quickly.

1. Senta was attracted to the young man as soon as she saw his superb skill on the ice.
   The young man was a wonderful, graceful skater! ( )

2. Behind her on the wall were posters of her favorite entertainers. The entertainers were the Beatles, Loretta Lynn, and Charlie Daniels. (:)

3. An adequate diet should contain some fiber-rich bran as well as foods that provide protein, fats, and carbohydrates.
   Fiber-rich bran is available in bran cereals or in bulk at some health food stores. ( )

4. These activities helped Melissa maintain her good health and trim figure.
   Swimming fifty laps every day, bicycling several miles on weekends, and playing volleyball twice a week after school were the activities. (:)

5. In writing a comparison essay, it is a good idea to choose two items that share some elements and then show their similarities and differences.
   The items are perhaps two poems on death. (—, —)

6. Dell's interest in movies began when he was a child watching Disney films, and it has grown ever since.
   The Disney films were *Snow White*, *Bambi*, and *Pinnochio*.

7. Take this letter to the front office for confirmation of your employment.
   No signatures are needed.

8. These were the traits that made her so likeable.
   A good sense of humor, a warm personality, and a sensitivity to the needs of other people were the traits.

9. Five vehicles suffered front- or rear-end damage when they ran into each other in the swiftly moving expressway traffic.
   The five vehicles were all late model cars.

10. The visitors had to smile when they saw the animals in the zoo nursery window.
    The animals were a two-week-old spider monkey nursing on a doll-sized bottle, a baby cheetah trying to chew off a bandage on its paw, and a newborn African kudu that pressed its nose softly against the glass.

Writing Practice: *Joining Sentences with Special Relationships*

Choose an appropriate paragraph from one of the expository essays you have written for this chapter. Revise the paragraph, using dashes, parentheses, and/or colons to join sentences that have special relationships. If necessary, add details to your sentences. Work to achieve a variety of sentence lengths and patterns.

5 Imaginative Writing

Defining Imaginative Writing

The term *imaginative writing* encompasses stories, novels, plays, and poetry.

In imaginative writing, elements from the real world (such as actual places, character traits, and experiences) often combine with elements that the writer invents. Imaginative writing takes these real and/or invented elements and presents them in a new way. This new creation—whether it is a story, play, novel, or poem—gives the reader an experience of the world through the mind of the writer.

In this chapter you will learn to apply your own imagination to the writing of short stories, plays, and poetry. The skills that you learn would definitely be applicable to the writing of novels as well.

Writing Poetry

The term *poetry* covers a wide range of imaginative writing. Although much poetry follows formal patterns of rhyme and rhythm, poetry can also be written with no formal patterns and can even be composed in paragraph form like prose. What do these highly different forms of poetry have in common? In all poetry the reader is aware not only of what the poet is saying but also of the special language being used to express specific thoughts and feelings. In this section you will learn about the elements that make the language of poetry distinct from other imaginative writing. You will also learn various techniques of composing several types of poems yourself.

Poetry written in paragraph form is called *prose poetry*. *Free verse* refers to poetry without rhyme or rhythm. *Blank verse* means that the poetry has rhythm only. *Lyric poetry* refers to poetry written with both rhyme and rhythm. Sound patterns in lyric poetry are similar to the sound patterns of repeated notes and phrases in music. The pattern of repeating sounds is called *rhyme*, the pattern of repeating rhythm is called *meter*, and the patterns of repeating lines are called *stanzas*.

The Element of Structure

W hen the lines of a poem are divided into groups, each grouping is called a *stanza*. The number of lines in each stanza can form a pattern that repeats throughout the poem. For example, both the Stevie Smith poem on page 147 and the Yeats poem on page 151 use three stanzas of four lines each. The way a poem is divided into stanzas is part of its overall form or structure. The structure reflects and enhances the overall meaning of the poem.

Poets may also divide their poems into stanzas of unequal length. Usually, this indicates a grouping of ideas, with each stanza devoted to one major idea.

Model: *Poetic Structure – Stanza Breaks*

In the first two stanzas of "Dover Beach" by Matthew Arnold, the stanza breaks serve a definite purpose. What is the subject of the first stanza? Of the second?

[from] Dover Beach

The sea is calm tonight,
The tide is full, the moon lies fair
Upon the straits;—on the French coast the light
Gleams and is gone; the cliffs of England stand,
Glimmering and vast, out in the tranquil bay.
Come to the window, sweet is the night-air!
Only, from the long line of spray
Where the sea meets the moon-blanched land,
Listen! you hear the grating roar
Of pebbles which the waves draw back, and fling,
At their return, up the high strand,
Begin, and cease, and then again begin,
With tremulous cadence slow, and bring
The eternal note of sadness in.

Sophocles long ago
Heard it on the Aegean, and it brought
Into his mind the turbid ebb and flow
Of human misery; we
Find also in the sound a thought
Hearing it by this distant northern sea.

—Matthew Arnold

Matthew Arnold uses the stanza structure to indicate a change of thought and setting. In the first stanza a contemporary speaker watches and listens to the sea on a moonlit night from a window overlooking Dover Beach in England. In the second stanza the scene and time both change. The setting is ancient Greece in the time of Sophocles. Sophocles, too, thinks about life's sadness, ". . . ebb and flow/Of human misery."

Two other important elements of structure in poems are *line length* and *line breaks*. The choices that poets make about the length of line to use in a poem, and where to break off each line and start another, have an important influence on their poems.

Model: *Poetic Structure – Line Length and Line Breaks*

The following poem by British poet Ken Smith uses short lines to give the effect of a list jotted down. As you read, notice how the short lines fit the meaning of the poem.

Inventory/Itinerary[1]

Illinois, Iowa
Dead grass & maize stalks
Miles, miles, 4 1/2 thousand
Timeshift 7 hours
2 continents, 1 ocean
Travelling, 4 days
1 good time, much being quiet
200 cigarettes, 1 bottle brandy
1 arrive in Iowa City
March 25th 1969, 6:00 p.m.
$3.38c in my pocket
1 cab-ride into the clapboard wilderness
1 return on foot carrying 2 bags
9 phone calls, 2 wrong numbers, 1 reply
Waiting, waiting
1 poem written quickly holding things down
The durations of wind, cold, grainfields
Endless, helpfulness, cheerfulness, on the nail
The bland faces, America America
And silence. And night
And wind blowing, right through the heart

—Ken Smith

Think and Discuss

The title of the preceding poem "Inventory/Itinerary," tells you that the poem will be a kind of list, a record of things the poet takes with him and places he goes. The short lines emphasize these items and places by focusing the reader's attention on one thing at a time. Notice that when Ken Smith starts writing about emotions and observations in America the line length grows. The longer lines give a flowing, continuous effect. For example, the final line would have a very different feeling if it were written in the following way.

And wind blowing
Right through the heart

The line break would create a pause that would interrupt the flow of thought.

1. Look for other instances in the poem of the importance of line length.

2. What other subjects or feelings do you think would be appropriate for short lines of poetry?

---

[1]"Inventory/Itinerary" from *Work, Distances* by Ken Smith. Copyright © 1973 by Ken Smith. Originally published by Swallow Press, Chicago. Reprinted by permission of the author.

Writing Practice 1: *Poetic Structure*

Write an unrhymed poem, paying close attention to structure. Let your poem be about a journey. Use the shape of the poem for effect, making the structure of stanzas and the length of your lines appropriate to the poem's content. Like Ken Smith, you can suggest the short, staccato quality of a fast journey by listing things you took, people you saw, things you said, observed, and so on. Or you can write about a long, leisurely journey, shaping your lines and stanzas accordingly.

Figurative Language in Poetry

The purpose of *figurative language* is to go beyond the literal meaning of words in order to create a sense of correspondence between dissimilar things. This discovery—the correspondence between things that are apparently different—can help the reader as well as the writer experience the world in a new way. *Simile, metaphor,* and *personification* are widely used types of figurative language. You will find figurative language in prose and even in daily speech, but in poetry figurative language is often the primary means of expression.

Simile

A simile states a comparison between two unlike items.

Similes contain words such as *like, as, than, seems,* and *appears.* "Love *is like* a rose" is an example of simile.

Model: *Figurative Language – Simile*

Similes can create surprising comparisons, as in the following stanza by Scottish poet Hugh MacDiarmid.

[from] Esplumeoir[1]

'It was an amazing discovery, like the inside of your head being painlessly scraped out. There was an amazing clarity, like the brilliant moon falling into it and filling it neatly.'

—*Hugh MacDiarmid*

---

[1]From "Esplumeoir" from *Collected Poems of Hugh MacDiarmid*. Rev. Edn. © Christopher Murray Grieve 1948, 1962. Copyright © 1967 by Macmillan Publishing Co., Inc.

Think and Discuss

Hugh MacDiarmid begins his poem with a startling description of a discovery so amazing that he compares it to "the inside of your head/being painlessly scraped out."

1. What is the second simile in the poem?

2. How does it relate to the first?

Metaphor

A *metaphor* is an implied comparison between two unlike items.

A metaphor is stated without the linking words used by similes. "Love *is* a rose" is an example of metaphor. Poets use metaphor to show resemblances in more concentrated language than that of similes.

Model: Figurative Language–Metaphor

Look for the metaphor in the following excerpt of a poem by Stevie Smith.

[from] Black March[1]

I have a friend
At the end
Of the world.
His name is a breath

Of fresh air.
He is dressed in
Grey chiffon. At least
I think it is chiffon.
It has a
Peculiar look, like smoke.

It wraps him around
It blows out of place
It conceals him
I have not seen his face . . .

—Stevie Smith

---

[1]Stevie Smith. *The Collected Poems of Stevie Smith.* Copyright © 1972 by Stevie Smith. Reprinted by permission of New Directions Publishing Corporation.

Think and Discuss

The metaphor about the strange friend ("His name is a breath/Of fresh air.") has a more concentrated effect than if Smith had written it as a simile: "His name is like a breath of fresh air." "Black March" also contains a simile in its description. What is the simile?

Personification

Personification **is the attribution of the appearance, feelings, or thoughts of a living thing to a nonliving subject. Of the many variations of metaphor, personification is one of the most frequently used.**

Model: Figurative Language–Personification

The following poem by Ted Hughes uses personification to describe the experience of inspiration. You have probably shared the experience of trying to write something, waiting for the right idea, and then suddenly having it come into your head. Hughes portrays the thought he is waiting for as a fox, "The Thought-Fox." As you read, notice how the identification of the thought with the fox continues through the poem.

The Thought-Fox[1]

I imagine this midnight moment's forest:
Something else is alive
Beside the clock's loneliness
And this blank page where my fingers move.

Through the window I see no star:
Something more near
Though deeper within darkness
Is entering the loneliness:

Cold, delicately as the dark snow,
A fox's nose touches twig, leaf;
Two eyes serve a movement, that now
And again now, and now, and now

Sets neat prints into the snow
Between trees and warily a lame
Shadow lags by stump and in hollow
Of a body that is bold to come

Across clearings, an eye,
A widening deepening greenness,
Brilliantly, concentratedly,
Coming about its own business

Till, with a sudden sharp hot stink of fox
It enters the dark hole of the head.
The window is starless still; the clock ticks,
The page is printed.

—*Ted Hughes*

Think and Discuss

1. What is the metaphor in the first line of "The Thought-Fox"?

2. How does Hughes imagine the fox approaching him as the poem progresses?

3. What descriptive words does he use to convey the appearance and movement of the fox? How do they also apply to thought?

---

[1]"The Thought-Fox" from *Selected Poems,* 1957-1967 by Ted Hughes. Copyright © 1957 by Ted Hughes. Reprinted by permission of Harper & Row, Publishers, Inc. and Faber and Faber Ltd.

Writing Practice 2: *Figurative Language in Poetry*

Write a poem based on simile, metaphor, and/or personification. As you write, remember to fit the structure of the poem to its content. The following suggestions may be helpful in writing your poem.

1. In "Esplumeoir" Hugh MacDiarmid begins with two unusual similes to describe an experience. You could write a poem about an experience by making a list of unusual similes. You may want to write about an action, such as ice skating, or jumping into a cold river; or you may want to write about a mental activity, such as looking at a painting or listening to music or day-dreaming. This poem can be humorous or serious. Include a simile in each line.

—or—

2. In "The Thought-Fox" Ted Hughes links an animal with the human attribute of thought. You could write a poem making another link between an animal and a human attribute. For example, you might want to write about dreaming: What animal do you associate with the act of dreaming? Thoughts seem to come into the mind instantly, while dreams have a slower, more gradual quality. What animal do you associate with that quality? Write a poem describing a dream coming to you by personifying it as an animal, or a poem using personification in another way.

The Element of Rhyme

Words *rhyme* when they share similar sounds.

Words can rhyme exactly, as in the rhyme *light/sight*, or words can rhyme approximately, as in *light/time*, or *light/out*. The first type of rhyme is called *exact*, or *perfect*, *rhyme*. The second type is called *half*, or *slant, rhyme*.

Model: Rhyme in Poetry

The following poem by the British poet Stevie Smith uses exact rhyme in combination with half rhyme. The combination gives a musical feeling to the poem, and the rhymes help knit the lines of poetry together. Identify the exact and half rhymes after reading the poem.

Not Waving but Drowning[1]

Nobody heard him, the dead man,
But still he lay moaning:
I was much further out than you thought
And not waving but drowning.

Poor chap, he always loved larking
And now he's dead.
It must have been too cold for him his heart gave way,
They said.

Oh, no no no, it was too cold always
(Still the dead one lay moaning).
I was much too far out all my life
And not waving but drowning.

—Stevie Smith

Think and Discuss

1. What is the scene in this poem? Who are the characters? What happens?

2. What is exact rhyme in "Not Waving but Drowning"?

3. What is the half rhyme?

4. In formal rhyming patterns the words at the end of each line rhyme. It is also possible for words within a poem to rhyme exactly or to make a half rhyme. When repeating sounds occur

---

[1]Stevie Smith. *The Collected Poems of Stevie Smith*. Copyright © 1964 by Stevie Smith. Reprinted by permission of New Directions Publishing Corporation.

within a poem, the effect is called *internal rhyme*. For example, Stevie Smith uses internal rhyme to emphasize meaning in the line "Oh, no no no, it was too cold always." The repeating *o* sound has a moaning quality that emphasizes the importance and the meaning of the line. What other examples of internal rhyme do you find in "Not Waving but Drowning"?

Consonance, Assonance, and Alliteration

Notice that each of Stevie Smith's stanzas in "Not Waving but Drowning" has the same rhyming pattern, with the rhyme on the final word of the second and fourth lines. This type of half rhyme is called *consonance*. *Consonance* is the repetition of final consonant sounds, but not vowel sounds, in a pair of rhyming words. *Wing/song, right/out, moaning/drowning*—all are examples of consonance. Another type of half rhyme is called *assonance*. Assonance is the repetition of vowel sounds in a poem. Whereas *seethe* and *breathe* are exact rhymes, *seethe/he* is an example of assonance. *Light/time, boat/shone,* and *half/apple* are all examples of assonance.

Another rhyming pattern that occurs within a poem is called *alliteration*. Words *alliterate* when they begin with the same sound rather than end with the same sound. The phrases "deeper within darkness" and "the window is starless still" in Ted Hughes' "Thought-Fox" (page 145) are examples of alliteration.

Writing Assignment I: *Rhyme in Poetry*

Write a poem of at least eight lines, using exact rhyme, half rhyme, consonance, assonance, alliteration, or a combination of these. Do not use the same rhyming sound for the last word in each line. Instead, alternate rhymes in a pattern you choose throughout the poem. Use the prewriting, writing, and postwriting steps to help you with ideas for your poem.

A. Prewriting

When you write a poem using a formal element such as rhyme, it is important to think about the subject of the poem first rather than to think of the rhymes. In "Not Waving but Drowning," Stevie Smith writes about an impossible speech. A dead man speaks to the living, who do not understand him. You might want to use an impossible speech as the subject of your poem; give a voice to someone or something that cannot speak. This speech can come from a person who would like to express a thought or feeling but cannot, or it can

come from something that has no voice. For example, you might imagine what the wind or rain would say if it had a human voice, or the ocean, the moon, the winter, a fire, death, or a long highway.

Suppose, for example, that you want to write about the voice of the snow. Imagine yourself in a place you know, looking at a snowy field or street, or watching the snow come down. Stevie Smith begins her poem, "Nobody heard him, the dead man." You may begin your poem in a similar fashion: "Nobody heard the snow," or find some phrase to tell the reader that the snow will speak. Next, think about the snow itself. The snow is speaking because it is not understood, like the drowned man in Stevie Smith's poem. Why is it not understood? What does it want to say to people or to the earth? What does it feel? How does it envision itself? Think about all these questions as they apply to your subject. What your subject has to say is the heart of the poem.

B. Writing

As you think about what your subject has to say, jot down the ideas that come to you. Then use brainstorming or a rhyming dictionary to create rhymes for some of the words you have chosen. For example, if you find many words that rhyme with *snow*, use *snow* as one of your end rhymes. You can rhyme every other line, as the Stevie Smith poem shows, or you can use the rhyme pattern of the Ted Hughes poem on page 145.

C. Postwriting

When you have finished your poem, give it a title. Exchange your poem with your classmates; read each other's poems for enjoyment.

The Element of Meter

Meter **is a formal rhythmic pattern in a poem.**

There are many ways to organize patterns of rhythm into formal meters. The meter most commonly used in English poetry is called *accentual-syllabic* meter. To understand accentual-syllabic meter, look at the following line by the Irish poet William Butler Yeats:

> When yóu are old and gréy and full of sléep

In the preceding line the marked syllables are the ones your voice would emphasize as you read. The line makes a pattern. An unaccented syllable (starting with *When*) is followed each time by an accented syllable (starting with *you*). You can hear the same pattern in these words: *reléase, enjóy, decéive, allów.* This unaccented/accented pattern is the metrical unit most common to English: the *iamb.*

Model: *Meter in Poetry*

The line by Yeats also follows a second pattern of organization: the number of syllables used adds up to ten, with five accented syllables in each line. As you read the rest of the poem, "When You Are Old," notice how the metric pattern works in each line. Read the poem aloud or listen to it being read so that you can hear the metric pattern.

When You Are Old[1]

When you are old and grey and full of sleep,
And nodding by the fire, take down this book,
And slowly read, and dream of the soft look
Your eyes had once, and of their shadows deep;

How many loved your moments of glad grace,
And loved your beauty with love false or true,
But one man loved the pilgrim soul in you,
And loved the sorrows of your changing face;

And bending down beside the glowing bars,
Murmur, a little sadly, how Love fled
And paced upon the mountains overhead
And hid his face amid a crowd of stars.

—*W. B. Yeats*

Think and Discuss

Each line of Yeats' poem uses the iambic pattern: an unstressed syllable followed by a stressed syllable. There are a few variations, to add emphasis or to prevent the poem from becoming too regular. For example, in the second line, the phrase "take down this book" is a variation. Usually you would not say "take down this book." The words *take* and *down* are both accented, which emphasizes the meaning of the words. There is no variation, however, in the number of syllables used in each line. Thus, in accentual-syllabic meter, the syllable pattern remains the same throughout the poem.

1. "When You Are Old" also follows a regular rhyming pattern. Does Yeats use the exact rhyme or a half rhyme at the end of each line?

2. Name examples of internal half rhyme that you find.

3. When you read a formal poem, always think about how the formal pattern of rhyme and meter fits the meaning of the poem. For example, in Yeats' poem the speaker addresses a woman he loves as he imagines her in the future, as an old woman. The regular, steady meter gives a quiet feeling to the poem that enhances its meaning; it is a poem about memory. What do you learn from this poem about the poet who loves the woman?

---

[1] "When You Are Old" from *Collected Poems* of William Butler Yeats. (New York: Macmillan, 1956) Reprinted by permission of Macmillan Publishing Co., Inc., M. B. Yeats, Anne Yeats, and Macmillan Landon Limited.

4.   What specific words does the poet use to describe the woman? How does he want her to think of him in the future?

Writing Practice 3: *Meter in Poetry*

Write one or more stanzas of a poem that uses regular, iambic meter in each line. You may use Yeats' pattern of five accented syllables to a line or choose another number. It may be helpful to reread the Yeats poem before you begin. You may include rhyme in your poem if you wish. The following ideas can be used as suggestions for the subject of your poem.

1.   Write a poem to someone in the future, as Yeats does in "When You Are Old." Imagine what the person will be like then. It will help to visualize the person in a definite setting, as Yeats imagines the woman nodding by her fire over a book. Tell this person what you would like him or her to remember of earlier times.

—or—

2.   Write a poem to someone who has not been born yet and tell that person something about the earth as it is now, when you are living. For example, you could talk about sights and sounds that are beautiful or pleasurable to you, experiences that a future person might not share.

—or—

3.   Imagine that you yourself are old, and write a poem about an important memory that you have kept all your life. You might want to begin your poem by envisioning yourself in a particular place: sitting in a chair, staring out the window, walking through the park, or being someplace quiet where you can call up your memories. Include details about where you are and what you see in the present as well as what it is you remember.

Writing a Short Story or Play

Short fiction and plays share many basic elements. Both are constructed by combining *characters,* the people involved in the action; *setting,* the time(s) and place(s) of the action; *plot,* the action itself; and *conflict,* the element of struggle in the plot. The way in which these elements work together, plus other choices the writer makes about the language, ideas, and feeling conveyed in the short story or play, all constitute the writer's individual *style.*

Establishing Characters

The opening of a short story, like the first scene of a play, is especially important, because it is at this point that the reader will either become involved and read further or decide that the story is not interesting.

One way that short stories involve the reader from the beginning is to present the characters in a compelling way.

Model: Characters in a Short Story

The paragraphs that follow open a short story by Katherine Mansfield titled "Mr. Reginald Peacock's Day." Instead of describing her main character to the reader, Katherine Mansfield begins this story in the middle of the character's train of thought as he wakes up in the morning. As you read, notice what the character Reginald says about being wakened by his wife. Notice the way that he expresses himself.

If there was one thing that he hated more than another it was the way she had of waking him in the morning. She did it on purpose, of course. It was her way of establishing her grievance for the day, and he was not going to let her know how successful it was. But really, really, to wake a sensitive person like that was positively dangerous! It took him hours to get over it—simply hours. She came into the room buttoned up in an overall, with a handkerchief over her head—thereby proving that she had been up herself and slaving since dawn—and called in a low, warning voice: "Reginald!"

"Eh! What! What's that? What's the matter?"

"It's time to get up; it's half-past eight." And out she went, shutting the door quietly after her, to gloat over her triumph, he supposed.

He rolled over in the big bed, his heart still beating in quick, dull throbs, and with every throb he felt his energy escaping him, his—his inspiration for the day stifling under those thudding blows. It seemed that she took a malicious delight in making life more difficult for him than—Heaven knows—it was, by denying him his rights as an artist, by trying to drag him down to her level. What was the matter with her?[1]

---

[1]Excerpt from "Mr. Reginald Peacock's Day" in *Collected Stories of Katherine Mansfield* by Katherine Mansfield. Copyright 1920 by Alfred A. Knopf, Inc., renewed 1948 by John Middleton Murry. Reprinted by permission of Alfred A. Knopf, Inc.

Think and Discuss

1. In the preceding paragraphs, Katherine Mansfield tells the story from Reginald's *point of view*; everything that happens is seen through Reginald's eyes. Reginald's train of thought—what he observes and how he feels—all these inform the reader about him. For example, Reginald believes that his wife deliberately wakes him up abruptly because she knows he hates being awakened that way. He imagines that she must "gloat over her triumph" of making him miserable. What other thoughts does Reginald have about his wife's attitude?

2. When Reginald says, "But really, really, to wake a sensitive person like that was positively dangerous! It took him hours to get over it—simply hours," the reader can imagine him speaking in a fussy, excited tone of voice. What does Reginald's manner of speaking tell you about him as a character?

By beginning in the middle of a character's train of thought, Katherine Mansfield pulls her readers into the story through curiosity. A reader might want to know, for example, what sort of artist Mr. Peacock is, whether or not his feelings about his wife are justified, and what his feelings for her will cause him to do.

Writing Practice 4: *Characters in a Short Story*

Imagine that you are writing a short story from a character's point of view. The first paragraph of your story will follow that character's train of thought about something, perhaps your character's reaction to a specific situation. Select one of the following characters and situations, or use one of your own, and write an opening paragraph from that character's point of view. Save your work.

1. A young child, usually very practical and rational, wakes up at night and starts seeing or hearing strange things.

2. A waiter or waitress setting up tables before work remembers being yelled at the day before by the boss.

3. A young woman at a party, angry at being taken for granted by her boyfriend, imagines what she would like to say to him.

4. A humanoid robot on a long journey from one space station to another fantasizes about what it would be like to be a respected human being.

Use the prewriting section that follows to help you with ideas for your paragraph.

Prewriting: When you write from the point of view of a character, you need to imagine exactly what your character is like. Appearance, personality, childhood background, activities—all these elements combine to make a real character. Even though you will not use all of these elements in your paragraph, thinking about them will help make your character seem real to you.

Take a few moments and imagine that you are the character you want to write about. You can get ideas for your character from many different sources: observation of people you know, details you notice about people you pass in the street, stories about your childhood or other people's childhoods, and any other sources that prove useful. On a separate sheet of paper, write the name you choose for your character at the top and jot down your responses to the following questions about the character. Use these notes to help get a complete sense of your character's identity before beginning the paragraph.

1.   What was my childhood like? (Do I come from a large family, or am I an only child? Do I get along well with my family? Was there anything unusual about my childhood: for example, was I extremely poor or rich? What did my parents do for a living? What did they want me to be when I grew up?)

2. Where did I grow up? (What do I remember most about my childhood? Walking through the woods in the snow? Sitting on a hobbyhorse in a dusty attic? Getting in trouble by turning on the water hydrants in the summer?)

3. Where do I live now, and what do I do? (What brought me to this place? Do I still live in the town where I grew up, or have I traveled many places to arrive here? What do I do during the day? Do I have a job, am I unemployed, am I a student? How do I feel about what I do? Would I do something else if I could? How does my family feel about what I do?)

4. How do I feel about myself? (What do I look like? Do I feel pleased with my appearance? What is my most noticeable physical trait: a facial feature, the way I walk, the way I speak?)

5. What is the most important thing in my life? (What am I committed to: my work, another person, being successful? Do others think of me as a dedicated person, as an energetic person, or as a drifter? What would happen to me if I had to give up the most important thing in my life?)

Setting

Setting **refers to the time and place of a story.**

In "Mr. Reginald Peacock's Day," the main focus is on the character Reginald rather than on the setting of the story. Many short story writers, however, weave in descriptions of the setting with character descriptions.

Model: *Setting in a Short Story*

In the opening paragraphs of the story "The Wheelbarrow" by V. S. Pritchett, the writer introduces the main characters and the setting together. He presents them from the general, or *omniscient*, point of view. As you read, notice how V. S. Pritchett combines descriptive details of the setting, the bonfire in particular, and the characters.

"Robert," Miss Freshwater's niece called down from the window of the dismantled bedroom," when you have finished that, would you mind coming upstairs a minute? I want you to move a trunk."

And when Evans waved back from the far side of the rumpled lawn where he was standing by the bonfire, she closed the window to keep out the smoke of slow-burning rubbish—old carpeting, clothes,

magazines, papers, boxes—which hung about the waists of the fir trees and blew towards the house. For three days the fire had been burning and Evans, red-armed in his shirt sleeves and sweating along the seams of his brow, was prodding it with a garden fork. A sudden silly tongue of yellow flame wagged out: some inflammable piece of family history—who knew what?—perhaps one of her Aunt's absurd summer hats or a shocking year of her father's day dream accountancy was having its last fling. She saw Evans pick up a bit of paper from the outskirts of the fire and read it. What was it? Miss Freshwater's niece drew back her lips and opened her mouth expectantly. At this stage all family privacy had gone. Thirty, forty, fifty years of life were going up in smoke.

Evans took up the wheelbarrow and swaggered back with it across the lawn towards the house, sometimes tipping it a little to one side to see how the rubber-tyred wheel was running and to admire it. Miss Freshwater's niece smiled. With his curly black hair, his sun-reddened face and his vacant blue eyes, and the faint white scar or chip on the side of his nose, he looked like some hard-living, hard-bitten doll. "Burn this?" "This lot to go?" was his cry. He was an impassioned and natural destroyer. She could not have found a better man. "Without you, Robert," she said on the first day with real feeling, "I could never have faced it."[1]

Think and Discuss

The preceding paragraphs open in the middle of an activity: Miss Freshwater's niece and her helper, Robert Evans, have built a bonfire to destroy the "old carpeting, clothes, magazines, papers, boxes" that the niece does not want to save from her aunt's house. The *place* of the setting is the house itself and the lawn in front, where the fire has burned for three days.

1. What details tell the reader about the *time* the story is set in: the approximate time in history? The time of year?

2. V. S. Pritchett describes the bedroom the niece calls from as "dismantled." What does that one word tell you about the scene?

3. How does Pritchett describe the lawn where Evans tends the fire?

4. The writer also mentions specific items that the niece imagines burning in the fire. What do these details, such as the "absurd summer hat," tell you about the niece's family and her attitude toward them?

---

[1]From "The Wheelbarrow" from *Selected Stories* by V. S. Pritchett. Copyright © 1978 by V. S. Pritchett. Reprinted by permission of Literistic, Ltd. and Random House, Inc.

Writing Practice 5: *Setting in a Short Story*

Imagine that you are writing a short story and that your opening paragraph or paragraphs will introduce the setting as well as the main character. Use the character you created for the previous Writing Practice. First, decide if you are going to write from your character's point of view, as in the passage by Katherine Mansfield, or from a general point of view, as in the passage from V. S. Pritchett. Next, read the following suggestions to help imagine your setting, and, on a separate sheet of paper, write down the details that come to you.

1. Where does this scene take place? Indoors or outdoors? City, suburbs, or country? A home or a public place? Describe the surroundings in detail, starting with what is nearest the character and working outward.

2. When does this scene take place? At what time in history? What day of the week? What time of year? What point in the character's life?

3. What objects in the scene are most important to the character? How are they important?

Finally, select the most important details and write a one- or two-paragraph description introducing your main character and the setting of your story. Save your work.

Characters and Setting in Plays

When you read a play, you first learn about characters and setting from the notes the playwright makes at the beginning of the play. These notes describe where the action of the play will take place and give brief descriptions of the characters involved.

Model: Characters and Setting in a Play

The following notes are taken from the beginning of a play by Tom Stoppard titled *Enter a Free Man*. As you read, notice the specific details given about the setting and about each character.

> Stage Right is the living-room of RILEY's home . . . a dining-table with chairs, a settee, a grandfather clock, a portrait of the Queen, a transistor radio (the only thing that does not look vaguely out of date). Everything is spick and span. There are lots of potted plants, on sills, shelves and tables, and almost everywhere where there is a plant there is some plumbing above it, quite discreet. Stairs to the bedrooms can be seen beyond the door.
>
> PERSEPHONE is responsible for the tidiness. She is matronly, plump, plain, nice, vague, usually vaguely distracted. She is a real duster and emptier of ashtrays. Her daughter LINDA is in pyjamas. She is eighteen, self-assured, at least on the surface, and can be as cruel or warm as she feels like being. She is *never* sentimental, and often anti-sentiment: sharp, abrasive, cool, when her guard is up, and rather childlike when it drops.
>
> Stage Left is the bar, the public bar of a slightly old-fashioned unfashionable pub in what is probably a seedy urban suburb . . .
>
> RILEY is a smallish untidy figure in a crumpled suit (when he appears)—a soiled fifty with a certain education somewhere in the past: it gives him a tattered dignity now. He is certainly not mad but he is definitely odd. Unsinkable, despite the slow leak.[1]

Think and Discuss

1. The preceding character descriptions help the reader envision how the characters will interact. The tidy character of Persephone is set against the "untidy figure" of her husband Riley, and when their daughter Linda is described as "sharp, abrasive, cool," the reader can imagine that she will not be in harmony

---

[1]From *Enter a Free Man* by Tom Stoppard. Reprinted by permission of Faber and Faber Ltd. and Grove Press, Inc.

with either of her parents. What other descriptive details about the characters does Stoppard give as clues to the nature of the play?

2. The setting is given as two distinct places: a living room and an "old-fashioned unfashionable pub." The action of the play will shift between these two places. What specific details does Stoppard use to describe each place?

3. What might be the significance of the fact that, in the living room, potted plants are set under plumbing pipes?

Dialogue

In plays, and in much short fiction as well, the reader learns about characters mainly through *dialogue*: conversation between characters. Dialogue can be used to reveal the personality of characters by showing how they speak, how they interact with others, and what others say about them.

Model: Dialogue

The following dialogue from *Enter a Free Man* takes place between George Riley, the main character, and a casual acquaintance named Harry. Riley is an unsuccessful inventor, who believes that some day he will make it big. Harry is around thirty, "flashy, sharp, well-dressed." Earlier in the scene Riley announces that he has walked out on his family, but no one takes him seriously. As you read, notice how Stoppard uses conversation to give information about each character.

RILEY: A man must resist. A man must stand apart, make a clean break on his own two feet! Faith is the key—faith in oneself. (*Producing out of his pocket an envelope which he waves about.*) I have in here a little idea—one of many—that will take me away from all this. I'm saying good-bye to it all, Harry, just as I said good-bye to Persephone.

HARRY: It rings a bell. Let's have a look at it.

RILEY: What the creative mind needs is respect for its independence.

HARRY: Exactly! Respect. That's what we've got for you. We all have. Right, Carmen?

CARMEN: What?

HARRY: You see—respect. You've been coming in here, and we like it. Raises the tone. Right, Carmen?

CARMEN: Eh?

HARRY: Because of what? Because we're common. I mean, what have we got to give the world? Nothing. But you're—well, you're a genius! An inventor! You're a clever bloke, sitting there in your workshop, pioneering you might say, from your blood and your sweat for the lot of your fellow man.

RILEY: The lot of my fellow man!

HARRY: It's people like you who made this country great.

RILEY: You've got something there, Harry. That's very good.

HARRY: I had to say it.

RILEY: Thank you, Harry.

HARRY: *Able* thinks you're somebody—don't you?

ABLE: What?

HARRY: Don't you think George here is a clever bloke?

ABLE: 'Course he's a clever bloke. He's an inventor, isn't he?

HARRY: My very point. An inventor. That's your job. Amazing. I don't know if you've ever thought, George, but if you took away everything in the world that had to be invented, there'd be nothing left except a lot of people getting rained on.

RILEY: *(excitedly):* You're right! Progress is the child of invention! . . . *(Soberly.)* Harry, I have been touched by what you have said. *(He brandishes his envelope.)* My own resources are limited, but simplicity is the hardest thing to achieve—the simple idea that is a revolution. And I have achieved it, Harry. I would like you to have the honour of being the first to see it.

HARRY: Oh, I'd be very honoured, George. I'll remember this. (RILEY *opens the envelope and takes out a smaller, ordinary letter-envelope. He hands this to* HARRY, *who inspects it and turns it over dumbly.)* Yes . . . Yes, I can see this going over very big. A lovely job. A nice piece of work. An envelope. But—well, George, I must confess to a slight sense of—how should I put it?—

CARMEN: Disappointment—

HARRY: Disappointment. Yes, disappointment. An envelope—oh, I'm not saying it's not good, but it's not new, George, not new. An invention is better if it's new.

RILEY: You haven't noticed. Look at it. Something's different. You see? Gum on both sides of the flap! You see what that means?

HARRY: Yeah, yeah . . . what?

RILEY: You can use it twice. (HARRY *stands up. Walks around his stool, speechless with admiration and wonder.* RILEY *watches him expectantly.)*

HARRY: Genius . . . genius . . .

RILEY: You've got it. An envelope you can use twice. For instance, I write you a letter. I use one side, and then *you*—turn it inside out, write my address on it—and there's your gum on the flap!

HARRY: *(almost beyond words):* Simplicity. The simplicity of it. First the wheel, now this.[1]

Think and Discuss

The preceding conversation shows two characters with completely different attitudes. The reader learns very early that Harry does not take Riley seriously, that Harry is quietly mocking him. For example, when Harry exaggerates about Riley's labors, "your blood and your sweat for the lot of your fellow man," he is obviously poking fun. Riley, however, is totally serious. From this dialogue the reader learns that Riley wants to believe in himself so much that he does not see the way Harry makes fun of him.

1. What else do you learn about Riley's character from the conversation with Harry?

2. What sort of person is Harry? What parts of the dialogue lead you to this conclusion?

3. What do you think his reason is for making fun of Riley?

Writing Practice 6: *Dialogue*

Imagine that you are writing a story or play and that you want to create a dialogue between two characters. Begin with the character and setting you described for the previous two Writing Practices. Then create a second character, using the same techniques you used for the first. Answering the following questions may help you find ideas for your dialogue.

1. What is the relationship between your characters? Are they members of the same family? If not, how do they know each other?

2. How do your characters feel toward each other?

3. What has occasioned this conversation between them? What is each doing? Why?

---

[1]From *Enter a Free Man* by Tom Stoppard. Reprinted by permission of Faber and Faber Ltd. and Grove Press, Inc.

At the top of a sheet of paper, write the name of each character with a one-paragraph description of each. Add one more paragraph describing the setting. Then write at least one page of dialogue, indicating when each character speaks by writing the name on a new line as the dialogue in the previous model shows. Save your work.

For Your Writer's Notebook

For information on adjectives, see pages 398-411.

Good imaginative writing relies on the writer's powers of observation to make scenes and characters come alive for the reader. You can practice your own skills of observation by writing descriptions of places and people you encounter. (They do not have to be strange or unusual to be interesting.) Select one place or one person to observe closely. Then write a description, using specific details and adjectives to record your impressions of the place: its sounds, tastes, smells, and textures as well as its visual details. Write a description of the person, noting important details of appearance and behavior.

Plot and Conflict

A *plot* is a story-line: a plan of action that centers on a conflict and that is brought to some kind of resolution.

The element of struggle between opposing forces in a plot is called *conflict*. Without conflict a plot becomes simply a series of connected events, with nothing special to compel the reader's attention. Conflict helps create tension; within a story it makes the reader ask, "How will this be resolved?"

Although there are several types of conflict, conflict most often occurs between characters. However, conflict can also refer to a character's struggle against external circumstances or to a character's inner battle.

Model: Plot and Conflict

In V. S. Pritchett's story "The Wheelbarrow" the real conflict takes place within the mind of Miss Freshwater's niece. She feels that she has no attachment to her past and wants to burn it all in the huge bonfire. When she comes upon an old trunk with her private things in it, however, the sight overwhelms her. In the following passage from the story, notice how the niece's reactions to photos in an old album emphasize her internal conflict.

> . . . She was looking painfully through the album, rocking her head slowly from side to side, her mouth opening a little and closing on the point of speech, a shoulder rising as if she had been hurt, and her back moving and swaying as she felt the clasp of the past like hands on her. She was looking at ten forgotten years of her life, her own life, not her family's, and she did not laugh when she saw the skirts too long, the top-heavy hats hiding the eyes, her face too full and fat, her plainness so sullen, her prettiness too open-mouthed and loud, her look too grossly sly. In this one, sitting at the cafe table by the lake when she was nineteen, she looked masterful and at least forty. In this garden picture she was theatrically fancying herself as an ancient Greek in what looked like a nightgown! One of her big toes, she noticed, turned up comically in the sandal she was wearing. Here on a rock by the sea, in a bathing dress, she had got thin again—that was her marriage—and look at her hair! This picture of the girl on skis, sharp-faced, the eyes narrowed—who was that? Herself—yet how could she have looked like that! But she smiled a little at last at the people she had forgotten. This man with the crinkled fair hair, a German—how mad she had been about him. But what pierced her was that in each picture of herself she was just out of reach,

flashing and yet dead; and that really it was the *things* that burned in the light of permanence—the chairs, the tables, the trees, the car outside the cafe, the motor launch on the lake. These blinked and glittered. They had lasted and were ageless, untouched by time, and she was not.[1]

Think and Discuss

1. Turning through the leaves of the photo album, Miss Freshwater's niece discovers "ten forgotten years of her life." Remembering them is painful to her. She sees herself critically, and even her prettiness as a girl seems "too open-mouthed and loud." What other negative details describe how she sees herself in the photographs?

2. What does the niece's response to the old photos reveal about her feelings toward her past?

3. The niece's realization (that the *things*, rather than herself in the photos, are what seem real and permanent) gives readers a clue about what may come next in the story. How do you imagine the niece will feel about having burned up all the many things from her past?

Writing Practice 7: *Plot and Conflict*

The following suggestions are for conflicts between two characters in a play or short story, or conflict within a character.

---

[1]From "The Wheelbarrow" from *Selected Stories* by V. S. Pritchett. Copyright © 1978 by V.S. Pritchett. Reprinted by permission of Literistic, Ltd. and Random House, Inc.

1. Two friends are walking together. That day one noticed the other cheating on something important. The friends argue.

2. An older person warns a younger one not to do something. The younger person responds emotionally to the warning.

3. A character walks home alone after a failure. The character has serious doubts about his/her abilities.

Select one of these conflicts, or substitute one of your own, and write a page of prose or play dialogue that explains and describes the conflict. Use the characters you created for previous Writing Practices in this chapter. Save your work.

Resolving the Conflict

In fables and fairy tales, conflicts are usually resolved by a single simple action, and the characters live happily ever after. The Prince wakes Sleeping Beauty with a kiss, and the enchanted castle awakes; Jack kills the evil giant and saves his family from poverty. Conflict in most plays and short stories requires a more complex resolution. There are many ways to resolve a struggle, but all depend on a number of factors rather than on one simple act, and most leave the reader with a sense of what will happen to the characters in the future.

The word *resolution* does not necessarily mean that the conflict will end. Sometimes, the characters are involved in a conflict they will not be able to change. In this case the resolution is simply the characters' understanding that, in the future, the nature of the struggle will remain the same.

The most clear-cut type of resolution occurs when a character makes a major change. Something happens in the plot to make the character change behavior or point of view. This change can come from a personal realization, from the efforts of another character, or from a combination of the two.

Writing Practice 8: *Resolution*

In one sentence, write a summary of the conflict you created for the last Writing Practice. Then brainstorm five possible ways that the conflict could be resolved. (Remember that, in brainstorming, not all your ideas need be practical.) List your five ideas. Next, choose one and write a paragraph describing how each of your characters would

be affected if that resolution occurred. Finally, write a paragraph describing how each character would be affected if no resolution occurred. Save your work.

Writing Assignment II: *A Short Story or Play*

Write a short story or a short one-act play. Use the following steps for prewriting, writing, and postwriting.

A. Prewriting

Begin by gathering the material you have written for this chapter's Writing Practice exercises on Characters, Setting, Dialogue, Plot and Conflict, and Resolution. On the basis of that material, make a *story* or *play map*. Divide a sheet of paper into four equal parts. Label the parts SETTING, MAIN CHARACTERS, CONFLICT, and RESOLUTION. In the center of the page, write the tentative title of your story or play and circle it.

Under SETTING, write a brief summary of the environment you will portray in your story or play. Include not only the time and the place, but also descriptions of weather, significant objects, etc.

Under MAIN CHARACTERS, list the main characters' names. Jot down phrases that summarize the looks and personality of each character.

Under CONFLICT, summarize the conflict that will occur in your play or story. Note what part each character has in it.

Under RESOLUTION, describe the way the conflict will (or will not) be resolved. Mention how each of the main characters will be affected.

B. Writing

Begin the first draft of your story or play in the middle of some kind of action. As you write, use your story or play map as a guide. Work in the material you wrote for this chapter's Writing Practice exercises on Characters, Setting, Dialogue, Conflict, and Resolution. You will probably want to cut some parts of that material and add to other parts of it. Add words, phrases, or sentences as needed to connect the various parts and to develop your plot.

Writing a story or play involves both description and narration. Remember that a key to strong descriptive writing is judicious use of specific sensory details; a key to strong narrative writing is the use of transitions that keep the readers oriented in time.

For the end of your story or play, you may want to write a sentence that reminds the reader of how the piece began. For instance, the last sentence might refer once more to objects or events mentioned in the very first sentence. Or you may want to end with an image of your main character either performing some action or experiencing some emotion.

C. Postwriting

Let three or four of your classmates read what you have written. Ask each to answer these questions.

1. What is the most vivid part?

2. What part(s) do you wish there was more about? Why?

3. What part(s) could be shortened? Why?

4. What parts, if any, are unclear? How could they be improved?

Taking their answers into account, revise what you have written. Use the proofreading checklist in Chapter 1 to proofread your work so that it conforms to Edited Standard English.

Sentence Combining:
Using Subordinators

Connecting Sentences with Subordinators

Words called *subordinators* can be used to join two sentences of unequal importance.

For more information on subordinating conjunctions, see page 433.

Subordinators connect a sentence of lesser importance (the subordinate sentence) to a major sentence (the base sentence) by indicating the relationship between the two sentences. The following are the most common subordinators. These words are also called *subordinating conjunctions*.

after	before	until
although	even though	when
as if	just as	whenever
as long as	just when	where
as soon as	since	wherever
as though	so that	whether
because	unless	while

For more information on subordinate clauses, see page 511.

By placing a subordinator in front of a sentence, you create a *subordinate clause* that cannot stand alone but is dependent on the base sentence. For example, when the subordinator *although* is added to the sentence *He began life as a slave*, the resulting clause, *Although he began life as a slave*, is no longer an independent sentence.

Sentences: He began life as a slave. (*although*)
Booker T. Washington became president of the first black college.

Joined: *Although* he began life as a slave, Booker T. Washington became president of the first black college.

For more information on punctuating subordinate clauses, see page 523.

In the preceding example the subordinate clause is attached to the beginning of the base sentence, but you can also attach clauses to the end of a base sentence. A subordinate clause is usually separated from the base sentence with a comma when the clause is attached to

169

the beginning of a sentence. A subordinate clause at the end of a sentence usually does not require a comma. The following example illustrates the options.

Sentences: The barbecue was ready.
The kids returned from the lake. (*when*)

Joined: The barbecue was ready *when* the kids returned from the lake.
When the kids returned from the lake, the barbecue was ready.

Exercise 1: Connecting Sentences of Unequal Importance

Combine the following pairs of sentences by using subordinators. In each of the first five exercises the subordinator is given immediately *after* the sentence that will become the subordinate clause. In the last five exercises you must choose the subordinators you think are appropriate, remembering that the subordinate clause may be placed before or after the base sentence for variety and style. Punctuate your combined sentences correctly.

Examples

a. The mountain residents are evacuating.
   The volcano may erupt at any time. (*because*)
   The mountain residents are evacuating because the volcano may erupt at any time.

   or

   Because the volcano may erupt at any time, the mountain residents are evacuating.

b. The personnel manager called me for an interview.
   She read my application.
   The personnel manager called me for an interview as soon as she read my application.

   or

   As soon as she read my application, the personnel manager called me for an interview.

1. The camera crew arrived at the fire.
   The helicopters arrived to rescue people from the roof. (*just as*)

2. Shoplifting is really a serious crime. (*although*)
   Some people consider it little more than an innocent game.

3. Some species of whale may become extinct.
   Two countries refuse to ban whale hunting. (*because*)

4. In his writing Geoffrey Chaucer captured the spirit of medieval England.
   He lived at the close of the Middle Ages. (*even though*)

5. Members of Congress can ill afford to give themselves a substantial pay raise.
   The government is asking the public to hold down wages and prices. (*when*)

6. The winters remain dry.
   The New England states will have to conserve water.

7. Andy will not graduate.
   He passes the proficiency tests.

8. Vitamin supplements probably are not necessary.
   You maintain a well-balanced diet.

9. She turned fifteen.
   Christine got a Social Security card.

10. No part of the United States is immune from tornadoes.
    They usually occur in the Midwest.

Exercise 2: *Joining Sentences with a Variety of Connectors*

As a review of the sentence-combining strategies you have studied so far, use connectors to combine these sentence sets in the order they appear. The first four sets have signals. For the last four sets, decide how best to join the sentences. Before you begin, study the example sentences and the paragraph that results. Write your combined sentences as a complete paragraph.

Examples

(Adapted from "To Build a Fire" by Jack London)

   a. He plunged in among the big spruce trees.
      He found a faint trail. (*and*)
      He plunged in among the big spruce trees and found a faint trail.

   b. A foot of snow had fallen.
      The last sled had passed over. (*since*)
      A foot of snow has fallen since the last sled had passed over.

c. He was glad he was without a sled.
He preferred to travel light. (*because*)
He was glad he was without a sled because he preferred to travel light.

d. He left his pack at camp yesterday. (*after*)
He now carried nothing but the lunch wrapped in the handkerchief.
After he left his pack at camp yesterday, he now carried nothing but the lunch wrapped in the handkerchief.

e. He rubbed his numb nose and cheekbones with his mittened hand. (*just as*)
He concluded that it certainly was cold.
Just as he rubbed his numb nose and cheekbones with his mittened hand, he concluded that it certainly was cold.

f. He was a warm-whiskered man.
The hair on his face did not protect the high cheekbones and the eager nose. (*but*)
They were thrust so aggressively into the frosty air. (*since*)
He was a warm-whiskered man, but the hair on his face did not protect the high cheekbones and the eager nose, since they were thrust so aggressively into the frosty air.

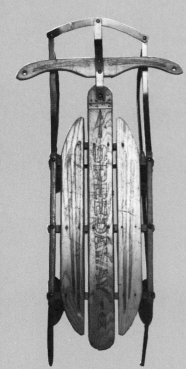

Paragraph Form

He plunged in among the big spruce trees and found a faint trail. A foot of snow had fallen since the last sled had passed over. He was glad he was without a sled because he preferred to travel light. After he left his pack at camp yesterday, he now carried nothing but the lunch wrapped in the handkerchief. Just as he rubbed his numb nose and cheekbones with his mittened hand, he concluded that it certainly was cold. He was a warm-whiskered man but the hair on his face did not protect the high cheekbones and the eager nose, since they were thrust so aggressively into the frosty air.

1. Life is complex.
Life is also fun. (*yet*)

2. It is complicated. (*because*)
Think of life in this way.

3. Life is not a lot of happy endings and somewheres.
It is a long, never-ending pathway stretching out ahead of you. (*but*)

4. You are on one pathway now. (*just as . . . so*)
    There are many other pathways leading off to either side.

5. The pathway you are on now represents the life style you are now living.
    The side pathways represent new directions you might take.
    You will find new jobs, new hobbies, new places to live.

6. One pathway might be labeled "be a cartoonist."
    You might choose to start down that pathway.

7. Soon you will reach a fork.
    One branch would be labeled "free-lance cartoonist," and the other, "regularly employed."

8. You will have to choose.
    Your choice will have considerable influence on your future options.
    The side pathways leading off the two branches will not always be the same.

Writing Practice: *Joining Sentences*

Look again at the paragraph you wrote for Writing Practice 5: Setting in a Short Story. Improve the variety of your sentence patterns by using subordinators to join sentences. Work to achieve a smooth-flowing combination of sentence lengths and patterns.

173

6 Critical Writing

Writing About Literature and Film

Writing critically about literature or film does not necessarily mean finding fault. It means reading and reviewing carefully, with an understanding of how literature and films are structured. It also means analyzing, evaluating, and then commenting upon selected elements of the work.

Almost all stories share common elements. First, there are *characters*, humans or nonhumans, who think, feel, act, and respond in their fictional world. These characters perform actions based on *motives*, or reasons. These motivated actions, which make up the *plot* of the story, frequently arise from a *conflict*, or problem, and take place against a background of time and place, called a *setting*. Finally, the way the story is told, its *style*, helps readers to interpret its significance.

Analyzing Characters

Many stories have two kinds of characters: major and minor. *Major characters* carry the burden of the plot and take part in most of the action. One of the major characters may be a *protagonist*, someone who has a problem to solve or a conflict to resolve before there can be a satisfactory ending. The protagonist's problems may be caused by an *antagonist*, someone against whom the protagonist struggles to resolve the conflict. Sometimes, the antagonist is not a person at all, but a force of nature, an animal, or circumstance.

Minor characters enrich a story or play by providing the major characters with further complications and by reflecting character traits that amuse, puzzle, entertain, and inform readers about the main ideas of the story.

Characters, whether major or minor ones, can be either *round* or *flat*. A *round character* is one that is dynamic, capable of growth and change. A *flat character* is static, frequently *stereotyped*, and does not grow or change during the story. If this character is a stereotype (such

as the hanging judge of old Westerns or the street-wise, gum-chewing, joke-cracking newspaper reporter), you need to try to determine what the character contributes to the story. Writers can describe characters either directly (by telling how they look and act) or indirectly (by having other characters describe them).

Model: Direct Character Description

In the following passage from "The Infant Prodigy" by Thomas Mann, the central character is introduced through *direct description*. As you read, notice the details of appearance and background that help you see the infant prodigy.

> The infant prodigy entered. The hall became quiet.
> It became quiet and then the audience began to clap, because somewhere at the side a leader of mobs, a born organizer, clapped first. The audience had heard nothing yet, but they applauded; for a mighty publicity organization had heralded the prodigy and people were already hypnotized, whether they knew it or not.

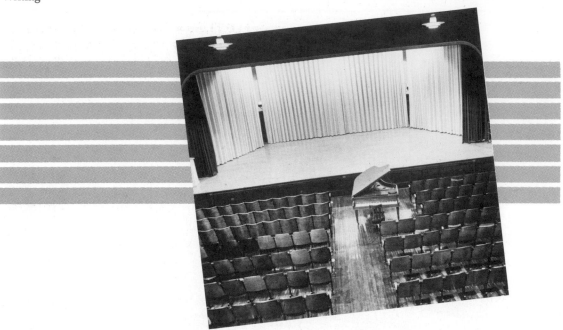

The prodigy came from behind a splendid screen embroidered with Empire garlands and great conventionalized flowers, and climbed nimbly up the steps to the platform, diving into the applause as into a bath; a little chilly and shivering, but yet as though into a friendly element. He advanced to the edge of the platform and smiled as though he were about to be photographed; he made a shy, charming gesture of greeting, like a little girl.

He was dressed entirely in white silk, which the audience found enchanting. The little white jacket was fancifully cut, with a sash underneath it, and even his shoes were made of white silk. But against the white socks his bare little legs stood out quite brown; for he was a Greek boy.[1]

Think and Discuss

1. Notice the air of anticipation as the young performer enters the room. What details in the first two paragraphs describe the atmosphere in the concert hall?

2. What picture of the infant prodigy do you have as you read the third paragraph? How do "diving into the applause as into a bath" or "advanced to the edge of the platform and smiled as though he were about to be photographed" help you visualize the boy?

---

[1]Excerpt from "The Infant Prodigy" in *Stories of Three Decades* by Thomas Mann, translated by H. T. Lowe-Porter. Copyright 1936 and renewed 1964 by Alfred A. Knopf, Inc. Reprinted by permission of Alfred A. Knopf, Inc.

Indirect Character Description

A writer may also introduce a character to you indirectly, through what other characters say about him or her. You may not even be introduced to the character, but instead become familiar with him or her through the eyes of others.

Model: Indirect Character Description

In the opening scene of the play *Hedda Gabler* by Henrik Ibsen, two characters who have kept house for the previous occupants are talking about the arrival of the new ones. As you read their conversation, notice what bits of information and description you get about two major characters, Hedda and George Tesman.

BERTA. Well, but there's another thing, Miss. I'm so mortally afraid I shan't be able to suit the young mistress.

MISS TESMAN. Oh, well—just at first there may be one or two things—

BERTA. Most like she'll be terrible grand in her ways.

MISS TESMAN. Well, you can't wonder at that—General Gabler's daughter! Think of the sort of life she was accustomed to in her father's time. Don't you remember how we used to see her riding down the road along with the General? In that long black habit—and with feathers in her hat?

BERTA. Yes, indeed—I remember well enough! But good Lord, I should never have dreamt in those days that she and Master George would make a match of it.

MISS TESMAN. Nor I. But, by-the-bye, Berta—while I think of it: in future you mustn't say Master George. You must say Dr. Tesman.

BERTA. Yes, the young mistress spoke of that too—last night—the moment they set foot in the house. Is it true, then, Miss?

MISS TESMAN. Yes, indeed it is. Only think, Berta—some foreign university has made him a doctor—while he has been abroad, you understand. I hadn't heard a word about it, until he told me himself upon the pier.

BERTA. Well, well, he's clever enough for anything, he is. But I didn't think he'd have gone in for doctoring people too.

MISS TESMAN. No, no, it's not that sort of doctor he is. (*Nods significantly.*) But let me tell you, we may have to call him something grander before long.

BERTA. You don't say so! What can that be, Miss?

MISS TESMAN (*smiling*). Wouldn't you like to know! (*With emotion.*) Ah, dear, dear—if my poor brother could only look up from his grave now, and see what his little boy has grown into! (*Looks around.*) But bless me, Berta—why have you done this? Taken the chintz covers off all the furniture?

      BERTA. The mistress told me to. She can't abide covers on the chairs, she says.

      MISS TESMAN. Are they going to make this their everyday sitting room then?

      BERTA. Yes, that's what I understand—from the mistress. Master George—the doctor—he said nothing.[1]

Think and Discuss

1.   What do you learn about Hedda and George from the conversation?

2.   Do Berta and Miss Tesman seem to be enthusiastic about the young couple's arrival? How can you tell?

3.   Although Hedda has not yet entered the action of the play, what do you think she may be like from the few details you have in this short scene?

Writing Practice 1: *Analyzing Characters*

For this assignment select a favorite short story or play from your literature anthology or a library book. Then make a list of the major characters in the story or play and a list of the character traits each possesses. For instance, in the short story "Flight" by John Steinbeck, the young boy Pepe has character traits of trustworthiness, tenderness, determination, and fear of the unknown. Write down on a sheet of paper as many character traits as you can for each of the major characters. Finally, decide whether each character is round, flat, or stereotyped, and write several sentences explaining and supporting your answer for each. Save your work to use in an assignment later in this chapter.

Analyzing Action

The plot of a story proceeds in a series of events. The plot is often started on its way through one or more complications or problems that affect the protagonist and other characters. As the plot becomes more complex and perhaps interwoven with other minor plots, a *climax*, or *turning point*, is reached. This turning point may be an unexpected discovery, a crucial decision, or a resolution of

---

[1]Excerpt from *Hedda Gabler* from *Henrik Ibsen: The Complete Major Prose Plays*, translated by Rolf Fjelde. Copyright © 1965, 1970, 1978 by Rolf Fjelde. Reprinted by arrangement with The New American Library, Inc., New York, New York.

the conflict. The reader finishes the story with a sense of release from the tension created by the plot. In many stories, however, just as in real life, the conflict is not completely resolved. Instead, the resolution finds the protagonist changed as a result of the conflict.

Plots do not always proceed from Day 1 to Day 20 in orderly fashion. Writers may employ techniques called the *flashback* and the *flash forward* to give readers glimpses of what happened before or what will happen in the future. Knowledge of earlier events helps the reader interpret and understand the motivations of characters. Seeing what lies ahead gives the reader a different perspective on present action and allows him or her to understand more fully how actions or circumstances contribute to the ending.

Writing Practice 2: *Analyzing Action*

For this assignment, use the same short story or play you used for the previous Writing Practice. On a sheet of paper, write down the major events, or actions, that happen in the story. Try to arrange them in the order in which they happen. Now think about the turning point in the plot. Which event, decision, or act eventually led to a resolution? Write a short paragraph explaining what the climax was and why you think it was the turning point in the story. Save your work.

Analyzing Motivation

Most well-written stories are not simply a series of happenings; rather, the actions arise from characters. Things happen because people in a story respond to ideas, other people, and situations. Characters may be motivated by emotions—fear, pain, love, guilt—and by deliberate decisions. As a reader you can take into account what other characters say, what they do, what others say about them, and what others do in relation to them. All these supply information about characters' motivations. You can also be aware of *foreshadowing*, the technique of hinting about events to come through description of setting, minor characters, conversations between characters, and the tone of the story's narrator. For instance, in the short story *The Fall of the House of Usher*, Edgar Allan Poe foreshadows the supernatural disaster at the end of the story by mentioning gloomy details of setting near the beginning. The story takes place on "a dull, dark, and soundless day . . . when the clouds hung oppressively low. . . ."

Model: Motivation and Foreshadowing

In Robinson Jeffers' retelling of the ancient Greek tragedy *Medea*, Jason, who sought the legendary Golden Fleece, has cast off his foreign wife, Medea, and married a Greek princess. In the following scene Medea is preparing to send wedding gifts to Jason's new wife. Actually, Medea seeks revenge and has poisoned the gifts. In the dialogue, unnatural events in nature are discussed.

MEDEA. These are the gifts I am sending to the young bride; this golden wreath
And this woven-gold veil. They are not without value; there is nothing like them in the whole world, or at least
The Western world; the God of the Sun gave them to my father's father, and I have kept them
In the deep chest for some high occasion; which has now come
I have great joy in giving these jewels to Creon's daughter, for the glory of life consists of being generous
To one's friends, and—merciless to one's enemies—you know what a friend she has been to me. All Corinth knows.
The slaves talk of it. The old stones in the walls
Have watched and laughed.
(MEDEA *looks at the gold cloth, and strokes it cautiously with her hand. It seems to scorch her fingers.* THIRD WOMAN *has come nearer to look; now starts backward.)*
MEDEA. See, it is almost alive. Gold is a living thing: such pure gold.
(NURSE *enters from up Right; crosses to foot of steps.)*
But when her body has warmed it, how it will shine!
(*To the* NURSE.)
Why doesn't he come? What keeps him?
NURSE *(evidently terrified).* Oh, my lady: presently.
I have but now returned from him. He was beyond the gate watching the races—where a monstrous thing
Had happened: a young mare broke from the chariot
And tore with her teeth a stallion.
MEDEA (*stands up, shakes out the golden cloak, which again smoulders. She folds it cautiously, lays it in the leather case. The light has darkened again. She looks anxiously at the clouded sun*). He takes his time, eh? It is intolerable
To sit and wait.
(*To the* SERVING WOMEN.)
Take these into the house. Keep them at hand
For when I call.
(*They take them in.* MEDEA *moves restlessly, under extreme nervous tension; speaks to the* NURSE. NURSE *crosses below steps to stage Left, then up two steps.)*
You say that a mare attacked a stallion?
NURSE.   She tore him cruelly.

I saw him being led away: a black racer: his blood ran down
From the throat to the fetlocks.

MEDEA.	You're sure he's coming? You're sure?
NURSE.	He said he would.
MEDEA.	Let him make haste, then!

SECOND WOMAN (*she crosses to Left below* NURSE).
        Frightening irrational things
Have happened lately; the face of nature is flawed with omens.
        FIRST WOMAN (*crosses to Left, joining* SECOND WOMAN).
        Yesterday evening a slave
Came up to the harbor, carrying a basket
Of new-caught fish: one of the fish took fire
And burned in the wet basket with a high flame: the thing was witnessed
By many persons.
        THIRD WOMAN (*crosses Left of other* TWO WOMEN, *joining
                them*). And a black leopard was seen
Gliding through the marketplace—
        MEDEA (*abruptly, approaching the* WOMEN). You haven't told
                me yet: do you not think that Creon's daughter
Will be glad of those gifts?
        FIRST WOMAN.   O Medea, too much wealth
Is sometimes dreadful.
        MEDEA. She'll be glad, however. She'll take them and put them
                on, she'll wear them, she'll strut in them.
She'll peacock in them. I see him coming now—the
        (THREE WOMEN *retire to up Left corner.* NURSE *sits below
                Left pillar.*)
                                        whole palace will admire
        her. Stand away from me, women,
While I make my sick peace.[1]

Think and Discuss

1. If you have read *Medea*, you know that the gold cloth burns the new wife's skin and causes her to die painfully. What lines in the dialogue foreshadow this event? To answer this question, look at how the gold cloth is described.

2. What lines in the dialogue give clues about Medea's motivation for killing Jason's new wife?

Writing Practice 3: *Analyzing Motivation*

Think about the conflict or problem in the story or play you used for the previous two Writing Practices. What was the conflict or problem,

---

[1]Excerpt from *Cawdor and Medea* by Robinson Jeffers. Copyright 1928, 1956 by Robinson Jeffers. Reprinted by permission of New Directions Publishing Corporation.

and why did the protagonist react to it as he or she did? Also, think about what other characters did and what they said about the protagonist. When you can answer the question *Why did events happen as they did?*, write a brief explanation of what happens and why each major event happens. Save your work.

Analyzing Setting

The *setting* of a story or play may be as important to the meaning as the characters themselves. As you analyze a story, decide the time and place in which it takes place. You can do this easily if the story includes place names and dates, but you can also determine the setting by looking carefully at how characters speak, dress, and behave; and at the writer's description of places, such as homes, fields, forests, towns, and schools. However, a story may take place in an unspecified time and place, perhaps even inside a character's mind. You will need to look for clues in the context of the story itself to determine setting in these cases.

Model: *Setting*

In her novel *Jane Eyre*, Charlotte Brontë describes Jane's arrival at Ferndean, the home of her employer, Mr. Rochester. As you read the following description from that scene, notice how details of the physical setting suggest a foreboding, gloomy atmosphere.

> To this house I came, just ere dark, on an evening marked by the characteristics of sad, cold gale, and continued small, penetrating rain. The last mile I performed on foot, having dismissed the chaise and driver with the double remuneration I had promised. Even when within a very short distance of the manorhouse, you could see nothing of it; so thick and dark grew the timber of the gloomy wood about it. Iron gates between granite pillars showed me where to enter, and passing through them, I found myself at once in the twilight of close-ranked trees. . . .
>
> I proceeded: at last my way opened, the trees thinned a little; presently I beheld a railing, then the house—scarce, by this dim light, distinguishable from the trees; so dank and green were its decaying walls. Entering a portal, fastened only by a latch, I stood amidst a space of enclosed ground, from which the wood swept away in a semicircle. There were no flowers, no garden-beds; only a broad gravelwalk girdling a grass-plot, and this set in the heavy frame of the forest. The house presented two pointed gables in its front: the windows were latticed and narrow: the front-door was narrow, too, one step let up to it. The whole looked, as the host of Rochester

Arms had said, "quite a desolate spot." It was as still as a church on a week-day: the pattering rain on the forest leaves was the only sound audible in its vicinage.

"Can there be life here?" I asked.

Think and Discuss

1. What specific details help you determine where and when this story takes place?

2. Mr. Rochester's house is dark and isolated. What words or phrases in the second paragraph suggest the isolation and apparent lack of life?

Writing Practice 4: *Analyzing a Setting*

Use the same piece of literature you have used for the previous Writing Practices. This time, think about its setting. On a sheet of paper, identify the time and place in which the story takes place. If the scene changed from place to place or from time to time, note the background of the major part of the action. As you recall the background, jot down the clues you can remember that told you where and when the story took place. For example, specific places, people, and events may be named to tell viewers about time and place. The clothing and the objects used by characters are further clues to establish the story's setting. Save your work.

Analyzing Style

For more information on style, see pages 540-546.

When you look at a writer's *style*, you analyze imagery, point of view, and other identifiable uses of language.

Imagery

Imagery is the use of language to appeal to the senses and to make ideas, actions, and characters vivid. Images are frequently found in comparisons, especially in figures of speech such as *similes* and *metaphors*. In the passage from *Jane Eyre*, the narrator says that the manor house of Mr. Rochester "was as still as a church on a weekday." This simile compares the house to an empty church, thus emphasizing its isolation and emptiness.

Point of View

Although writers *write* their stories, someone else *tells* them. That someone is a narrator, and the narrator may tell a story from any one of several *points of view*. A narrator may tell the story from *first-person point of view*. In first-person narration a character who refers to herself or himself as *I* both narrates the story and plays a part in it.

Model: First-Person Narrator

In the following passage from Alice Walker's story "Everyday Use," a successful daughter, Dee, returns with her boyfriend to visit her mother and sister Maggie, who have remained on the farm where they grew up. As the story opens, the mother is thinking about Dee's visit and about Maggie's reaction to it. Notice how the narrator describes her own feelings. How is the narrator able to say how Maggie will react to her sister's visit?

> I will wait for her in the yard that Maggie and I made so clean and wavy yesterday afternoon. A yard like this is more comfortable than most people know. It is not just a yard. It is like an extended living room. When the hard clay is swept clean as a floor and the fine sand around the edges lined with tiny, irregular grooves anyone can come and sit and look up into the elm tree and wait for the breezes that never come into the house.
>
> Maggie will be nervous until after her sister goes: she will stand hopelessly in corners homely and ashamed of the burn scars down her arms and legs, eyeing her sister with a mixture of envy and awe. She thinks her sister has held life always in the palm of one hand, that "no" is a word the world never learned to say to her.[1]

The mother is able to describe Maggie's reaction to her visit because she knows her daughter so well. A first-person narrator does not have magical powers. He or she cannot know the thoughts and feelings of other characters unless that knowledge is based on observation, as it was in the preceding example.

The *third-person point of view*, in which the narrator is not a character in the story, has several versions, depending upon how involved the narrator is with the characters in the story. At one extreme is the *omniscient* (all-knowing) *narrator*, who knows everything that happens in the story and can describe what all the characters think and feel. Since this narrator knows everything, he or she may pass judgment on what happens, may at times speak directly to the reader, and may interpret meanings.

Another third-person narrator, sometimes called a *selective omniscient narrator*, speaks through the thoughts of one of the characters

---

[1] From "Everyday Use" from *In Love and Trouble* by Alice Walker. Copyright © 1973 by Alice Walker. Reprinted by permission of Julian Bach Literary Agency, Inc. and Harcourt Brace Jovanovich, Inc.

but understands the thoughts of other characters from the outside only. In such stories the view of the world comes through the mind and senses of one character, usually a major one. The reader can only go where the narrator goes.

Model: Selective Omniscient Narrator

In the following excerpt from a short story by John Galsworthy, for example, the narrator shows readers Mr. Nilson's limited world only through his words and feelings. What words and phrases in the selection identify the narrator as a selective omniscient narrator?

> As Mr. Nilson, well known in the City, opened the window of his dressing room on Campden Hill, he experienced a peculiar sweetish sensation in the back of his throat, and a feeling of emptiness just under his fifth rib. Hooking the window back, he noticed that a little tree in the Square Gardens had come out in blossom, and that the thermometer stood at sixty. "Perfect morning," he thought; "spring at last!"
>
> Resuming some meditations on the price of Tintos, he took up an ivory-backed handglass and scrutinized his face. His firm, well-coloured cheeks, with their neat brown moustaches, and his round, well-opened, clear grey eyes, wore a reassuring appearance of good health. Putting on his black frock coat, he went downstairs.
>
> In the dining room his morning paper was laid out on the sideboard Mr. Nilson had scarcely taken it in his hand when he again became aware of that queer feeling. Somewhat concerned, he went to the French window and descended the scrolled iron steps into the fresh air. A cuckoo clock struck eight.[1]

The words, "he experienced a peculiar sweetish sensation in the back of his throat," identify the narrator as omniscient. Since nowhere in the story does the narrator reveal thoughts and feelings of other characters, he can be classified as a selective omniscient narrator. Unless he had access to the thoughts of Mr. Nilson, the narrator could not know that the character was experiencing a feeling of emptiness.

Another kind of third-person point of view presents a narrator who simply records what is said and what happens. This narrator functions something like a sound camera, picturing events and recording dialogue, but doing so *objectively*. Such a narrator does not comment or enter any character's mind. A narrator cannot be

---

[1]From *Caravan* by John Galsworthy. Reprinted by permission of The Society of Authors as the literary representative of the Estate of John Galsworthy.

completely removed from the story, of course, for just as a camera selects and limits what viewers see and hear, so does the narrator select what readers learn about the characters and events. This point of view generally has the most action. Since it does not interpret, the reader is allowed to do his or her own interpreting.

Writing Practice 5: *Analyzing Point of View*

For this assignment, use the same literary work you have used in the previous Writing Practices in this chapter. Write a brief explanation of the point of view from which the story is told. Identify the narrator by name, if there is one, and define the kind of point of view as first or third person. If it is a third-person point of view, further identify it as *omniscient, selective omniscient,* or *objective.* Then give examples of the narrator's point of view by citing words and phrases. Save your work.

Reading a Review

In reviewing a work of literature or a film, a critic must analyze characters, plot, motivation, setting, and style. It is on these analyses that the critic bases his or her overall opinion of the work. This opinion is not just a judgment of "good" or "bad"; rather, it evaluates the strengths as well as the weaknesses of the work and suggests what aspects of it audiences might appreciate.

Usually, a review is structured as an expository essay. The reviewer's overall opinion is stated in the essay's thesis sentence, usually in the introductory paragraph. In subsequent paragraphs, analyses of characters, motivations, plot, setting, and style supply the details that develop the thesis.

Model: A Review

As you read *Newsweek* critic Harry F. Waters' review of "Tinker, Tailor, Soldier, Spy," a TV miniseries based on a novel by John le Carré, notice where character, motivation, plot, and setting are mentioned.

> Viewers who are into James Bondage, or who actually believe that real spies behave like Charlie's Angels, should be warned away from this six-part adaptation of John le Carré's best-selling thriller. Its hero is a dumpy, bookish and melancholy middle-ager, forever fiddling with his spectacles or brooding about his adulterous wife. There are no car chases, no kung fu demolitions. The hideously complex plot is

as demanding as a London Times crossword. Yet anyone who sticks with this BBC import will discover the most mesmerizing, ingeniously crafted whodunit ever designed for the small screen.

Sir Alec Guinness plays George Smiley, a retired British spy who is recalled to duty to ferret out a "mole"—a Russian double agent who has infiltrated the top echelons of British intelligence. Smiley's suspects number four, all old colleagues. The maze through which we follow him teems with false exits, ambiguous flashbacks and claustrophobic menace. Almost everyone could be someone else, an effect le Carré mischievously enhances by giving his operatives such innocent trade labels: "baby-sitters" [for bodyguards], "lamplighters" [surveillance experts] and "bad boys" [professional muscle men]. The series' denouement, in which the mole reveals the chilling rationale for his treachery, may be the most subtly nuanced of this genre.

Memory: Public TV has commissioned Robert MacNeil to serve as a sort of plot-decoder for the American audience. Even so, each episode presents a maddening memory test; at least readers of the novel could flip back the pages. Turn away for just a few minutes—or what it takes to write a check to PTV—and you'll be as lost as Smiley when he takes the case. Still, none of that miffed British viewers; the which-one's-the-mole mystery was debated in pubs almost as hotly as the who-shot-J.R. Perhaps that's because the story is based, in part, on that of Kim Philby, Donald Maclean and Guy Burgess, the notorious British spies who defected to Moscow during the cold-war period but whose duplicitous legacy is still making headlines.

Once again, Alec Guinness turns in an elegantly effortless performance, playing George Smiley almost as if he had invented him. The role calls on Guinness to spend almost all of his time listening to others. Only his eyes, and an occasional offhand gesture or sign, convey a mind that is sifting and connecting with computerlike ease. The closest Guinness comes to histrionics is in the climactic scene, when he confesses to his wife . . . that he had momentarily considered shooting his quarry. "Poor George," she dryly scolds. "Life is such a puzzle to you, isn't it?"

"Tinker, Tailor" is chess played with human pieces, the lights off and the opponent unknown. Viewers patient enough to figure out the moves, however, will come away feeling like winners over Anatoly Karpov.[1]

—Harry F. Waters

Think and Discuss

1. How does the introductory paragraph of this review get the reader's attention?

[1]Column on "Tinker, Tailor, Soldier, Spy" by Harry F. Waters in *Newsweek*, October 6, 1980. Copyright 1980 by Newsweek, Inc. All Rights Reserved. Reprinted by Permission.

2. What is Harry F. Waters' overall opinion of "Tinker, Tailor, Soldier, Spy?" Where in the review do you find it stated?

3. Since this is a review of a filmed work, the critic analyzes acting instead of analyzing writing style. How does he feel that the acting contributes to the general effect of the series?

4. What main characters does Waters analyze? Where does he mention motivation? Setting? Plot? To which of those four aspects does Waters devote most space in his review?

Writing Assignment I: *Writing a Review*

Using your material from previous Writing Practice exercises in this chapter, write a review of the work of literature or play you have chosen. Follow the steps for prewriting, writing, and postwriting.

A. Prewriting

Gather and reread the short analyses of characters, plot, motivation, setting, and point of view that you have written for this chapter's Writing Practice exercises. In order to develop a thesis statement for your review, think about 1) which literary aspect of the work you have chosen is most striking, 2) which audience the work will especially interest, and 3) which features of the work might decide its appeal.

Next, take out a pen and a clean piece of paper, and spend the next five minutes brainstorming possible thesis sentences for your review. Each possible thesis sentence should summarize your analysis of the literary aspects of the work and your ideas of its audience appeal. Write every sentence that you come up with. When five minutes are up, choose the thesis sentence you like best.

Write your thesis sentence near the top of a new piece of paper. Beneath the thesis sentence, jot down ideas from your Writing Practice exercises that will support and explain it. Put these supporting ideas in an order that makes sense to you. Your review should mention all the literary aspects of the work you are reviewing, but you may choose, as Waters did, to concentrate on only one of those aspects.

B. Writing

Write your review in the present tense. This is standard procedure for all professional reviews.

Decide who will be reading your review (your teacher may tell you to direct it toward a specific audience), and begin the review with a sentence that will capture your audience's interest. You will

probably want to state your thesis near the end of your introductory paragraph.

Follow your prewriting notes as you compose the body of your review. Support each of your main points by citing specific details from the work you are reviewing. Remember to use quotation marks when quoting directly from a piece of literature.

Conclude your review, if possible, with an evaluation that will stay in your readers' minds. You may want to create a striking metaphor; Harry F. Waters, for instance, wrote, "'Tinker, Tailor' is chess played with human pieces. . . ."

C. Postwriting

Use the checklist on page 190 to revise your review; then write a second draft. Use the Checklist for Proofreading at the back of the book to be sure that your review conforms to Edited Standard English. Then, you may wish either to let members of your class read your review and comment on it, or to submit your review to your school newspaper or literary magazine.

> ## *Checklist for the Critical Essay*
>
> 1. The essay reflects your analysis of the story or film.
>
> 2. The essay is focused on one main topic.
>
> 3. The first paragraph contains a thesis sentence that sets forth your evaluation of the work and summarizes your analysis.
>
> 4. You have used sufficient specific detail from the work itself to support and develop your thesis.
>
> 5. If you have used direct quotations, they are enclosed in quotation marks or indented, depending on their length.
>
> 6. The essay is in present tense.
>
> 7. The essay is organized with an introduction that contains your thesis, a body that develops and supports the thesis, and a conclusion that summarizes or rephrases the thesis to emphasize it.

Other Responses to Literature and Film

Besides writing reviews, you can write other kinds of expository essays in response to films or works of literature. When you know you will be assigned an expository essay on a work you are reading, your Writer's Notebook can be especially useful. At periodic intervals as you read, use your notebook to record thoughts and reactions that the literature brings up. Note any patterns you detect in the literature, and think about what will happen next.

An essay about literature may be about any aspect of it: plot, character, setting, motivation, conflict, or style. When you have reviewed the story and your notebook entries, ask yourself what you liked most about the story, what affected you most strongly, and what you would like to explain to others about it. Then you will be better able to decide what the purpose of your essay will be: to compare, explain, analyze, describe, or evaluate.

Suggestions for Responses

For papers that compare:

The roles of two characters in the same story, such as Viola and Olivia in Shakespeare's *Twelfth Night*, or Brutus and Cassius in *Julius Caesar*

Two characters or groups of characters in different works by the same author, such as Jim in Joseph Conrad's *Lord Jim*, and the young captain in *The Secret Sharer*

Two works of literature that explore similar themes, such as *A Separate Peace* and *Catcher in the Rye*

Two versions of the same story, such as *Romeo and Juliet* and *West Side Story*

For papers that analyze and evaluate:

The role of setting in developing the theme in Emily Brontë's *Wuthering Heights*
The importance of light and dark imagery in *Oedipus the King* or *Romeo and Juliet*

Symbolism in *The Glass Menagerie*

The effectiveness of comic scenes in *Hamlet*

Coincidence in *The Return of the Native*

Significance of "the beast" in *Lord of the Flies*

For papers that explain and describe:

The meaning of the ending of *2001: A Space Odyssey*

The function of the chorus in Greek tragedy

Elements of the Chivalric Code in the Arthurian legends

Animal Farm as a parable and warning

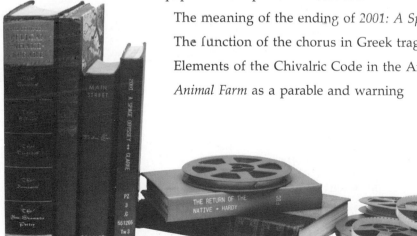

191

Sentence Combining:
Inserting Modifiers

Inserting Modifiers

For more information on adjectives and adverbs, see pages 398-409 and 412-425.

Besides joining sentences, writers can also expand a *base sentence* by inserting modifiers from other sentences, called *insert sentences*.

Modifiers are adjectives, adverbs, prepositional phrases, and other words used to describe. Several modifiers can be inserted into a base sentence as long as each is clearly connected to the word it modifies.

For more information on prepositional phrases, see pages 490-491.

Base Sentence: Rosie's explanation of the traditional dance was interesting and informative.

Insert: Rosie's explanation was lively.

Insert: The dance was from Mexico.

Combined: Rosie's lively explanation of the traditional dance from Mexico was interesting and informative.

Because the word *lively* and the phrase *from Mexico* modify (or describe) words in the base sentence, they can be inserted into the base sentence without altering its meaning. In fact, the combined sentence is more interesting and economical than the original sentences.

For more information on using commas to separate adjectives preceding a noun, see page 552.

Frequently two or more modifiers describe the same word. In this situation the modifiers may be separated by a comma or the word *and*. The following example illustrates modifiers that are separated by commas and the word *and*. Notice that the position of the modifiers can vary.

Base Sentence: Early joggers run along the sea's edge.

Insert: The joggers run effortlessly.

Insert: The joggers run gracefully.

Insert: The joggers run silently.

Combined: Early joggers run effortlessly, gracefully, and silently along the sea's edge.

> **or** Early joggers run <u>gracefully, effortlessly, and silently</u> along the sea's edge.

Although modifiers can be inserted into different places in the base sentence, they must be clearly attached to the words they modify so that readers correctly understand the writer's meaning. The first example that follows illustrates how modifiers can be correctly inserted in different places, while the second illustrates how misplaced modifiers change or confuse meaning.

For more information on misplaced modifiers, see pages 505-506.

Base Sentence: We drove cousin George to the bus station.

Insert: We drove <u>through the fog</u>.

Insert: The fog was <u>dense</u>.

Insert: The fog was <u>dangerous</u>. (*and*)

Combined: <u>Through the dense and dangerous fog,</u> we drove cousin George to the bus station.

> **or** We drove cousin George <u>through the dense and dangerous fog</u> to the bus station.

Base Sentence: The coach jumped up from the bench to protest the foul, and the referee threw her out of the game.

Insert: The coach was <u>irritated</u>.

Insert: The referee threw the coach out of the game <u>without a warning</u>.

Combined: <u>Irritated</u>, the coach jumped up from the bench to protest the foul, and the referee threw her out of the game <u>without a warning</u>.

but not   Without a warning, the coach jumped up from the bench to protest the foul, and the referee threw her out of the game irritated.

In the second combination *irritated* cannot be moved to the end of the sentence because it describes how the coach felt; it should be placed next to the word it modifies. Also, the phrase modifier *without a warning* cannot be inserted at the beginning of the sentence because these words describe the referee's actions.

Sometimes, an insert sentence can be made into a modifier by changing it to a "with . . ." phrase. The following examples show how this combination works.

Base Sentence:	The girl is my cousin.
Insert:	The girl has <u>long hair</u>. (*with*)
Combined:	The girl <u>with long hair</u> is my cousin.

Base Sentence:	The peacock strutted around the yard.
Insert:	<u>Its long, flowing tail trailed behind it</u>. (*with*)
Combined:	<u>With its long, flowing tail trailing behind</u>, the peacock strutted around the yard.

Exercise 1: *Inserting Modifiers*

Combine the following, using the first sentence in each set as the base sentence. Signals are given for sets 1–5 only.

Examples

a. A man was sleeping on the park bench.
The man was <u>dirty</u>.
The man was <u>ragged</u>. (,)
The man was <u>hungry</u>. (, *and*)
The park bench was <u>in the playground</u>.
A dirty, ragged, and hungry man was sleeping on the park bench in the playground.

b. Winds chased the leaves from the branches.
The winds were autumnal.
The leaves were brown.
The branches were bending.
The autumnal winds chased the brown leaves from the bending branches.

1. The boys failed to recognize the nature of Uncle Jeffrey's comments about the water shortage.
The boys were <u>giggling</u>.
The boys were <u>talking</u>. (,)
The nature of Uncle Jeffrey's comments was <u>serious</u>.
The water shortage is <u>imminent</u>.

195

2. The rescuer of the child received an award.
   The rescuer was brave.
   The rescuer was persistent. (,)
   The child was small.
   The reward was well-deserved.

3. The car stalled, leaving John alone in a town.
   The car was old.
   The car stalled on a street.
   The street was dark.
   The street was deserted. (,)
   The town was strange.

4. A farmer digging a well found several pieces of pottery and a stone weapon, a discovery that led to the excavation of a burial site.
   The farmer was from California.
   The farmer found the pottery and stone weapon in 1978.
   The pieces of pottery were broken.
   The stone weapon was carved.

5. Heroes have achieved an immortality as constellations.
   The heroes are ancient.
   The heroes are mythological. (,)
   The constellations are brilliant.
   The constellations are majestic. (,)
   The constellations are in our night skies.

6. Although the city sprayed every neighborhood and treated swamps, the mosquitoes continued to swarm.
   The city was sprayed routinely.
   The swamps were treated chemically.
   The swamps were nearby.
   The mosquitoes were pesky.
   The mosquitoes were dangerous.

7. Even though historians credit the Vikings with the discovery of America, some feel that an Irish expedition to this continent was possible and even likely.
   The historians are American.
   The historians are European.
   The discovery was the first.
   The discovery was Western.
   The Irish expedition was legendary.

8. During the reign of Charles I, the peace was shattered.
   The reign of Charles I lasted twenty-five years.
   The peace was of the Elizabethan era.
   The peace was shattered by a civil war.

The civil war was long-threatened.
The civil war was devastating.

9. The dentist probed her mouth, looking for plaque deposits.
   The dentist was concerned.
   The dentist probed carefully.
   The dentist probed thoroughly.
   Her mouth was wide open.
   The plaque deposits are destructive.
   The plaque deposits are between the gums and teeth.

10. Awaiting her arrival, Carlos arranged the bouquet.
    Carlos was awaiting her anxiously.
    Her arrival was from the office.
    Carlos arranged the bouquet tenderly.
    Carlos arranged the bouquet nervously.
    The bouquet was of a dozen roses.
    The roses were red.
    He arranged the bouquet in a vase.
    The vase was antique.

Writing Practice: *Inserting Modifiers*

Take out the plot analysis you wrote for Writing Practice 2: Analyzing Action. Revise it by inserting modifying words and phrases into some of the sentences. Strive for a variety of sentence lengths and patterns.

7 Writing the Research Paper

The Research Paper

The *research paper* is an extended, formal composition presenting information gathered from a number of sources.

Although a research paper is similar to a long expository essay, it includes more library resources and also identifies those sources in parenthetical documentation and a bibliography. While some research papers remain strictly informational, others draw a new conclusion from the facts they reveal. Typical of the informational kind would be a report on career opportunities in computer technology, the current employment status of women in the labor force, or a study of the Appalachian dialect. Papers that attempt to reach a conclusion often seek an answer to a question: How will computer technology affect education in the next two decades? Has the increase in number of women executives altered the business world? What new food sources can be made available to feed an expanding world population? How does an approaching presidential election affect the business of government?

Because writing a research paper requires careful, independent, and responsible work, it is important to understand each step in the research process before you begin to write. You will find the paper easier to write, and you will produce a better final product, if you schedule enough time to carefully complete each of these steps.

1. Choose and limit a topic.

2. Survey resources.

3. Develop a preliminary thesis statement and working bibliography.

4. Gather information.

5. Reevaluate.

6. Write a final thesis statement and formal outline.

7. Write the rough draft.

8. Write the final draft with parenthetical documentation and bibliography.

Alexander Calder, Circus, *1926–31, Mixed media. wire, wood, metal, cloth, paper, leather, string, rubber tubing, corks, buttons, sequins, nuts, bolts, bottle caps, 54" × 94¼" × 94¼". Collection of Whitney Museum of American Art.*

Choosing and Limiting a Topic

Some teachers consider the choice of topic so important to the success of the final paper that they assign topics they know students can manage. If you are free to make a choice yourself, choose a topic that will interest you, since you will be spending much time and effort learning about it. If your teacher indicates a certain length for the assignment, keep that guideline in mind.

Remember that your topic must be general enough that you can locate sources providing pertinent information, yet limited enough that ideas can be discussed in some depth.

A quick check of *library resources* will help you decide whether a topic is adequately limited or narrowed. Suppose you have always enjoyed art and decide you want to write about *The work of artists.* However, since your local and school libraries carry several books on that topic, you realize you must limit your emphasis even more. Tentatively, you decide on a more specific aspect of art: sculpting, the invention of the mobile, or the artist Alexander Calder. Since you can locate only one chapter on the invention of the mobile and no magazine articles, that topic is too limited. After further investigation, you decide on *The artist Alexander Calder* as a limited topic because you can locate some sources, but the amount of information is not overwhelming.

Also, consider the *scope* of a topic before you make a decision. Topics that cover long time spans (*The history of painting* or *Sculpture from its beginning to the present day*) are too general, as are topics that cover many categories or groups (*Art museums throughout the world* or *Famous portrait artists*). On the other hand, beware of topics that are too limited in time or scope: *How sculpture is displayed at the San Diego Museum of Art* or *The restoration of a Renaissance masterpiece*.

Writing Practice 1: *Limited Topic*

Divide a sheet of paper into two columns with the headings *Subjects* and *Limited Topics*. In the first column, list five general subjects that appeal to you. In the second column write five limited topics for a short research paper developed from the subjects in the first column. Use subjects from the following list, or choose your own. Save your work.

1. Migrant workers in America

2. Alternative schooling in America

3. History of a major business or industry in your area

4. History of photography

5. Famous Hispanic-American writers

6. Development of criminology

7. Problems of public transportation in the United States

8. Theories about the aging process

9. Patent medicines in early America

10. Famous women in science

Surveying Resources

For more information on using library and reference resources, see pages 630-645.

Next, take time to get an overview of your topic and to locate the resources you will need, such as reference books, periodicals, and other information sources in your school or public library.

An *overview*, or broad understanding of the topic gained from scanning several general background sources, will eliminate wasted or incomplete research. For example, if you have decided to write about some aspect of modern sculpture, you might read the entry on *sculpture* in the *World Book Encyclopedia*. Be sure to check the yearbooks of encyclopedias, too, because these annual volumes update all entries annually and feature special articles on timely subjects.

The *Readers' Guide* will also help you locate information, but remember that your goal now is to gain a general background. Choose articles addressed to the general public and articles under broad topic headings. If your topic is *Alexander Calder*, a general article about the artist's work in *Time* magazine will be more valuable than an *Instructor* article about the complexities of teaching mobile construction in a high school classroom.

Also, spend some time examining the library shelf containing books on your topic. Quickly look at individual works, noting the chapter headings and major divisions. If a book contains a general introduction or preface about your topic, skim that section quickly. Avoid taking lengthy notes early in your research. It is more important to get a thorough overview at this stage. Later, you will be able to choose your focus.

Writing Practice 2: *Overview*

Use the card catalogue and the *Readers' Guide to Periodical Literature* to find at least three articles that provide general background information about your research topic or an alternative topic you might choose for this assignment. (Refer to Chapter 27, Library Resources, if you need information on using the card catalogue and *Readers' Guide*.) On a separate sheet of paper, list these sources. Then, in a paragraph, summarize what you learned from reading the selected articles to get an overview of the topic. Tentatively organize the information you have gathered. Save your work.

Developing a Preliminary Thesis Statement

At this point in the writing process you may be ready to give your paper a single focus, or preliminary thesis statement. How will you select a focus for your paper?

A student interested in the work of Alexander Calder might choose one of the following as a preliminary thesis statement. Read each carefully. Notice that each of these ideas also suggests something about the paper's organization and how it will be developed.

1. The notion of the artist as tortured soul was laid to rest by the wit, wisdom, and breakthrough artistic concepts of Alexander Calder. (This suggests an attitude toward the artist's work that the writer will support and prove in the paper.)

2. Alexander Calder made a lasting contribution to the world of art with his inventions of the mobile and the stabile. (This suggests that the student will explore two specific art forms, perhaps contrasting them with the previous concepts of art.)

3. Alexander Calder's playful art mirrors his own energy and interests. (This suggests that the student will focus on the relationship of the artist to his work.)

As your research progresses and you become more knowledgeable about the topic, reevaluate and, if necessary, revise your thesis.

Writing Practice 3: *Preliminary Thesis*

On a sheet of paper, write four possible preliminary thesis statements for your research paper topic. Base them on what you learned from your overview. Save your work.

Preparing a Working Bibliography

A *working bibliography* lists, in alphabetical order by the author's last name, all the books, magazines, and newspaper articles, pamphlets, and other information sources you might use for research. Each source is given a number; this will simplify later note-taking. Preparation of a working bibliography ensures that adequate sources have been located.

In a bibliography a standard form governs the order in which author, title, and publishing details are listed and separated by marks of punctuation. You will save time later by listing these items correctly in your working bibliography. Check with your teacher about the bibliography form you should use, as there are several acceptable ones. In this chapter the MLA form, developed by the Modern Language Association and explained in the *MLA Handbook*, is used.

A good approach is to record the necessary information about the author, title, publisher, and publication date of each source on a separate note card. Using this method for the working bibliography makes the preparation of a final bibliography easier.

The following source card is a sample. Notice the circled number in the upper-right corner identifying this title as Source 1. Using this source number later on note cards prevents having to recopy bibliography details on each note card.

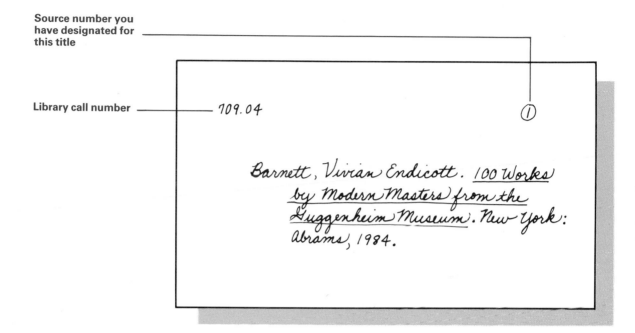

Source number you have designated for this title

Library call number

709.04

①

Barnett, Vivian Endicott. *100 Works by Modern Masters from the Guggenheim Museum*. New York: Abrams, 1984.

The following list shows the MLA bibliography form for various sources.

Model: *Bibliographic Forms*

Book by One Author

Pennycook, Andrew. Codes and Ciphers: Amazing Ways to Scramble

and Unscramble Secret Messages. New York: McKay, 1978.

(Notice that the subtitle is included as part of the complete title.)

Book by More Than One Author

Crerar, Thomas, and David King. Choice of Words. New York: Oxford

UP, 1969.

A Work in Several Volumes or Parts

Abrams, M. H., et al., eds. The Norton Anthology of English Literature.

3rd ed. 2 vols. New York: Norton, 1974. Vol. 1.

Work Within a Collection of Pieces by Different Authors

Welty, Eudora. "A Worn Path." By and About Women: An Anthology

of Short Fiction. Ed. Beth Kline Schneiderman. New York:

Harcourt, 1973. 317–325.

Article from a Critical Edition or Casebook

Widmer, Kingsley. "Black Existentialism: Richard Wright." Modern

Black Novelists: A Collection of Critical Essays. Ed. M.G. Cooke.

Englewood Cliffs, N.J.: Prentice, 1971. 79–87.

Edition of a Work of Literature

Clemens, Samuel Langhorne. Adventures of Huckleberry Finn: An

Authoritative Text, Backgrounds and Sources, Criticism. Ed.

Sculley Bradley, et al. 2nd ed. New York: Norton, 1977.

Article in an Encyclopedia or Other Reference Work (No Author Given)

"Wright, Frank Lloyd." Encyclopaedia Britannica: Macropaedia.

1979 ed.

Article from an Encyclopedia or Other Reference Work

Marty, Martin E. "Resurgent Fundamentalism." Encyclopaedia

Britannica: 1980 Book of the Year. 606–607. (Articles in

references arranged alphabetically need not be identified by

volume and page.)

Article from a Monthly Magazine

Hahn, Emily. "Eleventh Hour." The New Yorker 1 Sept. 1980: 37–69.

Article from a Newspaper (No Author Given)

"Minimum Wage to Rise Again." Decatur Herald 10 Oct. 1979,

sec. 1: 2.

Article from a Newspaper

Stevens, Michelle. "Home or Hospital Birth? Center Offers

Alternative." Chicago Sun-Times 2 Mar. 1981: 7.

Review of a Film, Book, or Play

Raynor, Vivien. "Picasso, of Course, Is Everywhere." Rev. of The

Shock of the New, by Robert Hughes. The New York Times

Book Review 15 Feb. 1981: 3.

A Source Not in Print Format

McCluskey, Paul. Personal interview. 28 Feb. 1981.

Frost, Robert. Frost Reads His Poetry. Caedmon, XC 783, 1952. (Use

this format for records.)

Pamphlet

The MLA Handbook. 2nd ed. New York: MLA, 1970.

U.S. Bureau of Labor Statistics. Productivity. Washington, D.C.: GPO,

1958.

If an item of information is not available, record that fact by writing *no author, no date of publication, no place, etc.,* on the bibliography card. Later, when you organize the final bibliography, you will know you did not forget to record this information.

Writing Practice 4: *Working Bibliography*

Using materials in your library, prepare a working bibliography for your research paper by filling out a card for each source you plan to use. (If you are not writing a paper, select a topic for this assignment and prepare five bibliography cards.) Save your work.

Formulating Basic Questions

Taking notes will be easier if you formulate a list of basic questions to guide your research. The techniques described in Chapter 1 can be used to develop a list of basic questions. For example, the *Pentad* might lead to the following basic questions relating to the topic of the artist Alexander Calder.

1.   *Action:* What did the artist make?

2.   *Actors:* Who and what influenced Calder?

3.   *Agent:* What materials and techniques did Calder use to create artworks that show playfulness?

4.   *Scene:* In what country and in what time period did Calder live and work?

5.   *Purpose:* What is the reason Calder created the works he did?

When your list of basic questions is complete, you can arrange the questions as a preliminary outline if you wish. Although this outline will help you anticipate the important questions your paper will have to answer, it will probably require some revision as your research progresses. If you discover new points that need to be included, add them. If a point later seems unrelated to the scope of the final paper, remove it from the outline.

Writing Practice 5: *Basic Questions*

Keeping in mind the focus of your paper and the information you gained from the overview of your topic, write a list of basic questions on your research paper topic. Use one of the information-gathering techniques in Chapter 1 as an aid. Save your work.

Taking Notes

Taking notes will be easier if you use file cards, recording one item of information from a particular source on each card. The examples on pages 207 and 208 are note cards for a paper on *The Artist Alexander Calder.* The circled number in the upper-right corner indicates the source of this information; since the bibliography card with the same number lists all information about title, author, and publication, there is no need to repeat it on each note card. The *slug,* or topic heading, in the upper-left corner identifies the main idea of the note and allows the writer to organize the cards later without rereading each one.

Recording notes on cards in this manner has several distinct advantages. A final paper on Alexander Calder might contain a lengthy paragraph on the invention of the mobile; the supporting details for this paragraph might come from four different sources. Shuffling through pages of notes from a source to locate the necessary information is difficult and time consuming. With the information recorded on cards, the writer can simply pull out those carrying the slug *The mobile* and arrange and rearrange them to produce the best order.

Evaluating Sources

You will probably use both *primary* and *secondary sources* in your paper.

Primary sources are firsthand documents.

For example, an entry in the artist's notebook, the memoir of the artist, or an interview with the artist would all be primary sources.

A *secondary source* is one written about some aspect of the primary source.

For example, the biography of the artist Alexander Calder, or a magazine article written from interviews with Calder are both secondary sources.

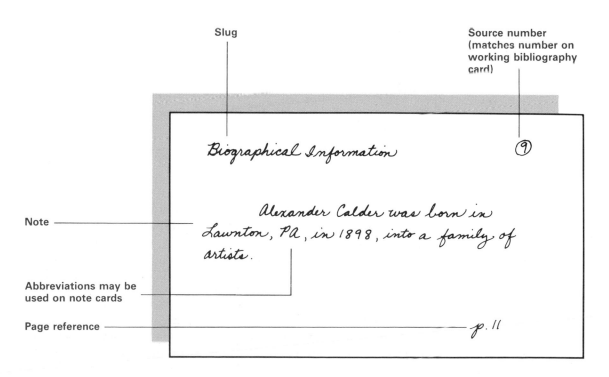

Slug

Source number (matches number on working bibliography card)

Biographical Information

⑨

Alexander Calder was born in Lawnton, PA, in 1898, into a family of artists.

Note

Abbreviations may be used on note cards

Page reference

p. 11

Source number

Slug

Page reference

Note combines
quotation and
paraphrase

⑨

The mobile

p. 51

As author Lipman observes, "The never-
failing Calder playfulness and humor are
noticeable even in his totally abstract
kind of work." One mobile, _Gongs_, even
rings as brass pieces hit together.

Not all sources are equally reliable or valuable. If your topic is *The Work of Alexander Calder*, you might limit your sources to those written specifically about his art. For this reason, Anthony Padovano's *The Process of Sculpture*, which discusses sculpting techniques, is not a valuable resource. The author's reputation and expertise should also be considered. Sometimes, you can discover which authors are most respected by noting references to them in other sources. The bibliographies at the end of books and articles often reveal which works are most respected or most important to understanding a topic. Also consider the audience for which a source was intended; articles in popular general magazines often do not have the authority of articles written for specialized journals. A quotation about Calder from *ARTnews,* a publication about contemporary art, carries more weight than a feature about making mobiles found in a family magazine.

Reading Efficiently

Survey a resource before you begin taking notes, and use your overview or preliminary outline to guide your reading. First, locate the sections that provide specific information on your topic. Then scan for the main idea, noting headings, subheadings, and *italicized* words. Finally, read the material before you take notes rather than recording as you read; you may discover the author's first explanation of a term is not the best one or that an entire chapter is quickly summarized in the last few pages.

Before you write a note on a card, put the circled bibliography card number for that source in the card's upper-right corner. If

Calder's Universe is source number *8*, every note card with information from this source should have the circled number *8* in the upper-right corner. Under the source number place the page number(s) covered by that note. You may also want to put a topic heading in the upper-left corner of the card.

Notation

Usually a note card summarizes or paraphrases information found in a primary or secondary source.

To *paraphrase* information, read the source several times and then write a version that restates the ideas in your own words. Since your note cards are for your use, you may want to use abbreviations (*ex.* rather than *example*) and phrases rather than complete sentences. However, the note must be complete enough that you will understand it later.

The *summary* is a shortened version of a long work or passage. The summary concentrates on main ideas only. It eliminates most descriptions, details, and examples.

Model: Source, Paraphrase, and Summary

The following selection is an original passage from the book *Alexander Calder and His Magical Mobiles* by Jean Lipman with Margaret Aspinwall. It is followed by both a paraphrase and a summary.

> For Sandy's later mobiles, though some of them were still about real things, like an elephant or a cat, or kept the idea of real things, like suns and moons, or snowflakes or spiders, it was the abstract shapes and colors, and especially movement, that he cared about most. He said one time, "Just as one can compose colors, or forms, so one can compose motions."[1]

Paraphrase: Some of Calder's later mobiles represented actual objects or animals, but most were abstract, composed of shapes, colors, and movement—with the emphasis on movement. He believed that movement could be

---

[1]From *Alexander Calder and His Magical Mobiles* by Jean Lipman with Margaret Aspinwall. © 1981 by the Whitney Museum of American Art.

used artistically in the same way that color and form are.

Summary: Calder's later mobiles were often abstract, composed of shapes and colors, with an emphasis on movement.

The process of paraphrasing or summarizing information is important; recording information in your own words will help you understand the topic and write a better paper. The final paper should be your work in your words, not a hodgepodge of borrowed passages. Submitting a paper with the words or the ideas of another presented as your own work is *plagiarism*, a dishonest practice you should avoid.

Direct Quotations

Although quotations should be used sparingly, when an author states information especially clearly or forcefully, you may want to quote those words exactly. If you are writing about a work of literature, you can quote lines from the work to support your ideas. Also, if a writer is particularly associated with a phrase, even of one or two words, the phrase should be quoted. (Example: *Lincoln spoke of a government "for the people."*)

Always record an author's words exactly and place quotation marks around the words on the note card. If you abbreviate the quote by omitting a portion of the original, use an ellipsis (three spaced periods) to indicate the omission. Notice the ellipsis on the note card on this page.

Source number

Slug

Page reference

Ellipsis indicates
omission of words
from quote

Direct quote enclosed
in quotation marks

⑥

Inspiration for work

p. 208

"*Sandy's association with toys had been continuous and pleasurable. They were never something to put on a shelf . . . but something to manipulate, to use imaginatively.*"

Brackets can be used to indicate that you have changed a word in the original quotation; however, this is done only rarely. The quotation on this page originally used the pronoun *his*. The student has inserted the word *Sandy's* in brackets to avoid quoting the previous sentence.

Writing Practice 6: *Note Cards*

Write note cards for your research paper from sources you have located. Paraphrase or summarize information, using quotations only when they are especially appropriate. Save your work.

Source number ──────────

Slug ──────────

Pages on which quote appears ──────────

Abstract Art

⑥
pp. 260-261

Brackets indicate change in original word ──────────

Direct quote enclosed in quotation marks ──────────

"From the beginning, [Sandy's] constructions related to the organic world; it was to nature that he turned for elements of abstract form."

Reevaluating Your Work

Before you settle on a thesis statement, prepare your formal outline, and begin writing your research paper, review the headings of your note cards. If applicable, reevaluate your preliminary thesis statement and your list of basic questions. If you have discovered important new material or if the purpose of your paper has changed, make revisions now. To reevaluate your work, consider the following questions.

1. Have you discovered new information that changes the emphasis of your paper? Should you modify your preliminary thesis to reflect this new focus?

Alexander Calder, White Lily, 1944–45, Sheet metal, wire, 41¾". The
Saint Louis Art Museum, Museum purchase. 144:1946

2. Is there a topic in your overview or preliminary outline that is
not adequately treated by your note cards? Should you eliminate
the topic or locate more information to develop it adequately?

3. Have you recorded information unrelated to your topic? If so,
set these note cards aside; perhaps you can use this material to
develop an interesting introduction or conclusion.

Organizing the Formal Outline

If you use the slugs, or topic headings, on your note cards to
group related cards in stacks, writing the formal outline should
not be difficult. Rearrange the cards, eliminating any that do not
fit, until you have the best sequence for developing the thesis.

For more information on
thesis statements, see
pages 112-113.

Some instructors ask students to include a thesis statement at
the beginning of the outline. Even if your teacher prefers an outline
without a thesis statement, now is a good time to revise your
preliminary thesis statement, or finally develop a thesis statement
based on your research. It should be a single declarative statement
that presents the central idea of your research paper.

The *formal outline* uses Roman numerals (I, II, III), capital letters
(A, B, C), and Arabic numbers (1, 2, 3) to show the relationship of
major and minor ideas in the paper. Notice that there are always two
or more divisions under a heading or none at all; an *A* requires at least
a *B*, a *1* requires at least a *2*. Divisions (or subheadings) are used when
a broad topic is broken down into smaller topics. When the major
topic cannot be subdivided into two or more parts, there is no reason
for a subheading.

All the headings in a formal outline share a similar grammatical structure. In a *sentence outline* each point, major or minor, is stated as a complete sentence; in a *topic outline* all the headings are written as words and phrases. Do not mix these two forms in the same outline.

The sample research paper on pages 221–226 was written from the following topic outline.

Thesis Statement: The widely accepted notion of artist as tortured soul was laid to rest in the 1930s by the wit, wisdom, and breakthrough artistic concepts of Alexander Calder, inventor of the mobile and stabile.

I. Influences of his youth

    A. Artists in family

    B. Encouraged to experiment

    C. Happy personality

II. Fascination with sense of action and order

    A. The universe

    B. The circus

III. The mobile and the stabile

    A. Influence of Mondrian

    B. Mobiles became popular

        1. Unique and amusing

        2. Adorn many buildings

    C. Encouraged new artists

The following example shows how the first division of the previous outline would look in a sentence outline.

I. Calder's experiences as a youth influenced his career.

    A. His mother, father, and grandfather were artists.

    B. He was encouraged to experiment in his work.

    C. His happy personality was reflected in his art.

Writing Practice 7: *Formal Outline*

Using information from your note cards, write either a sentence outline or a topic outline for your research paper. Be sure to include the thesis statement. Save your work.

Writing the Rough Draft

Writing the first, or rough, draft will be easier if your note cards are organized to correspond with your outline. If you discover that some notes do not fit the final organization of the paper or that you need more details to develop your topic, take time to delete or add more information.

The research paper possesses all the characteristics of a well-developed expository essay. The introduction should catch the reader's attention and introduce the central idea, or thesis statement. Each paragraph in the body of the paper should be restricted to one idea. This central idea should be adequately and clearly developed with examples, facts and statistics, the steps in a process, or some other method of paragraph development. Transition devices should be used between sentences and paragraphs to help the reader move from idea to idea and to show the relationships between these ideas. The conclusion should restate the paper's central idea in an interesting way and reveal the significance of the research.

For more information on transition devices, see pages 82-88.

Research papers sometimes vary in formality. A paper about local history that includes personal interviews with local residents might be written in the first person. A more formal paper based completely on library research would probably be written without reference to yourself.

Two special aspects of writing your rough draft are incorporating quoted material and adding parenthetical documentation.

Using Quotations

Over the years researchers have developed standard methods for adding quotations to the research paper.

Long quotations, usually more than three lines of poetry or four lines of prose, are set off from the body of the paper and introduced with a short statement followed by a colon. Any of the following methods could be used to introduce a long quotation.

In <u>Alexander Calder and His Magical Mobiles</u> authors Jean Lipman and Margaret Aspinwall portray Calder as an artist whose happiness showed in his work:

In Maurice Bruzeau's Calder the author recounts, in Calder's words, the conversation with Mondrian:

Recorded in Ugo Mulas's Calder, the following is translated from a French exhibition catalogue:

Each line of a long quotation is also indented ten spaces from the left-hand margin. If you write your paper in longhand, emphasize that you are quoting directly by making the indentation obvious and by introducing the quotation. Because this special format identifies the quotation, the quotation marks at the beginning and end of the passage are omitted.

Because *short quotations* of four lines or less are not indented, quotation marks are used at the beginning and end of the passage to indicate that the words are a quotation. A short quotation should not upset the smooth flow of the sentence or paragraph in which it appears. Instead, the writer should create a smooth transition between the quoted material and the rest of the sentence. Notice how this transition is achieved in the following example of a short quotation.

In Alexander Calder and His Magical Mobiles, he is quoted as saying, "The underlying sense of form in my work has been the system of the Universe" (Lipman and Aspinwall 45).

Alexander Calder, Black Widow, *1959, Painted sheet steel, 7'8" × 14'3" × 7'5". Collection, The Museum of Modern Art, New York, Mrs. Simon Guggenheim Fund.*

Alexander Calder, The Cock's Comb, *1960, Painted sheet iron, 119¼" × 145¾" × 98½". Collection of Whitney Museum of American Art, Purchase, with funds from the Friends of the Whitney Museum of American Art. 62.18*

Documentation

Documentation is a reference to a source. *Parenthetical documentation* tells readers the sources for important information or direct quotations used in the paper. Because this type of documentation is enclosed in parentheses, it is called *parenthetical documentation*; individual notations are sometimes called *parenthetical references.* Parenthetical references have several important functions: (1) they give authors credit for unique facts, original theories, and words quoted exactly; (2) they provide enough information for the source to be located easily in the bibliography; (3) they cite specific page numbers that allow the reader to find the material quickly in the original source; and (4) they reassure readers that the material is not speculation or hearsay, but the result of the writer's sound research.

You may be unsure about what material to document. Direct quotations must always be documented even if the quotation is only two or three words. Information that is unique to a particular author is also documented, even if you do not quote that information word for word. However, if a fact or idea appears so frequently that giving credit to a particular source seems impossible, documentation is not necessary. For example, since critics generally acknowledge that Alexander Calder's art is playful, that information would not be followed by a parenthetical reference. You would also not document Calder's birth date; that information is undisputed fact.

Although the absence of a necessary parenthetical reference can be considered plagiarism, a research paper can also include excessive documentation. If several sentences or all the information in a paragraph is drawn from a single source, one parenthetical reference can be used at the end of the paragraph.

Include parenthetical documentation in your rough draft to ensure that no references are left out. Keep your note cards in the order you write your paper so that you can check for accuracy of the parenthetical documentation as you prepare your final copy.

Remember the following points as you write parenthetical documentation.

1. Parenthetical documentation appears in the text of your report, either at the end of a sentence or where a pause occurs in the sentence, and is *followed* by sentence punctuation (such as a comma or period). A parenthetical reference for a direct quotation follows the end quotation mark but precedes the sentence punctuation. When a reference is made at the end of an indented quotation, however, it comes after the last period or other end punctuation.

2. Parenthetical references are brief, usually containing only the author's last name and the specific page number or numbers from which a quotation or information was taken. Documentation gives only as much information as is necessary for the reader to locate the source in your bibliography and the specific page reference for the material used. Thus, any source you document in the text of your report must be included in your bibliography.

3. Each reference is enclosed in parentheses.

4. No comma follows the author's last name, and the page number is not identified by the word *page* or an abbreviation such as *p.* or *pp.* If the title of a source is needed to specify a work by a particular author, a comma separates the name and the title; again, no comma precedes the page number. If a title only is used, no comma separates the title and page number.

5. A title in parenthetical documentation may be shortened, using the main or key word or words, with the articles *the, a,* or *an* left out. Be sure to include the word under which the source is alphabetized in your bibliography, however. Underline the titles

of books and use quotation marks for the titles of articles.

The following sample parenthetical references illustrate the MLA form for various sources of information. Your teacher may ask you to use this or another form of documentation.

Model: Parenthetical Documentation

Note: The word *source* below refers to any text listed in your bibliography: a book, magazine article, or the like.

Source by One Author (Only One Source by This Author Listed in Bibliography)

(Pennycook 20)

Source by More Than One Author (Only One Source by These Authors Listed in Bibliography)

(Crerar and King 88-91)

Source When More Than One Title by the Same Author or Authors Appears in Bibliography

(Pennycook, Codes and Ciphers 20)

(Crerar and King, Choice of Words 88-91)

A Work in Several Volumes or Parts

(Parrington 2: 41)

Note: The number before the colon is the volume number; the number following the colon is the page number.

Edition of a Work of Literature

(Clemens 111; ch. 21)

Note: The number before the semicolon is the page number of the edition referenced in the bibliography. So that the reader may find the reference in another edition, the chapter of a novel is also provided. For plays, the act and scene may be cited. A classic play or long poem are referenced by act, scene, or part and lines without a page number given. Act 1, Scene 3, lines 2-8 of a play would be written this way: 1.3.2-8.

Article in an Encyclopedia or Other Source When No Author Is Given

("Wright, Frank Lloyd")

Note: Articles in references arranged alphabetically (such as encyclopedias) or contained on one page need not be identified by volume and page.

("Minimum Wage" 1: 2)

Note: If the pages of a newspaper are numbered separately by section as they are in this example, be sure to identify the section (shown here preceding the colon) as well as the page number. Many newspapers use letters for the sections, in which case you need not use a colon; simply use the letter and page number: *A12, B6,* and the like.

("Life Story" 17)

A Source Not in Print Format (an interview, recording, etc.)

(McCluskey)

Note: Use the name or title under which the source is listed in your bibliography.

There is no need to repeat the name of an author or source if you use it in the text of your paper. The documentation for such a reference would consist only of the page number in parentheses following the quotation or information, as the following example shows.

Dr. Smith believes that "many discoveries of this nature are occurring

every year" (68).

If you refer to an entire source rather than a specific page, simply note in the parenthetical reference the name or title under which the source is listed in your bibliography.

A whole science of the nature of these advances has emerged in

recent years (Smith).

When you quote something from an indirect source, you need to note this in the documentation with the words *qtd. in.* An indirect source is a secondary source that is itself referring to what someone else said. If an author's words are quoted in a critical article, for example, and you use the words as written in that article, you would use the phrase *qtd. in* in your parenthetical reference. The following is an example of this kind of reference.

Dr. Jones once said, "It's not how often you think that counts. It's

that you think" (qtd. in Groh 12).

Of course, you should always use the original source of a quotation if it is available.

The MLA format for research paper documentation presented in this chapter is the style most widely accepted and used in such humanities fields as English and history. However, it is not the only available style; almost every field of scholarship, from chemistry to psychology, has its own preferred format.

Writing Practice 8: *Parenthetical Documentation*

On a sheet of paper, write these references as parenthetical documentation, just as they would appear in the text of a research paper. You may not need all the information given for each reference; you must decide what to include and what to exclude.

1. Reference to page 117 of *The Americans: The National Experience,* by Daniel Boorstin, published in New York in 1965 by Vintage Books. This is the only book by Boorstin in the bibliography.

2. A reference to page 401 of *Illinois: A History of the Prairie State* by Robert P. Howard. This is the only source by Howard in the bibliography. Published by William B. Eerdmans Publishing Co., of Grand Rapids, Michigan in 1952.

3. A reference to Paul M. Angle's *Bloody Williamson: A Chapter in American Lawlessness,* a 1952 publication of Alfred Knopf, Inc., of New York. Another source edited by Angle is listed in the bibliography. The reference is to page 81.

4. A second reference to Howard's book. Reference is to page 400.

5. A reference to *Prairie State: Impressions of Illinois, 1673–1967, by Travelers and Other Observers,* published by the University of Chicago Press, located in Chicago, in 1968. The reference is to page 333. The book's editor is Paul M. Angle, the author of another source listed in the bibliography.

6. A second reference to *Prairie State: Impressions of Illinois, 1673–1967, by Travelers and Other Observers.* The reference is to pages 370–371.

7. A reference to page 14 of an anonymous article in the January 16, 1975, issue of the magazine *Senior Scholastic.* The article's title is "How Good Were the Good Old Days? Chicago in 1874."

8. A reference to page 75 of the article "Prairie Cattle Kings of Yesterday" by George Ade in the July 4, 1931, *Saturday Evening Post.* It is the only source by Ade in the paper.

9. A reference to Richard Sennett's book *Families Against the City: Middle Class Homes of Industrial Chicago, 1872–1900,* published in 1970 in New York by Vintage Books. This is the only source by Sennett listed in the bibliography. The reference is to page 141.

10. A second reference to Sennett's book. Reference is to page 140.

Reading a Research Paper

Model: Research Paper

As you read this research paper on Alexander Calder, notice how the author has used description and narration, as well as exposition, to keep the reader's interest.

Alexander Calder, Untitled, *1976, Aluminum and steel, 29' 10½" × 76'. National Gallery of Art, Washington, Gift of the Collectors Committee. 1977.76.1*

The Moving Shadows Of Genius

The public perception of artists and their work has always been a matter of personal taste. Fifteen people studying a work of art will likely result in fifteen different opinions as to what the artist was feeling when he or she was creating the piece. Through the centuries artists such as Van Gogh, Gauguin, Munch, and others have implanted in the public mind that suffering is an essential part of the process of creation. This widely accepted notion of the artist as tortured soul was permanently laid to rest in the 1930s by the wit, wisdom, and break-through artistic concepts of Alexander Calder, inventor of the mobile and stabile.

221

Born in 1898 in Lawnton, Pennsylvania, Alexander, nicknamed Sandy, exhibited signs of artistic interest and talent at a very early age. His talent may have been inherited, as Sandy grew up in a family that included a mother who painted and a father and grandfather who were highly regarded sculptors. Little did the family know at that time that young Sandy would someday take the Calder name to the very top of the art world.

If the Calder family had a creed, it was to improvise whenever possible (Hayes 31). Encouraged by his parents to create from his imagination, Sandy began to make objects out of whatever he could get his hands on. He used wood, wire, and all sorts of odd items to make animals and jewelry. Anything that could be glued, twisted, hung, or otherwise lifted was fair game for his fertile mind. His happy personality and sense of humor were beginning to manifest themselves in his art. The amusing outlook that would later become his trademark was taking shape almost daily. In Alexander Calder and His Magical Mobiles authors Jean Lipman and Margaret Aspinwall portray Calder as an artist whose happiness showed in his work:

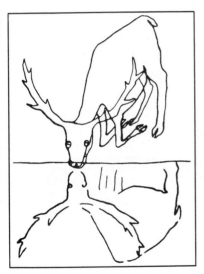

Alexander Calder, Calder's Animals, *1931, Drawings for* Aesop's Fables. *Spencer Collection of The New York Public Library.*

> Sandy was never, in all his long life, unhappy. He himself said that he had "a big advantage" as he was "inclined to be happy by nature." You can see from his work that the pure pleasure of combining interesting shapes and colors and lively motion is a great deal of what it's about, and that's why it gives us instant pleasure to look at. He wrote in a letter to his grandniece: "Above all, I feel art should be happy." Very few works of art can make us feel light-hearted the way Sandy Calder's do. (18)

During his formative years Calder became fascinated by two things: the universe and the circus. The movement of the moon and sun and the relationship of the heavenly bodies permeated his thinking and grew into a conceptual inspiration for his art. In Alexander Calder and His Magical Mobiles, he is quoted as saying, "The underlying sense of form in my work has been the system of the Universe, or part thereof. For that is a rather large model to work from" (Lipman and Aspinwall 45).

Likewise the circus, with all of its action and well-ordered sense of zaniness, greatly affected him. He began to use circus performers and animals as models for his work with wire and wood. While living in Paris in the mid-1920s Calder created and exhibited a miniature circus—fashioned out of wire—much to the appreciation of the art world.

As Calder's art became celebrated, his name grew in prominence and he made friends with many artists who would influence the direction of his work. On one memorable visit to the studio of artist Piet Mondrian, Calder wondered out loud how movement would enhance Mondrian's abstract art. At the time Mondrian let Calder know that he was less than thrilled about the idea. In Maurice Bruzeau's Calder the author recounts, in Calder's words, the conversation with Mondrian:

> I liked his paintings well enough. But those little black or colored rectangles pinned to the wall—I should have liked to see them move. When I mentioned this to Mondrian, he replied: "...Quite the opposite. My paintings are restless enough just as they are. They don't need to move!" ... From that moment on ... I plunged headlong into abstraction, but always with the intention of making things move. Even my wire figures. (13)

Calder's abiding passion for movement in art had become crystallized. He began making and exhibiting motorized sculptures, termed "mobiles" by his friend, artist Marcel Duchamp. Calder's stationary constructions were given the name "stabiles" by Jean Arp, another artist/friend. Through his mobiles and stabiles Calder found the perfect vehicles for expressing his feelings of wonderment and humor.

The public and critics alike embraced the spirited imagination in Calder's mobiles. These unique creations were soon finding their way into prestigious museums and the private collections of serious art patrons. The man who created these wondrous, living mobiles was becoming a very popular subject of discussion. What sort of person could infuse his art with such amusing intelligence? Recorded in Ugo Mulas's Calder, the following is translated from a French exhibition catalogue:

> Smiling and curious he sways in the air as part of nature itself....Nothing escapes him. He sees everything....He has amalgamated and coordinated everything. With them he has

created plastic objects, then still smiling he puts his finger on a magic push button and quietly and gracefully everything moves! Mobile sculpture has been invented.... Calder's work is bound to stay popular. Why not? (57)

Stay popular indeed. The demand for his services came from a variety of countries and institutions. His work adorns banks, opera houses, restaurants, airlines (he painted a jet), and open spaces in front of many modern buildings. Calder had rightfully assumed his position in the upper echelon of the art world. His influence spread around the globe and encouraged a new generation of artists to seek out unexplored avenues of expression.

The few who questioned the artistic merit of Calder's work were most likely viewing it from the wrong angle—with their hearts closed—for the heart was the source of inspiration for Calder throughout his career. He created what he felt. Were he alive today, Calder would probably appreciate the following conversation overheard between two visitors at an exhibition of his work: "Nine red saucers and two balls that bounce around and hit them. What's so wonderful about that?" The reply: "That's just the point. It isn't wonderful. But with this guy we can see the beauty and fun in the simplest things around us. It isn't wonderful, he is" (Hayes 295).

Calder died in 1976, but the spirit of his genius lives on in his mobiles and other creations. He left behind a legacy that speaks to the child in all of us. The next time you view a piece of Calder's art, close your eyes and listen; you just might hear echoes of laughter from the man whose visual magic makes you think and laugh at the same time.

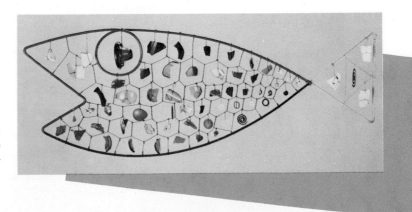

Alexander Calder, Fish Mobile, *1940, Glass, metal, wire, and cord, 16¼" × 46" × 3". Hirshhorn Museum and Sculpture Garden, Smithsonian Institution, Gift of Joseph H. Hirshhorn, 1966.*

Alexander Calder, Lobster Trap and Fish Tail, *1939, Hanging mobile: painted steel wire and sheet aluminum, 8'6" × 9'6". Collection, The Museum of Modern Art, New York, Commissioned by the Advisory Committee for the stairwell of the Museum.*

Bibliography

Barnett, Vivian Endicott. 100 Works by Modern Masters from the
   Guggenheim Museum. New York: Abrams, 1984.

Brommer, Gerald F., and George F. Horn. Art in Your Visual Environment.
   2nd ed. Worcester, MA: Davis, 1985.

---. Art in Your World. Dallas: Hendrick; Worcester, MA: Davis, 1977.

Bruzeau, Maurice. Calder. New York: Abrams, 1979.

Flint, Lucy. The Peggy Guggenheim Collection. New York: Abrams, 1983.

Hayes, Margaret Calder. Three Alexander Calders. Middlebury, VT:
   Eriksson, 1977.

Heron, Patrick. The Changing Forms of Art. London: Routledge, 1955.

Lipman, Jean. Calder's Universe. New York: Viking, 1976.

Lipman, Jean, and Margaret Aspinwall. Alexander Calder and His
  Magical Mobiles. 1st ed. New York: Hudson Hills, 1981.

Morman, Mary Jean. Art: Of Wonder and a World. Blauvelt, NY: Art
  Education, 1978.

Mulas, Ugo. Calder. New York: Viking, 1971.

Thalacker, Donald W. The Place of Art in the World of Architecture. New
  York: Chelsea; New York: Bowker, 1980.

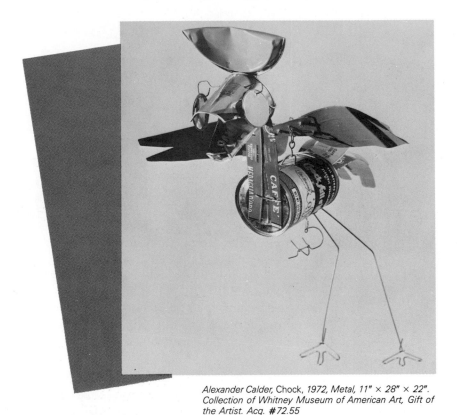

Alexander Calder, Chock, *1972, Metal, 11" × 28" × 22".
Collection of Whitney Museum of American Art, Gift of
the Artist. Acq. #72.55*

Think and Discuss

1. In the first paragraph of "The Moving Shadows of Genius," has the writer used descriptive, narrative, or expository writing?

2. Where is the thesis of "The Moving Shadows of Genius" stated?

3. What main points does the author of "The Moving Shadows of Genius" use to develop and explain the thesis?

4. What paragraphs in the body of the report contain description? Narration?

5. List two examples each of parallel structure, repetition, paraphrase, and transitions used for coherence.

6. How is the conclusion of "The Moving Shadows of Genius" related to the introduction?

Writing Practice 9: *Rough Draft*

With the aid of your note cards and formal outline, write the rough draft of your research paper. Remember to add parenthetical documentation where it is needed and to insert quotations correctly. Save your work.

Writing the Final Bibliography

The *final bibliography* includes only those sources you used in gathering information for your research paper.

After checking the information on your bibliography cards for accuracy, arrange them alphabetically by the author's last name. If no author is listed for a source, alphabetize it by the first major word in the title. In very lengthy bibliographies, sources are also subdivided by types: books, articles, films, pamphlets, each alphabetized under a separate heading.

Write the bibliography on a separate sheet of paper under the heading *Bibliography*. If an entry requires more than one line, indent the second and all other lines five spaces. If two sources were written by the same author, the author's name is not repeated in the second listing; three hyphens are used instead for all other sources by that author. The following example shows how two works by Gerald F. Brommer and George F. Horn are listed in the bibliography.

> Brommer, Gerald F., and George F. Horn. Art in Your Visual Environment. 2nd ed. Worcester, MA: Davis, 1985.
> ---. Art in Your World. Dallas: Hendrick; Worcester: Davis, 1977.

Notice that the name of the publisher is shortened, including only the major word in the name and, sometimes, abbreviations of other important words. For example, *Davis Publications, Inc.* is shortened to *Davis, W. W. Norton and Company, Inc.* is shortened to *Norton*, and the *University of Chicago Press* becomes *U of Chicago P*.

Look at the sample bibliography on pages 203–205. Notice that the listings for magazine and newspaper articles, as well as works within a collection of pieces by different authors in the same book, include the page numbers on which the article or work can be found. This bibliography conforms to the MLA style, although your teacher may prefer that you use another accepted style.

Writing Practice 10: *Final Bibliography*

On a separate sheet of paper, organize and write your final bibliography, using the working bibliography you created in Writing Practice 4 as well as any other bibliographic sources you found as you continued your research. Remember that your bibliography must be arranged in alphabetical order by the authors' last names. Follow the MLA bibliography style presented on pages 203–205, unless you have been instructed to follow another format. Be sure to follow the correct order for presenting author, title, and publishing details. Also check to be sure that your bibliographic entries are correctly punctuated. If you are not writing a paper, write final bibliography entries for the sources listed below.

1. A book by Paul M. Angle entitled *Bloody Williamson: A Chapter in American Lawlessness.* This work was published in New York by Alfred Knopf, Inc., in 1952.

2. A work published by William B. Eerdmans of Grand Rapids, Michigan in 1952. The book is *Illinois: A History of the Prairie State* by Robert P. Howard.

3. A work called *Prairie State: Impressions of Illinois, 1673–1967, by Travelers and Other Observers.* Paul M. Angle edited the book, which was published by the University of Chicago Press in Chicago in 1968.

4. An anonymous article in *Senior Scholastic* titled "How Good Were the Good Old Days? Chicago in 1874." The article appeared on pages 14–15 in the January 16, 1975, issue of the magazine.

5. An article called "Where Gangsters Fell—Then and Now" on pages 42–46 of the *Chicago Tribune,* sec. 9, for Februray 11, 1979. The article was written by W.K. Murray.

Writing Assignment I: *Research Paper*

A. Prewriting

Read the checklist that follows and think about how you could improve your rough draft. Make notes on your manuscript to indicate changes that would increase the effectiveness of your organization and wording.

Checklist for Revising a Rough Draft

1. Is the thesis stated near the beginning of the paper?
2. Does the introduction catch the reader's interest?
3. Is it clear how the topic sentence of each subsequent paragraph relates to the thesis?
4. Is it clear how all facts and details in each paragraph relate to the topic sentence?
5. Is each unfamiliar term or idea explained in simple language?
6. Is there any unnecessary repetition?
7. Are sentence patterns varied?

Notice the improvement that results with the revisions in the following paragraph from a research paper on Alexander Calder.

If the Calder family had a creed, it was to improvise whenever possible (Hayes 31). ~~His~~ Encouraged by parents ~~encouraged him~~ to create from his imagination, ~~so~~ Sandy began to make objects out of whatever he could get his hands on. He used ~~all~~ wood, wire, and sorts of odd items to make animals and jewelry. ~~Animals were one of his favorite subjects.~~ ~~This came from his delight with the circus; he painted~~ ~~and drew animals as well as used them as the subjects~~ ~~for other works. He used~~ anything that could be glued, twisted, hung or otherwise lifted. ~~These were all~~ was fair game for his ~~good~~ fertile mind. His happy personality and sense of humor were beginning to manifest themselves in his art. The ~~happy~~ amusing outlook that would become his

trademark was taking shape almost daily. In <u>Alexander</u>
<u>Calder and His Magical Mobiles</u> the authors portray
Calder as an artist who showed happiness in his work:

(handwritten annotations: "Jean Lipman and Margaret Aspinwall" above "the authors portray"; "whose" above "who showed")

B. Writing

Using the notes you have made on your rough draft, write a final
version of your research report. Remember that revision is not a
patchwork process. When they read the final draft, readers should
find your changes smoothly incorporated.

C. Postwriting

Use the following list to check your paper; then proofread it, using the
Checklist for Proofreading at the back of the book.

Checklist for the Final Draft

1. Each item of information in the final paper explains or develops the topic in some way.

2. Important theories, unusual or specific facts, and quotations are documented parenthetically.

3. If quotations are used, they are placed correctly in the paper.

4. Information in parenthetical documentation is ordered correctly and follows a standard form, such as MLA.

5. Information in the bibliography is ordered correctly according to a standard form.

Sentence Combining:
Inserting Participial Phrases

Inserting Participial Phrases as Modifiers

For more information on participial phrases, see pages 493-494.

Writers often create vivid and compact images by using participial phrases to modify words in a base sentence. The present participle is made by adding *-ing* to the basic verb form. The past participle is the verb form used with *has* or *have*. A participle is often supported by additional words built around it, making a *participial phrase*. The following example illustrates how an insert sentence can be added to a base sentence by forming a participial phrase.

Base Sentence: The Reverend Jesse Jackson directs a successful program that develops a positive self-concept among young black students.

Insert: The Reverend Jesse Jackson works mainly with inner-city high schools. *(ing)*

Combined: Working mainly with inner-city high schools, the Reverend Jesse Jackson directs a successful program that develops a positive self-concept among young black students.

Notice that the verb *work* from the insert sentence is changed to its *-ing* form when added to the base sentence as a participial phrase. In this example, the signal *(ing)* indicates that the verb must be changed to this form. The underlining signal shows what part of the insert sentence will be added to the base sentence.

The signal *(ing)* is not used when a past participial phrase is inserted, although changes in the verb may be necessary. The following example illustrates how a past participial phrase is inserted into a base sentence.

Base Sentence: I was late for my appointment.

Insert: I was delayed by very heavy traffic.

Combined: Delayed by very heavy traffic, I was late for my appointment.

In the preceding set, notice that the helping verb *was* from the insert sentence is not used in the combined sentence.

For more information on punctuating participial phrases, see page 504.

When two or more participial phrases are added to the base sentence, they are separated by commas, by a conjunction, or by a comma and a conjunction. The signal will indicate how to join the phrases.

Base Sentence: The President prepared the State of the Union Address.

Insert: The President is confined to the Oval Office.

Insert: The President read the advice of his counselors. *(ing)*

Combined: Confined to the Oval Office, reading the advice of his counselors, the President prepared the State of the Union Address.

Base Sentence: The young woman broke her wrist.

Insert: She fell in her haste. *(ing)*

Insert: She threw out her arms to protect herself. *(ing + and)*

Combined: Falling in her haste and throwing out her arms to protect herself, the young woman broke her wrist.

For more information on placing phrases correctly, see pages 505-507.

You may insert participial phrases at the beginning, in the middle, or at the end of the sentence. However, each phrase should be closely attached to the word or words it modifies in order to avoid confusing or nonsensical statements, as the following example shows.

Base Sentence: The woman slowly reeled in the prize marlin.

Insert: The woman was strapped to the swivel chair at the stern.

Combined: Strapped to the swivel chair at the stern, the woman slowly reeled in the prize marlin.

or The woman, strapped to the swivel chair at the stern, slowly reeled in the prize marlin.

but not The woman slowly reeled in the prize marlin strapped to the swivel chair at the stern.

As the example illustrates, inserted participial phrases are usually set off by commas.

Exercise 1: Inserting Participial Phrases

Combine the following sentence sets by inserting participial phrases into the base sentences. For sets 1–5 only, the phrases to be inserted are underlined; sets 6–10 have no signals. Insert phrases where they make the best sense and add commas where necessary. Study the examples before you begin.

Examples

a. We watched the lead guitarist.
   He twisted and jumped on the stage. *(ing)*
   He was singing our favorite cut.

   We watched the lead guitarist, twisting and jumping on the stage, singing our favorite cut.

b. The cat ran across the yard.
   The cat heard us coming.

   Hearing us coming, the cat ran across the yard.

1. The satellite passed over the city.
   The satellite shined brightly. *(ing)*

2. The fire fighters found a gasoline can in the charred hallway.
   The fire fighters conducted an arson investigation. *(ing)*

3. Robert walked into the manager's office.
   Robert straightened his tie. *(ing)*
   Robert buttoned his coat. *(ing + and)*

4. Robert Louis Stevenson also wrote poetry.
   He is remembered first as a writer of adventure novels.

5. The students waited for the teacher to begin the exam.
   The students thought they were prepared. *(ing)*
   The students crammed to the last minute. *(ing + but)*

6. The mother robin searched for her baby.
   The mother robin flew down from her nest.
   She looked around the grass below.
   She wondered if the cat was about.

7. The artist spread black paint over the canvas.
   The artist realized that the original idea would not work out.

8. Thomas Alva Edison enjoyed the company of fellow inventor Henry Ford.
   Edison never realized the financial success of his friend.

233

9. Karen began planning her wedding for early July.
   She thought about the guest list.
   She remembered the relatives out west.

10. The quarterback staggered off the field.
    He was sacked by the defensive cornerback.
    He gasped for air as he reached out for the oxygen mask.

Exercise 2: *Inserting Participial Phrases*

Combine each of the following sentence sets by inserting participial phrases. For unsignaled sets, you must decide which sentence works most effectively as the base. Remember that you may have to change the verb form to *-ing* or add commas or connectors when you insert a phrase. Study the examples before you begin.

Examples

a. The cabbie pulled over to the curb.
   The cabbie noticed a man frantically waving and yelling. *(ing)*
   Noticing a man frantically waving and yelling, the cabbie pulled over to the curb.

b. The labor market is swollen with members of the postwar baby boom.
   The labor market is depressed by high inflation and tight money.
   The current labor market reflects a very high unemployment rate.
   Swollen with members of the postwar baby boom and depressed by high inflation and tight money, the current labor market reflects a very high unemployment rate.

1. Ella Grasso was the first woman to govern a state who did not succeed her husband.
   She was elected governor of Connecticut in 1974.

2. He was born in poverty.
   George Washington Carver is especially known for his research on industrial uses of the peanut.

3. Patches was covered with mud. *(and)*
   Patches was shivering.
   Patches sat curled up on the doormat.

4. Sidney Poitier was nominated for his role in *Lilies of the Field*.
   Sidney Poitier was the first black performer to receive an Oscar for best actor.

5. Joe and his son <u>prepared for the cold winter.</u> *(ing)*
   They chose mature trees near the cabin.
   They cut down the oldest ones.
   They chopped the wood.
   They piled it near the door. *(and)*

6. The parachutist descended rapidly.
   The parachutist pulled the cord.
   The parachutist opened the parachute.

7. The coroner did not know the victim.
   The coroner suspected foul play.
   The coroner began to examine the body.
   The coroner looked carefully at the two puncture marks on the neck.

8. They congratulated each other.
   They knew their opponents had conceded.
   They anticipated the next match.

9. Kiyo decided to apply to medical school.
   She realized that it would be very expensive.
   She made an appointment with the financial aid office.

10. Tommy noticed an old horse.
    Tommy turned as he heard an odd noise.
    An old horse was drawing a rickety wagon.
    The old horse was breathing with difficulty.

Writing Practice: *Inserting Participial Phrases*

Choose two paragraphs from one of your Writer's Notebook entries. Revise them by inserting participial phrases to achieve greater sentence variety. Let the inserted participial phrases add detail to your paragraphs.

8 Logic and Writing

Uses of Logic

Logic **means clear and orderly thought.**

In writing, logic is necessary to support an argument in any kind of persuasion, in answering an essay question, and in supplying evidence to support an opinion. In this chapter you will learn about two kinds of logical thought: *deductive reasoning* and *inductive reasoning*. You will also learn to recognize *fallacies,* or errors in logical thinking.

Deductive Reasoning

Deductive reasoning begins with a generalization, adds a related statement, and ends with a conclusion that is necessarily drawn from the two statements.

The three-statement argument in deductive reasoning is called a *syllogism.*

Major Premise: All seniors at Shaw High School must take a course in government.

Minor Premise: Floyd Bly is a senior at Shaw High School.

Conclusion: Floyd Bly must take a course in government.

In a deductive argument the statements move from the general (*all seniors at Shaw High School*) to the specific (*Floyd Bly*). You can see that if the first two statements in the syllogism are true, the conclusion must necessarily be true.

Truth and Validity

A syllogism may look like a perfectly good argument, and yet the conclusion may be false. In order for the conclusion to be true, two requirements must be met.

1.   The major premises and the minor premise must both be true.

Major Premise: All red flowers are roses.

Minor Premise: This geranium is red.

Conclusion: This geranium is a rose.

You can see immediately that the major premise of the preceding syllogism is false: it *is not* true that all red flowers are roses. Therefore, the conclusion drawn from the premises is necessarily false. You cannot arrive at a true conclusion when one or both of the premises are false.

2.   The argument must be *valid*—that is, the argument must follow the rules of logic.

One rule of logic is that no conclusion can be drawn unless the major premise states a *universal*. This means that the major premise must state (or imply) the words *all, every, no* or *none*. The statement

237

made in the major premise must be true of every person or thing that the major premise mentions. The following are some examples of premises that make universal statements.

All suns are stars.

No mammals have gills.

All insects have six legs.

In deductive reasoning a statement that contains a limiting word (such as *many, most, some, several, few, usually,* or *sometimes*) cannot lead to a valid conclusion. For example, the following nonuniversal statements cannot be used as either a major or minor premise in a syllogism.

Most commercial breads contain preservatives.

Some spiders have four eyes.

Professional musicians usually play more than one instrument.

Many Kiowa live in California.

The following syllogism has a nonuniversal major premise.

Premise: Most freshmen take four courses.

Premise: Julie Sizuki is a freshman.

Conclusion: ?

Both of the premises in the preceding syllogism are true, yet no valid conclusion is possible because the major premise contains the limited word *most.* You do not know whether Julie Sizuki is one of the "most freshmen" who are taking four courses or one of the other freshmen who are taking three or five courses.

A second rule of logic is violated in the following syllogism. Can you tell why the conclusion is not valid?

Major Premise: All members of the Key Club visited the Northeast Nursing Home on Saturday morning.

Minor Premise: Jeffrey Ruiz visited the Northeast Nursing Home on Saturday morning.

Conclusion: Jeffrey Ruiz is a member of the Key Club.

The syllogism is not valid because the conclusion does not *necessarily* follow from the two premises. Jeffrey Ruiz may have visited the nursing home for any number of reasons. Perhaps a friend or relative is a patient there, or perhaps he had decided to volunteer some time to visiting patients in the nursing home. The fact that Jeffrey's visit coincided with that of the Key Club does not necessarily mean that he is a member of that club. In fact, no conclusion is possible from the premises as stated.

Consider the following syllogism.

Major Premise: All members of the Key Club visited the Northeast Nursing Home on Saturday morning.

Minor Premise: Jeffrey Ruiz is a member of the Key Club.

Conclusion: Jeffrey Ruiz visited the Northeast Nursing Home on Saturday morning.

The preceding argument is valid because the conclusion must necessarily be true if the first two premises are true.

Writing Practice 1: *Deductive Reasoning*

Write the conclusion that follows from the two premises of each of the following sets. Then tell whether the argument is valid and whether the conclusion is true, and explain why. If no conclusion is possible, tell why.

1. Premise: All violins have four strings.
   Premise: This instrument is a violin.

2. Premise: A person who serves as President of the United States must have been born in the United States.
   Premise: Franklin D. Roosevelt was the thirty-first President of the United States.

3. Premise: Applications to the University of Cincinnati must be received by February 1.
   Premise: Jeanette Valentino is applying to Kenyon College.

4. Premise: In order to register to vote, a person must be eighteen and must have lived in an election district for six months.
   Premise: Juan Rivera has just registered to vote.

5. Premise: All people who pilot airplanes must have pilot's licenses.
   Premise: Janet pilots an airplane.

6. Premise: All tuna are amphibians.
   Premise: The albacore is a type of tuna.

7. Premise: Many of the counselors at Hi-Y Camp have attended the camp as campers.
   Premise: Ron Chin is a counselor at the Hi-Y Camp.

8. Premise: All frogs are animals.
   Premise: All fish are animals.

9. Premise: Few people who live in this neighborhood have children.
   Premise: Mr. and Mrs. Cerraila live in this neighborhood.

10. Premise: Since 1964 no quarter contains silver.
    Premise: This quarter was minted in 1958.

Evaluating a Deductive Argument

A long argument, as in a speech or an essay, usually does not have the neat three-step makeup of the syllogisms you have been studying. It may list several reasons to support the conclusion and may contain a lot of padding. Some of the premises may not even be directly expressed; the writer or speaker may simply make assumptions that the reader or listener will have to identify. In evaluating a deductive argument, always try to pare the argument down by asking such questions as:

1. What is the conclusion of the argument?

2. Does the argument contain a universal statement? If so, what is this statement?

3. What reasons are given to support the conclusion?

4. Are all of the reasons true? How can I find out whether they are true?

5. What, if any, assumptions are made but not stated directly?

6. Does the conclusion necessarily follow from the premises?

7. Does the argument contain any fallacies? (See pages 246–252 for a discussion of fallacies.)

Writing Practice 2: *Evaluating Deductive Arguments*

Use the list of questions on the preceding page to evaluate the following arguments. Write your answers to each question.

1.

The newsroom of the *Daily Planet* has just received an anonymous letter saying that Joan Xavier, the city's mayor, has been seeing a psychotherapist for the past six months. The letter contains a photograph of the mayor leaving the therapist's office and a detailed log of her visits. Lew Ryan, the city editor, tosses the letter and photograph into the wastebasket and decides not to print the story. "Every individual has a right to privacy, even public officials," he says, "and whether or not someone is seeing a therapist is strictly a personal matter."

2.

"I'm going to die someday anyway," says Cheryl. She has been smoking a pack of cigarettes a day since she was fifteen. "So what," she says of the Surgeon General's warning on the cigarette package. "They say that everything we eat and drink causes cancer."

3.

Everyone can use all the help and training he or she can get on how to cope with life's problems. *Psychology* is the study of human beings from the viewpoint of child development, personality theory, learning theory, and abnormal behavior. *Anthropology* is the study of groups of people and their different cultures. Jefferson High has excellent courses in psychology and anthropology, but they are electives, and few people get the benefits of these courses. I think that these courses help students become better parents and develop more respect for themselves and for others. I think that psychology and anthropology should be required courses so that everyone graduating from Jefferson has a better idea of what it means to be human and of the different ways of solving life's problems.

Inductive Reasoning

In *inductive reasoning* a general conclusion is reached at the end of a process in which a whole series of facts or evidence is gathered and weighed.

Inductive reasoning, then, moves from specifics to a general statement; in this it is opposite to deductive reasoning, which moves from a general premise to a specific conclusion.

Assume, for example, that Jenny Gagarin was trying to decide how cacti are different from other kinds of plants. Jenny visited several florist shops and plant nurseries and made the following observations.

Evidence: The ball cactus has spines.
The prickly pear cactus has spines.
The Indian fig cactus has spines.
The crown of thorns cactus has spines.
The tuna cactus has spines.

On the basis of what she saw, Jenny made the following generalization: "All cacti have spines." This is an example of inductive reasoning. In this example, the evidence is a series of personal observations. Most sound inductive arguments contain a mixture of personal observations, published statistics, and opinions of authorities. In the case of the cactus argument, for instance, Jenny should also have checked a reference book, because not all cacti do have spines.

Working With Evidence

In inductive reasoning the word *population* is used to refer to the group or class of things that is being studied.

Jenny's population is "all cacti." Anything in the world—from seventeenth-century English poetry to white dwarf stars to Americans living in Tokyo today—may be the population (for the subject under study) in an inductive argument.

The conclusion in an inductive argument is reached by making what is called the *inductive leap*.

This leap is the process of moving from the specific evidence to a generalization about the entire population. The inductive conclusion is never certain, because you can never study every single member of the population.

The *sampling* is the number of specific cases of the population that are examined as evidence.

In order to ensure a sound inductive argument, two criteria must be met. First, the sampling must be large. When a sampling is too small, as in the case of Jenny's cacti study, you cannot reach an accurate conclusion. (A too-small sampling is a fallacy called a *hasty generalization*.) If Jenny had gone on to examine perhaps forty or fifty different kinds of cacti, she would probably have discovered that some species of cacti do not have spines. Reference works are good sources of support for inductive arguments because they report the results of large samplings. Second, the sampling must be random. This ensures the chances of gathering accurate evidence. People involved in public opinion polls, television ratings, or market research are especially concerned about getting a random sampling of the population.

The evidence in an inductive argument can never be considered as absolute proof that the conclusion is true.

Consider the following example.

Model: Inductive Reasoning

Eleven minutes after Flight 629 took off from Denver at 6:52 P.M., November 1, it crashed on farm land north of Denver. Wreckage was strewn over an area five miles long and two miles wide. The tail section and nose section were found virtually intact, far apart, but the engines, wings, and main cabin section were destroyed. Many bits of metal looked like shell fragments. Some remnants of the plane had the acrid smell of gunpowder. A thorough investigation turned up no indication of malfunction of the plane or of the crew. Farmers in the area told of hearing loud reports just before the crash. Officials of the Civil Aeronautics Board and the FBI properly concluded that a bomb had been placed in the luggage compartment and that its explosion had caused the crash.[1]

---

[1] From *Thinking Straight: Principles of Reasoning for Readers and Writers,* 4th Ed., by Monroe C. Beardsley, p. 24 © 1975. Reprinted by permission of Prentice-Hall, Inc., Englewood Cliffs, N.J.

In this argument the conclusion is probably true and is strongly supported by evidence, but it is impossible to be certain about what happened. You must still make the inductive leap—and hazard the chance of being wrong.

The conclusion in an inductive argument is often worded to reflect exactly the evidence that has been presented and to show that the conclusion is suggested, not proved, by the evidence. Limiting words and expressions, such as the following, are used.

> *On the basis of this survey, it seems that* workers prefer job security over chances for advancement.

> *The evidence suggests that* the number of stray cats in the city *has probably* increased threefold over the past year and a half.

> *According to conversations with representative legislators, approximately* thirty per cent of the legislators have made up their minds on how they will vote.

Soundness of Inductive Conclusions

You use the inductive method when you make generalizations based on your own experiences and on what you read and learn from others. The scientific method is often called the *inductive method* because it, too, uses the inductive approach in its three basic steps:

1. Gather the data.

2. Weigh the evidence carefully.

3. State the conclusion.

Research scientists know that it is difficult to discover new "truths" that everyone will acknowledge as true. A scientist, for example, may run the same experiment over and over again, amassing thousands of figures over a course of several years. Finally, the scientist makes a generalization based on the evidence. But before others are willing to accept the scientist's conclusion as sound, the following requirements must be satisfied.

1. The explanation (or conclusion) must account for all the facts.

2. The evidence must be observable by others and reproducible by others.

3. The evidence must strongly support the conclusion.

4. All other plausible explanations must be excluded.

Writing Practice 3: *Inductive Reasoning*

From the following list, choose the word that you think will make each of the following generalizations a true statement.

All   Several   Some   Many   Most   No   Few

Then list what kind of evidence, and how much, you could gather to support each generalization. Note that some of the statements are opinions, not facts.

1. _____ children need love and discipline.

2. _____ automobile drivers must have licenses.

3. _____ women are capable of becoming good scientists, engineers, and doctors.

4. _____ mothers go back to working full time when their children are a few months old.

5. _____ green plants contain chlorophyll.

6. _____ people care about helping others.

7. _____ dogs can talk.

8. _____ teenagers respect their parents.

9. _____ people need to spend some time alone.

10. _____ people take criticism well.

Evaluating an Inductive Argument

In evaluating an inductive argument, question the soundness of both the conclusion and the evidence leading up to it. Sometimes, especially in a long speech or essay, it is not easy to identify the conclusion and reasons. A good speaker or writer emphasizes them, but sometimes the argument gets muddled. The following words are often clues that a conclusion will follow: *therefore, in conclusion, hence,* and *consequently.* Reasons are sometimes signaled by the words *first, second, since, because, for,* and *as shown by.* One way to find the main points of an inductive argument is to outline it briefly.

The following checklist will be helpful.

Checklist for Evaluating an Inductive Argument

1. What is the conclusion of the argument?

2. What evidence is offered to support the conclusion? List each main reason (or type of evidence) separately.

3. What is the source of the evidence? Is the sampling random?

4. How much evidence has been gathered? Is the sampling sizable?

5. Does the evidence lend strong support to the conclusion, or is the evidence weak?

6. Is the conclusion carefully worded to reflect the evidence, or does it seem to make a statement for which there is no adequate evidence?

7. Does the argument contain any fallacies? (See pages 246–252.)

Fallacies: Errors in Logic

Being aware of common errors that people make in logical thinking will help you evaluate the soundness of arguments you hear and read, as well as those you write. These errors in reasoning, called *fallacies,* are found in both deductive and inductive arguments.

Post Hoc, Ergo Propter Hoc

The Latin name for this fallacy means, "After this, therefore because of this." This fallacy occurs when one event is assumed to have caused a second event just because the two events occurred in sequence. The following is an example of *post hoc* reasoning.

Evidence: On Tuesday afternoon I got my hair cut.
On Tuesday evening my goldfish died.

Conclusion: My goldfish died because I got my hair cut.

It is obvious that the preceding two events are unrelated; therefore, one cannot be considered the cause of the other, and the conclusion is ridiculous. However, *post hoc* reasoning is not always so apparent. Remember that a cause-effect relationship is usually quite difficult to establish. Whenever something is said to be a cause, the argument should be examined carefully.

Only-Cause Fallacy

It is an oversimplification to name a single cause for a complex situation. Consider the following example of the only-cause fallacy.

> We can keep peace in the world only if every other country is afraid of being destroyed by our superior nuclear power. All we would have to do to ensure world peace is to drop a nuclear bomb—just once—on a country that gets out of line and invades another country. That would teach the whole world that we mean business and that they'd better keep the peace.

In the preceding argument only one thing causes the absence of peace in the world: the lack of fear of destruction by nuclear force. Look for the only-cause fallacy whenever the causes—and solutions —of complicated problems (such as inflation, unemployment, and injustice) are discussed. None of these complex problems has a single cause or a single solution.

Non Sequitur

This Latin expression means, "It does not follow." Whenever a conclusion does not logically and necessarily follow from the premises or evidence, a *non sequitur* occurs. Examine this deductive *non sequitur*.

Premise: All living things require water.

Premise: An automobile requires water.

Conclusion: An automobile is a living thing.

An inductive conclusion may also be a *non sequitur* if the evidence given is not sufficient to support the conclusion. Look at the following argument.

Evidence: Lisa has chicken pox.
Wendy has chicken pox.
Charlie has chicken pox.

Conclusion: The schools should be closed because there is an epidemic of chicken pox in the city.

Hasty Generalization

A conclusion based on too small a sampling is called a *hasty generalization*. This is one of the most widespread fallacies, appearing frequently in arguments as well as in individuals' thinking. Assume, for example, that your cousin took you to your first Mexican restaurant, where she suggested you order tacos. You thought the tacos were too spicy and refused to try any other Mexican food. If you spent the rest of your life avoiding Mexican food as too spicy, you would be guilty of a hasty generalization based on a single experience. Remember that generalizations should only be made after an adequate and random sampling.

Stereotype

A hasty generalization about groups of people is called a *stereotype*. Stereotypes are almost always negative. Unfortunately, racial, religious, economic, and ethnic stereotypes continue to exist in this culture. The way to combat stereotypes is, first of all, to recognize them when they appear in advertising, in jokes, and in everyday speech. A second way is to get to know and respect individuals from every kind of racial, religious, economic, and ethnic background.

Unreliable Authority (Ipse Dixit)

Sometimes, a person will quote an authority in order to strengthen an argument. If authorities are qualified experts with respected credentials, their opinions may be useful as evidence—provided that the experts are talking about the field in which they are experts. For example, the head of a tax accounting firm should be listened to seriously when he or she is talking about income tax tips. A movie star, however, is not a qualified expert on income tax, nor is a baseball player a qualified authority on the nutritional value of cereals. *Ipse dixit*, meaning "He said it," is the fallacy of citing an unreliable authority, a person who is not an expert in the field being discussed. The *ipse dixit* fallacy appears in the following advertisement for an adult condominium community.

According to Don Xenophone, world-renowned comedian, "Life is a lot of laughs at Sunshine Village. If you've worked hard all your life and now it's time for you to have fun full-time, buy a condominium at the place where you'll be happiest— Sunshine Village. Folks who live at the Village say they're busy all day long and happy 85 per cent of every day. So when were you ever 85 per cent happy before?"

Irrelevance or Distraction

For information on misleading uses of language, see pages 618-622.

A sound argument has the same kind of unity found in a well-written paragraph. Every reason contributes meaningfully to the argument; none of the reasons are unrelated or distracting. In any argument, look out for reasons or facts that are not really related to the argument. Such reasons are irrelevant and distracting, and weaken the argument. Often the irrelevance or distraction involves emotional appeals, which have no place in a logical argument.

Assume, for example, that a woman lawyer has written a letter to the President. She argues that too few women judges have been appointed by the President to federal judgeships and that the number of female judges should reflect the number of female lawyers. Which of the following would be irrelevant to her argument?

a. The opinion of a member of the Supreme Court on having more women appointed as federal judges.

b. The opinion of members of her family on having more women as federal judges.

c. The present number of women and of men holding positions as federal judges.

d. The present number of women lawyers and men lawyers in the nation as a whole.

e. The percentage of women judges on various state, county, and local levels.

f. Biographical data about a woman who has served as a federal judge for the past ten years.

The opinion of an expert (Item *a*) and the relevant figures (Items *c*, *d*, and *e*) are sound evidence to support the writer's conclusion, but Items *b* and *f* have no place in that argument.

Attacking the Person and Not the Issue (Ad Hominem)

Ad hominem means "against the man." *Ad hominem* arguments often appear in election campaigns and in debates, when one candidate attacks the other's personal life, rather than his or her stand on the issues.

Candidate Y: We have heard Candidate X speak eloquently on the issue of inflation and on his specific proposals to curb inflation. Yet I ask you to take a look at Candidate X's personal situation. Inflation doesn't affect him—he's a millionaire. His financial disclosure form reveals that he's got nothing to worry about—no matter how expensive hamburger and gasoline get to be. And according to his last year's income tax return, Candidate X has found so many tax shelters that even though he's very rich, he paid less taxes last year than the average hard-working citizen.

A strong personal attack such as the preceding one is also called *poisoning the well.*

Argument by Analogy

An *analogy* is a comparison in which two things are shown to have at least one quality in common.

A human brain is like a computer. Because the brain can be programmed to think in a certain way, whoever controls the input into the human brain has tremendous power to shape the individual. Psychologists have told us that a child's first five years are the most crucial in the development of personality and mind. Therefore, children should start going to public schools at age three—before their brains are programmed too rigidly and finally by their parents and their community.

The brain is indeed like a computer in many ways. In fact, the first computer was developed by a scientist trying to imitate the workings of the human brain, so the analogy is a good one. However, even if several similarities are pointed out in an analogy, the comparison itself *proves* nothing. The argument about school for three-year-olds is weak because it is supported only by an analogy, and arguing by analogy is a fallacy.

False Analogy

A comparison that is shown, on close examination, to be farfetched is called a *false analogy.*

> An ideal human society would be like the society of the bees. Every individual has a job to do and knows what the job is and performs it well. There is no waste, no doubt, no insecurity.

An ideal human society cannot be compared meaningfully to life in a bee colony, where individuals have no choice of the kind of role they will perform. The colony is dominated by a single individual—the queen bee—and worker bees live for only six weeks. Is there happiness or creativity or fulfillment in a bee colony? Would people want an ideal human society in which these things did not exist? Can a bee colony and an ideal human society really be compared? False analogies are often found in arguments. Whenever you hear or read an argument containing an analogy, think about the comparison carefully. Is it really a sound comparison? Does it help in any way to make the writer's or speaker's argument clearer?

Begging the Question, or Circular Thinking

Both of these names identify the same fallacy: arguing that a conclusion is true without providing any evidence or reasons. Consider this example.

> The law requiring students to attend school until the ninth grade is unjust. I think the law should be changed because it is unfair to those students who want to drop out of school and can't do it legally.

The writer here is arguing that students be allowed to leave school before the ninth grade—but if you examine the argument carefully, you will see that no reasons are given. The writer simply restates in other words that he thinks the law is unjust.

A Priori

Similar to circular thinking is *a priori* reasoning, in which the person stating the argument assumes that a statement is true and expects the reader or listener to believe that it is true simply because the writer or speaker says so. *A priori* means "based on the previous statement."

> I'm absolutely sure that Maria is the best-qualified candidate for the Student Senate. So take my advice and vote for Maria.
> I feel confident that Solution B is the only solution that can solve our problem. Therefore, we must choose solution B.

Both of these statements would be perfectly acceptable as a summary conclusion, offered at the end of an argument in which reasons were given to support the conclusion. However, if they are offered alone, without any reasons or evidence, the writer or speaker is guilty of *a priori* reasoning.

Excluded Middle, or Either-Or

When this fallacy occurs, the person who is arguing claims that only two alternatives are possible in a given situation. All other possible choices or actions are ignored. Can you see the *either-or* fallacy in Jeff's argument?

Jeff: Marcia, we've been dating for a month now, and I really like you a lot. But I don't like you going out with other guys, too. Either you and I go steady, or we have to stop seeing each other completely.

Marcia points out the fallacy:

Marcia: Jeff, I like you a lot, too, but we're just getting to know each other. We shouldn't have to choose between going steady and not seeing each other at all. I'd hate to lose your friendship, but I'm not ready to commit myself to dating just one person. We could see each other often— maybe more often—and continue to date others. Or we could just be friends and stop dating. Or maybe we could keep on getting to know each other and talk about how we feel and see if things change as time passes. I just don't see why it has to be one or the other of the choices you suggested—and no other possibilities.

Writing Practice 4: *Identifying Fallacies*

Choose six of the following fallacies and write an argument containing each fallacy. Circulate the arguments among your classmates and see if they can identify the fallacy in each argument. Be ready to identify all of the fallacies mentioned in this section.

Post hoc, ergo propter hoc	Ad hominem
Only-cause	Arguing by analogy
Non sequitur	False analogy
Hasty generalization	Begging the question
Unreliable authority	A priori
Irrelevance	Either-or

Sentence Combining:
Inserting Clauses and Appositives

Inserting Adjective Clauses

For more information on adjective clauses, see page 515.

Inserting adjective clauses is another strategy for adding specific information to a base sentence. An *adjective clause* contains a subject and verb, but it cannot stand alone as a sentence. The adjective clause is dependent on the noun or pronoun it modifies in the base sentence.

An adjective clause usually begins with a relative pronoun, an adjective, or an adverb that replaces a word in the insert sentence. The following example shows how a clause containing additional information about Albert Einstein is inserted into the base sentence.

For more information on relative pronouns, see pages 335 and 350.

The relative pronoun *who* replaces the words *Albert Einstein* from the insert sentence to form the adjective clause. In the combined sentence *who* attaches the clause to the noun it modifies: *Albert Einstein.*

Base Sentence: Albert Einstein profoundly changed and deepened basic concepts of space, time, matter, and energy.

Insert: Albert Einstein was also a philosopher and humanitarian. (*who*)

Combined: Albert Einstein, who was also a philosopher and humanitarian, profoundly changed and deepened basic concepts of space, time, matter, and energy.

The following words usually mark the beginning of adjective clauses.

who, whom, that	relate to people
whose	relates to possessives
which, that	relate to things
where	relates to place
when	relates to time
why	relates to a reason

The preceding words replace a noun or pronoun from an insert sentence and relate the inserted clause to a base sentence. The following examples show that the signal word introducing the adjective clause is clearly attached to the noun or pronoun it modifies in the base sentence.

Base Sentence: The SAT/ACT tests do not measure real intellectual ability.

Insert: Colleges and universities use the tests to screen applicants for admission. (*which*)

Combined: The SAT/ACT tests, which colleges and universities use to screen applicants for admission, do not measure real intellectual ability.

Base Sentence: The club officers will meet in the room.

Insert: They met in the room last week. (*where*)

Combined: The club officers will meet in the room where they met last week.

For more information on punctuating adjective clauses, see pages 523-525.

When the adjective clause is not essential to the meaning of a sentence, it is set off by a comma or paired commas. However, when a clause is essential to the meaning of a sentence, as in the preceding example, it is not set off by commas.

Exercise 1: *Inserting Adjective Clauses*

Combine each of the sentence sets by adding adjective clauses to the base sentence. For unsignaled sets, decide which words best introduce the adjective clauses. (Remember to use commas where necessary.) Study the examples before you begin.

Examples

a. Sir W. Arthur Lewis received the Nobel Prize for Economics in 1979.
Sir W. Arthur Lewis was the first black person to win a Nobel award other than the Peace Prize. (*who*)

Sir W. Arthur Lewis, who was the first black person to win a Nobel award other than the Peace Prize, received the Nobel Prize for Economics in 1979.

b. The Space Shuttle was transported from California to Cape Canaveral.
The space shuttle will make its first flight from Cape Canaveral.

The Space Shuttle was transported from California to Cape Canaveral, where it will make its first flight.

1. Mary was admitted to the hospital yesterday.
   Mary has a history of severe headaches. (*who*)

2. Anna applied for a job at Zion National Park.
   Anna has a degree in archaeology. (*who*)
   She hopes to work on some Indian digs at Zion National Park. (*where*)

3. The cleaning deposit must be paid with the first month's rent.
   The cleaning deposit may be refunded when you move. (*which*)

4. Some say John Wayne was the last American hero.
   John Wayne's real name was Marion Morrison. (*whose*)

5. Services from the Library of Congress are available to many schools and institutions.
   The Library of Congress has over 1,000 employees. (*which*)
   The Library of Congress is the largest repository of information in the U.S. (*and + which*)
   Schools and institutions subscribe to its services. (*that*)

6. Langston Hughes was one of the foremost interpreters to the world of the black experience in the U.S.
   Langston Hughes is remembered as a major American poet.

7. Henry told a joke.
   Henry is usually very serious.
   I had not heard the joke before.

8. Chinese New Year is celebrated by the Chinese, Korean, and Vietnamese people.
   Chinese New Year is based on a lunar calendar.

9. The pizza had anchovies.
   We ordered the pizza.
   Few people like anchovies.

10. The river was rising rapidly yesterday afternoon.
    The river flooded last winter.
    The rains stopped yesterday afternoon.

Inserting Appositives

For more information on appositive phrases, see pages 499-500.

Another strategy for adding information to a base sentence is inserting an appositive or appositive phrase. An appositive, with or without additional modification, is used as a noun and placed near another noun or pronoun to further explain it.

The appositive phrase *the league's leading scorer* in the example on the next page renames and further explains the noun *Melissa Johnson*.

Base Sentence: Melissa Johnson just received a scholarship from Oregon State.

Insert: Melissa Johnson is <u>the league's leading scorer.</u>

Combined: Melissa Johnson, <u>the league's leading scorer,</u> just received a scholarship from Oregon State.

In this lesson, underlining identifies the word or phrase you will insert in the base sentence.

For emphasis and variety, an appositive is sometimes placed at the beginning of the base sentence, in front of the word it explains or identifies.

Base Sentence: Alaska contains America's largest oil and gas reserves.

Insert: Alaska was <u>once a booming gold rush territory.</u>

Combined: <u>Once a booming gold rush territory,</u> Alaska contains America's largest oil and gas reserves.

or Alaska, <u>once a booming gold rush territory,</u> contains America's largest oil and gas reserves.

Appositives are set off by commas when they express information not essential to understanding the meaning of a sentence.

For more information on placing and punctuating appositive phrases, see pages 503-506.

Exercise 2: *Inserting Appositives*

Combine each of the following sets of sentences by inserting appositives or appositive phrases into the base sentence. Follow the underlining signals in the first five sets; the last five sets are unsignaled. For variety remember that you can shift some appositives to the beginning of a sentence. Study the examples before you begin.

Examples

a. The *Concorde* was the world's first supersonic passenger plane.
The *Concorde* is <u>a British and French project.</u>

The *Concorde*, a British and French project, was the world's first supersonic passenger plane.

b. "Sir Duke" is a tribute to Duke Ellington.
"Sir Duke" is <u>a popular song by Stevie Wonder.</u>

A popular song by Stevie Wonder, "Sir Duke" is a tribute to Duke Ellington.

1. Mr. Yee came to this country only three years ago.
   Mr. Yee is the new plant manager.

2. The surgical team will be led by Dr. Cynthia Meyers and Dr. Jason Mathews.
   Dr. Cynthia Meyers is a renowned heart specialist.

   Dr. Jason Mathews is the inventor of the artificial valve.

3. His new book received complimentary reviews.
   His new book is a review of the American economy today.

4. The house was designated a historical landmark.
   The house is perhaps the oldest in the state.

5. Yesterday I went ice-skating.
   That's something I hadn't done for ten years.

6. Four American Presidents have been assassinated.
   They are Lincoln, Garfield, McKinley, and Kennedy.

7. The ancient Chinese gave the world many important tools and machines.
   The ancient Chinese were a people of inventors and discoverers.

8. The Amazon flows almost 4,000 miles across northern Brazil.
   The Amazon is the second largest river in the world.
   Brazil is the largest country in South America.

9. The Super Bowl is the championship game between the National and American Football Conferences.
   The Super Bowl is the most watched of any sports event.
   The National and American Football Conferences are both part of the National Football League.

10. Spaghetti was originally brought to Europe from the Orient by Marco Polo.
    Spaghetti is a type of pasta popular all over the Western world.
    Marco Polo was an explorer who made the first official European contact with China.

Writing Practice: *Inserting Adjective Clauses and Appositives*

Choose one of the arguments you wrote for Writing Practice 4: Identifying Fallacies, and expand it by inserting adjective clauses and appositives into some of the sentences. Your expanded argument should contain a variety of sentence lengths and patterns.

9 Persuasive Writing

The Purpose of Persuasion

The basic purpose of exposition is to give readers information. The purpose of persuasive writing, on the other hand, is to bring about either changes of opinion or actions in the reader. When you write exposition, you give information so that your readers can form opinions and draw conclusions. When you write persuasion, you may also give information, but your main purpose is to change minds and bring about actions.

Model: Exposition and Persuasion

Each of the following passages is about the eruption of Mount St. Helens in 1980. The first is from Richard L. Williams' article, "Phenomena, Comments and Notes," in *Smithsonian* magazine. The second is a newspaper editorial. As you read, decide whether the articles meet the definition of exposition or persuasion.

1

The other day I went out to George Mason University in northern Virginia to hear Dr. David W. Johnson, an ecologist (he also had been on the Smithsonian panel), talk about what survived and what did not. On leave from the University of Florida to direct ecological studies at the National Science Foundation, he has coordinated research at St. Helens, and has visited it three times since May.

To me, the most interesting thing he talked about was not trees (200 billion board feet of lumber worth more than $500 million, looking today "like a giant game of pickup sticks" which could have built 200,000 homes "or a billion bluebird boxes") but the bees.

"Honey bees," he said, "spend a great deal of their time grooming themselves; ash fell on their wings and bodies as well as on everything else, and when they brushed themselves clean the abrasive ash took away their protective cuticle. Also, ash clogged their tracheas, and they died." Whether more bees will be around in the spring to pollinate any plants they find is anybody's guess.[1]

---

[1] From "Phenomena, Comments and Notes" by Richard L. Williams from *Smithsonian* Magazine, January 1981. Reprinted by permission.

2

The senior senator from this state has said that he will vote against a bill to provide funds for the cleaning up and rehabilitation of the area around Mount St. Helens. Everyone who is concerned with ecology and with the national economy should write to the senator, urging him to change his stand and support the bill.

With the funds appropriated, the federal government could salvage a large portion of the 200 billion board feet of lumber that now lie around the mountain like giant pickup sticks. The value of this lumber is estimated to be $500 million.

Aside from the economic value of the lumber, the government needs to do something to restore the ecological balance of the area. The plight of the honey bees is an example. Like many other insects, honey bees spend much time grooming themselves. When Mount St. Helens erupted, their wings and bodies were covered with abrasive volcanic ash. When they groomed themselves, the ash removed their protective cuticle and clogged their tracheas, and they died. Without these bees, how will the plants be pollinated in the spring?

From both the economic and ecological standpoint, the bill to provide funds for rehabilitating the Mount St. Helens area makes good sense. So don't postpone. Write to the senator today.

In the preceding examples the article from the *Smithsonian* is exposition. It gives information about Mount St. Helens, but it does not urge or suggest any action. The second passage is also informative, but it uses its data as reasons for taking action. This difference in purpose is the real difference between exposition and persuasion.

In this chapter you will study the art of persuasive writing. First, you will learn two basic approaches to persuasion: appeals to emotion and appeals to logic. Then, you will examine a particular kind of persuasion called *propaganda*. Finally, you will learn to write a persuasive essay based both on appeals to emotion and appeals to logic.

Appeals to Logic

The chapter "Logic and Writing" discusses inductive reasoning, deductive reasoning, and logical fallacies. A persuasive essay usually uses a combination of inductive and deductive reasoning. You can see that in constructing an argument (a series of reasons and facts) designed to support a conclusion, persuasive writing follows the basic procedures of inductive reasoning. However, the reasons given to support the writer's position may include general principles, which the writer may apply to a specific situation, as in deductive reasoning.

In persuasive writing, the writer's challenge is to build a logical, tightly knit argument with enough evidence to be convincing. This means defining terms, giving clear reasons, supporting reasons with facts and data, and citing authorities.

Appeals to Emotion

Appeals to emotion are not, in themselves, bad. In fact, persuasive writing at its best often combines appeals to logic and appeals to emotion. However, important decisions should be made rationally—not emotionally—so it is necessary to be able to recognize emotional appeals when they occur.

Television and magazine advertisers want to persuade you to buy a certain product or to think well of their company. Because advertisers know that they have only a few seconds or a quick glance to convince you, they rely primarily on emotional appeals. Advertisers have learned from psychologists that besides the basic physiological needs (such as food, drink, and shelter), everyone has powerful psychological needs. These include the need to be loved, the need to feel attractive, the need to feel well-liked and respected, the need to feel successful, the desire to be like everyone else, and the desire to remain young-looking. Advertisers plan their messages and visuals carefully to appeal to these needs and convince you to buy their products. For example, can you identify the emotional appeals in the following ad?

> A beautiful young woman is standing in a lush green meadow filled with wildflowers: "I feel confident and know I look my best when I use SPRING-FRESH soap."

Most women want to look like, and most men want to be with, the beautiful young woman (need to feel attractive; need to feel young-looking). Most people would like a guarantee of self-confidence (need to be well-liked), and most people would like to get away from problems and stand in a meadow filled with wildflowers (need to play and relax; need to stop worrying). The words *spring* and *fresh* are loaded words (see page 263), signifying rebirth, joy, newness, youth, and innocence.

Other emotional appeals are directed toward distinct emotions, such as love, guilt, loyalty, and fear. This type of appeal occurs more frequently in political campaign speeches—for example, as an appeal to patriotism or an appeal to fear. You can also find such emotional appeals whenever one person is trying to persuade another.

261

Writing Practice 1: *Analyzing Persuasion*

Most advertisements try to persuade the reader to buy the advertised product. Some ads, however, try to persuade readers to change their opinions about companies or products. (These are called public relations ads.) In a magazine or newspaper, find an example of a product advertisement and a public relations advertisement, and bring them to class. Use the following questions to analyze each ad.

1.   What exactly does the ad try to persuade the reader to do?

2.   What sort of reader is the ad aimed at? (Where you found the ad will provide a clue to the audience for which the ad is intended.)

3.   What devices does the ad use to persuade? Promises? Bribes? Appeals to emotion?

4.   What visual appeals does the ad make? (Consider the use of photographs, colors, design, and typography.)

Propaganda

Persuasive materials put out by an organized group to further its purpose are called *propaganda*.

The word *propaganda* usually has negative connotations because propagandists sometimes use devices that deceive the reader or distort the truth. However, propaganda is not all bad. For example, the United States government broadcasts propaganda daily in its Voice of America programs directed to Europe and Asia. Also, letters to state representatives, a visit to the state capitol to meet with legislators, television and newspaper editorials, lobbying by mental health experts and doctors—all of these can be part of a propaganda campaign for a good cause.

You should be able to recognize the following propaganda devices, used by advertisers and persuaders of all kinds.

Loaded Words

Besides having dictionary meanings, many words arouse feelings— either positive or negative. Such feelings are called *connotations*. Words such as *freedom, democracy, friendship,* and *justice* have strongly positive connotations; *evil, dishonest,* and *unethical* have negative connotations. For example, how many loaded words can you find in the following paragraph?

> My opponent's claim is utterly dishonest. I have had the utmost loyalty to my government, putting the interests of each and every citizen far above my own personal interest. I have sacrificed daily by working long hours above and beyond the call of duty. The evidence that my opponent purports to have gathered is as malicious as it is false, and his accusation is completely unethical.

Positively Loaded Words (for the speaker)	**Negatively Loaded Words** (against the speaker's opponent)
utmost loyalty	utterly dishonest
each and every citizen	purports
sacrificed daily	malicious
long hours	false
above and beyond the call of duty	completely unethical

Glittering Generality

A *glittering generality* is a loaded word or phrase with strong positive connotations such as *the American Dream, mother love,* and *ethnic pride.* Patriotism and family or group loyalty are usually appealed to in these vague yet powerful devices for persuasion.

Writing Practice 2: *Identifying Loaded Words*

Identify all of the loaded words in the following passages.

1. Does your house smell moldy and stale? Can you smell dust, grime, and yesterday's dinner? Are you ashamed and worried when friends come over? Try using OZONE fresh-air spray. OZONE makes your house smell like a spring morning—with sunshine and buds in bloom. Yet the scent is light and natural. All winter long OZONE makes you remember fresh, clean air, sunny breezes, and a spring day.

2. Anyone who believes in decency, justice, and the American way will vote for this bill. It gives every American citizen an equal opportunity to a decent college education. Free college education will in turn provide better educated, proud, and self-supporting Americans.

Card-Stacking

Withholding pertinent information in order to persuade an audience is called *card-stacking.* For example, suppose that you were trying to sell a house and knew, but did not tell prospective customers, that in five years an expressway would be built in front of the house. That would be card-stacking. Or suppose that an advertisement for a new novel quotes only reviews that praise the novel, while negative reviews are omitted. That is another example of card-stacking—one that happens frequently in publishers' advertisements.

In any argument it is rare that all of the facts in the case will support a single point of view. Instead of omitting evidence that does not support your argument, deal with such contradictory evidence directly. Try to point out why the apparently contradictory evidence still does not defeat or negate your argument.

The Bandwagon

The *bandwagon* appeal is an emotional appeal to the need to be like everyone else. When "everybody else" is doing something, most people will join in. Advertisers use this appeal in ads such as those on the next page:

Don't be the last person in the world to try new Delicioso Potato Chips!

Ninety percent of all dog owners keep their dogs happy and comfortable with Magic Dust Flea Powder.

Hurry, hurry, hurry! All but 8 of the 500 new automobiles on the lot have been sold to people who know a good buy when they see one.

Plain Folks

Political candidates and advertisers know that people tend to like and trust others who seem "just like" themselves. That is why images of middle-class, healthy-looking, cheerful people in ordinary clothing and everyday surroundings appear so often in television commercials and print media advertisements. In Florida a millionaire campaigned his way to governor by working for a day at a time at many different blue-collar jobs, such as waiter, cab driver, and garbage collector. His plain folks approach was a successful attempt to convince the voters that he knew and understood their problems because he had experienced them himself and had talked to other workers on his jobs.

Snob Appeal

You must have seen many ads showing "the beautiful people"—obviously wealthy, well-dressed, driving expensive cars and wearing expensive jewelry. The desire to be like these carefree, beautiful men and women helps sell things like perfume, automobiles, vacations, credit cards, and watches. The unstated sales pitch goes like this: "If you buy what these people own, your life will be happier, better, and more romantic." Snob appeal, the opposite of the plain folks approach, arouses the desire to achieve status and wealth, the desire to be superior to most people. For obvious reasons snob appeal is not used often in political campaigns, since most campaign material is aimed at the average voter—"the common man and woman."

Transfer

Advertisers hire popular sports figures and entertainment stars to persuade people to buy their products. Such advertisements are effective because viewers and readers transfer their feelings about the star to the product itself. For example, in a series of television ads, a respected actor who plays the part of a doctor in a long-running television series endorses a brand of decaffeinated coffee. Not only does the actor lend his prestige as an actor to the product he is selling, but he also lends his fictional authority as a doctor, established in the minds of his series' viewers. Sometimes, the transfer device is used for a good purpose, as when a sports star or well-known entertainment figure urges the public to contribute to a charity.

Writing Practice 3: *Identifying Propaganda*

In each of the following arguments, identify the propaganda techniques by name.

1. Author of a nationally acclaimed, best-selling book on running: "I eat Wholesome Brand cereal every morning. It's the best way to start my day."

2. All over the world people are starving to death every day. A contribution of less than three cents a day—a little more than ten dollars a year—can mean the difference between a child's life or death. You have so much—won't you share a bit of your food with those who have nothing at all? Send a contribution for any amount to this food relief agency.

3. A student candidate for city council in a university town speaks to a rally on campus: "For the past fifteen years, no one under fifty has served on the city council. We really need someone who can represent your interests, who can introduce legislation and look out for student concerns. For example, if you've tried to live off campus, you know that rents are out of sight. This city needs a strong rent control law. And what about more city parking lots around campus? Vote for me for city council, and I'll take care of you."

4. The city has offered to subsidize the cost of shade trees on the right of way in front of homes provided that eighty percent of the residents on any given block agree to pay for, plant, or care for two trees on their property. "On our block, seventy-five percent of the homeowners have already signed a statement agreeing to plant the trees. Don't be the one who will stop our block from becoming beautiful. Sign here please."

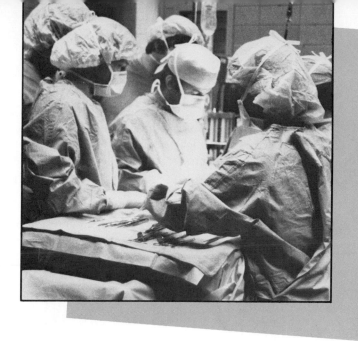

Writing a Persuasive Essay

Writing a persuasive essay is similar in many ways to writing an expository essay or a research paper. In the remaining sections of this chapter, you will study the following steps in writing a persuasive essay.

1. Choose a topic or proposition.

2. Gather evidence to support your proposition.

3. Outline your argument.

4. Write a first draft.

5. Revise and then write the final draft.

6. Proofread.

Choosing a Proposition

In persuasive writing the term *proposition* refers to the statement of the writer's position—that which the writer wants the reader to believe or to do.

For more information on developing propositions, see pages 662-675.

A proposition, which is equivalent to a thesis statement in expository writing, must meet the following requirements.

1. The proposition must be arguable.

An arguable proposition is a specific statement that can be debated by people with opposing viewpoints.

For example, people may either agree or disagree with each of the following propositions.

Laws should be passed to severely limit the import of foreign cars.

The United States government should offer a voluntary national health insurance plan, available to citizens of all ages.

The President and Vice President of the United States should be elected by direct popular vote, and the Electoral College should be abolished.

Besides being debatable, each of the preceding propositions is specific. One cannot debate vague, general statements, such as, "People should be kinder to each other." Neither can one debate factual statements, such as "One hundred centimeters make a meter." By definition a fact is true and is therefore not arguable. Each of the preceding three propositions is an opinion, not a fact. Notice the verb *should* in each. What *should be* is a matter of opinion, and opinions are arguable.

Which of the following is more suitable as a proposition for a persuasive essay? Why?

–High school students should choose the most useful courses.

–Students in career education should be required to take at least six literature courses.

The first proposition is too vague and too general. Which students? What courses? It is impossible to build an argument to support such a nonspecific statement. The second proposition, however, names specific students (those in career education) and a specific number (six) of a specific type of course (literature). This proposition is arguable and specific.

2. The proposition must be uncertain.

With few exceptions (such as determining causes for major historical events), it is useless to be persuasive about the past. To be meaningful an argument must deal with an issue that is yet to be decided or one that involves changing an existing condition. Which of the following two propositions meets the requirement of uncertainty?

–Each of the states in the United States should be represented by a star on the flag.

—If the draft is reinstated, young women should be drafted as well as young men.

The second proposition meets the requirements of uncertainty and is also arguable. The first proposition states an existing condition and is therefore unsuitable as the topic for a persuasive essay.

Writing Practice 4: *Choosing a Proposition*

For each of the following topics, write an arguable proposition that meets the requirement of uncertainty. Your proposition may propose a solution or a way of dealing with a problem. Word your proposition carefully in order to be specific. Save your work.

1. Mandatory school attendance laws

2. Mandatory seat belt laws

3. Growth of nuclear energy

4. Legalized gambling

5. Longer jail sentences for convicted criminals

Gathering Evidence

Once you have chosen an issue and defined your views by stating a proposition, you are ready to begin gathering evidence to build your argument. For some kinds of persuasive essays, you can come up with all the evidence you need by simply thinking about your proposition. This might be true especially of essays that concern school situations with which you are very familiar. Most topics, however, will require you to do some research in order to assemble the facts and evidence you will use to support the proposition. Television and radio shows, the daily newspaper, current magazines, recent books, and pamphlets are all rich sources of material.

Ideally, the evidence that you gather will contain facts as well as opinions of authorities. Take notes as you read recent books and magazine articles. It will be helpful in organizing your essay to outline arguments that you read or hear—even those that oppose your views. Always be sure to use more than a single source for your research, since a book or magazine may have some bias that you are not able to detect.

Discussing your topic with relatives, teachers, and friends may also be helpful. Find out what others think about the issue—and why. You will discover that people give a variety of reasons to support their opinions. These discussions may provide you with reasons for your essay and help you clarify your own views as well. If you have already formulated some clear reasons to support your proposition, try convincing someone of your view. An informal discussion—and immediate feedback from the person with whom you are talking—will give you an idea of the effectiveness of your argument.

Writing Practice 5: *Gathering Evidence*

Select a proposition from Writing Practice 4, or write a new one, on which you would like to base a persuasive essay. List the sources you would consult and the kind of evidence you would look for if you were writing a persuasive essay. Then consult at least three sources, and take notes. Save your work.

Outlining Your Argument

Before you begin your essay, you need a clear idea of your audience. How much background information you present and which reasons are most effective depend in large part on the makeup of your audience. For example, assume that you were writing an essay on the need for government-subsidized day-care centers for working mothers. Your argument would not be the same if you were addressing a group of working mothers (who would be favorably disposed) as it would if you were addressing a group of nonworking mothers (who may be hostile to the idea). A group of legislators addressed on this issue would probably need more convincing than either of the groups of mothers.

Go over your notes and choose the reasons and opinions that you think are best for your audience. You should have at least three reasons to support your proposition, and each of these should be supported with specific examples, statistics, illustrations, and quotations. The more evidence you give to support your statements, the more convincing you will be. Examine your reasons critically to be certain that you have not included any that weaken your argument. If a reason does not provide strong support for your proposition, drop it and look for a better one.

The next step is to make an informal sentence outline for your essay. Let your proposition be the thesis sentence. Then decide in what order to present your reasons. You may want to put the strongest reason first, or you may want to save it for last. After each reason, list supporting facts, expert opinions, and details.

Writing Practice 6: *Outlining the Argument*

Outline the argument for your persuasive essay. Use the form on the next page.

Thesis statement (proposition)
   First reason
      Fact, expert opinion, or detail
      Fact, expert opinion, or detail
      Fact, expert opinion, or detail
   Second reason
      Fact, expert opinion, or detail
      Fact, expert opinion, or detail
      Fact, expert opinion, or detail
   Third reason
      Fact, expert opinion, or detail
      Fact, expert opinion, or detail
      Fact, expert opinion, or detail

Continue with as many reasons as you have. Save your work.

Reading a Persuasive Essay

In evaluating an argument in a persuasive essay, your first step should be to determine the writer's position. What is he or she trying to persuade you to do? Then you should be able to identify all of the reasons given to support the writer's position. What evidence is offered to support each reason?

Be sure to keep in mind those aspects of persuasive writing that you have been studying. Be aware of how language is used to appeal to your emotions. Do the reasons used to support the writer's position appeal to your reason or to your emotions? Be alert to fallacies—flaws in the reasoning process—and to the use of persuasive devices such as card-stacking and glittering generalities. Are terms clearly defined? Is the author's language easy to understand? What questions do you have about the issue that the writer does not answer? Before you decide whether or not to be persuaded, what other information do you need?

Model: Persuasive Essay

Using what you know about evaluating an argument, read the following persuasive essay by Gloria Steinem, which first appeared in *Ms.* magazine. As you read, try to determine the writer's position and the reasons she uses to support that position. Look also for evidence she uses to support each reason. Be prepared to discuss the questions that follow.

Introduction

(1) Almost every week now, we open our newspapers and read the story of an exceptional woman, some courageous "token" who has survived all odds and become the first woman vice-president of a large company, the first rabbi or priest, the first commercial pilot, truck driver, opera conductor, or TV anchorwoman. While we celebrate, extend support (which any "token" will no doubt need), and hope that some image-breaking results in the minds of readers who might have thought females couldn't do such things, we are also painfully aware of a fact that the newspaper reports never reflect. These invasions of "male" professions have no impact on the lives and economic problems of most women.

Body

(2) In fact, the motive for printing the story sometimes seems to be an updated version of the motivation for covering some huge, atypical alimony settlement: if women can be convinced that we already have power, or the chance of power, as individuals, then perhaps we'll stop agitating on the issues of women as a group.

(3) Unfortunately, the media emphasis on tokenism probably does give us some false sense of well-being, even those of us who should know better. Many women have a vague sense that "things are getting better," even though a look at the growing female unemployment rates, the number of women and dependent children on welfare, and the increasing male-female salary differential shows clearly that—while token victories are important for raising aspirations—the economic situation of women as a group is remaining constant, or even getting worse.

273

(4) A major reason for this uncomfortable truth is that the great majority of women workers are ghettoized in traditionally female occupations. In those areas, "equal pay for comparable work" and "equal chance for advancement" have very little meaning. Equal to whom? Advancement to where? These giant pools of cheap female labor—whether they are sales work or food service; typing for corporations or for government agencies—share many characteristics. First, they are paid according to the social value of the worker, not the intrinsic nature of the work. (A barber, for instance, performs less complicated tasks than a beautician, just as an assembly-line worker usually needs fewer skills than a secretary; yet the first two groups are paid and honored more, simply because they are men.) Second, the work areas traditionally occupied by women are usually nonunionized. Even existing unions that should or could organize such workers are rarely helpful. Third, the female work force is encouraged to be temporary by lack of advancement, pension, and sometimes even full-time opportunities. (Though women are said to be less employable because of family responsibilities, the subterranean truth seems to be that employers encourage the part-time worker, the young woman who leaves to care for children, and the older woman coming back into the labor force in an entry-level job.)

(5) Fourth, even the few men who are in traditionally female work areas are at the high end of the pyramid, leaving women workers still ghettoized at the bottom. (Here, too, there's no logic to job divisions. High-tip restaurants employ white males, while women, as well as minority men, are confined to cheaper restaurants, though the trays are just as heavy. Women sales personnel sell men's underwear while men sell kitchen ranges; the crucial difference is the higher commission, not who uses the product.)

(6) In an important new book called *Pink Collar Workers*, Louise Kapp Howe exposes this ghettoization of women workers. The sobering statistical analysis is all there; for instance, that there is at least as much restriction of women to poorly paid "female" jobs now, with many more women in the salaried work force, as there was in the 1900s. But the unique feature of the book is the long, in-depth, and intimate interviews with women in these professions; interviews that make clear the need for massive movement to honor and humanize the "female" occupations, as well as to form unions that can force employers to pay decent salaries, even at the expense of high profits. The chapter on beauticians . . . as well as Louise Kapp Howe's subsequent chapters on salesworkers, waitresses, officeworkers, and housewives, are the personal expressions of a deep political caste system that tokenism cannot change, and that women workers everywhere will recognize. An additional analysis is provided by economist Juanita Kreps, a longtime expert on women in the work force and currently Secretary of Commerce, who suggests that changed work patterns for both women and men may help to break down the female job ghetto, and change the social definitions of work.

(7) In a patriarchy, even suffering is valued according to the identity of the sufferer. We have heard a great deal about the plight of the blue-collar worker, for instance, in part because most of those workers are males. The few women in blue-collar professions are actually better paid than many if not most of their salaried sisters. But to raise the concerns of women working in traditionally female jobs is not to denigrate the problems of male workers. In fact, the threat of competition and absorption by women's cheap labor is a crucial factor in keeping many male workers in their place. For the sake of all workers, we need to look at the problems of that majority of women now working in the pink collar ghetto; a number of us that is growing more numerous, better educated but less well paid as the service sector of the economy increases.

Conclusion
(8) The work revolution we need isn't the toleration of a few women in "male" professions. It will begin with the rise of the pink collar worker.[1]

(Paragraph numbers added)

Think and Discuss

1.   Describe the audience for whom the essay is intended. Would you say the audience is likely to be hostile or sympathetic (or something in between) to Gloria Steinem's message?

2.   What is the problem that the writer discusses? Which sentences state the problem most clearly? Do you agree that the problem exists, or do you disagree? Tell why.

3.   What is the purpose of the first paragraph?

4.   Which paragraphs give analysis of the reasons for the problem? State the four reasons the author gives to explain the existence of the problem.

5.   What is Ms. Steinem's proposed solution to the problem? Which sentences state the proposed solution most clearly? What reasons does Gloria Steinem give to support her proposed solution?

6.   What purpose does the book *Pink Collar Worker* play in the writer's argument? If you had a chance to look at this book, what information would you want to read in it?

---

[1]From "Where the Women Workers Are: The Rise of the Pink Collar Ghetto" by Gloria Steinem in *Ms.* magazine, 1977. Copyright © 1977 by the Ms. Foundation for Education and Communication. Reprinted by permission.

Writing Assignment I: *Persuasive Essay*

Using the material you have saved from the Writing Practice exercises in this chapter, write a persuasive essay. Follow the steps for prewriting, writing, and postwriting.

A. Prewriting

Before you begin to write, keep in mind that the tone of a persuasive essay should be formal. Informal usage, slang, and even contractions are inappropriate. Avoid highly technical terms, unless they are absolutely necessary. If they are, be sure to define the terms. Loaded words can be used for effect, especially when trying to motivate an audience to take some action. However, make sure that your argument is not based on emotional appeals alone. In general, the tone of a persuasive essay should be factual and objective, depending much more on appeals to logic than on appeals to emotion.

B. Writing

Introduction: The beginning of a persuasive essay should capture the reader's attention. When you try to persuade someone, find a point of agreement as a place to begin. For example, suppose that Angela is writing a paper in support of the proposition that the school year should be extended through the summer with only two weeks for vacation. Her essay will appear as an editorial in the school newspaper. Since she knows that most students oppose the idea of a twelve-month school year, Angela anticipates that her readers will be hostile at the outset. Before presenting her argument, she finds a common meeting ground:

> Life in the 1980s is much more complicated than it was in the '50s or even in the '60s and '70s. For example, computers are becoming as common as adding machines and typewriters once were. Ordinary citizens must understand basic economic theory or run the risk of having their savings depleted by fluctuations in the economy. Only informed people can take advantage of advances in medicine and health care. The list of examples could go on and on, but the point is this: As life becomes more and more complex, citizens need more and more "basic training" in order to cope. On this point we can all agree. Among several possibilities for teaching modern "survival skills," one stands out as the most economical, least complicated, and most effective: extending the school term through the summer, with two weeks for student vacations.

Angela begins her editorial by noting a common problem and common concerns. She wins over the audience enough to get them to listen to her proposition, which she then states. Besides capturing the reader's interest and establishing some common point of agreement, the introduction must clearly state your proposition or thesis statement. Readers should know your point of view from the outset so that they can judge the merits of your argument.

Body: The body of a persuasive essay contains your reasons and the supporting material. Cover all of the major points in your outline in the order in which you have decided to present them. In general, devote a paragraph to each of your reasons. Be sure to state each reason clearly and develop it with specific details and examples. Remember that every statement you make in a persuasive essay—unless it is blatantly obvious—needs to be supported. Offer proof to back up your claims, cite sources for your facts, and identify authorities whom you quote.

To be most effective a persuasive essay should deal with the opposing point of view in a serious and respectful way. It is inappropriate to say, "The people who oppose this view do not know what they are talking about." Choose two or three of the opposition's main arguments and try to refute them logically. Again, use evidence, facts, and quotations to support your statements.

Conclusion: The concluding paragraphs should summarize your argument, repeating the proposition and each of the main reasons. Keep the summary brief by omitting the details and statistics that you have used to support each reason. Avoid the temptation to go on and on; remember that the argument in a persuasive essay should be tightly knit—without wasted words.

If you want your readers to perform a certain action, your final paragraphs should tell specifically what you want them to do—providing, of course, that they agree with your viewpoint. At this point many writers use appeals to emotion to overcome the readers' inertia and move them to action.

C. Postwriting

Allow at least half a day before writing the final draft. Being away from your paper for a while will give you a fresh perspective and enable you to read it critically. As you reread the first draft, use the following checklist to improve your essay.

Checklist for a Persuasive Essay

1. The beginning captures the reader's interest and states the proposition clearly.

2. The reasons used to support the argument are clearly stated and backed up with facts, examples, illustrations, or some other kind of supporting detail.

3. The reasons are arranged in the most effective order.

4. The argument does not contain any logical fallacies. It does not use emotional appeals that distort the truth or deceive the reader.

5. The argument deals directly with the opposing viewpoint.

6. There is a clearly worded summary at the end. If the reader is meant to perform a specific action, that call to action is clearly stated.

7. Each paragraph has unity. There are no sentences or paragraphs that do not contribute meaningfully to the argument.

8. The tone of the essay is appropriately formal. The argument is geared toward the audience for which it is intended.

Then revise your persuasive essay. (Your teacher may wish to see it first.) Make changes on the first draft by adding, deleting, rearranging, or substituting words, phrases, and paragraphs. When you finish, rewrite the first draft for a final copy. As a last step check your writing against the Checklist for Proofreading at the back of the book.

Sentence Combining:
Inserting Clauses and Phrases

Inserting Noun Clauses

For more information on noun clauses, see pages 520-521.

Inserting noun clauses into a base sentence is another sentence-combining strategy. A *noun clause* contains a subject and verb, but when inserted into a base sentence cannot stand alone as a sentence. The noun clause functions as a noun in the combined sentence. In this lesson the base sentence contains the signals *something* or *someone*, which are replaced by a noun clause made of all or part of the insert sentence.

Base Sentence: Henry thought *something*.
Insert: Her advice about the proposal was wrong.
Combined: Henry thought her advice about the proposal was wrong.

The signals (*who*), (*what*), (*when*), (*where*), (*why*), (*that*), and (*how*) indicate how to attach the noun clause to the base sentence. The following examples illustrate these signals.

Base Sentence: This booklet by the Internal Revenue Service explains *something*.
Insert: You are to prepare your tax return. (*how*)
Combined: This booklet by the Internal Revenue Service explains <u>how you are to prepare your tax return</u>.

Base Sentence: *Something* was as much a mystery as *someone*.
Insert: The airplane crashed somewhere. (*where*)
Insert: Someone was the pilot. (*who*)
Combined: <u>Where the airplane crashed</u> was as much a mystery as <u>who the pilot was</u>.

As in the second example, notice that the word order may change when a noun clause is inserted.

Other signals such as (*it . . . that*), (*the fact that . . .*), (*how long*), or (*how far*) are sometimes used to insert noun clauses. In the following examples notice the word order of a sentence may change when it is inserted as a noun clause.

Base Sentence: *Something* was strange.
Insert: All the whales beached themselves without apparent injury or disease. (*it . . . that*)
Combined: <u>It</u> was strange <u>that all the whales beached themselves without apparent injury or disease</u>.

Base Sentence: *Something* didn't seem to affect their relationship.
Insert: He had been away. (*how long*)
Combined: <u>How long he had been away</u> didn't seem to affect their relationship.

The signal (*join*) indicates that you should insert the noun clause directly into the *something* slot. The following example illustrates this combination.

Base Sentence: We thought *something*.
Insert: It was a good idea. (*join*)
Combined: We thought <u>it was a good idea</u>.

Exercise 1: Inserting Noun Clauses

Combine the following sets of sentences by inserting noun clauses into the base (first) sentence. The first five sets have signals; the last five sets are unsignaled, and you must decide the best way to combine them, using a noun clause. Study the examples before you begin.

Examples

a. The doctor suggested *something*.
I slow down and not worry so much. (*join*)
The doctor suggested I slow down and not worry so much.

b. *Something* was certain.
The hotel disaster was a result of arson. (*it . . . that*)
It was certain that the hotel disaster was a result of arson.

1. Before leaving on their trip, our neighbors told us *something* and *something*.
The dogs should be fed. (*how much*)
They should run every day. (*how long*)

2. José quickly learned *something*.
The new computer terminal worked. (*how*)

3. *Something* is a mystery to Europeans.
A great many Americans are reluctant to learn foreign languages. (*why*)

4. *Something* suggests Carolyn will get the promotion.
The supervisor has asked her to handle the special projects. (*the fact that . . .*)

5. A good résumé should tell *something*, *something*, and *someone*.
You have studied and worked. (*where*) (Note: *Where* replaces the word *something* when you combine the sentences; *who* replaces the word *someone*.)
You have studied. (*what*)
Someone can attest to your performance. (*who*)

6. You should bring warm clothing, but *something* is not necessary.
You bring a raincoat and umbrella.

7. Scientists are trying to determine *something*.
Researchers think the escape of radon gas from the ground relates to earthquakes.

8. *Something* didn't seem to influence the judge's decision.
Cindy slipped once on the ice.

9. The newscaster explained *something*.
Unfortunately, the hostages were not released after the ransom was paid.

10. *Something* must be decided before *something*.
We can take our vacation sometime.
We can take our vacation somewhere.

Inserting Absolute Phrases

Another strategy for adding more variety and detail to your sentences is to use the *absolute phrase*. An absolute phrase adds related meaning to a sentence, but it does not modify a specific word. Form absolute phrases by omitting the *to be* verb from the insert sentences, as in the following example.

Base Sentence: The young child still refused to sleep.
Insert: All her dolls were positioned on the bed.

Insert: Her hall light was on. (*and*)

Combined: Her hall light on and all her dolls positioned on the bed, the young child still refused to sleep.

For sentence variety and emphasis, absolute phrases can go at the beginning, middle, or end of a sentence. They are always set off by a comma or paired commas.

For information on punctuating and placing phrases, see pages 503-506.

Exercise 2: *Inserting Absolute Phrases*

Combine each of the following sets of sentences by inserting absolute phrases. The first five sentence groups have underlining signals; the last five are unsignaled. Remember that absolute phrases are set off by commas and that they can be attached to the beginning, middle, or end of a sentence. Study the examples before you begin.

Examples

a. Standing at the pulpit, the minister began the ceremony. A glass of cool water was on her right.

A spray of flowers was on her left. (*and*)

Standing at the pulpit, the minister began the ceremony, a glass of cool water on her right and a spray of flowers on her left.

b. The old apartment building was razed by the city. Its lower floors were gutted by looters.

Its facade was tired with age.

The old apartment building, its lower floors gutted by looters, its facade tired with age, was razed by the city.

1. The newspaper office was shut down by a strike.
   Its workers were angry over the new automation program.

2. The photographer caught the winner just as she crossed the finish line.
   His camera was focused.

   His body was stretched out over the rail. (*and*)

3. The judge gave instructions to the jury.
   His face was lined with exhaustion.

4. The cat waited for the mouse to appear.
   Its body was hunched in the striking position.

   Its eyes were fixed on the small opening. (*,*)

5. From the hill, the neighborhood looked deserted.
   All the houses were dark.

   No one was stirring about. (*and*)

6. Jim was nervous as he entered the principal's office.
   His palms were sweaty.
   His legs were wobbly.

7. Jenny finished the report without interruption.
   Her office was closed.
   Her phone was off the hook.

8. A few hours later I made my way back to the car.
   Packages were under my arm.
   My feet and legs were aching.

9. The farmer sat on the ground and smiled.
   His last truck was loaded.
   His trees were bare.

10. Chris walked up to Sarah.
    An anxious smile was on his face.
    Two tickets to the concert were in his hand.

Writing Practice: *Inserting Noun Clauses and Absolute Phrases*

Choose a paragraph from your persuasive essay to revise by inserting noun clauses and absolute phrases. Let each clause or phrase that you insert add details or facts to the sentence. Work to achieve a balanced variety of sentence lengths and patterns.

10 Business Letters and Forms

Business Writing

I n this chapter you will review some of the basic skills for writing business letters. You will practice writing consumer complaints and letters to elected officials. You will also practice writing a résumé and a cover letter. Finally, you will practice filling out an application for admission to a university.

Checkup Quiz: Form of a Business Letter

Number a separate sheet of paper 1–10 and write the correct answers to the items that follow.

1. Unlike a friendly letter, a business letter must always contain (a) a salutation, (b) a heading, (c) an inside address.

2. A business letter should be written on (a) plain, white paper, (b) colorful stationery, (c) ruled paper to keep the lines even.

3. In a business letter the salutation is followed by a (a) comma, (b) semicolon, (c) colon.

4. Between the name of the state and the ZIP code, there should be (a) no punctuation, (b) a comma, (c) a colon.

5. An appropriate closing for a business letter is (a) As always, (b) Yours truly, (c) Respectfully I remain yours sincerely.

6. The signature in a business letter appears directly below the (a) salutation, (b) body of the letter, (c) closing.

7. The return address on the envelope belongs (a) just below the middle of the envelope and slightly to the right, (b) in the upper right-hand corner, (c) in the upper left-hand corner.

8. If you are writing a business letter to Mrs. Katie Daniel, Director of Admissions at Metropolis University, the salutation should read: (a) Dear Katie: (b) Dear Mrs. Daniel: (c) To whom it may concern:

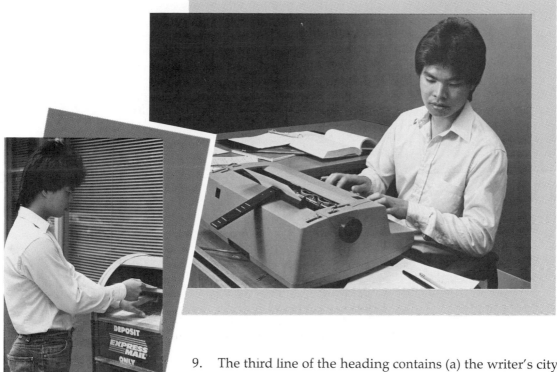

9. The third line of the heading contains (a) the writer's city, state, and ZIP code, (b) the city, state, and ZIP code of the person who will receive the letter, (c) the date on which the letter is written.

10. If a business letter is more than one page long, the second page should (a) begin on a new page, (b) be written on the back of the first page, (c) be deleted so that the letter fits on a single page.

The answers to this checkup quiz are on page 301. If you answered all the questions correctly, you may (with your teacher's permission) skip the next part of this chapter, on the forms of a business letter. Turn to the section *Writing a Consumer Complaint Letter*. However, if you missed even one question, take the time to read the section on business letters and to do the writing practices. Your business letters must be perfect, with no mistakes at all, if you want them to have the best possible results.

For more information on capitalization and punctuation, see pages 582-594 and 548-581.

Reviewing the Form of a Business Letter

A business letter should be written on standard-sized, plain, white paper (8½ by 11 inches or 5 by 7 inches). Use a typewriter if possible. If you cannot type your letter, write legibly in blue or black ink. Your left margin should be absolutely straight, and the right margin should be as even as possible. The margins above and below the letter should be equal.

Never write on the back of a business letter. If your letter has a second page, always begin a new page. Across the top of the second page, write as a single-line heading the name of the person you are writing to, the page number 2, and the date:

Ms. Georgia Owolski 2 May 9, 1988

Proofread your letter carefully to make sure that you have avoided all mistakes in punctuation, grammar, and spelling. If you must make one or two corrections, make the corrections neatly so that they are not obvious. A smudged, messy letter with many obvious corrections is not acceptable.

A business letter has six parts: heading, inside address, salutation, body, closing, and signature.

1. The three lines of the *heading* contain this information.
   a. The writer's street address and apartment number (if any)
   b. The writer's city, state, and ZIP code
   c. The date on which the letter is written

> 16902 Birchwood Avenue, Apt. 203
> St. Paul, MN 55110
> June 5, 1988

Do not make the mistake of putting commas at the end of each line of the heading or between the name of the state and the ZIP code.

2. The *inside address* contains the name and/or title of the person you are writing to and the company name, street address, city, state, and ZIP code.

> Mr. John Chin
> Director, Summer Programs
> American Youth Hostels, Inc.
> 132 Spring Street
> New York, NY 10012

If you do not know the name of the person who will read your letter, you may address it to a title (such as *Director of Admissions* or *Personnel Manager*) or to a department (such as *Customer Service Department* or *Credit Department*). The inside address always begins at the left margin about four spaces below the heading.

3. The *salutation* (or greeting) is always followed by a colon.

If you are writing to a specific person, the salutation should include that person's name and title.

Dear Dr. Lorenzo:

Dear Miss O'Neal:

Dear Professor Orlinsky:

Dear Mayor McLaughlin:

Dear Mr. Kutun:

In recent years the abbreviation *Ms.* has become acceptable in addressing a woman when you do not know whether she is married or single.

Dear Ms. Simond:

When you do not know the name of the person who will be reading your letter, you may repeat the title used in the inside address:

Dear Credit Manager:

You may also use *Dear Sir:* or *Dear Madam:* or *Gentlemen:* as your salutation.

4. The *body* begins two spaces below the salutation.

Paragraph your letter as you would an essay, beginning a new paragraph when you begin a new topic or thought. In block form all paragraphs begin at the left-hand margin. In semiblock form, however, paragraphs are indented five spaces.

5. The *closing* appears at the end of the letter just before the signature.

The following closings are appropriate for business letters: *Very truly yours, Yours truly, Respectfully yours,* or *Sincerely yours.* Notice that the closing is followed by a comma and that only the first word is capitalized. The closing is always aligned with the heading.

6. Your *signature* should always be written in ink.

If you are typing your letter, type your name below your signature, just to make sure that the person reading the letter can see the correct spelling of your name. Notice that a title may be typed below the typewritten name but is not used as part of the signature.

Very truly yours,

Dr. Robert D. Ingraham

Yours truly,

Elaine Thompson
Senior Editor

Writing Practice 1: *Business Letter Form*

On a sheet of paper, set up forms for two of the following business letters. Draw lines to symbolize the body of the letter and write all of the other parts in their proper places according to the information provided. Use today's date or a future date.

1. Mrs. Olivia Hawthorne, who lives at 2869 Palo Alto Drive in Albuquerque, New Mexico 87112, is writing to Miss June Warshaw, Vice President, Olympic Sporting Goods Company, 104 Scaneatles Avenue, Hempstead, New York 11552.

2. Ms. Carole Ryan, 411 Sandpiper Avenue, Canton, Ohio 44718, is writing to Mr. K. J. Searles, President, M & M Upholstery Company, 500 East Texas Road, Allentown, Pennsylvania 18106.

3. Mr. Kevin Weiss, 21 East Burningtree Road, Charleston, South Carolina 29412, is writing to Mrs. Sarita Vasquez, Director, Island Tours, Inc., 4301 Villa Andalucia, San Juan, Puerto Rico 00926.

Folding the Letter

If you are using a long envelope for a letter on 8½-by-11-inch paper (or a short envelope for 5½-by-8-inch paper), first fold the letter in thirds (fold the bottom third of the letter toward the top; next, fold the top third down). Then insert the letter into the envelope with the open end of the letter at the top of the envelope.

If you are using a small envelope with 8½-by-11-inch paper, first fold the letter in half, bringing the bottom half up. Next, fold the right third of the letter toward the left, and then fold the left third over the right third. Insert the letter into the envelope with the open end of the letter at the top of the envelope.

Addressing the Envelope

Begin by writing the return address in the upper left-hand corner of the envelope. Write three lines, using (1) your first and last name but no title, (2) your street address and apartment number, and (3) your city, state, and ZIP code.

Just below the middle of the envelope and slightly to the right, write the name, title, company name, address, city, state, and ZIP code of the person (or department) you are writing to. Always use a

Alice Morikame
562 Arroyo Drive
Amarillo, TX 79107

Mrs. Grace Winover
Manager, Credit Department
Connors Department Store
428 Old Point Avenue
Hampton, VA 23669

title (*Miss, Mrs., Ms., Mr., Dr.*) before the name of the person you are addressing. If you do not know the ZIP code, learn to use the ZIP code directory found in every post office and public library.

Abbreviations

The United States Post Office has approved two-letter abbreviations for states, possessions of the United States, and Canadian provinces to be used with ZIP codes. (See the list on page 290.)

Writing Practice 2: *Business Letter Envelopes*

On a sheet of paper, draw outlines for four envelopes. Address the envelopes for the four names and addresses on the following page, using your name and address for the return address.

1. You are writing to Lois Moran, editor of *American Craft* Magazine, 22 West 55th Street, New York, New York 10019.

2. You are writing to the Box Office Manager, Superjet Stadium, 3920 Navaho Avenue, Spokane, Washington 99208.

3. You are writing to Frank Beale, Director, Institute of Natural Resources, 309 West Washington Street, Chicago, Illinois 60606.

4. You are writing to Mrs. Donna Tully, Manager, Discount Stereo, 2500 Whalen Lane, Madison, Wisconsin 53713.

Alabama **AL**	Mississippi **MS**	Washington **WA**
Alaska **AK**	Missouri **MO**	West Virginia **WV**
Arizona **AZ**	Montana **MT**	Wisconsin **WI**
Arkansas **AR**	Nebraska **NE**	Wyoming **WY**
California **CA**	Nevada **NV**	Canal Zone **CZ**
Colorado **CO**	New Hampshire **NH**	District of Columbia **DC**
Connecticut **CT**	New Jersey **NJ**	Guam **GU**
Delaware **DE**	New Mexico **NM**	Puerto Rico **PR**
Florida **FL**	New York **NY**	Virgin Islands **VI**
Georgia **GA**	North Carolina **NC**	Alberta **AB**
Hawaii **HI**	North Dakota **ND**	British Columbia **BC**
Idaho **ID**	Ohio **OH**	Manitoba **MB**
Illinois **IL**	Oklahoma **OK**	New Brunswick **NB**
Indiana **IN**	Oregon **OR**	Newfoundland **NF**
Iowa **IA**	Pennsylvania **PA**	Northwest Territories **NT**
Kansas **KS**	Rhode Island **RI**	Nova Scotia **NS**
Kentucky **KY**	South Carolina **SC**	Ontario **ON**
Louisiana **LA**	South Dakota **SD**	Prince Edward Island **PE**
Maine **ME**	Tennessee **TN**	Quebec **PQ**
Maryland **MD**	Texas **TX**	Saskatchewan **SK**
Massachusetts **MA**	Utah **UT**	Yukon Territory **YT**
Michigan **MI**	Vermont **VT**	Labrador **LB**
Minnesota **MN**	Virginia **VA**	

Content of a Business Letter

The content and tone of a business letter are very different from those of a friendly letter or an essay. Keep your business writing clear, simple, and to the point.

Before you begin writing, ask yourself the following three questions:

1. What do you want the reader to do? (In other words, what is the purpose of your letter?)

2. What does the reader have to know in order to do this? (What information do you need to include in your letter so the reader can respond?)

3. How can you get the reader to do this? (What is the best way of wording what you want to say?)

If you spend a few minutes thinking about purpose, information, and presentation before you begin writing, you will find it easier to write an effective business letter.

When writing any kind of business letter, three rules govern the content:

1. *Be complete.* Include all of the information the person reading your letter needs to know, such as dates, places, sizes, prices, account numbers, and so on. You may want to include photostat copies of bills or other relevant documents that pertain to the business of your letter. Never send the original of any important document—you may need it later.

2. *Be clear and concise.* Say everything that you need to say as clearly and briefly as you can. Don't confuse the reader with unnecessary information.

3. *Be courteous.* You should always create a pleasant tone in your business letter if you want to get results from the letter. Put yourself in the place of the reader.

Writing Practice 3: *Content of a Business Letter*

Rewrite the letter on the next page, correcting all errors in form. You may reword the letter as much as you think is necessary, deleting unnecessary information and creating any details you need to supply missing information. Remember to follow the rules stated above.

7569 West Honey Creek Parkway
Milwaukee, Wisconsin 53219

Wisconsin Bell Telephone Company
14995 West Central Street
Milwaukee, Wisconsin 53218

Dear Customer Service Representative,

My telephone bill arrived today, and it has three
long-distance telephone calls that I never made.
Nobody else made those calls either. I live with my
sister and her husband, but I have my own phone.

I refuse to pay my telephone bill until this matter is
taken care of.

As always,

Wendy Ryan

Wendy Ryan

Proofreading a Business Letter

Before you mail a business letter, proofread it carefully to be certain that it is complete, follows standard form, and is free from errors. Use the following checklist as a guide in proofreading your business letters.

Checklist for Proofreading Business Letters

Form and Appearance

1. The letter is neatly written in ink or typed with no smudges or obvious corrections.

2. The letter is centered on the page, with each part having the correct amount of spacing above and below.

3. The margins are even.

4. Your signature is legible and written in ink.

Punctuation

1. In the heading and inside address, a comma comes between the city and state. There is no comma between the state and ZIP code.

2. A comma comes between the day of the month and the year in the heading.

3. A colon follows the salutation.

4. A comma follows the closing.

Capitalization

1. The names of streets, cities, and states in the heading and inside address are capitalized.

2. The name of the month in the heading is capitalized.

3. The title of the person to whom you are writing and the names of the department and company listed in the inside address are capitalized.

4. The word *Dear* and all nouns in the salutation are capitalized.

5. Only the first word of the closing is capitalized.

Writing a Consumer Complaint Letter

Unless you are very lucky, you may have to write some letters of complaint about merchandise or services that you have purchased. Proceed according to the steps on the next page.

1. Decide what you think would be a fair settlement of the problem. Do you think the company should replace the product or repair it? Do you think you should get your money back?

2. Go back to the salesperson who sold you the product. Take with you all your receipts (canceled check, repair slip, warranty). State the problem and tell that person how you think the problem should be solved.

3. If you are not satisfied with the salesperson's response, ask to see the department manager or store manager. Repeat the facts and state what you want.

4. If you are not satisfied with the store manager's response and the company is a national one, write to the company president. You can obtain the name of the company president and the address of the company by calling the company's local office and asking for the information. Or you may go to the public library and consult a reference book called *Standard & Poor's Register of Corporations, Directors, and Executives*, which lists more than 37,000 American businesses. If you know only the product's name but have no idea of the name of the manufacturer, you can look up the name and address of the company in a book called the *Thomas Registry*.

5. Write a letter to the company president, stating your problem clearly, giving all necessary information. Enclose photocopies of important documents, such as the sales slip and warranty. Ask the company president for a solution to your problem (the action you want the company to take) within a reasonable period of time. Keep a copy of your letter.

Model: Consumer Complaint Letter

Heading

1987 Kemball Lane
Cambridge, MA 02140
June 12, 19—

Inside Address

Mr. Gregg Nolan, President
Nolan Tires, Inc.
61 Pryor Mountain View Drive
Billings, MT 59101

Salutation

Dear Mr. Nolan:

Body

On May 10, I purchased four new steel-belted radial tires at the sale price of $69.95 each from Nolan Tires in Medford. I had the tires on the car for two weeks when I noticed a balloonlike bubble on the whitewall of the right front tire. I immediately brought the car to the Medford store along with my receipt and warranty.

Mr. Leonard Goodsaver, the manager of the Nolan Tires in Medford, had the tire removed from the car and inspected. He informed me that the tire was in no way defective but that it had been injured upon an impact—presumably by scraping against a curb. Mr. Goodsaver offered to give me a twenty-five per cent discount on the purchase of another new tire.

I am the only driver of my car, and I know that there was no impact to this tire during the two weeks I had it. Even if I had scraped against a curb (which I didn't), I believe that a $69.95 tire should not be ruined in this way. The tires have a two-year or 15,000-mile guarantee. I want Nolan Tires to replace my faulty tire with a new tire of the same quality, and I want the tire put on my car at no charge.

I am enclosing photostat copies of my sales receipt and warranty. I will appreciate hearing from you in this matter and will wait three weeks before seeking help from the Cambridge Department of Consumer Affairs. You may contact me at the above address or by phone (home: 653-0798; office 565-4000).

Closing

Yours truly,

**Signature
and Typed Name**

Gina Walters

Miss Gina Walters

Writing Practice 4: *Consumer Complaint Letter*

Write the following consumer complaint letter, making up any details that you need.

Two weeks ago you bought a pair of Viking sneakers for $31.95 from Lombard's Sporting Goods store at 81 Nugget Court, Boulder, Colorado 80302. The rubber at the tips of the soles and heels has completely worn through, but the store manager refuses to replace the shoes. Write to the president of Viking Shoes, Inc., 3480 Calle Corta, Bakersfield, California 93309.

Writing to an Elected Official

When you write a letter to the editor, you are expressing your opinion to readers of the newspaper or magazine—the public in general. You can express your opinion even more effectively, however, when you write to your elected representatives: your city or county commissioner, mayor, governor, state senator and representative, United States senators and members of the House of Representatives. All of these people respond to mail they receive from their constituents, the people who live in their election district.

Letters about laws that are soon to be voted on carry a good deal of weight. The staffs of senators and representatives tally such letters carefully to see how the public feels on any bill. If you are writing to an elected representative about a bill, time your letter so that it arrives before the vote is taken. Express your opinion clearly. Tell how the proposed law (or change in law) will affect you personally, your community, and the people that you know. If you know the name of the legislation or the number of the bill, state it. As a voter, you are entitled to know your representative's opinion on the issue you are writing about. Ask your representative to tell you his or her position on the issue. Later, take the time to write a letter of thanks to your representative for a job well done or for specific work on a particular issue.

Model: Letter to an Elected Official

6021 LaTijera Blvd.
Los Angeles, CA 90056
February 11, 19—

The Honorable S. I. Hayakawa
United States Senate
Washington, D.C. 20510

Dear Senator Hayakawa:

I know that the Senate will soon be considering a bill to lower the cost-of-living increase in Social Security payments. I have followed news reports about the proposed bill and have read several magazine articles about it. I urge you strongly to vote against this bill when it comes into the Senate.

My grandparents, who are in their early seventies, are having a hard time making ends meet with their Social Security checks. Given the present inflation rate, they would find it impossible to maintain their own home if there were a cutback in Social Security payments. They would probably have to ask for some kind of public assistance or even go into a nursing home, paid for by Medicare and Medicaid. This would cost the taxpayers more money than keeping up their Social Security payments.

Many of the elderly persons I talk to—neighbors and relatives—have had to cut back more and more on essentials like food, clothing, and heating. They just can't seem to manage on the payments they receive now. I think we owe these elderly citizens the feeling of security that they can get with cost-of-living increases in the Social Security system. I would greatly appreciate knowing your views on this issue.

Sincerely yours,

Cynthia Talbot

Cynthia Talbot

For names and addresses of your local government officials, check your telephone book for listings under city, county, and state governments. Address a mayor, governor, senator, or representative by the title *The Honorable:* The Honorable Mayor Dianne Feinstein.

The following are addresses and salutations for the President and for members of the Senate and House of Representatives.

The President
The White House
Washington, D.C. 20015

Dear Mr. President:

The Honorable [*first and last name*]
United States Senate
Washington, D.C. 20015

Dear Senator [*last name*]:

The Honorable [*first and last name*]
House of Representatives
Washington, D.C. 20015

Dear Representative [*last name*]:

Writing Practice 5: *Letter to an Elected Official*

Read the front section of your newspaper every day for several days. Choose an issue that is being discussed by government officials—local, county, state, or national. Before you decide what your views are, you may need to do some additional research. Consult your librarian for recent articles. Find the name and address of your representative, write a letter expressing your views, and mail the letter.

Writing a Résumé and Cover Letter

A résumé is a summary of personal data, background, and experience in an outline form. Many prospective employers prefer to receive a résumé, which is easier to read than a long letter of application. Once you have prepared a résumé, you should be able to use it many times, updating it as needed.

A brief cover letter should accompany your résumé, telling what job you are applying for and asking for an interview. Do not repeat in the cover letter information that is found in the résumé.

Model: Résumé and Cover Letter

Robert Alan Gordon

Address:	11802 Edgewater Drive Lakewood, Ohio 44107
Telephone:	831-6098
Personal:	Born: May 17, 1970, in Akron, Ohio Marital status: Single Health: Excellent Height: 5'8" Weight: 160 pounds Social Security number: 085-44-3290

Education:	Senior at Lakewood High School,
	    college preparatory course
	Grade point average: 3.5 (B+)
	Member Lab Program of Cuyahoga
	    County schools for two years
	Attended two-week program for gifted
	    science students, Summer 1985

Extracurricular Activities:	President, Science Club Member, debating team Captain, swimming team Member, National Honor Society

Skills:	Can handle laboratory animals
	Can compile and analyze results of
	    laboratory experiments
	Can operate centrifuge and other lab
	    equipment
	Can program computer

Work Experience:	Mt. Sinai Medical School, Cleveland,
	    Ohio
	Lab assistant in study of lung diseases,
	    using animals for research
	Summer 1985, after school 1985–86
	
	Corner Book Shop, Shaker Square, Ohio
	Clerk on Saturdays from 1986 to date

References:	Mr. Larry Wyzckowski, Lab Director,
	    Mt. Sinai Hospital, Cleveland,
	    Ohio, 795-6000
	Mrs. Jenny Owens, owner, Corner
	    Book Shop, Shaker Square, Ohio,
	    442-8756

11802 Edgewater Drive
Lakewood, Ohio 44107
March 8, 19—

Mr. Jonathan Scalley
Director, Marine Life Research Laboratory
2640 West 147th Street
Cleveland, Ohio 44111

Dear Mr. Scalley:

 I would like to apply for a job as a lab assistant in the Marine Life Research Laboratory during the coming summer. I would also be interested in after-school work and work on Saturdays if such a job were available.

 I am enclosing a résumé of my skills and background. I am very interested in pursuing a career in marine biology and have applied to several colleges where I can specialize in this field.

 Whenever it would be convenient for you, I would be happy to come to the laboratory for an interview. You can reach me at the above address or by phone, 831-6098.

Very truly yours,

Robert Gordon
Robert Gordon

Writing Practice 6: *Résumé and Cover Letter*

Write your own résumé and cover letter for a job that you choose. Write a rough draft first and proofread both your letter and résumé carefully. Remember to include everything about yourself that is relevant to your qualifications for the job.

Filling Out Forms

From now on, you will be filling out many important forms: applications for jobs, college, loans, credit, licenses, insurance, and so on. Before beginning to fill out any form, read the directions carefully and then follow them exactly. Be sure to fill out the form completely; do not leave any spaces blank except those

designated for office use. Print neatly in ink or use a typewriter so that the information you write is legible.

A sample form is included on pages 302–304. It is similar to many college application forms and applications for financial aid. Use the information on the form to answer the questions below.

Writing Practice 7: *Filling Out Forms*

1. Which section of the form may you choose to fill out or to leave blank?

2. Which tests are required or suggested for application and acceptance to these colleges?

3. Information about education should begin at what grade?

4. Which years of extracurricular activities are the colleges interested in? Write your extracurricular and personal activities on a separate sheet of paper.

5. How would you fill out the section entitled "Work Experience"?

6. Is writing in blue ink acceptable?

7. If you are applying for financial aid, where on the form do you indicate this? What do you have to do if you are applying for financial aid?

Answers to quiz on pages 284–285

1.c	2.a	3.c	4.a	5.b	6.c	7.c	8.b	9.c	10.a

Agnes Scott • Alfred • Allegheny • American University • Amherst • Antioch • Bard College • Bates • Beloit • Bennington • Boston University • Bowdoin
Brandeis • Bryn Mawr • Bucknell • Carleton • Case Western Reserve • Centenary College of Louisiana • Claremont McKenna • Clark University • Coe
Colby • Colby-Sawyer • Colgate • Colorado College • Davidson • Denison • University of Denver • DePauw • Dickinson • Drew • Earlham • Eckerd
Elmira • Emory • Fairfield • Fisk • Fordham • Franklin and Marshall • Furman • Gettysburg • Goucher • Hamilton • Hampden-Sydney • Hampshire
Hartwick • Haverford • Hobart • Hood   Kalamazoo • Kenyon • Knox • Lafayette
Lawrence • Lehigh • Lewis and Clark   Linfield • Macalester • Manhattan
Manhattanville • Mills • Mount Holyoke   Muhlenberg • Newcomb   College

COMMON APPLICATION

New York University • Oberlin • Occidental   Ohio Wesleyan • Pitzer • Pomona
University of Puget Sound • Randolph-Macon   Randolph Macon Woman's College
University of Redlands • Reed • Rice   University of Richmond • Ripon
University of Rochester • Rollins • St. Lawrence • Salem • Sarah Lawrence • Scripps • Simmons • Skidmore • Smith • University of the South • University of
Southern California • Southwestern at Memphis • Stephens • Stetson • Susquehanna • Swarthmore • Texas Christian University • Trinity College
Trinity University • Tulane • Union • Valparaiso • Vanderbilt • Vassar • Wake Forest • Washington College • Washington University • Washington and Lee
Wells • Wesleyan • Western Maryland • Wheaton • Whitman • Willamette • William Smith • Williams • Wooster • Worcester Polytechnic

APPLICATION FOR UNDERGRADUATE ADMISSION

These colleges and universities encourage the use of this application. The accompanying instructions tell you how to complete, copy, and file your application to any one or several of the colleges. Please type or print in black ink.

PERSONAL DATA

Legal name: _____
                  Last   *First*   *Middle (complete)*   *Jr., etc.*   *Sex*

Prefer to be called: _____ (nickname)   Former last name(s) if any: _____

Are you applying as a freshman ☐   or transfer student ☐ ?   For the term beginning: _____

Permanent home address: _____
                                             Number and Street

_____ State of legal residence _____
    City or Town   *County*   *State*   *Zip*

If different from the above, please give your mailing address for all admission correspondence:

Mailing address: _____
                                  Number and Street

_____
      City or Town   *State*   *Zip*

Telephone at mailing address: _____ / _____ Permanent home telephone: _____ / _____
                Area Code   *Number*   *Area Code*   *Number*

Birthdate: _____ Citizenship: U.S. ☐ Permanent Resident U.S. ☐ Other ☐ _____ Visa number _____
      Month Day Year   *Country*

Possible area(s) of academic concentration/major: _____ or undecided ☐

Special college or division if applicable: _____

Possible career or professional plans: _____ or undecided ☐

Will you be a candidate for financial aid?   Yes _____   No _____   If yes, the appropriate form(s) was/will

be filed on: _____

The following items are optional: Social Security number, if any: ☐☐☐ ☐☐ ☐☐☐☐

Place of birth: _____ Marital status: _____ Height: _____ Weight: _____

Parents' place of birth: Mother _____ Father _____

What is your first language, if other than English? _____

How would you describe yourself: (Please check one)
☐ American Indian or Alaskan Native   ☐ Hispanic (including Puerto Rican)
☐ Asian or Pacific Islander (including Indian subcontinent)   ☐ White, Anglo, Caucasian American (non-Hispanic)
☐ Black (non-Hispanic)   ☐ Other (Specify)

EDUCATIONAL DATA

School you attend now _____ ACT/CEEB code number _____

Address _____ Date of secondary school graduation _____

Is your school public? _____ private? _____ parochial? _____

College advisor: _____ School telephone: _____ / _____
                Name   *Position*   *Area Code*   *Number*

1983–84   **APP**

Please list all other secondary schools, including summer schools, programs, and institutes you have attended since 8th grade.

Name of School	Location (City, State, Zip)	Dates Attended
_____	_____	_____
_____	_____	_____
_____	_____	_____

Please list all colleges at which you have taken courses for credit and list names of courses on a separate sheet. Please have a transcript sent from each institution as soon as possible.

Name of College	Location (City, State, Zip)	Degree Candidate?	Dates Attended
_____	_____	_____	_____
_____	_____	_____	_____
_____	_____	_____	_____

If not currently attending school, please check here: ☐   Describe in detail, on a separate sheet, your activities since last enrolled.

TEST INFORMATION. Be sure to note the tests required for each institution to which you are applying. The official scores from the appropriate testing agency must be submitted to each institution as soon as possible. Please list your test plans below.

	Scholastic Aptitude Test (SAT)	Achievement Tests (ACH)	Subject	American College Test (ACT)
Dates taken or	_____	_____ _____	_____ _____	_____
to be taken	_____	_____ _____	_____ _____	_____

FAMILY

Mother's full name: _____ Is she living? _____

Home address if different from yours: _____

Occupation: _____
(Describe briefly)   *(Name of business or organization)*

Name of college (if any): _____ Degree: _____ Year: _____

Name of professional or graduate school (if any): _____ Degree: _____ Year: _____

Father's full name: _____ Is he living? _____

Home address if different from yours: _____

Occupation: _____
(Describe briefly)   *(Name of business or organization)*

Name of college (if any): _____ Degree: _____ Year: _____

Name of professional or graduate school (if any): _____ Degree: _____ Year: _____

If not with both parents, with whom do you make your permanent home: _____

Please check if parents are separated ☐   divorced ☐

Please give names and ages of your brothers or sisters. If they have attended college, give the names of the institutions attended, degrees, and approximate dates:

_____

_____

ACADEMIC HONORS

Briefly describe any scholastic distinctions or honors you have won since the eighth grade:

_____

_____

_____

EXTRACURRICULAR AND PERSONAL ACTIVITIES

Please list your principal extracurricular, community, and family activities and hobbies in the order of their interest to you. Include specific events and/or major accomplishments such as musical instrument played, varsity letters earned, etc. Please (√) in the right column those activities you hope to pursue in college.

Activity	Grade level or post-secondary (p.s.) 9 10 11 12 P.S.	Approximate time spent Hours per week / Weeks per year	Positions held or honors won	Do you plan to participate in college?

WORK EXPERIENCE

List any job (including summer employment) you have held during the past three years.

Specific nature of work	Employer	Approximate dates of employment	Approximate no. of hours spent per week

Sentence Combining:
Inserting Gerunds and Infinitives

Inserting Gerunds

For more information on gerunds, see pages 495-496.

When the *-ing* form of a verb is used as a noun, called a gerund, it can be inserted into a base sentence. Below, the verb *leaves* is changed to the gerund *leaving* and is inserted with its modifiers into the base sentence.

Base Sentence: *Something* was a good idea because the rains came that afternoon.

Insert: We left the campground early. *(ing)*

Combined: Leaving the campground early was a good idea because the rains came that afternoon.

In the preceding example, the subject of the insert sentence is not included in the combined sentence. In many sentences, however, the subject is changed to a possessive and inserted directly in front of the gerund. Both possessives and gerunds are used in the following sentence combinations. The signal *(pos)* directs you to make a noun or pronoun in the insert sentence possessive.

Base Sentence: *Something* gave strength and intelligence to an otherwise weak production.

Insert: Maria acted in the play. *(pos + ing)*

Combined: Maria's acting in the play gave strength and intelligence to an otherwise weak production.

Base Sentence: *Something* most definitely annoyed the concert promoters.

Insert: We waited in line all night. *(pos + ing)*

Combined: Our waiting in line all night definitely annoyed the concert promoters.

In the last example the pronoun *we* was changed to the possessive *our*. The following list contains all of the possessive pronouns.

Pronoun	Possessive Pronoun
I	my
she	her
he	his
it	its
we	our
you	your
they	their

For more information on using possessive pronouns with gerunds, see page 351.

Both possessive pronoun and gerund changes are made in the following example.

Base Sentence: Tony's downfall was *something*.

Insert: He studied all night before the exam. (*pos + ing*)

Combined: Tony's downfall was <u>his studying all night before the exam</u>.

An additional change allows you to insert an adverb from the insert sentence into the base sentence as a gerund modifier. The signal (*ly*) tells you to drop the *ly* ending from words such as *carelessly*, *happily*, and *slowly*. The following example illustrates how this combination works.

Base Sentence: *Something* impressed the audience.

Insert: She skated gracefully. (*pos + ~~ly~~ + ing*)

Combined: <u>Her graceful skating</u> impressed the audience.

An (*of*) signal also works with (*pos*), (*ing*), and (*~~ly~~*) to produce the following combination.

Base Sentence: *Something* was pitiful.

Insert: The woman mourned her loss ceaselessly. (*pos + ~~ly~~ + ing + of*)

Combined: <u>The woman's ceaseless mourning of her loss</u> was pitiful.

Exercise 1: Inserting Gerunds

Combine each of the following sets of sentences into one sentence. Signals for inserting possessives and gerunds are given in the first five sentences; the last five sentences lack signals but can also be combined with possessives and gerunds. Study the examples before you begin. (There may be more than one way to make a combination.)

Examples

a. Stephanie made it to class on time by *something*.
   She ran across the football field. *(ing)*
   Stephanie made it to class on time by running across the football field.

b. I was irritated by *something*.
   Alexandra threw the ball constantly against the garage wall. *(pos + ~~by~~ + ing + of)*
   I was irritated by Alexandra's constant throwing of the ball against the garage wall.

c. *Something* was the only way Clover could get any food.
   She waited patiently for the large German shepherd to finish eating.
   Her patient waiting for the large German shepherd to finish eating was the only way Clover could get any food.

1. Your mistake was *something*.
   You sent cash through the mails. *(ing)*

2. The teacher forbids *something*.
   We talk during class. *(pos + ing)*

3. Researchers feel that someday it may be possible to replace destroyed brain cells with healthy brain cells by *something*.
   They will carefully transplant cells from a healthy human brain into a brain with neurological disorders. *(pos + ~~by~~ + ing + of)*

4. *Something* kept you out of trouble.
   You were honest. *(pos + ing)* *(Note: Were is the past tense of the verb be; its -ing form is being.)*

5. *Something* changed his entire life.
   He read the book *Roots*. *(pos + ing + of)*

6. By *something*, Dr. Don Young solved two ecological problems, *something* and *something*.
   He removed sulfur from gasoline.
   He reduced the pollutants emitted when gasoline is used as fuel.
   He created a soil additive that greatly improves the productivity of alkaline soil.

7. *Something* was the gift the ancient Phoenicians gave to the world.
   They created an alphabet in which each letter represented a sound rather than a word or an idea.

8. *Something* costs billions of municipal dollars each year.
   The city removes garbage.

9. *Something* is a truly unfortunate but necessary part of life in Los Angeles, California.
   Commuters drive on the freeways.

10. *Something* and *something* are her favorite pastimes.
    She watches movies avidly.
    She eats popcorn constantly.

Inserting Infinitives

For more information on infinitive phrases, see page 497.

One sentence can be inserted into another as an *infinitive phrase*. An infinitive phrase is the word *to* plus a verb. To combine two sentences with an infinitive phrase, the *(to + verb)* combination replaces the signal *something* in the base sentence, as in the following example.

Base Sentence: *Something* is good exercise.

Insert: Jogging is exercise. *(to + verb)*

Combined: To jog is good exercise.

If there is a helping verb in the insert sentence, remove it when you form the infinitive.

Base Sentence: During his visit to the college, Frank wants *something* and *something*.

Insert: Frank will inquire about dorm rooms. *(to + verb)*

Insert: Frank will talk to the athletic director about a tennis scholarship. *(to + verb)*

Combined: During his visit to the college, Frank wants to inquire about dorm rooms and to talk to the athletic director about a tennis scholarship.

Sometimes, the verb will change form when it is inserted into the base sentence as an infinitive phrase. In the next example *fishes* becomes *to fish*.

Base Sentence: Her favorite sport is *something*.

Insert: She fishes for marlin.

Combined: Her favorite sport is to fish for marlin.

In some base sentences you will see the words (*to do*) in parentheses. They appear simply to help you understand the meaning of the base sentence. When you insert an infinitive phrase, remove the words (*to do*).

Base Sentence: The twins felt they would have (to do) *something* in order to develop as individuals.

Insert: They would attend different colleges. (*to + verb*)

Combined: The twins felt they would have <u>to attend different colleges</u> in order to develop as individuals.

Base Sentence: For Estella (to do) *something* is quite unlikely.

Insert: She gives up her dream of becoming a film set designer. (*to + verb*)

Combined: For Estella <u>to give up her dream of becoming a film set designer</u> is quite unlikely.

Exercise 2: Inserting Infinitives

Combine each of the sentence sets on the following page into a single sentence by following the (*to + verb*) signal. In the first five sentences the signals are included; in the last five sentences no signals are given, and you must decide how to combine the sentences by inserting infinitive phrases. Study the examples before you begin.

Examples

a. *Something* was Simon's goal.
   He becomes a fire fighter. (*to + verb*)
   To become a fire fighter was Simon's goal.

b. For the United States (to do) *something* or (to do) *something* is a dilemma facing us today.

309

The United States initiates a national medical services program. *(to + verb)*
The United States maintains its present mix of private and public medical services coverage. *(to + verb)*

For the United States to initiate a national medical services program or to maintain its present mix of private and public medical services coverage is a dilemma facing us today.

1. *Something* was the dream of Martin Luther King, Jr.
   He ensured equality for all Americans. *(to + verb)*

2. A good citizen does not refuse *something*.
   A good citizen votes in elections and serves on juries. *(to + verb)*

3. For you (to do) *something* is wasteful.
   You throw away empty cans and bottles. *(to + verb)*

4. My brother prefers *something* because he is afraid of heights.
   He sleeps on the bottom bunk. *(to + verb)*

5. Would you choose *something* or *something*?
   You take the summer off. *(to + verb)*
   You earn money for the fall semester. *(to + verb)*

6. If Josie wants *something*, she will have (to do) *something*.
   She attends cosmetology school.
   She sends in her application now.

7. Traveling allows us *something*.
   We better understand people from different countries and cultures.

8. Sky divers like *something*.
   They live dangerously.

9. *Something* is *something*.
   (People) consider the experiment a failure.
   (People) admit the failure of the entire project.

10. For people (to do) *something* requires endless patience.
    People train parrots.
    Parrots talk.

Writing Practice: *Inserting Gerunds and Infinitives*

Choose one business letter you have written. Revise it, combining sentences by inserting gerunds and infinitives. The revised letter should contain sentences of varied lengths and patterns.

2
Grammar and Usage

11 Nouns

Understanding Nouns

Nouns are words that name—people, places, things, and even ideas. In this section you will learn ways to identify nouns: by their definition, by the classes into which they can be divided, and by the features that distinguish them from other parts of speech. In addition to working through this section now, you might want to use it later as a handy reference on common usage problems with nouns when you work in the section *Using Nouns*.

Defining Nouns

A *noun* is often defined as the name of a person, place, thing, or idea.

Tina wants to go to law school.	[name of person]
On our vacation we went to *Dallas*.	[name of place]
Ricardo jogs a *mile* around the *track*.	[names of things]
The statue symbolizes *truth*, *justice*, and *liberty*.	[names of ideas]

Exercise 1: *Identifying Nouns*

Write out the following sentences and underline all nouns. Above each noun write whether it names a person, place, thing, or idea.

Example

a. Leontyne Price was considered a great singer both in the United States and in Europe.

        person   thing

    <u>Leontyne Price</u> was considered a great <u>singer</u> both in the

      place   place

    <u>United States</u> and in <u>Europe</u>.

1. Della keeps a journal in which she writes down her thoughts and emotions.

2. Zeke the hound snored in the shade, the picture of perfect peace.

3. The politician spoke about law and order in England and about how police there carry no firearms.

4. The area of the United States that first emerged from beneath prehistoric seas is the Ozark Plateau, a section of land rich in fossils.

5. Two sparrows sat on the fence, ruffling their feathers to protect themselves against the chilly wind and freezing drizzle.

6. The phoenix is a mythical bird that dies in flames but springs reborn out of its own ashes.

7. The villain claimed to be interested only in truth and justice, but she really loved only power, money, and fame.

8. Terry yearned to buy the old convertible and restore it to its former glory; such a car would be a rare antique.

9. The Sweetwater River earned its name when an explorer's mule slipped while crossing it and lost several bags of sugar to the rushing waters.

10. Mary Teresa Norton was the first woman to be chairperson of the Democratic party in New Jersey.

Classifying Nouns

Nouns fall into four general classifications.

Nouns are either *proper* or *common*.

Proper nouns name specific persons, places, things, or ideas; nouns that are not specific names are called *common nouns*.

Proper Noun	Common Noun	
Sarah Vaughan	singer	[person]
Alaska	state	[place]
Brooklyn Bridge	bridge	[thing]
the Four Freedoms	freedom	[idea]

Proper nouns are capitalized; common nouns are not.

The *building* is immense.	[common noun]
The *World Trade Center* is immense.	[proper noun]
The *doctor* performed the operation.	[common noun]
Dr. Rosa Diaz performed the operation.	[proper noun]

Nouns may be classified as either *concrete* or *abstract*.

Concrete nouns name objects that can be perceived by the senses—seen, touched, tasted, heard, or smelled. *Abstract nouns* name ideas, qualities, feelings, and so forth, entities that cannot be seen, touched, etc.

           concrete   abstract
The <u>United States Constitution</u> stresses the legal <u>equality</u> of all

  concrete
<u>citizens</u>.

    concrete   abstract   abstract
All <u>people</u> are endowed with the <u>right</u> to pursue <u>happiness</u>.

Every noun may be classified as either common or proper, concrete or abstract. *Ethel Kennedy,* for instance is a proper noun and a concrete noun. *Motherhood* is a common noun and an abstract noun.

Two or more words joined to name one person, place, thing, or idea are called a *compound noun*.

Many proper nouns are compound nouns: *Diana Ross, Nitty Gritty Dirt Band, Boston Celtics, Empire State Building, Boy Scouts of America.*
    Not all compound nouns are proper, however; many common nouns are compound as well. They may be closed (spelled as one word), open (spelled as two separate words), or hyphenated. If you are unsure whether a compound noun should be closed, open, or hyphenated, use a dictionary to find the accepted spelling.

Closed:	landlady, motorboat, shinbone, searchlight
Open:	minus sign, relay race, saddle horse, outer space
Hyphenated:	sister-in-law, self-control, merry-go-round

Some compound nouns have more than one acceptable spelling:

rock 'n' roll, rock-and-roll

drug store, drugstore

A *collective noun* names a group.

---

choir	committee	group
class	crowd	organization
club	jury	team

Exercise 2: Classifying Nouns

Write out the following sentences, underlining each noun. Then beneath each sentence, list the nouns and the classes to which they belong: *proper* or *common, concrete* or *abstract, compound, collective.* Remember that a noun may belong to several different classes.

Example

---

a. O. J. Simpson, famous for his ability in football, was well liked by the team.

O.J. Simpson, famous for his ability in football, was well liked by the team.

O.J. Simpson—proper, concrete, compound; ability—common and abstract; football—common, concrete, compound; team common, concrete, collective

1. The yucca, a kind of cactus, is sometimes called "Adam's needle" because of its long, sharp thorns.

2. Aunt Carol has a large collection of old records, including boogie-woogie, rhythm and blues, and early rock.

3. A *cat's-eye* is a semiprecious stone, but a *cat-o'-nine tails* is a type of whip.

4. The most dramatic moments of a launch are the countdown and the takeoff, the moment the great rocket finally rises into the air.

5. *A Raisin in the Sun,* a play by Lorraine Hansberry, was a success on Broadway and later a critically acclaimed motion picture.

6. The lawyer for the defense conducted a brilliant cross-examination of the witness, and the courtroom was filled.

7.   Anglo-Norman was the language spoken by the Scandinavians who invaded and settled in early England; Anglo-French was a dialect spoken by French settlers.

8.   Uncle Smedley makes a terrible dish he calls chili; he uses chickpeas, chili sauce, garlic powder, and ground liver.

9.   A "bread-and-butter" letter is a note written to thank a person who has been your host, whether for a meal or for an extended visit.

10. Stories of spies and intrigue are especially popular among young adults.

Finding a Noun by Its Features

Nouns have four characteristics that help you distinguish them from other parts of speech. Not all nouns have all four characteristics, but most nouns will have at least one of the following identifying features.

Nouns often follow determiners.

Determiners signal that a noun will soon follow. The most common determiners, the words *a, an,* and *the,* always indicate a noun will soon appear; these specialized words are sometimes called *articles.* Besides the articles, other words may sometimes work as determiners as well, words like *her, his, many, my, this, that, these,* and *some.*

a village	*many* cars
an apple	*some* countries

Sometimes, the determiner and noun will be separated by one or more words. The determiner still signals that a noun is on its way and will eventually arrive.

the battered, old guitar
an unripe apple
her newest cashmere sweater
some newly emerged countries

Nouns are singular or plural.

Another feature of nouns is that they show number. Most nouns have a form to show they are singular and another form to show they are plural. A few nouns, however, do not have different forms for singular and plural.

Singular	*Plural*
one toad	two toads
a doghouse	several doghouses
an octopus	eleven octopuses or octopi
the goose	two geese
a deer	many deer

Nouns may change form to indicate possession or ownership.

To form the possessive of a noun, you usually add an apostrophe (')
and an -s or an apostrophe alone. A noun's possessive form shows
that the possessive noun has a special relationship to another noun:

Amy's trumpet   Muhammad's beliefs
the city's problems   the pitcher's handle

**Nouns may be formed with certain *noun suffixes*, such as
-ance, -ation, -ence, -ism, -ment, and -ness.**

When a noun suffix is added to a word, the resulting word is a noun.
You can recognize nouns by learning these suffixes.

guide + ance = guidance   national + ism = nationalism
invite + ation = invitation   place + ment = placement
confer + ence = conference   sick + ness = sickness

Exercise 3: Identifying Nouns by Their Features

Many of the nouns in the following paragraph are preceded by a
determiner. Write the paragraph and draw a circle around each
determiner. Then underline the noun that follows the determiner.

Example

---

a. Sharon Washington is helping a group of people in her town
   work on the special centennial project.

   Sharon Washington is helping ⓐ group of people in ⟨her⟩
   town work on ⟨the⟩ special centennial project.

317

The centennial marks the town's one-hundredth anniversary, and the group Sharon is helping is a genealogical society. A genealogical society is an organization composed of people who have an interest in tracing their ancestors and preserving the records of the past. Sharon is taking part in a special project that involves many hours of work and some traveling as well. This project involves visiting the county cemeteries, recording the locations of the graves and the names on the stones, and noting the stones that are illegible and those graves that have never been marked. This information will be put into order and printed in a special booklet. Sharon is glad to be involved with the project; her interest in genealogy was sparked by Alex Haley's book *Roots*.

Review: Understanding Nouns

The following passage about working conditions during the 1800s is from the book *The Good Old Days—They Were Terrible!* by Otto L. Bettmann. Using what you have learned about identifying nouns, find the nouns in the selection and list them on a sheet of paper in the order they appear.

History offers a yardstick by which to measure the status of the American worker. Today he has dignity and protection; less than a hundred years ago he was poor, debased and unprotected. Industrialists of the period regarded labor as a commodity—a raw material like ore or lumber to be mined of its vitality and flushed away. Profits were enormous against meager wages—''Never before have the rich been so rich and the poor been so poor''—an imbalance that helped 1 percent of the population by 1890 to own as much as the remaining 99 percent put together. Marshall Field's income was calculated to be $600 an hour, while his shopgirls, at a salary of $3 to $5 a week, had to work over three years to earn that amount. Virtually unopposed by any organized front—by 1900 only 3.5 percent of the work force was unionized—employers hired and fired at will. A New England shoe manufacturer sacked outright all of his workers and replaced them with Chinese laborers he brought from the West Coast who were willing to work for $26 a month. To survive in the absence of social benefits, workers endured wretched conditions. The huge labor pool, augmented by a massive influx of foreigners, created a rivalry for even the most repugnant jobs. And if labor unrest caused an occasional stir, industrialist Jay Gould was confident he had the solution for it: ''I can hire one half of the working class to kill the other half.''[1]

---

[1]From *The Good Old Days—They Were Terrible!* by Otto L. Bettmann. Copyright © 1974 by Otto Bettmann. Reprinted by permission of Random House, Inc.

Applying What You Know

From a favorite poem, short story, or piece of nonfiction, select a passage at least five sentences long. Then using your knowledge of the definition, classes, and features of nouns, find the nouns in the selection and list them on a sheet of paper in the order they appear. (Your teacher may ask you to explain how you identified each noun.)

Using Nouns

In this section you will practice using nouns: forming noun plurals, both regular and irregular; forming possessives; and using concrete and proper nouns to add clarity and life to your writing.

Forming Regular Plurals

Form the plural of most nouns by adding the suffix -s.

Singular	*Plural*
one jacket	ten jackets
one tire	a dozen tires

Form the plural of nouns ending in *s, sh, ch, x,* or *z* by adding the suffix -es.

Singular	*Plural*
a hiss	several hisses
one crash	two crashes
a switch	a number of switches
a hex	three hexes

Form the plural of nouns ending in *o* preceded by a vowel by adding the suffix -s. Form the plural of nouns ending in *o* that have to do with music by adding the suffix -s.

Singular	*Plural*
one stereo	two stereos
one solo	three solos
one arpeggio	two arpeggios

Form the plural of most nouns ending in *o* preceded by a consonant by adding the suffix -*es*.

Singular	*Plural*
hero	heroes
potato	potatoes

Exception: Some nouns that end in an *o* preceded by a consonant form the plural by adding either -*s* or -*es*. If you are unsure how a certain plural should be formed, check your dictionary. The following entries tell you that both spellings are acceptable for *hobo, mosquito,* and *zero.*

> ho·bo n., pl. **hobos, hoboes**
> mos·qui·to n., pl. **mosquitos, mosquitoes**
> ze·ro n., pl., **zeros, zeroes**

Exercise 4: Forming Regular Noun Plurals

Write out the following sentences, changing each *italicized* noun to its plural form by adding either -*s* or -*es*. Underline the nouns that you make plural.

Example

---

  a. The *chemist* had been startled by the loud *hiss* and strange *fizz* of the *mixture*.

  The chemists had been startled by the loud hisses and strange fizzes of the mixtures.

1. The *cargo* consisted of the *box* of *metal,* the *burro,* and the pack *saddle.*

2. The student wrote about the *hero* of the *rodeo,* the *clown* who saved the *rider* from the *bull.*

3. In the store *window* were the *stereo, piano, radio, guitar,* and *tuba* that were on sale.

4. The show was rather strange; for instance, the *soprano* sang the big *solo* in the *silo* at the back of the stage.

5. The *box* containing the *switch,* the *watch,* the *lantern*, and the *key* to the *church* had been misplaced.

6. The *crunch* and *crash* told us that the *burro* and *mule* must be escaping from their *stall.*

7. Weird *moss* hung from the *arch* that formed the *entryway* to the *tower* on which the *witch* had cast the *hex.*

8. The *chef* felt outraged when the *swatch* of *chintz* had been discovered in the stewed *tomato.*

9. The *flash* of light from the *match* helped us open the *latch* of the *gate* that led into the cemetery.

10. The *screech* of the *owl* and the *buzz* of the *mosquito* kept the *camper* awake and uncomfortable until the first *ray* of dawn came over the *hill.*

Forming the Irregular Plurals of Nouns

Some nouns do not form a plural with the addition of *-s* or *-es;* their plurals are formed through changes in their basic spelling. Such plurals are called *irregular plurals.*

For most nouns that end in *y,* change the *y* to *i* before adding the suffix *-es.*

Singular	*Plural*
one story	two stories
a democracy	several democracies
one artery	a number of arteries

For nouns that end in *y* preceded by a vowel, add the suffix *-s* to the singular form.

Singular	*Plural*
a donkey	many donkeys
one Tuesday	four Tuesdays

Form the irregular plurals of some nouns by changing an internal vowel sound.

Singular	Plural
foot	feet
goose	geese
man	men
tooth	teeth
woman	women

For many nouns ending in *fe* or *f,* change the *f* to *v* before adding the suffix *-es.*

Singular	Plural
calf	calves
elf	elves
half	halves
hoof	hooves
leaf	leaves
life	lives
loaf	loaves
self	selves
sheaf	sheaves
thief	thieves
wife	wives
wolf	wolves

For some nouns ending in *fe* or *f,* simply add the suffix *-s.*

Singular	Plural
belief	beliefs
dwarf	dwarfs
puff	puffs
roof	roofs

Some nouns have the same form for both singular and plural. Many of these nouns name fish, game birds, or other animals.

Same Singular and Plural Forms

shrimp	pike	grouse
elk	salmon	quail
fish	sheep	carp
moose	trout	deer

Some nouns that name nationalities also use the same form for both singular and plural.

Singular	Plural
one Chinese	10,000 Chinese
a Japanese	several Japanese
one Portuguese	three Portuguese
a Swiss	a million Swiss
one Vietnamese	a hundred Vietnamese

Form the plural of some nouns by a change in spelling.

Many words from Old English or from Latin and Greek form plurals with a spelling change.

Singular	Plural
alumnus	alumni
basis	bases
crisis	crises
datum	data
louse	lice
hypothesis	hypotheses
index	indexes or indices
medium	media
ox	oxen
parenthesis	parentheses
radius	radii or radiuses

If you are in doubt about the plural form of any noun, check your dictionary. If the dictionary gives no plural form, it means the noun forms its plural regularly.

Exercise 5: *Forming Irregular Noun Plurals*

The *italicized* nouns in the following sentences all have irregular plurals. Write out each sentence, changing the *italicized* noun to its plural form. If you are unsure how the plural is formed, check your dictionary. Underline the nouns you change.

Example

a. The *foot* of the *calf* showed some *injury*, but the *sheep* seemed unharmed.

The feet of the calves showed some injuries, but the sheep seemed unharmed.

1. The scientist wanted *datum* on the *life* of the *grouse*, *quail*, and *ostrich* in the zoo.

2. The *alumnus* of the college awarded the *child* the *trophy*.

3. The *man* could not explain the *phenomenon* of the mysterious disappearance of the *tooth* of the *ox*.

4. The *Swiss* and the *English* met with the *Vietnamese* and the French *woman*.

5. On Wednesday the zoo keeper bathes the monkey, the *wolf*, the *goose*, and the *grouse*.

6. The *basis* of the *crisis* had been discovered, and the *man* and *woman* had saved the *life* of the *child*.

7. The Thanksgiving decorations were the *loaf* of bread, the *sheaf* of grain, and the colored *leaf*; the Christmas decorations were the *elf* and the angel with the *halo*.

8. The *moose* and the *elk* grazed peacefully beside the *deer* and the *buffalo*.

9. The *thief* stripped the *shelf* of the *battery*, the rare *dictionary*, and the valuable *penny*.

10. I hated the book because it was about the little *fairy*, the adorable *dwarf*, the cute little *elf*, and the disgustingly sweet little *pixie*.

Forming the Plurals of Compound Nouns

Form the plurals of compound nouns written as one word by adding the suffix -s.

Singular	*Plural*
one *cupful*	two *cupfuls*
a *doorknob*	three *doorknobs*
the *stronghold*	the *strongholds*

Follow the appropriate rule to form the plural of a compound noun written as one word that ends in a word with an irregular plural.

Singular	Plural
a *chairwoman*	several *chairwomen*
the *grandchild*	four *grandchildren*
one *werewolf*	several *werewolves*

Form the plurals of compound words written as separate or hyphenated words by making plural the most important word.

Singular	Plural
one *merry-go-round*	two *merry-go-rounds*
the *hound dog*	the *hound dogs*
a *brother-in-law*	seven *brothers-in-law*

If you are unsure how to form the plural of a compound noun, check your dictionary.

Exercise 6: *Forming Compound Noun Plurals*

Each of the following sentences contains one or more compound nouns in their singular forms, as well as other nouns with irregular plurals. Rewrite the sentences, changing each *italicized* noun to its plural form. Underline the nouns you make plural.

Examples

a. The *apple blossom* were in bloom, and the *jack-in-the-pulpit* were up.

The apple blossoms were in bloom, and the jack-in-the-pulpits were up.

b. The worst *enemy* of *king cobra* are *mongoose*.
The worst enemies of king cobras are mongooses.

1. The poem "Beowulf" is about one of the *hero* of a tribe called the *Spear-Dane* who aids another tribe called the *Ring-Dane*.

2. The king of the *Ring-Dane* built the largest of *mead-hall*, a large building to house himself and his warriors, his family and *in-law*.

3. *Elf* and other supernatural creatures lived in the *swampland* near the hall; the most fearsome of these was Grendel, the marsh-stalker, most savage of *blood drinker*.

4. Grendel terrorized the *Ring-Dane* until Beowulf came, braving the *sea-current* with his fellow *hero*, garbed in their *mail coat* and carrying their *battle spear*.

5. No *war-shield* were strong enough to protect the *man* from the *tooth* of Grendel, stealer of *life*.

6. Beowulf, best of *warrior-prince*, must defeat Grendel without *battle spear* or *war sword*, for the monster had cast *magic spell* on all weapons.

7. Beowulf killed Grendel with his bare hands but then had to fight Grendel's mother, the most savage of *monster-wife*, cruelest of the *water dweller*, one of the creatures called *mere-woman*.

8. He pursued her underwater and seized *handful* of her slimy hair; she struck out at him with *fingernail* like *knife*.

9. The *seafarer* celebrated when Beowulf emerged from the lake; he had slain both *water monster* and brought back *trophy* of his *success*.

10. The king rewarded Beowulf and his fellow *swordsman* with *trunkful* of treasure; *war weapon*, gold, and *heirloom*.

Forming the Possessives of Nouns

A noun's possessive form may show ownership or possession:
The film was about Harriet *Tubman's* career.
The *dog's* new collar has an identification plate on it.

A noun's possessive form may show origin or relationship.
The *neighbor's* noisiness was getting on our nerves.
Amelia Earhart's disappearance remains a mystery.

Form the possessive of a singular noun by adding an apostrophe (') and an -*s*.

the death of the *tree*	the *tree's* death
an edge on the *box*	the *box's* edge
the speech by *Standing Bear*	*Standing Bear's* speech

When a singular noun ends in *s* and has more than one syllable, the possessive may also be formed by adding only the apostrophe.

Dropping the *s* after the apostrophe eliminates the second -*s* sound, which is sometimes difficult to pronounce.

the *mattress'* cover
Gwendolyn Brooks' poem
the *abyss'* depth
Paris' streets

Note: It is also considered correct to add both an apostrophe and an *s: mattress's* cover, Gwendolyn *Brooks's* poem, *abyss's* depth, *Paris's* streets.

Form the possessive of a plural noun ending in s by adding only an apostrophe.

---

the team of the *girls*   the *girls'* team
the den of the *lions*   the *lions'* den

Form the possessive of a plural noun that does not end in s by adding an apostrophe and s.

---

the honking of the *geese*   the *geese's* honking
the liberation of *women*   *women's* liberation
the hardness of the *teeth*   the *teeth's* hardness
the nest of the *mice*   the *mice's* nest

Exercise 7: *Forming Noun Possessives*

Write out the following sentences, supplying the possessive form of each noun given in parentheses. (Before you form the possessive, check whether the noun is singular or plural.) Then underline the possessive nouns.

Examples

---

a. The _____ fragrant blossoms drew swarms of foraging bees. (bushes)

The bushes' fragrant blossoms drew swarms of foraging bees.

b. The _____ honking disturbed the young _____ sleep. (geese) (woman)

The geese's honking disturbed the young woman's sleep.

1. The _____ violence was unexpected, and the rains caused some damage to the _____ facilities. (storm) (zoo)

2. The _____ den was flooded, and in the eastern part of the zoo, the water was as high as the tallest _____ knees. (wolves) (giraffe)

3. The _____ cage had a foot of water in it, and the beast kept filling its trunk and squirting water in the _____ faces. (elephant) (rescuers)

4. The _____ pond was also flooded, but the creature didn't notice; the _____ disgust was evident, though, as they gingerly trod the spongy soil and avoided puddles. (hippopotamus) (camels)

5. The _____ pen was a muddy mess, with muck and water up to the _____ belly; the _____ legs were caught in the mire. (rhinoceros) (rhino) (beast)

6. In the Australian exhibit the _____ pen and the _____ yards were damaged, but the _____ field was unhurt. (kangaroos) wallabies) (ostriches)

7. In the polar exhibits the _____ den and the _____ pool were unhurt, but the _____ pen and the old bull _____ cage received slight flooding. (bear) (penguins) (arctic foxes) (walrus)

8. In the monkey house the cage that was most seriously flooded was the spider _____; the _____ cage was filled with water but was easily drained, and the _____ dwellings were undisturbed. (monkey) (rhesus) (chimpanzees)

9. In the insect and reptile house the _____ exhibit was slightly damaged, the _____ more seriously damaged, and the _____ glass case was completely destroyed; the _____ cage was undamaged, so its disappearance was a mystery. (butterflies) (praying mantises) (tarantulas) (daddy longlegs)

10. The most tragic occurrence was the giant ground _____ death; the _____ name was Cosmo, and _____ innate laziness kept him from climbing out of the _____ path. (sloth) (animal) (Cosmo) (water)

Review: Using Nouns

Rewrite the following sentences, making each of the nouns in parentheses plural. Underline the plurals that you form.

Example

a. The (hoof) of the (sheep) showed (trace) of disease.

The hooves of the sheep showed traces of disease.

1. The (child) opened the (box) of (toy).

2. All the news (medium) covered the (story) about the prehistoric (tooth) discovered in the volcanic (ash).

3. By the (bush) a group of (jack-in-the-pulpit) grew, and at the (edge) of all the (flower bed), ornamental (moss) grew.

4. Linda's mother lives with her (sister-in-law) and her two (teenager), Linda and Jody, as well as with two (four-year-old) who are her twin (niece).

5. When we go to (rodeo), sometimes we meet the (Valdez), who also like to watch the (rider) on the (bronco) and the (Brahman bull).

6. On (Saturday) we go fishing for (bass), (trout), (bluegill), and (bullhead).

7. In the polar exhibit at the museum, there are stuffed (seal), (walrus), (polar bear), and (wolf).

8. In the (lobby) of the (office) were (bench), (sofa), and low (table).

9. The (basis) of the (hypothesis) were drawn from (datum) on a certain strain of (bacterium).

10. When the (concerto) reached their (crescendo), the (alumnus) of the college shouted their (bravo).

Rewrite each of the following sentences, putting each of the nouns in parentheses into its possessive form. Underline the possessive nouns you form.

Examples

a. (Charles) brother cleaned the (cockatoo) cage.

Charles' brother cleaned the cockatoo's cage.

b. The (children) favorite program was not shown so that the (politicians) speeches could be broadcast.

The children's favorite program was not shown so that the politicians' speeches could be broadcast.

11. It is said that (geese) cries alerted Romans of their (enemy) approach.

12. A (goose) honk is as loud and effective as a (watchdog) bark.

13. The (gas) distinctive odor made (Mavis) eyes water.

14. In a (year) time they might forget the mistake; in a hundred (years) time they will certainly not remember it.

15. (Cheech and Chong) new comedy album isn't nearly as funny as (Joan Rivers) new one.

16. The (Mayberry Accordion Company) president is also the president of the (world) largest kazoo company.

17. (Women) liberation put an end to the notion that a (woman) place is in the home and nowhere else.

18. (Ray Charles) recording of that song is better than the (Beatles) original version.

19. The Steinberg (family) Hanukkah party was a huge success; it's too bad all (families) reunions can't be so perfect.

20. (Ross) answer to the problem was different from (Corliss).

Writing Focus: *Using Specific Nouns*

Good writers use nouns to present a clear, specific picture to the reader, ordinarily avoiding dull or general nouns, such as *stuff, junk, things, elements*. Instead, such writers use concrete nouns that add vitality and clarity:

My brother's room is full of *stuff*.	[vague]
My brother's room contains one *bed*, one *dresser*, one *lamp*, five *aquariums*, two *radios*, a complete electric *train layout*, a life-sized *poster* of Dracula, *a unicycle*, a *pogo stick*, and a *set of stilts*.	[improved]

Proper nouns also make writing more precise and informative.

Several women were pioneers of blues music.	[vague]
Bessie Smith and *Ma Rainey* were pioneers of blues music.	[improved]

Assignment: *The Car of Your Dreams*

An eccentric millionaire has just announced that you will be given the car of your dreams. In one or two paragraphs, describe the car you will have: its looks, features, and capabilities.

Your audience will be your classmates, and your purpose will be to describe your new car as vividly as possible. Your paragraphs will be evaluated for the use of specific nouns.

Use the following steps to complete this assignment.

A. Prewriting

Use clustering, described in Chapter 1, to generate ideas and material for your paragraphs. For help with organization, review Chapter 3.

B. Writing

Write your paragraphs, using your word cluster. As you write, pay attention to the nouns you use; go into specific detail, using concrete and proper nouns as much as possible.

C. Postwriting

Use the following checklist to revise your paragraphs.

1. Does each paragraph have a clear topic sentence?

2. Is it clear how each supporting sentence relates to the topic?

3. Does the paragraph have enough specific details?

4. Have I used concrete and proper nouns effectively to make my writing more precise?

Proofread your paragraphs, using the checklist at the back of the book. Then share your writing with the members of your class.

12 Pronouns

Understanding Pronouns

Generally thought of as words that take the place of nouns or other pronouns, pronouns help writers avoid repetition and add variety to writing. In this section you will learn ways to identify pronouns: by their definition, by the classes into which they can be divided, and by the features that distinguish them from other parts of speech.

Defining Pronouns

A *pronoun* is often defined as a word that takes the place of a noun or another pronoun.

The noun or pronoun that the pronoun replaces and refers to is called the *antecedent* of the pronoun. In the following examples the pronouns are in *italics*, and an arrow points to the antecedent.

Mari Sandoz spent *her* youth in Nebraska.

Cochise was the leader of *his* people.

Here is the picture *that* Mary painted.

A single noun may be the antecedent of several pronouns.

Tammy wondered if *she* should take *her* jacket with *her*.

The antecedent of a pronoun may also appear in a preceding sentence.

Julio stared at the *snake*. *It* was a natrix, a harmless water snake.

Sometimes, a pronoun may take the place of another pronoun.

A few of the customers complained about *their* dinners.

Exercise 1: *Identifying Pronouns and Their Antecedents*

Write the following sentences, underlining the pronouns. (Some sentences have more than one pronoun.) Then draw an arrow from each pronoun to its antecedent.

Examples

a. Maria found the lost book, which had fallen behind the sofa.

Maria found the lost book, <u>which</u> had fallen behind the sofa.

b. The camel stared at the people with a wise expression on its face.

The camel stared at the people with a wise expression on <u>its</u> face.

1. The worst thing about the movie was its inconclusive ending.

2. The shamrock is the plant that people connect with Ireland.

3. There are many people who have allergic reactions to milk or who lack the enzymes to digest milk properly.

4. The first woman physician in America was Elizabeth Blackwell. She and her sister helped train nurses during the Civil War.

5. Helen Keller and Anne Sullivan were remarkable women; many people have read about their inspiring story.

6. Carbon, nitrogen, oxygen, and hydrogen are the most numerous elements in the universe; they make up ninety-nine per cent of all matter, and they are the basic matter of stars.

7. Bobby Leech was the man who survived going over Niagara Falls in a barrel, but he later died when he slipped on a banana peel.

8. The first woman who was elected to the Senate was Hattie Caraway, who was a Democrat from Arkansas.

9. *The Mousetrap* is a play that Agatha Christie wrote for Queen Mary of England. It became the longest-running play in the world.

10. Larry Doby, Jackie Robinson, and Roy Campanella played their first All-Star game together in 1949.

Classifying Pronouns

Most pronouns can be divided into five classes: personal, relative, interrogative, demonstrative, and indefinite pronouns.

A *personal pronoun* refers to one or more persons or things.

Except for the pronoun *you*, personal pronouns have separate singular and plural forms.

	Singular	*Plural*
First Person:	I/me/my/mine	we/us/our/ours
Second Person:	you/your/yours	you/your/yours
Third Person:	he/him/she/her/it	they/them/their/theirs
	his/hers/its	

The *person* of a pronoun indicates the relationship of that pronoun to the speaker.

First-person pronouns (I, me, we, us) refer to the speaker or to a group of which the speaker is a part.

I sat on *my* lunch accidentally.	[the speaker]
We finished *our* assignment.	[the speaker and others]

Second-person pronouns refer to the person or persons being spoken to. Notice that the singular and plural forms of the second-person pronouns are the same.

You are the only person to get the answer right.	[one person]
You have succeeded because all of *you* have worked together.	[more than one person]

Third-person pronouns refer to persons or things other than the speaker or the speaker's listeners.

She is an excellent tennis player.	[one person]
They have the best spaghetti in town at this restaurant.	[more than one person]

Marcia poured a glass of milk and drank *it*.	[one thing]

Personal pronouns have reflexive forms that are formed by adding the suffix *-self* or *-selves* to the pronoun base.

Singular	*Plural*
myself	ourselves
yourself	yourselves
himself herself itself oneself	themselves

Note: The words *hisself* and *theirselves* are not a feature of Edited Standard English.

The reflexive forms of personal pronouns may be used in two different ways. In one way they may be used to refer to the person or thing named as the subject, showing the subject doing something to itself.

I cut *myself* on the letter opener.

Carlotta asked *herself* how she could have forgotten such an important appointment.

The reflexive forms may also be used to show emphasis.

Queen Elizabeth *herself* made this request.

This football was autographed by Mean Joe Green *himself*.

A *relative pronoun* introduces a subordinate clause, connecting it to some other word in the sentence.

My cousin is the girl *who* is wearing the yellow sweater.

The three-toed sloth, *which* is native to South America, has a much better disposition than its cousin the two-toed sloth.

When the following words are used to introduce subordinate clauses, they function as relative pronouns.

which   who   whose   that   whom

335

An *interrogative pronoun* introduces a question.

The following words function as interrogative pronouns when they stand alone to introduce a question.

who   whose   what   whom   which

When one of the words in the preceding list modifies a noun, however, it is no longer considered an interrogative pronoun but rather a modifier. The words *what, which,* and *whose* may function as either interrogative pronouns or as modifiers.

What is a quark?	[interrogative pronoun]
What vitamins are water soluble?	[modifier]
Which is the right answer?	[interrogative pronoun]
Which color looks best?	[modifier]
Whose is this?	[interrogative pronoun]
Whose coat is that?	[modifier]

A *demonstrative pronoun* points out a specific person, place, thing, or idea.

This is a recording by Roberta Flack.

That is Mount Rainier in the distance.

These are the peach trees we planted.

Those are mockingbirds.

There are only four demonstrative pronouns:

this   that   these   those

When one of these words is used before a noun, it is no longer considered a demonstrative pronoun but a modifier.

These were my great-grandfather's cuff links.	[demonstrative pronoun]
These papers are illegible.	[modifier]

Have you noticed *this*?	[demonstrative pronoun]

Would you hold *this* carton?	[modifier]

An *indefinite pronoun* does not refer to a specific person or thing.

Indefinite pronouns may take the place of a noun in a sentence, but they frequently have no antecedents.

Somebody will probably call about the lost watch.

Both of us knew what we had to do.

Most indefinite pronouns are either singular or plural.

Singular Indefinite Pronouns

anybody	everyone	no one
anyone	much	one
each	neither	somebody
either	nobody	someone
everybody		

Everybody *is* here.

One of these pens *is* yours.

Plural Indefinite Pronouns

both	few	many	others	several

Both *are* here.

Several of these pens *are* yours.

The following indefinite pronouns can be either singular or plural, depending on how they are used in a sentence.

all	any	most	none	some

None of the book *was* very interesting.	[singular]
None of the articles *were* very interesting.	[plural]
Some of the land *is* swampy.	[singular]
Some of the berries *were* ripe.	[plural]

Exercise 2: Identifying and Classifying Pronouns

On a sheet of paper, write the following sentences, underlining the personal, relative, interrogative, demonstrative, and indefinite pronouns. Beneath each sentence identify the class to which each pronoun belongs.

Examples

a. The first native American woman who was a candidate for sainthood was an eighteenth-century woman of the Mohawk nation.

The first native American woman <u>who</u> was a candidate for sainthood was an eighteenth-century woman of the Mohawk nation.

who—relative

b. Are these the pictures that all of the controversy is about?

Are <u>these</u> the pictures <u>that all</u> of the controversy is about?

these—demonstrative; that—relative; all—indefinite

1. This is Max, who is from Switzerland, and who is our exchange student this year.

2. These are the election results that everyone has been waiting to hear.

3. Gina called her parents and told them about the job offer.

4. Everyone who heard the news was stunned, but nobody was sure yet that the information was true.

5. Which of these is the one that Lydia wants?

6. Who was the astronomer who predicted the existence of the planet Pluto long before anyone else suspected it was there?

7. Many of the people who saw the incident gave conflicting accounts; this was not unusual.

8. These are the documents that contain most of the information that the report calls for.

9. "What is this?" the archaeologist asked. "None of these bones look like any that have ever before been seen."

10. Someone who has a warped sense of humor has put goldfish in most of the office's water coolers.

Finding a Pronoun by Its Features

Pronouns have three features that distinguish them from other parts of speech. Most of the personal pronouns exhibit all three features; most other kinds of pronouns have at least one of the features.

A pronoun may be singular or plural.

Personal, reflexive, demonstrative, and indefinite pronouns have singular and plural forms.

Singular	Plural
I	we
he, she, it	they
myself	ourselves
himself, herself, itself	themselves
this, that	these, those
each, neither, everybody	both, many, several
anybody, no one, one	few, others

Relative pronouns and interrogative pronouns do not show number; the same forms are used with both singular and plural antecedents.

Pronouns may change form to show their function in a sentence.

Only personal pronouns and the relative and interrogative pronoun *who* have this characteristic. The personal pronouns and *who* have both subject forms and object forms.

Subject Forms	Object Forms
I, we	me, us
you	you
he, she, it, they	him, her, it, them
who	whom

The *subject form* is used when the pronoun functions as the subject or complement of a clause.

Subject: *She* will be elected mayor.

Complement: The mayor will be *she*.
                      It is *I*.

The *object form* is used when the pronoun functions as a direct object, indirect object, or object of a preposition.

Direct Object: The sudden noise startled *them*.

Indirect Object: My aunt gave *me* a Confederate dollar bill.

Object of Preposition: When you see Dawn, give this note to *her*.

In addition to subject and object forms, the personal pronouns and *who* have possessive forms as well.

Possessive Forms

my, mine, our, ours
your, yours
his, her, hers, its, their, theirs
whose

Pronouns may have gender.

Personal and reflexive pronouns may be masculine, feminine, or neuter.

Masculine: he, him, his, himself

Feminine: she, her, hers, herself

Neuter: it, its, itself

Pronouns like *I*, *me*, and *myself* can be either masculine or feminine, depending on the user. Words like *they*, *them*, *we*, and *us* may refer to either sex or to mixed groups of both sexes, depending on the context.

Exercise 3: *Identifying and Classifying Pronouns*

Write the following sentences, underlining the pronouns. Beneath each sentence indicate the class to which each pronoun belongs.

Examples

a. Which of the whales that the scientists studied was the most intelligent?
Which of the whales that the scientists studied was the most intelligent?

which: interrogative; that: relative

b. Sheila bruised herself when she was putting the steer back into its stall.
Sheila bruised <u>herself</u> when <u>she</u> was putting the steer back into <u>its</u> stall.

herself: personal, reflexive; she: personal, possessive; its: possessive

1. Oberlin College, which is in Ohio, was the first American college that granted women the same education as men.

2. My scientific friend says that there were several serious scientific errors in the movie *Star Wars*, but I don't know what they are.

3. This is the essence of the new law: anyone who burns trash within the city limits will be fined.

4. Only a few of the trees that we planted last spring survived the long winter with its abnormally low temperatures and fierce winds.

5. The Republic of San Marino honored someone unusual on one of its commemorative stamps when it pictured Mickey Mouse on a special issue.

6. One of the extraordinary things about the camel is the number of noises it can make.

7. When O. Henry began publishing short stories, few of his readers knew that he was writing while at the same time serving a prison term.

8. Queen Elizabeth I of England was a strong monarch who could be ruthless if she had to be; most of her subjects appreciated her courage and strength.

9. What did she do to protect herself?

10. "You won't catch many fish today," the guide told her clients. "The heavy rains that fell last night have roiled the water and made it too muddy for the fish to bite."

Review: Understanding Pronouns

Use your knowledge of the classes of pronouns and their features to locate at least twenty-five pronouns in the following passage from Graham Greene's "Across the Bridge." List the pronouns on a sheet of paper in the order they appear; beside each pronoun identify the class to which it belongs: *personal, relative, interrogative, demonstrative,* or *indefinite.*

> "They say he's worth a million," Lucia said. He sat there in the little hot damp Mexican square, a dog at his feet, with an air of immense and forlorn patience. The dog attracted your attention at once; for it was very nearly an English setter, only something had gone wrong with the tail and the feathering. Palms wilted over his head, it was all shade and stuffiness around the bandstand, radios talked loudly in Spanish from the little wooden sheds where they changed your pesos into dollars at a loss. I could tell he didn't understand a word from the way he read his newspaper—as I did myself, picking out the words which were like English ones. "He's been here a month," Lucia said. "They turned him out of Guatemala and Honduras."
>
> You couldn't keep any secrets for five hours in this border town. Lucia had only been twenty-four hours in the place, but she knew all about Mr. Joseph Calloway. The only reason I didn't know about him (and I'd been in the place two weeks) was because I couldn't talk the language any more than Mr. Calloway could.[1]

Applying What You Know

From an essay or other piece of writing you have recently completed, select a passage about three paragraphs long. Using your knowledge of the definition, classes, and features of pronouns, identify the pronouns in the selection and list them on a sheet of paper in the order they appear.

Using Pronouns

One of the characteristics of Edited Standard English is the way in which pronouns are used. In this section you will learn to use pronouns in conformity with ESE—pronouns that agree with their antecedents in number and gender and pronouns with the proper subject or object forms. You will also learn to increase the clarity of your writing by avoiding ambiguous, general, and indefinite pronoun

---

[1]From "Across the Bridge" in *Collected Stories* by Graham Greene, Copyright 1947, renewed 1975 by Graham Greene. Published by The Bodley Head and William Heinemann. Reprinted by permission of Viking Penguin Inc. and Laurence Pollinger Limited as agent for the author.

reference. As you work through this section, refer to the preceding section, Understanding Pronouns, for any help you may need in identifying or classifying pronouns.

Agreement with Antecedent

A pronoun must agree with its antecedent in number. When the antecedent is singular, the pronoun used to refer to it must be singular.

Even if the antecedent is followed by a prepositional phrase containing a plural noun, the antecedent remains singular and a singular pronoun is used.

Neither of the boys has memorized *his* part.

Everyone in the girls' locker room has found *her* place.

When the antecedent is plural, a plural pronoun is used to refer to it.

Many of the representatives answer *their* mail faithfully.

Both of the calves had broken *their* halters.

The pronouns *all, any, some,* and *none* may be either singular or plural in meaning, depending on their use in a sentence.

Singular: None of the diet had lost *its* appeal.

Plural: None of the students liked *their* test scores.

When two or more singular antecedents are joined by *and,* they take a plural pronoun.

Mrs. Highwater and her son enjoyed *their* tour of New York.

Bill and I looked mournfully at *our* lunches.

When two or more singular antecedents are joined by *or* or *nor*, a singular pronoun is used to refer to them.

Neither Kim nor Juanita has gotten *her* pictures back yet.

Imat or Malcolm must have left *his* sweater here.

A pronoun must agree with its antecedent in gender.

When a singular antecedent is clearly masculine, use the pronouns *he, him,* or *his.* When a singular antecedent is clearly feminine, use the pronouns *she, her,* or *hers.* When the antecedent is neuter, use the pronouns *it* or *its.*

The man stood with *his* hand in *his* pocket.

The girl finished *her* lab experiment.

The tree was losing *its* leaves.

Formerly, students were taught to use a singular masculine pronoun when the antecedent is an indefinite singular pronoun.

Everybody has *his* own problems.

Some critics believe that such use of language is unfair to women, since the indefinite pronoun often refers to a mixed group of both men and women. In such sentences it may be better to use the expression *his or her* or else reword the sentence so that the problem is avoided.

Everybody has *his or her* own problems.
All people have *their* problems.
Everybody has problems.

Exercise 4: Using Pronouns That Agree With Their Antecedents

Write the following sentences, choosing the pronoun in parentheses that agrees with its antecedent or antecedents. Underline the pronoun you have chosen and be prepared to point out the antecedents of all pronouns.

Examples

    a. Each of the girls makes (their, her) own clothes.
        Each of the girls makes <u>her</u> own clothes.

    b. Neither Carlos nor Eddie had cast (their, his) vote yet.
        Neither Carlos nor Eddie had cast <u>his</u> vote yet.

1. Either Ms. Lee or Miss Gold will lend you (their, her) keys.

2. Each of the young men groomed (their, his) animals before the livestock show began.

3. Nobody in the senior class had received (their, his, his or her) yearbook yet.

4. Neither the pine nor the larch loses (their, its) foliage now.

5. Everyone is responsible for (their, his or her) own property.

6. Both glass and brick employ sand as (their, its) basic ingredient.

7. All of the speakers in the debate contest waited politely for (their, his) turn to come.

8. Neither Mike nor Max has heard anything about (their, his) job application yet.

9. Some streets had sycamores along (their, its) borders.

10. One of the full-time members and several of the part-time members presented (their, his) reports.

Using Subject Pronouns

The following personal pronouns are subject form pronouns, or pronouns in the nominative case.

Singular	Plural
I, you, he, she, it	we, you, they

When a pronoun is the subject of a group of words, use the subject form.

The Washingtons and *they* are coming late.

Karen and *I* will be there early.

When a pronoun follows a linking verb (such as a form of the verb *be*) and renames or describes the subject, use the subject form.

It is *I*.

The winners are Julio and *she*.

In informal speaking the expression "It's me" is acceptable. In formal situations or in Edited Standard English, however, the subject form is used.

It is *they* who must deal with this problem.

"I know the perpetrator of this crime," said Holmes, his eyes gleaming, "and it is *he*!"

Most problems in using the subject form of the pronoun will most likely happen when the pronoun is part of a compound subject or complement. Read the following sentence and decide which pronoun is correct.

Mollie and (she, her) watched the program.

Try each pronoun alone as the subject of the sentence to see which sounds correct to you. (An asterisk [*] indicates a sentence with a feature that is not part of Edited Standard English.)

She watched the program.	[sounds correct]
*Her watched the program.	[sounds unnatural]

Try this method to find the correct pronoun in the following sentence.

Have you and (I, me) got the assignment down correctly?	
Have I got the assignment down correctly?	[sounds correct]
*Have me got the assignment down correctly?	[sounds unnatural]
Have you and *I* got the assignment down correctly?	

Exercise 5: Using Subject Pronouns

Write the following sentences, choosing the pronoun from the pair in parentheses that correctly completes each sentence. Underline the pronoun you select.

Examples

a. Dawn and (I, me) are in the forensic society.
Dawn and I are in the forensic society.

b. The leads in the play will be Imat and (her, she).
The leads in the play will be Imat and she.

1. Neither Renaldo nor (her, she) will be able to attend the meeting.
2. The yearbook editors will be Pat Whitefeather and (me, I).
3. Either Ms. Washington or (me, I) can take your ticket money.
4. You and (her, she) are invited over to our place tonight.
5. The police chief and (she, her) talked to our civics class about careers in crime prevention.
6. In spite of the doctor's apparent innocence, in the end the villain was (he, him) after all.
7. Are Sonia and (they, them) still planning to sign up for VISTA?
8. (Her and me, She and I) are going to the Halloween party dressed as Tweedledum and Tweedledee.
9. The winners of the art contest are (her and him, he and she).
10. Mr. Chavez and (us, we) discussed energy conservation in class today.

Using Object Pronouns

The object form of the personal pronoun is sometimes called the *objective case.* The following personal pronouns are objective form pronouns.

Singular	Plural
me, you, him, her, it	us, you, them

Use an object form when a personal pronoun is a direct object.

> The college interests Clair and *me*.

> The mechanic phoned *us* about the carburetor.

Use an object form when a personal pronoun is the indirect object.

> The college sent Clair and *me* copies of the student handbook.

> The mechanic sent *us* the bill.

Use an object form of a personal pronoun when the pronoun is the object of a preposition.

> The Washingtons sent postcards to *her* and *me*.

> The Lings live across the street from *us*.

Use the object form when the personal pronoun is the subject, object, or predicate pronoun of an infinitive. The *infinitive* is the form of the verb that begins with the word *to: to go, to search, to find, to keep.* Infinitive phrases may have subjects, objects, and complements, just as sentences do.

> Marv asked *me* to lend him five dollars.
> [*Me* is the subject of the infinitive *to lend*.]

> We were just coming to see *him*.
> [*Him* is the object of the infinitive phrase.]

> Everyone expected the high scorer to be *her*.
> [*Her* is the predicate pronoun following the infinitive *to be*; it renames the subject of the phrase, *high scorer*.]

Confusion over using the object form usually occurs when the pronoun is part of a compound construction. Try using the pronoun alone to see which form sounds better. (An asterisk [*] indicates a sentence with a feature that is not a part of ESE.)

Raoul met Pam and (me, I) at the game.	
*Raoul met I at the game.	[sounds wrong]
Raoul met me at the game.	[sounds right]
Raoul met Pam and *me* at the game.	

Exercise 6: Using Object Pronouns

Write the following sentences, choosing the pronoun from the pair given in parentheses that correctly completes each sentence. Underline the pronoun you select.

Examples

---

    a. Vlad explained the story of the ballet to Carol and (me, I).
       Vlad explained the story of the ballet to Carol and <u>me</u>.

    b. Bring Davis and (her, she) to the party when you come.
       Bring Davis and <u>her</u> to the party when you come.

1. Sharon called Glenn, Lola, and (me, I) about the class election.

2. The wrong grades were mistakenly sent to Jay and (her, she).

3. Whenever Sarah and Malcolm are at one of our parties, we always ask (they, them) to sing.

4. The paintings were by Romare Beardon and (her, she).

5. Ms. Washington gave Irv and (me, I) our make-up assignments.

6. Roger invited the Wongs and (we, us) to a baseball game.

7. The practical jokes were attributed to Carla and (he, him).

8. We spent all afternoon waiting for Bill and (she, her) to arrive.

9. Jill sent the Orlandos and (they, them) thank-you notes.

10. We are anxious for Lisa and (she, her) to return from the airport.

Using Pronouns Correctly

When you must decide between using the subject or object form of a pronoun, the following general rules apply.

1. Decide how the pronoun functions in the sentence.

2. If the pronoun is used as the subject or predicate pronoun in a clause, use the subject form.

3. If the pronoun is used as an object (direct object, indirect object, object of a preposition, part of an infinitive clause), use the object form.

The pronouns *who* and *whom* follow these same principles.

Use *who* when the pronoun is used as a subject; use *whom* when the pronoun functions as an object.

Who and *whom* are interrogative pronouns when they introduce a question. Although *whom* is not often used in informal conversation, it is still used in formal speech and in Edited Standard English.

Subject Function: *Who* wrote this essay?
[*Who* is the subject of the sentence.]

Aphrodite was *who*?
[*Who* is the predicate pronoun.]

Object Function: *Whom* have you told about this?
[*Whom* is the direct object of the verb phrase *have told*.]

To *whom* shall I make out this check?
[*Whom* is the object of the preposition *to*.]

Who and *whom* are relative pronouns when they are used to introduce a subordinate clause. To decide which pronoun to use, first determine the pronoun's function within the clause.

Subject Function: Sarah Hale is the woman *who campaigned to make Thanksgiving a national holiday*.
[*Who* is the subject of the *italicized* subordinate clause.]

Object Function: We exchanged addresses with some people *whom we met on the train*.
[*Whom* is the object of the verb *met* in the *italicized* subordinate clause.]

Use *we* before a plural noun if the noun functions as a subject. Use *us* before a plural noun that functions as an object.

Subject Form: *We* stamp collectors held our meeting last week at my house.

The winners were *we* seniors.

Object Form: The rumor gave *us* science fiction fans an unexpected jolt.

Here is a new magazine for all of *us* jogging addicts.

When a pronoun is an appositive, its form is determined by the function of the noun with which it is in apposition.

An *appositive* renames or explains a nearby noun or pronoun. If the noun or pronoun functions as a subject, use the subject form of the pronoun. If it functions as an object, use the object form of the pronoun.

Subject Form: The soloists—Lee and *I*—were getting nervous before the concert.
[The pronoun *I* is in apposition with the noun *soloists*, which functions as the subject of the sentence.]

Object Form: The coach sent the guards—Liebnitz and *me*—back to the bench.
[*Me* is in apposition with the noun *guards*, which functions as a direct object in the sentence.]

Use the possessive form of a personal pronoun before a gerund—a noun formed from a verb ending in *-ing*.

Two kinds of words formed from verbs end in *-ing:* participles and gerunds. Gerunds are nouns; participles are modifiers. The possessive form of the personal pronoun is always used when a pronoun precedes a gerund.

My singing sounds like the gargling of a bullfrog.

The coach criticized *our* catching.

Exercise 7: *Using Pronouns Correctly*

Rewrite the sentences on the next page, correcting pronoun usage that does not conform to Edited Standard English. Underline the corrections you make.

Examples

---

a. Whom is calling, please?
Who is calling, please?

b. Mr. Allingworth decided to give we French students a test.
Mr. Allingworth decided to give us French students a test.

1. For who did he say the package was left?

2. Us banjo players can be identified by the calluses on our fingers.

3. The two runners-up—Bonnie and him—received plaques.

4. The clerk asked the last ones—Robb and she—to check out.

5. These are the people for who we bought the mushrooms.

6. I don't mind them playing the radio; I mind them keeping the volume so high.

7. "Who do you wish to visit?" asked the nurse, who obviously disapproved of us skipping by the desk.

8. Anyone who scores well on the test will help the rest of we students in special study sessions.

9. The judge sent the speeders—Judy and I—to a two-hour class designed to prevent her and me from repeating the offense.

10. When us film fanatics, who would never leave in the middle of a screening, heard about his leaving, we couldn't believe it.

Making Pronoun Antecedents Clear

To write clearly, make sure your pronouns have clear antecedents. Three kinds of unclear pronoun reference should be avoided: the *ambiguous*, the *general*, and the *indefinite*.

Reword sentences in which the antecedent of the pronoun is ambiguous.

An *ambiguous* statement is one that can have more than one meaning. Ambiguous pronoun references mean that a pronoun seems to have more than one possible antecedent. Such ambiguous pronoun references can usually be remedied by rewording the sentence or by replacing the pronoun with a noun.

Ambiguous:	Marcia told Lisa *her* ride was going to be late. [Whose ride, Marcia's or Lisa's, will be late?]
Clear:	Marcia said that Lisa's ride would be late. Marcia told Lisa that Lisa's ride would be late.
Ambiguous:	Jack went to see Phil and worked on *his* car. [Whose car—Jack's or Phil's—was worked on?]
Clear:	Jack went to see Phil and worked on Phil's car.

Reword sentences in which the pronouns *which, this, that,* and *it* refer to ideas that are vaguely expressed.

The antecedent of a pronoun may be a whole series of ideas. If the pronoun's antecedent is not clear, the sentence should be rephrased.

General: My sister had borrowed my backpack without asking, had taken it for the weekend to the lake, and had brought it home sopping wet; she never explained or apologized, *which* made me angry.

Clear: My sister had borrowed my backpack without asking, had taken it for the weekend to the lake, and had brought it home sopping wet; she never explained or apologized. Her total lack of consideration made me angry.

General: The windows were shut, the room was overheated, and weird smells were seeping in from the chemistry lab next door. *It* kept me from studying.

Clear: The shut windows, the overheated room, and the weird smells seeping in from the chemistry lab next door kept me from studying.

Reword sentences in which the pronouns *it, they,* or *you* do not have a clear antecedent.

Speakers and writers often use expressions such as "It says . . . " or "They say . . . " to refer to some indefinite authority. Avoid such indefinite pronoun references by specifically naming who or what is the source of the information.

Indefinite: It says that the buffalo hunters and railroads destroyed the economy of the Plains tribes.

Clear: Our American history text states that the buffalo hunters and railroads destroyed the economy of the Plains tribes.

Indefinite: They say this restaurant has very good trout.

Clear: Jim and Peggy say this restaurant has very good trout.

Indefinite: You can tour President Truman's house in Independence, Missouri.

Clear: Visitors to Independence, Missouri, can tour President Truman's house.

Exercise 8: Making Pronoun Antecedents Clear

Rewrite the following sentences to eliminate ambiguous, indefinite, and overly general pronoun reference.

Examples

a. If you shop carefully, you can save yourself money.
   Shoppers who are careful save themselves money.

b. They say that lightning often strikes twice in the same place.
   Our science book says that lightning often strikes twice in the same place.

---

1. What did it say on the radio about the election returns?

2. They say that the new park will cost over a million dollars.

3. Howard told Dan he had won the science fair's top prize.

4. They are having a mammoth closeout at Bee's Yarn Shop.

5. You can get a good pet quite cheaply at the animal shelter.

6. Lisa told Kim the news about her sister.

7. Out at the Horseshoe Bend Marina, they have some tame carp that stay near the dock, waiting for food to be tossed to them.

8. Pete was practicing his tuba while the twins were trying to see if they could master yodeling. It was deafening.

9. On television it said that there was the possibility of flash floods in the area tonight.

10. Last night my dog ran off. This morning I lost the filling out of my tooth. This afternoon I discovered my car had two flat tires. This depressed me.

Review: Using Pronouns

Rewrite each of the following sentences, changing any pronouns that do not conform to Edited Standard English or that have ambiguous, general, or indefinite pronoun reference.

Examples

a. Nobody in the girls' choir had their robe yet.
   Nobody in the girls' choir had her robe yet.

   b. Gina and her sister worked on her art project.
      Gina and her sister worked on Gina's art project.

1. Somebody on the boys' swimming team left their books in the locker room.

2. Rubin told Scott he had lost his car keys.

3. In Omaha, Nebraska, they have the headquarters of the Union Pacific Railroad.

4. Each of the elephants in the zoo has their teeth checked twice a year by a dentist.

5. Everybody who sat at the game with the band members wore their "Beat Benton High" badge.

6. They say that the temperature may drop to freezing tonight.

7. Neither Raoul nor his brother wanted to quit their job.

8. Both Dena and Carrie wore her mittens to the skating party.

9. They can now perform miracles with plastic surgery.

10. None of the dogs would stop its frantic barking.

11. Nobody who sent for that record album has received their order yet.

12. In the newspaper it said that Indira Gandhi was not related to Mahatma Gandhi.

13. Either Hester or Gina can lend you their skills.

14. To build a truly good doghouse, you should put in at least one layer of insulation.

15. Somebody had left their catcher's mitt on the park bench.

16. Both Madame Curie and her daughter won her Nobel Prizes in the field of science.

17. None of the witnesses wanted his name mentioned in the newspapers.

18. If you get your hair cut at Fantastic Fred's, you get a free pass to the Saturday afternoon movie at the mall.

19. Don never changes the oil in his car, never checks the water in his radiator, and never changes his filters. This will eventually ruin his motor.

20. I have to mow the lawn, trim the shrubs, burn a tree stump, weed the garden, and pick raspberries, which depresses me deeply.

Writing Focus: *Using Pronouns in Your Writing*

Good writers use pronouns to avoid unnecessary repetition, which can detract from their writing. To use pronouns correctly in your writing, follow these two rules:

1. Pronouns must agree with their antecedents in number, gender, and form (also called *case*).

2. Pronouns must have clear antecedents.

Assignment: *A Retreat into the Country*

The photographs on this page and the following page show the kinds of places to which many Americans, caught up in the stresses of modern life, sometimes feel they would like to escape. Do you think you could make a life for yourself in such a place? Could you live comfortably without modern conveniences and comforts? What would you miss most about your present life? Least? Discuss these questions with your friends and classmates.

After you have some ideas, write one or two well-developed paragraphs describing your life in a place like the one depicted in the photograph. Your audience will be your classmates, and your purpose will be to describe the kind of life you imagine in such a place. Your paragraphs will be evaluated for correct use of pronouns.

Use the following steps to complete this assignment.

A. Prewriting

Make two lists, one on the advantages of living in a remote place and one on the disadvantages. Work with the ideas brought up during your discussions. For help in organizing your paragraphs, refer to Chapter 3.

B. Writing

Using your lists, write one or two paragraphs that describe your life in a remote place. Include a topic sentence that clearly states the main idea of each paragraph. Supply enough specific details so that you convey a clear picture to your audience. As you write, use pronouns to add variety to your sentences.

C. Postwriting

Use the following checklist to revise your first draft.

1. Does each paragraph have a clear topic sentence?

2. Does each supporting sentence clearly relate to the topic?

3. Does each paragraph include specific details?

4. Have I used pronouns effectively to avoid unnecessary repetition in my writing?

Proofread your revision, using the Checklist for Proofreading at the back of the book. Finally, share your writing with your classmates and discuss one another's ideas.

13 Verbs

Understanding Verbs

In this section you will learn three ways to identify verbs: by their definition, by the classes into which they can be grouped, and by the features that distinguish them from other parts of speech.

Defining a Verb

A *verb* is often defined as a word describing an action or a state of being.

Buffy St. Marie *composes* and *sings* songs.	[action]
The brown recluse spider *is* highly poisonous.	[state of being]

Verbs that describe states of being usually assert that something *is* or *exists*, or they describe something's *condition*. The most frequently used verbs that describe a state of being are *am, are, is, was,* and *were.*

Exercise 1: *Identifying Verbs*

Write the following sentences, underlining the verbs. (A sentence may have more than one verb.)

Example

a. The explosion of Mount St. Helens scattered volcanic ash over four states and halted tourism for several weeks.

The explosion of Mount St. Helens <u>scattered</u> volcanic ash over four states and <u>halted</u> tourism for several weeks.

1. Lisa Lu and Kam Tong were co-stars on a popular television series in the 1950s.

2. Loretta Lynn married at the age of fifteen and became a grandmother at twenty-nine.

3. Josh Gibson of the American Negro League hit 800 home runs in his career; he once knocked the ball out of Yankee Stadium.

4. In World War I British sailors rescued a fox terrier from the wreckage of a German ship; the dog became the mascot of the British Navy.

5. Palindromes are words or sentences that read exactly the same forward and backward; an example of a palindrome is "Was it a car or a cat I saw?"

6. Myth says that Pegasus, the winged horse, sprang from the blood of the gorgon Medusa.

7. Comedian Flip Wilson created a number of memorable characters; my favorites were Geraldine and Reverend Leroy, who were both comic masterpieces.

8. Calypso music swings and sparkles, and one of its composers was Rupert Grant, who called himself "Lord Invader."

9. Sequoya was the Indian name of George Guess, the Cherokee who invented the first American Indian syllabary.

10. The comic strip "Pogo" contained many amusing characters, but the one with the most unusual name was the bloodhound who was called "Beauregard Chaulmoogra Frontenac de Montmingle Bugleboy"—with a name like that, it is no wonder he always looked bewildered and sad.

Classifying Verbs

For more information on transitive and intransitive verbs, see pages 472-473.

There are four classes of verbs: *action, linking, main,* and *helping* verbs. Action verbs are further divided into *transitive* and *intransitive* verbs.

Action verbs describe physical or mental activity.

Most action verbs show physical movement, but some describe mental or emotional activity that cannot be seen by others.

| The horses *thundered* around the curve. | [physical action] |
| Marsha *believed* the story. | [mental action] |

Linking verbs join the subject of a sentence to a noun or adjective that identifies or describes it.

Her name *is* Lana Valdez.
[*Is* is a linking verb because it links the subject, *name,* with a proper noun that identifies the name.]

The record *sounded* scratchy.
[*Sounded* is a linking verb because it links the subject, *record,* with the adjective, *scratchy.*]

The most commonly used linking verbs are forms of the verb *be: am, are, is, was, were, been,* and *being.* Other verbs may also be used as linking verbs:

appear	look	sound
become	remain	stay
feel	seem	taste
grow	smell	turn

Verbs in the preceding list may be either action or linking verbs, depending on their use in the sentence.

The puppies *looked* frightened.
[*Looked* is a linking verb in this sentence because it links the subject, *puppies,* to an adjective describing them: *frightened.*]

The puppies *looked* at the lizard with curiosity.
[*Looked* is an action verb in this sentence because it does not link the subject *puppies* to a word that describes or identifies it; rather, it names an action of the puppies.]

Verbs may be either single words or verb phrases. *Verb phrases* consist of two or more verbs acting as a single unit. The last verb in the verb phrase is called the *main verb.* The other verbs in the verb phrase are called *helping verbs* or *auxiliary verbs.*

The following is a list of common helping verbs.

is	do	should
are	does	would
was	did	have
were	can	has
am	could	had
be	will	may
been	shall	might

We *are going* to Montana this summer.

The baby-sitter thought the children *should have been* asleep hours ago.

We *will be playing* Tech High in the semifinals.

Sometimes, a main verb is separated from its helping verb or verbs by other words, such as *always, ever, never, not,* or the contraction *n't.* Such modifiers are not part of the verb phrase. In questions another word may occur between parts of the verb phrase.

Have you *seen* Sheila's tennis racket?

Mr. Whitewater *has* always *lived* in South Dakota.

The lost watch *may* never *be found.*

In some sentences a helping verb may be contracted:

She*'ll be coming* around the mountain.
[*She'll* is a contraction of *she will.*]

Priborski has the ball; he*'s running* past the ten-yard line.
[*He's* is a contraction of *he is.*]

Exercise 2: Identifying Verb Phrases

Write the following sentences, underlining the verb phrases. (Be careful not to underline any other words that may modify the verb phrase or that occur between its parts.)

Examples

a. A single drop of water may contain 50 million bacteria cells.
A single drop of water <u>may contain</u> 50 million bacteria cells.

b. Saturn's rings are not always seen, due to the planet's tipping.
Saturn's rings <u>are</u> not always <u>seen</u>, due to the planet's tipping.

1. Plant life could not exist without lightning.

2. Nitrogen is required by plants.

3. Earth's atmosphere is formed of almost 80 percent nitrogen.

4. This nitrogen, however, is in a form that plants can't use; it is insoluble.

5. Lightning is always accompanied by intense heat.

6. High temperatures will force nitrogen to combine with oxygen.

7. Nitrogen oxides are formed by the lightning; these oxides can be dissolved in water.

8. The nitrogen oxides are mixed with rain, and a dilute nitric acid is formed.

9. This acid is mixed with minerals in the earth and becomes the nitrates that the plants must have to live.

10. If electrical storms did not occur, the world's vegetation would most certainly perish, and the world would become an unlivable desert.

Finding a Verb by Its Features

Most verbs have three distinct features.

Verbs show tense.

Every verb has three forms called the *principal parts*. These principal parts are the *present*, the *past*, and the *past participle*.

Present	*Past*	*Past Participle*
trim	trimmed	(have) trimmed
teach	taught	(has) taught
ring	rang	(had) rung

The third principal part of the verb can be used with a number of helping verbs. Together, the principal parts and helping verbs can form all the different tenses in English, describing a wide variety of times.

Present:	I *trim* the bushes.
Past:	I *trimmed* the bushes.
Future:	I *will trim* the bushes.
Present Perfect:	I *have trimmed* the bushes.
Past Perfect:	I *had trimmed* the bushes.
Future Perfect:	I *will have trimmed* the bushes.

In addition to the tenses formed by the principal parts of the verb, another sense of time can be conveyed by the *progressive forms* of the tenses. The progressive forms of the tenses use the *-ing* form of the verb. This *-ing* form, called the *present participle,* is used with a form of the verb *be* in the progressive forms of the tenses.

Present Participles

trimming	teaching	ringing

Progressive Forms of the Tenses

Present Progressive:	I *am trimming* the bushes.
Past Progressive:	I *was trimming* the bushes.
Future Progressive:	I *will be trimming* the bushes.
Present Perfect Progressive:	I *have been trimming* the bushes.
Past Perfect Progressive:	I *had been trimming* the bushes.
Future Perfect Progressive:	I *will have been trimming* the bushes.

Verbs change form to agree in number with the subject of a sentence.

Every present tense verb has two different forms, one to agree with a singular subject, and one to agree with a plural subject.

Singular Form

Alice *drives.*

The train *arrives* on time.

The woman *works* at the plant.

[The singular form ends in *-s* or *-es.*]

Plural Form

Alice and Lana *drive.*

The trains *arrive* on time.

The women *work* at the plant.

[The plural form does not add an ending. It is simply the present form of the principal parts.]

The singular form of the verb is used with the pronouns *he, she,* and *it* and with a singular noun.

He *drives.*	It *works.*
She *arrives.*	The battery *works.*

The plural form of the verb is used with the pronoun subjects *I*, *you*, *we*, and *they* and with a plural noun.

I *drive*.	We *work*.
You *drive*.	The girls *work*.

Verbs show mood.

Verbs may express three different moods: the *indicative*, the *imperative*, and the *subjunctive*.

The *indicative mood* asserts something as a factual statement. Most of the verbs you use in speaking and writing are in the indicative mood.

The bus *stops* at this corner.

Queen Guinevere's love for Sir Lancelot *destroyed* the kingdom of Camelot.

The *imperative mood* is used to make commands or requests.

Please *pass* the yogurt, Marsha.

Show me your driver's license and registration.

The *subjunctive mood* expresses a wish or makes a statement that is opposed to fact, usually following the words *if* or *as though*.

I wish this corn fritter *were* a piece of cherry pie.

If wood ticks *were* worth money, our land would be unbelievably valuable.

Exercise 3: *Identifying Verbs and Verb Phrases*

Using what you have learned about the features of verbs, identify the verbs and verb phrases in the following sentences. Write the sentences, underlining the verbs and verb phrases. Be prepared to explain how you identified each verb. (A sentence may have more than one verb or verb phrase.)

Example

a. The original Harlem Globetrotters were known as the Saucy Big Five because they had played games at the Saucy Ballroom.
The original Harlem Globetrotters were known as the Saucy Big Five because they had played games at the Saucy Ballroom.

1. Sports promoter Abe Saperstein organized the team in 1927.

2. Because they did not have a hometown sponsor, they toured the country in Saperstein's car.

3. They played exhibition games and were soon known for their skill on the court.

4. The Globetrotters weren't just excellent ball players, however; they were proving themselves great entertainers as well.

5. Their clowning and fantastic ball handling endeared them to audiences, and the Globetrotters were beginning to be famous.

6. Their early years were filled with hardships and offered them little financial reward.

7. They truly became "Globetrotters" when their fame spread to other countries and they were playing exhibition games abroad.

8. The team has drawn crowds as large as 75,000, and their audiences are always pleased.

9. The players simply amaze people; they make impossible and flamboyant shots; they dribble and pass with dazzling skill; and somehow they always manage to perform antics as spectacular as those of the best comics.

10. Although the team had a humble beginning, it has now performed on all seven continents of the world.

Review: *Understanding Verbs*

Using what you have learned about the definition, classes, and features of verbs, identify the verbs and verb phrases in the following selection about the artist Georgia O'Keeffe by Mary Lynn Kotz. List the verbs and verb phrases on a sheet of paper in the order they appear and be able to explain how you identified each one.

> It is noon and I drive O'Keeffe to her other house, at Ghost Ranch, part of a spread that she first discovered 50 years ago. She knows every inch of the way, every mesa, curve and vista, and points them all out to me—including "the first hill I ever painted here. I drove my Model A out here," she says, "took my canvas and sat in the back seat to paint." She tells me that she drove across the United States, almost everywhere. "I'd leave home in an open car, with paint and canvases. When I had some paintings, I'd come back."
>
> Her face has taken on a new light. There is something especially exciting for her about this world that she has painted so many times. . . .

I ask her when she realized that she had a great gift.

"I don't think I have a great gift," she replies. "It isn't just talent. You have to have something else. . . . It is mostly a lot of nerve, and a lot of very hard work."[1]

Applying What You Know

From a convenient source, such as a newspaper, magazine, or textbook, select a passage about two or three paragraphs long. Then, using what you have learned in this section, identify the verbs and verb phrases in the selection and list them on a sheet of paper. If you like, use a recently written paper of your own as the basis for this assignment.

Using Verbs

The features of verbs—that they show tense, that they have singular and plural forms, and that they show mood—cause some usage problems. In this section of the textbook, you will learn how to use verbs in Edited Standard English. As you work, you may wish to refer to the section Understanding Verbs for any questions you have about the definition, classes, and features of verbs.

Forming Verb Tenses

Verbs show tense, or time, with their three principal parts: the *present, past,* and *past participle.*

The wind *howls* up in these hills.	[present]
The sirens *howled* in warning.	[past]
He *had howled* in protest.	[past participle with helping verb *had*]

Verbs are classified as either *regular* or *irregular*, depending on the formation of their principal parts.

---

[1]From "Georgia O'Keeffe: An American Original" by Mary Lynn Kotz. © *ARTnews* 1977.

The past and past participle parts of regular verbs are formed by adding *-d* or *-ed* to the present form.

Present	*Past*	*Past Participle*
enjoy	enjoyed	enjoyed
ignore	ignored	ignored
hop	hopped	hopped
apply	applied	applied

Notice that some verbs, such as *hop* and *apply*, have spelling changes when *-ed* is added to the present form.

The past and past participle of *irregular verbs* are not formed in regular ways. For this reason, principal parts of irregular verbs must be memorized. The following list gives the principal parts of the most common irregular verbs.

Irregular Verbs

Present	*Past*	*Past Participle* (has, have, had)
become	became	become
begin	began	begun
break	broke	broken
bring	brought	brought
build	built	built
burst	burst	burst
buy	bought	bought
catch	caught	caught
choose	chose	chosen
come	came	come
cost	cost	cost
dive	dived or dove	dived
do	did	done
draw	drew	drawn
drink	drank	drunk
drive	drove	driven
eat	ate	eaten
fall	fell	fallen
fly	flew	flown
forget	forgot	forgotten

Present	Past	Past Participle
freeze	froze	frozen
give	gave	given
go	went	gone
grow	grew	grown
hit	hit	hit
keep	kept	kept
know	knew	known
lay	laid	laid
lie	lay	lain
ride	rode	ridden
ring	rang	rung
rise	rose	risen
run	ran	run
see	saw	seen
set	set	set
shake	shook	shaken
shrink	shrank	shrunk
sing	sang	sung
sink	sank	sunk
sit	sat	sat
slay	slew	slain
speak	spoke	spoken
spring	sprang	sprung
steal	stole	stolen
strive	strove	striven
swear	swore	sworn
swim	swam	swum
take	took	taken
teach	taught	taught
think	thought	thought
throw	threw	thrown
wear	wore	worn
write	wrote	written

If you are not sure how the principal parts of a verb are formed, check your dictionary, which uses the present form as the entry for all verbs. Some dictionaries do not list the principal parts of regular verbs. This means that the verb forms its principal parts in the usual way, with *-d* or *-ed* added to the present form. All dictionaries list the principal parts of irregular verbs:

grind (grīnd) vt. **ground, grind'ing**
par·take (pär tāk') vi. **-took', -tak'en, -tak'ing**

When dictionaries list the principal parts of irregular verbs, the forms are listed in the same order as they are on the preceding chart. In addition, some dictionaries list the present participle, or *-ing* form. Up to four forms may be listed:

Present Form	Past Form	Past Participle	Present Participle
write (rīt) v.t.	**wrote**	**written**	**writing**

When only three forms are listed, the past and past participle are the same:

Present	Past and Past Participle	Present Participle
spend (spend) v.t.	**spent**	**spending**

Sometimes, a dictionary will list alternate past or past participle forms. Either form is acceptable, but the one listed first is preferred.

Present	Past	Alternate Past	Past Participle	Present Participle
dive (dīv) v.i.	**dived** or	**dove**	**dived**	**diving**

Exercise 4: Using Irregular Verbs

The sentences on the following page contain irregular verbs. Write each sentence, supplying the appropriate principal part of the verbs given in parentheses. (Remember that the past participle form is always used with the helping verb *has, have,* or *had.*) Underline the verb or verb phrase.

Examples

a. LaDonna had _____ about soccer practice after school. (forget)
LaDonna <u>had forgotten</u> about soccer practice after school.

      b. Rita, Nicki, and Rosa all have _____ on jumbo jets. (fly)
        Rita, Nicki, and Rosa all <u>have flown</u> on jumbo jets.

1. John claims that he lost the report when he absent-mindedly _____ it on the top of his car, then _____ away. (set) (drive)

2. The luggage _____ in the Baggage Claim area for hours before its owners finally _____ for it. (sit) (come)

3. The dripping water had _____, and the icicles had _____ marvelously long. (freeze) (grow)

4. Mrs. Lewington has _____ her famous banana bread to every reunion her family has _____. (bring) (hold)

5. The forest fire had _____ their courage badly and had _____ some of them nightmares for weeks afterwards. (shake) (give)

6. The boat had first _____ a leak, and finally it had _____. (spring) (sink)

7. He had _____ to see the log cabin that Josie and Ed _____. (go) (build)

8. The children accidentally _____ the baseball through Mrs. McGrouchly's picture window and then _____ in terror. (throw) (run)

9. The defendant has _____ that he has never _____ anything in his life, and you know he is a man who has always _____ the truth. (swear) (steal) (speak)

10. Have you _____ what Margo has _____ to school? It is a poem that Gwendolyn Brooks has _____ in her own handwriting. (see) (bring) (write)

Using Verb Tenses

In this section you will learn to avoid common usage problems with verb tenses.

Simple Tenses

The three simple tenses are the *present tense*, *past tense*, and *future tense*.

    Verbs in the *present tense* express an action happening at the present moment or an action that occurs repeatedly.

Billie Jean King *returns* the serve.	[present action]
The calf *kicks* and *bellows*.	[present action]
The sun *rises* in the east.	[habitual action]
My pet tortoise *eats* tomatoes and lettuce.	[habitual action]

The *present progressive* form of the verb also shows action happening in the present or action occurring repeatedly.

| The ice *is melting* in the lemonade. | [present action] |
| We *are saving* our money to buy a houseboat. | [habitual action] |

Verbs in the *past tense* express action or a state of being that occurred in the past.

Marcie *studied* for the math test.	[past action]
The old cat *dozed* in the afternoon sunlight.	[past action]
Karen *was upset* about the party.	[past state of being]
We *were* champions for two years in a row.	[past state of being]

The *past progressive* form of the verb expresses an action in the past that was ongoing.

We *were fishing* for crawdads in the lagoon.

My mother *was working* in a law office then.

The *future tense* is formed with the helping verb *shall* or *will* added to the present form of the verb. Verbs in the future tense express an action that will occur in the future. Future tense verbs may also give orders or make predictions.

We *will hold* the next meeting three weeks from tonight.	[future action]
You *will study* harder from now on.	[order]
Little green people from space *will* soon *land* on earth.	[prediction]

The *progressive* form of the future tense also describes future action.

Next week we *will be swimming* in the Pacific.

If those dogs keep barking, the neighbors *will be calling* up.

Perfect Tenses

The three perfect tenses are the *present perfect*, the *past perfect*, and the *future perfect*.

The *present perfect tense* is formed with *has* or *have* and the past participle of the verb. Verbs in the present perfect tense may describe an action that began in the past and continued to the present.

Marcia *has had* a cold all week.

We *have wondered* what is wrong with our television.

The present perfect tense may also be used to describe an action completed at an unspecified time in the past.

Lisa *has seen* every episode of *Star Trek*.

The club members *have collected* over a thousand dollars for the Red Cross.

Like other tenses, the present perfect tense has a progressive form. The progressive form expresses an action begun in the past and continuing into the present.

My Uncle Ebenezer *has been saving* string for forty-eight years.

The girls' tennis team *has been practicing* all week.

The *past perfect tense* is formed with the helping verb *had* and the past participle. Verbs in the past perfect tense describe either an action that was completed before another action was begun or one that was completed before a certain specified time.

Linda called, but you *had left* for work.

We *had finished* our project the day before it was due.

The past perfect tense also has a progressive form. The progressive form of the past perfect tense describes an action that was ongoing in the past.

Leslie *had been mowing* the lawn when the company arrived.

The coach was angry because the players *had been missing* too many free throws.

The *future perfect tense* is formed with *will have* or *shall have* and the past participle of a verb. Verbs in the future perfect tense describe a future action that will be completed before another future action.

In December we *will have completed* work on the house.

My grandparents *will have been married* forty-five years this April.

There is a future perfect progressive form of the verb, but it is used less often than the other progressive forms.

This month Marcie *will have been dating* Tony for five years.

By the time you get this letter, we *will have been fishing* in Minnesota and will have returned home.

Conjugation of the Verb See

To *conjugate* a verb means "to show its different forms according to voice, mood, tense, number, and person."

In the following conjugation, the verb *see* is conjugated in the active voice, indicative mood. The verb is conjugated in each of the six tenses, singular and plural, as used with first, second, and third person. The progressive form of the verb in each tense is shown in *italics*. Use the conjugation as a study aid as you learn the tenses.

Principal Parts		
Present	**Past**	**Past Participle**
see	saw	seen

Present Tense				
			Progressive Form (present form of *be* + *-ing* form of verb)	
Singular	**Plural**	**Singular**	**Plural**	
I see	we see	*I am seeing*	*we are seeing*	
you see	you see	*you are seeing*	*you are seeing*	
he she it } sees	they see	he she it } *is seeing*	*they are seeing*	

Past Tense				
			Progressive Form (past form of *be* + *-ing* form of verb)	
Singular	**Plural**	**Singular**	**Plural**	
I saw	we saw	*I was seeing*	*we were seeing*	
you saw	you saw	*you were seeing*	*you were seeing*	
he she it } saw	they saw	he she it } *was seeing*	*they were seeing*	

Future Tense
(*will* or *shall* + present form of verb)

		Progressive Form (future form of *be* + *-ing* form of verb)	
Singular	*Plural*	*Singular*	*Plural*
I will see	we will see	*I will be seeing*	*we will be seeing*
you will see	you will see	*you will be seeing*	*you will be seeing*
he she } will see it	they will see	he she } *will be seeing* it	*they will be seeing*

Present Perfect Tense
(*have* or *has* + the past participle)

		Progressive Form (present perfect form of *be* + *-ing* form of verb)	
Singular	*Plural*	*Singular*	*Plural*
I have seen	we have seen	*I have been seeing*	*we have been seeing*
you have seen	you have seen	*you have been seeing*	*you have been seeing*
he she } has seen it	they have seen	he she } *has been seeing* it	*they have been seeing*

Past Perfect Tense
(*had* + past participle)

		Progressive Form (past perfect form of *be* + *ing* form of verb)	
Singular	*Plural*	*Singular*	*Plural*
I had seen	we had seen	*I had been seeing*	*we had been seeing*
you had seen	you had seen	*you had been seeing*	*you had been seeing*
he she } had seen it	they had seen	he she } *had been seeing* it	*they had been seeing*

Future Perfect Tense
(*will* [or *shall*] *have* + past participle)

		Progressive Form (future perfect form of *be* + *-ing* form of verb)	
Singular	**Plural**	**Singular**	**Plural**
I will have seen	we will have seen	*I will have been seeing*	*we will have been seeing*
you will have seen	you will have seen	*you will have been seeing*	*you will have been seeing*
he she it } will have seen	they will have seen	*he she it } will have been seeing*	*they will have been seeing*

Note: In formal English *shall* is used with the first person in future tenses.

Exercise 5: *Using Verb Tenses*

Write the following sentences, supplying the verbs in the tense indicated in parentheses. Underline the verb or verb phrases you supply.

Examples

a. My sister _____ to night school for six years and _____ in August. (*go*, present perfect; *graduate*, future)
My sister <u>has gone</u> to night school for six years and <u>will graduate</u> in August.

b. The newspaper office _____ the type for our yearbook, but another company _____ it. (*set*, past perfect; *print*, past)
The newspaper office <u>had set</u> the type for our yearbook, but another company <u>printed</u> it.

1. By the time you _____ to New York, we _____ to go home. (*get*, present; *leave*, future perfect)

2. The detectives _____ that the butler _____ the crime. (*believe*, past; *commit*, past perfect)

3. We _____ Ms. Winnetka if she _____ the French Club. (*ask,* present perfect; *sponsor,* future)

4. After we _____ Alaska, we _____ every state in the Union. (*visit,* present perfect; *see,* future perfect)

5. The Olsens _____ a complaint to the company, and the vice president herself _____ to investigate the matter. (*write,* past perfect; *come,* past)

6. In this novel a young writer _____ to a small town in Maine and _____ supernatural happenings. (*come,* present; *discover,* present)

7. The debate team _____ first place in every tournament this year; they _____ only one debate last year. (*win,* present perfect; *lose,* past perfect)

8. My sister _____ in every store in town, and she finally _____ a dress for the dance. (*look,* present perfect; *find,* present perfect)

9. Juliet _____ a sleeping potion, but Romeo _____ that she had poisoned herself. (*take,* past perfect; *believe,* past)

10. The Jackson twins _____ every scholastic award that the school _____ by graduation time. (*win,* future perfect; *give,* present)

Using the Moods of Verbs

The word *mood* in grammar refers to the speaker's attitude toward his or her statement—whether the statement is made as fact, as contrary to fact, as a wish, or as a command. In English all verbs are said to be used in one of three moods: the *indicative,* the *imperative,* or the *subjunctive.*

Statements in the *indicative mood* are statements that are expressed as facts.

Statements in the indicative mood assert that something happened, is happening, or will happen. Most of the verbs you use in speaking and writing are in the indicative mood.

The banjo *is* an instrument invented in America.

Mr. Jefferson *walks* his St. Bernard every night.

The La Flesche sisters *advocated* Indian rights.

The *imperative* mood is used to express direct commands and requests.

The imperative mood is used when a speaker or writer gives an order or makes a request. Even when the word *please* is used, the verb is still considered to be in the imperative mood.

Get out of Mr. Fudd's carrot patch right now.

Stop making that noise.

Please *do* the dishes.

Most native speakers of English have little trouble using the indicative and imperative moods. The subjunctive mood, however, may be troublesome for speakers and writers, even those who have used English all their lives.

The subjunctive mood is used to express wishes, possibilities, statements contrary to fact, and indirect commands, especially after such words as *insist, request, recommend*, and *urge*.

Most verbs show only one difference in the present tense between the indicative and subjunctive moods. This difference occurs in the forms used with *he, she, it* or a singular noun.

Indicative:	he *obeys*	she *goes*	it *stops*	Lisa *sings*
Subjunctive:	he *obey*	she *go*	it *stop*	Lisa *sing*

The third-person subjunctive form is most frequently used in stating commands or requests not addressed directly to a listener or reader.

The teacher insisted that Herb *obey*.

We urged that she *go* with us.

When my mother heard the loud music, she insisted that it *stop*.

Ms. Moffat requested that Lisa *sing* the solo in the Thanksgiving program.

In the present tense of the subjunctive, the verb *be* does not change form.

Indicative:	I *am*	you *are*	she *is*	we *are*	they *are*
Subjunctive:	I *be*	you *be*	he *be*	we *be*	they *be*

The use of *be* for the present tense of the subjunctive mood is usually encountered in only two places: older literature and rather formal statements.

> If this *be* treason, make the most of it.
>
> —Patrick Henry

> If music *be* the food of love, play on.
>
> —William Shakespeare

> I move that the amendment *be* approved.
> I ask that I *be* excused.

In the past tense the only subjunctive verb whose form differs from the indicative form is *be*. The differences occur only with *I, he, she,* and *it.*

Indicative:	I *was*	she *was*	it *was*
Subjunctive:	I *were*	he *were*	it *were*

This form of the subjunctive is often used to make statements contrary to fact or expressing a wish.

If I *were* President, I would cut taxes.	[contrary to fact]
If she *were* here, we could get this meeting started.	[contrary to fact]
I wish I *were* at the beach.	[wish]
I wish she *were* going with us.	[wish]

Exercise 6: Using the Moods of Verbs

Write each of the following sentences, supplying and underlining the appropriate form of the verb given in parentheses.

Examples

    a. _____ quiet, or please leave the theater. (*Be,* imperative)
        Be quiet, or else please leave the theater.

    b. Queen Victoria _____ monarch of England for over fifty years. (*be,* indicative)
        Queen Victoria was monarch of England for over fifty years.

1.   Steve Martin advised his audience: " _____ pompous, obese, and eat cactus." (*Be,* imperative)

2. We _____ down at the pond, fishing, when we heard the commotion. (*be*, indicative)

3. If I _____ rich, the first thing I'd buy would be a ticket to Paris. (*be*, subjunctive)

4. We requested that she _____ . (*stay*, subjunctive)

5. Debbie _____ home in the evening to study because she wants a scholarship. (*stay*, indicative)

6. When Mrs. Highwater cleans house, she zooms about as if she _____ a whirling dervish. (*be*, subjunctive)

7. My cousins insisted that my aunt _____ to school to finish her degree. (*return*, subjunctive)

8. A boomerang is a hunting stick that _____ to you if you throw it correctly. (*return*, indicative)

9. The landlord demanded that Inez _____ raising chinchillas in her apartment. (*stop*, subjunctive)

10. The entire bus rattles and shakes every time the vehicle _____ . (*stop*, indicative)

Making Verbs Agree with Subjects

A verb must agree with its subject in number. Singular subjects take a singular form of the verb; plural subjects take a plural form.

Singular	*Plural*
Pete leaves.	Pete and Stacey leave.
Cheese contains protein.	Fish and cheese contain protein.
Marcia does the dishes.	Marcia and Lance do the dishes.

With the present tense the singular form of the verb either ends in -*s* or -*es*.

The toaster works.

he works, she works

it works

that works, this works

(The verb *be* is an exception to this rule because it has two singular tense forms—*am* and *is*—as well as two past forms—*was* and *were*.)

Past and future tense verbs use the same form for both singular and plural subjects.

Past

I voted
you voted   } singular
he, she, it voted

we voted
you voted   } plural
they voted

Future

I will vote
you will vote   } singular
he, she, it will vote

we will vote
you will vote   } plural
they will vote

Agreement problems occur only when either the main verb or the helping verb of a verb phrase is in the present tense.

Singular

Sharon plays piano.

Sharon has studied four years.

Lila does not jog.

Plural

Sharon and I play piano.

Sharon and I have studied four years.

Lila and Malcolm do not jog.

The verb or verb phrase must agree with the true subject of the sentence.

Sometimes, the subject and verb of a sentence may be divided by a group of words. In such a case, special care must be taken to make the verb agree with the true subject of the sentence rather than with some intervening noun or pronoun.

One of the puppies has a patch over its eye.

[*One*, not *puppies*, is the subject of the sentence.]

The box that has the eggs in it has disappeared.

[*Box*, not *eggs*, is the subject of the sentence.]

When word order is inverted, as in questions, be sure to locate the true subject in order to make the verb agree with it in number.

Has the call of whooping cranes ever been recorded?

[*Call*, not *cranes*, is the subject.]

Where does he take his photographs to be developed?

[*He*, not *photographs*, is the subject.]

The subject also follows the verb in sentences beginning with the expletives *here* or *there*.

Here is a recipe for buttered snails.

[*Recipe* is the subject, not *here*.]

There were old license plates nailed to the garage wall.

[*License plates*, not *there*, is the subject.]

There was an exhibit of Zuñi silverwork at the museum.

[*Exhibit*, not *there*, is the subject of the sentence.]

Exercise 7: *Making Verbs Agree with Subjects*

Write the following sentences, choosing the verbs that agree with the subjects from the pairs of verbs given in parentheses. Underline each subject once and each verb or verb phrase twice.

Example

a. The technology of printing presses _____ advanced greatly in recent years. (has, have)

The technology of printing presses has advanced greatly in recent years.

1. Only one of the file cabinets _____ saved from the fire. (was, were)

2. Where _____ the San Andreas Fault? (is, are)

3. There _____ several good reasons why you should wear a seat belt while driving. (is, are)

4. That set of folk songs _____ recorded by Odetta. (was, were)

5. There _____ some people known as the Dogon tribe who have a surprising knowledge of modern astronomy. (is, are)

6. The stories written by Rudyard Kipling about India _____ a special place in my mother's library. (has, have)

7. Several types of exotic food _____ available at the new restaurant. (is, are)

8. Where _____ frogs, toads, and salamanders go in the winter? (do, does)

9. The books of Maya Angelou _____ exceptionally well-written. (is, are)

10. The presence of sharks _____ only one of the many reasons why I don't like swimming in the ocean. (is, are)

Subject-Verb Agreement with Indefinite Pronouns

A group of words known as the *indefinite pronouns* may cause speakers and writers some difficulty in subject-verb agreement. The following indefinite pronouns are always singular and take the singular form of the verb.

anybody	everybody	no one
anyone	everyone	one
each	neither	somebody
either	nobody	someone

Anybody who needs a library pass can get one from Miss Garcia.

Each of the twins has her own distinct set of likes and dislikes.

Somebody among the students is clicking a ballpoint pen.

Five indefinite pronouns are always plural and take the plural form of the verb.

both	many	several
few	others	

Several of my ancestors are Choctaw Indians.

Few of the old Model T Fords are left.

Many are called, but few are chosen.

The last five indefinite pronouns may be either singular or plural, depending on how they are used in a sentence.

all   most   some
any   none

This is the *only* situation in which a group of words coming between a subject and verb may determine the correct form of the verb. When these indefinite pronouns refer to a singular noun, they take the singular form of the verb.

All of the meatloaf has been eaten.

[*All* refers to the noun *meatloaf*, which is singular.]

Most of the flood damage was minor.

[*Most* refers to the noun *damage*, which is singular.]

None of the milk is left.

[*None* refers to the noun *milk*, which is singular.]

When these five indefinite pronouns refer to a plural noun, they take the plural form of the verb.

All of the aces were gone from the deck.

[*All* refers to the noun *aces*, which is plural.]

Most of the tomato plants were ruined by the hail.

[*Most* refers to the noun *tomato plants*, which is plural.]

None of the people named Jones were related to one another.

[*None* refers to the noun *people*, which is plural.]

Exercise 8: Making Verbs Agree with Indefinite Pronouns

Write each of the sentences on the next page, choosing the correct form of the verb from the pair given in parentheses. Underline the subject once and the verb or verb phrase in each sentence twice.

Examples

a. Neither of the girls (was, were) able to come to the party.
   Neither of the girls was able to come to the party.

b. Most of the book (move, moves) quickly, but the ending (seem, seems) slow.
Most of the book <u>moves</u> quickly, but the <u>ending</u> <u>seems</u> slow.

1. Either of those parking places (is, are) all right for you to use during the weekend.

2. Some of the students (was, were) taking the advanced test.

3. Both my sister and my cousin Coretta (is, are) going to the art museum on Saturdays for drawing lessons.

4. Each of the suspects (was, were) capable of the crime, and each of them had an excellent motive.

5. Someone in those lines of marching players (is, are) quite out of tune with the rest of the band.

6. Looking for a midnight snack, I discovered all the milk (was, were) gone, and most of the bagels (was, were) eaten.

7. Any of the ponds (seems, seem) good for fishing around here, but most of the river (yield, yields) few catches at this time of year.

8. Nobody among the students in the classes (know, knows) the answer to that problem.

9. None of the critics (like, likes) the movie, but all of the public (enjoy, enjoys) it nevertheless.

10. Both of the farms (cost, costs) a great deal, but one of them (seem, seems) an excellent buy.

Subject-Verb Agreement with Compound Subjects

Two or more subjects joined by the word *and* always take the plural form of the verb.

<u>Clea</u> and <u>Erin</u> <u>are</u> the outstanding students in science.

The <u>sleet</u> and <u>snow</u> <u>make</u> the roads hazardous tonight.

<u>Mrs. Washington</u> and <u>Miss Garcia</u> <u>were</u> both officers in the League of Women Voters.

Roses and raspberries are members of the same plant family.

Jackals and wolves are the ancestors of the modern dog.

When two or more singular subjects are joined by the words *or* or *nor*, the singular form of the verb is used.

Either Clea or Erin is the lab assistant.

Sleet or snow makes the mountain pass dangerous.

Neither Mrs. Washington nor Miss Garcia was in charge.

When two or more plural subjects are joined by *or* or *nor*, the plural form of the verb is used.

Lizards or turtles are good pets for apartment dwellers.

Either bees or wasps seem to be living in the old barn.

Neither trains nor planes have as many accidents as automobiles.

When one part of a compound subject is plural and one part is singular, and the subjects are joined by *or* or *nor*, the verb agrees with the subject closest to it.

Either cheese or nuts are a good source of protein.

Either nuts or cheese is a good source of protein.

Neither I nor my brother likes rhubarb.

Neither my brother nor I like rhubarb.

Either you or Sharon still has the car keys.

Either Sharon or you still have the car keys.

Exercise 9: *Making Verbs Agree with Compound Subjects*

Each of the sentences on the next page contains a compound subject. Write the sentences and choose the correct verbs from the pairs given in parentheses. Then underline each subject once and each complete verb or verb phrase twice.

Examples

a. Both the monkeys and the parrot (screech, screeches) when the door to the pet shop is opened.
Both the <u>monkeys</u> and the <u>parrot</u> <u>screech</u> when the door to the pet shop is opened.

b. Neither Cindy nor her sisters (attend, attends) public schools.
Neither <u>Cindy</u> nor her <u>sisters</u> <u>attend</u> public schools.

1. The chickens and the rooster (is, are) huddled on their perches in the dark henhouse.

2. Neither the ivy nor the ferns (need, needs) much sunlight.

3. Either the students or the teacher (was, were) confused about what the assignment had been.

4. Tusks, warts, and bristly hair (distinguish, distinguishes) the wild swine called the wart hog.

5. Either the Lin sisters or Tom (is, are) going to design stage sets.

6. Mrs. Hubbard and her daughters (was, were) horrified to discover that four baby skunks had taken up residence under their porch.

7. The moon and planets (shine, shines) with light reflected from the sun.

8. Neither my parents nor I (am, are) happy about our move.

9. Either the camera's shutter or batteries (is, are) not working.

10. Neither my brothers, my sisters, I, nor the family dog (like, likes) the woodchuck casserole Uncle Elliot made.

Some Common Problems in Subject-Verb Agreement

Collective Nouns

Words such as *committee, team, crowd, class, audience,* and *group* are called *collective nouns* because they name a collection, or group, of persons or things. Collective nouns may be either singular or plural in meaning.

When a collective noun is used to describe a unit acting together, the noun has a singular meaning and takes the singular form of the verb.

The band practices on the football field every morning.

The jury agrees unanimously.

When the collective noun refers to the individual members of the group, the plural form of the verb is used.

The band were wearing plumed hats and white boots.

The jury disagree among themselves and with the judge.

Singular Nouns with Apparently Plural Forms

Use the singular form of the verb with nouns that are singular in meaning even though their form appears to be plural.

athletics	genetics	news
civics	mathematics	physics
economics	measles	politics

No news is good news.

Nouns that have only plural forms take only plural verbs. Some nouns have no singular forms:

jeans	pants	slacks	tweezers
pliers	scissors	trousers	

The pliers were old and rusty and badly in need of oil.

If the word *pair* precedes one of these nouns, however, use the singular form of the verb.

The pair of pliers is missing.

This pair of jeans has seen better days.

Titles and Names of Countries

Use the singular form of the verb for titles of works of art or for the names of countries.

Bolts of Melody is a collection of poems by Emily Dickinson.

The Union of Soviet Socialist Republics contains the vast area known as Siberia.

Amounts

Use a singular form of the verb for words and phrases that express time and amounts (money, fractions, weight, volume).

Two quarts is approximately the same as two liters.

Three-quarters is equal to 75 percent.

When such amounts are thought of individually and not as a unit, the plural form of the verb may be used.

The last three days have been dreary because of the rain.

Eleven dollars were hidden between the pages of the book.

Predicate Nominatives

When the subject and the predicate nominative are different in number, use a verb that agrees in number with the subject.

Leon's most prized treasure is his rare coins.

[*Coins* is the predicate nominative.]

Maintenance and repairs are the duty of the janitor.

[*Duty* is the predicate nominative.]

Every *and* Many a

Use the singular form of the verb when the words *every* or *many a* precede the subject.

Every student knows about pre-final jitters.

Many a person has suffered the pangs of love.

Every nook and cranny was investigated.

Doesn't *and* Don't

Use *doesn't* with singular nouns and third-person singular pronouns. Use *don't* with plural nouns and pronouns and with the pronouns *I* and *you*.

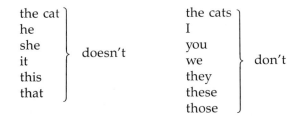

Exercise 10: *Making Verbs Agree with Subjects*

Write the following sentences, choosing the form of the verb that agrees with the subject. Underline the subject once and the verb you have chosen twice.

_____ *Examples* _____

a. The Oakton High School girls' basketball team (was, were) the state champion last year.
   The Oakton High School girls' basketball team was the state champion last year.

b. The United States (has, have) serious energy problems that need solving.
   The United States has serious energy problems that need solving.

1. Physics (offers, offer) the scientist many paradoxes.

2. The soccer team (has, have) a chance to play in the district tournament.

3. The majority of taxpayers (want, wants) lower taxes and simpler tax forms.

4. One-fourth of a dollar (is, are) the equivalent of twenty-five cents.

5. Many a mountaineer (has faced, have faced) the challenge of Everest, and every climber and guide (has faced, have faced) hardships on its cold steeps.

6. I (don't, doesn't) want to go; you (don't, doesn't) want to go; she (don't, doesn't) want to go; so it (don't, doesn't) seem we ought to go.

7. The audience always (listen, listens) appreciatively when the choir (sing, sings).

8. The scissors (is, are) lost; the pliers (is, are) misplaced; and the only pair of tweezers (have, has) disappeared.

9. *The Frogs* (is, are) a play by Aristophanes; *Seven Against Thebes* (is, are) a play by Aeschylus.

10. Three hours (is, are) the usual time it takes to fly to Chicago from here, but four hours (is, are) not unusual if there is fog or turbulence.

Using the Verb Be

Be is the most irregular verb in English. It has three present tense forms and two past tense forms. Since *be* is also the most commonly used verb, it is important that you learn to use it in accordance with Edited Standard English (ESE).

Present Tense

Singular	Plural
I am	we are
you are	you are
he/she/it is	they are

Notice that the word *be* itself is not listed as a present tense form. Although it is used in some spoken dialects, it is not used in Edited Standard English. (An asterisk (*) indicates a sentence with a feature that is not part of ESE.)

*I be sorry to hear that.
I *am* sorry to hear that.

*You be right about that problem.
You *are* right about that problem.

*She be asleep right now.
She *is* asleep right now.

Past Tense

Singular	Plural
I was	we were
you were	you were
he/she/it was	they were

Avoid using *was* with the pronouns *you*, *we*, and *they*, or with plural nouns.

*You was a member of the rifle team, wasn't you?
You *were* a member of the rifle team, *weren't* you?

*We was in a hurry when we left.
We *were* in a hurry when we left.

*They was anxious to start the game.
They *were* anxious to start the game.

*Weevils was in the cotton.
Weevils *were* in the cotton.

The past participle of *be* is *been*, which is used with a helping verb in Edited Standard English.

*I been sick.
I *have been* sick. [or] I've *been* sick.

Exercise 11: Using the Verb Be

Rewrite each of the following sentences, choosing the form of the verb in parentheses that is used in Edited Standard English. Underline the verb you select.

Examples

a. You (been, have been) rather cool toward Cheryl lately.
You have been rather cool toward Cheryl lately.

b. The Platters and The Supremes (was, were) two popular recording groups.
The Platters and The Supremes were two popular recording groups.

1. Someone (been, has been) telephoning for you all afternoon.

2. The Sioux, Cheyenne, and Pawnee (was, were) all tribes of the Great Plains.

3. "The Great Bear" (be, is) another name for the constellation usually called "The Big Dipper."

4. We (was, were) late, but you (was, were), too.

5. Arturo (been, has been) to California several times and says his trips (was, were) all pleasant.

6. I (be, am) sleepy today because all last night two cats (was, were) yowling beneath my window.

7. You (is, are) sure that they (was, were) invited, aren't you?

8. (Wasn't, Weren't) the Yankees the winners of the Series in 1978, and (wasn't, weren't) there some dissension on the team?

9. The cars (was, were) bigger in the 1950s because the gasoline prices (wasn't, weren't) so high.

10. The McCoys (be, are) our neighbors, and the Hatfields (was, were) our neighbors before.

Verbs That Are Frequently Confused

Three pairs of verbs—*lie/lay*, *sit/set*, and *rise/raise*—are frequently confused because they sound alike and have similar meanings. These verbs, however, are not interchangeable.

Lie and *lay* are probably the most confusing pair of verbs because they not only have similar meanings, but also share a common form.

Present	Past	Past Participle
lie	lay	(had) lain
lay	laid	(had) laid

Notice that the word *lay* is the present form of the verb *lay*, but is also the past form of the verb *lie*.

For more information on transitive and intransitive verbs, see pages 472-473.

Lie means "to recline" or "to be in a horizontal position." *Lie* is always intransitive. *Lay* means "to put something down" or "to place something." *Lay* is always transitive.

When you use the verb *lay*, tell what object is being put down or placed.

Hens *lay* eggs.

Masons *lay* bricks.

Each night we *lay* out our clothes for the next morning.

If you are confused about whether to use a form of *lay* or *lie* in a sentence, decide precisely what you are trying to say. If you can substitute the word *put* in the sentence, use the verb *lay*.

Lay: Marcia *laid* (put) her books on the table.
Darrin *had laid* (had put) out the cards for a game of solitaire.

Lie: The cow *lay* in the deep meadow grass.
The dollar bill *had lain* near the sidewalk all day.

In some dialects *set* means "sit down." In Edited Standard English, however, *sit* and *set* have distinctly different meanings.

Sit means "to occupy a seat" or "to rest." *Sit* is usually intransitive. *Set* means "to put down or place something." *Set* is usually transitive.

When you use *set* in a sentence, tell what object is being placed or put somewhere.

Present	Past	Past Participle
sit	sat	(had) sat
set	set	(had) set

Sit: The houses *sit* on a crest overlooking the river.
The cockatoo *sat* on its perch.

Set: Dawn *set* down her packages.
I thought I *had set* my book on the hall table.

Rise means "to go up" or "to get up." *Rise* is always intransitive. *Raise* means "to move something upward." *Raise* is always transitive.

The principal parts of *rise* are irregular, but the principal parts of *raise* are regular.

Present	Past	Past Participle
rise	rose	(had) risen
raise	raised	(had) raised

Rise: The audience *rose* to its feet, cheering.
Farmers *rise* early in the morning to begin their chores.

Raise: The scouts *raised* the flag at the Memorial Day ceremony.
The cobra *had raised* its body and begun to sway.

Exercise 12: Choosing the Correct Form of Frequently Confused Verbs

Choose the correct verb in parentheses to complete each of the following sentences. Write the sentences and underline the verb that you supply.

Examples

a. Ginger (lay, laid) out in the sun on her beach towel.
   Ginger <u>lay</u> out in the sun on her beach towel.

b. Ira Hayes was one of the men who (rose, raised) the flag on Iwo Jima.
   Ira Hayes was one of the men who <u>raised</u> the flag on Iwo Jima.

1. Alex didn't feel well, so he (lay, laid) down.

2. A huge copper-colored harvest moon (rose, raised) in the sky.

3. Marcia (had set, had sat) the basket too near the edge of the table.

4. Please (sit, set) down and fill out these forms.

5. My Aunt Consuela (had risen, had raised) early for the trip.

6. Doris couldn't remember where she (had lain, had laid) her glasses.

7. For centuries the pirate treasure (had lain, had laid) on the bottom of the sea.

8. The smoke from the signal fire (rose, raised) high above the trees.

9. We (have sat, have set) in this bus so long it seems like forever.

10. The setter (lay, laid) down the pheasant, then (lay, laid) by its master's feet.

Review: Using Verbs

Write each of the following sentences, choosing the form of the verb in parentheses that agrees with the subject. Underline the word you have chosen.

Examples

a. Sheila (don't, doesn't) like to play outfield.
Sheila <u>doesn't</u> like to play outfield.

b. Eleven days (is, are) slightly less than 1 million seconds.
Eleven days <u>is</u> slightly less than 1 million seconds.

1. The elephant (don't, doesn't) fear mice as the stories say.

2. Fifty-two playing cards (is, are) the number in an ordinary deck.

3. Both Phillis Wheatley and Anne Bradstreet (was, were) early American poets.

4. A carton containing boxes of seeds (was, were) left at the post office.

5. All of the breads (was, were) baked too long.

6. None of the flood water (has reached, have reached) our area.

7. Neither Rosa nor Kim (have seen, has seen) the final psychology scores.

8. A swarm of locusts (was, were) one of the Biblical plagues.

9. Everybody in all of the city's volunteer groups (was, were) eager to help.

10. Either the pliers or the tweezers (is, are) necessary for this type of job.

11. A pair of scissors (is, are) in the desk drawer.

12. Neither Shana nor her sisters (like, likes) sharing a room.

13. Either Miss Wallabee, Mr. Diaz, or the Johnson twins (is, are) going to be in charge of selling tickets.

14. Only a few of the team (was, were) graduating that spring.

15. As the gates are opened, the crowd (surge, surges) forward.

16. None of the lost treasure (has, have) ever been located.

17. None of the lost diamonds (has, have) ever been located.

18. After their boat tipped over, Nancy's jeans (was, were) wringing wet, and Pat's pair of shorts (was, were) ruined.

19. Either mayonnaise or yogurt (is, are) necessary for this recipe.

20. We (did, done) what we could for the wounded eagle; then a team of veterinarians (was, were) called in.

Writing Focus: *Using Vivid Verbs in Writing*

By choosing vivid verbs, you can make your writing come alive. In an article in *Writer's Digest*, written by Bill Kirtz, the historian Barbara Tuchman describes the effect that well-chosen verbs can have on a piece of writing: "I hate sentences that begin, 'There was a storm!' Instead, write 'A storm burst!'"

Limp, vague verbs result in limp, vague writing:

There *was* the sound of thunder.	[vague]
Thunder *mumbled* and *rumbled*.	[stronger]
The dog *came* down the street.	[vague]
The dog *bounded* down the street.	[stronger]
Leslie *looked* displeased.	[vague]
Leslie *frowned* and *wrinkled* her nose in distaste.	[stronger]

Assignment: *The United States One Hundred Years from Now*

What do you think the United States will be like in one hundred years? What will be changed and how? Will some things remain unchanged? What great advances will have been made? What will be the biggest problem? Discuss these questions in class.

After your class discussion, write two paragraphs describing America in one hundred years. Your classmates are your audience, and your purpose is to describe America in the future. Your writing will be evaluated for correct and effective use of verbs.

Use the following steps to complete this assignment.

A. Prewriting

Use clustering, described in Chapter 1, to get your ideas down on paper. Work with the ideas discussed in class and any other ideas that you have. For help in organizing your paragraph, review Chapter 3.

B. Writing

Using your word cluster, write a two-paragraph description of America 100 years from now. Provide enough specific details, using vivid verbs, to make your description interesting to your readers. As you write, be certain to use the correct form for each verb.

C. Postwriting

Revise your first draft, using the following checklist.

1. Does each paragraph have a clear topic sentence?

2. Are the ideas presented in a logical order?

3. Did I include enough specific details?

4. Did I use vivid verbs that convey exactly what I mean?

5. Is each verb in the proper tense, and does it agree in number with its subject?

Proofread your revision, using the Checklist for Proofreading at the back of the book. Share your writing with your classmates to learn about one another's expectations for the future.

14 Adjectives

Understanding Adjectives

Adjectives allow writers to describe colors, tastes, shapes, sizes, and a multitude of other qualities; they can add important details to a sentence. In this section you will learn how to identify adjectives through their definition, the classes into which they can be grouped, and the features that distinguish them from other parts of speech.

Defining an Adjective

An *adjective* is usually defined as a word used to modify a noun or pronoun.

Adjectives limit or qualify nouns or pronouns by telling *what kind*, *which one*, *how many*, or *how much*.

What Kind:	an *old* car, a *brick* building, a *heavy* package, a *red* rose
Which One:	*this* street, *that* boat, *these* plants, *those* books
How Many:	*three* cats, *ninety* years, *many* insects, *few* dollars
How Much:	*little* time, *more* intelligence, *less* gasoline

Exercise 1: Identifying Adjectives

Write the following sentences, underlining the adjectives. (*A*, *an*, and *the* are always adjectives.) Do not count the possessive pronouns, such as *mine*, *our*, *his*, as adjectives; they are considered pronouns.

Example

a. The hottest temperature on record occurred in the African country of Libya.

The hottest temperature on record occurred in the African country of Libya.

1. During the American Revolution many brides wore red gowns as a symbol of political rebellion.

2. The first nation to give women the right to vote was New Zealand, a member of the British Empire.

3. A French astronomer suggested the existence of black holes two centuries ago.

4. Handsome Dan is a bulldog, the famous canine mascot of Yale.

5. The first Congressional Medals of Honor were given to Union soldiers who hijacked a Confederate locomotive.

6. A memorial statue was erected to Balto, the lead dog of a team of huskies that braved a savage blizzard to deliver serum to fight a deadly epidemic among Alaskan Eskimos.

7. In the nineteenth century few people realized that a shy, reclusive woman, Emily Dickinson, would become a famous poet.

8. Pamela, a poor but virtuous servant, was the heroine of the first English novel, a great popular success.

9. "Blooper" is the name of a gold statuette presented to broadcasters that make the best—or worst—mistakes on the air.

10. The seven wonders of the ancient world included the Egyptian pyramids and the gigantic statue known as the Colossus of Rhodes.

Classifying Adjectives

Although many common adjectives (such as *hot, cold, happy, sad*) belong to no special class, others can be classified as articles, proper adjectives, predicate adjectives, pronouns used as adjectives, or nouns used as adjectives.

Articles

The most common adjectives are the articles *a, an,* and *the.*

A and *an* are called *indefinite articles* because they do not point out a definite person, place, or thing. *The* is called a *definite article* because it points out a specific person, place, or thing.

Indefinite Article: We'll have to take *a* bus.

Definite Article: Here comes *the* bus.

Indefinite Article: *An* aardwolf is not really a wolf.

Definite Article: *The* aardwolf at the zoo is named Aaron.

A is used before words that begin with a consonant sound; *an* is used before words that begin with a vowel sound.

a busy schedule	*an* impossible task
a rugby team	*an* airline attendant
a history exam	*an* honest answer

Proper Adjectives

Adjectives formed from proper nouns are called *proper adjectives.* A proper adjective begins with a capital letter.

Mexican artists	Chinese checkers
Ethiopian history	Guatemalan Indians
Korean restaurant	South African novelist

Predicate Adjectives

Adjectives usually precede the nouns they modify.

Sasha is an *extraordinary* and *beautiful* animal.

Some adjectives, however, are separated from the words they modify. An adjective that follows a linking verb and modifies the subject of the sentence is called a *predicate adjective.*

The table was *dusty.*

The hiking boots were too *tight.*

The cat seemed *nervous.*

Pronouns as Adjectives

Some words may function as either pronouns or adjectives, depending on how they are used in a sentence. The following words are adjectives when they modify a noun or pronoun. When they stand alone, however, they are considered pronouns.

all	few	one	this
another	many	other	those
any	more	several	what
both	most	some	which
each	much	that	
either	neither	these	

Pronoun:	*Which* was correct?
Adjective:	*Which* one was correct?
Pronoun:	A *few* of the boats were damaged by the storm.
Adjective:	A *few* boats were damaged by the storm.
Pronoun:	Tomorrow we'll pick *more* of the raspberries.
Adjective:	Tomorrow we'll pick *more* raspberries.

Nouns Used as Adjectives

A noun that modifies another noun is considered an adjective. Nouns used as adjectives always come directly before the nouns they modify.

> I hate hoeing the *vegetable* garden.
>
> Did you see the *hockey* game last *Friday* night?
>
> There are some *news* magazines on the top *closet* shelf.

Nouns used as adjectives can be easily confused with compound nouns that are written as two separate words. In the phrase *closet shelf,* for example, *closet* (a noun) modifies *shelf: closet shelf. Closet drama,* however, is a compound noun meaning "a play written mainly to be read, not staged." If you are uncertain about the classification of a word, consult a dictionary where you will find compound nouns listed as separate entries.

Exercise 2: Identifying Classes of Adjectives

On a sheet of paper, write the following sentences, underlining the adjectives. Beneath each sentence identify the class to which each adjective belongs. You will also find adjectives that belong to none of these classes. (Do not count possessive pronouns as adjectives.)

Example

---

a. Charles Fort was a newspaper reporter who liked to collect accounts of strange events that science could not explain.

Charles Fort was <u>a</u> <u>newspaper</u> reporter who liked to collect accounts of <u>strange</u> events that science could not explain.

a—article; newspaper—noun used as adjective; strange—adjective

1. Fort's relentless research and his wry wit attracted a number of followers.

2. Many Fortean Societies now exist, and events that science cannot explain are called "Fortean phenomena."

3. Such phenomena are numerous; some are comic, but others seem spooky and sinister.

4. Examples include such bizarre events as falls of red, blue, and black rains; Roman coins found in American Indian mounds; and sworn testimonies that large numbers of fully grown frogs have fallen out of an empty sky.

5. Some of Fort's theories were wild; he suggested, for instance, that certain animals were capable of traveling by mind power alone and crossing vast spaces in short periods of time.

6. This theory seemed sensible to Fort because it explained apparently unexplainable facts such as crocodiles that appeared suddenly in English gardens and the mysterious presence of swarms of adult African snails in Ceylon.

7. Many of Fort's findings read like science fiction; but his work, he claimed, was factual.

8. Some theories he proposed were fantastic, and a few were most certainly jokes, for Fort was a humorous man; nevertheless, he was serious about his main theory: modern science tends to ignore unexplainable phenomena.

9. Fort has been dead for fifty years now, but a large and strong American Fortean Society still exists and still investigates those unexplained events that Fort loved to fling in the face of science.

10. The society publishes a news and opinion magazine and collects data on such matters as sea serpents, the abominable snowman, flying saucer reports, and animal oddities.

Finding an Adjective by Its Features

Adjectives can be identified by certain features that distinguish them from other parts of speech.

Adjectives may change form to show degrees of comparison.

There are three degrees: *positive, comparative,* and *superlative.* The *positive degree* describes a quality or characteristic; it is the "plain form" of the adjective. The *comparative degree* is used to compare two persons or things. The *superlative degree* is used to compare three or more persons or things.

Positive:	Lisa is *tall.*
Comparative:	Lisa is *taller* than Sharon.
Superlative:	Lisa is the *tallest* member of the basketball team.

Positive:	This novel is *suspenseful.*
Comparative:	This novel is *more suspenseful* than the last one I read.
Superlative:	This novel is the *most suspenseful* one that I've ever read.

The comparative and superlative forms of adjectives are formed in two different ways.

Most adjectives of one syllable, and a few adjectives of two syllables, add *-er* to form the comparative degree and *-est* to form the superlative degree.

Positive	*Comparative*	*Superlative*
large	larger	largest
hot	hotter	hottest
kind	kinder	kindest
heavy	heavier	heaviest

Many adjectives of two syllables, and all adjectives of more than two syllables, form the comparative degree with the word *more* and the superlative with the word *most.*

Positive	*Comparative*	*Superlative*
bashful	more bashful	most bashful
essential	more essential	most essential
abundant	more abundant	most abundant

The words *less* and *least* are used before all adjectives to indicate less or least of a quality.

Positive	*Comparative*	*Superlative*
high	less high	least high
necessary	less necessary	least necessary

403

A few common adjectives form their comparative and superlative degrees irregularly.

Adjectives may follow intensifiers.

Words like *extremely, quite, rather,* and *very* are called intensifiers. They qualify the word that follows by telling "to what extent."

The job was *very* demanding.

The play was *quite* good.

The music was *rather* loud.

Adjectives may be formed with suffixes.

Certain suffixes, such as *-able, -en, -ful, -ish, -less, -like,* and *-ous,* are used to form adjectives. These suffixes signal that the word is an adjective.

dutiful	wooden	selfish
capable	industrious	penniless
lifelike	usable	mysterious

Exercise 3: Identifying Adjectives

Use your knowledge of adjectives to identify all the adjectives in the following passage from the short story "The New Dress" by Virginia Woolf. (Remember to count the articles *the, a,* and *an.*) Write at least twenty-five adjectives on a sheet of paper in the order in which they appear.

"I feel like some dowdy, decrepit, horribly dingy old fly," she said, making Robert Haydon stop just to hear her say that, just to reassure herself by furbishing up a poor, weak-kneed phrase and so showing how detached she was, how witty, that she did not feel in the least out of anything. And, of course, Robert Haydon answered something quite polite, quite insincere, which she saw through instantly, and said to herself, directly he went (again from some book), "Lies, lies, lies!" For a party makes things either much more real or much less real, she thought; she saw in a flash to the bottom of Robert Haydon's heart; she saw through everything. She saw the truth. This was true, this drawing room, this self, and the other false. Miss Milan's little workroom was really terribly hot, stuffy, sordid. It smelled of clothes and cabbage cooking; and yet, when Miss Milan put the glass in her hand, and she looked at herself with the dress on, finished, an extraordinary bliss shot through her heart.[1]

Review: *Understanding Adjectives*

Write the following paragraphs from a condensed version of *Broca's Brain* by Carl Sagan and underline at least forty-five adjectives. To determine if a word is an adjective, ask yourself whether it modifies a noun or a pronoun or whether it has any of the features of adjectives. Be sure to classify as adjectives any nouns or pronouns that modify nouns. In this selection Carl Sagan discusses the popular interest in unexplained phenomena such as the Bermuda Triangle, UFO's, and ancient astronauts.

The extraordinary should certainly be pursued; but extraordinary claims require extraordinary evidence—the burden of proof should fall squarely on those who make the proposals. In the meantime, the best antidote for pseudoscience lies, I believe, in the documented wonders of science itself:

—There is an African freshwater fish that is nearly blind. It generates an electric field that enables it to distinguish between predators and prey and communicates in a fairly elaborate electric language with other fish of the same species. This involves an organ system and sensory capability unknown to pretechnological human beings.

—Pigeons are now found to have a remarkable sensitivity to magnetism, evidently using this sensory capability for navigation and to sense their surroundings—a sensory modality never glimpsed by any human.

—Quasars seem to be violent galactic explosions that destroy millions of worlds, many of them perhaps inhabited. . . .

Such a list could be continued almost indefinitely. I believe that this smattering of findings in modern science is far more compelling and exciting than most of the doctrines of pseudoscience. Science is more intricate and subtle, reveals a much richer universe and powerfully evokes our sense of wonder. And it has the additional and important virtue of being true.[2]

---

[1]From "The New Dress" in *A Haunted House and Other Stories* by Virginia Woolf. Reprinted by permission of Harcourt Brace Jovanovich, Inc., the Literary Estate of Virginia Woolf and The Hogarth Press Ltd.

[2]Excerpt from "Astral Projection and the Horse Could Count" by Carl Sagan condensed in *Reader's Digest*, July 1979 from *Broca's Brain*. Copyright © 1979 by Carl Sagan. Reprinted by permission of Random House, Inc. and The Reader's Digest.

Applying What You Know

Select two or three advertisements from your local newspapers or from magazines. Clip out the ads and tape them to a sheet of paper. Then beneath each ad list the adjectives used to describe the product or service. Finally, look at your lists of adjectives and decide why those particular ones were selected for that audience. For example, if the ad is for nail polish, do the words give the ad a different tone from that of a car advertisement? To what audience is each ad directed? In what way are the adjectives suitable for that audience?

Using Adjectives

In this section you will practice using both regular and irregular forms of comparative and superlative adjectives.

Using Comparative and Superlative Degrees

When comparing only two things, use the comparative degree.

The kodiak bear is *larger* than the black bear.

This bicycle is *more expensive* than that one.

When comparing three or more things, use the superlative degree.

The kodiak bear is the *largest* of all bears.

This bicycle is the *most expensive* one in the shop.

Use the words *other* or *else* when comparing a person or thing with the rest of a group to which it belongs.

An asterisk (*) indicates a sentence with a feature that is not a part of Edited Standard English (ESE).

*Jupiter is larger than any planet in our solar system.
Jupiter is larger than any *other* planet in our solar system.

> *Chrissy is a better athlete than anyone in her school.
> Chrissy is a better athlete than anyone *else* in her school.

Avoid double comparisons in Edited Standard English. Do not use the *-er* or *-est* suffix with the words *more* or *most*.

> *I bought the most ugliest mask in the store.
> I bought the *ugliest* mask in the store.

> *Lon is feeling more better today.
> Lon is feeling *better* today.

Exercise 4: Using Comparative and Superlative Degrees

In some of the following sentences, adjectives are used in ways that do not conform to Edited Standard English. If a sentence has a feature that is not part of ESE, rewrite it so that it conforms to ESE. If a sentence is already in ESE, write *ESE* next to that number on your paper.

Examples

> a. Which of these four brands is more economical?
>   Which of these four brands is most economical?

> b. That reporter talks faster than anyone else on television.
>   ESE

1. Mo is a more smarter dog than Sophie.

2. Rhode Island is smaller than any state in the Union.

3. The cobra is one of the most deadliest snakes in the world.

4. We decided to sell the oldest of the two cars.

5. The house was more larger than we had expected.

6. Ross' poem was judged the best of the one hundred entries.

7. It is hard to say which of the three Brontë sisters was more remarkable.

8. Chico is the twin who is most outgoing.

9. Lucille Ball had a longer career than any comedienne on television.

10. Of all sports which is most safest?

Using Irregular Adjectives

Most adjectives form their comparative and superlative degrees either with the suffixes *-er* and *-est* or with the words *more* and *most*. A few common adjectives, however, have irregular comparative and superlative forms. To write Edited Standard English, you must memorize these forms.

Positive	Comparative	Superlative
bad	worse	worst
good	better	best
ill	worse	worst
little	less *or* lesser	least
many	more	most
much	more	most
well	better	best

I have *little* time and *less* money.

Married couples vow to take one another for *better* or *worse*.

Exercise 5: Using Irregular Adjectives

Write the following sentences, using either the comparative or superlative degree of the adjective in parentheses. Underline your choice.

Example

a. In 1980 Texas experienced the (bad) heat wave in recent history.

   In 1980 Texas experienced the <u>worst</u> heat wave in recent history.

1. Statistics show that (much) energy is consumed by industry than by citizens.

2. Booker T. Washington founded Tuskegee Institute so that black students could prepare themselves for (good) jobs than those available to them without education.

3. Sugar and honey are both sweeteners, but many people believe that honey is much (good) for your health.

4. Many people with allergies find pollen is their (bad) enemy.

5. Which has (few) calories—carrots or celery?

6. Sea travel makes me ill, and air travel makes me even (ill).

7. (Many) dogs are brown-eyed, but a few breeds have blue eyes.

8. Yesterday Carla didn't feel well, but today she is much (well).

9. Soybeans are much (little) expensive than meat and an excellent source of protein.

10. Many American rivers are treacherous, but the one that presents the (many) dangers is the Missouri.

Review: Using Adjectives

In some of the following sentences adjectives are used in ways that do not conform to Edited Standard English. Rewrite these sentences, bringing them into conformity. If adjective use follows ESE in a sentence, write *ESE* next to that number on your paper. Underline any changes you make.

Example

a. We looked over the two tents carefully and bought the one that was most durable.
We looked over the two tents carefully and bought the one that was more durable.

1. Of all the girls on the swimming team, Juanita has the more endurance.

2. Hydrogen is more common than any element.

3. For some reason the common cold is more commoner among well-educated people.

4. The beautiful Mata Hari was the more famous of all spies during World War I.

5. Franklin D. Roosevelt served a longer term than any U.S. President.

6. Wild strawberries bear littler fruit than domestic strawberries.

7. The effects of smoking are more bad on the heart than on the lungs.

8. One of the most important figures in the early exploration of America was the Indian guide Sacajawea.

9. Insects are the more numerous species on earth.

10. The women of North Dakota have the most high life expectancy in the United States—slightly over eighty years.

11. Catherine the Great was certainly the more colorful of all the Russian empresses.

12. Broiling, baking, or frying—which is the better way to cook meat and retain the natural vitamins?

13. The Atacama Desert in Chile is drier than any desert in the world.

14. At twilight our radio reception gets worser and worser.

15. The injured race horse was not completely well, but it was weller than it had been.

Writing Focus: *Using Fresh Adjectives in Writing*

Adjectives can add important specific details that make descriptions spring to life. A lack of adjectives may result in writing that gives few details of sight, smell, sound, taste, and touch. However, using too many adjectives or such overworked adjectives as *great, nice, cute,* or *fantastic* can be equally damaging. As a rule, avoid long strings of adjectives as well as vague and overused adjectives. Try to use specific, fresh adjectives to say exactly what you mean.

Assignment: *Inventing an Extraterrestrial Being*

Science fiction writers delight in creating beings from other planets. Imagine yourself as a science fiction writer and create a new kind of extraterrestrial being. How does the creature look and sound? How does its body differ from that of a human being?

Write a well-developed paragraph describing your imagined extraterrestrial being. Assume that your audience consists of readers of a science fiction magazine. Your purpose is to describe a unique creature for a science fiction story. Your paragraph will be evaluated for correct and effective use of adjectives.

Use the following steps to complete this assignment.

A. Prewriting

To develop ideas, try illustrating. On a blank sheet of paper, begin drawing possible shapes and features for your extraterrestrial. Try not to use figures you've seen before on book covers or in films. After you've drawn a few figures, look over them. Pick out the features that look best and begin combining these features into one figure.

Look at your composite illustration and list the creature's characteristics. What color is it? How tall is it? What distinctive features does it have? How does it move?

For help in organizing your paragraph, refer to Chapter 3.

B. Writing

Using your illustration and list, write a paragraph describing your creature. Begin with a topic sentence. As you write, use fresh, specific adjectives to give a clear picture of the creature.

C. Postwriting

Revise your first draft, using the following checklist.

1. Does my paragraph have a clear topic sentence?

2. Is my paragraph logically organized?

3. Do my adjectives describe the creature as I've imagined it?

4. Have I avoided using too many adjectives or adjectives that are vague and overused?

5. Do the adjectives conform to Edited Standard English?

Proofread your paragraph, using the Checklist for Proofreading in Chapter 1. Then share your writing with your classmates to see if they can visualize the creatures from the written descriptions.

15 Adverbs

Understanding Adverbs

Like adjectives, *adverbs* are modifiers. You will learn to identify adverbs by their definition, the classes into which they can be divided, and the features that distinguish them from other parts of speech.

Defining an Adverb

An *adverb* is often defined as a word that modifies a verb, an adjective, or another adverb.

Modifies a Verb:	The dog barked *frantically*.
Modifies an Adjective:	The land was *fairly* rocky.
Modifies an Adverb:	The elms grow *very* quickly.

Adverbs answer the question *how? how often? when? where?* or *to what extent?*

How:	The embers glowed *softly*.
How Often:	The century plant blooms *infrequently*.
When:	The package should reach you *tomorrow*.
Where:	The mothballs are kept *downstairs*.
To What Extent:	Our emergency supplies were *nearly* gone.

Exercise 1: Identifying Adverbs

Write the following sentences, underlining the adverbs. Beneath each sentence write the question answered by each adverb. Then draw an arrow to the word or words the adverb modifies.

Examples

a. Sometimes, Hal wished that he could graduate immediately.

Sometimes, Hal wished that he could graduate immediately.

sometimes: how often?

immediately: when?

b. Carlie was very proud that she played well.

Carlie was very proud that she played well.

very: to what extent?

well: how?

1. Today we drove slowly because of slick streets and heavy traffic.

2. Kio can skate forward or backward with equal ease.

3. Lorenzo will call you later tonight.

4. The Pasternak family often goes north for their summer vacations.

5. You should never approach a wild bear closely, even if it seems completely tame.

6. As the curtains slowly parted, the excited audience clapped loudly.

7. *We Have Always Lived in the Castle* is one of Shirley Jackson's highly suspenseful novels.

8. Billy Dee Williams is an extraordinarily gifted actor who still finds time for his favorite hobby, painting.

9. Too much Vitamin A can be very harmful to the body; an overdose can be fatal.

10. We seldom go into those woods because poison sumac grows everywhere.

Classifying Adverbs

Many adverbs fall into no special class. Others fit into one of four categories.

Interrogative Adverbs

The adverbs *how, when, where,* and *why* are *interrogative adverbs* when they introduce a question.

> *How* do you spell your name?

> *When* is the news special going to be on?

> *Where* is Timbuktu?

> *Why* do stars seem to twinkle?

Negative Adverbs

Not (and its contraction *n't*), *never, seldom, scarcely, barely,* and *hardly* are called *negative adverbs.* They deny or invert the statement being made, or they qualify it in a negative way.

Positive: He will be at play practice.

Negative: He will *not* be at play practice.

Positive: Rosa was through with her term project.

Negative: Rosa was*n't* through with her term project.

Positive: The governor makes long, boring speeches.

Negative: The governor *never* makes long, boring speeches.

Intensifiers

Intensifiers are adverbs that modify adjectives or other adverbs, but not verbs. They immediately precede the word they modify. Common intensifiers are *extremely, rather, somewhat, really, too, more, most, quite,* and *very.*

Modifies Adjective: Whooping cranes are *extremely* rare.

A *very* old oak stands in our yard.

Modifies Adverb: The storm arose *very* quickly.

Don't drive *too* quickly.

In writing avoid overusing the intensifier *very.* When used too often, it loses its force.

Nouns Used as Adverbs

Just as nouns are sometimes used as adjectives, so some nouns may be used as adverbs. A noun that answers the adverbial question of *when? where? how much?* or *to what extent?* should be classified as an adverb.

Sheila went *home* after lunch. [where?]

Chico will leave *Sunday*. [when?]

The next ice age could last *centuries*. [how long?]

Exercise 2: *Identifying Classes of Adverbs*

Write the following sentences, underlining the adverbs. If the adverb belongs to a special class, indicate that beneath the sentence.

Examples

a. Where did you go yesterday?
   Where did you go yesterday?

   where: interrogative; yesterday: noun used as adverb

b. We had not planned our trip very carefully.
   We had not planned our trip very carefully.

   not: negative; very: intensifier; carefully: adverb

1. How did the team do tonight?

2. Our oil reserves are not quite enough to meet every future emergency.

3. My cousin worked in the desert a year, prospecting for uranium without success.

4. Marcia doesn't work evenings now; she works the morning shift.

5. "It rains here too much," grumbled the tourist. "I'm never coming back."

6. We are going downtown tomorrow. What is the best way to go—by bus or car?

7. The pirate map indicated we should walk forty paces south, twelve paces east, and then we would see an extremely large boulder.

8. When and where did the very largest volcanic eruption in history take place?

9. Sarah wasn't home, so we went to the park and found her there.

10. Today will be rather cool, with that extremely low pressure center moving north.

Finding an Adverb by Its Features

Adverbs and adjectives are both modifiers and share the same three features. In order to distinguish an adjective from an adverb, you must look to see what word it modifies. Remember that adverbs modify verbs, adjectives, and other adverbs; adjectives can modify only nouns or pronouns.

Adverbs may change form to show degrees of comparison.

Some—but not all—adverbs show degrees of comparison: positive, comparative, and superlative degrees. Adverbs that end in *-ly* form their comparative and superlative degrees with the words *more* and *most*.

Positive	Comparative	Superlative
quickly	more quickly	most quickly
obviously	more obviously	most obviously
stubbornly	more stubbornly	most stubbornly

Most one-syllable adverbs form their degrees of comparison with *-er* and *-est* added to the positive degree. Most such adverbs may also function as adjectives.

Positive	Comparative	Superlative
far	farther	farthest
fast	faster	fastest
deep	deeper	deepest
hard	harder	hardest
late	later	latest
long	longer	longest
soon	sooner	soonest
wild	wilder	wildest

All adverbs that have degrees of comparison are compared in a negative way with the words *less* and *least*. *Less* is used to compare two items negatively, *least* is used to compare three or more items negatively.

Positive	*Comparative*	*Superlative*
quickly	less quickly	least quickly
obviously	less obviously	least obviously
far	less far	least far
soon	less soon	least soon

Adverbs may be used with intensifiers.

Intensifiers are a special class of adverbs that modify only other adverbs or adjectives. Intensifiers can be thought of as modifier signals because a modifier always immediately follows an intensifier. In the following sentences adverbs follow the intensifiers.

Dawn arrived *rather* late.

Malcolm finished *very* quickly.

Adverbs may be formed with suffixes.

The most common adverb suffix is *-ly* which means "in a certain manner" or "at a certain time."

slowly   recently   nervously

Not all words that end in *-ly* are adverbs, however; some, such as *homely, friendly, lovely,* and *kindly,* are adjectives.

Other adverb-forming suffixes include *-ward (upward, forward), -ways, (sideways, always),* and *-wise (crosswise, sidewise).*

Exercise 3: Identifying Adverbs

Use your knowledge of the definition and features of adverbs to identify the adverbs in the sentences on the next page. Write the sentences, underlining the adverbs.

Example

a. The roof has been leaking rather badly lately.
   The roof has been leaking <u>rather badly lately</u>.

1. Usually poison ivy occurs very rarely in highly populated urban areas.

2. We measured the fence wire lengthwise, then fastened it tightly with pliers.

3. Is it true that moss grows less thickly on the side of the tree that faces southward?

4. Because its orbit is quite eccentric, Pluto sometimes approaches nearer to earth than Saturn does.

5. The car hit the patch of ice too quickly, then skidded sideways off the road.

6. Snails sleep more heavily than most animals; sometimes they may snooze for three years.

7. Scientists maintain that nothing moves more quickly than light, but science fiction writers frequently ignore this law.

8. The elevator moved downward quickly, and the many passengers stood silently.

9. Unfortunately, for short distances alligators can run more swiftly than people.

10. The firecracker rose upward, then exploded most impressively into a shower of green stars.

Review: Understanding Adverbs

On a sheet of paper, list all of the italicized adverbs in the order they occur in the selection. Next to each adverb write the verb, adjective, or adverb it modifies. These paragraphs are taken from *Walden* by the nineteenth-century American naturalist and writer Henry David Thoreau. (Not all of the adverbs are italicized.)

When I went to get a pail of water *early* in the morning I *frequently* saw this stately bird sailing out of my cove within a few rods. If I endeavored to overtake him in a boat, . . .he would dive and be *completely* lost, so that I did *not* discover him *again*, sometimes, till the latter part of the day. But I was more than a match for him on the surface. He *commonly* went off in a rain.

As I was paddling along the north shore one *very* calm October afternoon, for such days *especially* they [loons] settle on to the lakes, like the milkweed down, having looked in vain over the pond for a loon, *suddenly* one, sailing out from the shore toward the middle a few rods in front of me, set up his wild laugh and betrayed himself. I pursued with a paddle and he dived, but when he came *up* I was *nearer* than before. He dived again, but I miscalculated the direction he would take, and we were fifty rods apart when he came to the surface this time, for I had helped to widen the interval; and *again* he laughed *long* and *loud*, and with more reason than before. He maneuvered *so cunningly* that I could not get within a half dozen rods of him. Each time, when he came to the surface, turning his head this way and that, he *coolly* surveyed the water and the land, and *apparently* chose his course so that he might come up where there was the widest expanse of water and at the greatest distance from the boat. It was surprising how *quickly* he made up his mind and put his resolve into execution. He led me at once to the widest part of the pond, and could *not* be driven from it. While he was thinking one thing In his brain, I was endeavoring to divine his thought in mine. It was a pretty game, played on the smooth surface of the pond, a man against a loon.

Applying What You Know

From your community or school newspaper, select an article describing a recent sports event. Then, using what you have learned about identifying adverbs, read the article to find the adverbs and list them on a sheet of paper. When you have finished, read the article to yourself, leaving out the adverbs. What effect did the adverbs have on the writing? On your perception of the event?

Using Adverbs

In this section you will practice using comparative and superlative forms of adverbs, both regular and irregular. Also, you will learn to distinguish between some adjective and adverb word pairs that are often confused, and you will learn that double negatives are not a feature of ESE.

Using Comparative and Superlative Forms of Adverbs

When two items are being compared, the comparative degree of the adverb is used.

Morty swims *faster* than Max does.
Morty swims *less fast* than Max does.

Kim studies *more often* than Maria.
Kim studies *less often* than Maria.

When three or more items are being compared, use the superlative degree of the adverb.

Morty swims *fastest* of all the competitors.
Morty swims *least fast* of all the competitors.

Kim studies *most often* of the sisters.
Kim studies *least often* of the sisters.

Exercise 4: Using Comparative and Superlative Forms of Adverbs

Write the following sentences, using the correct comparative or superlative form of the adverb given in parentheses. So long as it fits the sense of the sentence, the comparison may be either positive or negative. Underline the adverb you have used.

Example

---

a. Valery reads (frequently) than Pat.
Valery reads <u>more frequently</u> than Pat.
    or
Valery reads <u>less frequently</u> than Pat.

1. The planet Mercury moves around the sun (quickly) than the planet Venus does.

2. Of all classes the seniors scored (high) on the final achievement tests.

3. The cockroach has survived (successfully) than most other species.

4. Of all nineteenth-century novelists, Helen Hunt Jackson wrote (effectively) on behalf of Native American rights.

5. Trains use fuel (efficiently) than planes.

6. Which breed of dogs learns tasks (easily)?

7. Some scientists claim that of all food additives, sugar (frequently) injures our health.

8. Our daily paper reports events (accurately) than the radio station does.

9. Of all European explorers the Vikings appear to have visited America (early).

10. The willow grows (swiftly) than the oak tree, but the oak endures (long).

Using Irregular Forms of Adverbs

Most adverbs ending in *-ly* use the words *more* or *most* to form their degrees of comparison, while one-syllable adverbs usually add *-er* or *-est*. A few common adverbs form their comparative and superlative degrees irregularly. These forms must be memorized.

Positive	Comparative	Superlative
badly	worse	worst
far	farther	farthest
little	less	least
much	more	most
well	better	best

Some of the words in the preceding list may also be used as adjectives. Remember that they are adverbs only when they modify a verb, adjective, or another adverb.

Adverb: We have to travel *farther*.

The car ran *worse* after we fixed it.

Adjective: This is the *best* score I've made yet.

Please give me *less* salt this time.

Exercise 5: Using Irregular Forms of Adverbs

Write the sentences on the next page, supplying the comparative or superlative degree of the adverb in parentheses. Then underline each adverb and draw an arrow to the word that it modifies.

Examples

a. These nails will work (well) for the job than those will.

These nails will work better for the job than those will.

b. Of all injuries burns hurt (much).

Of all injuries burns hurt most.

1. Of all NASA's rockets which one has traveled (far) from the earth?

2. The expert said fish bite (much) when it is cool than when it is hot.

3. Of all chemicals I think sulphur stinks (badly).

4. Of all diets the one that works (well) is simply saying no to second helpings.

5. Nowadays, you have to make every dollar stretch (far) than you used to.

6. A body weighs (little) at the North or South Pole than it does at the equator.

7. The higher you climb above sea level, the (little) easily water boils.

8. Magnets attract nickel somewhat, but attract iron (much).

9. Robins use their sight (little) than their hearing to locate worms to eat.

10. Poison ivy infection itches badly, but poison oak infection itches (badly).

Choosing Between Adjectives and Adverbs

In writing and speaking you often have to choose between an adjective or an adverb. If you are uncertain which modifier you should use, check to see what word is being modified. Use an adverb to modify a verb, adjective, or another adverb; use an adjective to modify a noun or pronoun.

Adverb: The scientist watched the white rat *closely*.
[modifies verb *watched*]

Adjective: The race was *close*. [modifies noun *race*]

In many cases you will have no difficulty deciding whether to use an adjective or an adverb in a sentence. Problems sometimes arise, however, when an adjective is so frequently misused that the wrong choice sounds natural. Three such adjective-adverb pairs—*bad/badly, good/well,* and *slow/slowly*—are discussed in the following paragraphs.

Bad **is an adjective that modifies a noun or pronoun. It is frequently used after linking verbs such as** *feel, look, taste, smell.*

We felt *bad* about the mistake.

Mildew makes things smell *bad*.

Badly **is an adverb that tells how an action is performed.**

Tech High beat our team *badly* in the play-offs.

Good, **an adjective, is not used as an adverb in ESE.**

Good boots are essential to the hiker.

The apple blossoms smelled *good*.

Well **is a troublesome modifier because it can be used as both an adjective and and adverb.** *Well* **is an adjective when it means "healthy," "attractive," or "satisfactory." It is an adverb when it tells how an action is performed.**

Adjective: Marcia should be *well* by Friday.

Adverb: A "mudder" is a racehorse that runs *well* on a muddy track.

Slow is an adjective that means the opposite of *fast*.

The traffic is *slow* during rush hour.

Because of its use on highway signs, however, *slow* has become accepted as an adverb in some situations:

Drive *slow*.   Go *slow*.

The adverb *slowly*, however, should be used after action verbs other than *drive* and *go*.

The boat chugged *slowly* toward its destination.

The black snake crept *slowly* toward the robin's nest.

Exercise 6: Choosing Between Adjectives and Adverbs

Write the following sentences, choosing the correct modifier from the pair in parentheses. Underline the modifier you have chosen.

Example

---

a. Terry had a serious operation, but she is almost (good, well) again.
   Terry had a serious operation, but she is almost <u>well</u> again.

1. Freshly baked bread always smells (good, well).

2. I don't play tennis (good, well) because my reflexes are (slow, slowly).

3. The liquid trickled (slow, slowly) into the beaker; the experiment was going (good, well).

4. I felt (bad, badly) about forgetting to call Carol; I hope she doesn't take it (bad, badly).

5. The swordfish steaks tasted surprisingly (good, well), but the squid looks (bad, badly) to me.

6. Sharon is (good, well) at sports, sings (good, well), but makes friends (slow, slowly).

7. A rose smells (good, well), but a perfume tester smells perfume (good, well).

8. If you want to do (good, well) with your exercise program, begin (slow, slowly).

9. Sharon dresses (good, well), and she always smells (good, well)—she never goes out without squirting on a bit of cologne.

10. When they saw their test scores, Eddie felt (good, well) and Miriam felt (bad, badly).

Using Negatives

When two negative words are used where only one is needed, the construction is called a *double negative*.

Avoid double negatives in speaking and writing.

An asterisk (*) indicates a sentence with a feature that is not a part of ESE.

*I don't know nothing about it.
I don't know anything about it.
I know nothing about it.

*I don't have no pen.
I don't have a pen.
I have no pen.

Remember that the adverbs *barely, scarcely,* and *hardly* are also considered negative when used with other negatives.

*I was so confused, I couldn't hardly think.
I was so confused, I couldn't think.
I was so confused, I could hardly think.

The words *but* and *only* have negative meanings in such expressions as "haven't but," "can't help but," and "haven't only." Avoid these double negative expressions when speaking and writing.

*I don't have but two dollars left until payday.
I have but two dollars left until payday.

*When Gwen takes notes, she can't help but doodle in the margins of her notebook.
When Gwen takes notes, she can't help doodling in the margins of her notebook.

Exercise 7: Eliminating Double Negatives

Each of the following sentences contains a double negative. Rewrite each sentence so that it conforms to Edited Standard English.

Examples

a. We can't hardly change our minds at this point in the science project.
   We can hardly change our minds at this point in the science project.

b. We haven't got hardly enough gas to get home.
   We haven't got enough gas to get home.

1. No white person never knew where the grave of Crazy Horse could be found.

2. The store doesn't carry but one brand of seeds.

3. It seems some people can't help but talk too much.

4. The rickety bridge couldn't barely hold the weight of the cattle truck.

5. My teacher claims I don't know nothing about using double negatives.

6. It seems as if Grandmother's appearance hasn't scarcely changed since we were children.

7. We haven't got but enough supplies to get us to the next camp along the mountain.

8. There's never hardly enough time in the day to finish my work at school.

9. We don't have but sixteen dollars in the fund; that's not scarcely enough.

10. Nothing can't be done about the problem unless citizens are willing to admit that a problem exists.

Review: Using Adverbs

Write the following sentences, choosing the correct modifier from the pair in parentheses. Underline the word you have chosen.

Example

a. When the buzzer sounded, I gathered up my books (quick, quickly) and headed for my locker.
When the buzzer sounded, I gathered up my books <u>quickly</u> and headed for my locker.

1. The car's engine started (quick, quickly) even in winter.

2. Which of these three packages is the (better, best) buy?

3. Kevin didn't feel (bad, badly) about not making the first team.

4. Do you know which of Mars' two moons orbits the planet (more, most) swiftly?

5. Donna (has, hasn't) only fifty cents to buy lunch.

6. I don't (never, ever) want to eat parsnip pudding again.

7. The dead frog I had to work on in biology didn't smell very (good, well).

8. Carlos (can, can't) hardly wait to graduate.

9. There (is, isn't) but one aspirin left in the bottle.

10. After I broke the school record for eating dill pickles, I didn't feel too (good, well).

11. Things were going very (good, well) for our team until Tina tripped and hurt her ankle (bad, badly).

12. John grew (slow, slowly) until tenth grade, and then he shot up (quick, quickly).

13. "The fish is starting to smell (bad, badly)," my sister complained.

14. Of all the people who addressed the convention, Barbara Jordan spoke (more, most) effectively.

15. I (have, haven't) got enough money to buy only one record album.

16. Ham and eggs always go (good, well) together.

17. The peaches looked (good, well), but they didn't sell very (good, well).

18. We (could, couldn't) hardly ignore the noise outside the language room.

19. After I read for six straight hours, I felt rather (bad, badly) and my eyes didn't focus (good, well).

20. I like Ms. Jackson (better, best) of the two candidates.

Writing Focus: *Using Exact Adverbs in Writing*

Just as adjectives help the reader visualize a person, place, or thing, adverbs help the reader visualize action. Use exact adverbs to describe an action. Consider, for example, the action described in the following sentences.

> The fire burned *savagely*.
>
> The fire burned *weakly*.
>
> The fire burned *softly*.

Assignment: *Making the Perfect Sandwich*

Imagine that you've gone to visit your aunt who owns a delicatessen. She invites you to help yourself to any of the food in her store and to fix the perfect sandwich for yourself.

Write a paragraph giving specific, step-by-step directions for making your sandwich. Your audience will be your classmates, and your purpose will be to explain how to make the perfect sandwich. Your paragraph will be evaluated for correct and effective use of adverbs.

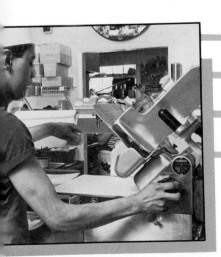

Use the following steps to complete this assignment.

A. Prewriting

To develop a recipe for your sandwich, make a list. Note all the ingredients you like best in a sandwich. Then number these ingredients in the order you would use them when making the sandwich.

B. Writing

Using your numbered list, write step-by-step directions for making your ideal sandwich. In the first sentence, state what your paragraph is about. Then write clear instructions, using exact adverbs as appropriate.

C. Postwriting

Revise your first draft, using the following checklist.

1.   Does the first sentence tell what your instructions are for?

2.   Are the instructions clear and in proper order so that the reader can follow them easily?

3.   Have you used exact adverbs to clarify the directions?

4.   Do the adverbs conform to Edited Standard English?

Proofread your paragraph, using the Checklist for Proofreading at the end of the book. Then share your recipe with your classmates and see if you can follow one another's directions.

16 Conjunctions
Understanding Conjunctions

Conjunctions, like prepositions, join sentence parts. In the lessons that follow, you will learn to recognize the three kinds of conjunctions and how these conjunctions are used in various types of sentences.

Defining a Conjunction

A *conjunction* is usually defined as a word that connects words or groups of words.

Some of the smallest and most common words in English are conjunctions. Words such as *and, but, or, for, nor,* and *yet* may join either single words or groups of words.

Jane Austen and Emily Brontë were early English novelists.

Roberto will letter the place cards, and Marissa will make the centerpieces for the banquet.

Vonnegut's novels are funny but thought-provoking.

Milk contains important nutrients, but many people are allergic to it.

Conjunctions like *either . . . or, neither . . . nor, both . . . and,* and *not only . . . but also* work together as pairs.

Either hamburger or sausage may be used in this recipe.

Both Wyatt and Surrey influenced the development of the English sonnet.

Some conjunctions may join groups of words to independent clauses. Conjunctions such as *after, because, before, when, since,* and *where* join dependent word groups to independent clauses.

We left before the concert was over.

Jerry always takes his first-aid kit when he goes backpacking or camping.

Exercise 1: Identifying Conjunctions

Write the following sentences, drawing one line under the conjunctions. Be prepared to identify the words they connect. (A sentence may contain more than one conjunction; some sentences may have conjunctions that work in pairs.)

Examples

a. Working independently of one another, both Soviet and American scientists discovered the laser in the 1950s.
Working independently of one another, both Soviet and American scientists discovered the laser in the 1950s.

b. Lasers are one of our country's most versatile and awe-inspiring discoveries; they can be used for either good or evil.
Lasers are one of our country's most versatile and awe-inspiring discoveries; they can be used for either good or evil.

1. Ordinary light diffuses as it travels; laser beams neither dissipate nor lose their strength.

2. Unlike ordinary light, laser beams can be aimed and focused; they are the most powerful lights on earth.

3. Laser beams can be used by artists to create holographs or by doctors to perform delicate eye surgery.

4. They can be used both to transmit signals and to generate steam power.

5. Because of the laser's power, it can be used as a precision cutting tool for substances as dense as steel or concrete.

6. In addition, the geologist can use it to detect signs of impending earthquakes, and the meteorologist can use it to measure cloud covers.

7. The possibilities for the peaceful use of the laser are heartening, yet the laser as a weapon has produced possibilities that are frightening.

8. Because lasers can transmit very clear photos, the beams are used to transmit photos of enemy installations and movements.

9. Since the war in Vietnam, many laser weapons have been developed, including bombs and ballistic missiles.

10. Before the invention of the laser, a "death ray" existed only in science fiction; lasers may well make this devastating weapon not only possible, but also inevitable.

Classifying Conjunctions

Conjunctions can be divided into three classes: *coordinating conjunctions*, *correlative conjunctions*, and *subordinating conjunctions*.

Coordinating conjunctions are *and, but, or, nor, yet, so,* and *for*.

Coordinating conjunctions join single words, phrases, or clauses. When one or more sentence parts are joined by a coordinating conjunction, the parts should be parallel in structure.

For more information on parallel structure, see page 436.

The recipes were economical, yet nutritious. [two adjectives]

Edna St. Vincent Millay or Sara Teasdale wrote that poem. [two nouns]

We subscribed to the news magazine, but not to the sports journal. [two prepositional phrases]

Cedar chips or pine needles in a doghouse will discourage occupancy by fleas. [two noun phrases]

I haven't heard Raphael's new joke, nor do I want to. [two independent clauses]

Correlative conjunctions are used only in pairs.

---

either . . . or   not only . . . but also
neither . . . nor   whether . . . or
both . . . and

Sentence parts joined by correlative conjunctions must also be parallel in structure.

Either <u>mozzarella</u> or <u>provolone</u> cheese is good on a pizza.

[two adjectives]

The wasps were <u>not only</u> <u>numerous</u>, <u>but also</u> <u>unfriendly</u>.

[two adjectives]

Both <u>a drama</u> and <u>a musical</u> have been based on the novel *I Am a Camera*. [two nouns]

Subordinating conjunctions are used to introduce adverb clauses.

A subordinating conjunction expresses the relationship of a subordinate clause to the main clause by showing time, place, cause, purpose, limitation, or condition. A list of the most common subordinating conjunctions follows:

after	because	in order that	than	when
although	before	provided that	that	whenever
as	how	since	though	wherever
as much as	if	so	unless	whether
as soon as	inasmuch as	so that	until	while

As much as I would like to, I won't be able to go to the beach.

The pageant will be held *wherever* the committee decides.

The newspaper reporters waited outside *while* the meeting was in session.

Exercise 2: *Classifying Conjunctions*

Write the sentences on the following page, underlining the conjunctions. Beneath each sentence list each conjunction and its class: *coordinating (coor.), correlative (cor.),* or *subordinating (sub.)*.

Examples

a. Either the band or the orchestra will perform at graduation.
Either the band or the orchestra will perform at graduation.

either . . . or—cor.

b. Vera has planned on being a television reporter since she was a sophomore.

Vera has planned on being a television reporter <u>since she was</u> a sophomore.

since—sub.

1. Wolves are neither as destructive nor as dangerous as many people imagine.

2. Although everyone dreams, many people do not recall their dreams.

3. Both Sigmund Freud and his daughter were influential in the development of psychiatry.

4. Since my youngest sister started playing the drums in her school's marching band, our household has had neither peace nor quiet.

5. The high school graduation exercises will be held in the football stadium provided that no rain is forecast for that afternoon.

6. Both magnesium and calcium aid the body in proper utilization of Vitamin C.

7. Neither age nor infirmity could deter actress Sarah Bernhardt; she continued to act although she was often unwell, even after her leg was amputated.

8. Let us know when the Pep Club party will be, and we'll organize two committees to help you with the cleaning and refreshments.

9. Because fiberglass is extremely tough, yet lightweight and flexible, it is quite often used for the bodies of speedboats and racing cars.

10. Although Pete wanted a pizza or a hamburger, he was too tired to cook, so he settled for a peanut butter sandwich and a glass of milk.

Review: Understanding Conjunctions

In the following paragraphs the contemporary American writer Ralph Ellison discusses his childhood bewilderment about being named for the poet and philosopher Ralph Waldo Emerson. Using what you have learned about conjunctions, identify the conjunctions in the passage and list them on a sheet of paper in the order they appear.

Beside each conjunction write the class to which it belongs: *coordinating (coor.), correlative (cor.),* or *subordinating (sub.).* Find at least fifteen conjunctions.

> From the start I was uncomfortable with it, and in my earliest years it caused me much puzzlement. Neither could I understand what a poet was, nor why, exactly, my father had chosen to name me after one. Perhaps I could have understood it perfectly well had he named me after his own father, but that name had been given to an older brother who died and thus was out of the question. But why hadn't he named me after a hero, such as Jack Johnson, or a soldier like Colonel Charles Young, or a great seaman like Admiral Dewey, or an educator like Booker T. Washington, or a great orator and abolitionist like Frederick Douglass? Or again, why hadn't he named me (as so many Negro parents had done) after President Teddy Roosevelt?
>
> Instead, he named me after someone called Ralph Waldo Emerson, and then, when I was three, he died. It was too early for me to have understood his choice, although I'm sure he must have explained it many times, and it was also too soon for me to have made the connection between my name and my father's love for reading. Much later, after I began to write and work with words, I came to suspect that he was aware of the suggestive powers of names and of the magic involved in naming.[1]

Using Conjunctions

Conjunctions help the writer combine and connect ideas and sentences coherently. In the following lessons you will practice combining sentences with conjunctions and punctuating these sentences correctly.

A series of short, choppy sentences can make writing seem childlike. By using coordinating, correlative, or subordinating conjunctions, you can combine such sentences and show the relationship between them.

---

[1]Excerpt from "Hidden Name and Complex Fate" in *Shadow and Act* by Ralph Ellison. Copyright © 1964 by Ralph Ellison. Reprinted by permission of Random House, Inc.

The following sentences use coordinating conjunctions to connect ideas of equal importance.

We could order invitations. We could make them ourselves.

We could order invitations *or* make them ourselves.

Bob is a good writer. He is not a very good editor.

Bob is a good writer, *but* he is not a very good editor.

Coordinating and correlative conjunctions join ideas of equal importance, expressed in sentence parts that are *parallel* in structure. Examine your writing to make sure it contains no *faulty parallelisms*. That is, all sentence parts joined by coordinating and correlative conjunctions must be similar in type, form, or structure.

An asterisk (*) indicates a sentence with a feature that is not a part of ESE.

I like to read. I like to ski. I like swimming.
*I like to read, to ski, and swimming.
I like to read, to ski, and to swim.
I like reading, skiing, and swimming.

Subordinating conjunctions express the specific relationship of a subordinate clause to a main clause.

Relationship	Subordinating Conjunction
Cause:	because, since, as, for, so
Purpose:	in order that, so that
Limitation:	though, although, in spite of the fact that, since
Time:	after, as, as soon as, before, since, until, when, while
Place:	where, wherever

The following sentences employ subordinating conjunctions to show the relationship of a subordinate clause to a main clause.

Salvador Dali is one of the most flamboyant twentieth-century artists. Many people are familiar with him.

Because Salvador Dali is one of the most flamboyant twentieth-century artists, many people are familiar with him.

Sandy decided she wanted to be a chemist. She had read about Madame Curie.

Sandy decided she wanted to be a chemist *after* she had read about Madame Curie.

Exercise 3: Combining Sentences with Conjunctions

Combine the following short sentences by using appropriate conjunctions. Underline the conjunctions you have used. Check each of your sentences for faulty parallelism.

Examples

a. None of the Brontë sisters lived very long. Each made a lasting mark on English literature.

Although none of the Brontë sisters lived very long, each made a lasting mark on English literature.

b. The store on the corner carries electronic supplies. It carries hobby items.

The store on the corner carries electronic supplies and hobby items.

1. Many people know about the disease of diabetes. Few are aware of a common, related disorder—low blood sugar.

2. We could not afford to have the literary magazine typeset. We typed it ourselves on the school typewriters.

3. I may go to the Halloween party as a vampire. I may go as a robot.

4. Coyotes are native to America. Raccoons are native to America.

5. I knew my answer must be right. Carrie had arrived at the same solution. Kim had arrived at the same solution.

Punctuating with Conjunctions

In a series of words, phrases, or clauses, a comma is used to take the place of each conjunction that is omitted. A comma also precedes the conjunction at the end of a series.

The Oglala, Hunkpapa, and Brulé are all tribes of the Sioux.

Our canoe trip will be on either the White, Mulberry, or Illinois River.

Commas are not necessary if no conjunctions are omitted, but this is not a frequently used construction.

John *and* Dave *and* Shelley are the club's new officers.
We could go water skiing *or* swimming *or* snorkeling.

A comma usually separates the subordinate clause from the main clause when the subordinate clause begins the sentence.

Because California is located on the San Andreas Fault, it has frequent earthquakes.

While Marcia typed the report, Tammy worked on the charts.

A comma is not usually necessary when the subordinate clause comes at the end of the sentence.

California has frequent earthquakes because it is located on the San Andreas Fault.

Tammy worked on the charts while Marcia typed the report.

Exercise 4: *Punctuating with Conjunctions*

Write the following sentences, adding commas wherever necessary. If the sentence is punctuated correctly, write *C* after it. Circle the commas you insert.

Examples

a. If you don't wear a seat belt in a car you substantially increase your chances of being hurt in an accident.

If you don't wear a seat belt in a car‚ you substantially increase your chances of being hurt in an accident.

b. When we think of colonial costumes we usually think of knee breeches tricornered hats and hoop skirts.

When we think of colonial costumes‚ we usually think of knee breeches‚ tricornered hats‚ and hoop skirts.

1. Since Mark was originally from Florida he didn't like driving in the Midwest during the winter.

2. Although everyone recognizes the actors who played Luke Skywalker Princess Leia and Han Solo few recognize the actor who played R2 D2 the android.

3. I would love to spend the whole summer loafing and reading and napping.

4. Tina bought a used car because she couldn't afford a new one.

5. Although many people are familiar with the phrase "blood sweat and tears" not many know that the original expression was "blood sweat toil and tears."

Review: Using Conjunctions

Combine the following short sentences by using appropriate conjunctions. Underline the conjunctions you have used.

1. Our national bird is the eagle. Benjamin Franklin wanted the turkey adopted as our nation's symbol. He felt eagles were nasty, predatory birds.

2. Some people felt Willie Stargell was too old to play in the 1979 World Series. He led his team to victory. He was chosen Most Valuable Player.

3. Calvin saw Sammy Davis, Jr., perform in Las Vegas. He wants to be a performer, too.

4. Siamese cats are beautiful. They are extremely noisy. They like a lot of attention.

5. I found it hard to study. My sister had her stereo going full blast. My brother was practicing on his drums.

Write the following sentences, adding commas wherever necessary. If the sentence is punctuated correctly, write C after it. Circle the commas you insert.

6. We couldn't leave to go shopping until the lawn was mowed the porch was cleaned and the mail had arrived.

7. The necklace was priceless because it contained flawless diamonds pearls and a huge star sapphire.

8. Because the sewing room was littered with needles and pins and scissors it was unsafe to sit down carelessly.

9. It was unsafe to sit down carelessly in the sewing room because it was littered with needles and pins and scissors.

10. Because drought continued for so long many cities began to ration water.

Writing Focus: *Using Conjunctions in Writing*

The proper use of conjunctions can make your writing flow more smoothly. Use conjunctions in your writing to combine sentences and ideas. Conjunctions tell readers exactly how one idea or event relates to another.

Assignment: *Analyzing Action in a Movie*

What's the best movie you've seen lately? Who is the major character? What key events trigger the character's actions, and what are those actions? How do these events and actions affect the movie's plot?

Think about these questions. Then, write a paragraph describing one important action taken by the main character, and analyzing its causes and effects. Your audience is a group of retired teachers and your purpose is to inform them about this movie, which they have not seen. Use the following steps to complete this assignment.

A. Prewriting

Begin by listing the main character's key actions in the film, leaving several lines blank after each action in your list. Then, after each action, jot down its causes and its effects. Next, read the notes you have made and choose one action to write about. Write one sentence that summarizes it. This will be the topic sentence of your paragraph.

B. Writing

First, write the topic sentence you have in your prewriting notes. After it, write sentences that explain it in detail; introduce the movie's main character, then describe the key action. Explain causes and effects of the action. As you write, use conjunctions to clarify rela tionships between events and ideas.

C. Postwriting

Revise your first draft, using the following checklist.

1. Does the topic sentence state the main idea accurately?

2. How have I made the paragraph both interesting and clear to my audience?

3. Have I used conjunctions effectively to show the relationship between ideas and events?

4. Are there sentence fragments or short sentences that can be combined by using conjunctions?

Finally, proofread your paragraph, using the Checklist for Proofreading at the back of the book. Then turn in your paragraph to your teacher.

17 Prepositions

Understanding Prepositions

Prepositions are one of the parts of speech that connect other words so that they work together in groups. By changing the preposition, a writer may radically change the meaning of a sentence.

A family of skunks lives *near* our house.
A family of skunks lives *under* our house.
A family of skunks lives *in* our house.

In the following lessons you will learn how to identify prepositions.

Defining a Preposition

A *preposition* is usually defined as a word that shows the relationship of a noun or pronoun to another word in the sentence.

The girl *with* the braids is Maureen.

In the preceding sentence the preposition *with* shows the relationship of the noun *braids* to the noun *girl*.

In Edited Standard English prepositions are not used alone. Instead, a preposition is part of a prepositional phrase that has two essential parts: the preposition (*P*) and the object of the preposition (*OP*). A prepositional phrase may also contain one or more modifiers.

$$\text{P} \qquad \text{OP} \quad \text{P} \qquad \text{OP}$$
The opera singer stood **in** the *center* **of** the *stage*.

$$\text{P} \qquad\qquad \text{OP} \qquad\qquad\qquad \text{P} \qquad\qquad \text{OP}$$
On the album's *cover* was a picture **of** a silver *unicorn*.

A single preposition may also have a compound object.

$$\text{P} \qquad\qquad\qquad \text{OP}$$
The college is famous **for** its science *division* and drama
$$\text{OP}$$
department.

                              P   OP   OP
We had a fine breakfast **of** *eggs* and *steak.*

The object of the preposition is usually a single word, but it may also
be a group of words.

                        P   OP
Sell the car **for** *whatever you can get.*

P   OP
After *seeing the double feature* we were all hungry.

The following is a list of commonly used prepositions.

about	besides	on
above	between	over
across	beyond	past
after	but	since
against	by	through
along	concerning	throughout
amid	down	to
among	during	under
around	except	underneath
as	for	until
at	from	unto
before	in	up
behind	into	upon
below	like	with
beneath	of	within
beside	off	without

Besides these one-word prepositions there are several compound prepositions that are made up of more than one word. Each of
these should be considered as a single preposition.

according to	because of	out of
along with	by means of	owing to
aside from	in front of	subsequent to
as to	in spite of	together with

Some words that function as prepositions, such as *across, down,
behind, in, under, up,* and so forth, may also function as adverbs.
Remember that a preposition introduces a prepositional phrase. If
you can find no object of the preposition, the word is probably being
used as an adverb.

Adverb: We had to go *on.*

                                   P   OP
Preposition: We had to go **on** the *bus.*

Adverb: The election results are *in.*

443

P   OP

Preposition: The election results are **in** the *paper*.

Do not confuse the infinitive *to* with the preposition *to*. The infinitive is the verb form that begins with the word *to*.

Infinitive: It takes persistence *to* succeed. [*to* followed by verb]

P   OP

Preposition: Are you going **to** the *rally*? [*to* followed by noun]

P OP

Preposition: Please give this **to** *her*. [*to* followed by pronoun]

Exercise 1: Identifying Prepositional Phrases

Write each of the following sentences, underlining the prepositional phrases. Above each preposition write *P*; above each object of the preposition, write *OP*. (Some sentences contain more than one prepositional phrase; some may have compound objects.)

Example

a. When assembly was over, students poured through the aisles and halls.

                                               P

When assembly was over, students poured <u>through the</u>

   OP   OP

<u>aisles and halls.</u>

1. Because of the heat our relatives won't be coming to visit.

2. On Tuesday the air raid sirens went off and nearly startled me out of my wits.

3. Mange is a common disease in dogs, caused by parasites in the animal's hair follicles.

4. Did you know that people with type A blood seem to be most susceptible to ulcers?

5. My brother always insists on practicing his tuba when I'm on the phone or trying to listen to the news.

6. Ms. Chavez has cast all the parts in the play except the part of the ballerina.

7. After all is said and done, writing is mostly a matter of persistence and of discipline.

8. When Dan was learning to play the banjo, all of us were subjected to his constant plinking and plunking.

9. The United States and a number of other countries did not send teams to the 1980 Olympics in the Soviet Union because they disapproved of Soviet actions in Afghanistan.

10. According to many sports writers, Muhammad Ali revived the ailing sport of boxing with his skill and flamboyant character.

Review: *Understanding Prepositions*

Using what you have learned about prepositions, list the prepositional phrases on a sheet of paper in the order they appear. Find at least forty-five.

I had just returned home from a lecture tour, tired and not feeling very well, and here I was tapping away at my typewriter, sipping a cup of hot tea and humming to myself.

My wife said, "If you don't feel so good, why don't you go up to bed?" and I replied, quite truthfully, "It makes me feel better to sit here working."

This is the beauty of doing work you enjoy, so that while it is a chore in one respect, it is a pleasure in another. And I earnestly urge all young people contemplating their careers to keep in mind that nothing in work is finally rewarding unless it is work you would be willing to do for nothing if you could afford to.

This is the ultimate test for lifelong congeniality in a career, of no matter what sort. Money is not the most important thing; fame is fleeting and uncertain; even status is irksome and uncomforting after a time. All that remains at the end is satisfaction—and occasionally delight—in the performance itself.

Do not do what does not please you; it does not pay, no matter how beguiling the material rewards may seem to be. The pot of gold that appears to be gleaming at the end of the rainbow is less gratifying than the rainbow itself.

The best recipe for a long and happy life is to be able to approach each new morning with anticipation and zest for the job, whatever it may be. This does not mean, of course, that we are not sometimes disgruntled or frustrated or even bored; but, over the long haul, these disaffecting moments are washed away by the tide of contentment, the swell of gratification, at doing well what one does best.

If you are engaged in work you like, even the drudgery and tedium involved in it seems worthwhile. The talented woodcarver who works patiently for hours, and whistles at his work, is getting more out of life—and of himself—than the affluent stockbroker who needs three martinis to get through the afternoon.

The people I have known who seem to rest most easily within themselves are those who have found, by design or lucky accident, the niche made just for them, in whatever field it may be, lofty or humble, so long as it gives them a sense of being needed, of being purposeful and of doing it a little better than most others can.

And those who seemed most unhappy, whatever their degree of external success, were the ones to whom the job was a *means,* not an end, a way of earning a living rather than a way of living. All they can look forward to is retirement, as boring, in a different way, as their jobs are. When the heart goes, the hands should still be tapping away happily.[1]

Applying What You Know

From a source such as a magazine, newspaper, or book, or from a paper you have recently written, select a passage about the length of that in the review exercise.

Using what you have learned about prepositions, identify the prepositional phrases in the selection and list them on a sheet of paper in the order they appear.

Using Prepositions

In this section you will study several prepositions that frequently cause writers and speakers trouble. Learn to use these prepositions correctly when writing Edited Standard English.

Beside means "by the side of."
Besides means "in addition to," "moreover," or "except."

The saltshaker is *beside* the napkins.

Besides chemistry I am taking English, history, and art.

There are few programs *besides* cartoons on Saturday morning television.

Between refers only to two persons or things.
Among refers to three or more persons or things.

This information must be kept *between* you and me.

The information was circulated *among* five committee members.

---

[1]From *Strictly Personal* by Sydney J. Harris. © 1981 Field Enterprises, Inc. Permission of News America Syndicate.

Between is sometimes used to compare the items within a group when each is considered individually.

What are the similarities *between* rock, country, and gospel music?

Use the preposition *from* after the adjective *different* instead of *different than*.

The program was *different from* what we had expected.

One kitten was *different from* others in the litter.

***Except* is a preposition that means "excluding."**
***Accept* is a verb meaning "to take" or "to receive." *Accept* should not be used as a preposition.**

Everyone could come to play practice *except* Rosita.

That restaurant will not *accept* checks or credit cards.

***In* means "inside" or "within."**
***Into* shows a movement from the outside to the inside of something.**

A stained glass ornament was hanging *in* the window.

A sparrow flew *into* our open window.

We have red and white corpuscles *in* our bloodstreams.

The veterinarian injected the serum *into* the bloodstream.

Exercise 2: Using Troublesome Prepositions

Write the sentences on the next page, choosing the word from the pair in parentheses that is used in ESE. Underline the word you have chosen.

Examples

a. The Rhodesians would not (accept, except) the terms of the treaty.
The Rhodesians would not accept the terms of the treaty.

b. Carla sits (beside, besides) Riko in biology class.
Carla sits beside Riko in biology class.

1. The petition circulated (between, among) the three classrooms.

2. Something about my band uniform seemed different (from, than) the others.

3. In the last furlong the race was (between, among) the bay horse and the gray.

4. What do you want for lunch (beside, besides) a hamburger?

5. There are a number of differences (between, among) insects and arachnids.

6. Linguists have noted distinct similarities (between, among) the English, German, and Danish languages.

7. Nobody preferred a skating party to a picnic (accept, except) Marie.

8. Was the Mayan culture very different (from, than) the Toltec?

9. Be sure that the life jackets are (in, into) the boat.

10. Be sure to put the life jackets (in, into) the boat.

Writing Focus: *Using Prepositions in Your Writing*

In this chapter you have learned the correct usage of such troublesome prepositions as *beside/besides, between/among, from* with *different, except/accept,* and *in/into*. Make it a practice to use these prepositions correctly in your writing.

Assignment: *Describing Differences Between Work and School*

How do you imagine working at a full-time job differs from attending high school? What kind of job could you obtain with your present skills? Would you prefer working or going to school?

Imagine a full-time job that you could obtain now, and write a well-developed paragraph describing the differences between working and attending school. Use such prepositions as *between/among* and *from* with *different* correctly in your writing. Your classmates are your

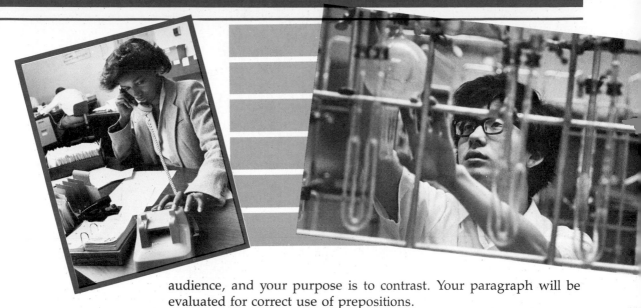

audience, and your purpose is to contrast. Your paragraph will be evaluated for correct use of prepositions.

Use the following steps to complete this assignment.

A. Prewriting

To gather ideas for your paragraph, interview someone who has a job like the one you imagine having. Take notes during the interview. If you need help in organizing your paragraph, refer to Chapter 3.

B. Writing

Use your notes to write a paragraph describing the differences between attending school and working full-time. Include a topic sentence that clearly states your main idea. Provide specific details to support your main idea. As you write, pay attention to your use of prepositions to make sure they conform to Edited Standard English.

C. Postwriting

Revise your first draft, using the following checklist.

1. Does my paragraph have a clear topic sentence?

2. Have I provided enough specific details to support the topic sentence?

3. Does my paragraph have a logical organization?

4. Does my use of prepositions conform to Edited Standard English?

Proofread your paragraph, using the Checklist for Proofreading in the back of the book. Then share your writing with your classmates and discuss the differences and similarities among your ideas.

18 Interjections
Understanding Interjections

Interjections are words that express strong feeling: surprise, pain, joy, anger.

Unlike other parts of speech, interjections have no grammatical relationship to the rest of the sentence. They stand apart, complete in themselves, as exclamations or expressions of emotion.

"Drat!" the professor said, "I've forgotten my umbrella."

Ouch! That handle is hot!

Some interjections express milder feelings, such as surprise or interest.

Well, look at that!

Oh, is this where you live?

The following is a list of some words commonly used as interjections.

ah	gee	hey	no way
aha	good grief	hooray	phew
alas	goodness	hurrah	ugh
congratulations	great	never	whew
dear me	help	nonsense	yippee

Notice that some of the words in the preceding list may also be used as other parts of speech.

Goya was a *great* painter.	[adjective]
You got an A? *Great!*	[interjection]

Exercise 1: Identifying Interjections

Write the following sentences, underlining each interjection.

Example

a. Rats, I dropped the keys in the mud!
   Rats, I dropped the keys in the mud!

1. Great Scott, Professor! A creature is emerging from the large meteorite!

2. Oh, I didn't know anyone was in here.

3. We're having boiled parsnips for supper? Ugh!

4. The actress sobbed and wrung her handkerchief, "Alas, we will lose the farm unless we can pay the mortgage."

5. Hurray! I passed my driver's test!

6. Well, things could be worse, but not much worse.

7. Did you smell the sulphur in the chemistry lab today? Whew!

8. He's hit the ball. Wow! It's going to go over the fence!

9. Congratulations, you have just won a year's supply of cat food.

10. Aha! I think I see how to solve this problem.

Using Interjections

Interjections, more than any other part of speech, go in and out of fashion. Your grandparents might have said *grand* or *swell*; your parents *great* or *neat*; an older brother or sister *wild* or *out of sight*. Because interjections often have a meteoric rise and fall in popularity, be careful about using them in formal writing. They can sound foreign to some readers and in a few years may seem dated or quaint.

Punctuating Interjections

Interjections may be followed either by an exclamation point or by a comma. An interjection followed by an exclamation point shows strong feeling, while a comma indicates milder emotion.

Yippee! The weekend is finally here!	[indicates strong feeling]
Well, I suppose we should get started.	[indicates milder emotion]

Notice that the word following the exclamation point is capitalized because it is the first word in a new sentence. When a comma is used after an interjection, however, the next word is not capitalized, for it does not begin a new sentence.

In a direct quotation use either a comma or an exclamation point, but not both.

"Wow!" Margaret said, "It's later than we thought."

"Mercy," said the trucker, "it looks like we've got ourselves a convoy."

Exercise 2: Punctuating Interjections

Write the following sentences, underlining each interjection. Then place an exclamation point after an interjection that shows strong or sudden feeling. Use a comma after an interjection that expresses a milder emotion. Remember to capitalize the first word following an exclamation point if that word begins a new sentence. Circle the punctuation you insert.

Example

   a. "Alas" cried the knight. "I wish I had never been born to see this tragic day."

   "Alas (!)" cried the knight. "I wish I had never been born to see this tragic day."

1. Oh I don't know whether I'll go or not.

2. Yipe that's a black widow spider crawling up the wall!

3. "Help" cried the swimmer. "I've been stung by a jellyfish!"

4. The pitcher sighed and sat down wearily. "Gee I thought we were going to win."

5. Hey this is a one-way street!

6. The nurse regarded the patient coolly. "Nonsense you will take this medicine or else!"

7. Wow did you see the size of that shark?

8. Grandmother said, "Well I suppose we ought to get out and do the chores."

9. "Whoopee we've won the championship!" the fan cried, embracing his wife and pounding her on the back.

10. Aunt Frances set the table, then said, "Oh gracious I forgot the cream."

Writing Focus: *Using Interjections in Your Writing*

Interjections are used primarily in dialogue. When you write dialogue, use interjections that express just the emotion you intend. In addition, use interjections that are appropriate for the speaker—a middle-aged man probably would not use the same interjections a teenager would.

Assignment: *An Ear for Speech*

How does the speech of your friends differ from that of your parents? What interjections and slang words do different groups of people use? For one day, pay particular attention to the way your friends speak. Note interjections, slang words, or unusual phrases they use.

"*gracious!*"

Write a short dialogue based on a conversation between an eleventh-grade student and a middle-aged person. In the dialogue use interjections that are appropriate for each person. Your paragraph will be evaluated for effective use of language and correct punctuation of interjections.

Use the following steps to complete this assignment.

A. Prewriting

Imagine that an exciting basketball game (or other sports event) is being watched by a teenager and a middle-aged person—perhaps a parent or a teacher. They discuss the event as they watch. Take a few notes, first jotting down a description of the situation. Give each person a fictitious name. Beside each person's name, list a number of interjections he or she might use in this conversation.

B. Writing

Using your notes, write a short dialogue for your two characters. Begin by writing one or two sentences describing the situation and

"HO HUM"

the characters. Then write the dialogue, using appropriate interjections for each person and punctuating the interjections correctly. Do not overuse interjections. Instead, try to realistically capture the speech patterns of each character.

C. Postwriting

Revise your first draft, using the following checklist.

1. Is my dialogue realistic?

2. Have I used interjections to accurately express the emotions of each character?

3. Have I overused interjections?

4. Have I correctly punctuated and capitalized the interjections and other elements of the dialogue?

Proofread your revision, using the Checklist for Proofreading in the back of the book. Then pair up with another classmate and perform your dialogue for the class.

GEE WHIZ!

19 Sentence Structure

Understanding Sentences

If you have been around children who are learning to talk, you know that their first utterances are single words, such as *Mama, Daddy,* and *kitty*. Gradually children learn to combine words to express more complex ideas. In their first few years they learn the rules for combining words to make sentences—no matter what language is their native one. It does not matter if you grew up speaking English, Spanish, or Chinese; you automatically learned how to put words into their proper order to make a statement or ask a question.

In this section you will learn about the structure of sentences. Even though you may have little trouble speaking in sentences, understanding sentence parts and how they work will help you write more clearly and effectively.

Defining a Sentence

A *sentence* is often defined as a group of words that expresses a complete thought.

Incomplete:	The woman in the hard hat. [What about the woman? Who is she, or what did she do?]
Complete:	The woman in the hard hat is the city's chief building inspector.
Incomplete:	Scuttled after the fleeing hunter. [Who or what chased the hunter?]
Complete:	The large alligator scuttled after the fleeing hunter.
Incomplete:	With the head of an eagle and the legs of a lion. [What?]
Complete:	The griffin was a fearsome mythical beast with the head of an eagle and the legs of a lion.

Groups of words expressing incomplete thoughts leave you with unanswered questions, such as *who? did what? what about it?* or *what happened?* Whenever you have such questions, the group of words is not a sentence because it does not express a complete thought.

Exercise 1: Identifying Sentences

Decide whether each of the following word groups expresses a complete thought. Then on a sheet of paper, write *S* for sentence and *NS* for nonsentence. If the group of words is not a sentence, add whatever words are needed to express a complete thought.

Examples

    a. The songs from the musical *Hair* were strongly influenced by African rhythms and melodies.
       S

    b. Since her broken leg hadn't healed yet.
       NS. Sandy couldn't ski in the race since her broken leg hadn't healed yet.

1. The girl over in the corner in the jeans and orange sweater.
2. Just when everyone was least expecting it.
3. Because the river was at flood stage and very swift.
4. A serigraph is a print made by a silk-screen process.
5. Hunting pythons in the jungles of Burma.
6. Groundhogs are also called "woodchucks."
7. Especially when I have to get up early the next morning.
8. While I was talking on the telephone to Pat.
9. A fern does not reproduce by seeds or shoots.
10. After eating six hot dogs with everything on them.

The Purpose of a Sentence

Sentences may be classified in two ways—by their purpose or by their structure.

Sentences can be formed for one of four purposes.

A declarative sentence makes a statement and ends with a period.

Maxine Hong Kingston is an excellent writer.

All leprechauns have a hidden pot of gold.

An interrogative sentence asks a question and ends with a question mark.

Are there really giant sharks?

Have you read any of the novels of Frank Yerby?

When will your sister's plane arrive?

An imperative sentence gives a command or makes a request and may be followed either by a period or an exclamation point.

The subject of an imperative sentence is always *you*, the person or persons being addressed. Even if the word *you* does not appear in the sentence, it is considered to be the "understood subject."

(You) Never stand under a tree during a lightning storm.

(You) Abandon ship!

An exclamatory sentence expresses strong feeling and is usually followed by an exclamation point.

We won the talent contest!

The dam has burst!

How lucky you are!

Exercise 2: *Classifying Sentences by Purpose*

On a sheet of paper, write the following sentences, ending each sentence with an appropriate punctuation mark. Then after each sentence indicate whether it is *declarative, interrogative, imperative,* or *exclamatory*. Circle the punctuation marks you insert.

Examples

---

a. Do you like Erica Jong's poetry

Do you like Erica Jong's poetry ? interrogative

b. Run for your lives

Run for your lives ! exclamatory

1. Did you know that Robert Redford was elected sewer commissioner of Provo, Utah

2. The dog's name *Fido* comes from the Latin word for *faithful*

3. What a disappointment that movie was

4. Please go through the metal-detecting apparatus before boarding the plane

5. Quasars are believed to be about 10 billion light years away from our planet

6. In what countries is cork grown

7. Don't touch that wire

8. Our motor is on fire

9. Does anyone know what started the great Chicago fire in 1871

10. The game of lacrosse is derived from an ancient Indian game called "baggataway"

The Parts of the Sentence

Every sentence has two essential parts: the *subject* and the *predicate*.

The *subject,* often a person or thing, is usually defined as that part of the sentence about which something is being said.

The *predicate* is usually defined as that part of the sentence that says something about the subject.

In the following sentences a slash divides the subject from the predicate:

Subject   Predicate
Badminton / originated in India.

Subject   Predicate
Mrs. Nancy Johnson / is credited with inventing the ice cream freezer.

Subject   Predicate
The digestive system of the pig / is remarkably like that of a human.

In most English sentences the subject precedes the predicate. In some sentences, however, the subject follows all or part of the predicate.

       Predicate   Subject
Under the pile of papers was / the lost check.

Exercise 3: *Identifying Subject and Predicate*

Write each of the following sentences and draw a slash separating the subject from the predicate. Then label each part *Subject* or *Predicate*.

Examples

  a. The coal miner's job is the most hazardous in America.

       Subject   Predicate
  The coal miner's job / is the most hazardous in America.

  b. In the Botanical Gardens in San Marino, California, is the world's largest collection of desert plants.

                         Predicate
  In the Botanical Gardens in San Marino, California, is / the

             Subject
  world's largest collection of desert plants.

1. Harriet Beecher Stowe's *Uncle Tom's Cabin* was a novel of great social impact.

2. The ancient Greeks painted their marble statues in several colors for realistic effect.

3. Brief and tragic was the career of Anne Boleyn.

4. A parrot in a national park in New Zealand learned to let the air out of the tires of parked cars.

5. Very few types of germs and bacteria can survive the cold of the South Pole.

6. Pepi II of the sixth Egyptian dynasty reigned for ninety years.

7. The first female boxing match took place in 1876 and was won by Miss Nell Saunders.

8. Deep in the cave slept hundreds of hanging bats.

9. Our word *dandelion* comes from a French phrase meaning "tooth of the lion."

10. A medieval suit of armor might weigh as much as a hundred pounds.

Complete Subject and Simple Subject

The *complete subject* tells who or what the sentence is about.

In the following sentences the complete subject is *italicized*.

> *Four of the band uniforms* have to be replaced.

> *The actress playing the part of Nancy* was Pearl Bailey.

> *The turkey with chestnut dressing* looked delicious.

The *simple subject* is the main word or words in the complete subject.

The simple subject is never part of a prepositional phrase, nor does it ever include modifiers.

In the following sentences the complete subject is *italicized;* the simple subject is underlined.

> *Four of the band uniforms* have to be replaced.

> *The actress playing the part of Nancy* was Pearl Bailey.

> *The turkey with chestnut dressing* looked delicious.

When the simple subject is a proper name, it may be made up of more than one word.

> *Stevie Wonder* is an extraordinary musician.

> *Westminster Abbey* is the burial place of many great poets.

In discussions of the parts of the sentence, the word *subject* usually refers to the simple subject, not to the complete subject.

Exercise 4: Identifying Complete Subject and Simple Subject

Copy the sentences on the following page, underlining each complete subject once and each simple subject twice.

Examples

a. An important figure in British legend and literature is King Arthur.

An important figure in British legend and literature is King Arthur.

b. Fiction, not fact, is the source of most Arthurian stories.

Fiction, not fact, is the source of most Arthurian stories.

1. Bits of information indicate the existence of a real King Arthur.

2. One of the ancient historians states that Arthur was a chieftain of the fifth or sixth century.

3. A very old manuscript in Latin states that Arthur died at the battle of Mount Badon in 518.

4. Several ancient poems, including the "Black Book of Carmarthen," mention a King Arthur.

5. The Arthur of these ancient poems is a supernatural king, almost a god.

6. A few researchers on the subject claim there may have been two King Arthurs.

7. One of these kings was a figure from ancient British folklore and was completely fictional.

8. The second Arthur, however, may have been an actual hero and warrior.

9. The characters of the two figures may have merged over the years.

10. A dashing figure with supernatural powers emerged to become the King Arthur of Camelot.

Complete Predicate and Simple Predicate

The *predicate* is the part of the sentence that tells something about the subject.

The *complete predicate* is made up of the verb and all its modifiers and complements.

In the following sentences the complete predicate is *italicized*.

The hummingbird *swiftly darted in and out of the blossoms of the trumpet vine.*

I *accidentally brushed my teeth with hair cream this morning.*

Marcia *is playing bass bugle in the drum and bugle corps.*

The *simple predicate* is the verb or verb phrase, the main word or words in the complete predicate.

In the following sentences the complete predicate is *italicized;* the simple predicate is *underlined.*

The hummingbird *swiftly darted in and out of the blossoms of the trumpet vine.*

I *accidentally brushed my teeth with hair cream this morning.*

Marcia *is playing bass bugle in the drum and bugle corps.*

In discussions of the parts of a sentence, the word *verb* or *verb phrase* is used more often than the term *simple predicate.*

Exercise 5: Identifying Complete Predicate and Simple Predicate

Write the following sentences, underlining the complete predicate once and the simple predicate (verb or verb phrase) twice.

Examples

---

a. *Frankenstein* was written by Mary Shelley in 1817.
   Frankenstein was written by Mary Shelley in 1817.

b. The historic book was originally subtitled *"or the Modern Prometheus."*
   The historic book was originally subtitled *"or the Modern Prometheus."*

1. The name *Frankenstein* actually refers to the scientist and not to the monster he created.

2. Dr. Frankenstein has learned the secret of endowing matter with life.

3. The doctor is like the legendary Prometheus, bringer of light to humanity.

4. Prometheus was punished by the gods for his gift to humans.

5. Dr. Frankenstein, like Prometheus, must suffer for his break-through.

6. He creates human life, but of a monstrous sort.

7. The creation is filled with loathing for its creator.

8. The monster murders the doctor's brother and the doctor's bride.

9. The monster ultimately causes the destruction of the horrified Dr. Frankenstein himself.

10. The gift of life has turned into the curse of death for the ambitious doctor.

The True Subject

In most English sentences the subject appears before the verb. Speakers or writers first identify who or what they are talking or writing about, and then complete the statement. (In the example sentences in this section, the subject is underlined once and the verb or verb phrase twice.)

The fly buzzed loudly against the windowpane.

In some sentences, however, all or part of the verb appears before the subject. Being able to identify the true subject of a sentence is essential in order to choose a verb that agrees in number with the subject. The verb may precede the subject in a question.

Is there any peanut butter in the cupboard?

Will you kindly step into the principal's office?

Have you seen my history books?

Does Karen like her job at the radio station?

Sometimes, sentences are inverted for effect. This means they are purposely written with the subject following the verb.

Under my lettuce leaf was a large insect.

Directly in our path was a large, brown bear.

In many sentences that begin with *there* and *here*, the subject follows the verb.

Here are my reasons for refusing.

There are few storms more powerful than a Pacific typhoon.

Sometimes, the word *it* is also used as an expletive. (An *expletive* is a word that signals that the subject will follow the verb.)

It is hard to concentrate with that television blaring.

To find the true subject of a sentence, first find the verb and then ask to *whom* or to *what* the verb refers.

Another way of locating the subject of a sentence is to change the inverted sentence or question into a statement with the subject preceding the verb.

You will kindly step into the principal's office.

Karen does like her job at the radio station.

My reasons for refusing are here.

Few storms are more powerful than a Pacific typhoon.

Remember that the subject of an imperative sentence is always the word *you*, the person or persons being addressed. When the word *you* does not appear in the sentence, it is understood as the subject.

(You) Help me with this package, please.

(You) Have some more mashed potatoes.

One last obstacle to locating the true subject of a sentence is the prepositional phrase. The subject of a sentence never appears in a prepositional phrase.

Several (of the choir members) were late for practice.

A number (of people) saw the mysterious flash in the sky.

Exercise 6: *Identifying Subject and Predicate*

Copy the sentences on the following page, underlining each simple subject once and each verb or verb phrase twice.

Examples

a. Somewhere beneath the sea may lie Atlantis.
   Somewhere beneath the sea may lie Atlantis.

b. Where is my physics notebook?
   Where is my physics notebook?

1. There is a myth about how the bear got its short tail.

2. Far in the west was a vague rumble of thunder.

3. The fear of heights is a very common phobia.

4. Here is an instance of poor engineering.

5. When will the next leap year occur?

6. Call me about the homework assignments.

7. There is a mysterious red spot on the planet Jupiter.

8. Down the path came a stray dog without a collar.

9. A box of broken tools and old flower pots sat in the garage.

10. How many of the seniors can graduate in January?

Compound Subjects and Verbs

Compound means "having two or more parts." Subjects and predicates may be compound.

A *compound subject* consists of two or more simple subjects joined by a conjunction.

The parts of a compound subject share the same verb.

Distemper, rabies, and parovirus are serious canine illnesses.

A carton of eggs and a quart of milk were in the cooler.

A *compound verb* consists of two or more verbs that are joined by a conjunction.

The parts of a compound verb have the same subject.

The audience laughed, applauded, and cheered.

The blizzard tied up traffic and brought all travel to a halt.

A sentence may contain both a compound subject and a compound verb.

Mrs. Rinaldo and Miss Chavez collected and counted the votes.

Exercise 7: Finding Compound Subjects and Verbs

Write the following sentences, underlining the simple subject once and the simple predicate (verb or verb phrase) twice. Remember to look for compound subjects and verbs.

Example

a. Kim is Korean-American and speaks two languages fluently.
Kim is Korean-American and speaks two languages fluently.

---

1. Bacon, eggs, and juice were set before the seasick passenger.

2. Hurricane Allen struck in 1980 and caused severe damage and flooding in the southern states.

3. A tank of tropical fish and a cage of finches stood in the pet shop.

4. Birds have no teeth and must use rocks and gravel to grind their food.

5. President Chester A. Arthur held a garage sale at the White House and sold twenty-five wagonloads of furniture.

6. Susan B. Anthony was fined a hundred dollars for attempting to vote, but refused to pay.

7. In 1972 a baboon escaped, jumped onto a passing bus, looked at the passengers, then ran all the way back to its cage.

8. Dorothy Dandridge, Sammy Davis, Jr., and Sidney Poitier starred in the movie version of *Porgy and Bess.*

9. A bushel of tomatoes and a crate of chickens fell from the truck and bounced across the highway.

10. A mouse or rat got into the cabin and ruined our supplies.

Subject-Verb Sentence Pattern

A few sentence patterns form the basis of all English sentences.

The simplest sentence pattern is the pattern *Subject-Verb*, abbreviated *S-V*.

In the S-V pattern the verb is always an action verb or one that expresses a state of being. Linking verbs occur only in other sentence patterns.

<pre>
S   V
</pre>
Jeans fade.

Modifiers do not affect the sentence pattern. Even though both the subject and the verb may have modifiers, the basic sentence pattern remains unchanged.

<pre>
               S   V
</pre>
Even expensive designer jeans often fade.

This sentence may be expanded still further without changing the S-V pattern:

<pre>
               S   V
</pre>
Even expensive designer jeans from the best stores often fade (after they are washed a few times).

Note: The group of words in parentheses is a subordinate clause, which does not affect the basic pattern. A verb phrase counts as a single verb.

<pre>
        S   V
</pre>
The roses *were wilting* swiftly.

<pre>
      S   V
</pre>
Miranda *had been dreaming.*

In any sentence pattern one or more of the elements may be compound.

<pre>
          S   V   V
</pre>
Several passers-by stopped and stared.

<pre>
      S   S   V   V
</pre>
The goose and gander honked and hissed at the dog.

A sentence is still considered *S-V* even though the verb may appear before the subject, as in a question or inverted sentence.

<pre>
        V   S
</pre>
Where is Timbuktu?

<pre>
           V   S
</pre>
Out of the basket rose a swaying cobra.

Complements

Sentences express complete thoughts by means of a subject (whom or what the sentence is about) and a predicate (what the subject is or does). Some sentences express a complete thought with only a subject and a verb. Many English sentences, however, contain a third necessary part—a complement.

A *complement* is usually defined as a word or group of words that completes the meaning of the verb and the subject.

Incomplete:	S V Carrie seems [seems what?]
Complete:	S V Comp. Carrie seems angry.
Incomplete:	S V José sent [sent what?]
Complete:	S V Comp. José sent his congratulations.

Complements, like subjects, are never found within a prepositional phrase.

    S   V
Barbara bounced into the room.
[*Into the room* is a prepositional phrase.]

    S   V   Comp.
Barbara bounced the basketball.

In the following lessons you will learn to identify several kinds of complements: predicate nominatives, predicate adjectives, direct objects, indirect objects, and objective complements. You will also learn the sentence patterns associated with these complements.

Predicate Nominatives

A *predicate nominative* is a noun or pronoun that follows a linking verb and renames the subject.
A sentence containing a predicate nominative has the sentence pattern *S-LV-PN*.

      S   LV   PN
"Fig-eaters" are beetles.

      S   LV   PN
"Fig-eaters" are the ones destroying the garden.

Adding modifiers does not change the basic sentence pattern.

<pre>
       S   LV   PN
</pre>
"Fig-eaters," a type of garden pest, are large beetles with iridescent wings.

Inverting sentence order to ask a question does not change the basic pattern:

<pre>
 LV   S   PN
</pre>
Are "fig-eaters" large green beetles?

Exercise 8: *Identifying Sentence Patterns*

Write the following sentences, underlining and labeling each part of the sentence according to its pattern. (Not all sentences contain predicate nominatives.)

Examples

a. Tina was my locker mate for a semester.

<pre>
  S   LV   PN
</pre>
Tina was my locker mate for a semester.

b. The lifeguard quickly swam to the struggling child.

<pre>
           S   V
</pre>
The lifeguard quickly swam to the struggling child.

1. Pit vipers are highly poisonous reptiles.

2. The last people in the band bus were Stacey and I.

3. The 1981 Scout Jamboree was held in Virginia.

4. Dorothy Sayers became one of the foremost mystery writers of our time.

5. "Nessie" is the nickname for the famous Loch Ness monster.

6. Our foreign exchange student this year is from Taiwan.

7. The actresses Margaux and Mariel Hemingway are the grand-daughters of Ernest Hemingway, the novelist.

8. At last soccer is becoming a popular game in the United States.

9. Isn't "Heart" an all-female rock music group?

10. My sister is a graduate of the music department of Howard University.

Predicate Adjectives

Predicate adjectives, like predicate nominatives, are complements that follow linking verbs. Predicate adjectives, as the name implies, are always adjectives; predicate nominatives are always nouns or pronouns.

A *predicate adjective* is usually defined as an adjective that follows a linking verb and modifies the subject of the sentence.

Laura was *happy* about her scholarship.

The clerk became *impatient* with the customer.

The campers looked *tired* and *dirty*.

Sentences with predicate adjectives have the pattern *S-LV-PA*.

     S   LV   PA
Laura was happy about her scholarship.

Exercise 9: Identifying Sentence Patterns

Write the following sentences, underlining and labeling each part of the sentence according to its pattern: S-V, S-LV-PN, or S-LV-PA.

Examples

  a. This book is a serious examination of religious cults and cult leaders.

          S LV   PN
     This book is a serious examination of religious cults and cult leaders.

  b. The baby quail looked toylike and helpless.

           S   LV   PA   PA
     The baby quail looked toylike and helpless.

1. The first woman candidate for the Presidency of the United States of America was Victoria Claflin Woodhull.

2. Sacajawea was a Shoshone woman and a guide for the explorers Lewis and Clark.

3. The Sahara is larger than any state and many countries.

4. The sun, moon, and stars appear larger when near the horizon.

5. Cheese is the oldest of all human-made foods.

6. A "red herring" is a slang term for a false or misleading clue.

7. Even in captivity zebras are wild and almost untrainable.

8. Soybeans are useful, versatile, and nutritious.

9. *Tess of the D'Urbervilles* is the tragic story of a young woman at the mercy of her environment.

10. In the tangled underbrush lurk many strange creatures of the night.

Direct Objects

Verbs are either linking verbs or action verbs. The complements used with linking verbs are the predicate nominative and the predicate adjective. In this and the next two sections you will study the complements used with action verbs. The first of these is the direct object.

A *direct object* **is usually defined as a word or group of words that receives the action of the verb.**

A direct object usually follows an action verb and answers the question *whom?* or *what?*

Conchita mailed the *invitations*.	[What did she mail?]
Jeff phoned his *sister*.	[Whom did he phone?]

Direct objects may be nouns, pronouns, phrases, or clauses.

Dan can ride a *unicycle*, but not very well.	[noun]
Marcia called *me* about the party.	[pronoun]
We liked *working with the movie equipment*.	[phrase]
Nobody wanted *to watch that program*.	[phrase]
Everyone knows *that germs cause disease*.	[clause]

Action verbs are classified as either *transitive* or *intransitive*.

A *transitive verb* is an action verb that takes a direct object. An *intransitive verb* is an action verb that does not take a direct object.

Many English verbs may be either transitive or intransitive, depending upon their use in the sentence.

Intransitive: The speaker *mumbled* unintelligibly.

Transitive: Sharon *mumbled* an apology.
[*apology* receives the action]

Intransitive: The violinist *performed* at Carnegie Hall.

Transitive: The violinist *performed* her own composition at Carnegie Hall.
[*composition* receives the action]

Sentences with direct objects have the pattern *S-V-DO*.

```
              S        V         DO
```
The governor released a statement to the press.
```
   S       V                     DO
```
(You) Remember your dentist's appointment at 9:30.

Exercise 10: *Identifying Sentence Patterns*

Copy the sentences on the following page, underlining and labeling each part of the sentence according to its pattern. For sentences with an understood subject, write *(you)* before the sentence. (Not all sentences have direct objects; some may have more than one.) Write a *T* after the sentence if the verb is transitive; write an *I* if it is intransitive.

Examples

---

a. Ursula LeGuin writes science fiction.

```
        S        V         DO
```
Ursula LeGuin writes science fiction.   T

b. The trained seal could play the horns and the xylophone.

```
           S        V          DO              DO
```
The trained seal could play the horns and the xylophone. T

1. The jets left vapor trails across the sky.

2. The 4-H Club members sold popcorn and peanuts at the football game.

3. Before entering politics, Ronald Reagan was a movie actor.

4. Kevin and Lucy can play either guitar or banjo.

5. Please buy a carton of eggs at the store.

6. In our creative writing class we wrote haikus, limericks, and ballads.

7. Melinda will be studying German and French in Europe this summer.

8. Gwendolyn Brooks is poet laureate of the state of Illinois.

9. Sheila telephoned every member of the band and pep club about the changes in the schedule.

10. Japan has discovered the charms of American bluegrass music.

Indirect Objects

A sentence containing a direct object may also have an indirect object.

An *indirect object* is usually defined as a word that tells *for whom* or *to whom* the action of the verb is done.

The indirect object usually comes immediately before the direct object. (In sentence patterns indirect objects are labeled *IO*.)

```
      S     V        IO     DO
```
The cat brought her *kittens* a mouse.

```
                    S     V   IO    DO
```
The gas station attendant drew *me* a map.

```
     S   V    IO              DO
```
We made *Rover* a two-story doghouse with three pillars and a veranda.

Indirect objects, like other kinds of complements, are never found in a prepositional phrase. When the word *to* or *for* is used, the noun or pronoun that follows is the object of a preposition, *not* an indirect object.

```
          S    V     DO
```
My father made a pizza for us.

      S   V   IO   DO

My father made us a pizza.

      S   V   DO

Mrs. Bush told her opinion on the issue to the reporters.

      S   V   IO   DO

Mrs. Bush told the reporters her opinion on the issue.

Remember that a sentence must contain a direct object in order to have an indirect object. No sentence may have an indirect object alone. Not all sentences with direct objects, however, have indirect objects.

Sentences containing an indirect object have the pattern S-V-IO-DO.

     S   V   IO   DO

Carla gave her horse an apple.

     S   V   IO   DO

Marcia tossed Jimmy his car keys.

Exercise 11: Identifying Sentence Patterns

Write the following sentences, underlining and labeling each sentence part. (Not every sentence contains an indirect object.)

Examples

---

a. We bought Grandmother a new tennis racket.

     S   V   IO   DO

We bought Grandmother a new tennis racket.

b. The clerks showed all the customers the entire new line of merchandise.

        S   V   IO   DO

The clerks showed all the customers the entire new line of merchandise.

1. Cammie made her cousin a funny get-well card.

2. The director gave the cast a few final words of encouragement.

3. The United States has sent several missions to the moon.

4. The magician told us the secret of his rope trick.

5. The rangers taught the younger campers some essential survival skills.

6. The chimpanzee in the zoo gave me a strange look.

7. The court awarded the victim of the accident $10,000.

8. Will the college offer adults any special night classes this spring?

9. Al carved his sister an ivory pendant.

10. Nobody had told either Clare or Rita of the change of plans.

Objective Complements

A special kind of complement that follows a direct object is called an *objective complement* because it describes or renames the object.

Objective complements follow only a few action verbs:

make	choose	appoint	voted	prove
consider	elect	name	think	find

Our joking made her *angry*.
We elected John *president*.

In order to have an objective complement, a sentence must also have a direct object. The sentence pattern for a sentence with an objective complement is *S-V-DO-OC*.

    S   V   DO   OC   OC
Congress considered the bill poorly *executed* and poorly *timed*.
    S   V   DO   OC
Carmen appointed Nick *treasurer*.

Exercise 12: *Identifying Sentence Patterns*

Write the following sentences, underlining and labeling each part of the sentence according to its pattern. (Not all sentences contain objective complements.)

Examples

a. Riko considers math her best subject.

    S   V   DO   OC
Riko considers math her best subject.

b. The motion of the roller coaster made Pam sick.

$$\underset{\text{S}}{\text{The motion of the roller coaster}} \quad \underset{\text{V}}{\text{made}} \quad \underset{\text{DO}}{\text{Pam}} \quad \underset{\text{OC}}{\text{sick.}}$$

c. The chairwoman appointed B.J. to the vacant office.

$$\underset{\text{S}}{\text{The chairwoman}} \quad \underset{\text{V}}{\text{appointed}} \quad \underset{\text{DO}}{\text{B.J.}} \quad \text{to the vacant office.}$$

1. We named our cocker spaniel Buffy.

2. Marcia considers soap operas stupid and boring.

3. The mayor thought the tax cut unwise at this time.

4. The team made Sherrie's English bulldog its mascot.

5. The detective proved Lady Tudberry the author of the crime.

6. Did we make Debby angry with our teasing?

7. Film critics have named that movie the best of the year.

8. The voters elected Ms. Johnson to be their delegate.

9. The jury found the man and woman innocent of the charges.

10. The Nitty Gritty Dirt Band was selected to tour Russia.

Active and Passive Voice

Transitive verbs (those that take direct objects) may be either active or passive.

For more information on the active and passive voice, see pages 543-544.

A verb is in the *active voice* when the subject of the verb performs the action. The verb is in the *passive voice* when the subject receives the action rather than performs it.

The following sentences illustrate the difference between active and passive voices.

Active: Ed *designed* the cover of the yearbook.
[The subject *Ed* performs the action.]

Passive: The cover of the yearbook *was designed* by Ed.
[The action is performed upon the subject *cover*.]

The passive voice of the verb tenses on the following page are formed by combining the appropriate tense of *be* and the past participle of the verb.

477

Present

Active:	Nipsey Russell *plays* the lead.
Passive:	The lead *is played* by Nipsey Russell. [present tense of *be* + *played*]

Past

Active:	Nipsey Russell *played* the lead.
Passive:	The lead *was played* by Nipsey Russell. [past tense of *be* + *played*]

Future

Active:	Nipsey Russell *will play* the lead.
Passive:	The lead *will be played* by Nipsey Russell. [future tense of *be* + *played*]

Present Perfect

Active:	Nipsey Russell *has played* the lead.
Passive:	The lead *has been played* by Nipsey Russell. [present perfect tense of *be* + *played*]

Past Perfect

Active:	Nipsey Russell *had played* the lead.
Passive:	The lead *had been played* by Nipsey Russell. [past perfect tense of *be* + *played*]

Future Perfect

Active:	Nipsey Russell *will have played* the lead.
Passive:	The lead *will have been played* by Nipsey Russell. [future perfect tense of *be* + *played*]

The Retained Object

Transitive verbs may have indirect objects as well as direct objects. When either of these objects continues to function as a complement in the passive construction, the object is called a *retained object*.

                    S   V   10   DO
Active: Rosa gave the newspaper staff their assignments.

When the preceding sentence is put into the passive voice, either the direct object, *assignments,* or the indirect object, *staff,* may serve as the subject of the sentence.

                        S   V   RO
Passive: The assignments were given the newspaper staff by Rosa.

                            S   V   RO
                The newspaper staff were given their assignments by Rosa.

Staff in the first sentence, and *assignments* in the second sentence are retained objects—objects of a verb in the passive voice.

Exercise 13: Identifying Active and Passive Voice and Retained Objects

Rewrite each of the following sentences. If the verb is in the active voice, change it to the passive voice. If the verb is in the passive voice, change it to the active voice. Then identify the voice of the sentence that you have written. Finally, if there is a retained object, underline and label it *RO.*

Examples

 a. The piece was recorded by the Preservation Hall Jazz Band.

                                                    DO
    The Preservation Hall Jazz Band recorded the piece.
    active voice
 b. The real estate agent showed the Lings the old mansion.

                                    RO
    The Lings were shown the old mansion by the real estate agent.
    passive voice

1. "Irene, Goodnight" was written by the folk artist Leadbelly.

2. The dust and mold in the old house gave Alison the sniffles.

3. Chief Red Cloud made an impassioned speech about Indian rights.

4. *Pride and Prejudice* was written by the English novelist Jane Austen.

5. Queen Elizabeth I considered Mary Queen of Scots a threat to her power.

6. Madeline was presented a scholarship by the Lions Club.

7. The experiment proved the theory false.

8. The starring role in *The World, the Flesh, and the Devil* was played by Harry Belafonte.

9. The British elected Margaret Thatcher Prime Minister.

10. Nuclear power is considered unsafe by some people.

Write a paragraph about music or film. Use the passive voice. Then rewrite the paragraph, changing the passive verbs to active ones. Which paragraph is stronger? Why?

Review: Understanding Sentences

Write each of the following sentences, underlining and labeling each part of the sentence according to its pattern.

Examples

a. The neoclassic period was a time of balance and harmony in literature.

                 S   LV   PN

The neoclassic <u>period</u> <u>was</u> a <u>time</u> of balance and harmony in literature.

b. The writers of the age admired careful structure and elegant language.

         S   V   DO

The <u>writers</u> of the age <u>admired</u> careful <u>structure</u> and elegant

   DO

<u>language</u>.

1. The world was a pleasant and orderly place to the neoclassic writers.

2. They considered the universe a perfectly ordered mechanism.

3. They gave reason and logic the utmost respect.

4. They were optimistic about the advances of science.

5. They admired the works of the ancient Greeks and Romans and patterned their own after them.

6. The height of the neoclassic period in England was in the eighteenth century.

7. Some people consider the poetry of this age cold and artificial.

8. A few young writers disliked the formality of the period.

9. Critics call their revolt against the age "the Romantic Rebellion."

10. "Romantic" writers did not necessarily write about love.

11. The word is associated with imagination, adventure, and intense emotion.

12. Two important early romantic poets were William Wordsworth and Samuel Taylor Coleridge.

13. Wordsworth wrote about ordinary people, not ancient gods or heroes or nobles.

14. His language was simple and unaffected.

15. Coleridge gave us the unsurpassable "Rime of the Ancient Mariner."

16. This poem is really not logical and orderly, but magical and imaginative.

17. Its form is simple.

18. Lord Byron was probably the most famous romantic poet.

19. He wrote passionate lyrics and long poems of high adventure.

20. His savage sense of humor gained him numerous enemies.

Using Sentences

In the following lessons you will learn how to avoid run-on sentences and sentence fragments, the two most common problems in writing sentences. You will also learn to improve your writing style by selecting appropriate words, by being concise, and by avoiding weak constructions.

Avoiding Run-On Sentences

When two closely related sentences are joined only by a comma or by no punctuation at all, the resulting group of words is called a *run-on sentence.*

Avoid using run-on sentences in your writing.

Run-On: Sally's favorite singer is Glen Campbell she has all of his albums.

Correct: Sally's favorite singer is Glen Campbell; she has all of his albums.

Run-On: Jan works for the police department, she is a dispatcher.

Correct: Jan works for the police department where she is a dispatcher.

Run-on sentences may be corrected by writing separate sentences or by changing the punctuation and wording.

The clauses of a run-on sentence can be written as separate sentences.

Run-On: Most poets cannot live on the income from their writing, they must have another job as well.

Correct: Most poets cannot live on the income from their writing. They must have another job as well.

A semicolon can be used to separate the two clauses when they are closely related in meaning.

Run-On: My little sister wants a special watch for her birthday it has a picture of Kermit the Frog on it.

Correct: My little sister wants a special watch for her birthday; it has a picture of Kermit the Frog on it.

A semicolon followed by a conjunctive adverb may be used to separate the parts of a run-on sentence. The adverb, which is always followed by a comma, shows the relationship of one part of the sentence to the other.

Run-On: Ferrets have a strong odor, some people don't like them for pets.

Correct: Ferrets have a strong odor; *therefore*, some people don't like them for pets.

A comma followed by a coordinating conjunction may be used to combine the two parts of a run-on sentence.

Run-On: We will have a centennial celebration next year all men who don't grow beards will be fined.

Correct: We will have a centennial celebration next year, *and* all men who don't grow beards will be fined.

One part of the run-on sentence may be changed to a subordinate clause or to a phrase.

Run-On: My aunt is a translator at the UN, she speaks three languages fluently.

Correct: My aunt, who is a translator at the UN, speaks three languages fluently.

Correct: My aunt, a translator at the UN, speaks three languages fluently.

Run-On: We set off for the movie early, we knew there would be a long line.

Correct: We set off for the movie early because we knew there would be a long line.

Exercise 14: Correcting Run-On Sentences

Using one of the methods discussed in the preceding section, correct each of the following run-on sentences. Write the corrected sentence.

Example

a. *Rendezvous* is a French word, it means "to get together again," "to meet."
   Rendezvous, which is a French word, means "to get together again," "to meet."

1. American fur trappers used the word *rendezvous* to describe their regathering in the spring, the members of the fur companies had gone their separate ways to trap throughout the winter.

2. Goods and furs were traded, there was much celebrating, eating, and drinking.

3. Today many people are still interested in the trapper's independent life style, they hold a modern rendezvous.

4. A rendezvous is an amazing sight you feel you have somehow traveled back in time to the previous century.

5. Those who attend the rendezvous obey strict rules, no modern tools, clothing, food, or shelter are allowed.

6. Most men dress in homemade buckskin clothing, women and children wear hand-sewn costumes of skins or cloth.

7. Participants live in tepees or wickiups, some of the shelters are brightly painted with designs and pictures.

8. All cooking is done over open fires with old-fashioned utensils, no canned food or refrigeration is allowed.

9. Furs, muzzle-loading rifles, and fine knives are traded, trade items are spread out on large hides before the shelters before they are sold.

10. There are contests in tomahawk throwing and shooting with black powder rifles, the competition is as fierce as at the rendezvous of old.

Avoiding Sentence Fragments

R un-on sentences need to be divided or rewritten because they contain too much information crammed together. Fragments, on the other hand, contain too little information and need words added to them to make them complete. Remember the three requirements for a complete sentence:

1. A sentence expresses a complete thought.

2. A sentence has a subject.

3. A sentence has a predicate verb.

In a sentence fragment one or more of these three requirements is missing.

Avoid using sentence fragments in your writing.

Incomplete:	While we were dancing.
Sentence:	I lost my watch while we were dancing.
No Subject:	Snores like a defective chainsaw.
Sentence:	Our large St. Bernard snores like a defective chainsaw.
No Predicate Verb:	The address written on the envelope.

Sentence: The address written on the envelope was illegible.

Remember that participles (verbs ending in *-ing, -en,* and so on) must have a helping verb to function as a predicate verb. Used alone, they function as modifiers.

Participle	*Verb Phrase*
playing	is playing
chosen	has been chosen

Phrases as Fragments

A *phrase* has neither a subject nor a predicate, nor does it express a complete thought. When a prepositional phrase, infinitive phrase, participial phrase, or gerund phrase is written as a sentence, it is a sentence fragment.

Fragment: I had left my term paper. In Stacey's car.

Sentence: I had left my term paper in Stacey's car.

Fragment: The tennis players were distracted by the sound of the jet. Roaring over the court.

Sentence: The tennis players were distracted by the sound of the jet roaring over the court.

Clauses as Fragments

A *subordinate clause* contains both a subject and a verb, but does not express a complete thought. Subordinate clauses must be attached to an independent clause; they cannot stand alone.

Fragment: I am now the proud owner of a stuffed owl. Because I got carried away at an auction.

Sentence: I am now the proud owner of a stuffed owl because I got carried away at an auction.

Fragment: Although the repair crews examined all the lines and equipment and worked throughout the night. The source of the power failure wasn't found.

Sentence: Although the repair crews examined all the lines and equipment and worked throughout the night, the source of the power failure wasn't found.

Appositives as Fragments

An *appositive* is a word or group of words that identifies a nearby noun or pronoun. An appositive cannot be punctuated as a sentence because it does not express a complete thought nor does it contain a subject and its verb.

Fragment: One of our family's favorite foods is kima. A spicy Indonesian dish of sauteed meat and vegetables.

Sentence: One of our family's favorite foods is kima, a spicy Indonesian dish of sauteed meat and vegetables.

Exercise 15: Correcting Sentence Fragments

Write the following sentences, correcting all sentence fragments.

Example

a. We always attend the War Eagle Arts and Crafts Fair. The biggest such fair in the United States.
We always attend the War Eagle Arts and Crafts Fair, the biggest such fair in the United States.

1. One evening last summer I decided to take a stroll with my sister. Down along the edge of the golf course.

2. It was a peaceful, pleasant evening with a faint breeze. A light mist forming on the green.

3. It seemed to us that there was a peculiar hush over everything. Because no birds were singing or crickets chirping.

4. We walked to our favorite spot. A large pond near the edge of the course.

5. Now, in the fading light, it looked rather sinister. With scarves of mist coiling over the dark water.

6. At almost the same moment we noticed bubbles boiling up in the water. Just a few yards away from us.

7. At first we thought a turtle or muskrat must be in the pond, but the bubbles became too large and violent. Far too large for any small animal to make.

8. Suddenly a huge, glistening black shape, as big as a person, rose from the water, and we both yelled. Thinking somehow, against all logic, that we were seeing a monster!

9. We were embarrassed but relieved to find it was only a scuba diver. Who had been collecting lost golfballs from the bottom of the pond.

10. My sister and I still are a little ashamed to admit that for one terrible moment we truly believed that we were going to be chased. By the Creature from the Black Lagoon.

Review: Using Sentences

Write each of the following sentences on this page and the next, correcting run-on sentences and sentence fragments.

1. There is a wealth of myth and legend about animals. Creatures that are both real and imaginary.

2. An old belief about geese was that a goose brought good luck to honest, innocent people, it brought bad luck to evil ones.

3. Germans believe that a stork nest on the roof brings good luck however Moroccans believe the opposite is true.

4. The Thebans thought crocodiles were sacred, they had pet crocodiles that wore bracelets and other jewelry.

5. A crocodile was supposed to weep as it devoured its prey, insincere crying is often referred to as "crocodile tears."

6. In the Renaissance it was thought that a toad's blood was lethal poison. Since toads were supposed to be venomous, like snakes.

7. Native American mythology sometimes shows the tortoise as the creator of the world. Which is similar to the Chinese legend of the tortoise and three other animals' bringing the world into existence.

8. Egyptian doctors carried snakes to the homes of ill people. To drive out disease or pain.

9. The snake figures in many stories of death it also is a central figure in stories about immortality.

10. Legends of India and China show great respect for the wisdom of apes, ancient Hebrews thought apes were unlucky.

11. The Greeks had a legend that the moon created the cat and that nighttime clouds are mice. Fleeing from the catlike moon.

12. Cats were respected and worshipped in Egypt they were even mummified after death.

13. Medieval Europeans connected cats with witchcraft cats were often burned as demons.

14. In Islamic religion the cat is a good friend to the prophet Muhammad, Buddhist folklore says that Buddha and the cat were enemies.

15. The panther has been favorably associated with numerous religious figures. Greek gods, including Dionysus.

Writing Focus: *Improving*

Sentence Structure

Good writers use complete sentences that are clear and concise. To improve your writing, avoid run-on sentences and fragments.

Assignment: *A Consumer Complaint Letter*

You have just learned that a local television station is canceling your favorite show and replacing it with a series on how to speak French. Write a letter in which you politely but firmly protest to the station manager, explaining what you like about your favorite show and why you think the substitution is a poor idea.

Keep in mind that your audience is the station manager and that your purpose is to persuade the manager to retain your favorite show. Your letter will be evaluated for correct and effective sentence structure.

Use the steps on the next page to complete this assignment.

A. Prewriting

Decide what your favorite TV show is. Then write a sentence that clearly states your position on the cancellation of the show and the substitution of the French series. Make two lists to support your position, one that states reasons for retaining your favorite show and one that states reasons for believing the substitution is a poor idea. Rank the reasons on each list by order of importance. Decide which reasons you will use.

B. Writing

Make up a name and address for the TV station manager. Use your position sentence and your lists of reasons to write your letter. Be sure the tone of your letter is formal and courteous. As you write, pay particular attention to the structure of your sentences. Avoid run-on sentences and sentence fragments.

C. Postwriting

As you revise your letter, use the following checklist.

1. Does the letter include a clear and precise statement of position?

2. Are the reasons arranged in logical order?

3. Is the tone of the letter polite but firm?

4. Are there sentence fragments or run-on sentences?

5. Is the letter written in correct business form? See the section Reviewing the Form of a Business Letter in Chapter 10.

Use the Checklist for Proofreading Business Letters in Chapter 10 to proofread your letter. Then, ask one of your classmates to assume the role of station manager and read your letter. Ask the reader to tell which of your reasons is the most convincing and why.

20 The Phrase

Understanding Phrases

Phrases, groups of words that work together as a unit, can add a great deal of information to a sentence:

The girl sat and wrote.

The girl *with the term paper assignment* sat *at the library table* and wrote *to the Agriculture Department, asking for information about beekeeping.*

In this section you will learn to identify the various kinds of phrases. More important, you will learn to understand how they function in a sentence.

Defining a Phrase

A *phrase* is usually defined as a group of words, without a subject and its verb, that functions as a single part of speech.

A phrase may function in a sentence as a noun, verb, adjective, or adverb.

Noun phrases are usually defined as a noun and its modifiers.

All students in the creative writing class must write *ten rhymed poems.*

The senator from Illinois became *a well-known orator in the Midwest.*

A *verb phrase* consists of a main verb plus one or more helping verbs.

A recycling project *will be held* the second week in March.

New science equipment for the lab *has been needed* for several years.

In the following sections you will study other kinds of phrases.

Prepositional Phrases

A *prepositional phrase* is made up of a preposition, its object, and any modifiers the object may have.

The object of a preposition is the noun or pronoun (or group of words functioning as a noun) that ends the prepositional phrase. In the following examples the prepositional phrases are in parentheses, and the object of each preposition is *italicized*.

We are going (to *Tulsa*) (on *Friday*) (for a field *trip*).

The otters cavorted and swam (in the stream's swift *water*).

A shaft (of *sunlight*) fell (on the brightly patterned *carpet*).

Prepositional phrases are modifiers, functioning either as adjectives or adverbs.

An *adjective phrase* is a prepositional phrase that modifies a noun or a pronoun. Like a single-word adjective, it tells *what kind, which one,* or *how many.*

Modifies Noun: The player *on the right* is Rosie Casales.
[The phrase *on the right* tells *which one.*]

Modifies Noun: The refrigerator contained only a box *of cheese.*
[The phrase *of cheese* tells *what kind.*]

Modifies Pronoun: One *of the baby jaguars* was in the petting zoo.
[The phrase *of the baby jaguars* tells *what kind.*]

In a series of prepositional phrases, an adjective phrase may modify the object of a preposition in the preceding phrase.

Sherry snapped a photo (*of the hippopotamus*) (*with the bird*) (*on its head*).

An *adverb phrase* is a prepositional phrase that modifies a verb, an adjective, or another adverb.

Adverb phrases answer the question *where? when? how?* or *how much?*

Modifies Verb:	Human beings have journeyed *to the moon*. [The prepositional phrase *to the moon* answers *where?*]
Modifies Adjective:	The coach became angry *in the afternoon*. [The prepositional phrase *in the afternoon* answers *when?*]
Modifies Adverb:	Our mail arrived late *in the afternoon*. [The prepositional phrase *in the afternoon* answers the adverbial question *when?*]

Two or more adverb phrases may be used in succession to modify the same word.

The fire roared (*through the forest*) (*toward the settlement*). [Both phrases modify the verb *roared*.]

Exercise 1: *Identifying Prepositional Phrases*

Write the following sentences. Underline each prepositional phrase and write above it *Adj.* for adjective phrase or *Adv.* for adverb phrase. Then draw an arrow from the prepositional phrase to the word or words it modifies.

Examples

a. The strange animal in the cage was an armadillo from Texas.

               Adj.   Adj.

   The strange animal <u>in the cage</u> was an armadillo <u>from Texas</u>.

b. We usually swim at the lake on weekends.

             Adv.   Adv.

   We usually swim <u>at the lake</u> <u>on weekends</u>.

1. The classical physics of Isaac Newton went unchallenged for two centuries.

2. The house on the corner of Eleventh and Poplar burned to the ground.

3. The unicorn is a horselike beast of mythology with a horn in the center of its forehead.

4. Hugh Glass was a trapper wounded by a bear and left for dead by his companions; he crawled over 400 miles across the prairie, recovered, and resumed his trapping career.

5. The bottom of the skillet was covered with burnt chili; we had to soak it for several hours and scour it with sand.

6. For years my parents have wanted to buy an old Victorian house with stained glass windows, gables, and a cupola.

7. Birdcage Walk and Constitution Hill are two London streets near Buckingham Palace; Victoria Street leads to Victoria Station, which is close to Westminster Cathedral.

8. The game went on in spite of the drizzle, and the miserable but loyal fans huddled under umbrellas or held sodden newspapers over their heads.

9. The hurricane moved across the Gulf of Mexico toward the Texas coastal towns, and weather forecasters warned residents about the potential dangers.

10. Hinduism is one of the most ancient of religions and also one of the most complex; many of its adherents live in India.

Verbal Phrases

Verbals—participles, gerunds, and infinitives are formed from a verb but do not function as a verb in a sentence. A *participle* is used as an adjective; a *gerund* functions as a noun; and an *infinitive* may function as a noun, adjective, or adverb.

When a verbal has a complement or a modifier, it becomes part of a *verbal phrase*. In the following sections you will learn to identify the three types of verbal phrases: *participial phrases, gerund phrases,* and *infinitive phrases.*

Participial Phrases

A *participle* is a form of the verb that is used as an adjective. Participles have present, past, and perfect forms.

Present: The river, *rising* rapidly, threatened to overflow.

493

Past: The bread dough, *risen* to twice its original size, was ready to be kneaded.

Perfect: *Having risen* early to catch my plane, I napped for most of the flight.

A *participial phrase* consists of a participle and its modifiers and complements. A participial phrase always functions as an adjective, modifying a noun or pronoun.

In the movie *Love Happy*, Harpo Marx, *having hidden inside a giant mechanical penguin*, eludes his pursuers.

Buddhism, *originating first in India*, spread to China, Japan, Sri Lanka, Vietnam, and many other Eastern countries.

Exercise 2: *Identifying Participial Phrases*

Write the following sentences. Underline the participial phrases and draw an arrow to the word each phrase modifies.

Examples

a. The mercury, already rising in the thermometer, indicated another scorching day was ahead of us.

The mercury, already rising in the thermometer, indicated another scorching day was ahead of us.

b. The vase fell to the floor, shattering into many fragments.

The vase fell to the floor, shattering into many fragments.

1. The diamond, seriously flawed, was not worth such a high price.

2. The dog, dreaming perhaps that it was chasing rabbits, barked and twitched its paws.

3. The truck, not having been used for two years, surprised us by starting immediately.

4. Searching for the mythical Bonaventura River, Jed Smith came upon the Great Salt Lake of Utah.

5. *Finnegan's Wake*, written over a period of thirty years, is one of the world's most complex novels.

6. The elephant, plagued by arthritis that kept it from lifting its feet from the damp straw, had to be outfitted with specially made boots.

7. We had to throw out the flour ruined by the mice and the corn meal infested with weevils.

8. The highways covered with sleet and snow made travel impossible, and a storm sweeping in from the northwest promised more bad weather.

9. Determined to get the best from his students, Mr. Boseman never settles for a mediocre performance.

10. Having studied English at a private school in Hong Kong, the exchange student surprised us with an excellent grasp of grammar.

Gerund Phrases

A *gerund* is a form of the verb that is used as a noun.

Gerunds may be used in the same way nouns are used—as subjects, objects, and predicate nominatives.

Subject:	*Dancing* is Joey's favorite recreation.
Object:	Marcia likes *fishing*.
Predicate Nominative:	Priborski's specialty was *punting*.

A *gerund phrase* is made up of a gerund and its complements or modifiers. In a gerund phrase the modifiers may be single words, phrases, or clauses.

Skipping breakfast is a bad habit.

We enjoyed *hearing that school would be let out a week early*.

Our art teacher demonstrated how to get some interesting effects by *painting with a goose quill*.

You will not confuse participial and gerund phrases if you remember how each phrase functions in a sentence.

1. A participial phrase always functions as an adjective.

2. A gerund phrase always functions as a noun.

Exercise 3: *Identifying Gerund Phrases*

Write the following sentences, underlining the gerund phrases. (Some sentences contain more than one gerund phrase.)

Examples

a. Some scientists credit animals with having ESP.
Some scientists credit animals with <u>having ESP</u>.

b. ESP, or extrasensory perception, is being able to know things beyond the range of our immediate senses.
ESP, or extrasensory perception, is <u>being able to know things beyond the range of our immediate senses</u>.

1. An example of ESP would be a dog's finding its way across many miles to be reunited with its owner.

2. There are many accounts of dogs and cats who have found distant owners by journeying for weeks or even months over strange territory.

3. Many people claim they first became aware of a supernatural event or a UFO by an animal's acting strangely.

4. A dog's eerie howling or a cat's sudden spitting and bristling are common devices in ghost stories.

5. Horses have been credited with refusing to cross a bridge or stretch of road that offered unseen danger.

6. Even the great psychiatrist Sigmund Freud is on record as admitting a belief in animal ESP.

7. Duke University is one of the most famous institutions involved in experimenting with ESP.

8. Findings by Duke's scientists and researchers suggest that strange, extranormal powers do exist, in spite of the scoffing of cynics.

9. Serious Russian experimenting with ESP indicates that the Soviet Union considers it an important phenomenon.

10. Learning to use and control this power is the dream of many scientists, and continued researching in the field may someday yield the secrets of ESP.

Infinitive Phrases

The *infinitive* is a form of the verb preceded by the word *to*.

Infinitives may be used as nouns, adjectives, or adverbs.

Noun: *To err* is human.

Adjective: John's hay fever gives him a tendency *to sneeze*.

Adverb: The formula for that chemical is hard *to remember*.

An *infinitive phrase* is made up of an infinitive, its modifiers, complements, and subject.

An infinitive may be used as the subject of the sentence, the direct object, the predicate nominative, or as an adjective or adverb.

Subject: To ski down a mountain at breakneck speed is not my idea of fun.

Object: Tracey hopes to win the tennis tournament.

Predicate Nominative: The way to succeed is to be honest and persistent.

Adjective: That was the perfect movie to give you nightmares.

Adverb: The sled dog was too old to be sent on another long, grueling expedition.

Unlike other verbal phrases, the infinitive phrase may also take a subject, which is part of the infinitive phrase. The subject of the infinitive phrase comes after the main verb and immediately before the infinitive.

The state trooper advised *the motorist to take the alternate route*.

We reminded *Mickey to bring her cymbals to the pep rally*.

The operator told *me to dial the number again*.

497

The subject of an infinitive follows only action verbs such as *urge, order, ask, tell, persuade, warn*, and so on.

Notice also that pronouns that function as subjects or objects in an infinitive phrase are always in the object form (*me, him, her, us, them*).

Subject of Infinitive:	The weather reports warned *us to drive slowly*.
Direct Object of Infinitive:	We needed *to see her*.
Indirect Object of Infinitive:	We have to *tell her the news*.

Exercise 4: *Identifying Infinitive Phrases*

Write the following sentences and underline the infinitive phrases. (Be sure to include any subject an infinitive phrase may have.) Then beneath the sentence write how each phrase is used: subject, object, predicate nominative, adjective, or adverb.

Examples

a. It is amusing to read about some of the strange inventions registered with the U.S. Patent Department.
It is amusing to read about some of the strange inventions registered with the U.S. Patent Department.

adverb

b. One inventor, for instance, designed spectacles to be worn by chickens.
One inventor, for instance, designed spectacles to be worn by chickens.

adjective

1. A water-squirting alarm clock certainly persuades a person to wake up on time.

2. Such a clock, however, would also probably persuade the person to throw the contraption out the nearest window.

3. For those who like to fly in balloons, there was a perfectly amazing invention, a balloon to be guided by eagles or vultures.

4. The birds would have to wear specially designed little corsets.

5. Then there are suspenders designed to be turned into a rope to help you escape from a burning building.

6. Another ingenious device could be used to grate and slice food and also to trap mice and flies.

7. For the person who wants to work while relaxing, there is a rocking chair designed to churn butter.

8. A horrible-looking device resembling a carpenter's drill was supposed to produce dimples.

9. It might be easy to convince people you are mannerly if you wear a hat designed to tip itself.

10. For people needing to jump out of windows or to hurl themselves from cliffs, there is this handy double invention: a parachute to attach to the head, and elastic-sole shoes to absorb the shock of landing.

Appositive Phrases

An *appositive* is a noun or pronoun that identifies or explains a nearby noun or pronoun.

Irish folklore tells of the pooka, *a supernatural animal.*

Margaret Meade, *an anthropologist*, wrote an important book about adolescence in Samoa.

An *appositive phrase* consists of an appositive and its modifiers, which may be single-word modifiers, phrases, or clauses.

The Sweet Adelines, *a singing group*, will perform at the fair.

The aspidistra, *a sturdy plant with long green leaves*, is also known as the "cast iron plant."

My car, *an old Edsel that is always needing repairs*, keeps me broke.

Exercise 5: Identifying Appositive Phrases

Write the sentences on the following page, and underline the appositive phrases. Then draw an arrow from the phrase to the noun or pronoun it modifies.

Examples

a. The Pea Ridge Battlefield, the scene of an important Civil War engagement, is now a national park.

The Pea Ridge Battlefield, the scene of an important Civil War engagement, is now a national park.

b. The Hollow Earth Society, a group that believes the center of the earth is not only hollow but also inhabited, has 400 members.

The Hollow Earth Society, a group that believes the center of the earth is not only hollow but also inhabited, has 400 members.

1. The tomato, a fruit often mistakenly classified as a vegetable, contains vitamin C.

2. Miss Piggy, the world's most glamorous swine, is my favorite Muppet character.

3. Alpha Centauri, the star that is nearest our own sun, often figures in science fiction stories.

4. The Sufis, a mystical sect of Persians, often use humorous stories to illustrate philosophical points.

5. *Paradise Lost*, an epic poem by John Milton, is about the fall of Lucifer from heaven and his temptation of Adam and Eve.

6. Pegasus, the winged horse of mythology, is the symbol of poetic inspiration.

7. One of Agatha Christie's most beguiling detectives is Miss Jane Marple, a deceptively innocent-seeming elderly woman who often knits while thinking out a murder case.

8. Sidney Moncreif, the highest-scoring player in the game, won the "Most Valuable Player Award."

9. Phrenology, a pseudoscience that claimed a person's character was indicated by the bumps of the skull, flourished in the nineteenth century.

10. Updoc, an odious mixture of corn syrup and peanut butter, is the creation of my Uncle Basil, who slathers it generously on his pancakes.

Review: Understanding Phrases

Write the following sentences, underlining the prepositional, participial, gerund, infinitive, and appositive phrases. Above each phrase write one of the following abbreviations:

Adj. adjective phrase   *Ger.* gerund phrase
Adv. adverb phrase   *Inf.* infinitive phrase
Part. participial phrase   *App.* appositive phrase

Examples

a. During the Renaissance the politics of England were often complex and brutal.

        Adv.   Adj.
During the Renaissance the politics of England were often complex and brutal.

b. Upon the death of Henry the Eighth (a powerful and scheming king) a long, relentless struggle for the throne began.

      Adv.   Adj.   App.
Upon the death   of Henry the Eighth   (a powerful and
                                                 Adj.
scheming king) a long, relentless struggle for the throne
began.

1. Edward, Henry's only son, took the throne at the age of nine.

2. Edward, having been weakened by illnesses, had a brief life and a brief reign, dying in his fifteenth year.

3. Before his death he had signed a will forbidding his two half-sisters to rule.

4. Parliament had to agree to this because Edward was quite capable of beheading anyone who opposed him.

5. He left the crown to his cousin, Lady Jane Grey, who became one of England's most pathetic victims in the long power struggle.

6. Jane Grey's "reign," lasting only nine days, ended in her imprisonment and death.

7. Edward's eldest half-sister, Mary of Scotland, seized the throne, accusing Jane Grey and her relatives of treason against the rightful heir.

8. Mary, later nicknamed "Bloody Mary," sent Jane Grey, only a sixteen-year-old girl, and all of her relatives to the executioner's block.

9. In addition, Mary, a religious fanatic, ordered 200 "heretics" to be burned at the stake.

10. Like her brother, Mary of Scotland was in ill health, suffering from a mysterious malady that caused her death in the fifth year of her reign.

11. Elizabeth, Bloody Mary's half-sister and the next queen, was no stranger to intrigue and violence.

12. Anne Boleyn, Elizabeth's mother, had been beheaded by Elizabeth's father primarily because she had been unable to produce a son for him.

13. During Bloody Mary's brief reign, she sent Elizabeth to prison, and Elizabeth narrowly escaped the fatal walk to the headsman's block.

14. Elizabeth, at the age of twenty-five, became queen, perhaps the strongest queen in English history.

15. Her subjects loved her, her ministers respected her, and her political enemies learned, to their sorrow, that they should not have tried to plot against her.

16. Condemning people to death was distasteful to Queen Elizabeth, but she was quite capable of it.

17. Seeing her power menaced by her cousin, Mary Queen of Scots, Elizabeth signed that unfortunate lady's death warrant.

18. Near the end of her long life, Elizabeth apparently fell in love with a much younger man, the Earl of Essex.

19. Essex committed the unpardonable sin, treason against the queen, attempting to seize power from her.

20. Elizabeth sent him to the tower prison and condemned him to death.

Applying What You Know

From a paper you have recently written or from another source, select a passage about two or three paragraphs long. Using your knowledge of the definition and types of phrases, identify the phrases in the selection and list them on a sheet of paper in the order they appear. Beside each phrase identify its type: adjective, adverb, participial, gerund, infinitive, or appositive.

Using Phrases

You can combine ideas and avoid short, choppy sentences by using phrases.

> The dog was barking. It was tied to the fence. It lunged futilely. It was lunging at the stray kitten.

> The barking dog, tied to the fence, lunged futilely at the stray kitten.

In the following lessons you will review how phrases are punctuated. You will also practice placing phrases within a sentence so that they communicate their meaning clearly and effectively, and you will see how phrases can be used to give variety to your sentence structure.

Punctuating Phrases

 phrase is not a sentence, because it does not contain a subject and its verb; therefore, a phrase cannot express a complete thought. A phrase should not be punctuated as if it were a sentence.

Avoid phrase fragments in your writing.

A phrase must be attached to the sentence to which it logically belongs.

Fragment: I wrote a note in the dust on the coffee table. Reminding myself to clean up the house. One of these days.

Sentence: I wrote a note in the dust on the coffee table, reminding myself to clean up the house one of these days.

Fragment: To sum up my opinions. I am against the proposed budget cuts because they will hurt the educational system.

Sentence: To sum up my opinions, I am against the proposed budget cuts because they will hurt the educational system.

In certain situations commas are used to set off phrases from the rest of the sentence.

Appositives are usually set off by commas.

Howard Hawks, *a Hollywood director*, was renowned for making great movies about the American West.

The long interval, *probably the best tactic in defensive driving*, can help you in many diverse situations.

Appositives are not set off when they are essential to the meaning of the sentence. Such appositives are usually a name or a one-word appositive.

My cousin *Dino* works at the hospital.

The conjunction *and* joins sentence parts together.

When introductory phrases are long or several introductory phrases are linked together, they are set off by a comma.

Shortly after the ringing of the burglar alarm, a police car pulled up to the store.

To make matters worse, I accidentally dropped my car keys in the sewer.

A short introductory phrase that precedes the subject is not set off by commas.

In July we are going to visit Mexico.

During October the monarch butterflies migrate southward.

An introductory participial phrase that precedes the subject is set off by a comma.

Gurgling horribly, the drain began to back up until the water overflowed.

Disgusted by the long line at the ticket window, we decided to skip the movie.

Nonintroductory phrases are set off by commas when they are not essential to the meaning of the sentence. (Such phrases are called *nonessential* phrases.) A phrase that is essential to the meaning of the sentence is not set off by punctuation.

Essential:	The artist *sketching with charcoal* is Rita Washington.
Nonessential:	The artist, *sketching with charcoal*, bent over her pad of paper in absolute concentration.
Essential:	All Americans are guaranteed the right *to pursue happiness*.
Nonessential:	His single desire, *to pursue happiness*, seemed shallow and immature.

Exercise 6: Correcting Phrases

Write the following sentences, correcting phrase fragments and errors in punctuation. If a sentence is correct as written, write C. Circle the punctuation you insert.

Examples

a. The principal wants to see you. In the office right now.
   The principal wants to see you in the office right now.

b. Howling balefully, the Hound of the Baskervilles stalked the fog-shrouded moors.
   C

1. The novel the story of a Polish girl who survived a Nazi concentration camp was nominated for the National Book Award.

2. Slipping from my hands the book dropped to the floor and bounced down the stairs.

3. The vegetable marrow, a type of large squash, is a favorite crop of British gardeners.

4. Bill Cosby the well-known comedian earned a doctoral degree in education.

5. Pedro trained for his ambitious goal. To compete in the next Olympics.

Placing Phrases

When phrases are used as modifiers, they usually come as close as possible to the words they modify; otherwise, confusion may result. Two kinds of problems sometimes occur when using phrases as modifiers: *misplaced modifiers* and *dangling modifiers*.

A modifier is *misplaced* when it seems to modify a noun or pronoun other than the one it was meant to modify.

Misplaced: I saw a moose *looking out of the cab of my truck.*

Corrected: *Looking out of the cab of my truck*, I saw a moose.

In your writing place a modifier as near as possible to the word it modifies.

Misplaced: Phyllis and her family saw the majestic Rocky Mountains *flying to Utah.*

Corrected: *Flying to Utah,* Phyllis and her family saw the majestic Rocky Mountains.

Misplaced: *Hanging by a long furry tail*, John watched the monkey eat the orange.

Corrected: John watched the monkey, *hanging by a long furry tail,* eat the orange.

A modifier is called *dangling* when a sentence contains no word or words for it to modify.

Dangling: *Listening to the news flash*, it was hard to believe the story was possible.
[Who was listening to the news flash?]

Corrected: *Listening to the news flash*, we found it hard to believe the story was possible.

Place phrases so that they clearly modify a word or words within the sentence.

Dangling: *Straining his tired eyes*, the pilot's visibility was very difficult.

Corrected: *Straining his tired eyes*, the pilot could barely see through the very dense fog.

Dangling: *Waiting for the train to pass*, the streets were blocked.

Corrected: *Waiting for the train to pass*, the cars blocked the streets.

Exercise 7: Correcting Misplaced and Dangling Modifiers

Rewrite the following sentences, correcting misplaced and dangling modifiers.

Example

> a. Coiled up in the rainspout, Grandmother saw a small copperhead snake.
>
> Grandmother saw a small copperhead snake coiled up in the rainspout.

1. In order to provide new students with essential information, a news sheet is sent to each one.

2. We ate a dessert made by my cousin called "Idiot's Delight."

3. Lying ear-deep in mud and contentedly chewing garbage, I watched the hogs.

4. Rummaging under the sofa cushions, a dime, two pennies, and four pencils were recovered.

5. By not reading the instructions on the box, the bicycle was put together incorrectly.

Review: Using Phrases

Rewrite the following sentences, correcting phrase fragments, errors in punctuation, misplaced modifiers, and dangling modifiers. If a sentence is correct as written, write C.

1. A large snapping turtle, nearly a foot across, sat hissing and shaking its head back and forth. Right in our path.

2. The musical comedy created in the nineteenth century is one of America's contributions to the world of theater.

3. Up until the very last second of the game with Texas A. & M. our team remained within one point of winning.

4. The actress playing the role of Suzie Wong was France Nuyen.

5. At the high point of the third act in the school play, I suddenly forgot my lines completely.

6. Disgusted by poor grades, the test was given again.

7. I saw several ancient mummies touring the museum.

8. I luckily escaped injury when I hit a cow on my motorcycle.

9. Completely upsetting the sportscasters' predictions, the tournament was won by Marcia Redhawk.

10. Looking through the microscope, the germs appeared large and ugly.

Writing Focus: *Using Phrases*

Good writers use phrases to add details, to combine sentences, and to vary the structure of their sentences. To use phrases effectively, be sure you place and punctuate them correctly. Place phrases as close as possible to the words they modify. To decide whether or not a phrase should be set off by commas, determine how the phrase functions in the sentence. Remember that the purpose of punctuation is to make sentences easier to read and understand.

Assignment: *Working with Details*

Imagine that you stroll over to your best friend's house for a visit, only to find no one home. As you are leaving, you notice a car with two people in it pulling up the alley behind the house. Suspicious, you look closely at the car and its passengers. Later that evening you discover that your friend's house was robbed shortly after you left the scene. You telephone the police, who think you might have seen the thieves.

Write two well-developed paragraphs, giving a detailed description of the car and its passengers. Your audience is a police officer, and your purpose is to present the facts about what you saw. Your paragraph will be evaluated for correct and effective use of phrases.

Use the steps on the next page to complete this assignment.

A. Prewriting

Pretend that you are in the situation described above. Imagine what the car and passengers looked like and what they did. Make up the kinds of details in which the police would be interested, such as the time you saw the car; the color, model, and license number of the car; and the sex, approximate age, clothing, and physical features of the passengers. Make a list of such information and any added details that would be helpful to the police. For help in organizing your paragraphs, refer to Chapter 3.

B. Writing

Using your list of details, write your two-paragraph description. Make it as clear and factual as possible. As you write, use phrases to add detail, to combine sentences, and to vary the structure of your sentences.

C. Postwriting

Revise your first draft, using the following checklist.

1. Have I included only facts, not opinions, in my paragraphs?

2. Are the sentences in each paragraph arranged in an orderly progression?

3. Do the paragraphs include enough specific details?

4. Have I used phrases effectively and correctly to add details, to combine sentences, and to vary the structure of the sentences?

Proofread your paragraph, using the Checklist for Proofreading at the back of the book. Finally, share your writing with classmates to enjoy one another's descriptions.

21 Clauses

Understanding Clauses

In the following lessons you will learn to identify clauses by definition and by categories. You will also learn to classify sentences according to the number and kinds of clauses they contain.

Defining a Clause

A *clause* is usually defined as a group of words that contains a subject and a predicate and that functions as part of a sentence.

Although the definition of a clause resembles that of a sentence (a clause and a sentence both have a subject and a verb, or predicate), a sentence differs from a clause in that a sentence must *always* express a complete thought. Some clauses, although they have both subjects and predicates, do not express a complete thought. All of the following are clauses.

$$\overset{\text{S}}{} \quad \overset{\text{V}}{}$$
because the streets were frozen

$$\overset{\text{S}}{} \quad \overset{\text{V}}{}$$
although the game was on Friday

$$\overset{\text{S}}{} \quad \overset{\text{V}}{}$$
The bowling ball fell on my toe.

Clauses may be divided into two main categories: *independent clauses* and *subordinate clauses*.

Independent Clauses

An *independent*, or *main*, *clause* is one that can stand on its own as a sentence.

E very sentence contains at least one independent clause. An independent clause can stand alone, expresses a complete thought, and contains a subject and its verb. It may also contain single-word modifiers, phrase modifiers, or both. Each of these sentences is one independent clause that contains a subject and its verb.

$$\overset{\text{S}}{}\qquad\qquad\overset{\text{V}}{}$$

The main chamber of the castle was gloomy and dank.

$$\overset{\text{S}}{}\qquad\overset{\text{V}}{}$$

The riders had dismounted from their horses.

A sentence may contain two or more independent clauses connected by a conjunction or semicolon.

The apples were ruined by the hail storm, but most of the pear crop survived.

Emily Brontë was an English poet and novelist; Emily Dickinson was an American poet.

Subordinate Clauses

T he word *subordinate* means "of lower rank." A subordinate clause is of lower rank than an independent clause because it cannot stand alone as a sentence. It needs to be attached to an independent clause in order for its meaning to be clear.

A *subordinate clause* is usually defined as a clause that cannot stand on its own as a sentence.

In the following examples the subordinate clauses are *italicized*.

Whenever the meter reader comes, the dogs bark wildly.

We saw the barns *that the tornado damaged*.

The pygmy rattlesnake ate mice, *which were plentiful*.

Exercise 1: Identifying Independent and Subordinate Clauses

On a sheet of paper numbered 1–10, write *S* if the *italicized* group of words in each of the sentences on the following page is a subordinate clause. Write *I* if it is an independent clause.

Examples

a. *An Englishman went to a cemetery* because he wanted to visit the grave of a friend.
I

b. He brought a small bouquet *that he laid upon the grave.*
S

1. The man stood at the grave *while he remembered his old friend.*

2. *When he looked up,* he saw another visitor at a neighboring grave.

3. The other man was a Chinese, *who was placing a bowl of rice on a grave.*

4. *The Englishman was startled and amused* because he had never seen such a sight.

5. "When do you expect *that your friend will come up and eat the rice?"* he asked.

6. *After the Chinese gentleman bowed politely,* he spoke.

7. "He will come up about the same time *that your friend comes up to smell the flowers,"* he replied.

8. *Although this story is probably fictional,* it illustrates an important truth.

9. We often accept familiar customs without question, *whereas we are astonished by customs that are strange to us.*

10. Our own actions and beliefs may seem as strange to others *as theirs do to us.*

Classifying Sentences by Structure

Sentences may be classified according to the number of independent and subordinate clauses they contain. According to structure, there are four types of sentences: *simple, compound, complex,* and *compound-complex.*

A *simple* sentence contains one independent clause and no subordinate clauses.

All of the mice in the laboratory escaped.

I bought myself a new record album.

A simple sentence may have a compound subject, a compound verb, or both.

Hinduism and Taoism are both eastern religions and are very ancient.

The forward and the guard from the same team both went for the ball and collided.

A *compound sentence* is made up of two or more independent clauses but no subordinate clauses.

I had to study, but people kept interrupting me.

A slight dew was on the field, and a gentle breeze stirred the grasses.

Crazy Horse was one of the most important Indian leaders, yet no photographs of him exist.

A *complex sentence* is composed of one independent clause and one or more subordinate clauses.

In the following examples the independent clauses are underlined once, the subordinate clauses twice.

We didn't go to the game because we lost our tickets.

Since I can't concentrate while the television set is on, I turn it off when I study.

If gasoline prices don't go down, I will have to travel on foot when I go to college.

A *compound-complex sentence* is composed of two or more independent clauses and one or more subordinate clauses.

In the following examples the independent clauses are underlined once, the subordinate clauses twice.

Because my sister likes to travel, she has been to Ireland and Hong Kong, but I prefer to stay home with a good book, since I hate planes and ships.

Although a small shark was found dead in the river, the authorities think that pranksters put it there, for this type of shark cannot live in fresh water.

Exercise 2: Classifying Sentences by Structure

Write the following sentences, underlining the independent clauses once and the subordinate clauses twice. After each sentence identify its type according to structure: simple, complex, compound, or compound-complex.

Examples

a. We saw that the river was up, but we didn't believe that it was nearing flood stage yet.

We saw that the river was up, but we didn't believe that it was nearing flood stage yet.

compound-complex

b. I let my brother borrow the car once, but I'll never do it again.
I let my brother borrow the car once, but I'll never do it again.

compound

1. Hypnosis, which is derived from a Greek word meaning "sleep," is familiar to most of us, but it is not well understood.

2. Hypnosis first began to be recognized in France, when the physician Mesmer began experimenting with magnets; he believed that magnets might have healing properties.

3. Although Mesmer seemed to heal some people with magnets, he began to believe that the power came from his own body.

4. He theorized that some people have a power, "animal magnetism," that could effect cures.

5. One of his followers who was performing experiments soon discovered that "animal magnetism" seemed to have nothing to do with magnetism.

6. By simply talking, he could put people into "trances."

7. Freud and other early psychologists experimented with hypnotism because they thought that it could open up the mind.

8. Today hypnotism is used in psychoanalysis, in medicine, and in police work to help witnesses recall details.

9. Hypnotism exists, and it often works, but we still do not know quite what it is or how it works.

10. Some experts say that there is no such thing as a "trance" and that the powers of suggestion and imagination bring about what we know as "the hypnotic state."

Adjective Clauses

According to their function in the sentence, subordinate clauses can be divided into three classes: *adjective, adverb,* and *noun.*

An *adjective clause* is a subordinate clause that modifies a noun or pronoun.

We saw the spot *where the tornado touched down.*

The Andrews Sisters, *whose first names were Pattie, Maxine, and LaVerne,* where the most popular singing group in the early 1940s.

We visited Red Cloud, Nebraska, *where Willa Cather lived.*

The adjective clause is usually introduced by a relative pronoun: *who, whom, whose, which, that* or *where.*

Relative pronouns refer to the noun or pronoun in the sentence that the adjective clause modifies. Within the clause the relative pronoun may function as the subject of the clause it introduces.

          S   V
She is a woman *who has accomplished much.*

          S   V
Air pollution is a problem *that affects us all.*

515

Relative pronouns may also serve as the object of the clause or as the object of a preposition within the clause.

DO   S V

Daisy Bates, *whom we met at the convention,* is a well-known civil rights worker.

OP S   V

I know someone *with whom I can ride.*

Where and *when* can also introduce adjective clauses.

I want to see the lake *where the sea serpent is supposed to live.*

The 1950s were the period *when rock-and-roll music became popular.*

Sometimes, a relative pronoun is omitted when the clause has its own subject and verb and the meaning is clear. In the following sentence the relative pronouns have been dropped.

The writer *I like best* is Maya Angelou.
[The relative pronoun *whom* has been dropped from the subordinate clause.]

I'll show you the truck *I want to buy.*
[The relative pronoun *that* has been dropped from the subordinate clause.]

Exercise 3: *Identifying Adjective Clauses*

Write the following sentences, underlining the adjective clause in each and drawing an arrow to the word the clause modifies. (A sentence may contain more than one adjective clause.)

Examples

a. Many young couples want a house that they can call their own.

Many young couples want a house that they can call their own.

b. They should find a reliable real estate agent on whom they can depend.

They should find a reliable real estate agent on whom they can depend.

1. Such an agent will not try to talk the customer into a house that is too expensive for him or her.

2. An agent who knows about houses can spot potential problems or hidden disadvantages in a certain home.

3. A pleasant-looking house may hide a number of flaws, of which termites, poor plumbing or wiring, and a leaky basement may be only a few.

4. The house a customer buys should be in a neighborhood that meets his or her needs.

5. A childless couple might not be happy in a neighborhood where a dozen preschoolers are playing noisily every day.

6. A house that is located far from the buyer's place of work or shopping may result in staggering gasoline bills.

7. The quiet soul who needs peace should not move next door to the animal lover whose eight beagles yodel all night long.

8. One point the buyer should remember is energy; a low-priced house that has huge gas and electric bills is no bargain.

9. A person who can't hammer a nail should probably not tackle a house that needs extensive repairs.

10. Novice house-hunters need an agent whom they can trust and who has their best interests in mind.

Adverb Clauses

An *adverb clause* modifies a verb, an adjective, or an adverb.

Like adverbs and adverb phrases, an adverb clause may answer the questions *why? where? to what extent?* or *under what conditions?*

We always fish a lot *when we go camping*.
[The clause tells *when*.]

You can't go overseas *unless you take a series of inoculations*.
[The clause tells *under what conditions*.]

Like single-word adverbs, adverb clauses may modify verbs, adjectives, and other adverbs.

You will fail *unless you study*.
[The clause modifies the verb *will fail*.]

As soon as we left, the rain began.
[The clause modifies the verb *began*.]

Ms. Polanski was certain *that she had left the tests on her desk*.
[The clause modifies the adjective *certain*.]

We were afraid *that the canoe would tip over in the rapids*.
[The clause modifies the adjective *afraid*.]

Kim can solve algebra problems more quickly *than I can*.
[The clause modifies the adverb phrase *more quickly*.]

The magician shuffled the cards faster *than the eye could follow*.
[The clause modifies the adverb *faster*.]

An adverb clause begins with a subordinating conjunction:

after	as though	since	when
although	because	so that	whenever
as	before	than	where
as if	if	though	wherever
as long as	in order that	unless	while
as soon as	provided that	until	

You may recognize some of the words in the preceding list as other parts of speech. For example, *since, until, before,* and *as* can be used as prepositions; *before* and *after* can be adverbs. In order to be classified as subordinating conjunctions, these words must introduce an adverb clause. Unlike the relative pronoun, the subordinating conjunction never functions as a subject or object within the clause.

The subordinating conjunction is important because it expresses the relationship of the ideas contained in the subordinate clause and the independent clause. Notice how changing the subordinate clause changes the meaning of the sentence:

I'll go *because I have to.*

I'll go *when I have to.*

I'll go *as soon as I have to.*

I'll go *wherever I have to.*

I'll go *if I have to.*

When two ideas are combined into a single sentence, either one may be subordinated to the other, depending on which idea the writer thinks is more important. Notice that the meaning of the following two sentences is somewhat different.

Although Linda didn't want to go to the party, she had a good time.

Linda didn't want to go to the party, although she had a good time.

Adverb clauses may be elliptical. An *elliptical clause* is one in which a word or words have been omitted. In elliptical clauses the omitted words are understood by both the speaker and the listener or the writer and reader. Notice that the omitted words, shown in brackets, may be the subject of the clause or the verb, or both.

When [she was] visiting Utah, Clare saw the Mormon Tabernacle.

When [I was] eating, I saw something moving in my salad.

Georgia is a larger state *than Tennessee [is].*

When [you are] in Rome, do as the Romans do.

Exercise 4: *Identifying Adverb Clauses*

Write each of the following sentences, underlining each adverb clause and circling the subordinating conjunction. If the clause is elliptical, write out the clause beneath the sentence and include in brackets the words that have been omitted.

Examples

a. The lake is lower than it has been for ten years

The lake is lower (than) it has been for ten years.

b. When leaving, be sure to turn out the lights.

(When) [you are] leaving, be sure to turn out the lights.

1. Since the late movie wouldn't be over until three in the morning, we decided to skip it.

2. While running to answer the phone, I tripped, knocked over the chair, and landed in a heap on the living room rug.

3. Although Marcia loves cats, she can't have one because they make her sneeze constantly.

4. When the Blazers played the Bucks, Moncrief made one of his stunning slam dunks.

5. Trailers cost less than houses, but they depreciate faster as well.

6. Willows and elms grow more quickly than oaks, but they are less sturdy than many other trees.

7. Because we didn't believe in ghosts, we tried to find some other explanation for the weird sounds in our attic.

8. My little sister will get her driver's license in May, provided that she raises her grades in math.

9. A pound of feathers is heavier than a pound of gold, because a "pound" of gold is only fourteen ounces.

10. Catherine looked as though she weren't feeling well after she rode the roller coaster.

Noun Clauses

A *noun clause* is a subordinate clause used as a noun.

A noun clause may be the subject of an independent clause, the direct object, the indirect object, the predicate nominative, the object of a preposition, or an appositive. In short, a noun clause may serve any function a noun can.

What I need is an extra day in each week.	[subject]
I believe *that flying saucers really exist.*	[direct object]
She gave *whoever called* the same message.	[indirect object]
My invention is *just what the world needs.*	[predicate nominative]
We will give help to *whoever needs it.*	[object of preposition]
Her theory, *that all is futile*, is ridiculous.	[appositive]

Adjective clauses usually begin with relative pronouns, and subordinating conjunctions introduce adverb clauses. Some of these same words introduce noun clauses, but they are not considered relative pronouns or subordinating conjunctions when they do. When any of the following begin a noun clause, they are considered introductory words.

that	whatever	where	whoever
what	when	who	whomever

In noun clauses, as in adjective clauses, the introductory word is sometimes omitted. For example, direct quotations that follow an expression such as *he said,* or *she answered* are really noun clauses with the introductory word *that* omitted.

He said, [that] *"The Jones sisters are the best teachers in the city system."*

I thought [that] *he was right.*

Grandmother knew [that] *a snake must be in the henhouse.*

Exercise 5: Identifying Noun Clauses

Write the following sentences, underlining the noun clause in each. (Some sentences may have more than one noun clause.) After the sentence indicate how each clause is used.

Example

a. Whoever sat next to me at assembly took my book.
   Whoever sat next to me at assembly took my book.

   subject

1. The trophy will be awarded to whoever climbs the greased flagpole first.

2. Whatever took my bait was very large and very fast.

3. We saw what appeared to be a large bluish light hovering over the swamp.

4. Sheila thought the bell would never ring.

5. For the party, dress in whatever costume expresses your secret fantasy.

6. More exercise and less rich food is what many Americans need.

7. Where I long to be is on a surfboard, riding the perfect wave.

8. Who the culprit must be suddenly flashed into the detective's mind.

9. A sudden thought, that I was not alone in the house, made me uneasy.

10. Give whoever needs extra paper one of these examination tablets.

Review: *Understanding Clauses*

Using what you have learned about identifying clauses, find the noun, adjective, and adverb clauses in the following paragraphs from *Adventures in English Literature*. List the clauses on a sheet of paper in the order they appear, labeling each clause *noun, adjective,* or *adverb.* For noun clauses identify its function in the sentence; for adjective and adverb clauses identify the word or words modified by the clause.

It is natural that we should be curious about the life of a writer who is almost unanimously considered to be the greatest figure in English literature. Fortunately, more facts are known about Shakespeare than about most Elizabethan playwrights. We know that he was born in Stratford-on-Avon in April (probably on the 23rd) 1564, and that his father John was a fairly prominent citizen of the town who eventually became an alderman and bailiff. Shakespeare was presumably educated at the local school in Stratford. He never attended a university. In 1582 he married Anne Hathaway. They had a daughter in 1583, and twins, a boy and a girl, in 1585. After this there is no factual information for seven years, but we know that by 1592 he was in London working as an actor and a playwright, for in this year he was attacked in writing by a resentful rival.

In 1593 the London theaters were closed because of an outbreak of the plague, and Shakespeare, temporarily out of work, needed the support of a private patron. He got such support from the Earl of Southampton, a wealthy young nobleman to whom Shakespeare dedicated two rather long narrative poems: *Venus and Adonis* (1593) and *The Rape of Lucrece* (1594). When the theaters reopened, Shakespeare became a member of the most successful company of actors in London, the Lord Chamberlain's Men.[1]

Applying What You Know

From a textbook or a paper you have recently written, select a passage about the length of that in the preceding review exercise. Then follow the instructions for the review exercise.

Using Clauses

The next few lessons will give you practice using clauses. Helpful writing skills you will study are punctuating clauses correctly and knowing when to use *who* and *whom.*

---

[1]From "William Shakespeare" in *Adventures in English Literature*, Heritage Edition, copyright © 1980 by Harcourt Brace Jovanovich, Inc. Reprinted by permission of the publisher.

Punctuating Clauses Correctly

Set off an introductory adverb clause from the rest of the sentence with a comma.

If you have any doubts, contact me.

After Washington struck out, we knew the game was lost.

(A comma is usually unnecessary, however, when the adverb clause follows the main clause.)

Contact me if you have any trouble.

We knew the game was lost after Washington struck out.

Do not use commas to set off an essential clause.

An adjective clause that is essential to the meaning of a sentence is called an *essential* (or *restrictive*) *clause*. Such a clause cannot be removed without changing or damaging the meaning of the sentence.

Essential: We saw a play *that won every award on Broadway.*
[Not just any play was seen; it was the play *that won every award on Broadway.*]

Essential: Every cabbage *that we've ever bought from Tudbury's Market* has been wormy.
[Not every cabbage in the world was wormy, not even every cabbage purchased was wormy; only those *that we've ever bought from Tudbury's Market* were wormy.]

A *nonessential clause*, on the other hand, does not add essential information. It adds additional information, but the sentence would still mean the same if the clause were dropped. Commas are used to set off nonessential clauses.

Nonessential: The troup visited the North Cape, *which is not easy to get to.*

Nonessential: Mrs. Gomez, *who lives next door*, is a certified public accountant.

Avoid making sentence fragments of subordinate clauses; do not punctuate them as if they were sentences.

A subordinate clause cannot stand alone; it must be attached to an independent clause.

Fragment:	Until the final ballots are counted.
Sentence:	We won't know who the next dog catcher will be until the final ballots are counted.
Fragment:	Because he thinks the moon is made of green cheese.
Sentence:	Because he thinks the moon is made of green cheese, he is not a very good candidate for astronaut training school.

Exercise 6: *Punctuating Clauses Correctly*

Rewrite the following sentences, adding commas where necessary and correcting sentence fragments. If a sentence is punctuated correctly, write C. Circle the commas you insert.

Examples

    a. Even if it rains or snows Ken jogs a mile each day.
       Even if it rains or snows⊙ Ken jogs a mile each day.

    b. The cat ate the lamb chops that were defrosting on the counter.
       C

1. The Zuñi who are a Southwestern nation are noted for their exquisite silverwork.

2. Of course I can go with you to the movies. After I do my eighteen pages of geometry.

3. My biology teacher who is rather cynical says that soon human beings will have one large eye for watching television and one large finger for pushing buttons.

4. The student government wants to turn the area that was supposed to be for storage into a student lounge.

5. The crowd laughed at the hypnotist's willing subject. Who was convinced she was the world's greatest hula dancer.

6. Whenever we let Rover into the house he immediately races through the kitchen and leaps onto the couch.

7. The house which had been built before the Civil War was beautiful but had no central heating system.

8. Nebraska a completely landlocked state has a mythical navy and bestows the honorary title of ''Admiral of the Nebraska Navy'' on some people as a joking tribute.

9. Since the invention of the automobile courting practices have changed drastically.

10. Although John McClure is an excellent mystery writer few Americans are familiar with his work. Because he is a South African.

Using Who *and* Whom *in Clauses*

Who and *whom* are used to introduce adjective clauses and noun clauses. Simple rules govern the use of *who* and *whom* in Edited Standard English.

Who is always used as the subject of a clause. Whom is used to function as an object, usually either a direct object or an object of a preposition.

The woman *who came to the door* was Ms. Feinberg.
[*Who* is the subject of the adjective clause.]

Chris is the person *whom I'd recommend for the job.*
[*Whom* is the direct object in the adjective clause.]

Do not ask *for whom the bell tolls.*
[*Whom* is the object of the preposition in the noun clause.]

Whom the police suspect has not yet been made public.
[*Whom* is the direct object of the noun clause.]

Notice that you must determine the use of *who* or *whom* as it functions within the clause, not within the sentence.

The words *whoever* and *whomever* follow the same rules. *Whoever* is the subject form; *whomever* is the object form.

Use whoever as the subject of the clause. Use whomever for an object within the clause.

Whoever passed the test must have been a genius.
[*Whoever* is the subject of the noun clause.]

The scholarship will be given to *whomever the coach recommends.*
[*Whomever* is the direct object of the noun clause that serves as the object of the preposition.]

Exercise 7: Using Who and Whom in Clauses

Write the following sentences, choosing and underlining the correct word from the pair in parentheses. Remember that you must first determine how the word is used within the clause.

Examples

---

a. Louis Armstrong is the singer (who, whom) made that song famous.

   Louis Armstrong is the singer <u>who</u> made that song famous.

b. Give these old magazines to (whoever, whomever) you want to have them.

   Give these old magazines to <u>whomever</u> you want to have them.

---

1. Mr. Mwangi is the teacher (who, whom) the students most respect.

2. (Whoever, Whomever) was trying to drive us from the castle would not succeed.

3. The housekeeper (who, whom) the agency recommended so highly was slovenly and ill-tempered.

4. We need to contact (whoever, whomever) is in charge of selling the tickets.

5. The player (who, whom) was on second base made a sprint to steal third.

6. The donation will go to (whoever, whomever) is the most deserving recipient.

7. (Who, Whom) shall I say is calling, please?

8. The organization will give $10,000 to (whoever, whomever) breeds a hamster marked like a panda bear.

9. (Who, Whom) did the committee elect as president?

10. Nobody knows (who, whom) will be selected for Groundhog Queen this year.

Review: Using Clauses

Write the following sentences, correcting any errors in punctuation or word choice. If a sentence is correct, write C. Circle the punctuation you insert and underline the corrections you make.

1. Send announcements to whomever is on the membership list.

2. If John Keats had lived longer he might have been one of our very greatest poets.

3. Transporting the fish and newts from our aquarium was our biggest problem when we moved to Chicago.

4. Give whoever the committee elects copies of the minutes of past meetings.

5. Since our cat has the bad habit of stalking birds we put several bells on its collar.

6. Marlie's favorite television program is *Soul Train* which is hosted by Don Cornelius.

7. The person who I most admire is Mother Teresa of India.

8. The book that won top honors for a first novel was *Song of Solomon* by Toni Morrison.

9. If a lightning storm begins while you are outside you should not take shelter under a tree.

10. The manager of the jewelry store who had no sense of humor threatened to fire Pat because of the prank.

11. When the Studebaker Company closed down in South Bend, Indiana, the city suffered a grave unemployment problem.

12. Della finally found the person for who she was searching.

13. Whenever Uncle Waldo decides to cook one of his gourmet delights the kitchen ends up looking like a disaster area.

14. The restaurant that specialized in health food dishes was closed down by the Board of Health.

15. I was only halfway through my test when the bell rang.

16. In honor of the students' favorite basketball player, the bookstore sells T-shirts, that say "Eugene, Eugene, the Dunking Machine."

17. When my sister went to college last fall she took her most treasured possession: a mounted moose head.

18. The local newspaper always contains so many printing errors, that it's called "The Daily Mistake."

19. Free entry blanks are available for whomever wants to enter the contest.

20. Because the cold rain poured down all day the dogs stayed in their houses and looked forlorn.

Writing Focus: *Using Clauses in Your Writing*

Like phrases, clauses are used by writers to add details, to combine sentences, and to vary the structure of sentences. You can strengthen your writing style by using clauses for these purposes. Be sure to punctuate clauses correctly. To decide whether a clause should be set off by commas, determine how the clause functions in the sentence.

Assignment: *Today's Generation*

Students of the 1950s were called the "Quiet Generation"; students of the 1970s were called the "Me Generation," described as self-centered and pleasure-seeking. How would you describe the generation of students to which you belong? What traits seem to characterize people of your age? What ideas, goals, problems, or concerns do you share? Discuss these questions with your friends and classmates.

After you have some ideas, write a well-developed paragraph describing your generation. Your audience will be your classmates, and your purpose will be to describe the unique characteristics of your generation. Your paragraph will be evaluated for correct and effective use of clauses. Use the following steps to complete this assignment.

A. Prewriting

Use clustering, described in Chapter 1, to get your initial ideas down on paper. Work with the ideas brought up during your discussions. For help in planning the organization of your paragraph, refer to Chapter 3.

B. Writing

Using your word cluster, write a paragraph that describes your generation. Include a topic sentence that clearly states the main idea of your paragraph. Add enough facts and specific details so that your audience will understand the characteristics that you ascribe to your peer group. As you write, vary your sentences by using clauses in different ways.

C. Postwriting

Revise your first draft, using the following checklist.

1. Does the paragraph have a clear topic sentence?

2. Is it clear how each supporting sentence relates to the topic?

3. Does the paragraph include enough specific details?

4. Have I used clauses effectively to vary the structure of my sentences?

5. Are there sentence fragments or short sentences that can be combined by using clauses?

Proofread your revision, using the Checklist for Proofreading at the back of the book. Finally, share your writing with your classmates and discuss one another's ideas and opinions.

22 Usage and Style

Advanced Usage

The following exercises review the use of irregular and confusing verbs as well as the use of singular and plural pronouns. Your mastery of English usage will help you write grammatically correct sentences.

Exercise 1: Using Irregular Verbs

Study the present, past, and past participle forms of the following irregular verbs:

Present	Past	Past Participle
be	was	(had) been
become	became	(had) become
begin	began	(had) begun
break	broke	(had) broken
bring	brought	(had) brought

Then write the following sentences, supplying the correct form of the verb in parentheses. Underline the verb you supply.

Example

a. We arrived at the theater a bit late, but the movie hadn't _____ yet. (begin)
We arrived at the theater a bit late, but the movie hadn't begun yet.

1. Surely I _____ in class for years, not just fifty minutes. (be)

2. That wretched cat has _____ another flowerpot. (break)

3. After we had hiked ten miles into the forest, we discovered nobody had _____ a can opener. (bring)

4. Mrs. Adams doesn't realize her darling little son Oliver has _____ a neighborhood pest. (become)

5. We _____ to suspect that the fire had been set deliberately. (begin)

6. The twins misbehaved until Uncle Osgood _____ so angry that he threatened to spank them. (become)

7. I'm trying to break the world's record; I've _____ sitting on this flagpole eighteen days. (be)

8. Lucy _____ the wrong notebook to class. (bring)

9. When the two players collided, Carlos _____ his glasses. (break)

10. And just where were you when all this trouble _____ ? (begin)

Exercise 2: *Using Irregular Verbs*

Review the forms of the irregular verbs *buy, catch, choose, come,* and *dive*. Then choose the word in parentheses that correctly completes each of the following sentences. Write the sentences, underlining the word you choose.

Example

a. Kim hasn't (buyed, bought) her class ring yet.
  Kim hasn't <u>bought</u> her class ring yet.

1. Who was (chose, chosen) for the team?

2. A bad strain of flu is going around, but I haven't (caught, catched) it yet.

3. Our neighbor (come, came) over last night to complain about my sister's dog.

4. When the starter fired the pistol, all the swimmers (dived, doved) into the water.

5. Have you (bought, boughten) your tickets yet?

6. The farmer finally (catched, caught) all the escaped cattle.

7. I (come, came) close to getting hit at that intersection.

8. I haven't ever (dived, dove) from the highest board at the pool.

9. Whoever (buyed, bought) that car made a terrible mistake.

10. Have you (chose, chosen) which sleeping bag you want?

Exercise 3: *Using Irregular Verbs*

Review the forms of the irregular verbs *do, draw, drink, drive,* and *eat.* Then write the following sentences, supplying the correct form of the verb in parentheses. Underline the verb you supply.

Example

a. The detective sighed, "I don't know who _____ it." (do)
   The detective sighed, "I don't know who <u>did</u> it."

1. Has Margo _____ her biology homework yet? (do)

2. Mrs. Jaworski has _____ a map of the library. (draw)

3. I'll _____ clams, but I don't like them. (eat)

4. After Juliet _____ the potion, she appeared to be dead. (drink)

5. Lisa never _____ a foul for goal-tending. (draw)

6. Have you ever _____ prune juice? (drink)

7. Lady Macbeth's guilt had _____ her mad. (drive)

8. We have _____ at the new Korean restaurant. (eat)

9. The doctors _____ everything they could to repair the injured elbow. (do)

10. We _____ cautiously down the winding road. (drive)

Exercise 4: *Using Irregular Verbs*

Review the forms of the irregular verbs *fall, fly, forget, freeze, give,* and *go.* Then write the sentences, choosing the verb in parentheses that completes each sentence. Underline the words you choose.

Example

a. Have you ever (gone, went) to a Ray Charles concert?
   Have you ever <u>gone</u> to a Ray Charles concert?

1. I felt as if my toes had (frozen, froze).

2. The reputation of that politician has certainly (fell, fallen).

3. We stopped at the office, but Ms. Garcia had already (went, gone) home.

4. The robins have all (flown, flew) south for the winter.

5. When I walked into the classroom, I (forget, forgot) everything I had studied.

6. I have never (forgotten, forgot) Chief Dan George's performance in that movie.

7. Suddenly a pheasant (flied, flew) up out of the brush.

8. The lake (freezed, froze) over, but not enough to skate on safely.

9. I have (gave, given) my decision to the coach.

10. Carey has (gone, went) to work for an oil company.

Exercise 5: *Correcting Errors in Verb Usage*

Some of the following sentences contain errors in verb usage. Rewrite the sentences, making any necessary corrections. If the sentence is correct, write C. Underline any corrections you make.

Examples

a. I knowed my irregular verb forms perfectly.
   I <u>knew</u> my irregular verb forms perfectly.

b. Marcia kept the secret to herself.
   C

1. Our cute puppy growed up into a huge, shaggy, obnoxious dog.

2. My little brother keeped peeking around the corner at us.

3. I hitted the ball with all my strength.

4. I've knew Dr. Arnez for three years.

5. Have you ever rode a Tennessee walking horse?

6. Hank Aaron has hit more home runs than any other American player.

7. Every time I've rid on the bus, I've got queasy.

8. You knowed better than to tease the bull; here's another bandage.

9. He has keep asking me for favors until I am tired of it.

10. Imat has growed a mustache.

Exercise 6: *Using Irregular Verbs*

Review the forms of the irregular verbs *ring, run, see, shake,* and *shrink.* Then choose the correct form of the verb in parentheses to complete each sentence. Write the sentences, underlining the correct forms.

Example

> a. Have you ever _____ the Harlem Globetrotters play? (see)
> Have you ever <u>seen</u> the Harlem Globetrotters play?

1. Someone has _____ the dismissal bell too early. (ring)

2. Not many Americans have _____ a live panda bear. (see)

3. The laundry _____ my favorite sweater. (shrink)

4. Denise wasn't hurt in the accident, only _____ a bit. (shake)

5. A raccoon got in our garbage, but the dogs _____ it off. (run)

6. Yesterday I _____ a great antique car. (see)

7. It seems that the true buying power of a U.S. dollar has _____ drastically. (shrink)

8. The church bells _____ after the ceremony. (ring)

9. The cat stepped onto the dewy grass, then _____ its paw. (shake)

10. The television station had _____ the wrong commercial. (run)

Exercise 7: *Using Irregular Verbs*

Review the forms of the irregular verbs *sing, sink, slay, speak,* and *spend.* Then choose the word in parentheses that correctly completes each of the following sentences. Write the sentences and underline your choices.

Example

> a. Josephine Baker had (sung, sang) in America before she became a star in Paris.
> Josephine Baker had <u>sung</u> in America before she became a star in Paris.

1. Our boat swamped and our fishing gear (sank, sunk) out of sight.

2. He was as proud as if he had (slayed, slain) a dragon.

3. We (sang, sung) some Osage songs at camp last summer.

4. I have (spoke, spoken) to the company about the problem.

5. Central didn't just beat us; they (slayed, slew) us.

6. I've (spend, spent) all my allowance and am poverty-stricken.

7. The congresswoman (speak, spoke) to the student body.

8. The tenor had (sung, sang) badly off-key.

9. The center had (sank, sunk) an almost impossible shot.

10. The golfer deftly (sunk, sank) the putt.

Exercise 8: *Correcting Errors in Verb Usage*

Review the forms of the irregular verbs *spring, steal, strive, swear,* and *swim.* Some of the following sentences contain errors in verb usage. Rewrite the sentences, making necessary corrections. If the sentence is correct, write *C.* Underline any corrections you make.

Examples

a. Several women have swam the English Channel.
   Several women have <u>swum</u> the English Channel.

b. The witness had sworn to tell the truth.
   C

1. Lester sprung out of the shadows, trying to scare me.

2. I swum in the river, but the current was dangerously strong.

3. We have striven to win this championship.

4. Chief Joseph had swore to fight no more.

5. Moncrief stoled the ball and made a great stuff shot.

6. Have you ever swam in a heated pool?

7. We sprang a surprise party for Cassie.

8. The dogs strived to catch the fleeing fox.

9. My grandfather sweared he once saw a hoop snake.

10. Somebody had stole most of the apples from the tree.

Exercise 9: Using Irregular Verbs

Review the forms of the irregular verbs *take, teach, think, throw, wear,* and *write.* Then write the following sentences, supplying the correct form of the verb in parentheses. Underline the verb.

Example

a. Somebody must have _____ my jacket by mistake. (take)
Somebody must have <u>taken</u> my jacket by mistake.

1. I've _____ my term paper for history class. (write)
2. The tires on my car are almost _____ out. (wear)
3. Have you _____ your vitamin pill today? (take)
4. I haven't _____ of a solution yet. (think)
5. Leslie _____ a class in belly-dancing. (teach)
6. Pat had _____ the ball too hard. (throw)
7. Conchita had _____ a note of apology. (write)
8. I accidentally _____ out the wrong papers. (throw)
9. We _____ our parrot how to talk. (teach)
10. Marcia must have _____ her knee out of joint. (throw)

Exercise 10: Using Lie and Lay

Review the forms of the verbs *lie* and *lay.* Remember that *lie* means "to recline" and that *lay* means "to place something" or "to put something down." Complete the following sentences by choosing the correct verb in parentheses. Write the sentences, underlining the verb you choose.

Example

a. I was (lying, laying) on the couch reading a mystery.
I was <u>lying</u> on the couch reading a mystery.

1. You look horrible, Selma, perhaps you should (lie, lay) down.
2. The keys had been (laid, lain) on the mantel.
3. Mel was in the backyard, (laying, lying) in the hammock.
4. The poker player (lay, laid) his cards down in disgust.

5. My uncle (lay, laid) the bricks for our patio.

6. Would you (lay, lie) those coats across the bed?

7. Zounds! The hen has (laid, lain) a blue egg!

8. I (lay, laid) down the book I was reading.

9. The cat was (lying, laying) on the front porch, asleep.

10. If a bear wanders into camp, just (lie, lay) still.

Exercise 11: Using Sit and Set

Review the forms of the verbs *sit* and *set*. Remember that *sit* means "to occupy a seat" or "to rest" and that *set* means "to put or place something." Complete the following sentences by choosing the correct verb in parentheses. Write out the sentences and underline the verb you choose.

Example

a. (Set, Sit) down and make yourself comfortable.
Sit down and make yourself comfortable.

1. The lion (set, sat) in its cage, yawning hugely.

2. Someone needs to (set, sit) down with him and have a talk.

3. She has (sat, set) in that chair all afternoon.

4. Just (set, sit) the groceries down on the counter.

5. Maureen will (set, sit) out some strawberry plants this spring.

6. I had just (sit, sat) down when the phone rang.

7. Marcia accidentally (set, sat) too many books on the desk.

8. A bird (set, sat) on the clothesline wire.

9. John was just (setting, sitting) down to write when you called.

10. Inez (set, sat) the trophy down with a thump.

Exercise 12: Using Rise and Raise

Review the forms of the verbs *rise* and *raise*. Remember that *rise* means "to go up." *Raise* means "to make something move up" and takes a direct object. Complete the sentences on the following page by choosing the correct verb in parentheses. Write the sentences, underlining the verb you choose.

Example

---

a. A hand (raised, rose) up and fumbled at the window latch.
   A hand <u>rose</u> up and fumbled at the window latch.

1. Prices have (risen, rose) again at the grocery store.

2. She (raised, rose) from her chair and went to the door.

3. Please (raise, rise) and salute the flag.

4. The Scouts (raised, rose) the flag for Memorial Day.

5. The snake (raised, rose) its head and flicked its tongue.

6. We'll have to (raise, rise) from our beds at dawn tomorrow.

7. Some questions have been (raised, risen) about the new school policies.

8. Miko's voice (raised, rose) with emotion.

9. The phone company's rates (raised, rose) last year by five percent.

10. The issue has been (raised, risen) and discussed already.

Exercise 13: Making Pronouns Agree with Antecedents

Review singular and plural pronouns. Then choose the pronoun that correctly completes each of the following sentences. Write the sentences and underline the pronoun you select.

Example

---

a. Neither of the girls had received (her, their) grades.
   Neither of the girls had received <u>her</u> grades.

1. Each of the choir members purchases (his or her, their) own robe.

2. Several of the boys had parked (his, their) cars in the faculty lot.

3. Only one of the boys had (his, their) car ticketed.

4. Somebody left (his or her, their) lunch in the biology lab.

5. Some of the apple trees had blight on (its, their) leaves.

6. Either of the girls might have lent you (her, their) tape recorder.

7. Everyone on the girls' softball team has improved (her, their) batting average.

8. None of the Boy Scouts wore (his, their) merit badges at the meeting.

9. All of the seniors have made (his or her, their) yearbook payments.

10. Everybody will bring (his or her, their) own food for the picnic.

Exercise 14: Making Pronouns Agree with Antecedents

Remember that when two or more singular antecedents are joined by *and*, a plural pronoun is used to refer to them. However, when two or more singular antecedents are joined by *or* or *nor*, a singular pronoun is used to refer to them. Complete the following sentences by choosing the correct pronoun in parentheses. Write the sentences, underlining the pronoun you select.

Examples

a. Either Kim or Estralita will bring (her, their) records.
Either Kim or Estralita will bring her records.

b. Mr. Blanco and Mr. Washington have seen (his, their) children become doctors.
Mr. Blanco and Mr. Washington have seen their children become doctors.

1. Neither Karen nor her mother wore (her, their) gloves.

2. The shortstop and the catcher both broke (his, their) records in that game.

3. Either the shepherd or the shepherdess lost (his or her, their) sheep.

4. Both Kevin and Mark got (his, their) letters in track.

5. Neither Archie Bunker nor Fred Sanford merited any points for (his, their) politeness.

6. Neither the collie nor the poodle liked (its, their) yearly visit to the vet.

7. Marge or Amanda will lend you (her, their) history notes.

8. Fran and Ruby have finished (her, their) short stories for creative writing class.

9. Neither Burt nor Rodney remembered (his, their) lines on opening night.

10. Carrie or Pat can use (her, their) artistic talents to help us.

Writing Effective Sentences

Good writing entails more than a grasp of the principles of grammar; it also demands clarity, grace, and a sense of what is appropriate. The following lessons offer guidelines for improving writing style.

Improving Style with Diction

Diction, in writing, is your choice of words.

The words you choose should be appropriate to the subject and tone of your writing and to the reader for whom you intend the writing—the wrong word can ruin the effect of a sentence. Consider, for example, the unfortunate poet who compared those he loved to drops of his heart's blood, then addressed his sweetheart as "one of my most treasured drips."

Some writers think long, "ten-dollar" words are the mark of a mature style; they are mistaken. Do not use a long word where a short one will do, unless you have a special reason for doing so. Good writing is a vehicle for expressing thoughts clearly, not for displaying the longest words you know. Notice in the following sentences how the impressive sounding words of the first example add up to a sentence that is distinctly *not* impressive.

Poor: Members of the populace who inhabit domiciles of a hyalescent character should eschew the propulsion of sedimentary, igneous, or metamorphic conglomerates.

Better: People who live in glass houses shouldn't throw stones.

The second sentence is clear, to the point, concise—and justly famous. The first sentence is both pompous and murky.

The words you choose should depend primarily on two considerations: the audience for whom you write and your purpose in writing. Even the most formal writing, however, should be simple and clear. To write simply means to use understandable words in clearly constructed sentences.

Poor: It is patently impossible to subjugate a human being without demeaning oneself as well.

Better: You can't hold a man down without staying down with him.

—Booker T. Washington

The use of large, ponderous words is not the only error of diction. Equally offensive is the sudden intrusion of slang or trite words and phrases into serious writing. Each of the following examples has a word that is inappropriate.

Perhaps Adolph Hitler was a cunning but warped politician with unusual gifts for persuasion and leadership; on the other hand he may have been simply nutso.

Othello is a remarkably constructed play with vital characters, a complex plot, and super language.

Exercise 15: *Improving Diction*

Each of the following sentences contains one or more problems in diction. Rewrite the sentences, changing the offending words or phrases to more appropriate ones. Use your dictionary for help with vocabulary.

Example

a. The arboreal growth about the edifice obfuscated it.
   The trees around the house nearly hid it.

1. Several creatures of the bovine persuasion masticated the foliage in the bucolic area.

2. Historians still dispute whether Custer's strategy at Little Big Horn was brilliant but misguided, or if it was goofy.

3. Allow canines under the influence of Morpheus to remain recumbent.

4. Branwell Brontë had genius equal to any of his famous sisters; it is lousy that he wasted it.

5. He evinced emotions of the deepest and most passionate and amorous category for her.

6. This particular novel by Jane Austen has been called her most ambitious; it shows great promise in the opening chapters, but unfortunately, she blows it in the later ones.

7. When Cleopatra appeared on her barge, she was as pretty as pretty can be.

8. I will elucidate the import of the information to my youngest sibling.

9. My maternal parent frequently emphasizes the necessity of my restoring my abode to a locale of greater hygienic quality and order.

10. Dear Dr. Brady: Please excuse me for rushing from the biology lab without permission this afternoon, but when I started to cut open my frog, I felt I was going to puke.

Being Concise

Wordiness is the enemy of good writing. Some writers think that the more words they use, the more impressive their writing becomes. Other writers, minds boggled at the idea of writing 500 words on a subject, pad their sentences or repeat the same idea in different words. As a good writer you must make your point and waste no words in doing so.

Conciseness is the opposite of wordiness; a concise statement expresses a thought clearly and cleanly.

Most first drafts, even carefully written ones, need revision—the cutting of extra words, repeated ideas, and unnecessary statements. The following examples show how sentences can be made more concise.

Poor: This phenomenon we call life seems to me to go on and on forever, very much calling to mind the incessant gnawing of a small mouse.

Better: Life goes on forever like the gnawing of a mouse.

—Edna St. Vincent Millay

Poor: My advice would be to avoid the tendency to turn one's glance behind one. The reason is that something may very well be gaining on one.

Better: Don't look back. Something may be gaining on you.

—Satchel Paige

Exercise 16: Making Sentences Concise

Rewrite the following sentences to make them concise.

1. In the modern world of today we must finally come to grips with the problems generated by the energy crisis.

2. We must resolve and end the crisis in the Middle East, and we must do so now, at this point in time.

3. In my opinion and my opinion only, for I am no expert on political matters, I would tend to believe the Electoral College should probably be replaced by another, more democratic process.

4. In this great country of ours, the United States of America, land of the free and home of the brave, there still exists, it is sad, perhaps even tragic, to say, poverty.

5. In the Civil War, or the War Between the States as some prefer to call the bloody ordeal, emancipation of the slaves, or those in bondage to the archaic institution of slavery, was but one of many, many issues.

6. The reason the color yellow is my favorite color of all is that it always tends to remind me of sunlight, summer flowers, and many other cheerful things of a similar nature.

7. When I take my pen in hand on occasions such as this, it is a frequent occurrence that I am incapable of finding anything in my mind that I can, in good faith, put down on paper.

8. In the novel the hero or protagonist, Carlos Garcia, is driving down a quiet, deserted road in his car when he suddenly sees before him a big, enormous spaceship hovering up in the air in front of him.

9. I like various role-playing games because I can imagine a state of being in which I am one of a number of characters that I want to be: a big giant, a secret agent, a space traveler, or a warrior.

10. Malcolm X has been perceived as a great and important leader by some people, but other people tended to think of him as a radical who was very dangerous.

Avoiding Weak Constructions

Action verbs have two voices: the active and the passive.

Active:	The horse bucked off the rider.
Passive:	The rider was bucked off by the horse.

Active:	Tina bought an old silver bracelet.
Passive:	An old silver bracelet was bought by Tina.

As the preceding examples show, the active voice is usually the shorter, more vigorous way of making a statement.

For more information on the active and passive voice, see pages 477-480.

Use the active voice when you write unless you have a good reason for using the passive.

Some sentences begin with an unnecessary expletive: "There is . . .," "Here is . . .," "It is . . .," and so on. If you can drop these phrases without hurting the meaning of your sentence and without creating an awkward construction, do so. The following examples show how such cutting can improve your writing:

Poor:	There were several cows grazing in the meadow.
Stronger:	Several cows grazed in the meadow.

The damage these two constructions (the passive voice and the "there is," "there are" constructions) can do is evident in the following passage.

If You Were Born in the Year of the Rooster

Poor:	Because dreaming is loved by him, the Rooster risks falling at times into laziness—though it is his nature to give everything to the job in hand once it is started by him, the reputation is had by him of being a hard worker. But there is the fact that he's forever biting off more than can be chewed by him, undertaking tasks that are beyond his strength. And if, after all his efforts, it still can't be made by him, there is nobody more disappointed than he.
Stronger:	Because he loves to dream, the Rooster risks falling at times into laziness—though his nature is to give everything to the job in hand once he starts it, and he has the reputation of being a hard worker. But he is forever biting off more than he can chew, undertaking tasks that are beyond his strength. And if, after all his efforts, he still can't make it, nobody is more disappointed than he.[1]

[1]From *Chinese Astrology* by Paula Del Sol. Reprinted by permission of Nat Sobel Associates, Inc.

The first paragraph limps along under the weight of useless words and unnecessary constructions. The second paragraph, using the active voice and cutting unnecessary introductory phrases, moves quickly and clearly.

Exercise 17: Strengthening Writing Style

Rewrite the following paragraph, eliminating weak constructions and making any other changes you feel will strengthen the style.

> There is a twisted, little-used road that leads to the town. It is seldom traveled by the residents of the county, almost never traveled by tourists. The town itself is situated in a valley that is green, gracious, and pleasant. There are ancient oaks and pines lining the hillsides, and there is a remarkably clear creek at the town's outer edge. But there are no people walking in the streets, sitting on porches, conversing in the deserted stores. Houses have been abandoned, store windows have been boarded up by the long-absent residents. The surrounding farms have been deserted by their farmers. There is only the motion of a tumbleweed being blown by the wind down the dusty main street.

Writing Focus: *Usage and Style in Writing*

Two hallmarks of good writing are correct usage and a strong style. Ensure correct usage by paying particular attention to the forms of verbs and pronouns. Then strengthen your writing style by carefully wording your sentences, by using the active voice whenever possible, and by cutting unnecessary words or phrases.

Assignment: *Taking a Stand*

The principal of your school has just issued an announcement that no more homecoming queens will be elected, since such elections are mere popularity contests at best, and at worst, teach people to prize and judge women on the basis of their looks. Write a letter in which you state your reasons for agreeing or disagreeing with your principal.

Keep in mind that your audience is the principal and that your purpose is to explain your opinion about the principal's decision. Your letter will be evaluated for correct usage and for strong writing style.

Use the following steps to complete this assignment.

A. Prewriting

Decide whether you agree or disagree with the principal's decision to cancel homecoming queen elections. Then jot down the reasons you agree or disagree. Rank these reasons in order of importance. Then decide which reasons you will use in your letter.

B. Writing

Using your list, write a letter to the principal in which you state your opinion about the cancellation of homecoming queen elections. Support your opinion with the reasons you have chosen from your list. As you write, pay particular attention to usage and style.

C. Postwriting

Revise your first draft, using the following checklist.

1. Have I stated my opinion clearly and concisely?

2. Have I used the correct forms of verbs and pronouns?

3. Have I used the active voice as much as possible?

4. Have I cut unnecessary words and phrases from my sentences?

5. Have I used the correct form for a letter?

Proofread your revision, using the Checklist for Proofreading at the back of the book. Finally, share your writing with your classmates and discuss one another's opinions.

3
Mechanics

23 Punctuation

Punctuation helps show the relationships between groups of written words. The period, for instance, clearly indicates where a sentence ends. It causes readers to stop and read a particular group of words as one complete thought. Other marks of punctuation, such as the semicolon or colon, show that there is a relationship between a word or a group of words and those that follow.

By mastering the punctuation rules of Edited Standard English, you will be able to write more clearly and accurately.

The Period

The *period* marks the end of a sentence or an abbreviation.

A declarative sentence ends in a period.

Conservationists voice concern about the pollution of our rivers by chemical wastes. Fortunately, many factories now have antipollution controls.

A mildly imperative sentence ends in a period.

Please park your car across the street.

Call home on Sunday.

A period follows many abbreviations.

Dr.	doctor	Capt.	captain
M.D.	doctor of medicine	Wm.	William
Inc.	incorporated	P.M.	post meridiem
Mr.	mister	A.M.	ante meridiem
Jr.	junior	Ave.	avenue
Sr.	senior	lb.	pound
U.S.	United States	i.e.	that is
B.C.	before Christ	cf.	compare

Some abbreviations, such as *Ms.* and *Mrs.*, cannot be spelled out. Some other abbreviations are not followed by a period: metric units (*10 ml, 2kg*), postal abbreviations for states in addresses (*PA, NY, NJ*), most government agencies (*NASA, FBI*), many large corporations (*CBS, NBC, IBM*), and some common abbreviations such as *TV, AM, FM,* and *mph.*

Dr. Carter and Mrs. Clark both worked for NASA.

Approximately 4 oz. of flour equals 112 g of flour.

Did you watch last night's TV special on NBC?

The Question Mark

A *question*, or *interrogative sentence*, ends with a question mark.

When is the party? I can't be there until after 9:00.

Who wrote that book? Is it someone we know?

Note: When a question is part of a declarative sentence, it is an *indirect question* and ends with a period.

Why aren't we going?	[direct question]
I wondered why we weren't going.	[indirect question]

A question mark is placed inside quotation marks only if the quotation is a question.

"Where is Albania?" Noah asked.

If the entire sentence is a question, the question mark is placed outside the quotation marks.

Who wrote "The Black Cat"?

When an interrogative pronoun or adverb such as *who, what, where, when, why,* or *how* is used alone to ask a question, it is followed by a question mark.

You made this yourself? How?

What? I did not hear that last question.

You missed the concert last night. Why?

The Exclamation Point

A strong imperative sentence is followed by an exclamation point.

Watch out!

Come quickly; we're late!

An exclamation point follows an exclamation.

How late I am!

What a great idea!

A mildly imperative sentence can end with a period. Similarly, a mild exclamation at the beginning of a sentence can be followed by a comma. Use an exclamation point, rather than a period or a comma, when you wish to convey stronger feeling. Likewise, a polite request can be followed by a question mark, a period, or an exclamation point. The end mark you choose depends on the meaning and emotion you want to convey.

Exercise 1: Using Periods, Question Marks, and Exclamation Points

Write each of the following sentences and use periods, question marks, and exclamation points as necessary. Be prepared to explain why you used each mark of punctuation. Circle punctuation marks you insert.

Examples

---

a. That raccoon is adorable Will it forage through our garbage cans

That raccoon is adorable (!) Will it forage through our garbage cans (?)

b. Has Dr Garcia ever been to St Kitts I must ask her

Has Dr (.) Garcia ever been to St (.) Kitts (?) I must ask her (.)

1. Ms Allen, Mr Janex, and Dr Cottler are looking for artists for their new gallery Send inquiries to this address:
   Modern Space Gallery
   4333 E Roosevelt Ave
   Reno, NV 85305

2. Help Where is Dr Lance's phone number Oh, how I hate this disorganized phone book

3. H J Castillo asked why it was snowing when the CBS 7:00 PM report had predicted fair weather "Who knows" replied Mrs Castillo. "How can anyone really predict the weather"

4. "When did the *SS France* take its last voyage" Capt L Jacobs asked. "Wow I would like to have piloted that ocean liner"

5. Sgt J J Newsome, US Army, barked orders to the new recruits. "Attention About face Forward march"

6. Did you see the writer P D James interviewed on the PBS show *Mystery* at 10:00 PM last night

7. Were you stationed at Ft Riley or at Ft Dix, Pvt Singer Did you, by any chance, know Dr W W Barnes What a coincidence

8. Bravo Bravo What an exciting performance Don't you think that the cast of Players, Inc, puts on a professional show, Prof Cours

9. How exciting that you've won a trip to Europe, Mrs Alonzo When will you go If you need more information, write to Walton Travel, Ltd, Ft Lauderdale, Florida

10. Please call as soon as you arrive That road is so bumpy it could have been built in 1950 BC instead of in AD 1950

The Comma

The *comma* separates words, phrases, or clauses within a sentence. Sometimes, the comma is used where a pause would occur in speech; at other times the comma is used as custom dictates.

Use a comma to separate words or groups of words in a series.

Ilena sings, dances, and acts.

Walter designed the table, cut the wood, and assembled it.

When items commonly go together, such as *bread and butter*, they can be paired as one item.

Jake added scallions, cheese, and salt and pepper to the omelet.

When the last two items in a series are joined by a coordinating conjunction (*and* or *but*), a comma precedes the conjunction. However, when all the items in a series are joined by conjunctions, do not use commas.

We ate chicken, salad, and carrots.

We ate chicken and salad and carrots.

In the following examples notice how the commas clarify the meaning of each sentence.

We ate chicken salad, potatoes, and carrots.	[three items]
We ate chicken, salad, potatoes, and carrots.	[four items]
Carlos invited Mary Beth, Sue Ann, and Kendra to the party.	[three people]
Carlos invited Mary, Beth, Sue, Ann, and Kendra to the party.	[five people]

Use a comma to separate two or more adjectives preceding a noun.

Six hundred talented, enthusiastic applicants answered the ad.

The high-paying, interesting, rewarding job was available.

Note: Do not use a comma between the last adjective and the noun that follows it. Sometimes, you should not use a comma between adjectives preceding a noun. Use a comma if the word *and* would make sense in its place.

The creaky wooden canoe seemed unsafe.
[No commas are necessary between the adjectives.]

The refreshing, salty air blew from the sea.
[An *and* makes sense between the adjectives; therefore, use a comma.]

Use a comma to separate independent clauses that are joined by the coordinating conjunction *and, yet, but, or, nor, for,* or *so.*

The house is inexpensive, but it requires a lot of repairs.

Juan is a good tennis player, yet he rarely plays.

I love warm weather, so I applied for a job in Hawaii.

Exercise 2: *Using Commas*

Write each of the following sentences, using commas where necessary. Circle the commas you insert.

Examples

a. Al Ann and Carl visited Austin San Antonio and Dallas.

Al ⊘ Ann ⊘ and Carl visited Austin ⊘ San Antonio ⊘ and Dallas.

b. José used to work for the San Francisco Chronicle but now he writes a syndicated column.

José used for work for the San Francisco Chronicle ⊘ but now he writes a syndicated column.

1. During March April and May the weather became warmer the rains ceased the buds appeared.

2. Pablo eats neither fish nor meat nor will he even kill an insect.

3. My sentimental sensitive romantic sister has saved every letter card and note that her husband has ever written her.

4. Helen Max and Juan chose green blue and beige fabric for the couch.

5. Hernando looked under the bed behind the dresser and in the closet for his favorite well-worn sneakers.

6. Fire is a constant hazard in Los Angeles County so the people post signs to warn visitors of the danger.

7. Every day Judy eats half a grapefruit before breakfast and lunch and dinner for she believes the grapefruits are healthful.

8. Tim and Jim and Kim live in the same apartment building but they work on different schedules and rarely see each other.

9. Janet designed the patterns bought the fabric and then sewed a skirt two shirts and a dress.

10. The narrow bumpy dirt road winds into the woods up the hill and around the reservoir; it must lead somewhere.

Use a comma to separate introductory adverb clauses, introductory participial phrases, and long introductory prepositional phrases from the rest of the sentence.

Introductory Adverb Clauses

When the concert ended, thousands of people jammed the exits.

Before she accepted the job, Mary Anne went on several interviews.

Introductory Participial Phrases

Running all the way, Janice reached the train station just in time.

Raised in Atlanta, Clarice never lost her Southern drawl.

Note: Be sure that a word ending in *-ing* is actually part of an introductory participial phrase and not the subject of the sentence.

Running is good exercise.
[*Running* is the subject.]

Long Introductory Prepositional Phrases

In a corner of the yard near the house, a beautiful lilac bush bloomed annually.

Without the benefit of a letter of introduction, Ken felt uncomfortable entering the personnel office of the large company.

Note: Use a comma with short introductory prepositional phrases only if the comma is necessary to make the meaning clear.

During May the company closes on Fridays.
[no comma needed]

By the sea, shore birds wade lazily.
[comma needed for clarity]

Use a comma to separate some short introductory elements from the rest of the sentence.

Use a comma after mild interjections and words such as *yes, no, well, why, still,* and *now* when they introduce a sentence or an independent clause.

No, I've never seen a cobra.

Why, it's pouring!

Bert lives in Chicago; still, he prefers living in the country.

Note: When these words are used as adverbs, they should not be followed by commas.

> *Now,* I'm sure you'll enjoy studying in Mexico. (not an adverb)

> She *now* studies in Mexico. (adverb)

Use a comma after a noun of direct address when it introduces a sentence or an independent clause. (When a noun of direct address occurs at the end of a sentence or clause, a comma precedes it.)

> Marika, please call your brother.

> I can't hear you, Rachel.

> Governor, where is your office?

Use a comma after introductory transitional and parenthetical expressions such as *however, accordingly, thus, consequently, therefore, besides, in fact, on the other hand,* and *by the way.* (When these appear at the end of a sentence, they are preceded by a comma.)

> By the way, Ellen has finished writing her book; however, she has not yet sold it to a publisher.

> Therefore, please call before midnight.

> I'm moving to Detroit, in fact.

In general, use a comma after any introductory expression that would be followed by a pause if you were speaking.

Use a comma to separate contrasting words, phrases, and clauses introduced by the word *not*.

> Carmine is a shade of red, not blue.

> Jack starred in the stage production, not the movie.

Exercise 3: Using Commas

Write each of the sentences on the following page and use commas where necessary. Circle the commas you insert.

Examples

> a. In fact Denise was born in Japan; however she speaks no Japanese.
>
> In fact⊙ Denise was born in Japan; however⊙ she speaks no Japanese.

b. The New Deal was enacted by Franklin Roosevelt not Theodore Roosevelt.

The New Deal was enacted by Franklin Roosevelt, not Theodore Roosevelt.

1. Levi Strauss originally went west to seek gold Mabel.

2. Having traveled west with canvas to sell for tents and wagons Strauss sold the fabric for pants instead; people needed sturdier pants not sturdier tents.

3. Called overalls or Levis these pants were durable clothing for the miners and farmers.

4. Strauss soon stopped using canvas however; as a matter of fact he began using denim.

5. When the Civil War ended Levi shipped his pants to Texas; thus they soon became the standard garb of cowhands.

6. Well Strauss wanted all of his pants to be the same color; therefore he dyed the pants with indigo so they would all be blue.

7. During the early days of Levis people wore the pants into the water and kept them on until they dried; as a result the pants fit perfectly!

8. Margo the original jeans had copper rivets on the back pockets; however the rivets scratched saddles and furniture. Consequently the manufacturer eliminated the pocket rivets.

9. In the collection of the Smithsonian Institute in Washington there is a pair of Levis canvas dungarees I think.

10. Well Levi Strauss would certainly be surprised to learn that his dungarees had become popular fashion not just sturdy work pants!

Paired Commas

Sometimes, words of direct address or transition appear within a sentence, rather than at its beginning or end. When this happens, enclose the interrupting word, phrase, or clause with commas, placing a comma both before and after the expression. These *paired commas* separate the expression from the rest of the sentence.

Use paired commas with nouns of direct address when they interrupt a sentence.

I think, Anita, that your drawing is lovely.

Why, Doctor, is my neck stiff all the time?

Use paired commas with transitional or parenthetical expressions that interrupt the sentence.

We stayed, nevertheless, until the game had ended and our team had won.

The painter Georgia O'Keeffe, by the way, took up pottery late in life.

Use paired commas with contrasting expressions when they interrupt the sentence.

Goats, not cows, graze on that hill.

Fleming, not Pasteur, discovered penicillin.

Note: Before placing commas, make sure that a word or phrase is really an interrupter.

Arthur Ashe, I think, has stopped playing tennis.

I think that Arthur Ashe has stopped playing tennis.

Exercise 4: Using Commas

Write out the sentences on the following page and place commas where necessary. Circle the commas you insert.

Examples

a. Mrs. Maggiore uses spinach flour not whole wheat flour to make her pasta.

Mrs. Maggiore uses spinach flour⊙ not whole wheat flour⊙ to make her pasta.

b. The Nile I think is the longest river in the world.

The Nile⊙ I think⊙ is the longest river in the world.

1. I believe that daffodils not roses are poisonous; I suggest however that you check with the botanical gardens.

2. Early movie entrepreneurs I believe moved west to escape legal problems in the East; Hollywood as a matter of fact became the home of the movie industry.

3. You know Sidney that Alfred Hitchcock not Anthony Perkins directed *Psycho*; Perkins on the other hand starred in the picture.

4. All the stores in London by the way will be closed on Thursday; Thursday it seems is the Queen's birthday.

5. Fares on the London subway Marika vary according to the length of the ride; a long ride costs more than a short one.

6. It is possible I suppose to enjoy a toy poodle. I wish however that those little poodles would bark not yelp when they get excited.

7. Alice by the way rarely makes a phone call after 7 o'clock in the evening; I on the other hand could talk on the phone all night.

8. Have you ever Bernardo visited the Brooks' farm in the winter? Julio claims that winter not summer is the most beautiful season there.

9. Last fall's rains as a matter of fact lasted for weeks; many homes as a result were flooded or washed away.

10. Silver not gold tarnishes; gold believe it or not keeps its shine for many years.

Use paired commas to enclose nonessential phrases and nonessential clauses and to separate them from the rest of the sentence.

Nonessential phrases and clauses are those that could be omitted from a sentence without changing its basic meaning. They are, in other words, not essential to the thought conveyed by the sentence.

Irene Warner, who lives across the street, is a physicist.
[*Who lives across the street* is a nonessential adjective clause; it does not affect the meaning of the sentence.]

Benito Juarez, panting and exhausted, just won the Boston Marathon.
[*Panting and exhausted* is a nonessential participial phrase.]

On the other hand, essential phrases and clauses are necessary to the meaning of a sentence. If they were eliminated, the meaning of the sentence would change; therefore, do not separate essential phrases and clauses with commas.

> The woman who lives across the street just got a job with the *Los Angeles Times*.
> [*Who lives across the street* identifies the woman and is essential to the sentence.]

> The man standing there just won the Boston Marathon.
> [*Standing there* identifies which man and is an essential participial phrase.]

Note: When a nonessential phrase or clause appears at the end of a sentence, only one comma precedes it.

> We attended the debut performance of Ken's youngest sister, who is a singer.

Use paired commas to enclose nonessential appositives that interrupt a sentence.

When an appositive merely explains the meaning of the noun or pronoun it refers to, it is nonessential and should be set off by paired commas. However, when an appositive distinguishes the noun or pronoun it explains from other people or things, it is essential and is not enclosed by commas.

> I. M. Pei, the noted architect, has designed New York's new Convention Center.

> Joanna Perkins, our accountant, just opened her own firm.

The appositives in both of the preceding sentences are nonessential. Since they do not affect the meaning of the sentences, they require commas. The appositives in the following sentences, however, are essential to the meaning of the sentences.

> Barbara's brother Paul is a data processor.
> [*Paul* identifies which brother.]

> The documentary film *Number Our Days* captures the life of elderly Jews in Venice, California.
> [*Number Our Days* identifies which film.]

Note: A nonessential appositive at the beginning of a sentence is followed by a comma. A nonessential appositive at the end of a sentence is preceded by a comma.

> An opera fan, Cara attends every performance she can.

> Marta studies at Reed College, a small school in Oregon.

Exercise 5: Using Commas

Write the following sentences and use commas where necessary. Be prepared to explain your reason for using each comma. Circle the commas you insert.

Examples

a. Mary Lou Williams a jazz pianist and composer performed last week with the Alvin Ailey dancers.

Mary Lou Williams⊙ a jazz pianist and composer⊙ performed last week with the Alvin Ailey dancers.

b. That is a photograph of Clara Barton who founded the American Red Cross.

That is a photograph of Clara Barton⊙ who founded the American Red Cross.

1. A talented singer and dancer Rita Moreno is now part of the cast of *The Electric Company* which is a television show for children.

2. Jack's dog Ken is a Saluki which is a nervous high-strung dog; however, Jack's other dog Luch is the sweetest mutt in the world.

3. The photographs that depict the earthquake were taken in 1886. That earthquake which occurred in South Carolina on August 31, 1886 was strong enough to derail locomotives!

4. A hat that has a wide brim offers good protection from the sun; on the other hand, a beret a brimless cap won't protect your face from the sun.

5. Margaret Corbin who fought bravely during the American Revolution is buried at West Point.

6. Did you know that Duke Ellington the composer and band leader used to live on West 106th Street in New York? In 1977, West 106th Street which runs between Riverside Drive and Central Park West was renamed Duke Ellington Boulevard.

7. Vermeil a mixture of gold and silver is frequently used to make jewelry instead of gold which has become very expensive.

8. In the Old West the chuck wagon a kitchen on wheels was the most popular vehicle on the trails; and the cook who often had to make much out of little was treated with a great deal of respect!

9. In a famous scene from *North by Northwest* a film by Hitchcock Cary Grant who starred in the film is chased by a crop-duster which is a small, two-winged propeller plane.

10. The woman who owns Kellogg Shoe Shop just wrote a book which will be published next spring; the book titled *Profits* is a well-written guide about managing a business.

Commas are also used to separate a variety of items that may or may not occur within a sentence.

Use a comma to separate parts of geographical names and dates.

Jerry was born on Thursday, March 14, 1970, at 5:55 P.M.

Meet me at Martin Luther King High School, 7503 Warwick Road, Detroit, Michigan 48233.

Otters live off the coast of Monterey, California.

Note: In addresses do not use a comma between the street number and the street name, nor between the state and the ZIP code. In dates a comma is unnecessary when only a month and a year are given in a date (*September 4, 1888; September 1888*).

When these items are joined by prepositions, commas are not necessary.

The museum is on Main Street in West Chicago, Illinois.

She was born in November of 1945.

Use a comma to separate a person's name (or a company's name) from the degree, title, or affiliation that follows it.

We bought these lamps from Lightoleer, Inc., in New York.

Connie Clark, M.D., is a pediatrician.

Dan Dowd, USAF, is an expert computer analyst.

Note: When used in a sentence, a degree or title is followed by a comma.

Julio Perez, M.D., just became president of the American Medical Association.

Use a comma after the salutation and the closing of a friendly letter.

Dear Bert,   Sincerely yours,

Exercise 6: Using Commas

Write the following sentences and use commas where necessary. Circle each comma you insert.

Examples

---

a. The Whartons drove from Denver Colorado to San Francisco California and back.

The Whartons drove from Denver⊙ Colorado⊙ to San Francisco⊙ California⊙ and back.

b. New bus fares will go into effect at 12:00 P.M. Saturday May 15 1981.

New bus fares will go into effect at 12:00 P.M.⊙ Saturday⊙ May 15⊙ 1990.

---

1. World Airlines Inc. announced a sale on flights between Newark New Jersey and Los Angeles California from April 15 1988 until May 15 1988.

2. If you're looking for a pet, go to the Best Pet Shop Ltd. 750 Wabash Road Bismarck North Dakota 58501.

3. Ann Miller M.D. consulted with Carl Rogers M.D. and Raina Fillipo M.D. regarding the injured patient.

4. On Thursday June 25 at 1:30 P.M. Colton Industries Inc. will announce the winner of their Employee of the Year Award.

5. Dear Aunt Helga

   I would like to order two plants from your catalogue of April 1981. Please send them to my friend Jonah Jakes Jr. 140 Walker Road Tampa Florida 31031.

   Fondly
   Kim

6. According to their ad, the Riviera Hotel at 333 Mission Drive San Diego California will lower its rates from May 15 1988 until February 1989.

7. Janis signed her complaint "Furiously yours" and sent it to Lance Lucky Sr. Sturdy Furniture Corp. 77 Park Avenue Jefferson Wisconsin.

8. Joel Yourk RAF and Bart Mars USAF owned a charter airline running flights between Boston Massachusetts and New Haven Connecticut.

9. The museum on the Parkway in Philadelphia Pennsylvania will have a special showing on Tuesday May 13 from noon until 5:00 and on Thursday May 15 from 1:00 P.M. until closing.

10. Carolyn Mendez M.D. will lecture to medical students in Paris France and London England and Hamburg Germany; her tour will begin on Friday November 12 1988 and continue until January 1989.

The Semicolon

You might think of the *semicolon* as a cross between a comma and a period. Although the semicolon is a stronger mark of punctuation than the comma, it does not signal as strong a break as does the period.

Use a semicolon to separate independent clauses not joined by a coordinating conjunction when the clauses are closely related.

José is an expert pianist; he has studied the piano since he was seven.

Irene never eats fish; she is allergic to it.

Use a semicolon between independent clauses when the second clause begins with a transitional expression such as *still, moreover, furthermore, otherwise, therefore, however, besides, in fact,* and *for example.*

The movie has already begun; besides, I'm too tired to go.

Last night's storm knocked down power lines; as a result, we had no electricity this morning.

Use a semicolon to separate items in a series when one or more of the items contains commas.

The awards read Alma Navarro, first place; Ken Yamah, second place; and Susie Castellano, third.

An Egyptian-Israeli peace settlement was negotiated by Jimmy Carter, President of the U.S.; Menachem Begin, Prime Minister of Israel; and Anwar Sadat, President of Egypt.

563

Use a semicolon between independent clauses when commas appear within the clauses.

Barbara Ling, who has relatives in Shanghai, will visit China next month; in addition to Shanghai, she'll travel to Peking and Manchuria.

For his aquarium Raoul bought snails, goldfish, angel fish, and guppies; but the angel fish, unfortunately, died within a week.

Exercise 7: Using Semicolons

Write the following sentences and place semicolons where they are needed. Circle the semicolons you insert.

Examples

---

a. Bart, a well-known animal handler, trains large animals for television, he is currently training a bear for an insurance company's commercial.

Bart, a well-known animal handler, trains large animals for television⨀ he is currently training a bear for an insurance company's commercial.

b. That book is filled with photographic firsts it includes the first photos ever taken of a dog begging, of the moon, and of a snowflake!

That book is filled with photographic firsts⨀ it includes the first photos ever taken of a dog begging, of the moon, and of a snowflake!

1. Ramon has just published a best-selling book as a result, he constantly appears as a guest on TV talk shows.

2. Cats, they say, have nine lives my cat, I'm sure, has already used seven of them.

3. Use a comma between independent clauses joined by a coordinating conjunction however, use a semicolon if the clauses contain commas.

4. Elizabeth Blackwell, the first woman doctor in the United States, founded the New York Infirmary for Women and Children that hospital still functions today.

5. Early photographers in the American West used portable dark-rooms in horse-drawn wagons there is, in fact, a famous photograph, taken in 1868, of a wagon darkroom traveling across the Nevada desert.

6. The evening lectures will be held in the following rooms: Art and Culture, Room 412 Hopi Architecture, Room 606 and Women of the '80s, Room 1000.

7. After George Washington Carver introduced the peanut to Southern farmers, they no longer had to depend solely on the cotton crop for income as a result, their economy boomed.

8. Everyone in the room had seen the UFO no one, however, had taken a picture!

9. The Banyons bought a camper for their cross-country drive still, they planned to stay with friends in Chicago, Illinois Denver, Colorado Winslow, Arizona and Sacramento, California.

10. Native Americans often made their canoes from the bark of large birch trees they sewed the pieces of bark together with white spruce roots.

The Colon

A *colon* calls attention to the word, phrase, or list that follows it.

Use a colon to separate a list of items from an introductory statement, which often contains the words *as follows, the following, these,* or a number.

> Monique speaks four languages: English, French, Spanish, and Dutch.
>
> Deciduous trees that fill Jake's yard are as follows: elm, maple, oak, and chestnut.

Note: The introductory statement that precedes a colon should be a complete sentence. Do not use a colon between a verb and its direct object or after a preposition. (An asterisk [*] denotes a sentence with a feature that is not a part of ESE.)

> *Kelly's dog eats only: liver and fish.
> [Unacceptable use of colon between verb and direct object]
> Kelly's dog eats only two things: liver and fish.

Use a colon to separate an introductory statement from an explanation, appositive, or quotation.

The crowd rose and yelled its cheer: "Bravo!"

Martha's Boston accent rang clear when she read these words: "Park your car in Harvard Yard."

The colon should also be used in three conventional situations:

Use a colon after the salutation of a business letter.

Dear Jane Coe: Dear Dr. Hart:

Use a colon to separate hour and minutes in expressions of time.

11:30 A.M.   4:00 this afternoon

Use a colon to separate chapter numbers from verse numbers in reference to chapters from the Bible.

Genesis 12:6   Matthew 2:10

Exercise 8: Using Colons

Write the following sentences and place colons where necessary. Circle the colons you insert.

Example

---

a. Buses depart for Newark at these times 830 A.M., 215 P.M., and 326 P.M.

Buses depart for Newark at these times⊙ 8⊙30 A.M., 2⊙15 P.M., and 3⊙26 P.M.

1. For her birthday Maureen received tickets to three Broadway shows *Barnum, West Side Story,* and *Children of a Lesser God.*

2. Which of these states has the largest population Texas, Massachusetts, or Illinois?

3. Before it was ravaged by civil war, Beirut had this nickname "Paris of the Middle East."

4. Having heard the concert, Julio had one response wonderful.

5. Liane, the movie plays at several times 300, 500, 700, and 900.

6. The dance involves four basic steps shuffle, kick, turn, bend.

7. Read the following excerpts from the Old Testament Genesis 3 7, Genesis 10 9, and Exodus 2 3.

8. The tour bus will make three stops between 1000 and 1100 A.M. Hotel Regency, El Toro Palace, and the Western Court Inn.

9. This sums up Jack's baby's vocabulary *pa, ma,* and *hi.*

10. Having traveled around the country, novelist Emmett Grogan said this of the United States "Anything anybody can say about America is true."

The Dash

The *dash* calls attention to the word or group of words that precedes it.

Use a dash to separate an introductory series or thought from the explanation that follows.

Lilacs and roses—those are my favorite flowers.

A twelve-inning game—that's exciting!

Use a dash to separate a sudden change in thought.

Dinner is ready—oh, I left my hat at the office.

June's birthday party is on Friday at—oops, I've lost the invitation.

Use a dash to show the omission of words in dialogue.

"It's thunderi—," Jack shouted.

When the elements separated by a dash occur within a sentence, use paired dashes to enclose the word or group of words and separate them from the rest of the sentence. Use dashes for parenthetical phrases that contain commas.

Betty's dog—it's an Australian sheepdog—won first prize!

Some peppers—jalapeños, for instance—are very spicy!

567

Exercise 9: Using Dashes

Write out the following sentences and place dashes where necessary. Circle the dashes you insert.

Example

a. Elizabeth's dictionary it's very old doesn't list the word *astronaut.*

Elizabeth's dictionary⊖it's very old⊖doesn't list the word

astronaut.

---

1. Terrified that's how I felt before the match.

2. Max was charged with littering throwing papers on the street and fined fifty dollars.

3. "Is the train com?" Joanne asked.

4. The Martinez's house a ranch, I think has a view of the sea.

5. Pat, I can't hear the baby is crying a word you're saying.

6. Georgia Coles I think that's her name just opened a boutique on Columbus Avenue.

7. There's a monument to the boll weevil it's a very destructive insect in Enterprise, Alabama.

8. Photographers who worked for the FSA the Farms Security Administration documented American life during the Depression.

9. Proud and tired mostly tired, I think was how I felt after having finished first in the marathon last weekend.

10. Those enormous dogs they're either Great Danes or mastiffs, I believe live across the street.

Parentheses

Parentheses, like commas and dashes, are used to enclose elements that interrupt a sentence.

Parentheses indicate a strong break in thought. Elements in parentheses, in fact, are really additional information. If these words were omitted, the meaning of the sentence would in no way change.

Estelle's mother (born in 1900) tells wonderful tales.

Dr. Michaels (our dentist) lives in Oakland.

Exercise 10: *Using Parentheses*

Write the following sentences and use parentheses where necessary. Circle the parentheses you insert.

1. Geronimo 1829–1909 was a well-known Apache chief.

2. The story of the prisoners' escape it's a really exciting tale will appear in three local papers tomorrow.

3. W. C. Handy the W. C. stands for William Christopher is known as "The Father of the Blues."

4. Didn't Lorraine Hansberry 1930–1965 write that drama?

5. Dorothea Dix 1802–1887 worked to improve the treatment of the mentally ill.

The Hyphen

The *hyphen* is used to link the parts of some compound words. It also links the parts of a word begun on one line and finished on the next. Consult a dictionary if you are uncertain about how to hyphenate a word.

Use a hyphen when a word is divided at the end of a line.

Place the hyphen only between syllables. Do not hyphenate a word if doing so would leave just one letter on either line. If a word already contains a hyphen (*self-control*), divide it only at the hyphen. Do not hyphenate proper nouns or adjectives or abbreviations.

Rome is a large, bustling, and cos-
mopolitan city.

Reporters swarmed about the President-
elect.

Use a hyphen to link the parts of compound nouns that begin with the prefixes *ex-, self-, all-,* and *great-* or that end with the suffix *-elect.*

---

ex-wife   president-elect   all-star

Use a hyphen to link all prefixes with proper nouns and adjectives.

---

pre-Columbian   pro-American   anti-American

Use a hyphen to link the parts of compound nouns that include a prepositional phrase.

---

father-in-law   jack-in-the-box

Note: Many compound nouns are not hyphenated. Some are two separate words (*tennis court*); others are one word (*baseball*). Check a dictionary if you are unsure about a word.

Use a hyphen to link the parts of a compound adjective when it precedes a noun.

---

muscle-building routine   up-and-down relationship
well-known author   high-paying job

Note: Do not use a hyphen when the adjective follows the noun (*The essay was well written*) or if the first modifier ends in *-ly* (*easily understood motive*).

Use a hyphen to link parts of a fraction used as an adjective.

---

one-half acre   two-thirds majority

Use a hyphen to link the parts of a compound number between twenty-one and ninety-nine.

---

sixty-three cents   forty-seven days

The Apostrophe

The *apostrophe* is used to show the omission of letters or numbers, to form the plurals of letters and numbers, and to form possessive nouns.

Use an apostrophe to show that letters have been omitted from a contraction.

can't [*cannot*]   don't [*do not*]

Use an apostrophe to show that the first two numbers have been omitted from a year.

the gold rush of '49   the hurricane of '22

Use an apostrophe to form the plurals of letters, numbers, and words.

"We have some *8*'s, but we're out of *10*'s," the salesperson informed us.

Mena pronounces her name as if it had two *e*'s.

Note: An apostrophe is not necessary when making centuries and decades plural (*1900s, the '30s*).

Add an apostrophe and an *s* to make a singular noun possessive or to make possessive most plural nouns not ending in *s*.

Maggie's whiskers   children's laughter

If a plural noun ends in *s*, show possession by adding only an apostrophe.

chickens' feed   the candidates' speeches

Note: The possessive forms of personal pronouns do not have apostrophes. Be careful, especially in the case of *its*, not to confuse the possessive forms with contractions.

its [possessive]	it's [contraction]
their [possessive]	they're [contraction]
your [possessive]	you're [contraction]

To show possession in hyphenated words and in words showing joint possessions, add an apostrophe and *s* only to the last word.

---

brother-in-law's company

Doyle Dane Bernbach's offices

Deborah and Bob's apartment

Note: When two or more people each possess something separately, make each of their names possessive.

men's and women's shoes

Julio's and Maurice's dreams

If the second word is a possessive pronoun, then the first word is also possessive.

Kendra's and my idea

When words of time, date, and money are used as possessives, they require an apostrophe.

---

ten minutes' worth of work

twenty-five cents' worth; one cent's worth

Exercise 11: Using Hyphens and Apostrophes

Write the following sentences and use hyphens and apostrophes where necessary. Circle the marks you insert.

Examples

---

a. Ive eaten so much deep fried chicken I feel like a two ton truck.

I⊙ve eaten so much deep⊖fried chicken I feel like a two⊖ton truck.

b. My daughter in laws house has a twenty one foot wall of windows in its living room.

My daughter ⊖in⊖law⊙s house has a twenty⊖one⊖foot wall of windows in its living room.

1. Barb and Julios collection of twenty three post Impressionist paintings hangs in a well lit and carefully guarded room.

2. Im sure that Hectors twenty three year old cat couldnt possibly scale that forty foot wall, arent you?

3. "If youre going to speak professionally, you must eliminate all the *I means* and *you knows* from your speech," Mindys self taught elocution teacher advised.

4. Manuels father signed a long term lease on a well run, carefully designed apartment, which was also well located.

5. Each one of the windows in Hectors and my second story apartment overlooked a rose filled garden, which was at least forty six feet long.

6. His son in laws new restaurant was terrible: its five course dinner consisted of sour tasting soup, day old bread, over-cooked meat and half cooked potatoes, dressing soaked salad, his great grandmothers stale cookies, and foul smelling cheese!

7. When she was in her twenties, my friends name was spelled *Judee* (with two *es*); in her thirties it was *Judy*; and by the '80s shed settled on the mature sounding *Judith*.

8. At the games excitement filled climax, a two thirds majority of the pro Dodger fans rushed toward the All Star teams dugout.

9. Carries mother in law gave her a mother of pearl necklace from the '30s, an old book, and her ex husbands gold filled watch.

10. Tims twin engined plane flew low over the palm lined shore; within twenty minutes time wed landed, set up our foldaway table and chairs, and unpacked our well stocked picnic baskets.

Quotation Marks

Quotation marks usually occur in pairs. They enclose a word or group of words and separate them from the rest of the sentence.

Use quotation marks to enclose a speaker's exact words.

Raoul reminded her, "Don't forget your tickets."

"When I earn my first million," Janet dreamed, "that's when I'll travel around the world."

In the preceding example the words *Janet dreamed* interrupt the direct quotation. Notice that the second part of the quotation does not begin with a capital letter. Use a capital letter to begin each quotation and each new sentence within a quotation.

Note: Remember to use quotation marks to enclose only a speaker's exact words. Do not use quotation marks in an indirect quotation.

> Sheryl advised that we should not underestimate Leo. [indirect quotation]

> "Don't underestimate Leo," Sheryl advised. [direct quotation]

Use quotation marks to enclose the titles of short stories, essays, short poems, songs, single television programs, magazine articles, and parts of a book.

> "Causes of the Russian Revolution" was a complicated chapter in the Russian history book.

> Have you seen "A Plague on Our Children," a show about toxic chemicals, which was shown on PBS's *Nova*?

Use quotation marks to enclose nicknames and slang expressions.

> "Lizard" LaRue is a devious character.

> What does "You dig" mean?

Sometimes, other marks of punctuation appear within quotation marks. Commas, for example, often separate a direct quotation from the rest of the sentence. The following rules explain how to place other marks of punctuation when they are used with quotation marks.

Always place commas and periods inside closing quotation marks.

> "Jefferson grew broccoli at Monticello," Denise told us.

> We left after Gloria sang "I Will Survive."

Place colons and semicolons outside closing quotation marks.

Toni Cade Bambara wrote "Raymond's Run"; she didn't, on the other hand, write "Bryon's Run."

Here's why that street is called "The Serpentine": it's very winding!

Place question marks and exclamation points inside closing quotation marks if just the quotation is a question or an exclamation. Place the marks outside the closing quotation marks if the whole sentence is a question or an exclamation.

Connie asked, "Is that a chicken?"

Was Rocky nicknamed "The Italian Stallion"?

Connie shouted, "What a catch!"

How Alicia loves the song "Call Me"!

In general, two end marks should never appear together. When you are considering using a comma and another mark of punctuation together, drop the comma and use the other mark. (An asterisk [*] indicates a sentence with a feature that is not a part of Edited Standard English.)

*"When does the shop open?", we wondered.
"When does the shop open?" we wondered.

*Manuel shouted, "Watch out!".
Manuel shouted, "Watch out!"

Exercise 12: Using Quotation Marks

Write the following sentences and use quotation marks as necessary. Circle the quotation marks you insert.

Examples

---

a. Please call, Jackie said, if you'll be late.

⟨"⟩ Please call, ⟨"⟩ Jackie said, ⟨"⟩ if you'll be late. ⟨"⟩

b. Our spirits fell when we read the sign: Closed for the winter.

Our spirits fell when we read the sign: ⟨"⟩ Closed for the winter. ⟨"⟩

1. Before checking in Chapter 7, Household Hints, Lorraine asked her friend, Do you know if club soda will remove berry stains?

2. Juan wrote three episodes for the television series: Caught in the Middle, Out on a Limb, and Long Walk on a Short Pier.

3. Did you know that these two songs have each been recorded in over 1,000 different versions: Yesterday and Tie a Yellow Ribbon Round the Old Oak Tree?

4. Paulo Lucky Santos and Paul Mr. Money Moran have opened a disco called Winners; they're sure it will be successful.

5. Remember when every other word Mickey said was a slang expression such as groovy, far out, pad, hip, or bummer? Well, now he's changed his act and sounds like an Oxford professor!

6. What an amazing discovery! June exclaimed. Would you ever have suspected that a clam was capable of all that?

7. Having prepared for your debut for all these months, Charlene moaned, you can't give up now. What's the matter? she asked. Have you panicked?

8. Who said, A nod is as good as a wink to a blind horse?

9. Ms. Androtti asked whether we'd read any of the following articles: Alternatives to the Automobile, Let's Cycle, or An Invigorating Hike.

10. How can I pretend that I know how to ski, Don asked, when I've never even seen snow?

Single Quotation Marks

Use single quotation marks to enclose a direct quotation or title that occurs inside another quotation.

Charles reminisced, "I remember hearing Ezio Pinza sing 'Some Enchanted Evening.'"

"Who," asked Pete, "was nicknamed 'The Phantom'?"

Notice that in the preceding example the direct quotation is a question; however, the nickname (*'The Phantom'*) within the quotation is not a question. Therefore, the question mark is placed *outside* the closing single quotation mark but *inside* the closing mark of the direct quotation. (The period in the first example is placed inside the closing quotation marks because periods always go inside the closing mark of a quotation.)

Writing Dialogue

When you write dialogue, you quote the words said by two or more people conversing. You enclose the words of the speakers in quotation marks. Speakers are often identified by phrases such as *Alex argued* or *Kim sobbed*. These words are not enclosed in quotation marks but are separated from the quoted material by commas or other marks of punctuation.

Liana said triumphantly, "We've won!"

"Where are we going?" John asked.

"Lilies close at night," Sue said, "and open in the morning."

When you write dialogue, begin a new paragraph whenever the speaker changes.

"Videotape is the wave of the future," declared Clarissa. "There's no doubt about it! Not only is it a popular medium for today's artists, but it has practical applications as well."

"You're right," Angelo agreed. "Video has been a boon to us on the swimming team—even when we don't like what we see! When we see ourselves on tape, however, we see immediately where our shortcomings are: a kick that's uneven or too much time lost at the turn."

"I work with emotionally disturbed children," mused Carmen, "and, now that you mention it, perhaps videotaping the teachers at work would be helpful. It would give us a chance to study our interaction with the children and see where we might improve or change our approach."

"Well, I guess we have our work cut out for us," Clarissa said. "If we all become masters of the video camera, we'll be on the road to success!"

Sometimes, one speaker's words run for more than one paragraph. When this happens, use quotation marks at the beginning of the quotation, at the beginning of each subsequent paragraph, and at the end of the whole quotation.

"I read a spell-binding mystery yesterday," Agnes said. "It gripped me on the first page, and I couldn't put the book down until I had finished.

"The plot is simple, almost classic. Five people are sitting in a room watching home movies. When the lights come on, one of the people is dead. Who did it? How was it done?

"Of course, no one has entered or left the room during the movies; thus, one of the other four people in the room has done it. I, of course, thought of poison—but that was wrong.

"Well, the detective arrives, the questioning begins. As the story unfolds, you learn that everyone has a motive. The plot thickens. The mystery isn't solved until the last page, and it had me fooled. Whew! I'm exhausted from the suspense!"

Underlining (Italics)

Underlining has several uses, but is used most frequently to indicate that a specific word or group of words is a title or name. While printers use special type (*italics*) for titles (*Huckleberry Finn*), writers use underlining (Huckleberry Finn).

Underline the titles of all the following:

Books, plays, and long poems	Pride and Prejudice
	Romeo and Juliet
	Paradise Lost
Newspapers, magazines, and pamphlets	The New York Times
	Today's Teen
	How to Can and Preserve Fruit
Films, radio and television series	Star Wars
	All Things Considered
	Masterpiece Theatre
Paintings, sculpture, and ballets	The Card Player
	Black Majesty
	Giselle

Underline the names of ships, aircraft, and spacecraft.

Queen Elizabeth II   Mariner

Underline words, letters, and numbers referred to as such and foreign words.

How many r's are there in the word occur?

The numbers 7 and 9 are frequently hard to read in your records.

Please define the Latin term carpe diem.

Exercise 13: *Using Underlining*

Write each of the following sentences and insert underlining wherever it is required.

Example

---

a. When is the drama club holding tryouts for roles in Don't Go Near the Water?

When is the drama club holding tryouts for roles in Don't Go Near the Water?

1. Last month's Science Fiction Facts contained an interesting interview with the author of Stranger in a Strange Land.

2. This article on advertising in the Daily Recorder used the phrase caveat emptor; what do you suppose that means?

3. Mr. Sanchez asked me to revise the essay and eliminate all the so's at the beginning of sentences.

4. According to Everyman's Almanac of Trivia, the first aircraft to successfully cross the Atlantic was called the Lame Duck.

5. Picasso's cubism is very evident in the painting The Card Player.

6. The youth symphony played a selection from Carmen and all of Berlioz' Symphonie Fantastique.

7. Here's the error in your algebra problem, Raoul; you wrote a 6 rather than a 5.

8. Janet interviewed one of the aeronautical engineers who worked on Skylab's landing gear.

9. I read Newsweek and the Tribune at the airport and watched the movie Star Wars during the flight.

10. Alexander Calder created the large sculpture Three Arches in 1963.

Review: Using Punctuation

Write the following dialogue and add all necessary marks of punctuation. Remember to check the placement of quotation marks with other marks of punctuation. Circle the marks you insert.

Much of Navaho family life Professor Moriarty explained centers around the hogan the traditional Navaho dwelling. One type of hogan the professor continued is called the cribbed roof A six sided building this hogan has six foot high walls made of logs and mud The door of the hogan always faces east and the rising sun.

Excuse me Professor Lucy interrupted. What is the roof like?

Professor Moriarty replied The roof too is made of logs and mud.

The professor continued During formal gatherings inside the hogan people sit in a traditional manner at the western side sits the husband facing the door. The other men sit on the south side of the hogan women and children sit on the right.

Hogans were usually set far apart for sufficient grazing land around the house. Since the land was arid many acres were needed to supply enough land for the sheep thus the hogans were often isolated. They became the center of each family's life the professor concluded.

Writing Focus: *Using*

Punctuation in Writing

Remember that the purpose of punctuation is to make the meaning of your writing clear. Correct punctuation helps your audience to read writing quickly and easily. Use punctuation correctly, and your writing will be much clearer.

Assignment: *Describing a Common Event*

Imagine that you have an overseas pen pal who does not know what an American homecoming parade is like. Write a short letter in which you vividly describe a typical homecoming parade.

Remember that your audience is a teenager from another country (decide which country) who knows little about American

customs. Your purpose is to describe a homecoming parade as vividly as possible. Your paragraph will be evaluated for correct punctuation. Use the following steps to complete this assignment.

A. Prewriting

Think about all the features of a typical homecoming parade and jot them down. Then pick the features that you would like to focus on and that you can adequately describe in a few paragraphs. For help in organizing your ideas, review Chapter 3.

B. Writing

Use your notes to write your letter. Include enough specific details so that your reader can get a clear picture of a homecoming parade. As you write, pay attention to your use of punctuation marks.

C. Postwriting

Revise your first draft, using the following checklist.

1. Does the letter include enough specific, descriptive details?

2. Does each detail clearly relate to the topic?

3. Are there sentence fragments or run-on sentences that should be corrected?

4. Have I used the correct punctuation marks throughout the letter?

Proofread your revision, using the Checklist for Proofreading at the back of the book. Finally, share your writing with your classmates to see how your descriptions differ.

24 Capitalization

By mastering the capitalization rules of Edited Standard English, you can make your writing clear and assure that your use of capitals is consistent. Capital letters indicate the start of new sentences, distinguish proper nouns and adjectives, and indicate titles. Capitals are also used, where tradition dictates, in certain abbreviations (such as C for *centigrade* or *Celsius*) or in the salutation of a letter. Although the use of capitals may vary a bit with style, the rules and examples that follow should guide you in your use of capitals.

Capitals That Set Off Groups of Words

Capitalize the first word of a sentence.

A capital immediately signals a new sentence and separates it from the sentence that precedes it.

> Because next Monday is a national holiday, all the banks will be closed.

> I have a check but can't deposit it. All the banks are closed.

Capitalize the first word of a direct quotation.

If a direct quotation is interrupted, capitalize only the first word of the quotation. Do not capitalize the word that begins the second part of the quotation.

> "We've just bought a new home," Anna announced.

> "We've bought a house," Anna explained, "which is not far from town." She added, "It's very convenient."

Capitalize the first word of a complete line of poetry.

> (Although the use of capitals in poetry might vary according to a poet's style, the first word of a line is usually capitalized.)

If music be the food of love, play on;
Give me excess of it, that, surfeiting,
The appetite may sicken, and so die.

—William Shakespeare

Capitalize the first word, the last word, and all other important words in the title of any work of art.

This rule applies to the titles of books, chapters, stories, magazines, poems, plays, movies, newspapers, musical works, works of art, historical documents, and so on. Do not capitalize prepositions and conjunctions that have fewer than five letters when they appear within a title. However, do capitalize *a, an,* or *the* (as well as all prepositions and conjunctions) when they are the first word of a title.

Isak Dinesen's *Out of Africa* tells about her life in Kenya.

William Faulkner, author of the American novels *Intruder in the Dust* and *As I Lay Dying,* also helped write the screenplay for the film *The Big Sleep.*

The record album *Music of the Civil War* contains two excerpts from Lincoln's Gettysburg Address and the "Battle Hymn of the Republic."

I located the poem "Is Wisdom a Lot of Language?" in a collection of Sandburg's poetry called *Honey and Salt.*

Exercise 1: Using Capital Letters

Write the sentences on the next page, using capital letters where necessary. Underline the words you capitalize.

Examples

---

a. "last night," Joanna said, "we went to the movies to see *the african queen* and *guess who's coming to dinner.*"
"Last night," Joanna said, "we went to the movies to see *The African Queen* and *Guess Who's Coming to Dinner.*"

b. although Fats Waller recorded and popularized "it's a sin to tell a lie," he didn't write the song. i'm not sure who did.
Although Fats Waller recorded and popularized "It's a Sin to Tell a Lie," he didn't write the song. I'm not sure who did.

1. according to an article in *playbill* magazine, some plays have had some strange titles. have you ever heard of *the devil in the cheese* or *a worm in the horseradish?*

2. frank Sinatra's album, *in the wee small hours of the morning,* is now popular with a whole new group of listeners. three generations of fans have admired "old Blue Eyes"!

3. "have you ever read *the wind in the willows?* Lucy asked. she added, "it's a classic."

4. the *chronicle* used to be the only paper in town, but now there are also the *daily gazette* and the *times.* at least there's more than one paper to read.

5. these words by Benjamin Franklin offer good advice: "dost thou love life? then do not squander time, for that is the stuff life is made of."

6. "we went to the opening of Paulo's show," Muhammad exclaimed. "it was wonderful. my favorite painting was entitled 'reflections inside a golden eye.'"

7. while researching for her sociology report, "feline fans—common personality traits among cat admirers," Helga read the books *cat people* and *working cats.* both books were filled with quotes from cat owners.

8. didn't Jack say that he had seen *the empire strikes back* four times? after seeing *star wars,* Jack declared, "if there are a million sequels to this picture, I'll see each of them at least four or five times."

9. "if you're planning to diet," Kim said, "read *shape up, thin from within,* and *get slim.* each book offers intelligent plans for diet and exercise."

10. "next week's film festival," the announcer said, "boasts some of the worst films ever made! two of the films that will be shown are *the attack of the killer tomatoes* and *plan nine from outer space.*"

Capitals That Set Off Proper Nouns and Adjectives

The following rules apply to the capitalization of proper nouns and adjectives.

Capitalize the names of specific people.

> While visiting New York, Bernie Cohen met Meryl Streep and Melba Moore.

> Last weekend Alice and Maxine stayed at the Cooper's house.

Note: Sometimes, capitals occur within a surname, such as *McCluskey* and *O'Henry*.

Capitalize a title preceding a person's name or a title replacing a person's name, as in direct address.

> One of the most active senators on the committee is Senator James.

> Do you expect, Governor, to run for another term?

Note: When the words *president* and *vice president* do not precede a person's name, they may be capitalized only when they refer to the highest officials of the government.

> The President [of the United States] is inaugurated in January.

> Vice President Ford later became President Ford.

> Juan's goal is to be president of the company within five years.

Capitalize the abbreviation for a person's name or title.

> Capt. Wm. Jordon will see you now, Prof. Clarke.

> Harry Brown, Sr., and Dr. Bertha Shapp own that building.

Capitalize words that show family relationships when they precede a person's name or when they replace a person's name.

> My sister went to Mexico with Aunt Irene.

> I wonder, Father, when you'll be ready to leave.

> I'm looking forward to meeting my long-lost cousin.

Capitalize *Miss*, *Mrs.*, *Ms.*, and *Mr.*

> Miss Ella Brown will head the special task force.

In American history Mrs. Eleanor Roosevelt is one of the most admired women.

Capitalize the names of specific places and proper adjectives formed from the names of special places.

Fifth Street in Plainfield becomes North Avenue in Westfield, but it's the same street.

The Caribbean islands of Aruba, Bonaire, and Curaçao are known as the "ABC Islands."

Five counties in southern New Jersey want to secede from the state. The new state would be called South New Jersey.

According to this map, Kahalui Bay is north of Haleakala National Park.

Note: Capitalize the names of compass directions only if they refer to a specific region or are part of an address.

Don't visit the Southwest in August!

If the museum is located at 75 East Huron, it is not on the northwest side of the city.

Exercise 2: Using Capital Letters

Write each of the following sentences and use capital letters where necessary. Underline the words you capitalize.

Examples

---

a. My aunt lives in cape may, a town at the southern tip of new jersey.

My aunt lives in Cape May, a town at the southern tip of New Jersey.

b. Jake's cousin, dr. wm. march, was elected president of the kiwanis club in jefferson, wisconsin.
Jake's cousin, Dr. Wm. March, was elected president of the Kiwanis Club in Jefferson, Wisconsin.

1. When asked if she could name all fifty state capitals, aunt Kim missed two—augusta, maine, and sacramento, california.

2. When did you move south to atlanta, reverend ames? I thought you lived in south carolina.

3. If don's cousin sherwin goes north to seattle this summer, chris and jenny will live in his house in los angeles.

4. Did you know, mother, that dr. yates, ms. aleta, mrs. knowles, and sen. coles met while traveling in south america? They visited venezuela, peru, and colombia.

5. When he visited washington, d.c., paulo morales, jr., who is the president of our student council, met the president and vice president of the United States at a restaurant in georgetown.

6. aunt ruth, uncle henry, and their daughter allison (my favorite cousin) took a mediterranean cruise, stopping in france, italy, sardinia, and tunisia.

7. Many old western trails began in texas and led north to the great plains, the rocky mountains, and california; for example, the shawnee trail ran between texas and kansas city, and the california trail led from texas to san francisco.

8. For his birthday my friend alonzo received a pair of fabulous cowboy boots made by the bootmaker tony lama, jr., whose company is located on tony lama street in el paso, texas.

9. Eleanor's cousin tommy lives on pudding street in bedford hills, a small town in westchester county just north of white plains and new york city.

10. Last summer jaimie's aunt, who is a professor at ohio state, taught a course in florence, italy, and then traveled with her sister, dr. celia ling, to rome and milan, and then across the english channel to london.

Capitalize the names of buildings, institutions, monuments, businesses, and organizations.

The American Medical Association has an office in the Speidel Building.

In 1912 Juliette Law founded the Girl Scouts of America.

Is Midwestern Mutual the insurance company that gave away plastic replicas of the Lincoln Memorial last year?

Capitalize the names of nationalities, religions, races, and languages. Also capitalize the proper adjectives formed from these nouns.

Jennie Lee has a French poodle and a Siamese cat.

Because he lived in North Africa, Alan speaks both French and Arabic and is a respected scholar in the Moslem faith.

This basket was made by a member of the Hopi nation.

Capitalize the abbreviations A.D., B.C., A.M., and P.M.

Tomorrow's sunrise is at 5:14 A.M.

Who won the Battle of Hastings, fought in A.D. 1066?

Note: Do not capitalize the abbreviations *am* and *fm* (pertaining to radio) or abbreviations for measurements such as *kg, cm, oz., sec.,* and *min.*

Capitalize the names of planets, stars, and other heavenly bodies.

Sailors used the North Star—Polaris—to guide them.

Which planet shines red in the sky—Mars or Venus?

Note: The words *sun, moon,* and *earth* are not usually capitalized. Never capitalize them when they follow the word *the.*

The term *heliocentric* refers to the belief of early scientists that the earth, not the sun, was the center of our solar system.

Exercise 3: Using Capital Letters

Write the following sentences, using capital letters where necessary. Underline the words you capitalize.

Examples

a. The american museum of natural history is across the street from the new york historical society.
The <u>American Museum of Natural History</u> is across the street from the <u>New York Historical Society.</u>

b. Which planet is larger, neptune or saturn?

Which planet is larger, <u>Neptune</u> or <u>Saturn?</u>

1. The african country of zaire—formerly the belgian congo—has rich deposits of copper and cobalt.

2. Did you know that New York's temple emanuel is the largest jewish synagogue in the world?

3. A fine example of japanese carpentry is the golden hall, a buddhist temple built in a.d. 679.

4. Don't forget that the league of women voters will sponsor a panel discussion on Tuesday night at 7:30 p.m. at the city center motor inn.

5. Last Saturday we ate at casa patron, a wonderful spanish restaurant around the corner from the minskoff theater.

6. The chinese have been practicing acupuncture since 3000 b.c.; recently american doctors have accepted acupuncture as a treatment for certain ailments.

7. Every year artists and writers apply for grants from organizations such as the national endowment for the arts, the national endowment for the humanities, and the ford foundation.

8. The exhibition at asia house includes japanese screens, chinese porcelain, chinese ivory, and korean silks.

9. French, mexican, spanish, italian, and canadian diplomats met at the white house to discuss trade agreements; the meetings, which ran from 9:00 a.m. until 9:00 p.m., were broadcast over fm radio.

10. Professors and administrators from boston university, emerson college, harvard university, simmons college, and amherst attended a meeting of the massachusetts association for continu ing education last week at the powell building.

Capitalize words referring to the Deity, holy families, and holy books of all religions. Capitalize personal pronouns when they refer to deities.

The evangelist urged, "Believe in the Lord and His power."

The prayer begins, "Blessed art Thou O Lord our God."

Our philosophy class compared sections of the Talmud with portions of the Old Testament.

Note: Do not capitalize the word *god* when it refers to a god of ancient mythology; capitalize the names of specific ancient gods.

The ancients attributed natural phenomena to their gods; for example, stormy seas might mean that Neptune, the god of the sea, was angry.

Capitalize the names of months, days of the week, holidays, and special events; capitalize historical events and periods.

Isn't Earth Day in April?

The Senior Prom is on Friday, June 3.

As a result of the Spanish-American War, the U.S. annexed Puerto Rico.

Unfortunately, I stated on my essay exam that Wordsworth was a Renaissance rather than a Romantic poet.

Note: The names of seasons are not usually capitalized.

That restaurant closes in winter.

Capitalize the names of school subjects that are formed from proper nouns or that name a specific course.

Since you plan to major in art, you must take Fundamentals of Drawing, a basic art course, before Design 204.

I believe that Literature III focuses on the American short story; it's an interesting literature course.

Note: Capitalize most nouns followed by a number or letter.

Isn't Room 422 in use on Tuesday afternoon?

Mrs. Ortega found Plan C met all of her insurance needs.

Capitalize the names of political parties, the names of government agencies, departments, and bureaus or their abbreviations.

When is the Democratic convention?

If you want information on national parks, you should write to the Department of the Interior. The ICC (Interstate Commerce Commission) has a helpful booklet on moving; why don't you send for a copy?

Capitalize the names of specific ships, trains, planes, and spacecraft.

Don's boat is called *Seaspray*.

Who was the commander of the starship *Enterprise?*

Agatha Christie wrote a mystery about the *Orient Express*, the luxurious European train that traveled between Calais and Istanbul.

Capitalize brand names of specific products.

Daisy detergent is the least expensive cleanser in this market.

Jell-O is one brand of gelatin dessert.

Capitalize the first word and each noun in the salutation of a letter. Capitalize the first word in the closing.

My dear Dr. Kramer,   Dear Mrs. Waller: Very truly yours,

Capitalize the pronoun *I* and the interjection *O*.

I don't know where I put my eyeglasses!

Where, oh where should I go, O Father?

Capitalize the first word of each topic of an outline.

I. Hollywood idols
   A. Stars of silent films
   B. Stars of "talkies"

Exercise 4: Using Capital Letters

Write each of the following sentences and use capital letters where needed. Underline the words you capitalize.

Examples

a. Marissa's course, yoga for beginners, meets on tuesday evenings, february through may, at 6 o'clock in room 750.
   Marissa's course, Yoga for Beginners, meets on Tuesday evenings, February through May, at 6 o'clock in Room 750.

b. My dog, i think, prefers bonz-o dog chow to bark bites.
   My dog, I think, prefers Bonz-O Dog Chow to Bark Bites.

1. You cannot, i understand, take modern art 12 without first having taken introduction to art 1.

2. Sometimes a Presidential candidate splits from the democrats or republicans to run on a third-party ticket; for example, Teddy Roosevelt formed the bullmoose party.

3. At the auction i attended last tuesday, lot 49 included a huge poster of the luxury liner *normandie.*

4. Yes, easter is always on a sunday, but it is not always the same date; it is, however, usually in april.

5. Next sunday, may 12, is mother's day; we're giving our mother a midnight cruise around the island on the ferryboat *glistening maiden* and a bottle of chanel perfume.

6. Jenny wrote, "dear aunt lynn, i'm writing—with my new jackson bros. pen—to let you know that i am coming on thursday, july 28, and will stay until saturday, august 15. i have reserved room 803 at the martin hotel, so i'll see you then. Oh, i can't wait! fondest regards, jenny."

7. Julio outlined his paper on the occult:
   I. unexplained events from may until august
      A. crying in room 412
      B. sinking of the *flying cloud* in the harbor
      C. hail on labor day

8. Religious thought 12 covers these holy books: old testament, new testament, koran, and tibetan book of the dead.

9. The mayor's department of consumer affairs (suite 3100) rates the following brands of typewriters as comparable buys: addison, adler, and march bros.

10. You'll have a long weekend for new year's day (january), washington's birthday (february), memorial day (may), independence day (july), labor day (september), thanksgiving (november), and christmas (december).

Review: Using Capital Letters

Write the following paragraphs and use capital letters where necessary. Underline the words you capitalize.

Ask any record company executives—whether from columbia records or a & m, inc.—to list important pop recording artists of the decade, and no doubt they will mention josé feliciano. Now a recognized star both in the united states and abroad, josé endured many hardships on his way to fame. After moving from puerto rico to new york, he had to fight to stake his claim; in addition, he had to overcome the problems of being blind.

José's father, who had been a farmer, left the caribbean to try his luck in manhattan. it was hard for five-year-old josé. He had no friends and had to learn english; so he spent much of his time indoors, by himself, listening to elvis presley and ray charles on the radio.

Inspired to become a musical star, José learned to play the concertina and the guitar. At first he played at school, and his performances at charles evans hughes high school on west 18th street won him fans.

His first job was in detroit, michigan. Then he returned to the east to perform in greenwich village. Encouraged by his wife, hilda perez, he kept working away. Then in 1968 his song "light my fire" secured his career.

With that hit, José began playing all over the country, from the atlantic to the pacific, from canada to mexico. Fans on both sides of the mississippi rushed to his concerts. Today, having won the music industry's grammy award, José continues to work hard. As usual, his next concert, june 24, will be before a sell-out crowd.

Writing Focus: *Using Capitalization in Writing*

The rules of capitalization are conventions that help clarify writing. In most of your writing you will use capital letters primarily for three reasons: to indicate the start of a new sentence, to distinguish proper nouns and adjectives, and to indicate titles.

Assignment: *Your Favorite Character*

Who is your favorite character from a television show, movie, or book? What distinguishing physical features does this character have? What traits does he or she have that appeal to you?

In two well-developed paragraphs, describe your favorite character from a TV show, movie, or book. Describe the character physically; then tell what this person's personality is like and what interests you about the character. Your classmates are your audience, and your purpose is to describe your favorite character as vividly as

possible. Your paragraphs will be evaluated for correct use of capital letters.

Use the following steps to complete this assignment.

A. Prewriting

Think about the attributes of the character you have chosen to write about. List these attributes under two headings: *Physical features* and *Personality*. From each list choose the attributes that you want to focus on. For help in organizing your paragraphs, refer to Chapter 3.

B. Writing

Use your lists to write two paragraphs describing your favorite character. Supply descriptive details that support each topic sentence. As you write, follow the rules of capitalization that you have learned.

C. Postwriting

Revise your first draft, using the following checklist.

1. Does each paragraph have a clear topic sentence?

2. Does each paragraph include enough descriptive details, and do the details support the topic sentence?

3. Are the sentences in each paragraph arranged in a logical order?

4. Have I avoided sentence fragments and run-on sentences?

5. Have I used capital letters correctly?

Use the Checklist for Proofreading in the back of the book to proofread your paragraphs. Then share your writing with your classmates.

4
Language Resources

25 Vocabulary and Spelling
Vocabulary

Your command of language affects your ability to communicate and so may affect your future. Vocabulary tests are a common device for measuring the aptitude of job applicants, college students, and entrants in training programs and the armed forces. The following sections on vocabulary building will help you gain mastery over words. You also will learn about the history of the English language and about ways to keep your language clear.

Words and Meanings

Determining Meaning Through Context

The *context* of a word is its environment—the other words that surround it.

Frequently a word's context gives clues to its meaning. Suppose, for instance, that a new word came into the English language: *fless*. By studying the contexts in which *fless* occurs, you could begin to understand its meaning:

I hope it snows this weekend because I want to *fless*.

Mona broke her leg while she was *flessing*.

Flessing is more fun than skiing, and the equipment is less expensive than ski gear.

I was going to *fless* this weekend, but I broke my *fless*board in a bad jump yesterday.

From the preceding contexts you know that *fless* means some sort of snow sport, rather dangerous, involving a board, perhaps something like a surfboard.

Words can also have different meanings in different contexts:

In geometry we learned about *obtuse* angles.
[An obtuse angle is greater than 90 degrees, but less than 180 degrees.]

I was too *obtuse* to learn much else in geometry.
[An obtuse person is dull, stupid.]

Exercise 1: Defining Words by Context

Read the following passage from a review by Brendan Gill of a recent production of Shakespeare's play, *Macbeth*. Then write a brief definition of each of the underlined words. If you cannot deduce the meaning of a word from its context, consult your dictionary and supply an appropriate definition.

Macbeth is a gory thriller written in exquisite verse. Blood gushes up at every turn of the plot, and so does poetry. The disparity between the barbaric story and the lyricism of language in which it is told provides a series of pleasing shocks to the ear. During the course of the play, we may be only half conscious of the commingling of vile deeds and melodious imagery, but as an aesthetic device the commingling is always poignantly, thrillingly at work, at once concentrating and magnifying our attention and causing us to feel an unexpected sympathy for the most contemptible of murderers—one who murders not out of jealousy or spite, or to avenge some grave social wrong, but simply in order to gain greater personal importance. At first, the villainous Macbeth and his wife appear to have little more on their minds than that they are Smiths and would like not only to keep up with the Joneses but to surpass them as well. Macbeth's ambitions are as loutish as they are commonplace, and yet in seeking to attain them he speaks some of the most ravishing lines ever written.[1]

Shades of Meaning

The explicit meaning of a word is called its *denotation*. The best-known denotation of *lemon* is "a small, egg-shaped, edible citrus fruit with a pale yellow rind and a juicy, sour pulp, rich in vitamin C." In another context *lemon* might be "a person or thing that is defective or undesirable," as in "The car that I bought turned out to be a lemon."

Words, however, can convey more than ideas; they can also convey attitudes and emotions. An *inexpensive canine* expresses an altogether different attitude from *cheap mutt*, and being a *sanitation engineer* sounds more dignified than being a *trash collector*. The associations of this sort that go with words are called *connotations*.

---

[1]From "Supping on Horrors" by Brendan Gill in *The New Yorker*, February 2, 1981, p. 62. © 1981 by Brendan Gill. Reprinted by permission.

Synonyms are words that denote nearly the same thing.

Even though two words have nearly the same meaning, they may have different connotations, and it is important to understand these differences. Connotations may be very close to one another, as in *car* and *auto*, but they may also be very far apart, as in *car* and *jalopy*.

A *thesaurus*, which is a dictionary of synonyms, is a valuable reference tool. When choosing a synonym, however, be sure that you choose one with appropriate connotations. As Mark Twain said, "There is as much difference between a right word and an almost right word as there is between lightning and a lightning bug."

Antonyms are words whose meanings are nearly opposite; *hot* is the antonym of *cold*; *up* is the antonym of *down*.

Many words form their antonyms with a prefix or a suffix; thus, *happy* can be turned into an antonym, *unhappy*; *guilty* into the antonym *guiltless*. Other antonyms are not related in form, and a word may have more than one antonym: *guilty's* antonym, for instance, could be either the related word *guiltless* or the unrelated word *innocent*. Knowing a word's synonyms and antonyms helps you better understand the word itself.

Exercise 2: Using Synonyms

Sportswriters and sportscasters need many synonyms to keep their stories from being too repetitive; thus, the *football* becomes the *pigskin* or the *spheroid*, and "The Tigers *beat* the Vikings" becomes "The Tigers *trounced* the Vikings." Rewrite the following scores, replacing the word *beat* with one more lively. Then rewrite the sports story that follows, using synonyms and fresh phrases for the underlined words.

Springdale beat Fayetteville   Nebraska beat Oklahoma
The Bucks beat the Hawks   The Bunnies beat the Bears
The Warriors beat the Wombats   New York beat Philadelphia
DePaul beat Indiana   Silverlake beat Aims
The Terriers beat the Mounties   Texas beat SMU

The Charleston Patriots beat the Winslow Wildcats tonight, 70–60. The Wildcats led by twelve points at the half, but a rally led by Willie Washington and Greg Forster tied the game. Then Clark Whitewater stole the ball and ran down the court to make a basket. Fouled on the play, he made another basket. The Wildcats turned over the ball, and Whitewater made another three-point play. In an incredible series of steals and turnovers, Washington made another basket, Forster made another basket, and Whitewater made another basket. The Patriots play the Buckingham Bucks next Friday night, in what promises to be an exciting game.

Examining Words

By examining the parts of words—their roots and affixes—you can often determine the meanings of the words themselves.

A *root word* is one from which others have been derived.

The words *meter, metric, metronome,* and *speedometer* are all derived from the root word *metron,* a Greek word meaning "measurement." One root may have many descendants, some bearing great family resemblance, some less. One way in which roots are transformed into new words is by the adding of *affixes.*

An *affix* is a word element, such as a prefix or suffix, that is added to the root and changes its meaning.

Some roots and affixes come from early English words; others have been borrowed from other countries, especially Greece and Rome. Familiarity with common roots and affixes can help you learn new words.

The following list contains the most common Greek roots used in the English language, their definitions, and examples of derived words.

Greek Roots

Root	Definition	English Derivative
-agog-	leader	demagogue
-anthrop-	man, human	anthropoid
-arch-	ancient, chief	archaeology
-aster-, -astr-	star	astronaut
-auto-	self	automatic
-bibl-	book	bibliography
-bi-, -bio-	life	biography
-chrom-	color	chromatic
-chron-	time	chronology
-cosm-	order, world	cosmos
-crac-, -crat-	govern	democrat
-crypt-	hidden	cryptogram

Root	Definition	English Derivative
-cycl-	wheel	bicycle
-dem-	people	democracy
-derm-	skin	dermatology
-dox-	belief	orthodox
-dyn-	power	dynamite
-erg-	work	energy
-gam-	marry	monogamy
-gen-	kind, source	genealogy
-geo-	earth	geography
-gon-	corner	hexagon
-gram-	write	grammar
-graph-	write	telegraph
-gyn-	female	misogynist
-hem-	blood	hemoglobin
-hetero-	other	heterogenous
-homo-	same	homogenize
-hydr-	water	hydrant
-lith-	stone	monolith
-log-	word, reason	logic
-mega-	large	megaton
-metr-, -meter-	measure	perimeter
-mono-	one	monogram
-morph-	shape	amorphous
-nom-	law	economic
-orth-	straight	orthopedist
-pan-	all	pantheism
-path-	feeling, sufferer	sympathetic
-phil-	love	philanthropy
-phos-, -phot-	light	photo
-poly-	many	polyhedron
-pyr-	fire	pyre
-soph-	wise, wisdom	philosophy
-theo-	god	theology
-therm-	heat	thermometer
-tom-	cut	atom
-zo-	animal, life	zoologist

Exercise 3: Using Greek Roots

Write each of the words on the following page and the Greek root
from which it is derived. Using your knowledge of the root, supply a
definition for the word and then check your definition with that in a
dictionary. Some words may be formed from more than one root.

1. polymorphous
2. protozoa
3. autocratic
4. synergy
5. cryptic

List and define two words drawn from each of the following Greek roots. Do not give words previously used as examples in the chapter.

6. -anthrop-
7. -dyn-
8. -path-
9. -mega-
10. -theo-

The following list contains the most commonly used Latin roots in the English language, their meanings, and examples of words derived from them.

Latin Roots

Root	Definition	English Derivative
-ag-, -act-	do	action
-cap-	seize	captive
-cede-, -ceed-	go	exceed
-clud-, -clus-	close	conclusion
-cur-	run	excursion
-dic-	say	dictate
-duc-	lead	conduct
-fac-, -fec-	make	factory
-fid-	faith	fidelity
-fin-	limit	finite
-form-	shape	formation
-gress-	go	regress
-junct-	join	junction
-pend-, -pens-	hang	pendant
-reg-, -rig-, -rect-	straight	regiment, rigor
-sent-, -sens-	feel	sensitive
-sequ-, -secut-	follow	sequence, consecutive
-spec-	look	speculate
-ten-, -tent-	hold	detention
-tract-	pull	traction

Root	Definition	English Derivative
-vert, -vers-	turn	divert, diversion
-volv-, -volu-	roll	revolve

Exercise 4: Using Latin Roots

Write the following words and the Latin root from which each is derived. Using your knowledge of the root, supply a definition for the word. Look in your dictionary to check and, if necessary, revise your definition.

1. preclude
2. perfidious
3. rectitude
4. ductile
5. sentience

Using your dictionary or drawing on your own vocabulary, list and define two words drawn from each of the following Latin roots. Do not give words previously used in the chapter as examples.

6. -ag-
7. -fac-
8. -fin-
9. -pend-
10. -reg-

Prefixes

Affixes that are put before the root are called *prefixes*.

The following is a list of common prefixes. Some have more than one spelling.

Prefix	Meaning	Example
ab-, a-	from, away	abstain
ante-	before	antecedent
anti-	against	antidote
auto-	self	automobile
bi-	two, twice	bicycle
circum-	around	circumstance
com-, con-	with	companion, contract
de-	down, from, away	depart
demi-	half	demitasse
dis-	negation, lack	distrust
en-, em-	in, among	engage
eu-	good, true	eulogy
ex-, e-	from, out of	expire
extr-, extro-	beyond	extraordinary, extrovert
fore-	previous	forecast

hemi-	half	hemisphere
hyper-	excessive	hyperbole
hypo-	under, below	hypothesis
in-, il-	not, against	invisible, illiterate
im-, ir-	not, against	impossible, irreplaceable
in-, il-	in, into	infest, illuminate
im-, ir-	in, into	immigrate, irritate
inter-	between, among	international
meta-	changed, later	metamorphosis
mis-	wrong, not	mismatch
para-	beyond, beside	paramedic
peri-	around, near	perimeter
post-	after	postpone
pre-	before	prepare
pro-	for, forward	promote
re-	back, again	recount
retro-	back	retrospect
se-	away	secede
semi-	half	semicircle
sub-	under, beneath	substandard
trans-	across	transplant
un-	not	unwise
ultra-	beyond, excessive	ultraviolet

Exercise 5: Using Prefixes

On a sheet of paper numbered 1–10, write the following words, underlining the prefix in each word. Then use each word correctly in a sentence, checking your dictionary if necessary.

1. abjure
2. euphemism
3. paradox
4. periscope
5. excoriate
6. ultramodern
7. transgress
8. prognosis
9. subsume
10. immolate

Suffixes

An affix that attaches to the end of a root word is called a *suffix.*

Sometimes, a suffix changes not only the meaning of the root word but its part of speech as well, as shown on the following page.

luck	[noun]	achieve	[verb]
lucky	[adjective]	achievement	[noun]
luckily	[adverb]	achiever	[noun]

The following suffixes are arranged according to the parts of speech they form.

Noun-forming Suffixes

Suffixes	Meaning	Example
-age	rank, process, state	bondage
-ance, -ancy	being, condition of	hesitance, hesitancy
-ation	action, state of	federation
-dom	state, condition	serfdom
-eer	doer, maker	auctioneer
-er	doer, action	reader
-ery	state	treachery
-hood	state, rank	motherhood
-ice	state	malice
-ine	dealing with	feline
-ism	act, doctrine	barbarism
-ist	doer, believer	guitarist
-ition	action, state	rendition
-ment	means, result, action	judgment
-mony	result, condition	alimony
-ness	quality, state	quietness
-or	doer, state	donor
-ory	pertaining to	memory
-tion	state	creation
-tude	quality, state	latitude
-ty	quality, state	scarcity
-ure	result, state	pleasure
-y	result, state	injury

Adjective-forming Suffixes

Suffixes	Meaning	Example
-able	able to, able to be	washable
-en	made of	oaken
-ful	having qualities of	delightful
-ish	like	foolish
-less	without	careless
-like	similar	lifelike
-some	apt to, showing	troublesome
-ward	in the direction of	windward

Verb-forming Suffixes	Meaning	Example
-ate	become, form, treat	separate
-en	cause to be	shorten
-esce	become, continue	convalesce
-fy	make, cause	liquify
-ish	do	finish
-ize	make, cause to be	fertilize

Exercise 6: Using Suffixes

Write each of the following words and underline the suffix. Define the word, and then use it correctly in a sentence.

Example

a. novice

novice—a person new to a particular activity or occupation

Being a novice at surfing, I spent more time under the waves than on them.

1. rectify
2. pulchritude
3. winsome
4. anarchist
5. acquiesce

6. parsimony
7. bellicosity
8. coercion
9. sanctimonious
10. porcine

The History of Language

Families of Language

In the same way that children of the same family may share a common characteristic inherited from their parents or grandparents (freckles or curly hair, for instance), modern languages share certain characteristics inherited from older parent languages. For example, from their study of the similarities of English, Swedish, Russian, Italian, Greek, and Sanskrit, linguists have learned that these languages and several other European and Asian languages belong to the same family; they are all modifications of an older parent language called *Indo-European*, which was spoken by groups of people living in central Europe around 4000 B.C.

Notice the similarities among the forms of the word *mother* in the following list. The languages in the list are all part of the Indo-European family.

Sanskrit: matar	Swedish: moder
Latin: mater	Danish: moder
Greek: meter	Dutch: moeder
Persian: mader	German: mutter
Icelandic: mōdhir	French: mère
Old Irish: mathir	Spanish: madre
Russian: mati	Portuguese: mae
Polish: matka	Italian: madre

Among the Indo-European languages, English is a western Germanic language closely related to Dutch, German, Flemish, Yiddish, Afrikaans, and Frisian.

Linguists are still in the process of positively identifying all language families. While the Indo-European family spread over a large geographic area as the original tribes moved east and west about 2000 B.C., some language families are confined to smaller areas. For example, there are over one hundred American Indian language families, and at least three families (Sudanese-Guinean, Bantu, and Hottentot-Bushman) can be found on the African continent.

The Old English Period (450 to 1066)

The history of English as a separate language begins around A.D. 410, when the Romans, who had invaded Britain 400 years earlier, abandoned their colony there and left the island's native inhabitants, the Celts, unprotected. Helpless, the Celts sought protection from three fierce Germanic tribes—the Angles, Saxons, and Jutes. Instead of protecting the Celts, these three tribes from northern Europe crossed the North Sea about A.D. 450 and conquered the Celts' homeland. These invaders brought with them their own West-Germanic language. This Anglo-Saxon dialect, soon referred to as "Angleish," developed into Old English.

The following example of Old English (OE) is a portion of the epic poem, *Beowulf*.

Old English

> De ā waes wundor micel/ Dæt se winsele.
> Wiotæfde headodērum,/ Dæ hē on hrūsan ne fēal,
> Fæger foldbold; . . .

Translation

> It was a marvel that the wine hall withstood the battlers,
> that it did not fall to the ground, beautiful building; . . .

Although the preceding example may seem strange as a foreign language, many basic, modern English words began in Old English. Common prepositions (*under, to, with, from*), the conjunction *and*, and the adverb *where*, and some pronouns (*his, I, we, your*) were all part of Old English. Some aspects of modern English grammar are also related to Old English; *was* and *were*, for example, are much like their Old English counterparts *waes* and *waere*. Even the words for certain weekdays, drawn from the names of Anglo-Saxon gods, are remnants of this time period: *Tuesday* comes from Tiw, the god of Venus; *Wednesday* comes from Woden, the chief god; *Thursday* from Thor, the god of thunder; and *Friday* from Frigga, the goddess of the home.

Three other languages also contributed to the English vocabulary during the Old English period. The native Celts retreated as the Anglo-Saxons invaded, but they left behind such place-names as Kent, Dover, and Thames. The early Romans, who left Britain in 410, and missionaries under St. Augustine, who brought Christianity to the Anglo-Saxon population around 597, introduced Latin words such as *altar, shrine, school,* and *paper.*

Finally, Viking invaders who settled in northern England provided everyday terms, such as *guess, leg, loose,* and *window*, that are still part of the English language.

Exercise 7: *Researching the Old English Period*

Using library resources, prepare a brief report on one of the following topics related to the development of Old English.

1. The Celts and their culture

2. The Angles, Saxons, and Jutes and their invasion of Great Britain

3. King Alfred

4. *Beowulf*

5. The runic alphabet

The Middle English Period (1066 to 1450)

The Old English period, which had begun with an invasion, also ended with an invasion in 1066 when William the Conqueror, also the Duke of Normandy, defeated the King of England at the Battle of Hastings. Under these Norman invaders (from Normandy in northwest France) the English way of life changed. For 200 years two languages coexisted in Britain—the French spoken by the ruling class and the English spoken by common people. After 1250, when the invaders' ties with the continent were severed, the Normans began to think of themselves as English. However, by the end of the Middle English (ME) period, over 10,000 French words had become a part of the English language. As a result, Modern English often has two words, one French and one from the older English, for the same item. For example, the French *village* has the same meaning as the English *borough*. In some cases a French word replaced an English one; the French *people*, for example, replaced the English *leod*.

These borrowed French words were not the only changes that marked the Middle English period. While it might be logical to assume that English would grow more complex as time passed, exactly the opposite was true. English grammar became simpler. In Old English a noun might have twelve different forms, six singular and six plural; during the Middle English period these forms were gradually eliminated until most nouns had only two singular forms and one plural form. Also, around 1400 a standard written language was developed. Before this time residents of different geographical areas in England who spoke different dialects spelled words as they were pronounced in their locale. After 1400, however, all English writers tended to use the dialect of London as a standard, making written communication clearer and easier.

As you read the following example of Middle English, a passage about King Arthur's death, notice the changes in spelling and grammar that make it easier to understand than the Old English passage from *Beowulf*.

> After was it monthes two,
>   As frely folke it undyrstode,
> Or ever Gawayne myght ryde or go,
>   Or had fote upon erthe to stonde;
> The thirde tyme he was full thro
>   To do batayle with herte and hande,
> But than was word comen hem to
>   That they muste home to Yngland.
> Suche mesage was hem brought,
>   There was no man that thought it goode;
> The kynge hem selfe full sone it thought
>   —Full moche mornyd he in hys mode
> That suche treson [in Ynglond] shuld be wrought—
>   That he moste nedys over the flode.

The Modern English Period (1450 to Present)

Students are often surprised to learn that writing such as the following passage from Shakespeare's *Macbeth* is considered Modern English.

SEYTON: The queen, my lord, is dead.
MACBETH: She should have died hereafter;
  There would have been time for such a word.
  Tomorrow, and tomorrow, and tomorrow,
  Creeps in this petty pace from day to day
  To the last syllable of recorded time,
  And all our yesterdays have lighted fools
  The way to dusty death. Out, out, brief candle!
  Life's but a walking shadow, a poor player
  That struts and frets his hour upon the stage
  And then is heard no more. It is a tale
  Told by an idiot, full of sound and fury,
  Signifying nothing.

Although Shakespeare's plays often contain unfamiliar words, the language in his work is closer to that used by English writers today than it is to Middle English. One reason for this similarity is the Great Vowel Shift of the late 1400s, which altered the pronunciation of many words. For instance, in the Middle English period *care* sounded like *car*, *sheep* like *shape*, and *boat* like *bought*. In the early years of the Modern Period, vowel sounds changed, and words acquired the pronunciation used today.

William Caxton's invention of the printing press also affected language during this period. Printing made books available to more and more people and increased the tendency toward standardized spelling. Print impresses a particular spelling on the mind, and once a word appeared in print spelled in a particular way, new writers felt constrained to adopt that spelling.

The invention of the press and the birth of the Renaissance also prompted more writing. In the Middle English period much writing was still done in Greek and Latin; however, the Renaissance fostered nationalism and a pride in the language of one's native country that promoted writing in English. When authors found the English language inadequate, they borrowed words from Latin and Greek, sometimes adding English endings. Words such as *education, esteem, theocracy,* and *dexterity* all found their way into English in this way. Increased trade and exploration of new lands also added more words to the English vocabulary, and as scientific knowledge expanded, new words were coined for the new inventions and technology that made life easier.

Exercise 8: *Determining Word Origins*

Using a dictionary, look up the following words to determine the period of language development in which each word entered the

English language. To record your findings, use the abbreviations *OE*, *ME*, and *Mod. E.* For help in reading word histories, consult the front of your dictionary under the heading "Etymology."

1. abbot	6. verdict
2. they	7. aesthetic
3. geology	8. poetry
4. druid	9. liberty
5. martyr	10. hostage

American English

Since the early days when parts of colonial America were settled by the English, some noticeable differences have developed between British and American uses of the same language.

These differences in spelling, vocabulary, and pronunciation have resulted in a distinct American English.

Some of these differences originated when Noah Webster, a young American schoolteacher, simplified the spelling of some English words for his *American Spelling Book* (1783) and the *American Dictionary of the English Language* (1828). Not all of Webster's changes were accepted, but today many American words have simpler spellings than their British counterparts.

British	*American*
cheque	check
humour	humor
programme	program
kerb	curb
defence	defense

Many words are also pronounced differently by British and American speakers.

Word	*British*	*American*
clerk	klärk	klərk
schedule	shed'-yü(ə)l	skej'-ü(ə)l
laboratory	lə-bär'-ə-t(ə-)rē	lab'-(ə)rə-tȯr-ē
lieutenant	le(f)'-ten-ənt	lü-ten'-ənt

Even greater differences exist between British and American English in vocabulary.

British	American
lift	elevator
petrol	gasoline
biscuit	cookie
chemist	druggist
underground	subway
flat	apartment

Exercise 9: *Finding American English Equivalents for British Terms*

Use a dictionary to find the American English equivalents for the following British terms.

1. draughts
2. spanner
3. lorry
4. torch
5. queue up
6. wireless
7. pram
8. post
9. trunk call
10. boot

Edited Standard English

While American dialect added an interesting color and richness to the language, it also created some problems. For example, in the early 1900s a major mail-order catalogue described one catalogue item as a *coal hod*, a *coal bucket*, *coal pail*, and *coal scuttle*, so that every potential customer, regardless of his or her regional dialect, would be reached. The need for a standard form for written English became apparent as businesses, newspapers, magazines, and literature developed. Such a form, called *Standard English*, developed to meet these needs.

In the United States today, Standard English is often referred to as the "language of the marketplace" because it is the English most accepted in business, industry, and commerce.

Written Standard English conforms to accepted rules that govern subject-verb agreement, pronoun reference, and so on. The written form of Standard English is referred to by the authors of this textbook as "Edited Standard English."

Growth in Vocabulary

One thousand years ago the English language contained only 37,000 words. Today English dictionaries often contain over half a million entries. During the Old English, Middle English, and early Modern English periods, new words added to the language were usually borrowed from other languages. Although borrowing still adds some new words to the language, in recent years other processes have accounted for more than half of the new words added to English dictionaries.

Compounds

Compounds are formed by combining two or more old words.

Such words as *downtown, football* and *alongside* are common compounds used in daily conversation. Compounds are either *open* (written as two words), *closed* (written as one word), or hyphenated, as is *brother-in-law*.

Exercise 10: *Compounds*

When people speak, it is sometimes difficult to determine whether a compound is open, closed, or hyphenated. Look up the following expressions in a dictionary and rewrite each in its correct form: as two separate words, as one word, or as a hyphenated word.

1. back yard
2. book keeper
3. butcher knife
4. court martial
5. forty two
6. news paper
7. next door
8. out doors
9. out of date
10. study hall

Blends

Blends, or *portmanteau* words, are created by combining two words and eliminating the unneeded letters to form a new word.

The following blends are extremely old; the dates in parentheses indicate when the words were used separately and at the time of the blend's entrance into the language.

bat (1205) + mash (1000) = bash (1641)

clap (1375) + crash (1400) = clash (1500)

flame (1377) + glare (1400) = flare (1632)

gleam (1000) + shimmer (1100) = glimmer (1400)

More recent examples of blending are *motel* (*motor* + *hotel*) and *smog* (*smoke* + *fog*).

Exercise 11: Blends

List each of the following portmanteau words on a sheet of paper. Then, beside each word, write the two older words that have been blended to create the new word. Use your dictionary if you need help.

1. telethon
2. squiggle
3. moped
4. paratroop
5. motorcade

6. brunch
7. splotch
8. chortle
9. splurge
10. whodunit

Clipped Words

Clipped words **are shortened forms of words.**

Speakers of English have a tendency to shorten long words by using only a part of the original. These *clipped words* (*auto* for *automobile*, *fan* for *fanatic*) occur so frequently that speakers often forget the longer, original form of the word.

Exercise 12: Clipped Words

The following list contains clipped words formed from longer words. Copy the list on a sheet of paper and beside each clipped word write the original longer form of the word. Use your dictionary for extra help.

1. gym
2. flu
3. dorm
4. bus
5. champ

6. lab
7. exam
8. lunch
9. sub
10. ad

Eponyms

Eponyms **are words derived from the names of people.**

After years of use, the capital letters used with a proper noun are often dropped from an eponym. For instance, the word *sandwich* was created in the 1700s to describe the special snack frequently requested by the Earl of Sandwich. The word *lynch* is believed to have also originated in the 1700s when John Lynch, a South Carolina planter, was hanged as a horse thief without the benefit of a fair trial.

Exercise 13: *Eponyms*

Copy the following list of eponyms on a sheet of paper. Using a dictionary for information about each word's origin, write the name of the person or place from which the word originated beside the eponym.

1. Ferris wheel
2. maverick
3. boycott
4. diesel
5. hamburger

6. tuxedo
7. Braille
8. watt
9. silhouette
10. leotard

Acronyms

Acronyms **are formed from the initials of a group of words.**

Some short acronyms are pronounced by saying each letter separately (*UN* for *United Nations*). However, most acronyms are pronounced as one word (*NOW* for the *National Organization for Women* or *radar* for *radio detecting and ranging*). Notice that the letters in some acronyms are all capitals.

As more and more agencies and organizations are formed and as more scientific and legal terminology become part of the general vocabulary, more acronyms are formed. For example, LEM (lunar excursion module), ZIP (zone improvement plan) code, and HUD (Department of Housing and Urban Development) are all recent additions to the growing list of acronyms in the English language. In fact, today there are more than 12,000 acronyms in the English language.

Exercise 14: *Acronyms*

Copy the following list of acronyms on a separate sheet of paper. Using a dictionary or encyclopedia for information, write the words each acronym represents next to the acronym.

1. SALT
2. NASA
3. CARE
4. WAC
5. CORE

6. NATO
7. VISTA
8. HUD
9. laser
10. SEATO

New Meanings for Old Words

Language changes can also involve giving new meanings to old words.

Over time word meanings change. For example, the word *eavesdrop* originally referred only to the ground beside a house, on which water from the eaves dripped. Later, used as a verb, *to eavesdrop* meant "to stand beneath the eaves and spy on a house." Today this verb refers to any situation in which one person secretly listens to another's conversation. The following list gives the old meanings of some common words.

Word	*Former Meaning*
closet	private room
girl	a child of either sex
villain	farm worker
silly	fortunate
carriage	things carried

Exercise 15: *New Meanings for Old Words*

Look up each of the following words in a dictionary of etymology, which provides information about word origins and changes. On a sheet of paper, write the oldest definition for each word and its current meaning.

1. marshal
2. cousin
3. nice
4. astonishing
5. skeleton

6. bravery
7. conceit
8. admirable
9. footmen
10. meat

Regional Dialects

In addition to the many ways in which language changes over time, it also varies in the way it is used at any one time. Some of these variations are the result of *dialects*—ways of speaking shared by people from a particular area or of the same social class, educational level, or occupation.

A resident of New England may speak of bringing home groceries in a *sack* and buying a *bag* of feed for livestock, while a Midwesterner carries a grocery *bag* and purchases a *sack* of feed. Differences in vocabulary, pronunciation, and grammar occur because residents of one geographical area share a regional dialect.

A *regional dialect* is a variation of a language shared by people in a particular geographic area.

American dialects did not come about from the corruption of an originally pure language; in fact, there was no standard for written or spoken English in colonial America. Instead, regional dialects grew from the haphazard circumstances that governed settlement, transportation, and communication in early America.

For example, the earliest residents of New England continued the pronunciations typical of their southern English dialect (*caht* for *cart*, *fahm* for *farm*) when they came to this country. Later immigrants from northern England and Europe pronounced their *r*'s more distinctly but tended to settle farther west on the frontier rather than in the populated New England area. The few immigrants who settled in New England learned English from the more numerous original settlers and, therefore, adopted their speech habits. However, on the western frontiers of Ohio and Indiana, the new immigrants' strong *r* sounds won out, and pronunciations such as *ahnt* for *aunt* or *bahn* for *barn* gradually faded.

Ironically, some dialects result not from change in language, but from the absence of change. For instance, the Appalachian dialect is actually very similar to Elizabethan English. Because the early settlers of Appalachia's mountainous, isolated areas had little contact with the outside world, some linguists believe their dialect changed very little.

Often accidents of transportation and settlement created strange patterns of dialect. In Illinois distinct Northern and Southern dialects exist side by side—a circumstance that dates back to the early 1800s when discontented residents from Kentucky, Tennessee, and St. Louis, sharing a similar Southern dialect, moved into the lower half of the state. Several decades passed before large numbers of New Englanders, lured by rumors of fertile land, used the newly completed Erie Canal to move west into northern Illinois. As a result of this pattern, travelers in Illinois today still notice a distinct change from Northern to Southern dialect as they reach the center of the state.

In many areas of the West, no such clear pattern of settlement occurred; Southerners, New Englanders, Midwesterners, and European immigrants lived side by side. As a result, there is no one Western dialect.

The following chart shows some of the differences in dialect in three large geographical areas: the South, the Midwest, and the North. As you read the chart, keep in mind that it lists only broad, general variations of dialect and does not apply to all speakers; within each area there are smaller dialectical pockets, such as Appalachia, Boston, and Brooklyn.

Variations in Vocabulary

Southern Dialect	Midland Dialect	Northern Dialect
skillet	frying pan	spider
corn pone	corn bread	johnnycake
cherry seed	cherry pit or seed	cherry pit
chicken pulley	wishbone	
polecat	skunk	wood pussy
a poke	paper *sack*, but *bag* of potatoes	grocery *bag*, but *sack* of potatoes

Variations in Pronunciation

Southern Dialect	Midland Dialect	Northern Dialect
his'n, her'n	his, her	his, her
greasy with a z sound	*greasy* with a z or s sound	*greasy* with an s sound
warsh for *wash*	*warsh* for *wash*	*wash*
coop and *hoop* may have the sound in *book*	*coop* and *hoop* may have the sound in *boot*	*coop* and *hoop* may have the sound in *boot*
fellow and *yellow* pronounced as *feller*, *yeller*		
	mourning and *morning* are pronounced the same	
	merry and *marry* are pronounced the same	
		car sounds like *cah*, *farm* sounds like *fahm*
		idea pronounced *idear*

Variations in Grammar

Southern Dialect	Midland Dialect	Northern Dialect
y'all	you	you
few pair, several bushel, ten pound	few pairs, several bushels, ten pounds	few pair, several bushel, ten pound
	quarter till six, quarter of six	quarter to six
We might could do that.	We might be able to do that.	We might be able to do that.
sick at one's stomach	sick at/to/in one's stomach	sick to one's stomach
I'm leaving. Do you want to come along?	I'm leaving. Do you want to come with?	I'm leaving. Do you want to come along?
	He give me a dollar. I seen that movie.	

Exercise 16: Regional Dialects

Write the lyrics from two different kinds of songs, such as a country-and-western song and a folk ballad. Using the dialect chart in the preceding section as a reference, underline the words and expressions that you think indicate a particular American dialect. If you prefer, use two poems instead of two songs. Many American poets, such as Robert Frost, James Dickey, Gwendolyn Brooks, Alice Walker, and Wendell Berry, incorporate features of American regional dialects into their writing.

Clarity in Language

Jargon

When a group of people from a particular profession talk about their jobs, they sometimes use a specialized language called *jargon*.

Jargon has real purpose when members of a profession or of a particular group speak with one another. Jargon can be a common vocabulary, a type of shorthand speech used to point out special features of work, such as tools, instruments, actions, procedures, and concepts.

Sports are well known for their jargon:

soccer	heading, save, sweeper, wall, marking, centering
baseball	RBI, twin bill, two-bagger, pinch hitter, steal
basketball	lay-up, foul, dribble, travel, shot clock

Professions and occupations also have their jargon:

editor	copy, proofs, galleys, boards
NASA employee	hold, systems, countdown, shutdown
builder	foundation, frieze, bridging, flashing

The media—television, film, and newspapers—have been influential in making the specialized language of jargon more familiar. In fact, many words that are considered jargon by some groups have become a part of everyday language, such as the following examples.

Word	Job	Job Meaning	General Meaning
feedback	computers	return of data	reactions between people; answers to questions
score	all sports	to make points	to be successful at something; to complete a goal
strike out	baseball	to miss hitting the ball and not get on base	to get nowhere
third degree	police	harsh questioning of suspects	any harsh questioning
zoom in	film	to focus on something	to direct your attention to something in particular

619

Word	Job	Job Meaning	General Meaning
grandstand	baseball	seating for spectators	to show off before people
hurdle	track	a frame to be jumped over in a running event	a barrier; an obstacle
pawn	chess	a chess piece that has the least power	a person who is unknowingly used by another person

Many jargon words that have become a part of everyday language are considered *slang* words that are only appropriately used in informal speech situations. Using jargon can cause problems in communication. When jargon excludes people from a conversation, it sets up a barrier that prevents understanding.

Exercise 17: *Jargon*

Choose one of the following occupations or professions and make a list of ten words that are a normal part of the jargon that this group of people would use in speaking to each other.

1. realtor
2. architect
3. swimmer
4. pilot
5. lawyer

6. electrician
7. mechanic
8. law enforcement officer
9. building contractor
10. journalist

Gobbledygook

Jargon that is used to confuse and exclude people is generally called *gobbledygook* or *doublespeak*.

Gobbledygook, also called *bafflegab*, *officialese*, and numerous other insulting names, pretends to be impressive and sophisticated. In its long, wordy phrases, it manages to conceal thought rather than reveal it. Can you understand what the following sentences are trying to communicate?

1. The realistic operational breakthrough produced a uniform growth reaction.

2. Global research dialogues are cost-benefit incentives for classified departmental commitments.

3. Optimal priority applications determine compatible maintenance dynamics for authoritative security parameters.

Sentences such as the preceding ones destroy meaning in their attempt to be impressive. Avoid this confusing use of jargon by making your language as clear and direct as possible.

Gobbledygook	Direct Language
He rendered a positive acclamation on the matter of my interrogation.	He said "Yes" to my question.
We proceeded to the dry cleaning facility where the proprietor acknowledged our presence.	We went to the dry cleaners where the owner greeted us.
I utilized your idea to finalize my project.	I used your idea to finish my project.
The usage of shinguards offers protectional advantages to players during the game.	The use of shinguards protects players during the game.

Euphemisms

Euphemisms are words that are substituted to make something that is offensive or unpleasant sound more agreeable or inoffensive.

In some cases euphemisms are harmless forms of courtesy used to avoid language that is offensive to many people. Euphemisms for swearing, for example, first developed in this country when Puritan laws prohibited the use of profanity. Such words as *darn, drat, doggone, blasted,* and *heck* are common euphemisms used to avoid swearing. Similarly, awkwardness is lessened for some people when they use the words *washroom, bathroom, lavatory, restroom, comfort station, powder room, ladies' room,* and *men's room* for "toilet."

Some forms of euphemism, however, go beyond courtesy and misrepresent the meaning of language. To call the janitor of a building a *maintenance facilitator* is misleading and deceptive, especially if that person is limited to sweeping floors. Elevating social status is becoming a common misuse of euphemism, but an even greater offense occurs when euphemisms are used to avoid the frightening facts of reality, such as in war. In 1977, for instance, the neutron bomb was described as a *radiation enhancement weapon*. Using the pleasant-sounding word *enhancement* with the destructive words *radiation* and *weapon* conceals the fact that such a bomb kills people within forty-eight hours.

Exercise 18: Gobbledygook and Euphemisms

Cut out an editorial from the newspaper or find an article in a news magazine and list or underline the phrases and words that you think conceal meaning behind gobbledygook and euphemisms.

Clichés

A *cliché* is an overused, stale term that no longer conveys a real sense of meaning.

Regular use of clichés represents dull, unimaginative language. How many clichés do you recognize in the following sentence?

Steve was just as cute as a button when he arrived on the first day of school all bright-eyed and bushy-tailed.

Clichés lack the original thinking that is needed to keep language alive and changing. In fact, some clichés even have a harmful effect when they are used to stereotype people and insult them.

Didn't you bring the little lady with you?

A woman's place is in the home.

You throw the ball like a girl.

Stop crying like a little girl.

Exercise 19: Clichés

Copy the following phrases on a sheet of paper, filling in the blanks to illustrate some of the common clichés in the English language. Next to each cliché write a word or phrase that conveys the same meaning more originally.

1. apple of _____ _____
2. birds of _____ _____
3. hook, line and _____
4. blind as a _____
5. strong as an _____

6. raining _____ and _____
7. boys will be _____
8. lock, stock, and _____
9. busy as a _____
10. gentle as a _____

Spelling

Learning the following basic spelling rules will help you spell hundreds of words correctly. Even though some words are exceptions, mastering the rules will help you avoid many unnecessary errors in spelling.

Words with ie *or* ei

In words containing an *ei* **or** *ie* **combination that sounds like the long** *e* **in** *feet***, use** *ie* **except after** *c***.**

---

ie sounded as long *e:* believe, niece, shield

ei after *c:* conceive, ceiling, deceitful

Exceptions: either, neither, leisure, protein, sheik, seize, financier, species

---

In many words containing an *ei* **or** *ie* **combination not sounded as long** *e* **(especially words with a long** *a* **sound as in** *weigh***), use** *ei***.**

---

ei sounded as long *a:* freight, reign, vein

ei not sounded as long *e:* forfeit, their, counterfeit

Exceptions: friend, handkerchief, science, pier, and words with a schwa (ə) sound: conscience, deficient, proficient, quotient.

The seed *Sound*

Words containing a syllable pronounced like the word *seed* **are spelled with one of the following forms.**

1	*2*	*3*
supersede	exceed	accede
	proceed	concede
	succeed	intercede
		precede
		recede
		secede

The only word in the English language spelled with the *-sede* form is *supersede*. Three very common words use the *-ceed* form:

exceed, proceed, succeed. All other words with a *seed* sound have the *-cede* form.

Exercise 20: *Spelling Words with* ie, ei, *or the seed Sound*

Write each of the following sentences, adding the correct *ei* or *ie* combination or *seed* sound that is missing in each blank. Underline the word you complete in each sentence.

Example

a. Working in a law firm during the summer improved Sam's profic _____ ncy in shorthand and typing.
Working in a law firm during the summer improved Sam's <u>proficiency</u> in shorthand and typing.

1. Because of her bel_____f in service for her constituents, Millicent Fenwick is often called "the consc_____nce of Congress."

2. Tonight's news report warned local businesses to beware of counterf _____ t twenty dollar bills.

3. The insuffic _____ ncy of operating funds super _____ ed all other problems at the school board meeting.

4. My fr _____ nd, I think you've had more than a small p _____ ce of that limburger cheese.

5. Benjamin Banneker's many ach _____ vements as an astronomer far ex _____ ed those of other men with years of formal education.

6. The new legal br _____ f super _____ ed the one prepared six months earlier.

7. The dental hyg _____ nist pro _____ ed to clean his patient's teeth.

8. Bes _____ ged with calls from the media, the famous film star finally con _____ ed to an interview.

9. Muhammad Ali, who rec _____ ved an Olympic gold medal early in his career, also won the world heavyw _____ ght championship twice.

10. Suc _____ ing to the throne after her father's death, Queen Elizabeth has r _____ gned since 1952.

Adding Prefixes

When a prefix is added to a root word, the spelling of the root word does not change.

---

ir + responsible   The *irresponsible* driver did not slow down even though the roads were icy.

un + certain   Tina is still *uncertain* about her career plans.

in + expensive   The young couple believed the remodeling would be *inexpensive* if they did the work themselves.

Exercise 21: *Spelling Words with Prefixes*

From the following list choose the prefix and root combination that correctly completes each of the following sentences, using a dictionary to define unfamiliar words. Write each of the sentences on a sheet of paper, inserting the correctly spelled word. Underline your inserts.

Example

---

dis + regarding   in + correctly
dis + similar   un + reliable

a. _____ the instructions, the applicant filled out the entire form _____

Disregarding the instructions, the applicant filled out the entire form incorrectly.

Prefix + Root List

---

dis + orderly	im + proved	over + rated
dis + satisfied	in + accurate	over + rule
il + legible	in + equality	re + mover
im + mature	mis + understood	re + organize
im + partial	non + violence	un + realistic
im + plausible		

1. Sojourner Truth devoted her life to speaking out against _____.

2. The lawyers questioned the woman to be sure she would be an _____ member of the jury.

3. The _____ customer wrote that the varnish _____ did not perform as expected.

4. Commenting that the film was highly _____, the critic said the plot was _____ and _____.

5. Because the chemist's experimental records were _____, valuable research time was lost.

6. Ms. Igrek, our new accountant, immediately suggested a way to _____ our bookkeeping system that _____ efficiency.

7. The secretary _____ the message because of the receptionist's _____ handwriting.

8. The Supreme Court can _____ the decision of a lower court.

9. Martin Luther King, Jr., never wavered in his devotion to _____ as a means of reform.

10. The seniors felt the _____ freshmen at the play were rude and _____.

Adding Suffixes

When a root word ends in an *e*, drop the *e* before adding a suffix beginning with a vowel.

survive + al   The infant's *survival* depended on an immediate blood transfusion.

regulate + ion   The contest *regulations* stated that the entries had to be submitted by midnight on March 3.

Exceptions: *serviceable* (service + able), *changeable* (change + able), *advantageous* (advantage + ous). In other words such as these, the final *e* is retained to create the soft *c* or *g* sound. Other words keep the final *e* for clarity: *acreage, dyeing, singeing.*

Do not drop the final *e* from the root word when the suffix begins with a consonant.

care + ful   *Careful* proofreading will help you avoid errors in your writing.

safe + ty   For *safety* the machine operators were required to wear goggles.

Exceptions: *argument* (argue + ment), *judgment* (judge + ment), *ninth* (nine + th), *truly* (true + ly), *introduction* (introduce + tion), *reduction* (reduce + tion).

Exercise 22: Adding Suffixes to Words with Final e

On a separate sheet of paper, write a sentence using the word formed by each of the following roots and suffixes. Underline the correctly spelled word in each sentence. Study the example before you complete the exercise.

Example

    a. please + ant

       Watching the blizzard from my window was a <u>pleasant</u> experience, since I knew school would be canceled.

1. advise + or
2. bare + ly
3. ridicule + ous
4. peace + able
5. outrage + ous
6. waste + ful
7. disintegrate + ion
8. price + less
9. confuse + ion
10. argue + ment

When a root word ends in a *y* preceded by a consonant, change the *y* to *i* before any suffix not beginning with *i*.

    hasty + ly   It is never wise to make a major purchase, such as a house, *hastily*.

    hurry + ed   She *hurried* through the crowd of commuters in the subway station.

    boy + hood   At fourteen, still in his *boyhood*, Charles Waddell Chestnut helped support his family by teaching school.

Exceptions: *drily* (dry + ly), *gaily* (gay + ly).
When a suffix begins with *i*, do not drop the *y*.

    try + ing   The historical society is *trying* to save the old church from demolition.

    study + ing   *Studying* all night is no way to prepare for semester exams.

Exercise 23: Adding Suffixes to Words with Final y

Write the following sentences, inserting in each blank the correctly spelled combination of the word and the suffix given in parentheses. Underline each word you form.

Example

a. Mom's comments as a master of ceremonies were even _____ than we expected. (funny + er)

Mom's comments as master of ceremonies were even <u>funnier</u> than we expected.

1. The day could not have been more _____; we visited the art museum, had a light lunch, and saw an excellent foreign film. (satisfy + ing)

2. _____ _____ the rim off the worn tire, Liz created an inner tube for the children. (Ready + ly), (pry + ing)

3. _____ discouragement and other obstacles, Althea Gibson _____ had the satisfaction of standing in the winner's circle at Wimbledon. (overcome + ing) (final + ly)

4. The form asked all applicants who _____ for the position to list their previous experience. (qualify + ed)

5. The length and _____ of the official greetings created _____ in the hot crowd standing in the summer sun. (wordy + ness), (uneasy + ness)

6. Alice Walker's *Revolutionary Petunias and Other Poems* presents incidents _____ her own ancestors. (involve + ing)

7. W. E. B. Du Bois did publish some poetry although it lacks the stature of his _____ and _____ writings. (historic + al), (sociologic + al)

8. We had to postpone my aunt's _____ birthday party because she was still _____ with the last details of a special assignment for the state police. (fifty + eth), (occupy + ed)

9. Typical of most _____ poetry, Phillis Wheatley's works contain numerous mythological references. (neoclassic + al)

10. _____ in her refutation of the plaintiff's facts, the elderly lawyer _____ _____ the defendant's case. (Mercy + less), (easy + ly), (justify + ed)

Double the final consonant before a suffix beginning with a vowel when both the following conditions are met:

a. The root word has one syllable, or the accent is on the last syllable.

b. The word ends in a single consonant preceded by a single vowel.

plan + ing	*Planning* each truck's route is part of her job as a dispatcher. [one-syllable root]
con·fer′ + ed	The principals and superintendent *conferred* about the rise in vandalism at several schools. [accent on the last syllable]

If both of these conditions are not met, the final consonant is not doubled before a suffix.

look + ing	*Looking* back at what she had written, she found several errors. [single consonant preceded by two vowels]
ben′·e·fit + ed	The neighbor's garage sale *benefited* the family who lost their home in the tornado. [accent is on the first syllable]

Exceptions: The accent on words such as *con·fer′, de·fer′, pre·fer′, re·fer′* sometimes shifts from the last syllable when a suffix is added.

Exercise 24: Doubling the Final Consonant

On a separate sheet of paper, write the correctly spelled word formed from each root and suffix combination. Then use that word in an interesting sentence, underlining the correctly spelled word. A dictionary will help you find the accent in words of more than one syllable.

Example

a. de·fer + ed

Lanston Hughes' poem questions the consequences of a dream deferred.

1. in·suf·fer + able
2. soak + ing
3. re·fer + al
4. de·vel·op + ment
5. con·trol + ed

6. for·got + en
7. hap·pen + ing
8. be·gin + er
9. de·fer + ence
10. re·mit + ance

26 Reference Works

Books that may be used to locate information or to find the answers to questions are called *reference books*. The *Readers' Guide,* encyclopedias, almanacs, and atlases are reference books. They can be found in the reference sections of most libraries. In this chapter you will learn how to use these reference works to locate specific information.

The Readers' Guide

Periodicals (magazines and newspapers) often contain recent information that may be valuable to your research. Because so many periodicals are published, containing so much diverse information, guides to their contents are regularly published. These guides are called *periodical indexes,* and the most famous is the *Readers' Guide to Periodical Literature.* The *Readers' Guide* indexes the contents of over a hundred widely read magazines and is published twenty-one times a year. Each new issue contains an index of the most recent copies of the magazines. So the library will not be burdened by a flood of small indexes, the *Readers' Guide* frequently publishes cumulative indexes, compiling information for recent months into one volume. At the year's end, a one-volume index containing all information is compiled, and every two years a two-year index is issued, so the researcher can cover many months of publishing information by using only the single-volume cumulative indexes.

All issues of the *Readers' Guide* index authors and subjects in alphabetical order. Beneath each subject heading is a list of recent articles on that subject and where they can be found.

The *Readers' Guide* uses many abbreviations. These are explained in special keys in the front of the index. Using the Key to Periodicals Listed and the Key to Abbreviations, you can easily decipher an entry. Consider, for example, the following entry:

Fading fall season [effects of actors' strike] H. F. Waters and J. Huck. il Newsweek 96: 72 Aug 18 '80

The preceding entry is for an article titled "Fading Fall Season," by H. F. Waters and J. Huck, in the August 18, 1980, issue of

Newsweek magazine (volume 96, page 72). The illustrated article is about the effects of the actors' strike. (Notice that only the first word of the article's title is capitalized in the entry; this is a special style used by the *Readers' Guide.*)

On page 632 you will find a sample page from the *Readers' Guide to Periodical Literature.*

Exercise 1: *Using the Readers' Guide*

Answer each of the the following questions in complete sentences.

1. Where is the *Readers' Guide* located in your library? How far back does your library's collection of *Readers' Guides* extend? Where is the list of periodicals found in your library?

2. To which of the following periodicals does your library subscribe: *Monthly Labor Review, Foreign Affairs, Car and Driver, Congressional Digest, Consumer Reports?* Does your library keep back issues of any of these magazines? If so, how far back do the issues go?

3. Using copies of the *Readers' Guide,* find at least two recent articles on the following topics: automotive repair, astronomy, nuclear reactors, cancer research. Copy the title, author, and page number of each article and write the issue of the periodical in which it appears.

4. Pick a topic from among the following: fashion, popular music, wildlife conservation, personal budgeting, home computers. Using the *Readers' Guide,* find an article on your topic. Write the title, author, and issue of the magazine in which the article appears. Then locate the article itself and write a one-paragraph summary of it.

Dictionaries

Dictionaries are usually classified as either abridged or unabridged. An *abridged dictionary* is the shorter of the two; it does not attempt to define all of the hundreds of thousands of words in the language. An *unabridged dictionary* is more comprehensive, containing many more entries, plus examples of usage; consequently, the unabridged dictionary may be a huge volume or, as in the case of the monumental *Oxford English Dictionary,* as many as thirteen hefty volumes.

entry by author ——————

entry by title ——————

title, issue, page ————
numbers and date
of magazine

subject heading ——————

secondary ————
subject heading

page numbers ————
of article

"see" cross ————
reference

WOOD pulp paper products. See Paper products
WOOD rats. See Rats
WOOD sculpture. See Wood carving
WOOD stove pollution. See Smoke
WOOD stoves. See Stoves
WOOD working. See Woodworking
WOODBURY, Robert S.
  Yen for a yacht [excerpt] [cont] il Motor B & S 147:76-7+ F; 67+ Mr '81
WOODCARVING. See Wood carving
WOODCHUCK hunting
  Chuck hunting is alive and well in Pennsylvania
  L. Atwill. il Outdoor Life 167:77-80 Ap '81
WOODCOCK, Leonard
  Friendly relations, but no U.S. alliance with Peking [interview by J. Wallace] por U.S.
  News 90:34 F 9 '81
  Inside China [interview by J. Flint] il por Forbes 127:31-2 Mr 16 '81
WOODEN dolls. See Dolls
WOODENWARE
    See also
  Cutting boards
  Lehn ware [reprint from February 1947 issue]
  V. M. Paul. il Antiques J 36:36+ F '81
WOODHOUSE, R. Y.
  Equality faces a dangerous decade [address. November 18, 1980] Vital Speeches
  4:242-6 F 1 '81
WOODLANDS, Goochland County, Va. See Plantations
The WOODLANDS, Tex.
  Nobody's laughing now. il por Forbes 127:84+ Mr 2 '81
WOODS, Craig
  Spring trout shortcut. il Outdoor Life 167:81-2 Ap '81
WOODS, James
  James Woods' guilty pleasures. il por Film Comment 17:60-3 Mr/Ap '81
WOODSIDE, William S.
  Why American Can is unloading so much. Bus W p48 Ap 13 '81
WOODSON, Carter Godwin
  I knew Carter G. Woodson. B. E. Mays. Negro Hist Bull 44:21 Ja/F/Mr '81
  Legend and legacy [excerpts from address. October 17, 1980] J. R. Picott. Negro
  Hist Bull 44:6-8 Ja/F/Mr '81 *
  Philippine challenge. A. Scally, bibl Negro Hist Bull 44:16-18 Ja/F/Mr '81 *
WOODWARD, Bob
  They were wrong about the brethren. R. M. Kaus. il Wash M 13:32-6+ Mr '81 *
WOODWORKING
    See also
  Carpentry
  Joints (carpentry)
  Miter boxes, gauges, etc.
  Saws and sawing
  Wood carving
              Projects
    See also
  Tables
  Weekend workshop [cont] il Pop Mech 155:140-2+ F; 26-7 † Mr '81
             Terminology
  Words woodworkers use. M. Algozin. il Pop Mech 155:28 Ja '81
WOODWORKING machinery
    See also
  Lathes
  Routing machines
WOODWORKING tools. See Tools
WOODY plants
    See also
  Shrubs
WOOL, Harold
  Coal industry resurgence attracts variety of new workers [excerpt from labor
  outlook for the bituminous coal mining industry] bibl f il M Labor R 104:3-8 Ja '81
WORCESTER Art Museum, Worcester, Mass. See Art galleries and
  museums—Massachusetts
WORD of God. See Logos (theology)
WORD processing
  Word machines for word people [authorship use] C. Courter. il por Pub W 219:40-3
  F 13 '81
WORD processing equipment industry
    See also
  Harris Corporation
  Word processing: a road to management. B. Scala. Work Wom 6:24+ F '81
  Word-processing boom. L. Glynn and others. il Newsweek 97:75 Ap 6 '81
WORDINESS. See Verbosity

A good dictionary will contain certain basic information: the word, its syllabication, pronunciation, and definition or definitions. In addition, it will supply a word's etymology, or origins, as well as variant spellings the word may have, and its inflections—for instance, if the word forms a plural or participle irregularly. The dictionary should also give *restrictive labels*, indicating whether the word has special meanings in different disciplines or instances (for example, the same word may mean one thing in chemistry and another in biology, or have another meaning that is slang or a colloquialism). The sample dictionary page on page 634 of this textbook shows how this information is arranged. The numbers and boxes on the sample dictionary page correspond to the numbered explanations of each feature on pages 633, 634, and 635.

Use the following list in conjunction with the sample from *Webster's New World Dictionary* on page 634. The numbers on the list correspond with the numbered items on the sample dictionary page.

1. Guide words are printed at the top of the page to show the first and last words on that page.

2. Word entries are printed in **boldface** type. Words are in alphabetical order.

3. Other forms of the word are also given. These forms may include plurals, principal parts of verbs, and comparative forms of adjectives and adverbs.

4. Syllables are indicated in word entries with a raised dot between them. These syllable markers indicate where words may be divided at the end of a line of writing.

5. Pronunciation is shown with diacritical marks and simplified spellings. These follow the word entry and are in parentheses.

6. Usage markers show whether or not the word is used in formal English. Meanings of abbreviations for usage labels can usually be found in the front of the dictionary.

7. The part of speech is shown by an abbreviation. The meanings of part-of-speech abbreviations are also listed in the front of the dictionary.

8. Word origins are shown in brackets, usually after the part-of-speech abbreviation. Look in the front of the dictionary for help in reading the history of a word.

9. When one entry has exactly the same spelling as the one that follows it, the two are distinguished by raised numbers.

10. Definitions of the words are numbered with Arabic numerals. Some dictionaries assign the lowest numbers to the oldest

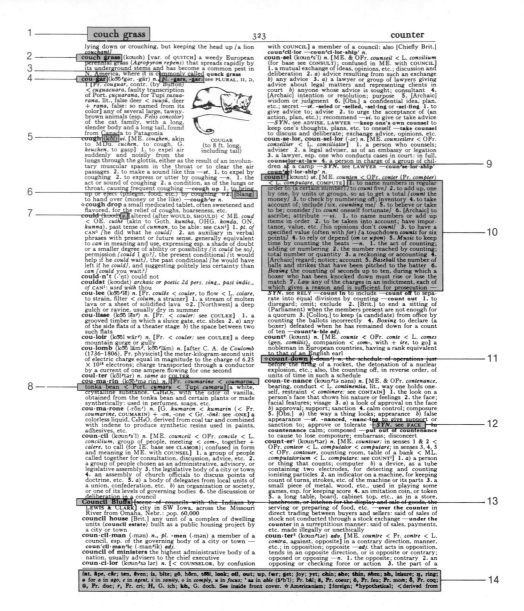

meanings. When a word has many definitions, the definitions are grouped according to the part of speech.

11. Phrases and compound words appear as entries.

12. Synonyms (words that have nearly the same meaning) often appear after definitions. *See* means "see the dictionary entry for the word."

With permission. Page 323 from *Webster's New World Dictionary*, Second College Edition. Copyright © 1982 by Simon & Schuster, Inc.

13. Information about people, places, and events is often given.

14. A pronunciation key is often found at the bottom of every other page. A more complete key can be found in the front of the dictionary.

Specialized Dictionaries

In addition to general dictionaries, there are specialized dictionaries on many subjects, such as *Black's Law Dictionary*. Dictionaries of synonyms include *Roget's International Thesaurus* and *Webster's New Dictionary of Synonyms*. Specialized dictionaries give more extensive information about specific categories of words. Most specialized dictionaries are organized alphabetically. *Roget's Thesaurus*, however, is organized in numbered categories. To use the thesaurus, look up the word in the index. Following the word will be the number of the category in which the word is grouped. If there are multiple meanings of the word, a number for each will be listed, along with a synonym for the words in that category. Find the category that most closely matches the meaning you want. Be wary, though: always check the definition of unfamiliar words. No matter how similar words may seem to each other, each has subtleties of meaning that must be considered.

Encyclopedias

Like dictionaries, encyclopedias are a basic research tool, and like dictionaries, most encyclopedias list their entries in alphabetical order. However, whereas the ordinary dictionary confines itself primarily to words and their meanings, the encyclopedia presents a condensation of human knowledge in all fields of general interest. In addition to articles on various subjects, most encyclopedias contain illustrations, maps, charts, graphs, and cross-references and bibliographies. One article may contain a cross-reference to other articles that will aid your research, as well as a bibliography of other reference works you may consult.

The modern age is in the midst of what is often called "an explosion of learning"; new information is constantly emerging. Encyclopedias keep up-to-date in three ways. First, many publish a yearly supplement that updates information and presents new developments. Second, each time the encyclopedia is reprinted, minor revisions are made. Third, at certain intervals the encyclopedia is completely revised and a new edition brought out.

Multi-Volume Encyclopedias

The following encyclopedias are found frequently in libraries.

Collier's Encyclopedia, composed of twenty-four volumes, is known for its readable style.

Compton's Encyclopedia, twenty-six volumes, is written for the younger student, but adults may find its simple style and organization helpful as an introduction to many subjects. *Compton's* is profusely illustrated, containing charts, graphs, and maps. Bibliographies follow the articles, and cross-references are given. A yearbook is published.

Encyclopedia Americana, thirty volumes, was the first encyclopedia published in America, its first edition appearing in 1829. It is also justly noted for its fine articles on science, technology, history, and biography. Containing illustrations, maps, glossaries, cross-references, and bibliographies, the encyclopedia is kept up-to-date through its yearbook, *Americana Annual.*

Encyclopaedia Britannica, thirty volumes, originally published in England, is now published in the United States. The most recent edition, in thirty volumes, orders information in a new way. The first volume, *Guide to the Britannica,* is introductory. It breaks human knowledge into different divisions, then lists articles pertaining to each subject, indicating where these articles are to be found in the other volumes. The next ten volumes, the *Micropaedia,* contain brief articles on many subjects. If a subject is too lengthy or complex for full treatment in the *Micropaedia,* it is summarized, and cross-reference is made to relevant articles in the *Macropaedia.* The nineteen-volume *Macropaedia* is composed of articles that treat subjects in depth. Extensive bibliographies follow the *Macropaedia* articles. Noted for its treatment of historical subjects, the *Encyclopaedia Britannica* is thorough, comprehensive, and scholarly. It is illustrated and contains maps, charts, and tables; it also includes a yearbook.

World Book Encyclopedia, twenty-two volumes, is designed for younger students although adults may find it a helpful reference early in research. It contains a research guide and index in Volume 22 and provides study aids on important subjects.

One- and Two-Volume Encyclopedias

"Desk encyclopedias," as one- and two-volume encyclopedias are sometimes called, are useful as introductions to subjects or for quick reference. Far less extensive than larger encyclopedias, they present basic facts on a multitude of subjects. Compact and readable, they can be a useful aid to both research and general learning.

The Concise Columbia Encyclopedia, a one-volume work, contains articles on numerous subjects.

The Lincoln Library of Essential Information is a two-volume work.

Exercise 2: *Researching the History of Encyclopedias*

Although modern researchers take encyclopedias for granted, these resources have not always been so widely accepted. In the following excerpt from an article in *The New Yorker* on the Eleventh Edition of the *Encyclopaedia Britannica,* Hans Koning describes early reactions to an encyclopedia. After reading the selection, complete the activity that follows.

The age of the modern encyclopedia began in August of the year 1751, in France, with the delivery of the first volume of the Encyclopédie to its subscribers. When, twenty-one years later, the work was completed, in seventeen volumes of text and eleven volumes of illustrations, a number of its original editors and contributors either had resigned in disgust, like Jean Le Rond d'Alembert, or had spent time in jail, like the chief editor, Denis Diderot, and the printer, André François Lebreton. On one occasion, some of the volumes were locked in the Bastille like criminals, and throughout those years police agents were running around Paris with orders to burn the manuscripts and impound the books. At one point, subscribers were instructed to hand in their sets at the nearest police post. But the Encyclopédie survived—because, according to Voltaire, during a supper in the Trianon Louis XV got into an unceremonious argument over the composition of gunpowder, and his Mme. de Pompadour said she did not know how such things as silk stockings and face rouge were made. The assembled company found that there was no way out but to have a servant chase down a copy of the banned Encyclopédie, which the King had never laid eyes on until that moment. After that evening, Louis was supposedly halfhearted about the proscription of the work, whose main enemy was his clergy.

Perhaps no other book, or set of books, has ever had the impact in its century of those twenty-eight volumes. They were called a War Machine, a Tower of Babel, the Gospel of Satan. Seventeen years after completion of publication, and as an unmistakable sequel, came the French Revolution.[1]

Use your school library's encyclopedias and other sources to prepare a report on the history of encyclopedias. In your report answer the following questions.

1. What accounts for the hostile reaction to early encyclopedias?

2. Besides increasing in size, in what other ways have encyclopedias changed over the years?

---

[1]From "Onward and Upward with the Arts" by Hans Koning; © 1981. Originally in *The New Yorker*.

27 Library Resources

A working knowledge of your library will help you track down many sorts of information with ease and efficiency. In this chapter you will learn how to find various kinds of books in your library.

Introduction to the Card Catalogue

One of the most helpful places to begin looking for information in a library is the *card catalogue,* a file of cards listing books and other reference materials. This file tells you if the library has a certain book or material on a certain subject, gives you basic information about the book, and indicates where you can find it. The file cards for fiction and nonfiction differ, since these two types of books are shelved separately from each other and are arranged according to different systems.

Catalogue Cards for Fiction

The card catalogue contains two cards for each work of fiction: a title card and an author (or editor) card.

In most libraries, fiction works are arranged alphabetically according to the author's last name. Therefore, if you know a book's title, but not its author, you will need to consult the card catalogue. If the library has more than one book by an author, these books will be alphabetically arranged according to the first *main* word in each title. Novels by Elizabeth Bowen, for instance, would be arranged as follows. (The first main word in the title is underlined.)

> The *Death* of the Heart
>
> The *Heat* of the Day

The Last September

A World of Love

Collections of short stories are alphabetized by the author's last name, if one author wrote all of the stories, or by the editor's last name if the collection contains stories by different authors. Short story collections may be shelved with novels, or they may be gathered in a group and placed at the end of the fiction section. Since practices may vary from library to library, check with your librarian on the placement of such collections.

Catalogue Cards for Nonfiction

Each nonfiction book or reference has three cards in the catalogue: one for the title, one for the author or editor, and one for the subject of the book. (See the sample title, author, and subject cards on page 640.)

Nonfiction books are shelved apart from fiction books and are arranged not by title, but by a *call number*, which appears in the upper left-hand corner of the cards.

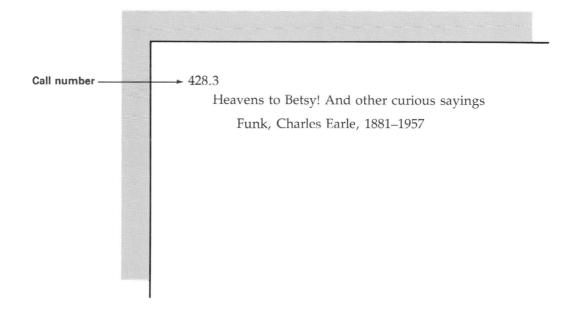

Call number ⟶ 428.3

Heavens to Betsy! And other curious sayings

Funk, Charles Earle, 1881–1957

The call number of each book is stamped on its spine, and books are arranged in numerical order according to the *Dewey decimal system,* or in larger libraries according to the *Library of Congress system.*

Title card

709.24   Alexander Calder and his magical mobiles.
LIPMAN   1st ed. New York: Hudson Hills Press in
         association with Whitney Museum of American
         Art, © 1981.
         96 p.: ill. (some col.); 26 cm. (50009599)

         ISBN 0-933920-17-2

Author card

709.24   Lipman, Jean, 1909–
LIPMAN   Alexander Calder and his magical mobiles.
         1st ed. New York: Hudson Hills Press in
         association with Whitney Museum of American
         Art, © 1981.
         96 p.: ill. (some col.); 26 cm. (50009599)
         Bibliography: p. 91.

         1. Calder, Alexander, 1898–1976.
         2. Artists—United States—Biography.
         3. Artists. I. Aspinwall, Margaret, 1945–
         II. Title.

Subject card

709.24   CALDER, ALEXANDER, 1898–1976
LIPMAN   Lipman, Jean, 1909–
         Alexander Calder and his magical mobiles.
         1st ed. New York: Hudson Hills Press in
         association with Whitney Museum of American
         Art, © 1981.
         96 p.: ill. (some col.); 26 cm. (50009599)

The Dewey Decimal System

The Dewey decimal system was created by American librarian Melvil Dewey. In this system nonfiction books are assigned a number according to their subject matter. Subject matter is divided into the following ten general categories.

000–099 General Works:	Includes encyclopedias, periodicals, book lists, and other reference books.
100–199 Philosophy:	Includes the fields of psychology, conduct, and personality.
200–299 Religion:	Includes Bibles and other religious texts, theology books, and mythology.
300–399 Social Sciences:	Includes economics, education, etiquette, fairy tales, folklore, legends, government, and law.
400–499 Language:	Includes grammars and dictionaries of different languages, including English.
500–599 Science:	Includes animals, astronomy, biology, botany, chemistry, geology, general science, mathematics, anthropology, and physics.
600–699 Technology:	Includes agriculture, aviation, business, engineering, health, home economics, manual training, and television.
700–799 The Arts:	Includes movies, painting, photography, sculpture, recreation, and sports.
800–899 Literature:	Includes poetry, drama, essays, criticism, and history of literature.
900–999 History:	Includes geography, travel, history, and collective biography.

The Dewey decimal system contains 999 numbers for various subjects, but classification is expanded with decimal subdivisions. For instance, the subject *Judaism* falls within the 200–299 category of religion and is assigned the number 296. However, Judaism is a complex subject, so decimal numbers are used to indicate books on specific aspects of the religion:

296.3	**Judaic doctrinal theology**
296.4	**Public service, rites, traditions**
296.8	**Sects and movements**

By using these numbers and decimal points, cataloguing agencies and libraries can assign a book its number and classify it correctly according to general and specific subject.

Exceptions to the Dewey Decimal System

One group of nonfiction books in the Dewey decimal system is not arranged numerically on the shelves: biographies and autobiographies. Collections of biographies, called *collective biographies*, are usually classified under *920*, then arranged alphabetically according to the writer's or editor's last name. *The Kings and Queens of England* by Jane Murray would be catalogued as $\frac{920}{M}$, the *M* signifying the initial of the author's last name.

Biographies and autobiographies are usually classified under number *921* and arranged alphabetically according to the *subject's* last name. For instance, Cornelia Otis Skinner's biography of Sarah Bernhardt would be alphabetized under *B* for *Bernhardt*. Libraries often stamp the spine of a biographical work with a *B* for biography, then place the last initial of the subject's name beneath. A biography of Pancho Gonzales, for example, might be stamped $\frac{B}{G}$. Check your school or public library to see how biographical works are labeled.

In many libraries books containing specialized information are taken from their usual places on the shelves and put in a special *reference section*. Encyclopedias, atlases, biographical dictionaries, and so on are frequently kept in reference sections. If you look up a book in the card catalogue and see the abbreviation *R* or *Ref.* above the call number, you will know you must consult the reference section, rather than the shelves containing general nonfiction. The reference section is like a mini-library, with books arranged in order according to their Dewey decimal numbers. Many libraries do not allow reference books to be checked out, so you must use them only in the library.

The Library of Congress System

Although the Dewey decimal system is used in many libraries, another classification system, the Library of Congress system, is spreading and is widely used in college and university libraries. It is more complex and comprehensive than the Dewey decimal system, containing twice as many general subject classifications. Each classification is assigned a capital letter; the *social sciences*, for instance, are classified under *H*. A second capital indicates a subdivision of the classification; *economic theory*, a subdivision of social science, is labeled *HB*. Numbers are added to make more specific distinctions about subject matter. Call numbers *HB3711–HB3840* deal with economic crises of various sorts.

Exercise 1: Understanding Library Systems of Classification

Use your library to answer the following questions.

1. What system of classification does your library use: Dewey decimal or Library of Congress?

2. Look in the biography section of your library. How are biographical books marked by the librarian? What numbers or letters are used?

3. Where are collections of short stories kept in your library? Are they marked in any way to distinguish them from other fiction?

Exercise 2: Using the Card Catalogue

Use your card catalogue to see if your library has the following books. If it does, write down each book's title, author, and (if it is nonfiction) its call number.

1.   A work by Katherine Mansfield

2.   A nonfiction work by James Baldwin

3.   A biography of Ho Chi Minh

4.   A copy of *Black Elk Speaks*

5.   A book on data processing

6.   A work by Gwendolyn Brooks

7.   A work on running or jogging

8.   A work about the American Civil War

9.   A copy of *All the President's Men*

10. A copy of *The Dragons of Eden*

Abbreviations and Terms Used in Card Catalogues

You may encounter the common abbreviations on the next page while doing research. Familiarize yourself with them so you can use them as aids.

anon.	author unknown
c.	copyright
cm.	centimeters (The catalogue card states the size of a book in centimeters.)
diagrs.	diagrams
ed.	editor or edition
et al.	and others (several authors or editors)
illus.	illustrated or illustrator
mounted pl.	mounted plates: full-page illustrations fastened to page
pseud.	pen name
rev.	revised (material has been updated)
tr. or trans.	translated or translator
v., vol., vols.	volume, volumes

The following terms refer to books or parts of books:

Appendix or Appendices:	Supplementary material at the end of the book that presents relevant information, such as statistics, quotations, tables
Bibliography:	A list of either (1) books and references the author consulted in writing the work, or (2) works the author recommends for further research on the subject
Copyright:	Copyright information is given on the back of a book's title page. It tells who copyrighted the book and when. Several copyright dates indicate that the book has been revised.
Glossary:	A list of key terms and definitions
Index:	An alphabetized list of people, places, and subjects treated in the book, with the number of the pages on which they appear
Introduction, Foreword, Preface:	Introductory material before a book's first chapter. The author or other writer may comment on the book's content, significance, and so forth.
Gazetteer:	A list of geographical places with brief descriptions of them or statistics about them
Text:	The main body of the book
Title Page:	A page at the book's beginning, stating title, author, and publication facts

Exercise 3: Finding Catalogue Cards

Find the catalogue cards for the following books. (For some questions, you will need to find the book as well.) Answer the following questions, and write the title of each book you describe.

1. Find a book of poems by Emily Dickinson. Who is the editor? Is there a preface or introduction? How many pages does the book have? What is the first entry in the Table of Contents?

2. Find a book by Alexandre Dumas. Who is its translator? What is its publication date? Does it have any illustrations?

3. Find a book about Pablo Picasso. Are there photographs or illustrations in the book? Are there any mounted plates? Is there an introduction?

4. Find a book by Adam Smith. Is there an appendix? Is there a bibliography? Who is the publisher?

5. Find a book on automotive repair. Are there any diagrams and illustrations? When was it copyrighted? Has the book ever been revised?

6. Look up *The Oxford Companion to English Literature*. Who is its editor? Does it have prefaces? If so, how many? Does it have appendixes? If so, how many?

7. Look up *The Annals of America*. How many volumes comprise it? Are there maps? Are there illustrations?

8. Find a copy of *Bulfinch's Mythology*. Is there a preface and, if so, by whom? Are there illustrations?

9. Find *The Amy Vanderbilt Complete Book of Etiquette*. Has it been revised or expanded since its first publication? If so, by whom? Are there illustrations? Find the index. Does it contain subheadings as well as main entries?

10. Find a book by Lewis Carroll. Lewis Carroll is a pseudonym; what is the author's real name? Does the book have an introduction? Is it illustrated? If so, by whom?

28 Preparing for Tests

In this chapter, you will find practice questions for standardized tests. By becoming familiar with the question formats for various kinds of tests, you increase your chances of performing well. Answers to the sample questions are found on page 661.

Tests of Vocabulary

Vocabulary tests usually examine a student's understanding of the sophisticated words found in formal writing—both fiction and informational nonfiction—rather than the common words used in conversation or informal writing. Familiarity with this vocabulary is thought to be an indication of the student's current reading ability and language experience; it is also viewed as a good predictor of the individual's ability to learn and use new words in advanced study.

Four common formats are used to test vocabulary: *vocabulary in context, synonyms, antonyms,* and *verbal analogies.*

Vocabulary in Context

Vocabulary-in-context questions often are presented as incomplete sentences that students complete by selecting the best response from four or five possible answers. Sometimes, students are asked to choose a synonym for a word in the incomplete phrase. In other questions the incomplete sentence includes a descriptive phrase, and the student completes the statement by selecting the word defined by that phrase. A third possibility is the reverse of the previous one—that is, the student selects the option that best defines a term in the incomplete sentence. The following is an example of a vocabulary-in-context question. (Answers to sample questions are marked with a dagger (†). All other answers are on page 661.)

A. Someone who is <u>loquacious</u> is:
  a reticent
  †b talkative
  c fervent
  d polite

Exercise 1: Answering Vocabulary-in-Context Questions

Read the beginning of each of the following sentences and all of the choices that follow it. Choose the answer that best completes the sentence.

1. A gregarious person is:

   a deviant
   b childish
   c introverted
   d sociable

2. An erudite article is one which is:

   a sarcastic
   b scholarly
   c controversial
   d simplistic

3. To work adroitly is to work:

   a willingly
   b carelessly
   c diligently
   d cleverly

4. A nebulous statement is one which is:

   a succinct
   b intelligible
   c vague
   d abusive

5. Things which are analogous are:

   a similar
   b opposite
   c transposed
   d convoluted

Synonyms

Two or more words or phrases that share essentially the same meaning are called *synonyms*. Sometimes, several words may have closely related meanings, although there are few instances in which two words are completely identical in meaning. Therefore, you will find that the "correct" answers in synonym tests are usually more accurately described as "best" answers. Careful reading of all the responses will help you choose the one that is better than the others.

   A. abate

   a release
   b increase
   c shrink
   †d subside

Exercise 2: *Choosing Synonyms*

For each of the following questions, choose the synonym (word most similar in meaning) for the underlined word.

1. meretricious
   - a sincere
   - b worthwhile
   - c gaudy
   - d genuine

2. germane
   - a relevant
   - b Teutonic
   - c developing
   - d insignificant

3. quell
   - a quibble
   - b foment
   - c immerse
   - d quiet

4. aversion
   - a prevention
   - b ability
   - c greed
   - d antipathy

5. leery
   - a suggestive
   - b distrustful
   - c rash
   - d lascivious

Antonyms

Words that have almost opposite meanings are called *antonyms*. Since there are very few true antonyms in English, you must look for the best answer. Remember that the negative form of a word often is not the best antonym. For example, something that is "*not* sour" (negative form) is not necessarily "sweet" (antonym of *sour*). By the same token, something can be "not sweet" without being "sour."

A. acute
   - a mild
   - †b chronic
   - c habitual
   - d occasional

Exercise 3: *Choosing Antonyms*

For each of the following questions, choose the antonym (word most nearly opposite in meaning) for the underlined word.

1. ambiguous
   a obscure
   b explicit
   c ardent
   d pretentious

2. taciturn
   a surly
   b quiet
   c anxious
   d talkative

3. inane
   a wise
   b silly
   c necessary
   d lively

4. esoteric
   a private
   b trivial
   c certain
   d well-known

5. crass
   a obtuse
   b helpful
   c discriminating
   d gentle

Verbal Analogies

Synonym and antonym vocabulary items require an understanding of the relationships between a pair of words. In analogies, the test taker must match two pairs of terms to demonstrate understanding of the relationships between those terms. Usually you will be given one pair of words or phrases. You must identify the relationship between those two terms and then find another pair of words with the same relationship. Sometimes, you will also be given the first word of the second pair, and will have to choose only the fourth term. The following is one example of a verbal analogy test item.

A. Pride is to lion as gaggle is to _____
   a bear
   b eagle
   †c goose
   d hawk

In this case *pride* is the term used for a group of lions. *Gaggle* is a parallel term applied to geese.

Sometimes only colons are used to suggest the relationship between the terms, as shown in the example on the next page.

B. QUARRY: STONE::
  a rock: mineral
  †b mine: ore
  c soil: field
  d oil: drill

Exercise 4: Identifying Verbal Analogies

In the following items, choose the pair of words whose relationship is most similar to that of the first pair.

1. **light: feather::**
   a hard: nails
   b lead: heavy
   c molasses: slow
   d grass: green

2. **bear: den::**
   a bird: cage
   b tent: camper
   c beaver: water
   d fox: lair

3. **lethargic: energetic::**
   a eager: lazy
   b mollify: soften
   c apathetic: enthusiastic
   d capricious: vigorous

4. **pleasure: pain::**
   a madness: sanity
   b happiness: sorrow
   c gentleness: amiability
   d intolerance: patience

5. **words: script::**
   a ink: pen
   b computer: digits
   c notes: score
   d letters: sounds

Reading Comprehension

Reading comprehension tests are used to assess a student's ability to read with accuracy and comprehension. On these tests, you will usually be asked to read a passage of some length—several hundred words, perhaps—and then to answer questions about what you have read. If the subject matter is unfamiliar, do not worry about that. The examiners are not interested in your previous knowledge of the subject. Rather, these tests are designed to measure how well you derive information from the passage itself and how well you draw appropriate inferences from the facts given to you.

Some questions are about specific information in the passage—literal or factual data. Other questions may ask you to define a term in the context in which it is being used. More often, the questions will require you to draw conclusions, synthesize a number of details, or evaluate the author's purpose or point of view.

Turning your regular reading assignments into practice tests is a good way to prepare for tests of this sort. Read a few paragraphs in your social studies or literature textbook and then do the following:

1. Briefly state the main idea or focus of the paragraphs.

2. Restate in your own words each important idea presented in the passage.

3. Look for words that can have more than one meaning and define each word in terms of its use in this passage.

4. Identify statements that are expressions of the author's opinion. Are they well founded and based on facts presented in the passage?

5. Identify value judgments, expressions of bias or prejudice, exaggerations, and understatements.

6. Try to identify the author's purpose or reasons for writing this particular passage. What is its tone? Is it descriptive, persuasive, argumentative?

7. What inferences can be drawn from what is stated?

English Mechanics and Usage

Tests of English mechanics and usage assess your understanding and use of the most basic skills of English composition. You may also be asked to write a short essay or writing sample, but more frequently, you will be given a multiple-choice test including sections on spelling, grammar, and usage. The test may also include exercises that evaluate your sensitivity to language and your ability to organize thoughts into a logical whole.

Spelling

Spelling test items usually assess your understanding of basic spelling rules or ask you to identify misspellings of frequently used words. The most common format is to present several words, one of which is misspelled. (Sometimes, one option is "no error.") Another format tests understanding of *homophones*—words spelled differently but sounding the same—such as *peace* and *piece* or *two* and *too*.

Exercise 5: Taking a Spelling Test

For each of the following questions, choose the one word that is misspelled. If no word is misspelled, mark *N* for "no error."

1. a cemetery
    b chastise
    c analyze
    d acommodate
    N

2. a current
    b medicine
    c possability
    d pejorative
    N

3. a category
    b innoculate
    c nickel
    d guidance
    N

4. a illicit
    b mischievous
    c height
    d fallacy
    N

5. a irresistable
    b knowledgeable
    c irrelevant
    d millionaire
    N

Error Recognition

Error recognition test items ask students to identify errors in short written passages. Sometimes, you may be asked to indicate the nature of the error. Other formats require only that you indicate the *presence* of an error. The following are examples of both these types.

Type 1
Mark your answer sheet:
(a) if the sentence contains an error in diction (choice of words)
(b) if the sentence is verbose or redundant (wordy)
(c) if the sentence contains a cliché or mixed metaphor
(d) if the sentence contains an error in grammar
(e) if the sentence is correct as it stands
    Example:
    A. The young man was fit as a fiddle. (c)

Type 2

Mark the letter of the line containing an error in spelling, punctuation, capitalization, grammar, or usage. If there is no error, mark *N* for "no error."

> *Example:*
>> B. †a the canadian flag has
>>> b a red maple leaf on a
>>> c ground of white.

Exercise 6: Taking an Error Recognition Test, Type 1

Mark your answer sheet:
(a) if the sentence contains an error in diction (choice of words)
(b) if the sentence is verbose or redundant (wordy)
(c) if the sentence contains a cliché or mixed metaphor
(d) if the sentence contains an error in grammar
(e) if the sentence is correct as it stands

1. After such a grueling game neither the player nor the coach are going to celebrate the victory.

2. Tourists taking extended journeys to the Far East that last a long time may become tired and exhausted.

3. The incumbent's campaign depended on most people thinking a bird in the bush was safer than changing horses in midstream.

4. Each complaint to the discotheque manager was followed by a temporary deduction in noise level.

5. Some of the eggs bought from the farmer last week is rotten.

Exercise 7: Taking an Error Recognition Test, Type 2

Mark the letter of the line containing an error in spelling, punctuation, capitalization, grammar, word choice, or usage. If there is no error, mark *N* for "no error."

1. a Less than half of the present
    b 152 member states were original
    c members of the United Nations.
    N

2. a Each of the women attending the
    b state conference were asked to
    c participate in the international assembly.
    N

3. a Due to the declining birth rate,
    b the amount of children attending elementary
    c school is decreasing each year.
    N

4. a After the fire it was discovered
    b that the flames had originated
    c in an electrical outlet in the school liberary.
    N

5. a Although she is as strong as, if not
    b stronger, than most of her teammates
    c she is not the best player.
    N

Organizing Paragraphs

Exercises involving scrambled paragraphs indirectly assess your ability to organize thoughts and present them logically. The test format usually consists of a passage with sentences in random order. You must organize these sentences into a coherent paragraph.

After reading the sentences, try to order the paragraph in your mind. Look for clues, such as transitional words or phrases within the sentences. Notice pronouns that refer to something in another (and therefore earlier) sentence. If necessary, jot down the order of the sentences on scrap paper. Then answer the specific questions you are asked. Study the following example.

P Myths, on the other hand, are born, not made.

Q A fable is a story, made to order, intended to be used for instruction.

R They owe their details to the imaginative efforts of generations of storytellers.

S A distinction must be made between myths and fables.

1. Which sentence did you put first?
    a Sentence P
    b Sentence Q
    c Sentence R
    d Sentence S

2. Which sentence did you put after S?
   a Sentence P
   b Sentence Q
   c Sentence R
   d None of the above. Sentence S is last.

The correct order of these sentences is *S, Q, P, R. S* is a topic sentence and makes sense only as the first sentence. As a final sentence it would be silly unless it included *therefore* or *thus* or some such phrase. Sentence *P* needs to come after *Q* because of the phrase *on the other hand*. The *they* in Sentence *R* refers to myths, not fables, so the order is established.

Exercise 8: Organizing Paragraphs

The following group of sentences is a paragraph presented in scrambled order. Each sentence in the group has a place in the paragraph. Read each group of sentences and decide the best order in which to put the sentences so as to form a well-organized paragraph.

P   An important step in taking a good photograph is to previsualize the result.

Q   One then thinks of possible improvements and makes necessary changes.

R   Essentially this means that while looking through the viewfinder the photographer visualizes or imagines how the shot will look when printed.

S   By making adjustments before the shutter is released, the actual photograph comes close to what was wanted and expected.

T   For professional photographers good photographs do not just happen; they are made.

1. Which sentence did you put first?
   a Sentence P
   b Sentence Q
   c Sentence R
   d Sentence S
   e Sentence T

2. Which sentence did you put after Sentence P?
   a Sentence Q
   b Sentence R
   c Sentence S
   d Sentence T
   e None of the above. Sentence P is last.

3. Which sentence did you put after Sentence Q?
   a Sentence P
   b Sentence R
   c Sentence S
   d Sentence T
   e None of the above. Sentence Q is last.

4. Which sentence did you put after Sentence R?
   a Sentence P
   b Sentence Q
   c Sentence S
   d Sentence T
   e None of the above. Sentence R is last.

5. Which sentence did you put after Sentence T?
   a Sentence P
   b Sentence Q
   c Sentence R
   d Sentence S
   e None of the above. Sentence T is last.

Writing Samples

Since the best test of a student's writing ability is to have the student write something, some tests of English composition skills ask students to prepare a writing sample. Because writing samples cannot be scanned by a machine or graded with complete objectivity, they are far more difficult to evaluate than multiple-choice test items.

There are two common methods used to evaluate writing samples. One approach is *holistic scoring*. Using this system, the trained reader/scorer reads your essay or paragraph quite rapidly and gives it a rating—perhaps on a scale of 1 (low) to 5 (high). The rating is based on an *overall* impression of the piece (hence the term *holistic*) rather than on any quantitative or even qualitative evaluation of specific elements. Spelling, punctuation, grammar, usage, organization, tone, even handwriting probably "count" to some degree, but they are not assessed or tallied separately. When writing samples are scored holistically, at least two readers will rate each sample independently. When the readers disagree, a third reader is often called on to make a final assessment.

A second method of scoring requires reading the writing sample several times and rating elements such as ideas, organization, wording, flavor, mechanics, and presentation (penmanship, neatness, spacing, etc.) separately. Each element may be rated 3 (excellent), 2 (average), or 1 (poor), and the ratings averaged to come up with a total score. If you have not had experience in writing short descriptive or persuasive pieces, you might practice writing "on demand" in preparation for this kind of test. The following is a short list of topics similar to those you might be asked to address in a writing sample.

1. Explain how to make an object.

2. Describe a favorite place you have visited.

3. Discuss improvements you would make in your high school.

4. Describe someone you like well.

5. Discuss your views on war.

6. A Job I Would Like to Have

7. Music I Enjoy

8. The World in A.D. 2000

9. An Autobiography

10. If I Were President

Preparing for Essay Examinations

An *essay examination* requires that you demonstrate your knowledge of a topic by writing about it.

Essay questions may be included as part of an examination in almost any school subject. The steps involved in writing essay answers are similar to those found in other types of exposition: work with a limited topic, development of a thesis statement, and support of the thesis with specific details. Sometimes, students are allowed to use their textbooks and notes as sources of supporting details such as examples, reasons, facts and figures, and so on.

The best way to prepare for an essay examination is to develop good study habits. The SQ3R (Survey, Question, Read, Recite, Review) method is one way to prepare for essay examinations. This method involves these steps.

1. Survey the material, noting the title, reading the introduction and summary, looking at illustrations, paying special attention to subject headings, marginal notes, and vocabulary words in **boldface** and *italicized* print.

2. Using chapter titles, topic headings, or hints from your teacher, formulate a list of questions that should be answered as you complete the reading assignment.

3. Read to find the answers to your questions.

4. Recite answers to the questions you have asked yourself and record your answers as reading notes.

5. Immediately after reading, review your list of questions and answers, trying to answer the questions without looking at your notes. After one week, review again.

Exercise 9: Practicing the SQ3R Method

Select a section or chapter from one of your textbooks to read and study using the SQ3R method. On a sheet of paper, write the questions you ask yourself in the *question* step and the notes you develop to answer those questions in the *recite* step.

Writing Essay Answers

The following suggestions will help you improve your performance on essay examinations.

Look over the test carefully before you begin.

Read the instructions to find out if you must answer every question or if you have a choice of topics. Then read the topics and decide which will be the easiest to discuss and which might offer you the most problems.

Schedule your time.

If you must write on three topics in an hour, allow fifteen minutes for each topic, ten minutes for note-taking, and five minutes for review. If one question carries more weight than the others, adjust your schedule to allow more time for that topic.

Analyze each essay topic carefully.

Most essay test items contain "clue words" that suggest how the essay should be written. Verbs such as *discuss, describe, compare, contrast, define, refute* suggest how a topic should be treated or developed. Notice the other development clues provided by the words in the following essay examination topics.

What *three services* does a life insurance agent provide for a buyer?

What *characteristics* of romanticism can be found in Wordsworth's poetry?

Explain the *major functions* of the United States Supreme Court.

Notice that sometimes a topic will specify a number of items that should be discussed:

Describe *three* major causes of water accidents.

Questions may also consist of several parts:

According to the definition of propaganda provided in this chapter, what modern occupations could be classified as propagandistic? Discuss each occupation's relationship to the spread of propaganda.

To answer this question students must discuss two things: (1) occupations that spread propaganda, and (2) how each occupation spreads propaganda.

Quickly gather information before writing your answer.

Jot down facts from reading and class discussions as rapidly as you can; if you have forgotten an important idea, go on to the next question and come back to your list later. The systems for gathering information (brainstorming, the Pentad, or the *who? what? why? when? where? how?* questions) are often helpful. (See Chapter 1.)

Briefly outline your answer and begin writing.

Remember that your essay should possess the qualities of an abbreviated expository essay. The essay question itself already tells you how the topic should be limited. Often the question can be restated as the thesis or main idea in your essay answer. Reread your list of notes, cross out irrelevant information, and number the remaining information in the order it should logically be presented.

Keep your time limitation in mind; if you must develop three points in your answer, divide your time equally among the three. Write concisely, stating the most important information first.

Save a few minutes of your scheduled time to reread your answer, making necessary changes and proofreading.

Your ideas will make a more favorable impression if they are stated clearly and correctly. Be especially careful to spell correctly any words and names given in the essay question.

Model: *Essay Question and Answer*

The essay examination answer in this section was written in response to the following question.

Question

In what ways do government services aid consumers and businesses? Illustrate your answer to this question by discussing the roles of three federal agencies or commissions.

Answer

Government services aid both consumers and businesses by shaping the direction in which the economy develops and by protecting the consumer's health and safety. For example, the FDA (Food and Drug Administration) carefully tests new drugs before they are made available to consumers to ensure that the drugs are effective and do not have harmful side effects. The FDA also sets up guidelines for food so that shoppers can purchase safe, carefully prepared, wholesome items in their local stores. The information about nutritional value that now appears on the packages of prepared foods is the result of FDA legislation.

Another government group, the FTC (Federal Trade Commission), oversees advertising and sales practices. The FTC protects the consumer from illegal price fixing by companies and dishonest advertising. In some cases, the commission has filed suits against companies and forced them to change deceptive magazine or television advertisements. The commission also investigates thousands of consumer complaints that are brought to their attention every year.

A third agency, the EPA (Environmental Protection Agency), protects consumers by setting standards for the pesticides that are used in American agriculture. The agency also sets standards for air, water, and noise pollution to ensure that businesses do not damage the environment in the process of manufacturing their goods.

While the FDA, FTC, and EPA were developed primarily to protect consumers, they also direct the economy by setting up guidelines that force American businesses to compete honestly and fairly, according to set regulations, for the consumer's dollar.

Exercise 10: Examining Essay Questions

On a sheet of paper, list the clue words in each of the following sample essay examination questions. Then indicate how many parts there are to each question and what they are.

1. Discuss the five approaches to the study of religion in terms of the contribution each makes to human understanding.

   —from Sociology: The Study of Human Relationships

2. Discuss the importance of the labor force to production, service, and distribution systems. What would happen to these systems if labor was not available?

   —from Sociology: The Study of Human Relationships

3. Compare the view of nature developed in "A Sunrise on the Veld" with the view developed in O'Flaherty's "The Wild Goat's Kid." Contrast the ways in which these views emerge.

   —from Adventures in English Literature

4. What are the advantages and disadvantages of each kind of life insurance below for a 20-year-old person?
   a. 5-year term insurance
   b. endowment insurance
   c. limited-payment life insurance

   —from The Consumer in America

Answer Key

Exercise	1	2	3	4	5	6	7	8
Item 1.	d	c	b	a	d	d	a	e (or a)
2.	b	a	d	d	c	b	b	b
3.	d	d	a	c	b	c	b	c
4.	c	d	d	b	N	a	c	b
5.	a	b	c	c	a	d	b	a (or e)

29 Speaking and Listening Skills

In this chapter you will learn how to debate—how to prove a statement, how logically to attack and defend an idea, and how to verbalize your thoughts quickly and clearly. You will also learn to analyze arguments as you listen to others and to evaluate the soundness of reasons given to support an idea. These are skills that you will need throughout your life, living in a society dependent on the spoken word.

Preparing for a Debate

Choosing Debatable Propositions

In debate terminology, a course of action that is supported by one side (the affirmative) and rejected by the other side (the negative) is called a *proposition*. It is a judgment about what should be done or believed.

Debate propositions can be labeled as one of the following three types.

Propositions of Fact

When debaters argue whether something is or is not true, or will or will not happen, they are arguing a *proposition of fact*.

Lawyers debate propositions of fact whenever they try to prove the guilt or innocence of a defendant. "Resolved: That Ron Kallas is guilty of fraud" is an example of a proposition of fact. The prosecutor (the affirmative side) will have to prove that Ron Kallas is guilty of fraud, while the defense attorney (the negative side) has the burden of proving Ron's innocence. The distinguishing characteristic of a proposition of fact is that a definite answer exists. The jury will find Ron guilty or innocent, and one lawyer wins the case while the other loses.

Propositions of Value

If you try to prove to someone that your opinion or value judgment about a certain issue is right, then you are arguing a *proposition of value*.

The affirmative side arguing a proposition of value contends that something is good, right, proper, desirable, or beneficial. When debating a proposition of value, you cannot absolutely prove that your position is correct or true as you can a proposition of fact. You can, however, try to prove your position beyond any reasonable doubt. An example of a proposition of value is: "Resolved: That American cars are better built than foreign cars." You could argue this statement all night in a "bull session" and still not be able to come up with a definite answer.

Propositions of Policy

When a debater suggests that a certain rule, course of action, law, or policy should be pursued, that debater is arguing a *proposition of policy*.

The debate in a proposition of policy centers around whether or not changes should be made in the way people do things, and this type of proposition characterizes all legislative debates. It also characterizes much of the debate that takes place in organizations, clubs, and businesses. Typical proposition-of-policy statements are: "Resolved: That the United States government should provide a free medical care system for all United States citizens" and "Resolved: That Anderson High School should establish an open lunch policy for all students." All propositions of policy statements suggest a change from what currently exists.

Wording the Debate Proposition

In most discussions speakers do not present their propositions in a formal manner, with the word *resolved* preceding the topic. The closest most people come to formalizing their request may be a statement such as, "I think that the government should pass legislation requiring the wearing of seat belts."

For formal debate, however, the basis for argument must be clearly defined and must be worded in a way that ensures a clash between two opposing sides. If the proposition is vaguely and improperly worded, then the debate will be unorganized and ineffective. To make the debate profitable, you should consider the following guidelines in choosing your proposition and in phrasing it.

The proposition should be controversial.

When you choose a topic, be certain that the topic is two-sided and that a difference of opinion exists about what should be believed or acted upon. If there is no conflict, then there is no need to debate. Thus, a proposition that states, "Resolved: That American democracy rests on the people's right to vote" is not very debatable. However, a proposition that states, "Resolved: That the Electoral College should be abolished" is debatable because it is controversial.

The proposition should involve only one main idea.

Confusion will reign if there is more than one debatable topic in a proposition. A proposition that reads, "Resolved: That the senior class sponsor a paper drive on December 26 and use the money toward the senior gift to the school" is too much. The debaters involved not only will clash over whether a paper drive is the best way to earn money, but they will also have to debate the date for the drive and the eventual use of the money. Each main idea demands a separate proposition and a separate debate.

The proposition should be worded affirmatively.

The proposition should always be worded so that the affirmative side supports the new idea stated in the proposition and so the negative side rejects it. In other words, the affirmative should always be put in a position of suggesting a change in the present situation, while the negative must defend what presently exists. A proposition that states, "Resolved: That compulsory education should be eliminated in the United States" fulfills this requirement because the affirmative is in a position of suggesting a change (supporting the proposition), while the negative must reject that change.

The proposition should be phrased in a single, neutral sentence that begins with the word *Resolved*.

Because a proposition should not give the edge to one side or the other, it should be written in the clearest possible language, and it should be free of bias. To state in a proposition, "Resolved: That the murderous, unethical, repressive act of capital punishment should be abolished" is unfair to the negative debaters. Let the arguments evolve from a fairly worded statement that reads, "Resolved: That capital punishment should be abolished."

Exercise 1: Writing Propositions

Working alone or in a group, create five propositions of fact, five propositions of value, and five propositions of policy. Share your ideas with your classmates.

Affirmative and Negative Obligations

O nce you choose a debatable proposition, the next step is to decide which side of the proposition you want to take. For the sake of the research you will do, limit yourself to propositions of policy. Neither propositions of fact nor of value lend themselves adequately to a research approach, since a proposition of fact is too easily settled and a proposition of value relies too much on personal opinion.

Before making your final decision about either supporting the proposition or opposing it, you need to understand some of the obligations both sides must fulfill.

First of all, the affirmative side has the obligation known as *burden of proof*. Since a proposition of policy suggests that a change should take place in the status quo (present system), the affirmative must prove that there is a need for that change. By proving beyond a reasonable doubt that certain problems exist in the status quo, the affirmative is accepting its burden of proof.

As the affirmative hammers away with the harm done by the present situation, the negative must be able to defend itself by fulfilling its obligation, known as *burden of rejoinder*. Basically, the negative must meet head-on each of the affirmative's attacks. Both affirmative and negative speakers are under the obligation of proving any statements they make.

Exercise 2: Understanding Affirmative and Negative Obligations

Divide into small groups and choose three propositions of policy that you have already drafted or that you will draft for this activity. Put each proposition on a separate sheet of paper and draw a line down the middle. In the left-hand column write the heading *Affirmative Attacks* and in the right-hand column write *Negative Responses*. As a group, think of as many affirmative arguments as possible that show problems with the status quo and prove that the proposition should be adopted. Write these arguments under the *Affirmative Attacks* heading. Then think of negative responses to those arguments and put them in the right-hand column.

Developing the Proposition

To prepare valid arguments backed by solid evidence and reasoning, consider research as having the following six components.

---

1. Read for background knowledge of the topic area.

Newspaper and magazine articles, chapters in a book, pamphlets, and encyclopedia entries can all help broaden your perspective on the topic by suggesting ideas for you to explore as you prepare your opinion and its defense.

---

2. Uncover the issues in the debate.

The *issues* are the main points about which the affirmative and negative disagree. They are the topics that must be analyzed by both sides and that will determine who wins the debate.

The essential issues in a debate should be phrased as questions to which the affirmative must answer *yes* and the negative must answer *no*. The following diagram illustrates how issues are uncovered about the proposition, "Resolved: That private firms be allowed to deliver first-class mail."

Affirmative Arguments	*Negative Arguments*
First Issue: Is the present system of delivering mail inefficient?	

Yes	*No*
a. The service is deteriorating.	a. The Postal Service is becoming more mechanized.
b. The cost of mail delivery continually rises.	b. Costs are rising due to inflation, not inefficiency.
c. The Postal Service always operates on a deficit.	c. The deficit is due only to a clumsy rate-making structure.

Second Issue: Would private firms create more jobs?	

Yes	*No*
Competition and reduced rates would mean expanded service and more jobs.	Jobs would be cut because there would be no union protection.

Third Issue: Is the Postal Service's monopoly of mail service harmful?

Yes

a. Because there's no competition, there's no incentive to improve.
b. Because there's no improvement, there have been cutbacks in deliveries and changes from doorstep to curbside delivery.

No

a. Rural areas would be harmed because private firms would serve only profitable urban areas.
b. A monopoly actually provides for an equality of service, which cannot be duplicated by private firms.

Fourth Issue: Would the proposed system of having private firms deliver first-class mail be more efficient?

Yes

a. Competition would cause companies to deliver mail more efficiently.
b. Competition would cut the cost of mail delivery.

No

a. The present system is already doing a good job, and there is no need to change.
b. The cost for transportation, employees, and maintenance would be the same for private firms as it is for the government.

Three general questions apply to almost all propositions of policy. These questions are called *stock issues*, and they can guide your thinking as you look for the specific issues dealing with your proposition.

Is there a need for a change?

Will the proposed change be practical, and will it solve any of the problems found in the status quo?

Will the change produce advantages over the status quo?

You can also discover your proposition's issues by answering questions like the following ones.

With what problems does the topic seem to be concerned?

What are the causes of these problems?

How harmful are these problems?

What are the effects of these problems?

Is the present method of solving these problems working at all? If not, why not?

Is there a way of improving the present system without drastically changing it?

Will the adoption of the proposition really solve the problems uncovered?

Will the adoption of the proposition be practical, inexpensive, and beneficial?

Will the adoption of the proposition do more harm than good?

Exercise 3: *Developing a Proposition*

Beginning with this exercise, you will research a proposition of policy that you will eventually debate for the class. First, divide into groups of four. Each group of four should choose an interesting proposition of policy. Then divide into pairs so that two of each group can debate the affirmative side while the other two debate the negative side. After sides of the topic are decided, begin your research. Each group member should read at least three general articles about the topic. Then each individual should develop a list of three to five issue questions that pertain specifically to the proposition. Share your lists. As a group, put all of your lists of issues together and pick the major three to five issues upon which the proposition rests.

3. Select the contentions you will use.

Since you and your opponents have now settled on three to five issues on which to focus the debate, you are ready to develop your *contentions,* which are the arguments used to support your side of an issue. Contentions, written as declarative sentences, are opinions that need to be proved to show that your side of the debate is right. In the diagram on pages 666–667, notice that both the affirmative and negative sides have made statements in response to each issue raised. These statements are the contentions that will actually be used during the debate. Several contentions are usually necessary to establish your side of an issue, and it always takes evidence and reasoning to establish a contention.

Exercise 4: *Listing Contentions*

Working with your partner, list the contentions you will need to prove to support the three to five issues you have already selected. These contentions should reflect your side of the debate and should be worded in simple declarative sentences.

4. Find evidence to support your contentions.

Finding specific evidence to prove your contentions is by far one of the most demanding tasks you will face in preparing for your debate. In fact, you may find that some of your contentions are unwarranted and must be replaced with other arguments that can be proved.

The library is your most important research tool. Interviewing knowledgeable people and corresponding with private and governmental agencies can also be useful.

Exercise 5: Finding Supporting Evidence

Dividing up the workload between you and your teammate, do a thorough search of the library sources that provide information about your proposition. List each source and its date so that you can return to it later to find specific information that supports your contentions. Do not, however, neglect sources giving information in support of your opponents' view. Finding out what others say against your position can help you strengthen that position when you debate.

5. Test the evidence you would like to use.

The evidence you look for will be of two types: *empirical evidence* and *opinion evidence*.

Whenever you find controlled scientific studies resulting in factual data or whenever you read about controlled observations of events, you are involved with empirical evidence. For example, studies showing that certain agents cause cancer can be accepted as proof if the studies follow proper scientific rules of experimentation, such as variables that are controlled and repeated experiments that generate the same results.

A more common type of empirical evidence is the evidence that is based on controlled observation of events. Opinion polls are good examples of this type of evidence, since they seek to draw conclusions about the way people think about issues. As long as the poll can prove validity (the pollsters actually observe what they claim to be measuring) and reliability (the same results would be gathered if the polls were repeated or if they had been gathered by another pollster at the same time), it can be accepted as evidence.

Even though empirical evidence is probably the strongest support you can gather for a contention, it is not always available. Instead, you may find yourself using opinion evidence. In using opinion evidence you rely on expert testimony to prove your point. If you quote an expert's opinion in an area in which he or she is qualified and competent, you are then using the weight of that person's authority to support your claim. In addition, if you quote a publication, such as a newspaper or magazine, that is noted for reliable, fair reporting, you are relying on that publication's reputation for supplying expert testimony. For example, a chemist may make a statement about the dangers of chemical warfare, and you may want to use that quotation as evidence. You are free to use the chemist's expert testimony or any empirical evidence you find as long as the evidence passes the tests described in the following statements.

a.   The evidence must be clearly written so that it can be understood by you and by your potential audience.

b.   The evidence must directly prove the contention, or it should not be used.

c.   The evidence must be consistent with other known evidence. (One study showing that cigarette smoking does not cause cancer is not credible, since all other studies indicate otherwise.)

d.   The source for the evidence must be free from bias and must be objective and responsible. (A geologist who works for an oil company may not be free from bias when reporting facts about oil recovery.)

e.   The evidence must be the most recent available.

f.   The evidence must be abundant. (The more evidence you have to prove the same idea, the stronger your argument will be.)

6. Record and file your evidence.

The final step in your research is to record and file your evidence so that you know what you have at a glance and so that it is easily retrievable. By using either 4×6 or 5×8 index cards, you can record one item of evidence per card, in a format that readily identifies it. Each note card should include a proposition heading that indicates whether your side is negative or affirmative, a subject matter heading, a citation heading (author's name, title of article and magazine or book, place and date of publication, and page number), and an exact quotation of the evidence you want to use. A typical evidence card might look like the one on the next page.

Exercise 6: Recording Evidence

Dividing up the workload between you and your teammate, begin recording evidence that supports the contentions you have developed. Record each piece of evidence on a note card. Include the proper headings.

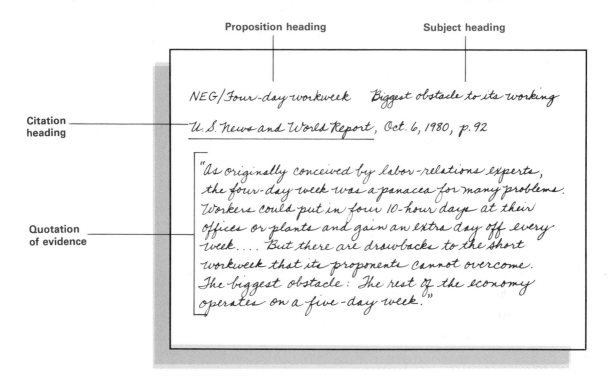

Proposition heading   Subject heading

Citation heading

Quotation of evidence

NEG/Four-day workweek   Biggest obstacle to its working

U.S. News and World Report, Oct. 6, 1980, p. 92

"As originally conceived by labor-relations experts, the four-day week was a panacea for many problems. Workers could put in four 10-hour days at their offices or plants and gain an extra day off every week.... But there are drawbacks to the short workweek that its proponents cannot overcome. The biggest obstacle: The rest of the economy operates on a five-day week."

Refuting Your Opponents' Arguments

During a debate you will be confronted with many arguments presented by your opponents. Since debate, however, rests on the premise of two sides clashing or arguing about the truth in a given matter, you will have to take each one of your opponents' arguments, analyze it quickly, and present valid objections to it. This process is known as *refutation,* and it is not an easy skill to learn unless you familiarize yourself with the ways to attack an argument and with the means to organize the attack.

Refutation involves three general strategies that can be used individually or together to refute an argument or to analyze any idea.

1. Attack the evidence used by your opponents.

Any evidence used should be analyzed carefully because it may provide a weak spot in your opponents' argument. When you listen to an argument, ask yourself the following questions to see if you can refute the argument by attacking your opponents' use of evidence.

a. Was there evidence used to support an argument?

b. Does the evidence directly relate to the argument it is to support?

c. Does the argument need more evidence to support it than was used?

d. Is the evidence too general to really prove anything?

e. Is the evidence outdated?

f. Is the evidence clearly written?

g. Is the evidence consistent with other reliable evidence?

h. Does the evidence have a bias? Is it from an unqualified source?

2. Attack the reasoning used by your opponents.

For more information on evaluating the soundness of arguments, see pages 246-252.

Evidence alone is not enough unless conclusions can be drawn from that evidence. The process of drawing conclusions from the facts is known as *reasoning*, and it, too, must be analyzed in a debate. Not all conclusions reached are valid, and you may be able to poke some holes in your opponents' arguments by attacking their methods of reasoning.

a. Do your opponents use hasty generalization when they jump to a conclusion without enough proof to support that conclusion? Example: "I've met three corrupt politicians in my life. That just goes to show that all politicians are crooks!"

b. Do your opponents commit the fallacy of *non sequitur* when they draw a conclusion based on facts that do not provide adequate, logical grounds for that conclusion? Example: "Washington is an excellent father. Therefore, he will make an excellent senator."

c. Do your opponents try to oversimplify a complex topic by arguing in terms too simple to take all issues into account? Example: "Slavery was the cause of the Civil War."

d. Do your opponents try to compare two situations that are not enough alike in all essential regards to make the comparison work? Example: "Nationalized health care works in Great Britain, so it will also work in the United States."

e. Do your opponents try to say that one thing caused another thing to happen when there may really be no relationship between the two or not a strong enough one to make a difference? Example: "The heavy amount of rain we had this summer must have been caused by that volcanic explosion out in Washington.''

f.   Do your opponents beg the question by assuming that something is true that requires proof, but yet they do not prove it? Example: ''Because the use of chemical weapons in warfare is morally wrong, it should be prohibited. Because the use of chemical weapons in warfare should be prohibited, it is morally wrong.''

---

3. Defend your own case.

You have probably heard the sports-related cliché that ''A good offense is the best defense.'' This bit of wisdom holds true for debaters too. One way to refute your opponents' case is to establish and defend your own. When you deal with an opponent's argument against your case, do not forget about the following refutation strategies:

a.   Use evidence that contradicts your opponents' evidence.

b.   Point out arguments that your opponents have dropped as the debate progresses.

c.   Minimize the significance of their arguments while maximizing the significance of your own.

d.   Point out inconsistencies in what your opponents have said in their argument.

e.   Dismiss their irrelevant arguments that have nothing to do with the real issues at hand.

f.   Point out emotional appeals that your opponents are using.

Once you have decided what strategies to use against an opponent's argument, you next have to organize your refutation. Unless you let your listeners know what you are trying to do, your refutation will be ineffective. Therefore, organize your refutation around the following four steps.

1.   State your opponents' argument that you intend to refute.

2.   Tell your listeners the objections you might have against that argument.

3.   Support with evidence or explain your objections.

4.   Explain how your objections weaken your opponents' case while strengthening yours.

Exercise 7: Presenting a Debate

Along with a group of four students, plan and present a debate to the class, using the evidence you have gathered from previous exercises in this chapter.

Evaluating a Debate

Even though you have prepared yourself for the debate, your success depends on one more skill—the ability to listen and take notes. You cannot refute an argument that you have not heard accurately or remembered completely. Most debates last about an hour. Without a note-taking system, it is almost impossible to remember everything that is said by both teams during that time.

As you listen to debates, or even to informal arguments, you should train yourself to listen for the speaker's proposition (or main idea) and for the argument set forth to support his or her position. Listening to a debate in order to follow the main ideas is similar to taking notes on the main ideas of a book that you are reading. You will find that speakers emphasize their main ideas, often by stating them first or with the words, "I believe that. . . ." In listening, transition words such as *first, second, finally,* and *in conclusion* help you identify the supporting arguments. Jot down notes to outline the main ideas of the argument.

If you are listening as an audience member to a speech or debate, you are expected to make a critical choice about which side most effectively presented its case. To do so, you need to have some criteria by which you can judge the speech or debate. Use the following six criteria in evaluating the arguments of a single speaker or of a debate team:

1. *Analysis.* How well did the speaker (or team) grasp the proposition and the opposing viewpoint?

2. *Reasoning.* How valid were the conclusions presented, based on the evidence? How strongly did the evidence support the conclusions?

3. *Evidence.* How believable was the evidence presented? Were the sources of the evidence cited?

4. *Organization.* How well organized was the argument? How easy was it to follow?

5. *Refutation.* How well did the speaker (or team) attack and refute the opposing viewpoint?

6. *Delivery.* How well did the speaker (or team) present the argument? Was the delivery clear, direct, and forceful?

Exercise 8: Evaluating Debates

Develop a rating sheet in which you use the six criteria for evaluating an argument. As your class debates, rate the speakers individually against the six criteria and then rate the teams against the criteria. Include on the sheet a place for comments about the team, and complete a sheet for each debate you hear in class. Share your evaluations with the debaters.

Glossary of Terms

Acronym A word formed from the initials of a group of words

Active voice The form of the verb when the subject performs the action

Ad hominem The fallacy of attacking a person instead of an issue; the Latin words mean, ''against the man''

Adjective A word used to modify a noun or pronoun

Adverb A word used to modify a verb, an adjective, or another adverb

Affix A word element, such as a prefix or suffix, added to a root to change its meaning

Analogy A comparison in which two things are shown to have at least one quality in common

Antagonist A character against whom the protagonist struggles to resolve the conflict

Antecedent A noun or another pronoun that a pronoun replaces or refers to

Apostrophe Punctuation mark used to show the omission of letters or numbers, to form the plurals of letters or numbers, and to form possessive nouns

Appositive A word or phrase that renames or explains a nearby noun or pronoun

A priori The fallacy of offering a conclusion without any evidence to support it; the Latin words mean, ''from the first''

Bandwagon appeal An appeal to the emotional need to be like everyone else

Begging the question The fallacy of arguing that a conclusion is true without offering any evidence or reasons

Bias The coloring of events or descriptions from a particular point of view

Brainstorming Stimulating creative thinking by letting one's mind wander freely over a subject

Card catalogue A file of cards listing books and other reference materials in a library

Card-stacking Withholding information in order to persuade

Central theme The main idea developed in a piece of writing

Clause A group of words that contains a subject and a predicate and functions as part of a sentence

Cliché An overused expression

Climax Turning point

Clincher sentence A sentence that provides a strong ending for a paragraph

Coherent paragraph A paragraph in which the links between sentences are made clear to the reader

Collective noun A noun that names a group

Colon Punctuation mark that calls attention to the word, phrase, or list that follows it

Comma Punctuation mark used to separate words, phrases, or clauses within a sentence

Commentary The writer's statements, reflections, and observations about the central theme

Comparison Identifying ways in which items are similar and ways in which they differ

Complement A word or group of words that completes the meaning of the verb and the subject

Complex sentence A sentence composed of one independent clause and one or more subordinate clauses

Compound Having two or more parts

Compound sentence A sentence containing two or more independent clauses and no subordinate clauses

Compound-complex sentence A sentence composed of two or more independent clauses and one or more subordinate clauses

Conjugate To show a verb's different forms according to voice, mood, tense, number, and person

Conjunction A word that connects words or groups of words

Connotation Feelings associated with a word

Critical writing Writing that analyzes, evaluates, and comments on selected elements of another's work

Dangling modifier A modifier that has no word or words for it to modify

Dash Punctuation mark used to call attention to a word or group of words that precedes it

Declarative sentence A sentence that states a fact

Deductive reasoning Reasoning that begins with a general statement, adds a related statement, and ends with a conclusion drawn from the two statements

Denotation The explicit meaning of a word

Dewey decimal system A method of dividing non-fiction works into ten categories

Diction Choice of words

Direct object A word or group of words that receives the action of the verb

Edited Standard English The written form of Standard English

Either-or fallacy The fallacy of arguing that only two alternatives are possible in a given situation

Euphemism A word or phrase substituted to make something offensive sound more agreeable

Exclamation point Punctuation mark used to end exclamatory sentences

Exclamatory sentence A sentence that expresses strong feeling

Expository writing Writing whose purpose is to explain

Facts Information that can be verified

Factual statement A statement that can be proved or disproved by measurement, experiment, or research

Fallacy An error in logical thinking

False analogy A farfetched comparison

Faulty parallelism An incorrect construction in which sentence parts joined by conjunctions are dissimilar in type, form, or structure

Final bibliography A list of all the sources actually used in writing a research paper

First-person narrator A character who refers to himself or herself as *I*, narrates the story, and plays a part in it

Flat character A character that is static and does not grow or change during a story

Foreshadowing The technique of hinting about events to come

Formal outline An outline showing the relationship of major and minor ideas with Roman numerals, capital letters, and Arabic numerals

Gerund A form of the verb used as a noun

Glittering generality A loaded word or phrase with strong positive connotations

Gobbledygook Jargon used to confuse and exclude others

Hasty generalization The fallacy of basing a conclusion on inadequate sampling

Hyphen Punctuation mark used to link the parts of compound words or to divide a word at the end of a line

Imagery The use of language to appeal to the senses

Imaginative writing Stories, novels, poetry, and plays

Imperative sentence A sentence that gives a command or makes a request

Independent clause A clause that can stand on its own as a sentence

Indirect object A word that tells *for whom* or *to whom* the action of the verb is done

Indo-European A parent language spoken in central Europe about 4000 B.C.

Inductive reasoning Reasoning that begins with a series of specific details and ends with a conclusion based on those details

Infinitive A form of the verb preceded by the word *to* and used as a noun, adjective, or adverb

Interjection A word that expresses strong feeling

Interrogative sentence A sentence that asks a question

Intransitive verb An action verb that does not take a direct object

Ipse dixit The fallacy of citing an unreliable authority; the Latin words mean, "He said it"

Library of Congress system A method of classifying books that is more comprehensive than the Dewey decimal system

Linking verb A verb that joins the subject of a sentence to a noun or adjective that identifies or describes it

Loaded words Words with strong connotations

Logic Clear and orderly thinking

Metaphor An implied comparison between two unlike items, stated without the use of linking words

Meter A formal rhythmic pattern of sound in poetry

Middle English The language developed from Old English, spoken from about A.D. 1066 to 1500

Modern English The English language developed from Middle English, spoken from about A.D. 1500 to the present

Mood The speaker's attitude toward his or her statement

Narrative The relating of incidents or experiences in chronological order

Nonrestrictive clause A clause that does not add essential information to the sentence

Non sequitur The fallacy of drawing a conclusion that does not necessarily follow from the evidence; the Latin words mean, "It does not follow"

Noun The name of a person, place, thing, or idea

Objective complement A complement that follows a direct object and describes or renames it

Old English A language developed from Anglo-Saxon, spoken from about A.D. 450 to 1066

Omniscient narrator A narrator who is not a character in the story but knows everything that happens and what all the characters think and feel

Only-cause fallacy The fallacy of naming a single cause for a complex situation

Opinion A belief about a subject

Outline A listing of the main points of a piece of writing

Parallel structure Similar wording or arrangement of words in a sentence or series of sentences

Paraphrase Rewording

Parentheses Punctuation marks that enclose elements within a sentence

Parenthetical documentation Internal documentation of sources in a research paper, enclosed in parentheses

Participle A form of the verb used as an adjective

Passive voice The form of the verb when the subject receives the action

Pentad A method of organizing writing by asking five questions (about *action, actors, scene, method,* and *purpose*)

Period An end mark following a sentence or an abbreviation

Personification A metaphor attributing human characteristics to nonhuman subjects

Persuasive writing Writing whose purpose is to change the opinions or actions of the reader

Phrase A group of words, without a subject and its verb, that functions as a single part of speech

Plot A story-line or plan of action that centers on a conflict and is brought to a conclusion

Population The group or class of things that is being studied in inductive reasoning

Post hoc, ergo propter hoc A fallacy that occurs when one event is said to be the cause of a second event because both occurred in sequence; the Latin words mean, "After this, therefore because of this"

Predicate The part of the sentence that says something about the subject

Predicate adjective An adjective that follows a linking verb and modifies the subject of the sentence

Predicate nominative A noun or pronoun that follows a linking verb and renames the subject

Prefix A syllable that is put before a root word

Preposition A word that shows the relationship of a noun or pronoun to another word in the sentence

Prepositional phrase A preposition, its object, and any modifiers of the object

Primary sources Firsthand documents

Process analysis Writing in which the author's purpose is to explain how something works

Pronoun A word that takes the place of a noun or another pronoun

Proofreading Correcting a manuscript before submitting it to another reader

Propaganda Persuasive materials put out by a group to further its purposes

Proposition The statement of the writer's position in persuasive writing

Protagonist A character who must solve a problem or resolve some conflict

Question mark Punctuation mark used to end interrogative sentences

Quotation marks Punctuation marks enclosing a word or group of words to separate them from the rest of the sentence

Readers' Guide An index to widely read magazines

Reference books Books used to locate information or to find the answers to questions

Regional dialect A variation of a language shared by people in a particular region

Research paper An extended, formal composition presenting information gathered from a number of sources

Restrictive clause An adjective clause that is essential to the meaning of the sentence

Résumé A summary of personal data, background, and experience in outline form

Retained object An object that continues to function as a complement in the passive construction

Review A critical evaluation

Revision The process of making changes to improve a piece of writing

Rhyme A pattern of repeating sounds at the ends of words

Root word A word from which others have been derived

Round character A character that is capable of growth and change

Run-on sentence Two closely related sentences joined only by a comma or by no punctuation

Sampling In inductive reasoning, the number of specific cases of the population that are examined as evidence

Secondary sources Documents written about some aspect of the primary sources

Semicolon Punctuation mark used to separate independent clauses not joined by a coordinating conjunction, items in a series when one or more of the items contain commas, and independent clauses when commas appear within the clauses

Sentence A group of words that expresses a complete thought

Simile A comparison between two unlike items using words such as *like, as, than, seems,* and *appears*

Simple sentence A sentence containing one independent clause and no subordinate clauses

Six basic questions A method of organizing writing by asking *Who? What? When? Where? Why?* and *How?*

Slang An informal language of words and phrases that carry a special meaning for members of a group

Slug A topic heading on a note card

Specialized dictionary A type of dictionary that gives more extensive information about a specific category of words

Standard English The form of English most accepted in business, industry, and commerce

Stanzas Patterns of repeating lines in poetry

Stereotype A hasty generalization about groups of people

Subject The part of the sentence about which something is said

Subjunctive mood The mood used to express wishes, possibilities, statements contrary to fact, and indirect commands

Subordinate clause A clause that cannot stand on its own as a sentence

Suffix A syllable added to the end of a root word

Syllogism The three-statement argument in deductive reasoning (major premise, minor premise, and conclusion)

Symbol A concrete object or place that suggests complex ideas and associations

Thesaurus A dictionary of synonyms

Thesis The point the writer intends to make

Tone The attitude of the writer toward his or her readers

Transitions Words or phrases that help link sentences

Transitive verb An action verb that takes a direct object

TRI pattern A method of paragraph development using Topic, Restriction, and Illustration

Turning point In a plot, an unexpected discovery, a crucial decision, or a resolution of the conflict

Unity The quality of wholeness

Verb A word that describes an action or a state of being

Verbals Participles, gerunds, and infinitives formed from verbs but not functioning as verbs

Vertical file A filing cabinet for storing reference materials that cannot be put on shelves

Working bibliography A list of all the possible sources for a research paper

Writer's Notebook A record of the writer's experiences, thoughts, and observations

Index of Authors
and Titles

Index

Bold numbers feature basic definitions and rules.

of a paragraph, **95**
Conclusion of expository essay, **119–120**
Conclusion of persuasive essay, **277–278**
Conclusions, true and false, **236**–240
Concrete nouns, **314**–316, **330**–331
Conflict, **164**–168
  resolving, **166–168**
Conjunctions, **430–441**
  classifying, **432**–434
  coordinating, **432–437**, **482–483**
  correlative, **432**–434
  joining word groups to independent clauses, **430**–432
  paired, **430–435**
  punctuating with, **437–438**
  subordinating, **169–173**, **432**–437
  writing with, **440–441**
Conjunctive adverbs, **482**
Connectives. *See* Transitional expressions.
Connecting pronouns, **89–90**
Connectors
  coordination, **33**
  paired, to join sentences, **66–67**
  using to join parts of sentences, **63–65**
  using to join sentences, **33–35**
Connotations, **597**
Consonance, **148**
Consumer complaint letter, writing a, **293–296**
Consumers, checklist for, **293–294**
Contentions, **668–670**
Context
  finding word meaning through, **596–597**
  vocabulary in, testing, **646–647**
Contractions
  apostrophe in, **571**
  of helping verbs, **361**
Contrast, developing paragraph with, **73–77**
Coordinating conjunctions, **432–437**, **482–483**
  list of, 432
  punctuation with, **437–438**

Coordination
  with adverbs, **98**–100
  with connectors, **33–35**
Copyright information in a book, **644**
Correlative conjunction, **432–435**
  list of, 432
Cover letter, **298**, 300
Critical essay
  model review, 186–188
  organizing, **188**
  prewriting, **188**
  revising, checklist for, **190**
  topics for, **190–191**
  writing, **188–189**
Critical review. *See* Critical essay.
Critical writing, **174–191**
  reviews, **186–190**

D

Dangling modifiers, 505–**506**
Dash, **567–568**
  joining parts of sentences with, **134–137**
  joining sentences with, **132**–134
  separating change in thought, **567**
  separating introductory elements, **567**
  showing omission of words in dialogue, **567**
  uses of, **567**
Dates
  commas separating parts of, **561**
  possessives, apostrophe with, **572**
  year, apostrophe in, **571**
Debates, listening to, **674–675**
Debating
  affirmatively, **662**, **664**–668
  burden of proof, **665**
  burden of rejoinder, **665**
  choosing debatable propositions, **662–663**
  contentions, **668**
  defense of own case, **673**
  developing the proposition, **666–670**
  issues, **666–667**
  negatively, **662**, 665–667

propositions, **662–665**
  refuting opponents' arguments, **671–673**
  uncovering issues, **666–668**
  wording the proposition, **663**–665
Declarative sentence, **457**
  punctuation of, **457**
Deductive reasoning, **236**
  evaluating the argument, **240**–241
  truth and validity in, **236–239**
Definite article, **399–400**
Definition, essay of, **123–126**
Degrees of comparison
  for adjectives, **402–404**, **406–407**
  for adverbs, **416–417**, **419**–420
  double, avoiding, **407**
Deity, capitalization of words referring to, **589**
Demonstrative pronouns, **336**–338, **339**
  list of, **336**
  singular and plural forms, **339**
Denotation, **597–598**
Dependent clause. *See* Subordinate clauses.
Description. *See* Details.
Desk encyclopedias, **636**
Details
  descriptive, 36–39, 49–50
  sensory, **410**
  specific, 43–45, **410**
Determiners
  articles as, **316**–318
  nouns following, **316**–318
Dewey decimal system, **641**–643
Dialects, regional, **615–618**
Dialogue
  dash used to show omission of words, **567**
  in plays, **160–163**
  punctuation in, **577–578**
Diary. *See* Writer's Notebook.
Diction, **540–542**
  See also Language.
Dictionaries, **631–635**
Different from, **447**
Direct address, set off by paired commas, **557**
Direct object, **472–473**
  personal pronoun as, **339–340**
  sentence patterns with, **473**–481

of transitive verbs, **478**–480
Indirect quotation, **574**
Indo-European languages, **605**–
    606
Inductive leap, **243**
Inductive method, **242**–246
Inductive reasoning, **241**
    defining terms in, **242**–243
    evaluating argument, **246**
    evidence and conclusion in,
        242–244
    in persuasive writing, **260**–261
    making generalization, **242**
    method, **242**–246
    sampling in, **243**
Infinitive
    combining sentences with,
        308–310
    inserting, **308**–310
    to, distinguishing from prepo-
        sition, 443–**444**
Infinitive phrases, **348**–349, **493**,
    497–498
    as sentence fragments, **485**
Informal essay. *See* Personal
    essay.
Informal outline, **109**–112
Information
    brainstorming for, **4**–5
    clustering, **6**–7
    gathering for expository
        essay, **108**
    ordering and outlining, **109**–
        112
    presenting in expository writ-
        ing, **117**–119
Insert sentences, **192**–195
Inside address of business let-
    ter, **286**
Instructions, writing, **102**–103
Intensifiers
    adjectives following, **404**
    with adverbs, **417**
    common, **404**, **414**
Intensive pronouns, 335
Interjections, **450**–455
    commonly used, **450**
    mild, comma following, **451**–
        452
    O, capitalizing, **591**
    punctuating, **451**–452
Interrogative adverbs, **415**
Interrogative pronouns
    list of, **336**
    who, whom, **525**–526

Interrogative sentence, **458**–459
Interrupters. *See* Commas.
Into, in, **447**
Intransitive verbs, **473**–474
Introduction in book, **644**
Introductions. *See* Specific types
    of writing.
Introductory elements, separat-
    ed by comma, **554**
Introductory participial phrase,
    commas with, **504**
Introductory phrases, **554**–555
    commas with, **504**
Introductory word, omitted
    from noun and adjective
    clauses, **521**
Ipse dixit fallacy, **248**–249
Irregular adjectives, comparative
    and superlative forms, **408**–
    409
Irregular adverbs, comparative
    and superlative forms, **421**–
    422
Irregular verbs
    be, **390**–392
    principal parts, **366**–370
    using, **530**–536
Irrelevance, **249**, 252
Issues in a debate, **666**–668
Italics, **578 579**
Item analysis, **127**–130

J

Jargon, **610 621**
Jobs. *See* Résumé.
Joint possession, apostrophe
    with, **572**–573
Journal. *See* Writer's Notebook.

L

Language, **605**–622
    clichés, **622**
    dialects, American, **615**–618
    Edited Standard English, **611**
    English, history of, **605**–618
    euphemisms, **621**–622
    families, **605**–606
    figurative, **142**–146
    French, **607**–608
    Germanic, **606**
    gobbledygook, **620**–621
    Greek, **599**–600
    growth in, **611**–618

imagery in, **183**
Indo-European, **605**–606
jargon, **618**–621
Latin, **601**–602
Middle English, **607**–608
Modern English, **608**–609
nonsexist, 344
Old English, **606**–607
regional dialects, **616**–618
Latin, roots from, **601**–602
Lay, lie, **392**–394, **536**–537
Less, least, **417**
Letters. *See* Business letters.
Levels of usage. *See* Usage.
Library
    atlases, **630**
    call number, **639**
    card catalogue, **638**–645
    Dewey decimal system, **641**–
        642
    fiction, **638**–639
    finding information in, **630**
    nonfiction, **639**–640
    parts of a book, **644**
    Readers' Guide, **630**–631
    reference books, **630**–637
Library of Congress system, **642**
Lie, lay, **392**–394, **536**–537
Like, as, in similes, **142**
*Lincoln Library of Essential Infor-
    mation*, **636**
Line breaks, **140**–141
Line length, **140**–141
Linking expressions. *See* Transi-
    tional expressions
Linking verbs, **360**, 362
    list of, **360**
    in sentence patterns, **469**–472
Listening, 662, **674**–675
Literary analysis, essay of. *See*
    Analysis.
Literature, writing about, **174**–
    191
Loaded words, **263**–264
Logic, **236**
    appeals to, **260**–261
    deductive reasoning, **236**–241
    fallacies, **246**–252
    inductive reasoning, **241**–246
    truth and validity in, **236**–239
    uses of, **236**
    and writing, **236**–252
Logical connections, as transi-
    tions, **86**–87
-ly ending, **417**

M

Magazine articles, listed in *Readers' Guide*, **630–631**, 632
Magazines. *See* Periodicals.
Main clause. *See* Independent clause.
Main idea. *See* Paragraphs.
Main verbs, **360–361**
Major characters, **174**
Major premise, **236–240**
Making connections (clustering), **6–7**
Many, number of, **337**
Many a or *every*, agreement of subject and verb, **388**
Metaphor, **143–144**
Meter, **150–152**
Method, Pentad question about, **11**, 17–18
Methods of paragraph development. *See* Paragraphs.
Middle English, **607–608**
Minor characters, **174**
Minor premise, **236–240**
Misplaced modifiers, **505–507**
MLA form
    for bibliography, **202–205**
    for footnotes, 217–220
Modern English, **608–609**
Modifiers
    adjective and adverb, **422–425**
    bad, badly, **423**
    combining sentences with, **192–197**
    dangling, **505–507**
    good, well, **423**
    inserting, **192–197**
    misplaced, **505–507**
    pronouns used as, **336–338**
    slow, slowly, **424**
Mood, **364–366**
    using, **376–379**
Most, number of, **337**
Motivation, writing about, **179–182**
Movie review, **174–191**
Myself, ourselves (reflexive pronouns), **335**

N

Names
    abbreviations, capitalizing, **585**
    capitalization, **584–591**
    of countries, singular form of verb with, **387–390**
    geographical, commas separating parts of, **561**
    separating from degree, title, or affiliation, **561**
    underlining, **578–579**
Narrative element in personal essay, **50–51**
Narrator
    first-person, **184**
    objective, **185–186**
    omniscient, **184**
    in personal essay, **52**
    selective omniscient, **184–185**
    third-person, **184**
Negative adverbs, **414**
Negatives
    double, **425–426**
    using, **425–426**
Neither, number of, **337**
Newspapers. *See* periodicals.
Nicknames, quotation marks enclosing, **574**
No, comma after, **554**
No one, number of, **337**
Nominatives, predicate, subject-verb agreement with, **388–390**
Non sequitur fallacy, **247–248**, 252
None, number of, **337**
Nonessential appositives, paired commas with, **559**
Nonessential clauses, **523**
    paired commas with, **558**
Nonessential phrases, paired commas enclosing, **504–505**, **558–559**
Nonfiction
    catalogue cards for, **639–640**
    number in Dewey decimal system, **641–642**
    number in Library of Congress system, **642**
Nonrestrictive clause. *See* Nonessential clause.
Nonsexist language, **344**
Nor, or, antecedents joined by, **344–345**
Note cards
    for research paper, **206–211**
    of sources for bibliography, 206–209
Note-taking

for expository essay, **108–109**
for research paper, **206–211**
Noun clauses, **520–521**, **525**
    combining sentences with, **279–281**
    inserting, **279–281**
    introductory word omitted, **521**
Noun suffixes, **317**
Noun phrases, **490**
Nouns, **312–331**
    abstract, **314**
    as adjectives, **401**
    as adverbs, **415**
    classifying, **313–315**
    collective, **315**, **386–387**
    common, **313–314**
    compound, **314–315**
    concrete, **314**, **330**
    features, **316–318**
    followed by number or letter, capitalizing, **590**
    following determiners, **316–318**
    formed with suffixes, **317**
    gerunds, **495–496**
    irregular plurals, **321–324**
    with no singular forms, **387–389**
    plural, **319–326**
    possessives, **317**, **326–328**
    proper, **313–314**, **330**
    regular plurals, **319–321**
    singular, **316–317**, **326–328**
    singular with apparently plural forms, **387**
    specific, using, **330–331**
Number, agreement of
    pronoun/antecedent, **343–345**
    subject/verb, **363–365**, **379–382**
Numbers, compound, hyphen in, **570**

O

O, capitalizing, **591**
Object complement. *See* Direct, Indirect objects.
Object forms of pronouns, **339–341**
    using, **347–349**
Objective complements, **476–477**
Objective narrator, **185–186**

generalization, 236
inductive, **241–246**
opponents' attacking, 672–673
syllogism, 236
Reasoning. *See* Logic.
Reasons, in persuasive writing,
271–272, 277–278
Rebuttal (refutation), **671–673**
Reference books
almanacs, 630
atlases, 630, 642
biographical, 642
dictionaries, 631, **633–635**
encyclopedias, **635–637**
Readers' Guide, 630–631, 632
Reference of pronouns. *See* Pronoun reference.
Reflexive pronouns, **335**
gender, **340**
list of, **335**
singular and plural forms, **339**
Refutation, **671–673**
Refuting the opposing argument, persuasive writing,
277
Regional dialects, **615–618**
Rejoinder, burden of, **665**
Relative pronouns, **335**
dropped from subordinate
clause, **516**
introducing adjective clauses,
515–516
list of, **335**
who and *whom*, **525–526**
Repetition, using to improve coherence, **91–92**
Reports, *See* Research paper.
Research paper
choosing and limiting topic,
199–200
direct quotations in, **210–211**
documentation in, **216–220**
final bibliography for, **227–228**
final draft, checklist for, **230**
final draft, writing, **230**
formal outline for, **212**–214
formulating basic questions
for, **205–206**
limiting the topic for a, **199–
200**
model, 221–226
organizing information for,
211–214

paraphrasing information for,
209–210
parenthetical documentation
for, 216–219
plagiarism, **210**
prewriting, **228**–230
reading, **208–209**, 221–227
reevaluating your work for,
211–212
revising, **228**–230
revising, checklist for, 229
rough draft, **214–215**
steps in writing, 228–230
surveying resources for, 200–
201
taking notes for, **206–207**
thesis statement, 201–202
using quotations in, **214–215**
working bibliography for,
202–205
Research report. *See* Research
paper.
Restriction sentence, 68–71
Restrictive clause, **523**
Résumé, 298–300
Retained object, **478**–481
Reverse TRI pattern, **72–73**
Review. *See* Critical essay.
Revising, 28
business letter, checklist for,
293
critical essay, checklist for,
190
expository composition, **119–
120**
final draft, checklist for, **230**
paragraphs, 95–**97**
paragraphs, checklist for, **97**
personal essay, checklist for,
62
persuasive essay, checklist
for, **278**
research paper, **229–230**
rough draft, checklist for, **229**
See also Specific type of writing.
Rhyme, **147–149**
Rise, raise, **393**–394, 537–538
Roget's International Thesaurus,
635
Root word, **599**
Roots of words, **599–602**
Greek, **599**–600
Latin, **601–602**

Rough draft. *See* Revising.
Round character, **174**
Run-on sentences, avoiding,
481–484

S

S-LV-PA sentence pattern, **471–
472**
S-LV-PN sentence pattern, **469–
470**
S-V sentence pattern, **467–468**
S-V-DO sentence pattern, **473–
474**
S-V-DO-OC sentence pattern,
476–477
S-V-IO-DO sentence pattern,
474–476
Salutation of business letter,
286–287
punctuating, **286–287**
Sampling, **243**
Scarcely, as negative word, **425**
Scene, Pentad questions about,
11, 15–17
School subjects, capitalizing, **590**
Second-person pronouns, **334**
Secondary sources, **207–208**
-Sede, -ceed, and *-cede*, spelling
rule for, **623–624**
See, conjugation of, **373–375**
Selective omniscient narrator,
184–186
Self-, hyphenation of words beginning with, **569**
-Self, -selves, pronouns ending
with, **335**
Semicolon, **563–565**
joining sentences with, **100–
101**
separating independent clauses, **511**
separating items in a series,
563
with quotation marks, **574–
575**
Sensory details, 38–39, 410
Sentence combining, **33–35,
63–67, 98–101, 132–137,
169–173, 192–197, 231–235,
253–257, 279–283, 305–310**
See also Combining sentences.

Skills Index

Writing

Business Letters and Forms

Critical Writing

Exposition

Logic and Writing

Paragraphs

Personal Essays

Persuasive Writing

Poetry

Prewriting Techniques

Proofreading

Research Papers

Checklist for Proofreading

1. Sentence structure is accurate. There are no fragments or run-on sentences.

2. Participial phrases, prepositional phrases, and dependent clauses are clearly attached to the words they modify, to avoid misunderstanding.

3. Verb tenses are correct, and verbs agree with their subjects.

4. Pronouns are the correct subject or object forms and agree with their antecedents. Singular pronouns such as *either, each, anybody, everybody,* or *nobody* are used with singular verbs.

5. The writer avoids unnecessary shifts in pronouns, such as *I* to *you,* or *they* to *you.*

6. Capitalization, punctuation, and spelling are correct.

7. Slang and other words or phrases not a part of Edited Standard English are used only when appropriate.

Symbols for Proofreading

Cap ≡	Capitalize	*Cap* everglades
lc /	Lowercase letters	*lc* a National Park
¶	New paragraph	¶ The Everglades covers an area of about 5,000 square miles.
no ¶	No new paragraph	*no* ¶ Once the home of the Seminole Indians, the Everglades today is a haven for such endangered species as the crocodile and the egret.
∧	Insert letter, word, or phrase; called a *caret;* also used to indicate where a change is to be made	The survival of the Everglade~e~ depends on a constant ~supply~ of fresh water. The large amount of construction in the Miami area may have endanger~ed~ this supply.
stet	Leave as is (from the Latin phrase meaning "let it stand"); used to indicate that a marked change is not to be made	Ramps built over the marshy areas enable visitors to come close to the wildlife and unusual vegetation that fill the area. ~which~ *stet*
∩	Transpose	As it blows across the sawgrass, the wind makes a low sound moaning.
⌒	Delete space	Signs through out the park remind visitors that the park belongs to the wildlife, and that it is the humans who are the visitors.
#	Insert space	A delicate balance must be preserved for wildlife to survive.

703

Acknowledgments

Credits

Key: (t) top, (c) center, (b) bottom, (l) left, (r) right.

Page 1, Jean-Claude Lejeune; 2, Thomas Hooke Photography; 3(l), Jean-Claude Lejeune; 3(r), Jim Whitmer; 10, 13(l), Frank Siteman/The Marilyn Gartman Agency; 13(r), 15(l), Jean-Claude Lejeune; 15(r), Frank Siteman/The Marilyn Gartman Agency; 16(l), 16(r), 19(l), 19(r), Jean-Claude Lejeune; 23(l), Thomas Hooke Photography; 23(r), Jean-Claude Lejeune; 29, V. Lee Hunter; 35, Frank Siteman/The Marilyn Gartman Agency; 36, Thomas Hooke Photography; 37(l), 37(r), 39, 42(l), Jean-Claude Lejeune; 42(r), Vito Palmisano; 43, Thomas Hooke Photography; 45(l), 45(r), Gregg Eisman; 46, Vito Palmisano; 55(tl), Jean-Claude Lejeune; 55(tr), 55(bl), Gregg Eisman; 57, 58, 59, Thomas Hooke Photography; 60(l), V. Lee Hunter; 60(r), Jean-Claude Lejeune; 62, 63, 65, Jean-Claude Lejeune; 68, Thomas Hooke Photography; 69(l), 69(r), Jean-Claude Lejeune; 70(l), Brent Jones; 70(r), Jean-Claude Lejeune; 73, Thomas Hooke Photography; 74(l), Frank Siteman/The Marilyn Gartman Agency; 74(r), Jean-Claude Lejeune; 76, Culver Pictures, Inc.; 79(l), Jean-Claude Lejeune; 79(r), Thomas Hooke Photography; 80, Eric Kroll/Taurus Photos; 84, Jean-Claude Lejeune; 86, Laimute Druskis/Taurus Photos; 90, Thomas Hooke Photography; 91, Jean-Claude Lejeune; 92, Thomas Hooke Photography; 93, Brent Jones; 96, Gregg Eisman; 102, Thomas Hooke Photography; 103(l), 103(r), Gregg Eisman; 114, Thomas Hooke Photography; 115(l), 115(r), Jean-Claude Lejeune; 118(l), 118(r), Frank Siteman/The Marilyn Gartman Agency; 120, 122, 126(l), Jean-Claude Lejeune; 126(r), Movie Still Archives; 129, 133, Frank Siteman/The Marilyn Gartman Agency; 135, 136, Jean-Claude Lejeune; 138, Thomas Hooke Photography; 139(l), Jean-Claude Lejeune; 139(r), Vito Palmisano; 144, Jim Whitmer; 146, 149, Jean-Claude Lejeune; 150, Bruce Powell; 155, Gregg Eisman; 157, Thomas Hooke Photography; 158, Gregg Eisman; 162, Jean-Claude Lejeune; 163, Gregg Eisman; 165, Jean-Claude Lejeune; 167, Jim Whitmer; 172, Thomas Hooke Photography; 173, Jean-Claude Lejeune; 174, Thomas Hooke Photography; 175(l), Culver Pictures, Inc.; 175(r), Jean-Claude Lejeune; 176, Gregg Eisman; 178, Gregg Eisman/Courtesy of The West Chicago Historical Society's Kruse House Museum; 182, Jean-Claude Lejeune; 187, Thomas Hooke Photography; 189(l), 189(r), Gregg Eisman; 191, Thomas Hooke Photography; 193, Vito Palmisano; 194(l), Jean-Claude Lejeune; 194(r), Thomas Hooke Photography; 197, Gregg Eisman; 198, UPI/Bettmann Newsphotos; 235, Myles E. Baker; 236, Thomas Hooke Photography; 237(l), 237(r), Jean-Claude Lejeune; 238, Frank Siteman/The Marilyn Gartman Agency; 239, Gregg Eisman; 241, 242, Vito Palmisano; 245, Jean-Claude Lejeune; 249, Gregg Eisman; 250(l), Jean-Claude Lejeune; 251(r), Thomas Hooke Photography; 256, Jean-Claude Lejeune; 258, Keith Gunner/West Sotck, Inc.; 259(l), Mary Kaye Desotelle/The Marilyn Gartman Agency; 259(r), UPI; 260, Bruce Powell; 262(l), 262(r), Vito Palmisano; 263(l), Jean-Claude Lejeune; 263(r), 264, Thomas Hooke Photography; 265(l), Brent Jones; 265(r), Thomas Hooke Photography; 267, Jim Whitmer; 269, Thomas Hooke Photography; 270(l), Frank Siteman/The Marilyn Gartman Agency; 270(r), Jean-Claude Lejeune; 273(l), Gregg Eisman; 273(r), Bruce Powell; 274, Vito Palmisano; 277, Jim Whitmer; 279, Jean-Claude Lejeune; 281, Thomas Hooke Photography; 282, Jean-Claude Lejeune; 284, Thomas Hooke Photography; 285(l), 285(r), Gregg Eisman; 294, Bruce Powell; 296, Thomas Hooke Photography; 298, Gregg Eisman; 301(l), Jean-Claude Lejeune; 301(r), Thomas Hooke Photography; 309, Gregg Eisman; 311, 331, Bruce Powell; 356, Jean-Claude Lejeune; 357, John Weinstein; 397, V. Lee Hunter; 411(tr), Jean-Claude Lejeune; 411(bl), John Weinstein; 428(l), 428(r), 429, Gregg Eisman; 440, 441(l), 441(r), Movie Still Archives; 448, Jean-Claude Lejeune; 449(l), Frank Siteman/The Marilyn Gartman Agency; 449(r), 453, 454, 455, Jean-Claude Lejeune; 489, Movie Still Archives; 508, 509, Gregg Eisman; 528, 529, 546, Jean-Claude Lejeune; 547, Bruce Powell; 581, Jean-Claude Lejeune; 594(l), 594(r), Movie Still Archives; 595, Jean-Claude Lejeune.

3 4 5 6 7 8 9 0 93 92 91 90 89 88